The Edinburgh Companion to Vegan Literary Studies

Edinburgh Companions to Literature and the Humanities

Recent volumes in the series

The Edinburgh Companion to Animal Studies
Edited by Lynn Turner, Undine Sellbach and Ron Broglio

The Edinburgh Companion to Contemporary Narrative Theories
Edited by Zara Dinnen and Robyn Warhol

The Edinburgh Companion to Ezra Pound and the Arts
Edited by Roxana Preda

The Edinburgh Companion to Elizabeth Bishop
Edited by Jonathan Ellis

The Edinburgh Companion to Gothic and the Arts
Edited by David Punter

The Edinburgh Companion to Literature and Music
Edited by Delia da Sousa Correa

The Edinburgh Companion to D. H. Lawrence and the Arts
Catherine Brown and Susan Reid

The Edinburgh Companion to the Prose Poem
Mary Ann Caws and Michel Delville

The Edinburgh Companion to Nonsense
Anna Barton and James Williams

The Edinburgh Companion to Virginia Woolf and Contemporary Global Literature
Edited by Jeanne Dubino, Catherine W. Hollis, Paulina Pajak, Celise Lypka and Vara Neverow

The Edinburgh Companion to Irish Modernism
Maud Ellmann, Sian White and Vicki Mahaffey

The Edinburgh Companion to the Essay
Mario Aquilina, Nicole B. Wallack and Bob Cowser Jnr.

The Edinburgh Companion to Vegan Literary Studies
Laura Wright and Emelia Quinn

The Edinburgh Companion to Modernism and Technology
Alex Goody and Ian Whittington

Forthcoming
The Edinburgh Companion to Charles Dickens and the Arts
Edited by Juliet John and Claire Wood

The Edinburgh Companion to the Brontës and the Arts
Amber Regis and Deborah Wynne

The Edinburgh Companion to Science Fiction and the Medical Humanities
Gavin Miller, Anna McFarlane and Donna McCormack

The Edinburgh Companion to W. B. Yeats and the Arts
Tom Walker, Adrian Paterson and Charles Armstrong

The Edinburgh Companion to Jane Austen and the Arts
Joe Bray and Hannah Moss

The Edinburgh Companion to Modernism in Contemporary Theatre
Adrian Curtin, Nicholas Johnson, Naomi Paxton and Claire Warden

The Edinburgh Companion to Women in Publishing, 1900–2000
Nicola Wilson, Elizabeth Gordon Willson, Alice Staveley, Helen Southworth, Daniela La Penna, Sophie Heywood and Claire Battershill

The Edinburgh Companion to British Colonial Periodicals
Caroline Davis, David Finkelstein and David Johnson

The Edinburgh Companion to First World War Periodicals
Marysa Demoor, Cedric van Dijck and Birgit Van Puymbroeck

The Edinburgh Companion to Don DeLillo and the Arts
Catherine Gander

The Edinburgh Companion to Literature and Sound Studies
Helen Groth and Julian Murphet

The Edinburgh Companion to Modernism, Myth and Religion
Suzanne Hobson and Andrew D Radford

The Edinburgh Companion to the Eighteenth-Century British Novel and the Arts
Jakub Lipski and M-C. Newbould

The Edinburgh Companion to Curatorial Futures
Bridget Crone and Bassam El Baroni

Please see our website for a complete list of titles in the series
https://edinburghuniversitypress.com/series/ecl

The Edinburgh Companion to Vegan Literary Studies

Edited by Laura Wright and Emelia Quinn

EDINBURGH
University Press

Edinburgh University Press is one of the leading university presses in the UK. We publish academic books and journals in our selected subject areas across the humanities and social sciences, combining cutting-edge scholarship with high editorial and production values to produce academic works of lasting importance. For more information visit our website: edinburghuniversitypress.com

© editorial matter and organisation, Laura Wright and Emelia Quinn 2022, 2025
© the chapters their several authors, 2022, 2025
Chapter 1 © Carol Adams, 1990/2015, The Sexual Politics of Meat, Bloomsbury Academic, an imprint of Bloomsbury Publishing Inc.

Edinburgh University Press Ltd
13 Infirmary Street
Edinburgh EH1 1LT

First published in hardback by Edinburgh University Press 2022

Typeset in 10/12 Adobe Sabon by
IDSUK (DataConnection) Ltd

A CIP record for this book is available from the British Library

ISBN 978 1 4744 9331 4 (hardback)
ISBN 978 1 3995 5708 5 (paperback)
ISBN 978 1 4744 9332 1 (webready PDF)
ISBN 978 1 4744 9333 8 (epub)

The right of Laura Wright and Emelia Quinn to be identified as the editors of this work has been asserted in accordance with the Copyright, Designs and Patents Act 1988, and the Copyright and Related Rights Regulations 2003 (SI No. 2498).

Contents

List of Illustrations	vii
Introduction *Emelia Quinn and Laura Wright*	1
Annotated Bibliography *Emelia Quinn and Laura Wright*	16

Part I: Themes and Theoretical Perspectives

1. Veganism and Women's Writing *Carol J. Adams*	41
2. Veganism and Modernism *Catherine Brown*	62
3. Veganism, Utopia, and Science Fiction *Joshua Bulleid*	77
4. Veganism and Animals *Sune Borkfelt*	93
5. Veganism and Race *Ruth Ramsden-Karelse*	107
6. Veganism, Gender, and Queerness *Rasmus R. Simonsen*	122
7. Veganism and Postcolonialism *Alexandra Isfahani-Hammond*	138
8. Veganism and the Monstrous *Emelia Quinn*	152
9. Veganism and Disordered Eating *Laura Wright*	167

Part II: Genres and Forms

10. Prose — 185
    Amy-Leigh Gray and Dana Medoro

11. Poetry — 193
    Stewart Cole

12. The Graphic Novel — 203
    Glenn Willmott

13. Adaptation — 212
    Christopher Sebastian

14. The Philosophical Essay — 222
    Josh Milburn

15. The Exposé — 231
    Sangamithra Iyer

16. Realism — 241
    Samantha Pergadia

17. Memoir — 250
    Armin Langer

18. Young Adult Fiction — 259
    Ali Ryland

19. Satire — 267
    Nicole Seymour

20. Utopian Fiction — 278
    John Miller

21. Speculative Fiction — 287
    Jovian Parry

Part III: Textual Histories and Contexts

22. Ancient Scripture — 301
    Lisa Kemmerer

23. Long Nineteenth Century Ephemera — 317
    James Gregory

24. Society Writings — 333
    Corey Wrenn

25. Modern Literary Production — 349
    Martin Rowe

Notes on Contributors — 365
Index — 370

List of Illustrations

Plate

Plate 1   Page 26 of Marjorie Liu and Sana Takeda's *Monstress* (2015)   208

Figures

Figure 24.1   Cover page for the first issue of the Vegan Society's newsletter (1944)   335
Figure 24.2   Cover of Freya Dinshah's 1965 cookbook, *The Vegan Kitchen*   341

Introduction

Emelia Quinn and Laura Wright

Introducing Vegan Literary Studies

VEGANISM IS ON the rise. As C. Lou Hamilton writes, "Veganism is hot" (2): a hot topic as much as a hot potato issue. Over the past few decades, the number of self-identified vegans has increased exponentially, particularly in the West. A 2016 survey indicated that the number of vegans in the UK alone had increased by 350 percent in the 10 years prior (Vegan Life). The COVID-19 pandemic and the international lockdowns it necessitated also correlate with a significant increase in the popularity of vegan foodstuffs. A study by the UK Vegan Society, for instance, suggests that during the first wave of the pandemic in 2020, one in four Britons ate less meat, with tofu sales increasing by 81.7 percent and oat milk by 113 percent (Vegan Society). In the US, retail sales data from 2021 "shows that grocery sales of plant-based foods that directly replace animal products have grown 27 percent in the past year to $7 billion" (Good Food Institute). Seemingly providing people with more time to invest in food preparation and meal-planning as well as for greater reflection on the harms perpetuated by animal agriculture, the pandemic has accelerated ongoing cultural shifts whereby concerns about the impact of industrial meat production and consumption on the environment combine with attention to animal welfare concerns to increase the number of people turning to plant-based diets.

However, the rise in veganism should not be reduced solely to statistics of plant-based consumption. As Eva Haifa Giraud writes, the increased focus on plant-based foodstuffs within a capitalist economic framework risks depoliticizing the vegan movement. For Giraud "Understanding veganism as a conversation for change, rather than consumerist, eating-focused movement" is necessary in order to shift perceptions of veganism away from "something that is about dietary purity and only available to a few, to a way of thinking about and engaging with the world" (*Veganism* 158). The risk of depoliticization is reflected in Ethan Varian's 2019 *New York Times* editorial, which details how "plant-based" offers health-conscious consumers a mode of eating that is "[f]ree from specific ethical constraints," increasingly used as "a way to distance oneself from the rigid ideology of veganism, which calls for abstaining from animal products of all kinds."

In such instances, it is necessary to note the implicit misogyny that underscores a recent spate of product placement and plant-based pontification. These entreaties are focused on the deletion of veganism from the history of so-called "plant-based" eating that has long been championed by women who view ethical veganism as an inherently ecofeminist act that necessarily recognizes the linkages between a lack of empathy for and oppression of the environment, animals, women, colonized subjects, and the planetary destruction facing us in the current moment (see, for example, Adams). As is apparent in a film like Louie Psihoyos's 2018 documentary *The Game Changers*, which strategically avoids the mere mention of "vegans" or "veganism," men like James Cameron, Michael Thomas, and Arnold Schwarzenegger get to *change the game*, to refuse to use the term "vegan" while managing to speak the same truths that ecofeminist vegans have been speaking since at least the 1970s. In the process the foundational work and contributions of women are erased, ignored, and rebranded.

Conversely, veganism does operate for many as a way of thinking about and engaging with the world, one that is experienced as a deeply felt and embodied response to suffering. Work in the emergent field of vegan studies takes seriously such modes of engagement. Laura Wright, for instance, has positioned veganism as a "delicate mixture of something both primal and social, a category . . . that constitutes for some people . . . something somewhat beyond one's choosing"; an orientation that is "much more deeply rooted than mere preference" (7). Akin to this sense of veganism as an orientation, Annie Potts and Jovian Parry's work on "vegansexuality" speaks to the ways in which veganism interacts with discourses of sexuality and constitutes a means by which to challenge heteronormative and heterosexist policing of female desire. A. Breeze Harper's *Sistah Vegan* project similarly positions veganism as a mode of resistance to institutionalized oppression, a form of dietary decolonization that is part of broader intersectional, anti-racist justice movements. Vegan studies is an interdisciplinary field that includes work concerned with the social, political, and economic possibilities of veganism. Mirroring the diversity of motivations for becoming vegan (including ethical, environmental, or health-based reasons), work within this burgeoning field is itself varied and wide-ranging.

Vegan Studies

Vegan studies is, much like veganism, on the rise. Texts published in 2021 alone, for instance, include Giraud's *Veganism: Politics, Practice and Theory*, Gary Francione's *Why Veganism Matters*, Catherine Oliver's *Veganism, Archives, and Animals*, Emelia Quinn's *Reading Veganism: The Monstrous Vegan, 1818 to Present*, and Corey Lee Wrenn's *Animals in Irish Society: Interspecies Oppression and Vegan Liberation in Britain's First Colony*, in addition to several edited collections, including Laura Wright's *The Routledge Handbook of Vegan Studies* and Cristina Hanganu-Bresch and Kristin Kondrlik's *Veg(etari)an Arguments in Culture, History, and Practice: The V Word*. These texts, drawing on the disciplinary conventions of geography, literature, rhetorical analysis, sociology, philosophy, and more, join the wide range of vegan studies work across the humanities and social sciences published over the past decade. The present moment is clearly a time in which vegan *studies* is hot.

However, vegan studies' cultural cachet is arguably confined within the relatively niche and insular academic communities among whom such research circulates. As Martin Rowe argues in his contribution to this volume, the unaffordability and limited reach of academic texts maintains a critical premium on knowledge that risks siloing important discussions about veganism. The high price-point of the present volume, and its limited affordability beyond the remit of academic libraries, is unfortunately no exception. While acknowledging the limited circulation of such academic texts, we nonetheless hope that the essays contained within this volume introduce ideas that will spur further thinking and action both within and beyond the academy and we maintain faith that academic vegan literary studies and theory constitutes a form of activism.

While vegan studies to date maintains a marginal status in the academy, the fact that it has attracted numerous vocal detractors in the right-wing press speaks to its disruptive potential. As Quinn notes in her contribution to this volume, many articles published over the past year show explicit hostility not simply to veganism (a long target of media disparagement) but to the emergent field of vegan studies itself: from the derogation of vegan philosophy in *The Sun* newspaper as "PC Poppycock" (Crowson), to the perceived threat to our understanding of British monuments posed by a vegan theoretical approach to art history, as feared by *The Critic* (Starkey). Such critiques form part of a broader movement, expressed particularly vocally in the US, against an assumed liberal bias in the university system and the social and political threat that is perceived to be posed by fields such as critical race studies. We propose here that the increasingly hostile reaction vegan studies faces in the right-wing media should act as incitement to further intersectional and interdisciplinary work, speaking as it does to the threat vegan studies is seen to pose to entrenched social systems.

Vegan Literary Studies

Vegan literary studies, the focus of the present volume, considers what veganism offers as a way of thinking about and engaging with literary texts. The work of vegan literary studies advances both literary studies and vegan studies by considering the role of literary texts in forming, shaping, developing, exploring, and challenging our relationship with nonhuman animals as well as with ourselves and other humans. Vegan literary criticism proposes not just a critical approach to veganism in texts but a critical lens through which to engage with literary texts. It draws on numerous existing disciplines, including work within animal studies, critical animal studies, human–animal studies, posthumanism, ecofeminism, ecocriticism, food studies, and moral philosophy. However, this volume asserts that vegan literary studies is also a distinct field of study in its own right.

Vegan literary studies may appear, on the surface, to be premised on a contradiction in terms. As Samantha Pergadia's essay in this volume notes, "As an interpretive strategy of how one should eat, vegan literary studies may seem like bad literary criticism, reducing complex or ambiguous meaning to a single political and ethical agenda" in contrast to "[g]ood literary criticism [which] has become synonymous with extending ambiguity, refusing political takeaway, and attending to questions of form or genre" (241). Quinn's contribution further reflects on the seeming disjuncture between literary studies' traditional embrace of ambiguity and the emphasis in work such as Carol J. Adams's *The Sexual Politics of Meat* on the importance of the recovery of the real, live animals made absent through metaphorical distortion. Rather than shy away from these difficulties, the present volume interrogates the contradictions and complexities that cohere in reading as a vegan, or through a vegan lens. The essays that follow this introduction make clear that vegan literary studies offers myriad ways of reading texts that expand rather than foreclose textual possibilities.

Vegan literary studies provides a mode of reading that grapples with the multiple contradictions and failings embedded in the enactment of a vegan life and as embodied by vegan readers and scholars, as well as with the utopian impulses and aspirations that sustain it. We choose not to reiterate the various origins of vegan studies here, since such introductions to the field can be found in numerous other places (see, for example, Giraud, *Veganism* 21–22; Quinn 1–27; Quinn and Westwood; Wright, *Vegan Studies* 1–27; and Wright, "Doing"). What follows provides an outline of what vegan literary studies is and does, or can and might do, through an elaboration of the key connective threads running through this companion. While we also do not offer here a comprehensive overview of developments in the field to date, since the annotated bibliography that follows this introduction contains detailed summaries of existing work, we do draw on existing work in and around vegan studies in order to illuminate points of theoretical alignment and tension across this volume as a whole.

Connective Threads

In our own respective past work, vegans themselves are the focus of our vegan literary analyses. Wright's foundational work in *The Vegan Studies Project*, for instance, seeks to theorize a specific post-9/11 US response to veganism. She considers the vegan vampire, the vegan zombie, and the ultra-masculine "hegan" as examples of emergent cultural figures in a political climate particularly hostile to veganism and its association with sexual, racial, and gendered deviancy. Quinn's work in *Reading Veganism: The Monstrous Vegan, 1818 to Present* also seeks to unpack the anxieties that coalesce around vegan bodies, identifying the trope of the "monstrous vegan" as a figure that recurs across the past 200 years of literary history. For Quinn, monstrous vegans provide an apt formal analogy of the contradictions and inconsistencies that, in vegan modes of life, offer a useful model for reconceiving of veganism, counter to its widespread perception as a movement premised on a desire for an impossible innocence or purity. However, a focus on individual vegans and the expression of vegan identity is not the sole remit of vegan literary studies. As Stewart Cole argues in his contribution to this volume, vegan reading practices should not be limited "*to engaging only with vegan authors or texts with explicitly vegan content*" (195, italics in original).

Evan Maina Mwangi's concept of the "vegan unconscious," as outlined in his *The Postcolonial Animal*, offers a particularly useful framework for understanding what it means to apply a vegan heuristic lens to texts ostensibly unrelated to veganism. For Mwangi, the corpus of postcolonial African texts he considers does not articulate any clearly defined or consistent vegan messaging, and further, he notes that there is no correlative term for "vegan" in any African language. However, this is not to say that such texts don't tell us anything about the kinds of relations between human and non-human animals that speak to the central concerns of veganism. For Mwangi, the job of vegan literary criticism is not to condemn or ignore those works that only partially fulfill vegan ideals. Instead, he looks at texts that present a vegan unconscious, defined as an "affirmative expression of potential ... a latent possibility that the societies portrayed in the text will embrace a future where animals will not be killed to satisfy human needs" (9). Mwangi's vegan literary approach to postcolonial African literary criticism is thus one invested in the conception of becoming-vegan as "aspirational, a process rather than an end in itself" (11).

Mwangi's concept of the vegan unconscious is engaged with in both explicit and implicit ways throughout this volume. Wright's essay, for instance, considers Tsitsi Dangarembga's *Nervous Conditions* (1988), the first English-language novel by a Zimbabwean woman, as a further example of a postcolonial African novel with a discernible vegan unconscious that simultaneously rejects accepted colonial modes of European education, gender enculturation, and diet. In addition, Sune Borkfelt's essay provides a blueprint for a vegan literary studies that is aligned with Mwangi's work through its close attention to ostensibly non-vegan scenes of meat-eating and slaughter. Many other contributors reinforce the need to look beyond texts concerned with explicitly vegan themes: from Catherine Brown's consideration of the elements of modernist literature that may conduce one towards veganism, to Glenn Willmott's analysis of vegan crisis points in the *Monstress* comics series (2015-), Ali Ryland's attention to the queer vegan resonances of Peter Dickinson's *Eva* (1988), and Christopher Sebastian's reading of the unconscious vegan sentiments of Gregory Maguire's *Wicked* (1995). Through these essays we learn that vegan literary studies is much more than just a study of texts explicitly about veganism.

However, for others, such as Armin Langer, turning to explicitly vegan texts can be just as productive an exercise for developing a complex and nuanced vegan reading practice. Langer considers the vegan voices articulated in Harper's *Sistah Vegan* as a way of rewriting the dominant discourses of veganism through the creativity and individuality afforded by the autobiographical essay form. Similarly, Ruth Ramsden-Karelse reads the vegan poetry of Black dub poet Benjamin Zephaniah as a necessary disruption to mainstream narratives of veganism. The aspirational element of vegan reading practices is connected, in Zephaniah's poetry, to a non-identitarian politics of veganism that aspires to radical solidarities across multiple categories, including race, gender, and species.

The idea of veganism as an aspirational, rather than fixed or stable, identity is a further connective thread running throughout this collection. John Miller's close reading of cultured meat in Mary E. Bradley Lane's feminist utopia *Mizora* (1890), for instance, complicates any straightforward sense of a technological "fix" to our current commoditization of animal bodies. Similarly, Jovian Parry draws a comparison between veganism and the utopian narratives of Octavia E. Butler to envision a mode of veganism that is "always-already in flux" (289). For Rasmus R. Simonsen, this sense of flux positions veganism as an aspirational transhuman approach to the world, one productively discerned in the posthumanist politics of Jeanette Winterson's *Frankissstein* (2019). And for Samantha Pergadia, the realist form of Ruth Ozeki's *My Year of Meats* (1998) resists any clear vegan didacticism, suggestive of the latent vegan possibilities to be found in the recognition of multispecies entanglements.

The concept of multispecies entanglement, most often associated with the work of Donna Haraway, is also a key idea engaged with by many essays in this volume. Haraway's posthumanist explorations of entanglement have had significant influence in the humanities, drawing attention to the ways in which our lives are inescapably entwined with other human and nonhuman actors, even as Haraway is highly skeptical of veganism, seen as antithetical to a recognition of one's messy entanglement with others. While her work promotes the need for "multispecies coflourishing" (105), for Haraway "nurturing and killing" are equal parts of our "inescapable mortal companion species entanglements" (105–06). Haraway associates veganism with moral absolutes that "would consign most domestic animals to the status of curated heritage collections or to just plain extermination as kinds and as individuals" (80). Haraway thus argues that we must "learn to live responsibly within the multiplicitous necessity and labor of killing, so as to be in the open, in quest of the capacity to respond in relentless historical, nonteleological, multispecies contingency" (80). Scholars such as Giraud ("Affirmative") have offered important rejoinders to Haraway's approach to veganism, and Parry's essay in the present volume draws on Giraud's work to demonstrate how authors such as Butler "soundly reject[s] a politics of purity while remaining deeply committed to a multispecies utopianism" (289). Similarly, Willmott's essay acts as an implicit rejoinder to Haraway's dismissal of veganism, embracing a recognition of entanglement as a productive state of "vegan crisis" (207). Quinn's essay also complicates Haraway's sense of veganism as seeking only moral purity. For Quinn, veganism is fundamentally monstrous, refusing to be contained by linguistic boundaries.

This transgression of veganism beyond linguistic borders is a further connective thread found throughout the volume. Amy-Leigh Gray and Dana Medoro, for instance, consider the ways that Han Kang's *The Vegetarian* (2007) challenges dominant narratives of meat, drawing attention to moments in the text in which the narrator challenges her confinement within pre-existing patriarchal discourses. The role of the textual and the literary as both modes of entrapment and forms of liberation from dominant meat narratives is also a theme running throughout Willmott's analysis of the graphic novel form. Sangamithra Iyer's essay grapples, in different ways, with the difficulty of the fact that mere awareness of the violence done to nonhuman animals, as recorded through the genre of literary exposé, does not always provide the desired effect on either readers or writers.

Nonetheless, all of the contributors collected here agree that the written word is a powerful medium for exploring further the complexities of vegan modes of being. As Rowe's essay demonstrates, the publication of vegan texts is itself a particular feat in a publishing industry under the stranglehold of a select few conglomerates, and is an important means of shaping public perceptions of veganism. The work advanced by Lisa Kemmerer, James Gregory, and Corey Lee Wrenn makes clear that we have much to gain from paying attention to the textual histories of vegetarian and vegan thought that exist beyond the realm of literary fiction. Rather than a modern fad diet, veganism is shown in these three chapters to be part of an evolving discourse with a significantly longer history in human thought than is often perceived. Furthermore, for Josh Milburn, philosophical writing, while perhaps lacking the nuance and imaginative possibilities found in literary fiction, is also essential in order to "interrogate, understand, justify, and explain ethical beliefs" (228), moving beyond mere conviction or faith. And for Alexandra Isfahani-Hammond, it is through her cross-genre experiment in autobiographical essay that she is able to come to terms with the intersections of race, gender, and species that shape her lived experience of human–animal kinships.

The volume as a whole makes clear that vegan literary studies is a cross-genre endeavor. Joshua Bulleid's essay in this volume establishes the vegetarian and vegan thought to be found throughout the history of the science fiction and utopian genres. Science fiction and utopian literature is often positioned as the most fitting medium for the exploration of vegan ideas. Sherryl Vint argues in *Animal Alterity: Science Fiction and the Question of the Animal* that science and speculative fiction "more than any other literature, can defy [the separation maintained between humans and animals] because its generic premises enable us to imagine the animal quite literally looking at and addressing us from a non-anthropocentric perspective" (6). Joshua Schuster has also suggested that veganism has a natural affinity with science fictional narrative conventions since "Being a vegan means living in a partially alternate world that has a science fiction feel because it involves continual cognitive estrangement from social norms" (219). The works of fiction considered in the essays of Miller, Parry, Ryland, Simonsen, and Willmott further emphasize the significance of science fiction to vegan literary criticism. However, this volume also makes clear that numerous other genres similarly have much to contribute to vegan studies, as in Adams's exploration of twentieth-century feminist anti-war novels and Wright's consideration of J. M. Coetzee's *Life & Times of Michael K*, as well as the range of genres and forms on display in Part II: from Cole's analysis of D. H. Lawrence's poetry, to Sebastian's consideration of Maguire's work of literary adaptation.

This handbook aims to provide an introduction to vegan literary studies as a discipline, for those interested in exploring what vegan studies is or those looking to use vegan studies in their research or teaching. The chapters that follow offer original and insightful close readings that also constitute an active contribution to vegan literary studies. The volume should therefore also interest students and scholars already familiar with vegan studies who are looking to engage further with its possibilities. Described above are just a small sample of the common threads running through the present volume and we invite our readers to discern and trace further connections and conflicts, ensuring that vegan literary studies remains a continually transforming and fluid constellation of ideas and debates.

Chapter Outlines

This volume begins with an introduction and an extended annotated bibliography. The annotated bibliography collects together some of the key works that make up vegan studies, providing the reader with concise summaries of major works in the field to date. It is intended as a reference to guide readers towards further pertinent resources. While not an exhaustive survey of available materials, we hope that this bibliography provides a springboard for those looking to pursue vegan studies in their own work. The rest of the volume is organized into three key sections: Part I, "Themes and Theoretical Perspectives"; Part II, "Genres and Forms"; and Part III, "Textual Histories and Contexts." The following section outlines and chapter summaries provide an overview of the material covered and should guide the reader towards specific sites of interest.

Part I: Themes and Theoretical Perspectives

Part I introduces some of the key themes and theoretical perspectives addressed in existing and ongoing work in vegan literary studies. These chapters, taken as a whole, offer a survey of some of the principal ideas and sites of discussion that recur within the emergent field. The chapters in this section are not comprehensive summaries of existing vegan studies work.[1] Instead, here we learn of the theoretical perspectives that emerge in vegan literature through the close reading of literary texts.

Carol J. Adams's chapter on veganism and gender is a reprint of "Chapter 7: Feminism, the Great War, and Modern Vegetarianism" from her groundbreaking 1990 work *The Sexual Politics of Meat*. In this chapter Adams traces a historical connection between feminism, pacifism, and vegetarianism at the turn of the twentieth century, a period in which vegetarianism was modernizing and appearing with increasing frequency in literary texts. For women writers, resistance to the Great War was frequently articulated through their ethical vegetarianism, in which the private space of the dining table was reconstituted as a front at which to articulate a resistance to warfare. Adams's chapter proceeds with a focus on a range of British and North American women's writing from the 1970s, including Margaret Atwood's *The Edible Woman* (1969), Mary McCarthy's *Birds of America* (1971), Marge Piercy's *Small Changes* (1973), and Isabel Colegate's *The Shooting Party* (1980); texts which demonstrate the historical continuity of the notion of the expanded front as a site through which to voice pacifist vegetarian resistance. Adams connects these texts through an analysis of their shared use of narrative interruptions, interruptions which create space in the narrative for vegetarianism to be voiced and heard.

Catherine Brown's and Joshua Bulleid's respective chapters provide histories of some of the other key literary developments as vegetarian and vegan diets and identities began to crystallize at the turn of the twentieth century. Their chapters assert the vegan sentiments to be found across modernist and science fiction literature, respectively, rooting the history of vegan literary studies in the growth of the Novel as the dominant literary form and the increasing democratization of the literary marketplace over the course of the nineteenth century. Brown's essay considers the unconscious vegan sentiments to be found in the literature of the modernist period and turns to scenes of slaughter and the hunt as sites particularly ripe for analysis. Her wide-ranging examples are contained by the temporal span between Thomas Hardy's *Jude the Obscure* (1895) and William Golding's *Lord of the Flies* (1954), and include reflections on these novels as well as Upton Sinclair's *The Jungle* (1906) and Henry Williamson's *Tarka the Otter* (1927). In considering the latent vegan sensibilities to be found across British and North American literature over this sixty-year-period, Brown reveals the imaginative utopias of the modernist period and argues for the need to continue to imagine the world differently in a world ever more hostile to nonhuman animals. Joshua Bulleid examines the increased interest in animal studies within the realm of science fiction and traces the historical development of vegan themes throughout modern Western science fiction – from the early nineteenth to the early twenty-first century – providing examinations of major examples in order to form a foundation for future studies into veganism and science fiction in other cultures and national contexts.

Sune Borkfelt's chapter considers how attention to nonhuman animal presences in vegan literary studies differs from existing work in literary animal studies. He offers three key approaches to vegan reading: reading texts for their depiction of relations between vegan characters and nonhuman animals; reading for latent vegan sensibilities seemingly unconnected to vegan practices; and paying attention to the dead animal presences represented by meat and other animal products. In demonstrating what each approach looks like in practice, Borkfelt turns to a diverse range of texts:

from Émile Zola's *The Belly of Paris* (1873), to Archie Hind's *The Dear Green Place* (1966) and Joseph D'Lacey's *Meat* (2008). Tethering vegan literary criticism to practices of de-objectification, it is the case that, as with Brown's essay, texts involving explicit depictions of meat-eating and slaughter take precedence. For Borkfelt, such texts allow for the application of a vegan heuristic that recovers the absent referent animal, first theorized by Adams, and allows for the recognition of latent vegan sensibilities through the discomfort felt by ostensibly non-vegan characters in the face of violent slaughter.

Ruth Ramsden-Karelse's essay considers the vexed question of race in a mainstream vegan movement frequently associated with whiteness. Unpacking the problematics of much popular vegan activism, and the limitations of a vegan identity in the face of capitalist systems and entrenched racial oppressions, Ramsden-Karelse's analysis is led by a close focus on the dub poetry of Black vegan poet Benjamin Zephaniah. Utilizing Zephaniah's poetry to consider the complex issue of veganism's entanglement with racial injustice, her essay foregrounds the literary "as a space in which the ambiguities, entanglements, and contradictions of a politics of veganism and social justice can be articulated in creative and meaningful ways" (109). Zephaniah's democratic vision of poetry, as a life-giving force for the oppressed that is rooted in oral traditions, is seen to advance a non-identitarian model of veganism that facilitates a process of continual ethical interrogation and aspiration for solidarities that extend across gender, species, and race lines.

Rasmus R. Simonsen's chapter on veganism and queerness also strives for solidarities across divisions of gender and species through the development of what he refers to as "trans-veganism." Drawing on trans, queer, and posthumanist theory, Simonsen provides the theoretical framework of a transhumanist veganism. Transhumanist veganism is developed through a close reading of Jeanette Winterson's 2019 novel *Frankissstein*. The central protagonist's transgenderism, posthuman sensibility, and vegetarianism offers a contemporary re-writing of Mary Shelley's iconic *Frankenstein* (1818) that aligns with Simonsen's sense of the trans-vegan and is supported, on a metatextual level, by the trans-historical nature of the novel's literary allusions. Using trans to envision an expanded sense of connection and kinship through a transfiguring, transgressing, and transversing of species boundaries, Simonsen asserts the fluid nature of life itself and envisions veganism as a radically queer way of negotiating one's humanity and the relationship between self and other.

Alexandra Isfahani-Hammond's chapter weaves her own narrative of personal loss, of her rescue dog Akbar, into an embodied analysis of André Alexis's 2015 novel *Fifteen Dogs* to provide a postcolonial critique wherein she foregrounds nonhuman animals that have generally been omitted from decolonizing work. Emelia Quinn's essay similarly engages a work that is not traditionally considered in the more established realm of literary animal studies, Vladimir Nabokov's 1962 novel *Pale Fire*, to unpack the seeming incompatibilities of veganism and literary criticism. In this chapter, Quinn furthers her conception of the "monstrous vegan" to explore the utopian underpinnings of vegan ideology and to argue the need for future vegan literary studies to embrace, rather than resist, monstrous excesses of meaning.

Laura Wright's essay builds on Quinn's conception of the monstrous in her engagement with literary depictions of vegan women, frequently figured in relation to mental and physical illness with veganism coded as a form of disordered eating. Comparing the heroic depiction of the starving male artist, as emblematized in Franz Kafka's 1922 short story "The Hunger Artist," to the depiction of veganism as a "precursor to insanity" (168) in Margaret Atwood's 1969 novel *The Edible Woman*, Wright's essay examines the gendered binary that exists in the literary depiction of veganism as resistance. Wright turns also to two postcolonial texts, J. M. Coetzee's *Life & Times of Michael K* (1983) and Tsitsi Dangarembga's *Nervous Conditions* (1988), as further iterations of the tendency to associate veganism with disordered eating that nonetheless complicate and challenge such coding, holding out possibilities for "new and potentially empowering ways of thinking about the revolutionary potential of nonstandard diets" (169).

Part II: Genres and Forms

Part II offers a series of short close readings of a wide range of genres and forms. The emphasis here is on enacting vegan literary criticism, with most contributors choosing to focus on reading a singular text. This section offers entry points into key works often discussed in the field as well as providing vegan readings of lesser known and unexpected texts. The wide range of texts covered across the section as a whole speaks to the amorphous nature of vegan literary studies and is resistant to attempts to construct a cohesive or definitive history of veganism or canon of "vegan texts."

Amy-Leigh Gray and Dana Medoro's chapter on prose texts offers a close reading of the possibilities provided by South Korean novelist Han Kang's *The Vegetarian* (2007) – a work of central concern for vegan literary analysis – of new ways of vegan being. They consider, for instance, how the subtle slippages between body and text, and between self and other, in the protagonist's experience of becoming-vegan sees her seep out of, and refuse to be held by, existing narratives of meat. Stewart Cole's essay establishes poetry as a further way of escaping discursive confinement, elaborating a vegan approach to reading poetry that is attendant to the utopian dimensions of poetic form and the capacity of poetry to acknowledge our shared vulnerability with other life forms. He uses this theorization of vegan reading to examine D. H. Lawrence's ostensibly non-vegan poem "Fish" (1923). While ambivalent in his approach to animals, Lawrence's poem is shown to offer much to vegan readers through its condemnation of the violent anthropocentrism of humankind.

Glenn Willmott's analysis of the graphic novel form takes up Cole's call for vegan readings of ostensibly non-vegan texts and offers subtle points of connection with Gray and Medoro's commentary on the way in which comics conventions seep into Kang's novel. For Willmott, comics represent a form that actively invites vegan reading practices. He walks us through the visual iconography of *Monstress*, a comics serial published from 2015 onwards, in order to articulate the vegan crisis developed through the aesthetic form of its storyworld, demonstrative of the anxieties of entanglement and the possibility of reimagining the divisions drawn between self and other, or human and animal. Christopher Sebastian's chapter also considers the politics of hierarchical categorization of human and non-human animals through his reading of Gregory Maguire's 1995 novel *Wicked*. The novel is an adaptation of L. Frank Baum's *The Wizard of Oz*, and Sebastian reflects on the unconscious vegan sentiments to be found in it and the ways in which literary adaptations and re-writings signal the continual re-working of texts in light of changing social and political landscapes.

Nicole Seymour considers a range of forms of vegan satire: from the satirical treatment of vegans as humorless killjoys to vegan satires of non-vegans and the self-satirization of veganism by individual vegans. The first half of her short essay considers a range of contemporary forms – including comedy sketches, memes, television shows, satiric news stories, and cookbooks – to consider the various affects of these satirical modes. The second half turns to a close reading of Olga Tokarczuk's *Drive your Plow Over the Bones of the Dead* (2009), a haunting novel by the Polish Nobel laureate author that is read as a provocative reflection on the role of the seemingly opposing affects of irony and pathos for the novel's elderly female protagonist and her traumatic encounters with human violence against nonhuman animals.

Jovian Parry considers Octavia Butler's *Xenogenesis* trilogy (1987–1989) as an example of speculative fiction that speaks to the complex politics of consumption and multispecies entanglements. Reading Butler in relation to the evolutionary theory of symbiogenesis, a theory that, in Donna Haraway's analysis, fundamentally troubles our sense of self as an autonomous subject, Parry forcefully counters Haraway's objection to veganism. He uses his symbiogenetic reading of Butler to enact a multispecies utopianism that does not shy away from the difficulties, complexities, and insufficiencies of a vegan positionality. John Miller similarly explores the difficulties and complexities of veganism through his reading of the relationship between cultured meat and utopianism. Turning to possibly the first literary representation of cultured meat, as found in Mary E. Bradley Lane's *Mizora* (serialized from 1880–1881), Miller considers the utopian promises and pitfalls of visions of a technologically mediated future without meat. In *Mizora*, for instance, the environmental benefits and utopian geography of Lane's feminist utopia conflict with a pernicious eugenic undercurrent that relies on the elimination of both nonhuman animals and undesirably raced bodies. For Miller, "The relationship between vegan literary studies and the history of meat technology seems likely to remain an informatively awkward one" (285) that requires ongoing debate and a refusal to shy away from the complexity of the issues at stake.

Josh Milburn invests in philosophical essays as a further way to grapple with complex ethical issues. His chapter opens by asking what it means to read philosophical texts *as* literature. By way of considering this question he turns to the work of Peter Singer, a philosopher of animal ethics who has had a significant influence within the field of vegan literary studies. Drawing on his disciplinary training in analytic philosophy, Milburn provides his own form of philosophical essay to make clear the limitations of mistaking philosophical argumentation for literary fiction, while accounting for the reciprocal exchange of ideas between fiction and philosophy.

Sangamithra Iyer's and Samantha Pergadia's essays consider the entanglement of fiction and reality in discourses around meat. Iyer turns to the meat exposé genre, exploring four texts: two written by omnivores – Michael Pollan's *The Omnivore's Dilemma* (2006) and Jonathan Safran Foer's *Eating Animals* (2009) – and two lesser known works by vegan writers interested in the stakes of bearing witness to violence: Timothy Pachirat's *Every Twelve Seconds: Industrialized Slaughter and the Politics of Sight* (2011) and Kathryn Gillespie's *The Cow with Ear Tag #1389* (2018). In exploring what it means to refuse to look at what one does not want to see, the essay itself functions as a form of exposé, drawing attention to the documented racism, homophobia, and misogyny of the agricultural hero of Pollan's narrative, Joel Salatan, and exposing the fictions of Foer's narrative through revelations gained through Iyer's personal connection to the anonymous animal rights activist "C" depicted in *Eating Animals*. Critical of the construction and fabrication of reality in Foer's work, Iyer sees fictional inventions divorced from the reality of animal activism as a missed opportunity to explore interconnected struggles for justice. Pergadia's essay considers, by contrast, the reciprocity between fiction and the real. Pergadia asks about the political demands made by realist fiction, in regards to the politics of eating, by looking at Ruth Ozeki's *My Year of Meats* (1998) and noting the novel's self-conscious refusal to neatly separate fiction from reality, or the literary from the political. Her reading of Ozeki's novel makes clear the importance of fiction as an intervention into the real, a means of recognizing both the structural violences and unequal systems of access that must be considered as part of an intersectional vegan politics.

The intersectional politics of veganism are also at stake in Armin Langer's essay. Langer focuses on A. Breeze Harper's *Sistah Vegan* project to elaborate "the power of memoir in deconstructing racialized ideas of veganism" (251). Langer elaborates the value of the diversity of vegan voices on display in the volume, complicating any simplified definitions of veganism and ensuring that veganism is invested in working towards intersectional justice for both human and nonhuman animals. As a collection of autobiographical essays, *Sistah Vegan* is seen to offer an important feminist revaluation of personal experience over rational abstraction.

Ali Ryland's essay is also invested in the project of feminist revaluation: seeking to rehabilitate Young Adult (YA) fiction from its relegation outside of the remit of "serious" literature. She considers the significant parallels to be drawn between veganism and YA fiction through the lens of contemporary queer theory, with both adolescents and vegans occupying liminal positions in society and proposing radical challenges to institutionalized norms. Ryland offers a reading of the vegan vampires of Blair Richmond's *Lithia* trilogy (2011–2014) to demonstrate that neither veganism nor YA are de facto queer or radical, with the former conforming to troublingly conservative iterations of the genre. However, Peter Dickenson's *Eva* (1988) is seen to fulfill YA's potential as a vegan medium, offering a radical rejection of normative models of rationality and maturity in order to advance interspecies identification and empathy.

Part III: Textual Histories and Contexts

Part III offers an expanded sense of the literary to consider the broader textual histories of veganism. While literary studies traditionally focuses its attentions on classic literary forms – novels, short stories, and poetry, for instance – the essays collected here demonstrate both the value of looking beyond these forms to ephemeral materials and historical texts – including newspaper articles, magazines, advertisements, and cookbooks – and the need to consider the broader climates of publication that come to shape the circulation of vegan texts.

A considerable temporal jump is enacted across these chapters: from ancient religious texts to the contemporary publishing industry. This volume is rooted in modern literature, primarily from the eighteenth century onwards, a period which witnessed a dramatic shift in Western reading habits and literary production. As such, there is little provided here for those interested in the resonances of veganism as found in the Middle Ages or Early Modern period, though this is not to say that such periods don't offer much of interest for the vegan scholar (as Erica Fudge's book on early modern cow ownership so amply demonstrates, for instance). Instead, we trace here the textual histories of direct relevance to developments in modern literature.

Lisa Kemmerer's expansive essay offers an introduction to the consideration of animal ethics and veganism as found in the five major world religions – Hinduism, Buddhism, Judaism, Christianity, and Islam – and is included in this history of modern literary veganism given the considerable and continued far-reaching impact of religious writings across modern world literatures. Focusing on specific sections of ancient texts and scripture that offer perhaps surprisingly vegan teachings to their practitioners, Kemmerer's work demonstrates that ancient texts have much to teach us about the pre-history of modern veganism as well as stressing the benefits of returning to ancient texts when considering religious approaches to nonhuman animals.

Gregory James's chapter on long nineteenth-century ephemera focuses on the concrete evidence of vegetarian and vegan thought in printed materials of the long nineteenth century. Focused on the US and UK, James offers an encyclopedic history of the physical traces of debates around what vegetarians were to eat and wear, and offers an analysis of anti-vegetarian satires and their role in shaping public perception of those abstaining from meat. The chapter thus provides a textual history of vegetarianism and veganism in print, not just among Vegetarian Society publications but in the wider press and associated movements. If vegetarianism and veganism rarely appeared in literary works of the nineteenth century, James demonstrates that they nonetheless sparked vocal debates and discussions in both the mainstream and vegetarian press.

Corey Lee Wrenn continues James's analysis of the literary traces of vegetarianism and veganism into the mid- to late twentieth century. She turns specifically to the productions of the official Vegan Society, looking at early issues of *The Vegan* and *Food, Home and Garden* magazines, among other literary productions across the UK and US. Wrenn makes clear that the textual legacies of The Vegan Society provide a necessary supplement to the study of more conventional literary texts, demonstrating the significance of literary production in the early days of the society, in which "its literary efforts were its primary emphasis for the purposes of conceptualizing and advancing veganism" (334). She demonstrates, for instance, the importance of such publications in sustaining group solidarity and in promoting and spreading vegan principles. Aligning herself with social movement history, Wrenn reflects too on contemporary shifts away from printed material towards online activism.

Martin Rowe draws on his experiences as co-founder of Lantern Books, a publisher invested in making room for vegan and animal advocacy texts. Rowe traces the surprising alignments between book publishing and veganism, as dual movements that have both been commercialized, commodified, and depoliticized. His chapter gives a behind-the-scenes look into what it means to be a vegan publisher in a climate of deep uncertainty for independent and academic book publishers. Through a reading of his own experience publishing *Sistah Vegan*, Rowe explores the way in which the publishing industry, and its domination by multinational conglomerates, can contribute to gatekeeping of veganism, preventing access to "an infinitely rich universe of veganisms" (254). He concludes with accounts from numerous other independent vegan publishers, including representatives of Sanctuary Press, Faunary Press, Vegan Publishers, Ashland Creek Press, Vegetarian Resource Group, and Book Publishing Company, with each reflecting on their experience of the publishing industry, and the difficulties of publishing both fictional and non-fictional vegan texts.

Note

1. For comprehensive summaries of how veganism intersects with queer theory, posthumanism, and other theoretical fields, the reader might turn instead to Laura Wright's *The Routledge Handbook of Vegan Studies* (2021).

Works Cited

Adams, Carol J. *The Sexual Politics of Meat: A Feminist-Vegetarian Critical Theory*. Polity Press, 1990.
Crowson, Isaac. "Dr Doolally. 'Woke' University Doctors Call for New Laws to Protect Animals from HATE SPEECH." *The Sun*, 17 June 2021.
Francione, Gary. *Why Veganism Matters: The Moral Value of Animals*. Columbia UP, 2021.
Fudge, Erica. *Quick Cattle and Dying Wishes: People and their Animals in Early Modern England*. Cornell UP, 2018.
Giraud, Eva Haifa. "Veganism as Affirmative Biopolitics: Moving Towards a Posthumanist Ethics?" *PhaenEx*, vol. 8, no. 2, 2013, pp. 47–79.
—. *Veganism: Politics, Practice and Theory*. Bloomsbury, 2021.
Good Food Institute. "U.S. retail market data for the plant-based industry." 2021.
Hamilton, C. Lou. *Veganism, Sex, and Politics: Tales of Danger and Pleasure*. Hammer/On, 2019.
Hanganu-Bresch, Cristina, and Kristin Kondrlik (eds). *Veg(etari)an Arguments in Culture, History, and Practice: The V Word*. Palgrave Macmillan, 2021.
Haraway, Donna. *When Species Meet*. U of Minnesota P, 2008.
Harper, A. Breeze. *Sistah Vegan: Black Female Vegans Speak on Food, Identity, Health, and Society*. Lantern Books, 2010.
Mwangi, Evan Maina. *The Postcolonial Animal: African Literature and Posthuman Ethics*. U of Michigan P, 2019.
Oliver, Catherine. *Veganism, Archives, and Animals: Geographies of a Multispecies World*. Routledge, 2021.
Potts, Annie, and Jovian Parry. "Vegan Sexuality: Challenging Heteronormative Masculinity through Meat-Free Sex." *Feminism & Psychology*, vol. 20, no. 1, 2010, pp. 53–72.
Quinn, Emelia. *Reading Veganism: The Monstrous Vegan, 1818 to Present*. Oxford UP, 2021.
Quinn, Emelia, and Benjamin Westwood. "Introduction." *Thinking Veganism in Literature and Culture: Towards a Vegan Theory*, edited by Emelia Quinn and Benjamin Westwood, Palgrave Macmillan, 2018, pp. 1–24.
Schuster, Joshua. "The Vegan and the Sovereign." *Critical Perspectives on Veganism*, edited by Jodey Castricano and Rasmus Rahbek Simonsen, Palgrave Macmillan, 2016, pp. 203–22.
Starkey, David. "See, the conqu'ring hero comes – to be ridiculed by vegans." *The Critic*, January/February 2021.
Varian, Ethan. "It's Called 'Plant-Based,' Look it up." *New York Times*, 28 December 2019.
Vegan Life. "Veganism Booms by 350%." *Vegan Life Magazine*, 18 May 2016.
Vegan Society. "Changing Diets during the COVID-19 Pandemic." *The Vegan Society*, May 2021.

Vint, Sherryl. *Animal Alterity: Science Fiction and the Question of the Animal.* Liverpool UP, 2013.
Wrenn, Corey Lee. *Animals in Irish Society: Interspecies Oppression and Vegan Liberation in Britain's First Colony.* SUNY Press, 2021.
Wright, Laura. "Doing Vegan Studies: An Introduction." *Through a Vegan Studies Lens: Textual Ethics and Lived Activism*, edited by Laura Wright, U of Nevada P, 2019, pp. vii–xxiv.
—. *The Vegan Studies Project: Food, Animals, and Gender in the Age of Terror.* U of Georgia P, 2015.
—. (ed.). *The Routledge Handbook of Vegan Studies.* Routledge, 2021.

Annotated Bibliography

Emelia Quinn and Laura Wright

VEGAN STUDIES AND vegan theory are fields of direct and urgent relevance to the present moment. And, as established in the introduction to this collection, work within these emergent areas of study is growing at a rapid rate. This annotated bibliography collects together the key works that make up vegan studies, providing the reader with concise summaries of major works in the field to date. While not an exhaustive survey of available materials, this annotated bibliography constructs a constellation of texts that exemplify and form the groundwork of the emergent discipline of vegan studies.

Vegan studies draws on the interdisciplinary insights of many fields, most notably those of animal studies, critical animal studies, ecofeminism, posthumanism, food studies, and moral philosophy.[1] However, providing comprehensive overviews of these fields is beyond the scope of this chapter. It is therefore with regret that the bibliography that follows does not include explicit reference to: foundational works of animal rights, ethics, and philosophy (as, for instance, that by Mary Midgley, Tom Regan, and Peter Singer); influential works of ecofeminism (including by Josephine Donovan, Greta Gaard, Lori Gruen, pattrice jones, Marti Kheel, Val Plumwood, and Karen Warren); related work in ecocriticism (including key works by Lawrence Buell, Graham Huggan and Helen Tiffin, Bruno Latour, Joseph Meeker, and Timothy Morton); Continental philosophy that has had a significant impact on vegan theoretical work (most notably the work of Jacques Derrida as well as later work by Matthew Calarco); works of posthumanist philosophy engaged with by many vegan theory scholars (such as by Donna Haraway and Cary Wolfe); work across literary animal studies (such as by Philip Armstrong, Erica Fudge, Anat Pick, Nicole Shukin, Tom Tyler, and Kari Weil); or intersectional work on animal liberation and interspecies justice (such as by Sunaura Taylor and Dinesh Wadiwel). Such work has undoubtedly been influential in the development of vegan studies and readers are encouraged to turn to the above authors and to explore further the rich fields from which they draw. However, we have chosen to focus here on texts that either explicitly situate themselves within the field of vegan studies or focus explicitly on veganism in order to establish vegan studies as a field in its own right, even as it draws on and contributes to existing fields of study.

The annotated bibliography that follows is divided into five key sections: texts specifically geared towards literary analysis, establishing the nascent field of vegan literary studies; works within the broader field of vegan studies; the wide array of work published in the past few years on meat and meat cultures; historical overviews of vegetarian and vegan identities; and an unannotated list of journal articles published in vegan studies, broadly conceived. While much of the work collected here is primarily rooted in European and North American academies, veganism, as identity and lived practice, comes to mean different things for different people beyond these contexts. We hope therefore that the cautious attempt to formalize the key texts of vegan studies is a useful one at this stage in the development of the field, providing scholars with a readily accessible range of texts that draw attention to the main concerns and issues in vegan literary studies and functioning as a springboard for those looking to pursue vegan studies in their own work.

Vegan Literary Studies

We discuss here books and edited collections that are specifically geared towards vegan literary study. This section is currently limited to only a handful of texts, in contrast to the numerous texts published within the related field of literary animal studies. The majority of vegan literary studies work has, to date, been found within broader interdisciplinary edited collections. We hope the present volume encourages further book-length literary studies that draw on the creative potentiality of literature to explore and complicate our understanding of veganism.

Adams, Carol J. The Sexual Politics of Meat: A Feminist-Vegetarian Critical Theory. *1990, Bloomsbury Academic, 2015.*

The Sexual Politics of Meat is a field-defining text of significant influence for vegan scholars. In this text Adams puts forward her concept of the "absent referent," a way of reading and re-membering nonhuman animals that has been central to work in the field of vegan literary studies. For Adams, the absent referent refers to the way in which the real, embodied presence of animals is negated literally (through meat-eating), definitionally (as in referring to "veal" or "meat" rather than dead animals), and metaphorically (in which the animal gains meaning only by reference to something else). The absent referent is the connective tissue linking the oppression of women and nonhuman animals within patriarchal, meat-eating cultures, and Adams encourages feminist-vegetarian reading practices that re-member these oppressed bodies. Other influential terms coined in Adams's text include "feminized proteins" to refer to eggs and dairy. In addition, Adams offers close readings of canonical literary texts, demonstrating the neglected vegetarian histories to be found in works such as Mary Shelley's *Frankenstein* and revealing the historical links between vegetarianism and feminist resistance to patriarchal culture. While Adams focuses on the politics of meat-eating and its relation to dismembered animal bodies, veganism is of central significance to her theory. Establishing *The Sexual Politics* as "truly a feminist-vegan critical theory" (63), the absence of veganism from the bulk of the text is proposed as a logistical matter due to veganism's relative lexical incomprehensibility at the time of writing and Adams's reluctance to anachronistically attribute a contemporary term to the historical texts under evaluation. Chapter 7 of *The Sexual Politics*, "Feminism, the Great War, and Modern Vegetarianism," is reprinted in this volume, as Chapter 1, "Veganism and Women's Writing."

Mwangi, Evan Maina. The Postcolonial Animal: African Literature and Posthuman Ethics. *U of Michigan P, 2019.*

Disrupting the white, Western bias found in much mainstream animal studies work, Mwangi's *The Postcolonial Animal* concerns itself with the possibilities and potentialities of non-exploitative relationships with nonhuman animals as found in works of postcolonial African fiction. From a consideration of well-known figures such as Chinua Achebe and former Kenyan Prime Minister Jomo Kenyatta to lesser known African authors, such as Yuda Komora, Mwangi's work offers an important disruption to Eurocentric animal rights discourses. Postcolonial animal studies is presented as an intersectional mode of critique that draws on posthuman philosophy in order to address the biases of both mainstream animal studies and postcolonial criticism without minimizing the central concern of either discipline. For Mwangi: "postcolonial critics should condemn any efforts to achieve the rights of one group at the expense of those in any of the other groups" (10), whether categories of race, gender, sexuality, or species. Mwangi asserts a clear and distinct vegan perspective but one that is cautious in its application of the term "vegan" to African contexts, as there is no correlative for the term in any African language. For Mwangi, the job of vegan literary criticism is not to condemn or ignore those works that only partially fulfill vegan ideals. Instead, he looks at texts that present a "vegan unconscious," defined as an "affirmative expression of potential . . . a latent possibility that the societies portrayed in the text will embrace a future where animals will not be killed to satisfy human needs" (9). Mwangi's vegan literary approach to postcolonial African criticism is thus one invested in the conception of becoming-vegan as "aspirational, a process rather than an end in itself" (11).

Quinn, Emelia. Reading Veganism: The Monstrous Vegan, 1818 to Present. *Oxford UP, 2021.*

Quinn's work provides new ways of reading a variety of canonical texts ranging across two centuries and multiple locations – Britain, Canada, and South Africa. Quinn's conception and establishment of vegan theory offers an academic lens through which to (re)examine literary texts, and serves to establish a clear roadmap for scholars interested in applying such a theoretical lens to their own scholarship. For Quinn, the monstrous vegan offers a means of reconceiving vegan identity as a state of strategic insufficiency: a mode of being that dwells with feelings of insufficiency, failure, and complicity while remaining invested in utopian visions of a future without harm. Beginning her study with Mary Shelley's *Frankenstein*, Quinn traces the iteration of what she terms "the monstrous vegan" through the work of H. G. Wells, Margaret Atwood, J. M. Coetzee, and Alan Hollinghurst. Quinn describes the monstrous vegan as a being defined by four traits – they do not eat animals, a characteristic that inspires anxiety in others; they are hybrid creatures, amalgamations of human and animal parts; they are not generated via heterosexual procreative acts; and they are intimately connected to acts of writing. This allows her to intersect queer and vegan theoretical readings of these authors' works. While Part I of the book traces a historical trajectory of iterations of the monstrous vegan figure, Part II considers reparative modes of reading that seek to rehabilitate the monstrous vegan through performance and camp aesthetics.

Quinn, Emelia, and Benjamin Westwood (eds). Thinking Veganism in Literature and Culture: Towards a Vegan Theory. *Palgrave Macmillan, 2018.*

Quinn and Westwood's edited collection is the product of the *Towards a Vegan Theory* conference they organized and hosted at the University of Oxford in May 2016, during which many of the scholars included in the collection worked to establish "what kind of place veganism and/or 'the vegan' should occupy in our theorizations of human–animal relations, animal studies, and the humanities in general" (1). In their introduction to the volume, Quinn and Westwood assert that they want to

> position this collection of essays as one not only about veganism, but about individual vegans; a project, then, concerned with the social and conceptual coherency of veganism, as well as with questions of self-definition and self-representation. Do we define veganism as an ethical principle, a set of practices, an identity, a "form of life?" To "think through veganism" . . . would therefore mean to cast a critical eye on the concept as such, and to conceive vegan practices as subject positions from which to think. (2)

The collection is comprised of four sections, each of which is concerned with engaging with veganism as a mode of viewing and understanding the world: "Politics," "Visual Culture," "Literature," and "Definitions." Essays include Laura Wright's consideration of how the US might find itself in an interregnum moment with regard to issues of race, politics, diet, and gender; Robert McKay's theorization of veganism via Wittgenstein as a "form of life"; and Anat Pick's theorization of vegan cinema. The "Literature" section includes Quinn's essay on vegan monstrosity in Margaret Atwood's *MaddAddam* trilogy, and Westwood's consideration of refusal as central to a vegan mode of existence through readings of Herman Melville's "Bartleby, the Scrivener," Franz Kafka's "A Hunger Artist," and Han Kang's *The Vegetarian*.

Wright, Laura. The Vegan Studies Project: Food, Animals, and Gender in the Age of Terror. *U of Georgia P, 2015.*

Wright's 2015 *The Vegan Studies Project* was the first academic monograph in the humanities to focus on veganism as an object study in its own right. The "project" of the title signals the experimental and, in Wright's terms, somewhat playful attempt to establish what it might mean to consider veganism as a subject of inquiry to be "explored, understood, and challenged" (1). The introduction to the book offers a foundational outline of the scope of vegan studies as a disciplinary field, considering both its intersections with and divergences from existing fields such as animal studies, critical animal studies, posthumanism, and ecofeminism. What follows is a consideration of vegan representation in the literature, as well as film, television, advertising, and print and online media, of the US in the decades preceding and immediately after the events of 9/11. Authors considered include Margaret Atwood, Cormac McCarthy, and Stephanie Meyer. Wright argues that the post-9/11 period marked a shift in vegan representation, triggering a widespread backlash against the perceived threat of veganism to a distinct racialized and gendered conception of American identity. Her close readings draw attention to the subsequent emergence of various vegan representational strategies in the mainstream Western imagination, from vegan vampires to vegan zombies, filicidal vegan mothers, ultra-masculine "hegans," and celebrity vegans. Significant attention is paid also to the imbrication of veganism with discourses of disordered eating and the female body. Her analysis offers an interdisciplinary cultural studies approach to understanding and deconstructing vegan representation in mainstream US culture that foregrounds the value of literary analysis as a methodological approach. The book lays the groundwork for the development of a vegan literary studies field that functions to "disrupt the presentation of a homogeneous notion of what it means to be vegan" (23).

Wright, Laura (ed.). Through a Vegan Studies Lens: Textual Ethics and Lived Activism. *U of Nevada P, 2019.*

This edited volume establishes veganism as a means by which to recognize enmeshed oppressions, with contributors drawing on postcolonial and ecofeminist theory to expand our understanding of veganism. The essays are offered as an opportunity to do theory *differently*, drawing on lived animal rights activism. The chapters are focused primarily on contemporary world literature, analyzing a range of new genres and forms of interest for vegan literary studies, including: Kathryn Kirkpatrick's examination of locavore literature, as epitomized by Michael Pollan's *The Omnivore's Dilemma*, Barbara Kingsolver's *Animal, Vegetable, Miracle*, and Noelle Carpenter's *Farm City*; John Yunker's elaboration of new environmental literature that is supportive of veganism, such as that published by Ashland Creek Press; Alex Lockwood's critique of new nature writing, such as Helen McDonald's *H is for Hawk* and Charles Foster's *Being a Beast*, for reinforcing existing structures of anthropocentric oppression; and Christopher Kocela's essay on "Buddhaphobic" novels, including Richard Powers's *The Echo Maker* and Jonathan Franzen's *Purity*, that posit a highly restrictive and socially alienating form of Buddhism as the undesirable but inevitable outcome of veganism. In addition to the primarily literary focus, other essays consider broader cultural shifts, including Carol J. Adams's chapter on the sexual politics of meat during the Trump era.

Vegan Studies

This section turns to books and edited collections situated within the broader interdisciplinary field of vegan studies. We include here both work that constitutes the study *of* veganism, as well as several academic works focused on arguing *for* veganism. This list comprises an interdisciplinary range of texts, though it is perhaps inevitably skewed towards our own humanities perspectives and our positions in the Anglophone academy. Further important work is to be found beyond the humanities such as in economics, politics, and law. We acknowledge that this list will inevitably be incomplete but hope that it nonetheless provides a helpful starting point in the collation of existing work in the field.

Brueck, Julia Feliz (ed.). Veganism in an Oppressive World: A Vegans-of-Color Community Project. *Sanctuary Publishers, 2017.*

This volume gives voice to a diverse range of vegans-of-color and is rooted in concrete practices of activism that work towards intersectional justice. Bringing together artists, activists, and scholars from a range of national, ethnic, and religious backgrounds, the collection puts forward an understanding of veganism that is focused on developing a consistent stance of anti-oppression that is actively intersectional in its practices. The collection as a whole is accessible beyond an academic context, targeted at the education of white vegans and animal rights activists, making clear the need to consistently support anti-oppression and to make room for vegans-of-color in order to avoid reducing veganism to a single-issue movement. The volume situates veganism as part of a broader justice movement that seeks to alleviate both human and nonhuman animal oppression. Rather than traditional essay forms, contributors offer a range of creative responses in articulating their own lived activist experiences of veganism, including poems, personal reflections, and multi-vocal interviews.

Brueck, Julia Feliz (ed.). Veganism of Color: Decentring Whiteness in Human and Nonhuman Liberation. *Sanctuary Publishers, 2019.*

Building on *Veganism in an Oppressive World*, this second collection from Brueck further illuminates the perspectives of vegans-of-color from a range of different national, racial, and religious contexts. This collection centers ongoing conversations across a diversity of oppressed communities, encouraging the forging of connections in their struggles for liberation. Connecting each contribution is the imperative to decenter whiteness in the vegan movement, critiqued as a form of white supremacy that fails to represent the voices and experiences of vegans-of-color. In the process, the volume advances a "veganism of colour" which situates veganism beyond a single-issue movement and roots it within broader anti-oppressive movements. The contributions develop intersectional social justice work and activism that challenges the ingrained racism of vegan and animal rights movements.

Castricano, Jodey, and Rasmus R. Simonsen (eds). Critical Perspectives on Veganism. *Palgrave Macmillan, 2016.*

This collection takes an interdisciplinary approach to consider the "ethics, politics, and aesthetics of veganism in contemporary culture and thought" (1). The foreword framing the volume as a whole, provided by Melanie Joy and Jens Tuider, establishes the overarching approach of the collection, with numerous chapters centering Joy's concept of "carnism" as a key concept to be challenged and unpacked in their analysis. Aiming for a more global perspective than that offered by other work in vegan studies, the volume takes a largely cultural studies approach, considering the impact and relevance of the role of sound art, visual art, literary texts, vegan cookbooks, mainstream television programming, celebrity chefs, and food blogs on the rise of veganism and its representation in contemporary culture. The challenges and risks of veganism's emergence into the mainstream are also considered, with two separate chapters, for instance, on the controversy surrounding vegan blog and cookbook *Thug Kitchen* and its implications for the whiteness associated with Western veganism. Literary texts are considered as part of the "Aesthetics and Representation" section, including Parag Kumar Deka's chapter on J. M. Coetzee's work and Joshua Schuster's essay on Philip K. Dick's *Do Androids Dream of Electric Sheep?*

Giraud, Eva Haifa. Veganism: Politics, Practice, and Theory. *Bloomsbury, 2021.*

Giraud's book draws on the methodological tools of media and cultural studies to demonstrate that veganism is more than just a diet. The text provides the most comprehensive assessment of the state of the field of vegan studies published to date, bringing together key issues and debates and constructing a broad picture of vegan studies that includes related work across critical animal studies, human–animal studies, sociology, and food studies. Therefore, her introductory chapters provide an invaluable outline of the state of the field. In later chapters, Giraud grapples with the vexed critical arguments surrounding veganism, including questions of activist tactics, anthropomorphism, intersectionality, and the contemporary popularization of veganism and its association with what she terms "plant-based capitalism." Taking popular culture seriously, the book illuminates existing debates in and around vegan studies with examples drawn primarily from British media and culture, as well as qualitative interviews with long-term vegans in the UK, in order to establish a "picture of veganism as something that is more multifaceted and complex than is often recognized in certain academic contexts or within mainstream media depictions" (2).

Hamilton, C. Lou. Veganism, Sex and Politics: Tales of Danger and Pleasure. *Hammer/On, 2019.*

A work of autotheory, Hamilton's book blends memoir with theoretical reflections and critical engagement with scholarly work. Her accessible mode of storytelling serves as an introduction to the pleasures and pains of living a vegan life. Hamilton details a mode of contextual ethical veganism that is driven by her queer and feminist commitments. For Hamilton this means moving away from an analytical rights-based tradition, or the universalist position of scholars such as Gary Francione, in order to recognize veganism as "a contextual and ever-changing practice, an aspiration rather than a moral absolute, an ongoing process of questioning one's place in the world rather than a secure sense of self" (14). The book offers a substantial and necessary critique of existing work in veganism, such as the anti-pornography stance Hamilton observes in Carol J. Adams's *The Sexual Politics of Meat*. Drawing primarily from British and North American material, Hamilton combines personal experiences with an analysis of cultural trends, to disrupt any easy or simplified model of what veganism is or can do. She draws out the problematic associations of an intersectional veganism that uncritically equates different forms of oppression and offers a multitude of ways of thinking differently about human relationships and entanglements with other animals. In the process she dismantles veganism's association with moral purity, positioning it in relation to radical queer and feminist subcultures in order to stress the joys and pleasures that can accompany an ethical vegan life.

Hanganu-Bresch, Cristina, and Kristin Kondrlik (eds). Veg(etari)an Arguments in Culture, History, and Practice: The V Word. *Palgrave Macmillan, 2021.*

This volume demonstrates the contribution to be made to vegan studies by rhetorical analysis. Using the term "veg(etari)anism" to capture the commonalities and shared histories of vegetarianism and veganism while resisting a conflation of the two movements, Hanganu-Bresch and Kondrlik posit veg(etari)anism as a social practice that "engenders discursive tensions related to its legitimacy" (xx). The volume therefore explores the rhetorical arguments used to legitimize, or delegitimize, veg(etari)anism in modern and contemporary culture. The chapters offer a global perspective, moving beyond the predominant focus on the US and UK in existing vegan studies work to consider the politics of veganism as they manifest in the meatlessness of fascist Italy, modern and contemporary Middle Eastern and North African Islamic cultures, contemporary Israeli politics, and postsocialist Serbia. The methodological focus on rhetorical strategies means that analyses are performed primarily on popular culture, including internet discussion boards, newspaper articles, and documentary films. Consideration of literary rhetoricity is also provided through Molly Mann's chapter on Djuna Barnes's *Nightwood* and Oren Abeles and Emma Lozon's chapter on Jonathan Safran Foer's *Eating Animals*. Other contributions elaborate veganism's intersectional relationships to anti-racism, anti-imperialism, and anti-sexism and offer reflections on the embodied experiences and entanglements that shift our rhetorical understanding of vegetarianism and the rhetoricity of the body.

Harper, A. Breeze (ed.). Sistah Vegan: Black Female Vegans Speak on Food, Identity, Health, and Society. *Lantern Books, 2010.*

This volume disrupts the common assumption of veganism as a white, middle-class lifestyle fad by foregrounding Black female vegan experience. The essays contained within draw on the autobiographical, prioritizing personal experience in order to give voice and visibility to individual Black vegan women's lives. The approaches taken by each contributor combine a reflection on the lived experience of their own veganism and the broader climate of racial inequality and food poverty as experienced by Black communities, primarily in the US. *Sistah Vegan* has been a highly influential text in the emergent field of vegan studies and Armin Langer's chapter in this volume considers *Sistah Vegan* in more depth, reflecting on the memoir form as a means through which to articulate an intersectional veganism that works in the service of decolonizing both the body and mind. Martin Rowe's essay in this volume offers further reflections on the publication and publicizing of *Sistah Vegan*, through his role as chief editor at Lantern Books.

Fox, Michael Allen. Deep Vegetarianism. *Temple UP, 1999.*

Michael Allen Fox's *Deep Vegetarianism*, while resisting veganism because of a supposed dearth of adequate nutritional studies at the time of writing, promotes vegetarianism as "helping to shape a way of life and to effect a shift in conscious awareness" (xix). Fox enacts a philosophical consideration of vegetarianism as a way of life and considers arguments in favor of vegetarianism alongside common rhetorical arguments against vegetarian diets. While infrequently cited in vegan studies, particularly in comparison to many of the other works noted in this annotated bibliography, Fox's book is an early example of vegan studies and theory, providing close, critical attention to vegetarianism and veganism as embodied modes of being-in-the-world.

Francione, Gary. Why Veganism Matters: The Moral Value of Animals. *Columbia UP, 2021.*

Francione is an often controversial and divisive figure in vegan circles, taking an absolutist stance on veganism as a moral baseline position. His abolitionist approach to veganism frequently takes aim at the work of those who are not vegan for their perceived ethical failings. In *Why Veganism Matters*, Francione forcefully asserts that if one believes that animals matter morally, then one has an obligation to be vegan. The book makes clear from the outset that the belief in the moral worth of animals is a prerequisite for reading the book, which aims to convert those already sympathetic to animal rights causes to veganism. What follows is an argument in favor of veganism that is built upon rational argumentation and situated in the tradition of analytic philosophy.

Ko, Aph, and Syl Ko. Aphro-ism: Essays on Pop Culture, Feminism, and Black Veganism from Two Sisters. *Lantern Books, 2017.*

This co-authored book by the Ko sisters emerges from their "Aphro-ism" website, launched in 2015, in which the sisters garnered much critical attention for their incisive blogging about their views on veganism, anti-racism, and feminism, and the interrelation of such "isms." Their eclectic essays represent a dialogue between the two sisters that merges personal reflection and activist commitments with cultural analysis and political commentary. Their predominantly US focus sees them broach a range of topics, from raising issues about the ways in which #blacklivesmatter and diversity initiatives risk reducing Black lives to only biological life, to considering debates in the Black community regarding the media response to the shooting of Cecil the Lion, and the value of confusion as a starting point for decolonizing knowledge and envisioning alternatives to the current system. Throughout the book they resist the problematic and reductive comparison of Black and animal oppression while insisting on the importance of thinking about a shared discourse of animality, the intertwined nature of binaries of White and Black, and human and animal, and the need to reclaim both blackness and animality. For the Ko sisters, Black veganism is about more than just being Black and vegan, and the book represents a process of ongoing thought and discussion that considers just what veganism has to do with race. Alongside the work of A. Breeze Harper (who provides the foreword to the text), *Aphro-ism* represents a key text in the growing body of work developing an anti-racist model of intersectional Black veganism.

Ko, Aph. Racism as Zoological Witchcraft: A Guide to Getting Out. *Lantern Books, 2020.*

In *Racism as Zoological Witchcraft*, Ko has written an accessible argument rooted in theory. In her argument for what she calls "epistemic ruptures," Ko offers a treatise against making current activist movements merge, arguing instead that our conception of "the animal," as a label for consumable and disposable bodies, is tied to the legacy of racism that operates by virtue of zoological, white supremacist witchcraft. Using examples from popular culture – including Jordan Peele's 2017 film *Get Out* – Ko examines the tension that exists between contemporary anti-racism and animal rights movements and argues for an examination of "raw" oppressions that can move the conversation beyond modern-day liberation movements in ways that intersectionality has been unable to do.

Linzey, Andrew, and Clair Linzey (eds). Ethical Vegetarianism and Veganism. *Routledge, 2019.*

Andrew and Clair Linzey's book is focused on how arguments in animal ethics and philosophical and theological debate about the rights of animals can support a move to vegetarian and vegan diets. The expansive volume of twenty-five chapters develops a three-part argument in favor of ethical veganism: moral arguments against the unnecessary killing of animals; arguments for the immorality of cruelty and violence; and arguments about the human and environmental costs of meat-eating. The volume as a whole offers an impassioned promotion of vegetarianism and veganism, elaborating the ethical imperative to give up meat. While the moral imperative of vegetarianism and veganism is stressed, contributors generally shy away from the moral baseline stance of Gary Francione's vegan ethics, noted above. The ambition is to promote and encourage vegan and vegetarian transitions among those interested in humanitarian and environmental concerns, presenting vegans to the reader as "moral pioneers" (12) with a role to play in future change for animals.

Oliver, Catherine. Veganism, Archives, and Animals: Geographies of a Multispecies World. *Routledge, 2021.*

Situating herself within the work of beyond-human or more-than-human geographies, Oliver takes veganism seriously as a way to forge a multispecies geography. Her book's geographical focus considers what effects a fluid but embodied sense of truth, regarding the reality of animal suffering, has on vegan navigations of space. The first half of Oliver's work provides theoretical reflection on the largely uncatalogued and unexplored papers of psychologist and animal rights activist Richard D. Ryder at the British Library, offering a feminist reading of the archives that resituates the importance of women's voices in the emergence of the modern animal rights movement. This charting of vegan activist histories is directed through a feminist revaluation of friendship, and Oliver offers the archive itself, and the archival memory it stores, as a theoretical space of possibility and friendship. The vegan theoretical approach of the work, rather than simply an analysis *of* veganism, is perhaps best epitomized in this theorization of friendship beyond the human as an opening-up to a mode of "thinking about the possibilities of a world beyond [animal pain], where animals are mutual co-constitutors in place and interspecies relationships" (54). Oliver also includes qualitative data from interviews with UK-based vegans and ends with an ethnography of chickens, considering the embodied experiences of the author, and her experiential as well as imaginative constructions of vegan knowledge.

Stephens Griffin, Nathan. Understanding Veganism: Biography and Identity. *Palgrave Macmillan, 2017.*

As a work of biographical research that values the lived experience of individual vegans, Stephens Griffin's book offers an empirical look at the lived experience of vegans through a series of twelve interviews. Taking a "critical biographical approach" to veganism, Stephens Griffin seeks to offer a more complex and nuanced sense of lived vegan identity than that provided by official definitions. Chapters account for individual experiences of veganism that intersect with questions of faith and belief, sexuality, and politics. The focus of his study is on UK veganism, with respondents derived largely from his own connections in British animal advocacy movements. Despite a stated ambition for critical intersectionality, situating the work within the broader political motivations of critical animal studies, the author himself acknowledges, with regret, the study's limited diversity, presenting "a largely white, hetero- and cisnormative picture of veganism" (124). Despite this acknowledged limitation, Stephens Griffin's analysis demonstrates the necessarily fluid nature of vegan identity and offers empirical accounts of the ways in which vegan identity is enacted through embodied performances.

Taylor, Nik, and Richard Twine. The Rise of Critical Animal Studies: From the Margins to the Centre. *Routledge, 2014.*

While not explicitly a vegan studies text, this collection contextualizes veganism within the broader discipline of critical animal studies (CAS). Taylor and Twine's introduction provides a useful introduction to CAS, as an academic discipline that strives to wed academic study with activist commitment. Taylor and Twine make clear that for them, veganism represents only an "ethico-political beginning" to addressing a broader intersectional web of oppressions (12). Intersectionality is key, here, to the critical approach taken. Several essays in the volume reflect in important ways on veganism as an identity category and mode of life. Sara Salih's "Vegans on the Verge of a Nervous Breakdown," for instance, offers an insightful disruption to ideas of veganism as premised on purity and good conscience, weaving personal reflections with theoretical insight to suggest veganism as a site of strategic breakdown. Numerous other chapters that proffer topics of key interest for vegan studies include Matthew Cole's essay on the historical formation of the Vegan Society, and Stephanie Jenkins and Richard Twine's consideration of the limits of food autonomy in relation to vegan praxis.

Wrenn, Corey Lee. Animals in Irish Society: Interspecies Oppression and Vegan Liberation in Britain's First Colony. *SUNY Press, 2021.*

Presenting a "vegan theory of Ireland" (xii), Wrenn's book considers the specificity of animals in an Irish context. Drawing on her sociological background, Wrenn provides a revisionist history of Ireland that positions animals as legitimate social actors. Conceiving of veganism in broad terms, not as a dietary preference but as "a political resistance to speciesism that resists the exploitations and oppression of other animals," Wrenn argues that "a sort of prototypical vegan Irish ethic has shaped Irish society for thousands of years" (7). Wrenn chronicles the shared oppression of human and nonhuman animals in Ireland, particularly under British colonialism, through an intersectional vegan feminist and Marxist theoretical lens. She charts, for instance, the animalization of the Irish under British control and the simultaneous growth of zoos, bloodsports, and pet-keeping. She also charts the development of animal rights in Ireland, drawing attention to forgotten figures of significance for the broader Western animal rights movement and detailing the significance of prominent Irish activists and literary figures, such as George Bernard Shaw. What results is a history of Irish human–animal relations through a vegan studies lens that sees recognition of entangled oppression across species lines as key to future liberation.

Wright, Laura (ed). The Routledge Handbook of Vegan Studies. *Routledge, 2021.*

This comprehensive volume covers an extensive range of disciplines and topics, providing a wide-ranging introduction to the key issues and ideas that have emerged in the formation of vegan studies. Contributors demonstrate the way in which veganism, as identity and lived praxis, is being considered and studied through a range of existing disciplines, including philosophy, law, sociology, psychology, food studies, linguistics, religious studies, media studies, film studies, and geography. A key thematic running throughout the volume is the need to recuperate and value emotional responses, and there is a polemical approach by several contributors that speaks to the sense, noted in chapters such as those by Matthew Cole and Kate Stewart, and Carmen Aguilera-Carnerero and Margarita Carretero-Gonzalez, that mainstream derogations have separated veganism from its powerfully felt ethical commitments. These chapters work to challenge and disrupt the traditions and restrictions of objectivity and dispassionate analysis associated with conventional academic scholarship. *The Routledge Handbook* provides a valuable introduction to the range of ideas and issues that are continuing to be thought through as the field of vegan studies develops. While there are several chapters that offer literary readings, this is not the central focus of the volume, which provides a broad overview of veganism's entry into the humanities and social sciences.

Meat Cultures

This section turns to the wide range of work published on meat cultures. There is a risk here of course of conflating veganism solely with what one eats, a conflation which this volume (along with the work of the vegan studies scholars outlined above) seeks to complicate. However, the growing body of work on meat cultures represents an important facet of contemporary vegan studies. In the words of Seán McCorry and John Miller, "meat critique" seeks "to unpack and to challenge the dominant narratives of meat-eating and conceptions of animals as resources" (2) and enacts a "similarly far-reaching endeavour to vegan studies and a form of critical practice that will . . . necessarily inform dissident perspectives on meat culture" (10). Many of the works detailed here also offer explicit reflections and analyses of veganism.

Bramble, Ben, and Bob Fischer (eds). The Moral Complexities of Eating Meat. *Oxford UP, 2015.*

This volume provides philosophical approaches to the question of meat-eating in our contemporary climate of industrial meat production, offering ethical and philosophical arguments in favor of vegetarian and vegan praxis. While broadly arguing in favor of vegetarian and vegan commitments, the volume offers multiple perspectives, with several chapters arguing for the moral permissibility of meat-eating in specific contexts, advocating, for instance, the consumption of roadkill. However, the primary focus of the volume is on vegetarian arguments, building on existing philosophical arguments in favor of vegetarianism, considering, for instance, questions of consequentialism and inefficacy objections. Particularly worth noting is the final section on possible futures, including a chapter on "Veganism as Aspiration" by Lori Gruen and Robert C. Jones that distinguishes between two ways in which people conceive of veganism: as a lifestyle or identity, and as an aspiration or goal. The former is seen as ineffective because to "ascribe moral purity and clean hands to veganism is to make a category mistake" (156). They offer instead a theorization of an aspirational veganism that, by contrast, has the power to make a difference, forging "a particularly empowering and grounded form of individual political commitment, [and] fostering a deeper understanding of intersecting injustices and oppressions" (169).

Chatterjee, Sushmita, and Banu Subramaniam. Meat!: A Transnational Analysis. *Duke UP, 2021.*

In this highly engaging and provocative collection, contributors consider the interplay of race, empire, gender, and power politics in the conception of "meat." Complicating our understanding of just what meat is, the authors explore meat as a global object that means different things in different contexts. Engaging with ideas from across queer theory, crip theory, and critical race theory, a truly transnational focus is adopted, from the geopolitics of contamination among Indigenous communities in Scandinavia, to contestations around fishing rights in the Arctic, and the history of reindeer herding in Alaska. South Asia is also a focus point, with several essays reflecting on the politics of beef bans and purity in India as a site that presents a specific disruption to Western narratives of vegetarianism and veganism. The introduction calls for vegan studies to engage with more complex transnational framings of meat and bodies that are enacted through caste politics and violence. In presenting the messy entanglements of meat with intersectional political struggles, the volume provides a necessary complication to any easy or simplistic accounts of veganism.

Cohen, Mathilde, and Yoriko Otomo (eds). Making Milk: The Past, Present and Future of Our Primary Food. Bloomsbury Academic, 2017.

This volume contributes a diversity of perspectives on the misogyny and racism of milk cultures, and the role of technology in dramatically shifting our relation to mammalian milk. The essays that make up this lavishly illustrated volume provide timely and important reading, showing us how "milk" has always been a fraught entity, entangled with and often inseparable from our ideas about gender, power, commodification, and cultural identity. The work navigates the nutritive, sociopolitical, cultural, and symbolic status of milk, a food that Melanie Jackson and Esther Leslie refer to as "an ur-substance, an originary substance" (63). In addition to the contribution of Jackson and Leslie, this collection features essays by international scholars and artists from a variety of fields, including law, literature, geography, political aesthetics, communication and media, history, media studies, sociology, art history, economics, and anthropology, all of whom grapple with the fraught and complex social, legal, political, and historical meaning of milk as food, mythological substance, and metaphor. Building on related work in food studies on the histories of milk, there is a strong vegan studies focus to this volume, with several chapters devoted to an examination of plant-based milks and milk futures, and the concluding chapters calling for greater attention to nonhuman animal suffering in our consideration of milk.

Donaldson, Brianne, and Christopher Carter (eds). The Future of Meat without Animals. Rowman and Littlefield, 2016.

This volume considers what a vegan future, or futures, might look like, detailing the paradigm shifts required to imagine what a future world without meat (or milk, cheese, and eggs) might look like. Contributors come from a diverse range of disciplines, and provide social, economic, and political perspectives on what it means to rethink our reliance on animals as the primary source of human food. This future-oriented focus sees a consideration of various creative strategies, whether through culinary innovation or imaginative over-conformity to existing meat-based narratives. The list of contributors includes prominent names in animal studies, including Carol J. Adams and Matthew Calarco, as well as giving voice to those directly involved in plant-based industries, with contributions by artisan vegan cheesemaker Miyoko Schinner, and Ethan Brown, CEO of Beyond Meat, among others.

Fiddes, Nick. Meat: A Natural Symbol. *Routledge, 1991.*

Nick Fiddes's *Meat* begins with a preface detailing a formative moment he experienced as a child, on first realizing the reality of the calf that had been killed to produce the indecipherable meat on his plate. In this recognition of what Carol J. Adams refers to as the "absent referent" animal, Fiddes continues with a similar trajectory to Adams in seeking to disrupt dominant narratives of meat. Fiddes's *Meat* was released almost simultaneously with Adams's *The Sexual Politics of Meat* and raises similar issues through its interrogation of the ways in which "meat" comes to mean and define itself as a symbol of human exceptionalism. He charts the cultural and discursive naturalization of the mythic status accorded to meat over the course of human history, as a symbol of masculinity as much as of human exceptionalism and domination over nature. This denaturalization of the myth of meat seeks to dismantle the social structures that allow the mass slaughter of animals for food to go on without question.

Joy, Melanie. Why We Love Dogs, Eat Pigs, and Wear Cows: An Introduction to Carnism. *Conari Press, 2010.*

Joy's book is addressed to a specifically American, meat-eating reader, employing thought experiments and accessible descriptions of psychological mechanisms to encourage a reconsideration of meat consumption and its ideological component. Aimed at a public rather than specifically academic audience, Joy's book employs often graphic descriptions of the conditions in factory farms, as well as the human consequences of industrial farming, to establish her concept of "carnism," a term that has been influential in much work in vegan studies. Carnism posits meat-eating as part of an ideological belief system. By naming this system, Joy aims to make carnist ideology visible and therefore denaturalize it. Like Carol J. Adams's concept of the "absent referent," carnism names an overarching social structure that explains Western culture's large-scale abuse of animals. The book concludes with a stress on the necessity of bearing witness to violence, and activating collective witnessing, in relation to animal exploitation. Countering dissociation, engaging with literature, and reading books such as Joy's are positioned as possible modes of bearing witness to animal suffering.

McCorry, Seán, and John Miller (eds). Literature and Meat since 1900. *Palgrave Macmillan, 2019.*

This collection fulfills what McCorry and Miller see as a lacuna in existing animal studies work regarding the textual history of meat. The volume focuses specifically on literary representations of meat and meat-eating in primarily European and North American texts from the turn of the twentieth century to the present, though it also treats other media including film, performance, and videogames as part of a broader sense of the literary texts of meat. The fourteen chapters look at the position of meat and meat-eating in relation to modernity, considering, for instance, the impact of neoliberal politics, overpopulation, industrial farming, food shortages, and climate change on our relationship to animal flesh. McCorry and Miller's introduction directly situates the book in relation to ongoing work in vegan studies. While not explicitly vegan in focus, the essays collectively engage in what the editors call "meat critique," work that seeks "to unpack and to challenge the dominant narratives of meat-eating and conceptions of animals as resources" (2) and that enacts a "similarly far-reaching endeavour to vegan studies and a form of critical practice that will . . . necessarily inform dissident perspectives on meat culture" (10). Authors considered include canonical writers such as W. H. Auden, Franz Kafka, George Orwell, W. G. Sebald, and Virginia Woolf, as well as the lesser known poets Selima Hill and Ariana Reines.

Potts, Annie (ed.). Meat Culture. *Brill, 2016.*

This volume brings together a range of scholars from across critical animal studies to elaborate on what Potts terms "meat culture." Meat culture is seen as the manifestation of Melanie Joy's concept of the ideology of "carnism," involving the culture and practice of mass meat consumption and production. Meat culture moves beyond the meat of its title to include mass production of dairy, eggs, and other animal products, and veganism is explicitly positioned in Potts's introduction as the opposite of the current global culture of meat production and consumption. The volume advances a distinct vegan theoretical approach throughout. Several essays, for instance, explicitly focus on veganism, including Richard Twine's empirical study of UK vegans and the effect of their veganism on relationships with family and friends; Matthew Cole and Kate Stewart's reading of the implicit vegan ethics of iconic British television series *Doctor Who*; and Greta Gaard's vegan ecofeminist critique of vegetal ecocriticism. Matthew Calarco and Carol J. Adams's co-authored contribution also reflects on veganism as part of their in-depth discussion of the links between Adams's work and that of Jacques Derrida. Additional chapters unpack discourses of racism, xenophobia, and sexism as they manifest in meat culture and consider prominent news scandals, including the European horsemeat scandal and Australian live export controversy. Kirsty Dunn's chapter also offers literary analysis of Michael Faber's *Under the Skin*. While Potts's introduction establishes the transnational scope and diversity of meat culture, contributors focus predominantly on Australian, European, and British contexts.

Rivera, Serena J., and Niki Kiviat (eds). (In)digestion in Literature and Film: A Transcultural Approach. *Routledge, 2020.*

This collection engages with the idea of digestion and indigestion as resistance across a variety of contexts, with work considering Brazil, Eastern Europe, France, Ireland, Italy, Japan, Mexico, South Korea, Taiwan, and the US. All of the essays herein question the nature of disordered eating practices as represented in transcultural film and literature. The essays in this collection work to trouble the notion of "disorder" as pathological acts of non-normative dietary practices, treating them, rather than as restrictive and taboo, as modes of resistance to restrictive hegemony. "Disorder" then becomes defined as actions against – as opposed to pathologized by – dominant socio-political dietary prescriptiveness and a means to deconstruct the norms that define specific dietary practices as pathological. The work is situated around the overall thesis that "eating, the refusal to eat, and the expulsion of food become acts against the patriarchy, organized religion, colonial powers, the atrocities of war, and even the publishing and film industries themselves" (4). To resist via refusal to eat or by choosing to eat certain things and not others is to place oneself at odds with capitalism writ large. Food and food choice or food rejection as forms of resistance against embedded institutions is of interest for vegan studies given that veganism, as Laura Wright's essay in the present volume (as well as her essay in Rivera and Kiviat's collection) makes clear, has long been associated with disordered eating. The book is divided into three sections, "Theoretical and Formal Contours," "Disordered Eating beyond the West," and "Disordered Eating in the West," which contain essays that range from examinations of class politics in Eastern European film, to pro-ana blogs, cannibalism in Japanese cinema, and transgressive hunger in James Joyce's *Ulysses*.

Historical Overviews

This section turns to book-length studies focused on tracing the history of vegetarian and vegan ideological beliefs and dietary practice. The history of non-normative modes of eating and living disassociates veganism from its contemporary associations with fad diets. These works demonstrate that an understanding and acknowledgment of the history of veganism is a vital part of building vegetarian and vegan futures.

Iacobbo, Karen, and Michael Iacobbo. Vegetarian America: A History. *Praeger, 2004.*

Vegetarian America: A History traces the way in which vegetarianism has evolved and been shaped by various other social movements that have taken place in the US and situates US vegetarianism as having occurred in three distinct periods: the 1830s and 1840s; 1900–1930; and the period from the 1970s to the book's present of the early 2000s. While William Metcalf organized the American Vegetarian Convention in 1850, which resulted in the creation of the American Vegetarian Society (AVS), during the 1830s and 1840s, the Iacobbos chronicle the lives of such foundational figures as the "Father of Vegetarianism" (23), Sylvester Graham, and physician William Alcott, co-founder of Fruitlands, a short-lived "vegan community in Harvard, Massachusetts" (60). This work also links vegetarianism to other social movements such as abolition and American feminism, noting that "unlike today, when social movements tend to stand apart from one another, during the Jacksonian era reformers of various causes were united in their views" (62). The second wave of vegetarian growth at the turn of the twentieth century is seen to have been initiated by the influence of Upton Sinclair's *The Jungle* (1905) on the passage of the Pure Food Act and the Meat Inspection Act, both of 1906. The Iacobbos note that between 1902 and 1921, "the annual consumption of flesh food ha[d] fallen from 225 pounds ... to 170 pounds ..., a decline of 24 percent" (154). Veganism emerges in the third wave of US vegetarianism identified by the authors. The establishment of the world wide web during this period not only allowed for greater access to information about vegetarianism and veganism but also for greater opportunities to actively engage in the discourse of defining and shaping those positions.

James, Gregory. Of Victorians and Vegetarians: The Vegetarian Movement in Nineteenth-Century Britain. *Taurus Academic Studies, 2007.*

James's text takes an in-depth look at the vegetarian movement of nineteenth-century Britain. Focused on the social history of the movement rather than vegetarian ideology itself, James draws on an expansive range of archival sources to flesh out the emergence and growth of vegetarianism in Victorian Britain. His study demonstrates the ways in which Victorian vegetarianism moved beyond simply concern for animals to broader health concerns and social justice issues, as with the vegetarianism movement's alignment with the anti-capital punishment movement which was revived at around the same time. The book also contains chapters focused on vegetarianism's relation to puritanism, medical orthodoxy, and spiritualism. Later sections of the book turn to the manifestation of the vegetarian movement in the form of restaurants and the press, and Chapter 7, "Representing the Vegetarian," traces representations of vegetarians in nineteenth-century literary fiction and poetry.

Preece, Rod. Sins of the Flesh: A History of Ethical Vegetarian Thought. *UBC Press, 2008.*

Preece, a political scientist and former chair of the Ontario Society for the Prevention of Cruelty to Animals, offers a history of vegetarian ideas that is principally concerned with those who have adopted vegetarianism based on the belief that eating animals is in and of itself unethical (as opposed to those who abstain from meat based on health, environmental, or religious grounds). Beginning this history with the pre-history of mankind, ruminating on the earliest origins of flesh-eating, full ethical concern for animals resulting in vegetarianism is not seen to emerge in human history until after the Aristotelian period in Greece. Aside from a few notable exceptions, it is then found repeated in Rome before disappearing until its revival at the start of the nineteenth century. As an attempt to explain and understand the incongruence between concern for animals and flesh-eating – in which increasing ethical concern has not necessarily led to an increased rejection of meat – Preece's broad trans-historical and transnational span charts how ethical vegetarian diets and philosophies have been debated and discussed across history. Relating historical instances of ethical vegetarianism to debates and issues around meat-eating in the present day, Preece traces how ethical vegetarianism has changed over time. Veganism is seen as the inevitable culmination of vegetarian ethics and Chapter 12 considers twentieth-century vegetarianism in conjunction with veganism.

Spencer, Colin. The Heretic's Feast: A History of Vegetarianism. *Fourth Estate, 1993.*

Spencer's study charts vegetarianism's progress across cultures and over vast expanses of time; it notes the ancient nature of what remains a contentious debate with regard to what one chooses to eat. Spencer offers a broad focus on the myriad reasons why people have chosen to abstain from flesh-eating across a historical span that ranges from human pre-history through Pythagoras, Plato, the Christian Gospels, the Manicheans, the Bogomils, and the Renaissance. In the process, Spencer examines the reasons why vegetarianism has consistently provoked resentment and ridicule from antiquity to the present; providing "a history ... of dissidence and revolt which often led to persecution and death, punishments which are only understandable once we comprehend the central and unifying role of meat within society" (xiii). Spencer does devote some analysis to veganism as a category distinct from vegetarianism. According to Spencer, "to many then and now veganism seems the logical outcome of vegetarianism, for in refusing all animal products . . . [vegans] are taking a stand against modern farming and all animal exploitation" (293). Spencer, who even argues that the sixth-century philosopher Pythagoras – the first recorded advocate of a vegetarian lifestyle – was likely vegan (38), views veganism as a "next step forward" and "an ideal to aim at" in the perpetuation of an ethic that seeks to reduce the suffering of animals (317). He notes that veganism is known both for being the diet "with the lowest report of the common afflictions like cancer and coronary complaints" and also "spiritually ideal in that there is no exploitation of animals by humans" (294).

Stuart, Tristram. The Bloodless Revolution: Radical Vegetarians and the Discovery of India. *Harper Press, 2006.*

Stuart's *The Bloodless Revolution* charts the history of vegetarianism in the West from 1600 to the present as an entity that was named in England in the 1840s and fully codified by the founding of the Vegetarian Society in 1847, the creation of which made "'vegetarianism' a fixed identity – indelibly associated with crankiness" (423), which, in turn, allowed for vegetarianism to be easily "pigeonholed and ignored" (xvii). Stuart's study situates vegetarianism as a philosophy rooted in the ancient past, with the West's "'discovery' of Indian vegetarianism" in the seventeenth century having a basis well before Alexander the Great reached India in 327 BC (40). Furthermore, he finds it an "extraordinary coincidence that roughly contemporaneous seminal and Greek philosophers, the Buddha and Pythagoras, both taught . . . that it was wrong for people to eat animals" (41). In his exhaustive and meticulously researched work, however, while he utilizes the terms "vegan" and "veganism" throughout, Stuart never examines veganism as a separate identity that may be dependent upon factors distinct from those that have influenced the cultural, religious, and social histories of vegetarianism. What Stuart's work does do, however, is present ethical vegetarianism as a paradox, at once interested in the preservation of life even as the vegetarian is implicated, like any other living creature, in the cycle of life and death.

Williams, Howard. The Ethics of Diet: A Catena of Authorities Deprecatory of the Practice of Flesh-Eating. *1883. U of Illinois P, 2003.*

This 2003 re-republication of Williams's 1883 encyclopedic history of vegetarian thought, which features an introduction by Carol J. Adams, works to recover this important text from relative obscurity. While ostensibly a historical survey of vegetarian ideas, Howard's text can now be seen as a significant document of vegetarian history in its own right, having been highly influential to Victorian vegetarians, being read, as Adams notes in her introduction, by figures such as Tolstoy and Henry Salt. Howard traces the history of vegetarianism through attention to key individuals and their espousals on the subject, from Hesiod to Schopenhauer. This biographical survey approach works to prove the presence of ethical vegetarian arguments throughout history and to draw connections and consistencies between vegetarian actors across millennia. This historical narrative does have its weaknesses, not least of which is, as Adams notes, the complete absence of women from the first edition. Nonetheless, as the oldest available history of vegetarian thought, Howard's text offers a rich resource to consult and to better understand historic vegetarian culture and thought.

Selected Journal Articles

Below we provide an unannotated list of journal articles published in vegan studies, broadly conceived. This is not an exhaustive list but a collation of a range of available published material. This section is primarily focused on articles in the humanities but also includes those published in other fields, such as the social sciences. Sociology has been a particularly productive discipline for work on veganism and vegan identity, and it is therefore worth collating here some of the major works published in this field. Vegan literary studies, while attuned to the literary particulars of veganism, is an interdisciplinary field that has much to gain from the insights of social scientific work and the findings of empirical research into veganism.

Adams, Carol J. "An Animal Manifesto: Gender, Identity, and Vegan-Feminism in the Twenty-First Century." *Parallax*, vol. 12, no. 1, 2006, pp. 120–28.

Adams, Matthew. "Communicating Vegan Utopias: The Counterfactual Construction of Human-Animal Futures." *Environmental Communications*, vol. 16, no. 1, 2022, pp. 125–38.

Alloun, Esther. "Veganwashing Israel's Dirty Laundry? Animal Politics and Nationalism in Palestine-Israel." *Journal of Intercultural Studies*, vol. 41, no. 1, 2020, pp. 24–41.

Ankeny, Rachel A., Michelle Phillipoy, and Heather J. Bray. "Celebrity Chefs and New Meat Consumption Norms: Seeking Questions, Not Answers." *M/C Journal*, vol. 22, no. 2, 2019.

Asher, Kathryn, and Elizabeth Cherry. "Home Is Where the Food Is: Barriers to Vegetarianism and Veganism in the Domestic Sphere." *Journal for Critical Animal Studies*, vol. 13, no. 1, 2015, pp. 66–91.

Avieli, Nir, and Fran Markowitz. "Slavery Food, Soul Food, Salvation Food: Veganism and Identity in the African Hebrew Israelite Community." *African and Black Diaspora: An International Journal*, vol. 11, no. 2, pp. 205–20.

Bailey, Cathryn. "We Are What We Eat: Feminist Vegetarianism and the Reproduction of Racial Identity." *Hypatia*, vol. 22, no. 2, 2007, pp. 39–59.

Berlant, Lauren, and Jordan Stein. "Cruising Veganism." *GLQ*, vol. 21, no. 1, 2015, pp. 18–23.

Brady, Jennifer, and Matthew Ventresca. "'Officially a Vegan Now': On Meat and Renaissance Masculinity in Pro Football." *Food and Foodways*, vol. 22, no. 4, 2014, pp. 300–21.

Buttny, Richard, and Etsuko Kinefuchi. "Vegans' Problem Stories: Negotiating Vegan Identity in Dealing with Omnivores." *Discourse & Society*, vol. 31, no. 6, 2020, pp. 565–83.

Calarco, Matthew. "Being Toward Meat: Anthropocentrism, Indistinction, and Veganism." *Dialectical Anthropology*, vol. 38, no. 4, pp. 415–29.

—. "Deconstruction is not Vegetarianism: Humanism, Subjectivity, and Animal Ethics." *Continental Philosophy Review*, vol. 37, 2004, pp. 175–201.

Cherry, Elizabeth. "Veganism as a Cultural Movement: A Relational Approach." *Social Movement Studies*, vol. 5, no. 2, 2006, pp. 155–70.

Clipsham, Patrick, and Katy Fulfer. "An Anti-Commodification Defense of Veganism." *Ethics, Policy & Environment*, vol. 19, no. 3, 2016, pp. 285–300.

Cole, Matthew, and Karen Morgan. "Vegaphobia: Derogatory Discourse of Veganism and the Reproduction of Speciesism in UK national newspapers." *The British Journal of Sociology*, vol. 62, no. 1, 2011, pp. 134–53.

Cole, Matthew, and Kate Stewart. "Speciesism Party: A Vegan Critique of *Sausage Party*." *ISLE: Interdisciplinary Studies in Literature and Environment*, vol. 24, no. 4, 2017, pp. 767–86.

Cushing, Nancy. "To Eat or Not to Eat Kangaroo: Bargaining over Food Choice in the Anthropocene." *M/C Journal*, vol. 22, no. 2, 2019.

Dean, Megan. "You Are How You Eat? Femininity, Normalization, and Veganism as an Ethical Practice of Freedom." *Societies*, vol. 4, no. 2, pp. 127–47.

Doyle, Julie. "Celebrity vegans and the lifestyling of ethical consumption." *Environmental Communication*, vol. 10, no. 6, 2016, pp. 777–90.

Fegitz, Ella, and Daniela Pirani. "The Sexual Politics of Veggies: Beyonce's 'commodity veg*ism." *Feminist Media Studies*, vol. 18, no. 2, 2018, pp. 294–308.

Fudge, Erica. "Why it's Easy being a Vegetarian." *Textual Practice*, vol. 24, no. 1, 2010, pp. 149–66.

Gaard, Greta. "New Directions for Ecofeminism: Toward a More Feminist Ecocriticism." *Interdisciplinary Studies in Literature and Environment*, vol. 17, no. 4, 2010, pp. 643–65.

Gambert Iselin, "Got Mylk? The Disruptive Possibilities of Plant Milk." *Brooklyn Law Review*, vol. 84, no. 3, pp. 801–71.

Gambert, Iselin, and Tobias Linné. "From Rice Eaters to Soy Boys: Race, Gender, and Tropes of 'Plant Food Masculinity.'" *Animal Studies Journal*, vol. 7, no. 2, pp. 129–79.

Giraud, Eva. "Veganism as Affirmative Biopolitics: Moving Towards a Posthumanist Ethics?" *PhaenEx*, vol. 8, no. 2, 2013, pp. 47–79.

Green, Leila. "Being a Bad Vegan." *M/C Journal*, vol. 22, no. 2, 2019.

Greenebaum, Jessica. "Questioning the Concept of Vegan Privilege: A Commentary." *Humanity & Society*, vol. 41, no. 3, pp. 355–72.

—. "Veganism, Identity and the Quest for Authenticity." *Food, Culture & Society*, vol. 5, no. 1, 2012, pp. 129–44.

—. "Vegans of Color: Managing Visible and Invisible Stigmas." *Food, Culture & Society*, vol. 21, no. 5, 2018, pp. 680–97.

Greenebaum, Jessica, and Brandon Dexter. "Vegan Men and Hybrid Masculinity." *Journal of Gender Studies*, vol. 27, no. 6, 2018, pp. 637–48.

Gruen, Lori et al. "Feminists Encountering Animals." *Hypatia*, vol. 27, no. 3, 2012.

Hamilton, Carrie. "Mourning Leather: Queer Histories, Vegan Futures." *Memory Studies*, vol. 14, no. 2, 2021, pp. 303–15.

—. "Sex, Work, Meat: The Feminist Politics of Veganism." *Feminist Review*, vol. 114, 2016, pp. 112–29.

Harper, A. Breeze. "Race as a 'Feeble Matter' in Veganism: Interrogating Whiteness, Geopolitical Privilege, and Consumption Philosophy of 'Cruelty-Free' Products." *Journal for Critical Animal Studies*, vol. 8, no. 3, pp. 5–27.

Horta, Oscar. "Discrimination against Vegans." *Res Publica*, vol. 24, 2018, pp. 359–73.

Jabs, Jennifer, Jeffery Sobal, and Carol M. Devine. "Managing Vegetarianism: Identities, Norms and Interactions." *Ecology of Food and Nutrition*, vol. 39, no. 5, 2000, pp. 375–94.

Joelle, Natalie. "Gleaning Lean Culture." *ISLE: Interdisciplinary Studies in Literature and Environment*, vol. 24, no. 4, 2017, pp. 737–52.

Johnson, Hope. "From 'Meat Culture' to 'Cultured Meat': Critically Evaluating the Contested Ontologies and Transformative Potential of Biofabricated Animal Material on Culture and Law." *M/C Journal*, vol. 22, no. 2, 2019.

Khara, Tani, and Matthew B. Ruby. "Meat Eating and the Transition from Plant-Based Diets among Urban Indians." *M/C Journal*, vol. 22, no. 2, 2019.

Linné, Tobias. "Cows on Facebook and Instagram: Interspecies Intimacy in the Social Media Spaces of the Swedish Dairy Industry." *Television & Media*, vol. 17, no. 8, 2016, pp. 719–33.

Lundahl, Outi. "Dynamics of Positive Deviance in Destigmatisation: Celebrities and the Media in the Rise of Veganism." *Consumption Markets & Culture*, vol. 23, no. 3, 2020.

McCorry, Seán. "'This Disgusting Feast of Filth': Meat Eating, Hospitality, and Violence in Sarah Kane's *Blasted*." *ISLE: Interdisciplinary Studies in Literature and Environment*, vol. 24, no. 4, 2017, pp. 753–66.

McDonald, Barbara. "'Once you know something, you can't not know it.' An Empirical Look at Becoming Vegan." *Society & Animals*, vol. 8, no. 1, 2000, pp. 1–23.

MacInnis, C. C., and G. Hodson. "It ain't easy eating green: Evidence of Bias towards Vegetarians and Vegans from both Source and Target." *Group Processes and Intergroup Relations*, vol. 20, no. 6, 2017, pp. 721–44.

McKay, Robert. "Metafiction, Vegetarianism, and the Literary Performance of Animal Ethics in J. M. Coetzee's *The Lives of Animals*." *The Journal of South African and American Studies*, vol. 11, no. 1–2, 2010, pp. 67–85.

Mann, Clare. "Can the Pain of Vystopia Help to Create a More Compassionate World?" *M/C Journal*, vol. 22, no. 2, 2019.

Markowski, Kelly L., and Susan Roxburgh. "'If I became vegan, my family and friends would hate me:' Anticipating Vegan Stigma as a Barrier to Plant-Based Diets." *Appetite*, vol. 135, 2019, pp. 1–9.

Milburn, Josh. "Should Vegans Compromise?" *Critical Review of International Social and Political Philosophy*, vol. 25, no. 2, 2022, pp. 281–93.

Milburn, Josh, and Bob Fischer. "The Freegan Challenge to Veganism." *Journal of Agricultural & Environmental Ethics*, vol. 34, no. 3, 2021, pp. 1–19.

Muller, S. Marek. "Archival Mocking as Feminist Praxis: A Rhetorical Repurposing of *A Vindication of the Rights of Brutes*." *Women's Studies in Communication*, vol. 44, no. 1, 2021, pp. 23–43.

Mycek, Mari Kate. "Meatless Meals and Masculinity: How Veg* Men Explain their Plant-Based Diets." *Food and Foodways*, vol. 26, no. 3, 2018, pp. 223–45.

Oliver, Catherine. "Vegan World-Making in Meat-Centric Society: The Embodied Geographies of Veganism." *Social & Cultural Geography*, 2021.

Ophélie, Véron. "(Extra)ordinary Activism: Veganism and the Shaping of Hemeratopias." *International Journal of Sociology and Social Policy*, vol. 36, no. 11/12, 2016, pp. 756–73.

Parry, Jovian. "*Oryx and Crake* and the New Nostalgia for Meat." *Society and Animals*, vol. 17, 2009, pp. 241–56.

Pick, Anat. "Turning to Animals Between Love and Law." *New Formations*, vol. 76, 2012, pp. 68–85.

Potts, Annie, and Jovian Parry. "Vegan Sexuality: Challenging Heteronormative Masculinity through Meat-Free Sex." *Feminism & Psychology*, vol. 20, no. 1, 2010, pp. 53–72.

Quinn, Emelia. "Notes on Vegan Camp." *PMLA*, vol. 135, no. 5, 2020, pp. 914–30.
—. "Vegan Attendance: Reading Gibbons' Animals." *Sculpture Journal* (special issue on Grinling Gibbons), vol. 29, no. 3, 2020, pp. 381–96.
Robinson, Margaret. "Veganism and Mi'kmaq Legends." *The Canadian Journal of Native Studies*, vol. 33, no. 1, 2013, pp. 189–96.
Rodan, Debbie, and Jane Mummery. "Animals Australia and the Challenges of Vegan Stereotyping." *M/C Journal*, vol. 22, no. 2, 2019.
Schwarz, Ori. "Identity as a Barrier: Claiming Universality as a Strategy in the Israeli Vegan Movement." *Social Movement Studies*, vol. 20, no. 5, 2021, pp. 600–18.
Simonsen, Rasmus Rahbek. "A Queer Vegan Manifesto." *Journal for Critical Animal Studies*, vol. 10, no. 3, 2021, pp. 51–80.
Stanescu, James. "Towards a Dark Animal Studies: On Vegetarian Vampires, Beautiful Souls, and Becoming-Vegan." *Journal for Critical Animal Studies*, vol. 10, no. 3, 2012, pp. 26–50.
Stănescu, Vasile. "'White Power Milk': Milk, Dietary Racism, and the 'Alt-Right.'" *Animal Studies Journal*, vol. 7, no. 2, 2018, pp. 103–28.
Stobie, Caitlin. "The Good Wife? Sibling Species in Han Kang's *The Vegetarian*." *ISLE: Interdisciplinary Studies in Literature and Environment*, vol. 24, no. 4, 2017, pp. 787–802.
Taylor, Chloë. "Abnormal Appetites: Foucault, Atwood, and the Normalization of an Animal-Based Diet." *Journal for Critical Animal Studies*, vol. 10, no. 4, 2021, pp. 130–48.
Turner, Ryan. "Veganism: Ethics in Everyday Life." *American Journal of Cultural Sociology*, vol. 7, 2019, pp. 54–78.
Twine, Richard. "Materially Constituting a Sustainable Food Transition: The Case of Vegan Eating Practice." *Sociology*, vol. 52, no. 1, 2017, pp. 166–81.
—. "Vegan Killjoys at the Table – Contesting Happiness and Negotiating Relationships with Food Practices." *Societies*, vol. 4, no. 4, 2014, pp. 623–39.
Williams, Deborah Kay. "Hostile Hashtag Takeover: An Analysis of the Battle for Februdairy." *M/C Journal*, vol. 22, no. 2, 2019.
Wrenn, Corey Lee. "Fat Vegan Politics: A Survey of Fat Vegan Activists' Online Experience with Social Movement Sizeism." *Fat Studies*, vol. 6, no. 1, 2017, pp. 90–102.
—. "Resisting the Globalization of Speciesism: Vegan Abolitionism as a Site for Consumer-Based Social Change." *Journal for Critical Animal Studies*, vol. 9, no. 3, 2011, pp. 8–27.
—. "Trump Veganism: A Political Survey of American Vegans in the Era of Identity Politics." *Societies*, vol. 7, no. 4, 2017.
—. "The Vegan Society and Social Movement Professionalization, 1944–2017." *Food and Foodways*, vol. 27, no. 3, 2019, pp. 190–210.
Wrenn, Corey Lee, and Rob Johnson. "A Critique of Single-issue Campaigning and the Importance of Comprehensive Abolitionist Vegan Advocacy." *Food, Culture & Society*, vol. 16, no. 4, 2013, pp. 651–68.
Wrenn, Corey Lee, and Alexus Lizardi. "Older, Greener, and Wiser: Charting the Experiences of Older Women in the American Vegan Movement." *Journal of Women & Aging*, vol. 33, no. 6, 2021, pp. 653–75.
Wright, Laura. "Introducing Vegan Studies." *ISLE: Interdisciplinary Studies in Literature and Environment*, vol. 24, no. 4, 2017, pp. 727–36.
—. "Vegan Studies as Ecofeminist Intervention." *Ecozon@*, vol. 11, no. 2, 2020, pp. 101–08.

Note

1. For more on the intersections with vegan studies and these fields see Laura Wright's introduction to *The Vegan Studies Project*, Quinn and Westwood's introduction to *Thinking Veganism*, and Eva Giraud's introduction to *Veganism*.

Part I

Themes and Theoretical Perspectives

1

VEGANISM AND WOMEN'S WRITING

Carol J. Adams

What is civilization? What is culture? Is it possible for a healthy race to be fathered by violence – in war or in the slaughter-house – and mothered by slaves, ignorant or parasitic? Where is the historian who traces the rise and fall of nations to the standing of their women?

Agnes Ryan, "Civilization? Culture?"

AFTER FRANKENSTEIN'S CREATURE describes its diet of acorn and berries, and its hope of retreating to South America with its companion, it remarks to Frankenstein, "The picture I present to you is peaceful and human."[1] The Creature's idyllic pacifist and vegetarian utopian vision intersects with the themes of a number of novels by twentieth-century women that in challenging patriarchal society hearken to a Golden Age of feminism, pacifism, and vegetarianism. The context against which these more recent novels must be read is World War I – for it was then that the peaceful, vegetarian life envisioned by the Creature and many others encountered its starkest contrast, catalyzing the assimilation of vegetarianism into the antiwar vision of women writers. As Edward Carpenter put it after World War I: "When we think of the regiments and regiments of soldiers and mercenaries mangled and torn . . . when we realise *what* all this horrible scramble means, including the endless slaughter of the innocent and beautiful animals, and the fear, the terror, the agony in which the latter exist," we must "pay homage" to Percy Shelley's androgynous vision, for he "saw that only a new type of human being combining the male and the female, could ultimately save the world – a being having the feminine insight and imagination to perceive the evil, and the manly strength and courage to oppose and finally annihilate it."[2]

Just as the Great War is the context for Carpenter's statement about the need for an androgynous vision to challenge war and animal slaughter, in the wake of World War I many modern women writers trace the causes of both war and meat-eating to male dominance. Events of the Great War yoked the heretofore sporadically linked notions of pacifism and vegetarianism. The Great War quickened vegetarianism, propelling it as a movement into the twentieth century and as a subject into the novels of women writers.

As an attribute of fictional characters, few literary examples of vegetarianism antedate the Great War, with the notable exception of Frankenstein's Creature. The modernization of vegetarianism occurred when it began to figure, as a theme or incidental element, in novels. The last chapter examined the significance of vegetarianism and its historical manifestations as it appears in one novel; this chapter applies that same approach to consider vegetarian themes that recur in a series of novels. As with *Frankenstein*, these novels, too, enact a narrative strategy that highlights vegetarian meaning.

In this chapter I will propose that the textual strategy of "interruption" allows modern women writers to introduce vegetarian incidents into their novels. Four themes arise when a vegetarian "interruption" occurs. These themes include rejection of male acts of violence, identification with animals, repudiation of men's control of women, and the positing of an ideal world composed of vegetarianism, pacifism, and feminism as opposed to a fallen world composed in part of women's oppression, war, and meat-eating.

The novels to be considered in this chapter adhere to patterns previously discussed in Chapter 5, "Dismembered Texts, Dismembered Animals." They bear the vegetarian word through allusion to earlier vegetarian ideas, through language that clearly identifies the functioning of the structure of the absent referent, and through the assumption that people who read vegetarian writings become vegetarian. We will see that the idea of meat is used as a trope for women's oppression; this trope identifies the overlap of the oppression of women and animals.

A feminist perspective in these novels links violence against people and violence against animals. It is this unique perspective that will be closely examined, for it demonstrates how vegetarian insights can be applied to analyses of other forms of political violence. The apparently unrelated critiques of women against war and vegetarians against meat-eating become intimately related. From this perspective of the interrelationships of violence, vegetarianism can be seen as a challenge to war, pacifism as a challenge to meat-eating. This interrelationship becomes visible when women articulate a connection with animals – beings who are also made absent referents by patriarchal society – thus correlating male acts of violence against people and animals. In deliberately bearing the vegetarian word, they challenge a world at war.

After briefly summarizing a feminist analysis of political violence and the ways by which the Great War effected the modernization of vegetarianism, we will consider the narrative strategies and thematic concerns of several illustrative works. This consideration will suggest the depths of the linkage between vegetarianism and pacifism in women's writings of the twentieth century and extend our understanding of the sexual politics of meat.

The Sexual Politics of War

During the Great War some anti-war feminists argued, like Edward Carpenter, that women had unique traits that caused them to be more peace-loving than men. This emphasis on gender distinctions, called by one historian the "argument for ameliorative influence," focused on women's role as nurturers and mothers. As historian C. Roland Marchand describes this viewpoint:

> Women embodied the "gentler traits of tenderness and mercy" and therefore had a special contribution to offer to government ... Destructive masculine ideas of physical force would only be overcome, militant suffragist Harriet Stanton Blatch argued, when the "mother viewpoint" forced its way into international diplomacy.[3]

In a chapter entitled "Woman and War," from her 1911 book *Woman and Labour*, Olive Schreiner provides an illustrative example of this argument for ameliorative influence. She posits that women oppose war *and* the killing of animals for sport because of their child-bearing:

> The relations of the female towards the production of human life influences undoubtedly even her relation towards animal and all life. "It is a fine day, let us go out and kill something!" cries the typical male of certain races, instinctively. "There is a living thing, it will die if it is not cared for," says the average woman, almost equally instinctively.[4]

Other feminists decried political violence by arguing that it was male domination, not male traits, and the absence of female power that caused war. Women's exclusion from powerful positions in patriarchal society provides Virginia Woolf with the opportunity to propose in her brilliant anti-war feminist essay, *Three Guineas*, the creation of an Outsider's Society. As she develops her argument linking male power, the exclusion of women, and bellicose militarism, she, like Carpenter and Schreiner before her, connects the deaths of people and of animals: "Scarcely a human being in the course of history has fallen to a woman's rifle; the vast majority of birds and beasts have been killed by you, not by us."[5]

Agnes Ryan and her husband Henry Bailey Stevens, both editors of *The Woman's Journal* and pacifists, became vegetarians during the Great War. They decided that the responsibility for both war and meat-eating rested with men, and were influenced in their analysis by their friendship with Emarel Freshel. Ryan describes Freshel's address on war and meat-eating to a 1915 Fabian Society meeting:

> Here was a new type of woman; here was a new spiritual force at work in the universe ... She clearly stressed the idea that wars will never be overcome until the belief that it is justifiable to take life, to kill – *when expedient*, – is eradicated from human consciousness.[6]

In 1917, Freshel, author of the definitive vegetarian cookbook for that time, *The Golden Rule Cookbook*, resigned from the Christian Science Church when it supported the entry of the United States into World War I.

If feminist vegetarians argued that killing animals becomes a justification for killing human beings, some who adhere to the dominant viewpoint persuade children to eat meat by justifying the necessity, at times, to kill even human beings. Lawrence Kohlberg, well-known scholar on the moral development of children, reports that his four-year-old son "joined the pacifist and vegetarian movement and refused to eat meat because, he said, it is bad to kill animals." Kohlberg's response was an attempt to "dissuade him by arguing about the difference between justified and unjustified killing,"[7] thus establishing a morality that recognizes some forms of killing as legitimate. It is as though the way to create a child's acceptance of animals' deaths is by convincing him or her that sometimes humans must be killed, too. "Just" wars then justify meat-eating. This phenomenon is figured in Walter de la Mare's "Dry August Burned": a small girl is weeping at the sight of the absent referent, a dead hare that lies lifeless on the kitchen table. A team of field artillery "thudding by" interrupts her mourning. She watches the wonderment and tumult of it all, returns to the kitchen and with flushed cheeks asks to watch the rabbit be skinned.[8] The soldiers have intervened; in their presence, the dead rabbit has now become an accepted fact, no longer mourned.

"Dry August Burned" figures a transition in an attitude toward an animal killed for food, a transition caused by the reminder of war. This response enforces a relationship between eating animals and killing humans. If the wartime killing of human beings is used to establish the legitimacy of meat-eating, then challenging meat-eating challenges a world at war.

Individual women took the insights of the connected brutalities of war and of meat-eating to heart. For instance Mary Alden Hopkins remarked: "I reacted violently at that time against all established institutions, like marriage, spanking, meat diet, prisons, war, public schools, and our form of government."[9] Many feminist-vegetarian pacifists can be found during World War I. During the Great War, feminist, pacifist, and vegetarian Charlotte Despard provided vegetarian meals at the cheap meals service she offered on her property.[10] At least four American vegetarian feminists traveled on the Ford Peace Ship in 1915.[11]

In the wake of the war, the position that the absence of female power caused war intersected with the view that meat-eating cultures were war cultures (even though not all meat-eating cultures were then at war). As feminists and vegetarians acknowledged their shared critical positions, they discovered that the destructive values of patriarchal culture were not limited to the battlefront.

The Great War: Modernizing Vegetarianism

When times are normal people and governments are inclined to pursue lines of least resistance; that is, to continue practices and customs not because they are best but because of habit, but it is during abnormal periods that we do our best thinking ... I have long had in mind a book on "Wheatless and Meatless Menus," but the time to bring it out was not ripe until now.
Eugene Christian, *Meatless and Wheatless Menus*, 1917[12]

Just as anti-war feminists believed that empowering women would end war, so vegetarians believed that eliminating meat-eating moved the world closer to pacifism. Indeed, they would say, the Vedic word for war "means 'desire for cows.'"[13] Anna Kingsford, when discussing Women's Peace Conventions of the nineteenth century bemoaned that "These poor deluded creatures cannot see that universal peace is absolutely impossible to a carnivorous race."[14] Percy Shelley thundered that "the butchering of harmless animals cannot fail to produce much of that spirit of insane and hideous exultation in which news of a victory is related alto' purchased by the massacre of a hundred thousand men."[15] In 1918 the Federation of Humano-Vegetarians in America wrote to President Woodrow Wilson seeking equivalent treatment for "adherents of the Vegetarian Cult" as for conscientious objectors because "we vegetarians, reaffirming our faith in the Universal Kinship of the 'Animal Kingdom' and the 'Brotherhood of Man,' adhere in our allegiance to the elementary human commandment, 'Thou Shalt Not Kill.'"[16] Douglas Goldring, in discussing the conscientious objectors who joined the 1917 Club, remarks that they "were certainly the oddest lot of people ever temporarily united under one banner. Some of them carried their dislike of killing so far that they existed only on vegetables."[17] Notably, after the Great War, insights into the possible connections between war and meat-eating can be found in writers other than ethical vegetarians.

One reason that insights into these connections are now found in other writers is because of the revelations of the war itself. During the war, soldiers' imaginations became alerted to what Bernard Shaw and other vegetarians had claimed for decades: corpses are corpses. How could the soldier avoid thinking of his commonality with animals as he sat in the trenches watching large black rats consume soldier and horse? The horrors of this war were also found in the slaughterhouse. The editor's introduction to L. F. Easterbrook's article on "Alcohol and Meat" explains,

> In 1918 the spectacle of a herd of scared and suffering cattle hustled together in a van, and being conveyed to a slaughter yard, struck the writer of this note as being at least as abominable, and as degrading to our civilisation, as anything he had recently witnessed on several hard fighting fronts in France and Italy.[18]

Philosopher Mary Midgley views the Great War as a turning point in attitudes toward animals, suggesting that after the war there was an upsurge of interest in and scientific proof of the continuities between the other animals and human beings. After citing examples of good-hearted tolerance of egregious acts of hunting, she writes, "For most of us, however, the light seems somehow to have changed – indeed, it probably did so during the First World War."[19]

The Great War also provided a positive, though transitory, vegetarian environment for civilians, especially women, through the rationing of food.[20] Civilians could turn to books such as *Meatless and Wheatless Menus* or *The Golden Rule Cookbook*. This rationing provided one researcher the largest survey population attainable, the entire nation of Denmark. Dr. Mikkel Hindhede describes it as "a low protein experiment on a large scale, about 3,000,000 subjects being available." After directing the rationing program necessitated by the war – "a milk and vegetable diet" along with bran bread, barley, porridge, potatoes, and greens – Hindhede, who had been conducting experiments on low-protein, mostly vegetarian, diets since 1895, found that it had improved the Danish people's mortality rates.[21] As a result of vegetarianism's increased attractiveness, the time between the Great War and World War II has been called the "Golden Era of Vegetarianism."[22]

While civilians encountered government encouragement for meatless diets, the epitome of the masculine men, soldiers, received meat, as I discussed in Chapter 1. Marty Feldman reported that during World War II when his father "was in the army, [he] could not eat meat because he was an orthodox Jew. He practically starved to death and was treated with great contempt by the other soldiers because a soldier should eat steak."[23] This emphasis on meat for the male population at the war front may have clarified connections between feminism, vegetarianism, and pacifism as well.

"The lesson of the past six years is this," Henry Salt observed in 1921: "As long as man kills the lower races for food or sport, he will be ready to kill his own race for enmity. It is not *this* bloodshed, or *that* bloodshed, that must cease, but *all* needless bloodshed – all wanton infliction of pain or death upon our fellow-beings."[24] In this observation, Salt expands the notion of the "front" at which deplorable killing occurs. Vegetarians are not alone in postulating an expanded front that includes animal victims. Some twentieth-century British and American women writers strategically expand the terrain of war while exploring the issue of male dominance. The front, they suggest, exists not only in traditionally viewed warfare, but also in what they view as the war against nonhuman animals, typified in hunting and meat-eating. Thus they apply insights about wars to the sexual politics of meat.

Women's Fiction and the Expanded Front

Wars will never cease while men still kill other animals for food, since to turn any living creature into a roast, a steak, a chop, or any other form of "meat" takes the same kind of violence, the same kind of bloodshed and the same kind of mental processes required to change a living man into a dead soldier.
Agnes Ryan, "For the Church Door," March 1943[25]

I expect after you have many times seen a deer or woodchuck blown to bits, the thought of a human being blown to bits is that much less impossible to conceive.
Medieval scholar Grace Knole in *The James Joyce Murders*[26]

Does a man revisit the Great War by recalling his days as a fox hunter? Yes, according to Siegfried Sassoon, whose *The Memoirs of George Sherston*, which culminates in 1918, begins with *Memoirs of a Fox-Hunting Man*.[27] Is sport a training for war, as Henry Salt argued in 1914?[28] How else should Robert Graves begin his farcical, satirical, humorous memoir – his book that turned the war and everything else on its end – but by introducing us to a vegetarian?[29] Can there be *A Case for the Vegetarian Conscientious Objector*, as Max Davis and Scott Nearing believed in 1945? Where else should a novel anticipating the Great War begin but with a male-only shooting party? All of these works suggest a connection between eating meat (and/or hunting) and war. This sense of connection was both verified and intensified once examined through a feminist lens. For then one saw that it was *Man* the Hunter and *Man* the Soldier – the phrases are Charlotte Perkins Gilman's from a poem that opens her penultimate book, *His Religion and Hers*, written after, and influenced by, World War I.[30]

Man the hunter, man the soldier: this refrain not only links disparate acts of violence – the killing of people and the killing of animals – but also focuses on the sex of the killer. The tradition of vegetarian feminist novels by women writers that I explore in this chapter recalls this approach. This tradition originates with the recognition of an expanded front that exists wherever animals are killed. A constellation of feminist insights seems to follow this recognition, which I have isolated into four distinct themes. (1) The theme of rejection of male acts of violence: While their complicity in meat-eating locates women *at* the front, a heightened sensitivity to the consumption of animal flesh also generates a comprehensive anti-war critique *from* the front. (2) The theme of identification with animals: Women are allied with animals because they too are objects of use and possession. Women's oppression is expressed through the trope of meat-eating. (3) The theme of vegetarianism as rejection of male control and violence: Through the adoption of vegetarianism women simultaneously reject a warring world and dependence on men. This dependence not only manifests itself in the need to be protected by men, but also the need to project on men tasks that women prefer not to think of themselves as doing, such as functioning as killers. (4) The theme of linked oppressions and linked ideal states: Human male dominance is seen to cause women's oppression, war, and meat-eating; conversely, in discussions of that perfect world before the Fall, vegetarianism and pacifism become linked with women's equality. While the works in this tradition are unified by their inclusion of animals, none of them attempts to include all four themes in any one text, nor is there any chronological order to the development of these themes. In essence, while the texts are united by a recognition of an enlarged war front, they vary according to the distinct themes evolving from the particular configuration they choose to explore.

Isabel Colegate's Great War novel *The Shooting Party* anchors the texts securely within the anti-war tradition. By exploring the connection between hunting and war from a woman's perspective, Colegate demonstrates, like Sassoon, that hunting is the perfect prelude and pattern for judging a warring world. Colegate provides a female twist, however, by including women in the expanded front. If hunting is the appropriate mirror against which to judge war, then women can gain a voice in judging what they do not share – the battlefront – by judging what they do share as spectators – the experience of the hunt.

Colegate's tightly constructed novel depicts the evening of the second and third days of a traditional shooting party. It is a stunning evocation of prewar innocence and a dark foreshadowing of a bloody war. But the shooting party – with its army of uniformed beaters following campaign plans, moving from the bivouac of lunch to the front line of the shooting, with the loaders scurrying in a no-man's-land retrieving the thickly strewn corpses – is not a mere intimation of things to come, but a depiction of a war itself. "War might be like this," thinks Olivia, "casual, friendly and frightening."[31] Indeed, male competition, culminating in the accidental death of a beater – who propelled the frightened pheasants forth to their slaughter at the guns of the upper-class shooters – represents the eternal cause of war. A hunter eager for the most animals "bagged" mistakenly shoots the beater.

Colegate places more spectators at the "front" than shooters. We find there the beaters, the upper-class women, an activist vegetarian, a young child worried about his pet duck, a maid. Their thoughts about the shooting act as counterpoints to the escalating competition of the male shooters.

By positioning her women at the shooting party, Colegate establishes their right to voice criticisms such as Olivia's: "And I am often aware at shooting parties how differently I feel from a man and how, more than that, I really would like to rebel against the world men have made, if I knew how to." Olivia articulates Colegate's theme of rejection of male violence. In Colegate's novel, women's presence in, but opposition to, the violent world men have made is constantly reiterated.

Through the analogy of the shooting party as war, Colegate expands the front to where women are, empowering their articulations. When the war is referred to as "a bigger shooting party [which] had begun, in Flanders," empowerment to speak of *this* front implicitly exists. Thus, *The Shooting Party* becomes one answer to the recurring twentieth-century question posed to women writers: how does a woman condemn war if she cannot be a soldier?[32] This issue is dissolved if she criticizes war by criticizing its equivalent, of which she *is* a part, as witness as well as subsequent consumer: the shooting party.

During the Great War the chasm between the soldier at war and the woman spectator was intentionally widened by soldier-writers who condescendingly dismissed – for lack of experience at the front – any writings by noncombatants. This legacy of condescension and dismissal carried into the Second World War as well. By showing that women, prior to the Great War, had a right to voice their perspective on war through the corollary experience of participating in, and responding to, a shooting party, Colegate brilliantly restores a right of articulation. The suggestion her novel leaves, therefore, is not that one must be at the war front to have the right to speak, but that one may speak by linking one's own experience *to* war, through making the connection between hunting and/or meat-eating and war. So, one can claim one's voice. Wilfred Owen and other writers of World War I erred not by restricting authentic experiences to the front alone, but by their too-limited definition of where the front can be found.

At the expanded front, the theme of identification with animals arises: with whom do the women located there align themselves, the hunter or the hunted? Identification with animals is a pivotal moment for two novels in this tradition of women writers. For Margaret Atwood's and Marge Piercy's characters, meat-eating becomes a trope of their own oppression. Women come to see themselves as being consumed by marital oppression at the domestic front; they realize that their bodies are battlegrounds and view animals with the new awareness of a common experience. The third theme, related to their identification with animals, expresses their sense of shared violation. Linking sexual oppression to meat-eating, Atwood's and Piercy's women forego the traditional romantic ending by giving up marriage and associating male dominance in personal relationships with meat-eating.[33] Thus, they give up meat as well.

The character who most successfully rejects both meat and marriage is Beth, in Marge Piercy's *Small Changes*. Newly married, she finds herself one night eating meat loaf at the kitchen table. Though shaken by a vehement argument during which her husband, angered by her apparent independence, had flushed her birth control pills down the toilet, she sits and contemplates her situation. As she chews the meat loaf she realizes her status as simultaneously victim and victimizer: "A trapped animal eating a dead animal."[34] She restores the absent referent:

> Remember the cold meat loaf. From the refrigerator she got the ketchup and doused it liberally. Then it was less obnoxious. Meat, a dead animal that had been alive. She felt as if her life were something slippery she was trying to grab in running water.

Grasping her life, she flees her domestic front, becoming a conscientious objector to the war against women and animals.[35] Beth undergoes numerous "small changes" on which Marge Piercy centers her novel. Beth's first and abiding change is her rejection of meat: "The revulsion toward eating flesh from the night of the meat loaf remained. It was part superstition and part morality: she had escaped to her freedom and did not want to steal the life of other warm-blooded creatures." (Her refusal of meat did not include fish.) Her insights of an expanded front catalyze her education into feminism, her evolution into lesbianism, and, finally, her important enactment of anti-war activism through a Traveling Women's Theater. Inevitably she denounces all war fronts.

Though Margaret Atwood's *The Edible Woman* takes place far from war it is in the midst of a war zone. Atwood's character, Marian, discovers there are no civilians there, only hunter or hunted, consumer or consumed. Marian's job is to assess the impact of a Moose beer ad that features hunting: "That was so the average beer-drinker, the slope-shouldered pot-bellied kind, would be able to feel a mystical identity with the plaid-jacketed sportsman shown in the pictures with his foot on a deer or scooping a trout into his net."[36] But Marian identifies with the victim and cries after hearing her fiancé describe his experience at the "front" as a hunter killing and eviscerating a rabbit.

An emotional argument over dinner propels Marian to realize that not only is she *at* the front, she is *the* front: She watches her fiancé skillfully cut his meat, and remembers the Moose beer ads, the hunter poised with a deer, which reminds her of the morning newspaper's report of a young boy who killed nine people after going berserk. Again she ponders her fiancé carving his steak and recalls her cookbook's diagram of a "cow with lines on it and labels to show you from which part of the cow all the different cuts were taken. What they were eating now was from some part of the back, she thought: cut on the dotted line." Then she casts her eyes at her own food.

> She looked down at her own half-eaten steak and suddenly saw it as a hunk of muscle. Blood red. Part of a real cow that once moved and ate and was killed, knocked on the head as it [*sic*] stood in a queue like someone waiting for a streetcar. Of course everyone knew that. But most of the time you never thought about it.

After this, Marian's unconscious attitude toward food changes: her body rejects certain foods and she realizes to her surprise that she is becoming a vegetarian, that her body has taken an ethical stand: "It simply refused to eat anything that had once been, or (like oysters on the half-shell) might still be living." Both meat-eating and first-person narration are suspended once Marian intuits her link to other animals, suggesting that a challenge to meat-eating is linked to an attack on the sovereign individual subject. The fluid, merged subjectivity of the middle part of the book finds mystical identity with things, especially animals, that are consumed.

Only when she can deal with her own sexual subjugation is Marian released from her body's refusal to eat. She confronts her fiancé with a truly edible woman, a cake she has made, and accuses: "You've been trying to destroy me, haven't you . . . You've been trying to assimilate me."[37] Domestic dynamics, a sexual war, led to vegetarianism. But so profound a challenge to the status quo seems too much to sustain: after breaking her engagement and freeing herself from subjugation to her fiancé, Marian both reclaims first-person narration and regains control over her body's selection of foods. Freed from domestic oppression, she has difficulty sustaining insights in opposition to the dominant worldview, and the pleasure of her own autonomy renders her less sensitive to others' oppression. Her consciousness of being (at) the front subsides. She begins to eat meat and to date men again.

If male dominance catalyzes the feminist insight of an expanded front and resultant vegetarianism, feminist vegetarianism offers men a way to reject war by rejecting meat-eating. As opposed to Piercy's and Atwood's controlling, masculine men, whose relationships with women catalyze the ineluctable insight that meat-eating and sexual oppression are linked, Agnes Ryan's unpublished novel "Who Can Fear Too Many Stars?" figures a romance of vegetarian conversion for a liberated man. Writing in the 1930s, Ryan introduced an unusual motivation for vegetarianism: love of a New Woman. Vegetarianism is the standard against which the new man is measured. As

Ryan described her work in a letter to the author of *The Golden Rule Cookbook*: "I would like to make it a ripping love story, hinging on meat-eating."[38]

Ruth, an independent, professional woman, is opposed to marriage yet finds herself in love with John Heather. Fearing that it will make their love "go asunder," Ruth withholds from John one vital piece of information. She will not "take anybody into [her] inner circle who can think and know – and still eat flesh." Unfortunately, John is a meat-eater. He struggles to become a vegetarian for the woman he loves, but, at Christmas, all romance collapses when he sends Ruth fox furs. Horrified by the gift and the lack of comprehension it reveals – John has not really understood her complete repugnance at exploiting animals – Ruth sends them back and flees. Deeply in love, John resolves to learn as much as possible about vegetarianism by reading, among others, nineteenth-century vegetarians Anna Kingsford and Bernard Shaw. The journal he keeps during this time reveals to Ruth that he is now fully a vegetarian, and as a result they can be married.

Vegetarianism and feminism act as antiphonal voices in this novel, not as a unified vision, except to demonstrate Ryan's theme "that there are many modern thinking women who mean to stiffen the case for men – or not marry."[39] While John reads vegetarian writings, Ruth receives a tract against marriage that warns "To be a bride is to become a slave, body and soul."[40] Ryan introduces vegetarian and feminist arguments into the novel through references to books, diaries, pamphlets; for her, texts mediate the conversion to vegetarianism and feminism. This adheres to the tradition of bearing the vegetarian word, believing that reading will bring about revelation and change. Whatever John and Ruth read, we must read as readers of Ryan's novel, thus we encounter both the literal and literary arguments for vegetarianism and feminism. But there is an imbalance there: while John reads his way into vegetarianism, Ruth avoids confronting the implication of romantic love. His fate as a male in love with a "modern thinking woman" is redemption. The word becomes flesh as he becomes a vegetarian. Ruth's fate as a modern thinking *married* woman will be to live in oppression. Ryan thus acknowledges there are some things that vegetarianism cannot redeem and that reading cannot accomplish. The text fails at this point: for what can be the fate of a woman in a ripping love story hinging on meat-eating? As a vegetarianism redeemed through romantic love is written into the text, *she* is written out of it. The novel collapses into itself and becomes a tract such as the ones that John and Ruth encounter.

Ryan's novel presents a variant formulation of vegetarianism as rejection of male control and violence. Rather than portray a woman who simultaneously rejects violence and dependence on a man, like Piercy's and Atwood's heroines, it figures a man who, through his love for a woman, discovers the ability to reject a warring world. John represents Ryan's husband, Henry Bailey Stevens, who held that humanity was initially vegetarian, goddess worshiping, and pacifist. These characteristics embody the fourth theme of the expanded front, the Golden Age of vegetarianism.

The Golden Age of Vegetarianism and Women's Fiction

Rynn Berry Jr.: *Do you think if more and more people become vegetarians, it will usher in a new Golden Age?* Brigid Brophy: No, not of itself. Bernard Shaw pointed out that human vegetarians were often very fierce people, and vegetarian animals also are often quite fierce. No, there is no direct connection. If, however, human beings work it out and decide to renounce violence then, obviously, if you renounce violence against chickens, cows, lambs, etcetera, you likewise renounce it against human beings. And then, yes – if we could all manage it – straight into the Golden Age.[41]

In *The Recovery of Culture*, Henry Bailey Stevens proposes that a plant culture – which he considers anthropologically and horticulturally verified – was replaced with a "blood culture." In a section entitled "The Rape of the Matriarchate" he writes: "The truth is that animal husbandry and war are institutions in which man has shown himself most proficient. He has been the butcher and the soldier; and when the Blood Culture took control of religion, the priestesses were shoved aside."[42] Novelists and short story writers join Stevens in locating the cause of meat-eating and war in male dominance; some twentieth-century women writers imagine a Golden Age before the fall that was feminist, pacifist, and vegetarian.

In the short story "An Anecdote of the Golden Age [Homage to *Back to Methuselah*]" Brigid Brophy suggests that men's behavioral change is at the root of war, women's oppression, and the killing of animals. Brophy's Golden Age is one in which immortals consume bounteous food from the garden. Naked women menstruate openly and their blood is admired by everyone for its rare beauty. However, men discover that they too bleed when two men engage in a blood-letting fist fight, and paradise is lost. Menstruation is tabooed and fruit, moments ago cherished food, is now disdained by one of the men, Strephon. He bombs another man's pagoda and offers this justification: "'Corydon was a murderer,' Strephon said sulkily. 'He was fair game. Which reminds me: I shall kill the animals next.'"[43] Strephon confines his menstruating woman to the house, "and preferably the kitchen, in which unglamorous setting she would be least attractive to other men." Brophy concludes her cautionary tale: "Strephon, the only one of the group to be truly immortal, is in power to this day."

Though obviously having a romp in this piece, Brophy's viewpoint is consistent with her other writings on the subject of the oppression of women and animals.[44] Brophy suggests that as long as men are in power, patriarchal violence and its attendant oppressions of women and animals will continue. This theme of the male overthrow of a pre-patriarchal vegetarian era also appears in June Brindel's *Ariadne: A Novel of Ancient Crete*. Blood sacrifice here is associated with male control. Ariadne, called by her author "the last Matriarch of Crete," attempts to introduce the ancient worshipful rituals featuring milk and honey but no blood. Brindel's feminist-vegetarian-pacifist mythopoesis figures a vegetarian time of powerful priestesses worshiping goddesses. The triumph of patriarchal control simultaneously introduces the slaughter of animals and the worship of male gods:

> Daedulus would ask a question about the ritual, cautiously. "The invocation to Zeus, when was that introduced into the ceremony? I do not find it in the oldest texts." Or, "The earliest records of offerings to the Goddess list only grains and fruit. When was the slaughter of animals added?"[45]

Brindel's dependence on early twentieth-century scholar Jane Harrison is evident in her description of the rituals followed by Ariadne. As women's power is displaced, Ariadne escapes to the mountains and pronounces that the labyrinth of Theseus is patriarchal thought that has killed the center, the Mother Goddess. Brindel continues this theme in *Phaedra: A Novel of Ancient Athens*, in which Phaedra, despite living in a hostile atmosphere, attempts to live a peaceful, vegetarian, goddess-worshiping life.[46] Brindel, like Brophy, evokes a female-centered Golden Age where there are no fronts and no wars.

Through diets for a peaceful vegetarian life, feminist utopias enact the critique of the expanded front, imagining a world without violence. This aspect of the fourth theme is initially depicted in the first feminist, vegetarian, pacifist utopia written by a woman, Charlotte Perkins Gilman's *Herland*, published during the Great War.[47] In *Herland*, we find menus recalling *The Golden Rule Cookbook*: "The breakfast was not profuse, but . . . this repast with its new but delicious fruit, its dish of large rich-flavored nuts, and its highly satisfactory little cakes was most agreeable."[48] Fruit- and nut-bearing trees, grains and berries, citrus fruits, olives and figs are carefully cultivated by the women inhabitants. Gilman's narrator, the American intellectual male of 1915, at once notices the absence of meat in *Herland* and queries: "Have you no cattle – sheep – horses?" In a novel that demonstrates the need for a feminine loving kindness, what Gilman called Maternal Pantheism, we might expect that their vegetarianism is one expression of mother love and the corollary belief that meat-eating causes aggressive behavior such as male dominance and war. But it is not. Instead, it is a politically astute and ecologically sound conclusion: wars can be avoided if meat-eating is eliminated. They did not have any cattle, sheep, or horses because they did "not want them anymore. They took up too much room – we need all our land to feed our people. It is such a little country, you know." What wartime had required of Denmark, the potential causation of war required of *Herland*.

Gilman's *Herland* is a feminist gloss on the ecological position enunciated in Plato's *Republic*.[49] Gilman's subtext about land use resulting in war is in opposition to the overt text, which suggests that motivations arising from Mother Love determine *Herland*'s policies. Through her use of the classical ecological argument of preventing wars through controlling diet, Gilman acknowledges that women living on their own would still have a potential for violence against each other *if* they left their diet uncontrolled. Thus women are not exempted from future wars, as Maternal Pantheism would imply. By extension, the Great War could not be the war that ends all wars if meat-eating continued. The issue of vegetarianism is an inevitable part of *Herland* because Gilman, while emphasizing women's strengths and abilities, deconstructs the essentials of patriarchal culture at its many fronts.

Whereas *Herland* is the initial text in which a modern woman writer posits the configuration of feminism, vegetarianism, and pacifism, Dorothy Bryant's more recent *The Kin of Ata are Waiting for You* extends Gilman's treatment by situating animals within the moral order. *The Kin of Ata* depicts an egalitarian utopian society in which men and women share child care, gardening, and cleaning. Dried fruits and nuts, grains and legumes, root vegetables and herbs provide great variety to the diet. And the reason for the diet is Bryant's 1970s equivalent to Maternal Pantheism: "I knew better than to suggest that we eat birds or animals, or even fish. They would have reacted the same way as if I had told them we should eat the children . . . No one would have thought of killing any of them."[50]

Because Gilman, Bryant, Ryan, and other women writers perceived connections between male dominance, war, and meat-eating, they figure men who demonstrate the ability to change. We find in their novels men who are adaptable, who forswear certain masculine and human-centered privileges, including meat consumption. In addition, sensitive male writers such as Shelley, Shaw, Salt, and Stevens explored the issues of animals' and women's otherness. Indeed, the conclusion to be drawn from their writings and their lives is that men as well as women can enact life-styles sensitive to issues of feminism, pacifism, and vegetarianism.

Rachel Blau DuPlessis comments that the "erasure of the dualism of public and private spheres is one part of the critique of ideology in women's writings."[51] Together the four themes arising from the insight of the expanded front exemplify this erasure. The meaning of the public front invades the private sphere, prompting a redefinition of the location of the front. Additionally, taken together these themes challenge the dualism separating the consequences of violence for animals and human beings. These works argue that domestic oppression and meat-eating, usually considered private occurrences, are vitally connected to waging war, while vegetarianism, an apparently private act, constitutes the public rejection of war as a method of conflict resolution. At the front, the connections between male dominance, the killing of animals, and the killing of human beings become clear.

The Narrative Strategy of Interruption

Central to all [Woolf's] thinking is the revelation of interruption, heralding change, and the growing expectation that society is on the verge of radical transformation.
Lucio Ruotolo, *The Interrupted Moment*[52]

The symbolism of meat-eating is never neutral. To himself, the meat-eater seems to be eating life. To the vegetarian, he seems to be eating death. There is a kind of gestalt-shift between the two positions which makes it hard to change, and hard to raise questions on the matter at all without becoming embattled.
Mary Midgley, *Animals and Why They Matter*[53]

We have examined novels in which feminist insights catalyze connections between vegetarianism and political violence. Each of these novels appears to employ the same literary technique for summoning these connections – a technique I call *interruption*. Interruption provides the gestalt shift by which vegetarianism can be heard. Technically, it occurs when the movement of the novel is suddenly arrested, and attention is given to the issue of vegetarianism in an enclosed section of the novel. The author provides signs that an interruption has occurred. Dots or dashes; the use of the word "interruption"; stammering, pauses, inarticulateness, or confusion in those who are usually in control; the deflection of the story to a focus on food and eating habits; or the reference to significant earlier figures or events from vegetarian history: all become the means for establishing an interruption, a gap in the narrative in which vegetarianism can be entertained.[54] Although the interruption is set apart, the meaning it contains speaks to central themes of the novel, unifying the interruption and the interrupted text through acute critical comments about the social order and meat-eating.[55]

In the works of modern women writers the intrusion into the text of a vegetarian incident announces a subversion of the dominant world order, enacted through the subversion of the text itself by the textual strategy of interruption. What was once silenced breaks into the text, deflecting attention from the forces that generally silence it, both thematically and textually. Interruption provides an opportunity for refocusing the trajectory of the text, as well as providing a protected space within the novel for expanding the front. Interruption does battle with the novel for meaning, wresting meaning from the dominant culture as represented in the text itself.[56] In essence, expanding the front requires extending the scope of the novel, taking it to new topical territory, and this is the function of interruption, which provides the needed space for such expansion. A vegetarian presence destabilizes patriarchal concerns.

Isadora Duncan's meditation on the connection between war and meat-eating in her autobiography *My Life* exemplifies the interruption of narrative. She interrupts a discussion about her life during the Great War to assert: "Bernard Shaw says that as long as men torture and slay animals and eat their flesh, we shall have war. I think all sane, thinking people must be of his opinion." From her wartime experience she concludes:

> Who loves this horrible thing called War? Probably the meat eaters, having killed, feel the need to kill – kill birds, animals – the tender stricken deer – hunt foxes. The butcher with his bloody apron incites bloodshed, murder. Why not? From cutting the throat of a young calf to cutting the throat of our brothers and sisters is but a step. While we are ourselves the living graves of murdered animals, how can we expect any ideal conditions on the earth?[57]

Duncan's interruption is clearly announced to readers by her beginning reference to Shaw and her ending with a literal invocation of what she believed to be his words.[58] However, she provides a distinctly feminist interpretation to Shaw's insights. By positioning the masculine pronoun between the butcher and the bloody apron, she implicitly indicts male behavior.

The most notable interruption in a text occurs during a Thanksgiving dinner in France, described in Mary McCarthy's *Birds of America*, a novel referred to briefly in Chapter 1. The novel moves forward without much regard to any specific ethics of consumption. Suddenly, a vegetarian speaks, attention becomes riveted to what the vegetarian is saying and not eating. The interruptions occur on many levels. Roberta Scott, a young American, refuses both dark and light meat from her host, a NATO general. Shocked, he must set down his carving knife before he can say, "*No turkey?*" With the carving knife he has arrogated power, and each slice of speared meat reinforces his military presence. Her refusal challenges his use of these symbolic implements and thus his power. His implements remain unused as he learns of her vegetarianism, and he must resort to playing "impatiently" with them as he solemnly informs his guest, "This is Thanksgiving!"[59]

Later, his wife asks, "What made you decide to take up vegetarianism? I don't mean to be intrusive, but tell us, do you really think it's cruel to kill animals?" Again, the general's actions are arrested by the presence of vegetarianism: "The general, who was carving seconds, paused with his knife in mid-air to await the verdict." In the midst of this interruption we find Miss Scott's precise echoing of the vegetarian position on warfare, artfully introduced into the text prior to a heated argument about the war in Vietnam:

> Why, some people actually claim that it's a flesh diet that's turned man into a killer of his own kind! He has the tiger's instincts without the tiger's taboos. Of course

that's only a hypothesis. One way of testing it would be for humanity to practice vegetarianism for several generations. Maybe we'd find that war and murder would disappear.

McCarthy's chapter uses domestic events to figure the claim that meat-eating causes war, as it traces the slowly escalating rage of the general for whom carving recalls his military might. He announces that he is "in command here," and discounts Miss Scott's refusal by giving her turkey anyway. But she will not eat it, nor any of the gravy-polluted foods he proffers. Her refusal implies that if meat-eating and war are related, as *some* people claim, then the dining-room table is a part of the extended front; her vegetarianism functions as a condemnation of war. The table soon becomes a site of simulated warfare, as an enlistee makes the sounds of an automatic machine gun. Meanwhile, the general perceives the subtle condemnation and escalates the verbal battle as he argues for the bombing of Hanoi. Pinpointing the cause of his bellicosity his wife confides, "Between you and me, it kind of got under his skin to see that girl refusing to touch her food, I saw that right away." McCarthy's novel pursues the question of how far moral obligations should extend; this interruption suggests that they extend to the quintessential bird of America.

The interruptions of *The Shooting Party* are caused by the appearance of Cornelius Cardew, who actually interrupts the shooting by bearing the vegetarian word through picketing. He shoulders his "Thou Shalt Not Kill" banner and marches "straight down the line in front of the guns."[60] Some of the shooters refuse to cease their firing, especially the most competitive one: "The interruption had not caused him to lose a single shot," but for the others, "their concentration had been broken by the interruption." By Cardew's interruption, the historical alliance between feminism and vegetarianism is suggestively summoned; he hands out his own pamphlet which, as we saw in Chapter 5, evokes past writers of vindications – Mary Wollstonecraft's *A Vindication of the Rights of Woman* and Percy Shelley's *A Vindication of Natural Diet*.

As these examples demonstrate, the interruptions contain their own legitimating mechanism by summoning historical figures who endorsed what the interruptions convey – the message of the expanded front. Essentially, vegetarian tradition provides the authority for interrupting the text with vegetarianism. Shaw is summoned by Duncan and Brophy, Salt by Colegate, the Doukhobors (Russian pacifist-vegetarians who migrated to Canada) by McCarthy and Atwood, and Kingsford by Ryan. It is striking that two different texts linking vegetarianism and pacifism insert the name of the Doukhobors, who maintained their vegetarianism and pacifism in rigorous circumstances, persecution, and banishment in Russia as well as migration as a group (estimated as high as 7,500 individuals) to Canada. The Doukhobors become grounding figures. This tradition of providing additional authority through historical references is a version of what any embattled group does – that is, evoke touchstone figures who in feminist terms we might consider "role models."

This historical invocation of past vegetarians imprints a distinctly feminist hermeneutic: Duncan's view of male butchers as inuring the world to bloodshed; McCarthy's female challenge to male bellicosity through dietary choice; Colegate's allusions to Wollstonecraft and Shelley as well as Salt. Situating historical reference within the interruption suggests that the notion of an expanded front is one that recurs in history. And through the feminist hermeneutic brought to vegetarian history, a causal link with male dominance and war is effected. Interruption destabilizes the text and the culture it represents.

Overcoming Dominant Viewpoints

There is not always encouragement and acceptance for those who try to introduce meanings for which there is no conceptual space in the social order.

Dale Spender, *Man Made Language*[61]

There is a kind of seductiveness about a movement which is revolutionary, but not revolutionary enough.

Mary Daly, *Beyond God the Father*[62]

How can we explain the heightened sensitivity by twentieth-century women writers to violence against animals and the failure among literary critics to remark on this sensitivity? When female marginality is "in dialogue with dominance" it invokes the position of animals, who are also on the margins, who are also absent referents.[63] Part of the otherness with which women writers identify is the otherness of the other animals; both are caught in the overlapping structure of oppression in which each functions as absent referents for the other. The "assertive repossession of voice" includes the expression of voice through identification with those who have none.[64]

Through specific female identifications catalyzed by male oppression, the character reflects on the question "How would you like it if this were done to you?" When Margaret Atwood's Marian cannot think of herself as *I*, when her first-person-singular identity is interrupted, her body becomes alert to the oppression of the other animals. What evolves is a poetics of engagement between women and animals, and a belief that violence against other animals carries the same seriousness as violence against people; where meat-eating is, there is the front. Vegetarianism becomes, then, a necessary accompaniment to pacifism. Challenging the dominant ethos that animals exist for human consumption by extension challenges a world at war.

Generally women as well as men hold to the powerful, dominant ethos regarding animals, just as Marian returns to eating meat once she is able to think again in the first-person singular. This causes the muting of a tradition that does not hold to the dominant ethos.

The tradition in which modern women writers confront the meaning of meat-eating within the context of war is one of a dialectic between silencing and risking speech. It is a tradition that speaks through specificity (i.e., naming what is eaten): interrupting a meal, interrupting a man's control, interrupting the male tradition with female voices. When women writers raise the issue of vegetarianism, they touch upon their dilemma of being silenced in a patriarchal world. Vegetarianism becomes a complex female meditation on being both dominated and dominator.

While modern vegetarianism interrupts modern women's writing and hence disrupts it as a way of finding space and power to speak, on a deeper level it confirms women's work. By redefining the front and locating it wherever meat-eating is, modern women writers make a powerful statement on the rights of women and women writers to have a voice during wartime. And this feminist, vegetarian, pacifist tradition – tracing its genesis to the Great War – would argue that an aspect of the war that gave it voice continues today.[65]

Notes

Epigraph: "Civilization? Culture?" notes for *Vegetarian Pocket Monthly*. Box 2, file no. 33, "Vegetarian Writings, circa 1952–3." All correspondence and unpublished manuscripts by Agnes Ryan cited in this chapter are in the Agnes Ryan Collection of the Arthur and Elizabeth Schlesinger Library on the History of Women in America, Radcliffe College, Cambridge, MA. Permission to publish material provided by The Schlesinger Library and the late Henry Bailey Stevens.

1. Mary Wollstonecraft Shelley, *Frankenstein or, The Modern Prometheus The 1818 Text*, ed. James Rieger, Indianapolis: Bobbs-Merrill, 1974; Chicago and London: University of Chicago Press, 1982, p. 142.
2. Edward Carpenter and George Barnefield, *The Psychology of the Poet Shelley* (London: George Allen & Unwin Ltd., 1925), p. 19.
3. C. Roland Marchand, *The American Peace Movement and Social Reform, 1898–1918* (Princeton: Princeton University Press, 1972), p. 202.
4. Olive Schreiner, *Woman and Labour* (1911, London: Virago, 1978), p. 176.
5. Virginia Woolf, *Three Guineas* (London: The Hogarth Press, 1938, 1968), pp. 13–14.
6. Agnes Ryan, "The Heart to Sing," unpublished autobiography, pp. 314–15.
7. Kohlberg is so struck by this that he cites this interchange in three of his lectures in Lawrence Kohlberg, *Essays on Moral Development, Volume I: The Philosophy of Moral Development* (New York: Harper & Row, 1981), pp. 14, 46, 143. James Sully's *Studies of Childhood* details a similar transition. He describes a four-year old who objected to his parents eating animals, to the killing of seals, and the hunting of stags. He wants the police to stop such activities and is informed that "They can't do that because people are allowed to kill them."

    > C. (loudly and passionately). "Allowed, allowed? People are not allowed to take other people and kill them." M. "People think there is a difference between killing men and killing animals."

    Sully refers to this time period as a time when the boy was wrestling "with the dreadful 'must,' which turns men into killers," and refers to the fact that at this time the boy has also learned to accept as positive the existence of soldiers. (James Sully, *Studies of Childhood* [New York and London: D. Appleton and Co., 1914], p. 475.)

    Matthew Lipman's *Lisa*, a book to aid children in focused discussions of philosophical and ethical issues, begins at episode 1 with the question, "Can We Both Love Animals and Eat Them?" A debate about hunting is described: One side argues that killing people evolves from hunting; the other that killing people is different from killing animals. Lisa remarks, "Once we get in the habit of killing animals, we may find it hard to stop when it comes to people." (Matthew Lipman, *Lisa* [Upper Montclair, New Jersey: Institute for the Advancement of Philosophy for Children, 1983], pp. 1, 2.)
8. Walter de la Mare, "Dry August Burned," *The Complete Poems of Walter de la Mare* (New York: Alfred A. Knopf, 1970), p. 365.
9. Mary Alden Hopkins, "Why I Earn My Own Living," in *These Modern Women: Autobiographical Essays from the Twenties* (Originally published 1926–1927 in *The Nation*), ed. Elaine Showalter (Old Westbury, NY: The Feminist Press, 1978), p. 44.
10. Reported in Andro Linklater, *An Unhusbanded Life: Charlotte Despard, Suffragette, Socialist and Sinn Feiner* (London: Hutchinson, 1980), p. 179.
11. The four were Alice Park, Lucinda Chandler, May Wright Sewall and Mary Alden Hopkins.
12. Eugene Christian, *Meatless and Wheatless Menus* (New York: Alfred A. Knopf, 1917), pp. 6–7.
13. Quincy Wright, *A Study of War*, Volume 1 (Chicago: University of Chicago Press, 1942), p. 134.

14. Edward Maitland, *Anna Kingsford: Her Life, Letters, Diary and Work* vol. 1 (London: Redway, 1896), p. 28.
15. Percy Shelley, *On the Vegetable System of Diet*, in *The Complete Works of Percy Bysshe Shelley*, Volume 6, ed. Roger Ingpen and Walter E. Peck (New York: Gordian Press, 1965), p. 343.
16. Quoted in Max Davis, *The Case for the Vegetarian Conscientious Objector* with a Foreword by Scott Nearing (Brooklyn, NY: Tolstoy Peace Group, 1944), p. 13.
17. Douglas Goldring, *The Nineteen Twenties: A General Survey and some Personal Memories* (London: Nicholson and Watson, 1945; reprinted by Folcroft Library Editions, 1975), p. 140.
18. L. F. Easterbrook, "Alcohol and Meat," *Nineteenth Century and After* 95 (February 1924), p. 306. One recent vegetarian, a true inheritor of this position, traced his abandonment of meat-eating to viewing "posters that showed the devastation of people and property in Vietnam." In response he asked himself, "What am I doing eating meat? I'm just adding to the violence." The *New York Times*, interview with Frederick P. Salvucci, March 21, 1975, p. 33. Dick Gregory writes of the connection between vegetarianism and the nonviolent civil rights movement:

> Under the leadership of Dr. King I became totally committed to nonviolence, and I was convinced that nonviolence meant opposition to killing in any form. I felt the commandment "Thou shalt not kill" applied to human beings not only in their dealings with each other – war, lynching, assassination, murder and the like – but in their practice of killing animals for food or sport. Animals and humans suffer and die alike. Violence causes the same pain, the same spilling of blood, the same stench of death, the same arrogant, cruel and brutal taking of life.

Dick Gregory's Natural Diet for Folks Who Eat: Cookin' with Mother Nature ed. James R. McGraw (New York: Harper & Row, 1973), pp. 15–16.
19. Mary Midgley, *Animals and Why They Matter* (Athens: The University of Georgia Press, 1983), p. 15.
20. The more extensive appeal to English women to become vegetarians during World War II is detailed in Raynes Minns, *Bombers and Mash: The Domestic Front 1939–45* (London: Virago, 1980).
21. Mikkel Hindhede, "The Effect of Food Restriction During War on Mortality in Copenhagen." *Journal of the American Medical Society*, 74 no. 6 (February 7, 1920), p. 381. Similar studies after World War II confirmed a relationship between a drop in mortality and the rationing of food. Axel Str#tom, M.D. and R. Adelsten Jensen, M.D. "Mortality from Circulatory Diseases in Norway 1940–1945," *The Lancet* 260 (Jan. 2, 1951), pp. 126–29.
22. Mervyn G. Hardinge and Hulda Crooks, "Non-Flesh dietaries. 1. Historical Background," *Journal of the American Dietetic Association* 43 (December 1963), p. 548.
23. Quoted by Rynn Berry, Jr., *The Vegetarians* (Brookline, MA: Autumn Press, 1979), p. 44.
24. Henry Salt, *Seventy Years Among the Savages*, quoted in George Hendrick, with the special assistance of John F. Pontin, *Henry Salt: Humanitarian Reformer and Man of Letters* (Urbana, Chicago, London: University of Illinois Press, 1977), p. 84.
25. Agnes Ryan, "For the Church Door," March 1943, Box 2.
26. Amanda Cross, *The James Joyce Murders* (New York: Macmillan Co., 1967), p. 89.
27. See Paul Fussell's discussion of these works, *The Great War and Modern Memory* (London, Oxford, New York: Oxford University Press, 1975), p. 91.
28. Henry Salt, "Sport as a Training for War," in *Killing for Sport: Essays by Various Writers*, ed. Henry Salt (London: G. Bell and Sons, Ltd. for the Humanitarian League, 1914).

29. In Graves's *Good-Bye to All That* (Jonathan Cape: 1929, Hammondsmith, Eng.: Penguin Books, 1957) the first paragraph of the first chapter ends: "or Mr Eustace Miles the English real-tennis champion and vegetarian with his samples of exotic nuts, I knew all about them in my way" (p. 9). See also Fussell, *The Great War*, pp. 203–20.
30. In his introduction to *The Home*, William O'Neill maintains that Gilman "published very little after the war," and attributes this to the fact that "World War I, and the changes that accompanied it, destroyed the moral foundation of her career" (William O'Neill, Introduction to *The Home* by Charlotte Perkins Gilman [Urbana: University of Illinois Press, 1972], p. x.) In contrast, I would argue that the war confirmed her claim of the need to involve women and women's values in decision making, and that *Herland* and *His Religion and Hers* suggest in opposite ways, first positively and then negatively, the conclusion that violence was a result of male dominance. *His Religion and Hers: A Study of the Faith of Our Fathers and the Work of Our Mothers* (London: T. Fisher Unwin, 1924).
31. Isabel Colegate, *The Shooting Party* (New York: The Viking Press, 1980, New York: Avon Books, 1982), p. 131. Other quotations cited in this chapter are found on pp. 20, 102, 188.
32. See for instance Susan Schweik, "A Word No Man Can Say for Us: American Women Writers and the Second World War" (PhD dissertation, Yale University, 1984) which examines the phenomenon that, especially during wartime, women are to be the receivers of information, objects who read, not objectors who write; repositories of meaning, not originators of meaning.
33. I am indebted here to DuPlessis's analysis, in *Writing beyond the Ending*, of women writers' strategy for challenging traditional romance. See Rachel Blau DuPlessis, *Writing beyond the Ending: Narrative Strategies of Twentieth-Century Women Writers* (Bloomington: Indiana University Press, 1985).
34. Marge Piercy, *Small Changes* (Garden City: Doubleday and Co., 1972, Greenwich, Conn: A Fawcett Crest Book, 1973), p. 41. The succeeding quotations in this paragraph are found on pp. 42, 48.
35. These metaphors are mine and not Piercy's. I use them to suggest that from her epiphanal moment in her kitchen, Beth evolves a systematic, ongoing rejection of a male, meat-eating culture that can be best represented by using metaphors from the anti-war movement.
36. Margaret Atwood, *The Edible Woman* (Boston: Little Brown and Co., New York: Warner Books, 1969), p. 25. Further quotations in this chapter are found on pp. 155, 183, 279.
37. Atwood reports that the idea for this scene came as she was looking "at a confectioner's display window full of marzipan pigs. It may have been a Woolworth's window full of Mickey Mouse cakes, but in any case I'd been speculating for some time about symbolic cannibalism." This scene, both as she experienced it as an individual and inscribed it as a novelist, exemplifies the structure of the absent referent. She saw a Marzipan pig or Mouse cakes; she imagines an edible woman cake. This association demonstrates the interchangeability of the categories of animal and woman. In addition, the relationship between symbol (cake animal or cake woman) and reality (consumed animal or consumed woman) suggests the alliance between what is really consumed and what is figured as being consumed. See Margaret Atwood, "An Introduction to *The Edible Woman*," in *Second Words: Selected Critical Prose* (Boston: Beacon Press, 1982), p. 369.
38. Letter to Freshel, October 14, 1936, Box 6, file no. 81.
39. Letter, March 23, 1937, Box 4, file no. 82.
40. "Who Can Fear Too Many Stars?", Box 3, file no. 35, p. 131.
41. Berry interview with Brophy in Berry, p. 88.
42. Henry Bailey Stevens, *The Recovery of Culture* (New York: Harper & Row, 1949), p. 105.
43. Brigid Brophy, "An Anecdote of the Golden Age [Homage to *Back to Methuselah*]," in *The Adventures of God in his Search for the Black Girl* (Boston: Little, Brown & Co., 1968), p. 35.

44. See for instance, "The Rights of Animals" and "Women" in Brophy, *Don't Never Forget: Collected Views and Reviews* (New York: Holt, Rinehart and Winston, 1966), pp. 15–21, 38–44; *Hackenfeller's Ape* (London: Allison and Busby, 1953, 1979); and "In Pursuit of Fantasy," in *Animals, Men, and Morals: An Enquiry into the Maltreatment of Non-Humans*, ed. Stanley Godlovitch, Roslind Godlovitch, and John Harris (London: Gollancz, and New York: Taplinger, 1972).
45. June Rachuy Brindel, *Ariadne: A Novel of Ancient Crete* (New York: St. Martin's Press, 1980), p. 76.
46. June Rachuy Brindel, *Phaedra: A Novel of Ancient Athens* (New York: St. Martin's Press, 1985).
47. It could be argued that Shelley's *Queen Mab* is the first feminist, vegetarian, pacifist utopia.
48. Charlotte Perkins Gilman, *Herland* (New York: Pantheon Books, 1979, p. 27). First serialized in the *Forerunner* 6 (1915).
49. As I summarized this position in chapter 6, Socrates tells Glaucon that meat production necessitates large amounts of pasture. Resultingly, it will require cutting "off a slice of our neighbours' territory; and if they too are not content with necessaries, but give themselves up to getting unlimited wealth, they will want a slice of ours." Thus Socrates pronounces, "So the next thing will be, Glaucon, that we shall be at war." Plato, *The Republic of Plato*, trans. Francis MacDonald Cornford, (New York and London: Oxford University Press, 1966), 2. 373, p. 61. See also Frances Moore Lappé, *Diet for a Small Planet: Tenth Anniversary Edition* (New York: Ballantine Books, 1971, 1982), pp. 67–74.
50. Dorothy Bryant, *The Kin of Ata are Waiting for You* (1971, Berkeley: Moon Books, 1976), originally titled *The Comforter*, p. 159.
51. DuPlessis, p. 113.
52. Lucio P. Ruotolo, *The Interrupted Moment: A View of Virginia Woolf's Novels* (Stanford: Stanford University Press, 1986), p. 16.
53. Midgley, *Animals and Why They Matter*, p. 27.
54. Dale Spender points out that "98 per cent of interruptions in mixed sex conversation were made by males." She continues, "Interruption is a mechanism by which (a) males can prevent females from talking, and (b) they can gain the floor for themselves; it is therefore a mechanism by which they engineer female silence." If women are not supposed to interrupt men in public, yet the presence of a vegetarian, especially at dinners, will call attention to the vegetarian and cause an interruption or disruption, then women have found a way of dislodging the conversation without being seen as verbally aggressive. Dale Spender, *Man Made Language* (London: Routledge & Kegan Paul, 1980), pp. 43–44.
55. In a similar vein, Lucio P. Ruotolo argues that finding meaning in interruption is important when considering the novels of Virginia Woolf. Ruotolo argues for the creative, positive nature of interruption because of the new direction it provokes, the new space it creates. "Those who allow the often-random intrusion of others to reshape their lives emerge at times heroically. Those who voice distaste for interruption fall back, invariably it seems, into self-supporting insularity." *The Interrupted Moment*, p. 2.
56. War images in this sentence remind us that the patterns of war have been adopted in the style and content of discourse.
57. Isadora Duncan, *My Life* (New York: Liveright, 1927, 1955), p. 309.
58. Emarel Freshel and others ascribe to Shaw a poem entitled "Living Graves," which begins:

> We are the living graves of murdered beasts,
> Slaughtered to satisfy our appetites.

As Janet Barkas reports: "It continues in a similarly violent vein to condemn animal slaughter as well as war. However, there are no references to this work in any of Shaw's manuscripts, notebooks, correspondence, or diaries. That it was created by Shaw as an

adventure in rhyming is possible but improbable." Janet Barkas, *The Vegetable Passion: A History of the Vegetarian State of Mind* (New York: Charles Scribner's Sons, 1975) p. 89.
59. Mary McCarthy, *Birds of America* (New York: Harcourt Brace Jovanovich, 1965, New York: New American Library, 1972), p. 166. Further quotations are from pp. 171, 172, 183.
60. Colegate, *The Shooting Party*, p. 92.
61. Spender, *Man Made Language*, pp. 82–83.
62. Mary Daly, *Beyond God the Father: Toward a Philosophy of Women's Liberation* (Boston: Beacon Press, 1973), p. 56.
63. See DuPlessis, p. 115.
64. DuPlessis, p. 107.
65. Jean Bethke Elshtain makes an observation about this fact as she concludes her preface to *Women and War*. "In thinking and sometimes dreaming about war over the past few years; in reading war stories and watching war movies; in composing portions of chapters on walks as well as on my word processor, I have gained a heightened awareness of the fleeting preciousness of life, including the lives we humans share with the other creatures with whom we have yet to learn to live in decency." Jean Bethke Elshtain, *Women and War* (New York: Basic Books, Inc., 1987), p. xiv.

Epigraphs to Part 3: Ruth Bordin, *Frances Willard: A Biography* (Chapel Hill and London: University of North Carolina Press, 1986), p. 122. Fran Winant, "Eat Rice Have Faith in Women," in Winant, *Dyke Jacket: Poems and Songs* (New York: Violet Press, 1980).

2

Veganism and Modernism

Catherine Brown

Modernism and Zoophilia

"Modernism" – an academic term used especially since the 1960s to denote avant-garde Western art forms of the early twentieth-century – has been used within Anglophone literary studies to refer especially to formally-innovative texts written between around 1910 and 1930. Recently "new modernism studies" has challenged this narrow focus, broadening the concept to include works of a range of styles which consciously respond to the conditions of late nineteenth- and early twentieth-century modernity. Their subjects include the nature and role of art as part of this modernity; consciousness and agency; physical health and degeneration; the relationship of ethics to science, new technologies, and mass production; new supra-national political and cultural movements; and new understandings of religion, race, class, gender, and species. All of these subjects inflect the period's "zoophilia" (the term is from 1894), as manifest in movements including vegetarianism (developing out of a strong Victorian tradition), anti-vivisectionism (which reached a peak in the Edwardian period), and anti-hunting sentiment (which reached a peak between the Wars).

Delimiting the investigations of this chapter to "vegan" authors of the long modernist period, even allowing the term to operate retroactively from 1944, would have left no canonical authors at all, while narrowing by vegetarian writers would have left only a well-trodden few. Rather, this chapter considers how a range of writers – almost none of them vegetarians, but all manifesting elements of a vegan consciousness as broadly conceived – have explored the category of the *human* in relation to the treatment of nonhuman animals.[1] Veganism is, after all, a human and ethical phenomenon, and with this focus the chapter aims to complement the considerable body of work that has already been done on modernist literary representations of nonhuman animals (notably by critics including Margot Norris and Carrie Rohman). It does so by concentrating on those human characteristics – especially the imagination – which may conduce towards veganism.

This chapter is further delimited by a focus on slaughter and hunting. By considering both we gain a binocular vision of how modernist writers have considered humanity through the lenses of the most violent aspects of its relationships with animals: slaughter relating to human practice since the agricultural revolution, hunting pre-dating it. Thomas Hardy's 1895 *Jude the Obscure* and William Golding's 1954 *Lord of the Flies* introduce these topics respectively and between them mark the outer boundaries of the period of my concern. Two further sections, on one topic each, consider texts temporally located between these boundaries, focusing respectively on

Upton Sinclair's 1906 *The Jungle* and Henry Williamson's 1927 *Tarka the Otter*. In concluding, my remit broadens to how authors' imaginative compensation to animals for humans' cruelty towards them functions in the works described, including a few extra works from the 1920s by D. H. Lawrence. The texts range from the realistic (*The Jungle* and *Tarka the Otter*) to the fabular (*The Wind in the Willows* and *Lord of the Flies*). As will become apparent, their vegan consciousness becomes most apparent when the former are read metonymically and the latter literally.

"'Where hast thou been, sister?' 'Killing swine'"[2]

Jude Fawley's imagining of his future as a Bishop is shattered first by derision: "Ha, ha, ha! Hoity-toity!", and then by the impact of a pig's penis – both flung by the woman who will shortly afterwards draw him away from theology and into sensuous experience (Hardy, *Jude* 43). From this point onwards *Jude the Obscure* enters vigorously into the exploration of humans' ontological status in the universe – an exploration which may at least in part be traced historically in the changing connotations of the species name. The Roman "humanitas" connoted the "civilized" behavior of those humans considered least to resemble nonhuman animals (thus "animality" was and has long been pinned onto "marginalized [human] others" [Rohman 30]). When the term surfaced in fifteenth-century English it asserted rather a contrast with divinity (*human, all too human*), yet the concomitant redirection of human thought to the "proper study" of itself in the "humanities" lent itself to a concern for human good that was to be found in various forms of "humanism," in "humane" behavior, and in what from the 1830s onwards was known as "humanitarianism."

But Jude lived in the age of Darwin, whose 1859 *On the Origin of Species* had "collapsed the cardinal distinctions between animal and human, arguing that they exhibit intellectual, moral, and cultural differences in degree only, not in kind" (Norris 3). At the same time Nature, previously envisaged variously as a neo-Classical machine, a constitutional lawyer, and a Romantic goddess, became "red in tooth and claw," and for some displaced gods of all kinds (Williams 219–24). Yet it was apparent at the level of lived experience that individual humans had a choice as to how red their teeth and claws were; indeed, their species had an apparently exceptional degree of choice over what or indeed whether to eat, just as they did over whether to reproduce. Not all social Darwinists advocated competition; others drew from Darwin an endorsement of cooperation, both within their species and beyond (Williams 224). Vegetarians of various motivations (from orthorexic to pacifist, utilitarian to utopian, Christian to spiritualist to socialist) represented a vocal if small minority of British society (Gregory 1–2).[3]

The owner of the pig's penis, Arabella Donn, is the daughter of a pig farmer (Jude's aunt, by symbolic contrast, is a baker). On the one hand she is presented as animal: she not only has "the rich complexion of a Cochin hen's egg" but hatches just such an egg in her cleavage, where it excites Jude to lust in "commonplace obedience to conjunctive orders from headquarters" (Hardy, *Jude* 44, 61, 45). These headquarters are what Freud was shortly to theorize as the "Unbewusstsein," which itself, as Rohman points out, was strongly allied with the concept of animality (23). On the other hand, this arousal of lust is significantly calculated towards achieving the financial advantage of Jude as a husband, and Arabella brings the same economic acumen to her exploitation of animals. During her first encounter with Jude she retrieves the hurled penis because it can be used for making dubbin (Hardy, *Jude* 43).

Their marital cottage is chosen such that "[Jude] might have the profits of a vegetable garden, and utilize her past experiences by letting her keep a pig" (64). This gendered division of labor between vegetables and animals is complicated when "The time arrived for killing the pig" (69). The professional pig-killer having been delayed, Arabella announces: "you must do the sticking . . . I'll show you how. Or I'll do it myself – I think I could." Jude insists that he do it, but, having tied the screaming pig up, declares: "Upon my soul I would sooner have gone without the pig than have had this to do!" (70). To this statement of a preference that many vegetarian campaigners assumed to be the default for all humans who had not been morally anaesthetized (Gregory 91), Arabella responds: "Don't be such a tender-hearted fool! There's the sticking-knife – the one with the point" (Hardy, *Jude* 70). Her words recall Lady Macbeth's injunction to her husband to "screw" his "courage to the sticking-place" when handing him the knives with which to kill Duncan, and subsequent declaration that it is "A foolish thought, to say a sorry sight" (Shakespeare 1.7.60, 981; 2.2.19, 982). The Macbeths, like the Fawleys, contest the nature of "manhood"; to Macbeth's assertion: "I dare do all that may become a man;/ Who dares do more is none" his wife responds: "What beast was't then/ That made you break this enterprise to me? . . . When you durst do it, then you were a man" (1.7.46–8, 981). At the end of this play, in which it is witches who kill swine, Malcolm associates butchers with devils in his reference to "this dead butcher and his fiend-like queen" (5.11.35, 999).

Jude himself repudiates the role of butcher as incompatible with manhood; after killing the pig he

> felt dissatisfied with himself as a man at what he had done, though aware . . . that the deed would have amounted to the same thing if carried out by deputy. The white snow, stained with the blood of his fellow-mortal, wore an illogical look to him as a lover of justice, not to say a Christian; but he could not see how the matter was to be mended. (Hardy, *Jude* 73)

The narrative goes no further in seeing how it could be mended than does Jude, and it, no more than Jude, perceives that the deed amounting "to the same thing if carried out by deputy" more consistently condemns than exculpates pig-killers both professional and amateur. Hardy had lived in the London of the 1860s and 1870s, which had several vegetarian restaurants, and Jude moves to Christminster in the 1860s, by which point provincial English towns also contained them (Gregory 134). But then, Hardy's is not a novel of solutions. Of the manifold motivations for contemporary vegetarianism one was the Christianity which informs Jude's revulsion from killing; another was the desire for "pure" food in order to avoid degeneracy. In the novel's tragic universe, degeneracy has freer rein than does a Christian God. Nonetheless, the nature of its tragedy rests on a conception of humanity which forbids the slaughter of a "fellow-mortal." Moreover, for all Arabella's sensuality, the aspect of her which is ready to kill pigs, or to throw Jude's *humane* books on the floor to create the space on which to make pig lard, is calculating and mechanical rather than animal; against this principle pig and human are united in protest (Hardy, *Jude* 73). The next day the marriage ends.

Hardy's choice of the pig as the animal which ends Jude and Arabella's marriage is not only socio-economically plausible (pigs predominating in working-class meat) but related to the particular guilt felt at the killing of long-term companion animals (pigs lived close to humans for ease of fattening and of the hygienic disposal of waste food). Kate Soper hypothesizes that the human propensity to project negative characteristics such as greed, overweening state force, and male chauvinism onto pigs may in part arise from a desire to allay the guilt that attached to the killing of these family members, along with an awareness of their anthropoid characteristics: intelligence, hairlessness, and anatomical proximity (87–88). It is awareness of this kinship, combined with the negative projections that may have arisen in order to mask it, that informs the choice of pigs as replacing humans in Orwell's 1945 *Animal Farm*.

"Kill the pig! Cut her throat! Spill her blood!"[4]

A decade later still, and we are a full six decades from *Jude the Obscure*. We have over-leapt modernism's core period to a work of late modernism which also makes the killing of pigs central to its meditation on humanity in the context of a failed Christianity, this time in relation to hunting. Indeed, in Golding's *Lord of the Flies* it is the shipwrecked choir boys who are fastest transformed into hunters, the tatters of their vestments flying behind as they pursue the island's pigs. Significantly, the most rational and least violent of the boys on the island is called "Piggy"; in his name his superior intelligence, plumpness, status as a mammal vulnerable to being killed (when fatally wounded "Piggy's arms and legs twitched a bit, like a pig's after it has been killed" [Golding 223]), and status as a pacific near-total vegetarian meet. He opposes neither hunting nor meat-eating on principle, but understands these practices to be incompatible with the maintenance of a sustainable society: with the systematic provision of shelter, or (through the maintenance of a fire) with the possibility of the boys' reintegration into wider society.

The novel's vegan sensibility is, it should be acknowledged, focused entirely on the pigs. The "odd fish or crab" with which the boys supplement their otherwise fruitarian diet have no attention paid to their killing (92). Essentially, the novel's thought experiment places its humans in the conditions of the period prior to agriculture, when – as the boys have doubtless been taught at school – humans were "hunter-gatherers." The narrative, however, breaks this hyphenation apart. This breaking had begun analytically with the Victorians, some of whom argued that the "paleolithic" diet was meat based, and others that humans were originally fruitarian.[5] *Lord of the Flies* presents the division psychologically and politically. Whatever the medium-term nutritional implications of fruitarianism, the hunters do not give its adherents the freedom to discover.

The boys are initially placed in an Eden. Within it, the forbidden fruit is the pigs. On their first exploration, when Jack and Ralph come across a piglet tangled in creepers, Jack "drew his knife again with a flourish . . . The pause was only long enough for them to understand what an enormity the downward stroke would be" (40). Committing this enormity produces, as in Eden, "knowledge"; after his first kill Jack's "mind was crowded with . . . the knowledge that had come to them when they closed in on the struggling pig, knowledge that they had outwitted a living thing . . . taken away its life like a long satisfying drink" (88). Against the *humanitas* which senses the enormity of pig-killing is counterposed bloodlust; the boundary between the predatory and the sexual is frequently lost in the hunting scenes, especially when the victim is female. The kill described in greatest detail, for example, is that of a sow, and the age of the hunting "bigguns," in relation to puberty, is salient. Roger impales her anus with his spear, and when "The sow collapsed under them . . . they were heavy and fulfilled upon her" (168). The narrator, Ralph, and Piggy at various times describe this lust in animal terms. When Simon is killed "There were no words, and no movements but the tearing of teeth and claws" (188). Ralph tells Piggy: "If I blow the conch and they don't come back; then . . . We'll be like animals" (115).

The condemnation resembles that of Mr. Scott to the organizer of dog fights in Jack London's 1906 *White Fang*: "you're not a man. You're a beast" (247). However, the identification is in both cases anthropomorphic, projecting onto animal predators the sexual sadism, delight in transgression, and masculine pride and competitiveness in violence that humans experience; moreover on the island, in contrast to London's Canadian wilderness, there are no animal predators against whom to compare them. Something similar applies to the discourse of "savagery." Piggy asks "What are we? Humans? Or animals? Or savages? What's grown-ups going to think? Going off – hunting pigs" (Golding 113). His racist implicit conflation of "savages" with children is followed up by his later question to Jack's "tribe": "Which is better – to be a pack of painted niggers like you are, or to be sensible like Ralph is? . . . to have rules and agree, or to hunt and kill?" (222). Again, unlike London's Canada the island lacks an indigenous human population, and Jack's tribe, performatively reaching towards a transgressively imagined "other," resembles any such as there might have been in nothing more than the quintessentially superficial aspect of face paint.

Meanwhile the "Beast" is multiply determined, including as "mankind's essential illness," or what Ralph apprehends to be "the darkness of man's heart," made flesh once humans kill animals (111, 248). Moreover, as pacifist vegetarians of the Romantic period onwards had argued to be the case, the killing of an animal is a gateway to the killing of humans (Gregory 113, 118). Ralph is finally forced to run along pig-tracks and think like a pig: "Hide, then. He wondered if a pig would agree" (Golding 141, 242). To assist with the hunting the entire island is set on fire; the novel's ending scales this up from the local to the global, as the boys' rescue by the British military re-absorbs them into a nuclear war which could destroy the planet as effectually as the boys destroy the island. The modern reader is likely to read the fire in relation to the virulent bushfires (such as those of 2019–2020 in Australia) which have resulted partly from climate change, just as she may read the novel's pig-eating as metonymic for the meat-eating which is a major contributory factor to that climate change. History since the 1950s has conduced progressively to a metonymic, rather than a metaphoric, reading of the novel.

Jude the Obscure was concerned with slaughter and *Lord of the Flies* with hunting. Both, in different ways, hypothesize a contradiction between humanity and animal killing, while also demonstrating it to be in practice all-too-human. The rest of this chapter will continue this investigation by considering a few texts which lie temporally between them and which offer examples of either practice – starting with slaughter.

"But I'm glad I'm not a hog!"[6]

Three years before Hardy published *Jude the Obscure*, Leo Tolstoy described his witnessing of an actual farmstead pig-killing in very similar terms to Hardy's description of Jude's. When the human-like squeals finally end, a fellow observer "sighed heavily. 'Do men really not have to answer for such things?' he said. So strong is man's aversion to all killing" (Tolstoy, "The First Step"). Tolstoy had converted to vegetarianism in 1888, soon after finishing *Kholstomer*, a novella about a horse who constitutes, like Swift's Houyhnhnms, a noble contrast to a corrupt humanity. But the main purpose of his 1892 essay "The First Step" (written as a preface to Howard Williams's 1883 anthology of vegetarianism, *The Ethics of Diet*) is to describe Tolstoy's visit to his local slaughterhouse in Tula. He observes that "It is built on the new and improved system practised in large towns, with a view to causing the animals as little suffering as possible." Nonetheless, many of the slaughters that he observes there are botched, prolonged, and painful. Tolstoy's particular objection is that

> man suppresses in himself, unnecessarily, the highest spiritual capacity – that of sympathy and pity towards living creatures like himself ... by example, by encouraging greediness, by the assertion that God has allowed it, and, above all, by habit, people entirely lose this natural feeling.

Just over a decade later Upton Sinclair spent seven weeks undercover in the meat-processing district of Chicago; his novel about this experience, *The Jungle*, was published in 1906. The Chicago stockyards (opened in 1865 and fully mechanized by the 1880s) represented the cutting edge of the industrial modernity which Tula sought to imitate; at Tula a hundred cattle were killed per day, at Chicago, ten thousand (Pacyga 153, 155; Sinclair 42). However, as the practice of slaughter had evolved from the solitary skilled work of Kholstomer's knacker and Jude's local pig-killer to Chicago's production line, the skill, pay, and autonomy of the slaughterers diminished sharply (Pacyga 153, 156). Several things follow from this decline in power, within the novel's socialist perception.

One is that, just as slaughterhouse mechanization proved paradigmatic for the development of other production lines such as that of car manufacture, as Carol J. Adams argues (52–53), and that of First World War slaughter, as Tromanhauser argues, the stockyard worker is presented as paradigmatic of exploited labor, and meat production of Darwinian exploitative capitalism: "it was especially true in Packingtown; there seemed to be something about the work of slaughtering that tended to ruthlessness and ferocity" (Sinclair 376). Scarcely any other legal mode of urban employment is represented in the novel, and those that do exist are represented as controlled by it ("With the millions of dollars a week that poured in upon it, it was reaching out for the control of other interests" [Sinclair 377]). As in *Lord of the Flies*, the "jungle" represents a society in which humans and animals are alike preyed upon by human "beasts of prey" (376). But the fact that in this case the latter are "the Beef Trust" enforces the irony that in this jungle there is scarcely any possibility of flight; the mainly immigrant workers are herded by economic necessity into the slums which surround the stockyards, as the animals are brought (equally by train) to their pens. A strike pushes this metaphor to literalism when the strike-breakers camp in the yards, "an army of fifteen or twenty thousand human beasts" (328). Whereas in *Jude the Obscure* Arabella's complexion resembles a cochin's egg, the men and women who work in Elzbieta's department are precisely the colour of the "fresh country sausage" they make, and are only a slip of the knife away from entering their own production line (156).

The "animality" of the novel's humans, therefore, focuses not, as in *Lord of the Flies*, on the predators but on the predated; not on the desire to kill but on the endurance of living standards which would be experienced by certain animals with less discomfort and detriment to their health ("the men ate as much raw blood as food at dinner-time" [123]). The title of Gerald Durrell's 1956 memoir *My Family and Other Animals* is comic in its conflation of human family members with animals. In *The Jungle* the same conflation occurs in a tragic key; the protagonist Jurgis's family live like animals, and his life consists of trying to keep those animals alive through killing the "other animals" of the stockyards. The workers are only described as resembling predators when they become criminals; when Jurgis's criminal career is thwarted "he was as literally crippled as any wild animal which has lost its claws"; "he must take his chances with the common herd" (335). As in *Lord of the Flies*, however, the analogy is anthropocentrically denotative of human, rather than animal, behaviors.

Moreover, the emphasis on the stockyards' mechanization complicates the analogy, meaning that the novel engages with the full range of what since World War II has been denoted by the Janus-faced term "posthuman": the natural or animal on the one hand, and the technological on the other. The stockyard machines render the workers nearly as vulnerable as the nonhuman animals they kill precisely by making them adjuncts to machines. This mechanization of humanity was deplored a few decades later by D. H. Lawrence, who in 1930 observed: "The dark, satanic mills of Blake / how much darker and more satanic they are now!", and asked "What is a man to do? . . . When the vast vast masses of men have been caught by the machine/ into the industrial dance of the living death, the jigging of wage-paid work, / and fed on condition they dance this dance of corpses driven by steam" – lines that apply with particular literalism to the Chicago stockyards (*Poems* 543, 545). Animal-like in relation to machines, machine-like in relation to animals, the workers are alienated not just from their labor but from the animals they kill.

Over the course of *The Jungle* the protagonist only gradually reaches alignment with the narrator and reader in his understanding of his likeness to the animals; when Jurgis and his family first tour the killing beds, "the sight suggested to them no metaphors of human destiny" (Sinclair 42). He rather more clearly apprehends, however, the animals' likeness to humans in their desire for life. In a passage colored by free indirect speech that is worth quoting at length, the narrator comments:

> It was porkmaking by machinery, porkmaking by applied mathematics. And yet somehow the most matter-of-fact person could not help thinking of the hogs; they were so innocent, they came so very trustingly; and they were so very human in their protests – and so perfectly within their rights! They had done nothing to deserve it; and it was adding insult to injury, as the thing was done here, swinging them up in this cold-blooded, impersonal way . . . It was like some horrible crime committed in a dungeon, all unseen and unheeded, buried out of sight and of memory.

> One could not stand and watch very long without becoming philosophical, without beginning to . . . hear the hog squeal of the universe . . . Each one of these hogs was a separate creature . . . And each of them had an individuality of his own, a will of his own, a hope and a heart's desire; each was full of self-confidence, of self-importance, and a sense of dignity. And trusting and strong in faith he had gone about his business, the while a black shadow hung over him and a horrid Fate waited in his pathway . . . Perhaps some glimpse of all this was in the thoughts of our humble-minded Jurgis, as he turned to go on with the rest of the party, and muttered: "Dieve—but I'm glad I'm not a hog!" (44–45)

Fernihough notes that modernists who believed that texts should be *chewed* (just as followers of Horace Fletcher believed that food should be lengthily masticated for maximum benefit) considered literary realism to resemble either pre-digested food or – especially if didactic – indigestible (238).[7] On such an analogy the realistic descriptions of the killing beds offer an alternative kind of moral orthorexia: the emetic.

Yet Jurgis is less shocked by the slaughter of the cattle which he witnesses thereafter than by that of the pigs, and he quickly becomes fascinated by the mechanization *per se* (slaughterhouse tours were run, and visitors' galleries built for them, because "it is a good advertisement," even though slaughterhouse tours were also a vegetarian campaign tactic [Gregory 91; Sinclair 43]).[8] Thereafter he is absorbed by his own struggle for survival; he loses Tolstoy's "highest spiritual capacity" which the slaughterhouse visitor, like the reader, may have greater power to exercise – and the narrative's vegan consciousness accordingly disappears for much of the novel. Neither Jurgis nor the narrator make a connection between the killing beds and the meat served at Jurgis's wedding a few weeks later. As J. M. Coetzee's vegetarian avatar Elizabeth Costello points out, the observation that the victims of the Holocaust were herded like cattle leaves unimplied the wrongness of treating cattle like cattle (20), and the human–animal analogy operates for much of the novel with a similar asymmetry; the scandal of treating workers like cattle effaces that of their treatment of cattle. Meanwhile the passage quoted above could be considered to remain in the novel's unconscious, making itself briefly felt when Jurgis obtains idyllic employment with a maker of "harvesting and mowing machines," the narrator euphemistically observing that "the work was free from many of the elements of filth and repulsiveness that prevailed at the stockyards" (Sinclair 237). Even when Jurgis comes to socialist consciousness at the end of the novel, he learns that the Beef Trust "had forced the price of cattle so low as to destroy the stock-raising industry, an occupation upon which whole states existed; it had ruined thousands of butchers who had refused to handle its products," and he joyfully envisages "taking possession of the Union Stockyards!" (377). In Tolstoyan terms, "habit" prevails.

Yet the novel's socialist campaigner Schliemann also considers: "it has been proven that meat is unnecessary as a food; and meat is obviously more difficult to produce than vegetable food, less pleasant to prepare and handle, and more likely to be unclean." "How would Socialism change that?" asks a student. Schliemann responds that free labor would not choose the work of slaughter, so "year by year the cost of slaughter-house products will increase; until eventually those who want to eat meat will have to do their own killing – and how long do you think the custom would survive then? –" (408). Like Hardy and Tolstoy, Schliemann, in a late resurgence of the novel's vegan consciousness after the novel has discovered an optimistic path for humanity, points to a contradiction between humanity and a willingness to slaughter.

Mother Earth's review of *The Jungle* qualified this assumption historically, asserting that:

> This author uses the squeal, or, rather, the wild death shrieks of agony of the ten millions of living creatures tortured to death every year in Chicago . . . to pander to the old brutal, inhuman thirst for a diet of blood . . . this cry of anguish from the "killing-beds" shall sound on until man, whose ancestors were once cannibals, shall cease to devour even the corpses of their murdered animal relatives. (qtd. in Fernihough 224)

That is, the reviewer presents humanity as evolving away from a willingness to kill first nearer and then more distant kin (overlooking the co-temporality of cultural cannibalism and cultural vegetarianism, and the historical preponderance of the latter). Yet the novel so stresses the kinship of oppressed humans and animals that the consumption of meat itself has the aspect of cannibalism. James Joyce's *Ulysses* (1922) makes a similar conflation, with its stress on metempsychosis, and its presentation of humans as animals whenever meat is concerned: "The ferreteyed porkbutcher folded the sausages he had snipped off with blotchy fingers, sausagepink" (61).[9] But in *The Jungle* the sausage-pinkness of fingers is caused by abusive working conditions, making what the narrator calls the "horrible crime" doubly cannibalistic.

There is a version of this perversity in many non-vegetarian works of modernist literature that are focalized through animals. Published two years after *The Jungle*, Kenneth Grahame's profoundly species-queer *The Wind in the Willows* is in several respects an inversion of *The Jungle*. Set in a rural idyll rather than an urban hellhole, in mild English countryside rather than an urban jungle, its animal protagonists resemble humans rather than the inverse. Their respective species' dwellings, such as rat holes, are adorned with human conveniences such as furniture, rather than such conveniences being denied to humans. Yet its protagonists also eat the meat of other animals. Individual rabbits are positive characters – but are also found without comment, and with unacknowledged cannibalism, in a "stew" of which Mr. Toad partakes (206–07). In its fairytale universe, then, the realism of *The Jungle* finds its mirror, as the explicit threat to animals of slaughter is replaced by the implicit threat of hunting and trapping. The next section considers hunting in another realist work that may be considered to invert *The Wind in the Willows*, but this time one that functions on that novel's home territory: rural England.

"Tally Ho!"[10]

When, in Chapter 7 of *The Wind in the Willows*, the otter child Portly temporarily disappears, his father is concerned that he might have been caught in a trap. It turns out that he is protected by the god Pan. Hunting and trapping are part of the novel's implied reality, but repressed from its view. Two decades later another novel came out which was to become a children's classic of animal life in the South of England, but with no such protections for either protagonists or readers: *Tarka the Otter: His Joyful Water-life and Death in the Country of the Two Rivers*. Like *Lord of the Flies*, this work meditates on hunting in poetically concentrated prose, and with a degree of detail that constitutes hyper-realism. Like *The Wind in the Willows*, it displaces humanity to the margins of its concern (otters are more individualized than that domesticated species, dogs, who are more individualized than humans), until such time as the latter suddenly exert overwhelming control (Toad imprisoned, Tarka killed). No ontological frisson attaches to them, and they are as matter-of-factly described as any other animal, decentering them still further (as Michael Bell notes, a "melodramatic, all-too-human, insistence on the inhuman" can itself open literature to the charge of "naïve anthropomorphism" [224]). Human language consisting mainly of sallies such as "*Tally ho! Yaa-aa-ee-io! Leu-in on 'm! Yaa-ee-oo!*" (Williamson 185), and otter vocabulary consisting of equally non-denotative "yikkering" and "tissing," levels them still further.

That said, the novel makes a greater attempt than any other modernist work to imagine (to adapt Thomas Nagel's question about bats) "What It Is Like to Be an Animal." As in *The Wind in the Willows*, Richard Adams's 1972 rabbit saga *Watership Down*, and many of the more realistic twentieth-century narratives centered on wild animals, there is a sense of arbitrariness in the choice of focalizing species (for Grahame otters are marginal if benign figures; for Grahame and Adams the otters' near relatives, weasels, are life-threatening antagonists). Evidently Williamson admired otters; his depiction of them recalls the assertion of the protagonist of Saki's 1914 story "Laura," who wishes to be reincarnated as one despite the risk of being hunted, that they are "elegant and lively, with a love of fun" (Saki 242). Nonetheless, there is a sense that the narrative's closely attentive eye might equally well have focused on owls, or harvest mice, or even fish (the animal which Lawrence's 1921 poem "Fish" considers paradigmatic of animal otherness [*Poems* 289–94; Rohman 97]).[11] Therefore *Tarka*, though as inevitably anthropomorphic as any human construct, exists at the extreme non-anthropomorphic end of the scale of representation of animals in literature of the period.[12]

As in London's *The Call of the Wild* (1903) and *White Fang*, the narrative is focalized through apex predators, but unlike in London's Yukon Territory the humans do not hunt in order to survive. Those who trap and hunt the otters neither eat nor wear them, nor are they shown as animated by a desire to protect their fish or poultry. Both "Laura" and *Tarka* were written during the late Victorian to interwar heyday of otter-hunting as a sport that was pursued principally, as on Golding's island, for fun. Among blood sports it was therefore peculiarly vulnerable to campaigns to ban it – although this was also for reasons centering on the otters (their association with courage, loyalty, and the hunting season's coincidence with their breeding season). Moreover the length and visibility of the kill excited a bloodlust that was considered by some to be incompatible with "humanity"; in 1905 the Reverend Joseph Stratton argued that "model men" would "find *pleasure* neither in torturing, nor annihilating any [animals]" (Allen 84).

Williamson did not present his novel as part of this campaign. On the contrary, he dedicated it "To William Henry Rogers," the master of the Devon otter hunt which Williamson followed by way of research (xi). Yet in numerous respects the novel is hostile to the hunt, and, despite exposing child readers to the kill, was not denounced by campaigners who deplored the fact that otter-hunting (being pedestrian rather than mounted) was peculiarly accessible to women and children (Allen et al. 88). The focalization is sensuously close to the hunted animal ("From far away there came a deep rolling sound, and a screaming cheer" [Williamson 22]), and the narration of the final, nine-hour hunt is exhaustingly and disturbingly prolonged (twenty-five pages, compared to twelve for *Lord of the Flies*' climactic hunt). The plot accords Tarka the dignity of killing his antagonist, the dog Deadlock, even as he is killed himself, underwater rather than in front of the hunters and readers (186). The novel twice creates welcome moments, involving humans, of pacific respite from the hunting with which nearly all of the novel's humans and nonhumans are otherwise engaged. A man enters a cave, leaves alone an otter seeking shelter there, and calms a temporarily abandoned baby seal by playing "soft tunes" on his wooden pipe, thus playing a similar role as Pan for Portly (76). During the final hunt a girl described as "gentle in thought to all her eyes beheld" notices Tarka in hiding: "For two minutes the maid sat silent, hardly daring to look at the river," but when Tarka sneezes, her accompanying "old man heard it: *'Tally Ho!'*" (184).

One anomalously meditative and conflicted passage presents humans as having achieved victory over animals, and the aristocracy as sentimentally preserving carnivores from extinction, before questioning hunting's naturalness, and associating instinct rather with imaginative pity. Finally it questions this instinct's relevance to survival:

> Once hunted himself, then hunting for necessity, man now hunts in the leisure of his time; but in nearly all those who through necessity of life till fields, herd beasts, and keep fowls, these remaining wildlings of the moor have enemies who care nothing for their survival. The farmers would exterminate nearly every wild bird and animal of prey, were it not for the landowners, among whom are some who care for the wildlings because they are sprung from the same land of England, and who would be unhappy if they thought the country would know them no more. For the animal they hunt to kill in its season, or those other animals or birds they cause to be destroyed for the continuance of their pleasure in sport – which they believe to be natural – they have no pity; and since they lack this incipient human instinct, they misunderstand and deride it in others. Pity acts through the imagination, the higher light of the world, and imagination arises from the world of things, as a rainbow from the sun. A rainbow may be beautiful and heavenly, but it will not grow corn for bread. (126–27)

The final sentence's turn functions as though reprimanding the preceding sentiment, and by implication the imaginative novel of which it is part, for the anti-hunting implications of this human-exceptionalist position by means of reaching for but missing a Darwinian imperative (since otter-hunting, too, grows no corn).

The novel nowhere presents hunting as re-engaging with an atavistic survival instinct (as when *The Call of the Wild*'s Californian dog protagonist Buck, suddenly placed in the far North, "remembered back to the youth of the breed, to the time the wild dogs ranged in packs through the primeval forest and killed their meat as they ran it down" [London 26]). Nor does the novel describe anything that corresponds to the justifications which Lawrence posited for hunting four years before: "The full eye of the deer or the rabbit or the horse would stagnate and lose its lustre, save for the keen, strange eye of the wolf and the weasel, and of man" (*Studies* 214); the novel affords no suggestion that Tarka's eyes would be any the less lustrous were he an unchallenged predator. Admittedly, Lawrence's justifications principally concern hunting for food. In *Tarka* the dispassionate descriptions of the hunting for survival in which the otters and other animals engage contrast with its evocations of the ceremonial culture, and enjoyment, of the human hunters. The killing of Tarka's son Tarquol resembles the killing of the sow in *Lord of the Flies*, which takes place in a glade of dancing butterflies:

> Among the brilliant hawkbits – little sunflowers of the meadow – he was picked up and dropped again, trodden on and wrenched and broken, while the screaming cheers and whoops of sportsmen mingled with the growing rumble of hounds at worry. Tarquol fought them until he was blinded, and his jaws were smashed. (Williamson 178)

The idea that the hunters are distorted versions of humans is pictorialized from Tarka's perspective in hiding: "From underwater he saw men and women, pointing with hand and pole, as palsied and distorted shapes on the bank . . . the huntsman's legs before him joined to the image of legs, and above the inverted image a flattened and uncertain head and shoulders" (the "head" which putatively harbors both "imagination" and "pity") (181–82, 184). Jeremy Gavron hypothesizes that the novel's vegan semi-consciousness is inflected by Williamson's experiences of World War I, citing the passage when the ground above Tarka's refuge is beaten by an iron bar ("On and on went the pounding" until they "could bear it no longer"), and the contrast between the hunt's inaugural festive spirit and its bloody development (xi, xx). He also argues that Williamson's later philo-German politics were influenced by his experience of the Christmas truce of 1914. The latter point, translated from the international to the interspecial plain, would also help explain the novel's *sotto voce* questioning of why it is that humans kill otters.

"We did not make creation, we are not the authors of the universe"[13]

Thus writes Lawrence in his 1925 essay "Reflections on the Death of a Porcupine," which, in one of its sections, retrospectively purports to justify his *crime passionnel* of the killing of a porcupine in retribution for injuring a dog by presenting the universe in Darwinian terms. The above quotation has the force of an excuse in response to an unvoiced accusation; "all creatures devour, and *must* devour the lower forms of life" is a diktat of which humans are not the authors. Yet in his 1921 poem, "Man and Bat," Lawrence's denial of having created the universe functions oppositely. After a bat has long resisted Lawrence's efforts to chase him out of a bedroom into Florence's sunlight, he finally collapses with exhaustion:

> What then?
> Hit him and kill him and throw him away?
>
> Nay,
> I didn't create him.
> Let the God that created him be responsible for his death
> (*Poems* 299)

Indeed, the "Porcupine" essay in fact adumbrates a bimodal vision of the universe: in what it calls the "fourth dimension," each individual "that attains to its own fullness of being" is "a nonpareil, a non-such" (*Reflections* 358). The quality of attention which Lawrence's artistry frequently pays to animals presents them in this dimension, and that apprehension is emotionally inconsistent with killing them, which is why Lawrence's characters and narrators are so frequently revolted by killing. Williamson's practical enactment of his own account of the relationship of imagination to pity has the same outcome, which is why the artistry of *Tarka the Otter* condemns the hunt; a similar dynamic may be found at certain moments in all of the works described in this chapter.

Conclusion

Whenever the concept of "humanity" is invoked in the works explored above, it is connected with this revulsion; and though the form of this position is exceptionalist (and indeed what Rohman calls "neohumanist" [160]), its content relies on an ontologically levelling recognition of kinship. Human exceptionalism operates nowhere in the opposite direction – granting humans the right to use animals as they choose (as accorded by Genesis 1.28 and 9.3, and as culturally entrenched as the speciesist discourse which Derrida calls "carnophallogocentrism") except, negatively, in *Lord of the Flies*' representation of "the darkness of man's heart" (Golding 248). Rather, wherever Christianity manifests itself (as it does in Jude's early faith, in the later Tolstoy's faith, and in much of the Victorian and early twentieth-century zoophile movement) it does so in a form that accords with Lawrence's perception of the "fourth dimension", which he also calls "the heaven of existence" (*Reflections* 358).

We see the island sow with her eleven piglets lying "sunk in deep maternal bliss" (Golding 166), and Tarka "in love with White-tip" playing "hide-and-seek" with her (Williamson 64), alike in this "heaven" of "fullness of being." The fact that we never see the animals of the Tula or Chicago slaughterhouses in this condition forces the narratorial perspective *of The Jungle* to the question:

> was one to believe that there was nowhere a god of hogs, to whom this hog personality was precious, to whom these hog squeals and agonies had a meaning? Who would take this hog into his arms and comfort him, reward him for his work well done, and show him the meaning of his sacrifice? (Sinclair 45)

Insofar as humans exercise a godlike role in relation to animals (in *Lord of the Flies* the eponymous deity is man's heart, and London's dog protagonists call men "gods"), then Sinclair, in the very writing of this passage, exercises the role that he hypothesizes. Saki compensates his hunted otter Laura by granting her reincarnation. Williamson's imagination hosts an otter afterlife when it observes that Tarka's son Tarquol, killed earlier in the hunt, "had gone home before Tarka," perhaps to the "Spirit that made it" (178, 61); and the world of *The Wind in the Willows* is guarded by Pan. These are all imaginative compensations to animals for the suffering inflicted on them by humans. Yet as Tolstoy and other vegetarians of the period knew, the dichotomy between Lawrence's Darwinian and "fourth dimension" worlds was not in fact conceptual and inevitable; they existed side-by-side, and most humans could, if they wished, choose to expand the realm of the latter. Jude "could not see how the matter could be mended," but Lawrence himself seems to see it in his "Autobiographical Fragment" of 1927, which presents a Lawrencianly utopian England of 2927 in which all men walk naked, live in peace, and are vegetarian (65–66).

The literature discussed in this chapter, albeit frequently morally conflicted, may through its effects on readers practically conduce towards, as well as imaginatively construct, a utopian world; we *may* be authors of the universe. We are a tenth of the way to 2927. Though otter-hunting was abolished in the UK in 1981, the factory farming of animals which took off in the late modernist period has risen steeply since then and continues to do so. Its effects on the environment, the climate, and the generation of viruses threaten multiple species including the human, rendering us not so much victims of our bloodlust as of a reluctance to face the "horrible crime . . . buried out of sight and of memory" that mechanized animal farming necessarily entails (Sinclair 45). The modern world, then, has still more need than did the "modernist" world of Williamson's "imagination."

Notes

1. The vegan consciousness of these authors is akin to the vegan *un*conscious noted by Evan Maina Mwangi in relation to African literature. As noted in the introduction to this volume, Mwangi's vegan unconscious is defined as an "affirmative expression of potential . . . a latent possibility that the societies portrayed in the text will embrace a future where animals will not be killed to satisfy human needs" (9).
2. Shakespeare 1.3.2, 977.
3. See also James Gregory's chapter in this volume for more on Victorian vegetarianism and veganism.
4. Golding 86.
5. H. G. Wells's 1895 *The Time Machine* projects this distinction into the future on a racial basis, in the dietary difference between the Morlocks and the Eloi, respectively.
6. Sinclair 45.
7. For more on this relationship between didacticism and literary realism, see Samantha Pergadia's chapter in this volume.
8. Ted Geier points out the parallels between Jurgis's willing surrender of himself to the machine of industrial meat production, and the self-sacrificial behavior of various of Kafka's protagonists (40).
9. Peter Adkins persuasively argues that *Ulysses* exhibits a vegetarian consciousness by pointing at this and other passages taken insufficiently seriously by Fernihough, who argues that the novel celebrates meat-eating (though Joyce certainly distrusted Irish nationalism's orthorexic strain of vegetarianism).
10. Williamson 184.
11. For a vegan reading of "Fish," see Stewart Cole's essay in this volume.
12. Moving along the scale, and making allowance for the human traits of dogs by definition, one passes through London's Buck and White Fang, Lawrence's St Mawr, Virginia Woolf's Flush, R. Adams's Hazel and friends, Mikhail Bulgakov's Sharik, Tolstoy's Kholstomer, the narrator of Kafka's "Investigations of a Dog," and Grahame's Badger, Mole, Ratty, and Toad.
13. Lawrence, *Reflections* 356.

Works Cited

Adams, Carol J. *The Sexual Politics of Meat: A Feminist-Vegetarian Critical Theory*. Polity Press, 1990.
Adams, Richard. *Watership Down*. Allen Lane, 1982.
Adkins, Peter. "The Eyes of That Cow: Eating Animals and Theorizing Vegetarianism in James Joyce's *Ulysses*." *Humanities (Basel)*, vol. 6, no. 3, 2017, p. 46.
Allen, Daniel et al. "'An incredibly vile sport': Campaigns against Otter Hunting in Britain, 1900–39." *Rural History*, vol. 27, no. 1, 2016, pp. 79–101.
Bell, Michael. *Open Secrets: Literature, Education, and Authority from J-J Rousseau to J. M. Coetzee*. Oxford UP, 2007.
Coetzee, J. M., et al. *The Lives of Animals*. Princeton UP, 1999.
Fernihough, Anne. *Freewomen and Supermen: Edwardian Radicals and Literary Modernism*. Oxford UP, 2013.
Gavron, Jeremy. "Introduction." *Tarka the Otter*, by Henry Williamson, Penguin, 2009, pp. v–xiii.
Geier, Ted. "Kafka's Meat: Beautiful Processes and Perfect Victims." *Literature and Meat Since 1900*, edited by Seán McCorry and John Miller, Palgrave Macmillan, 2019, pp. 19–34.
Golding, William. *Lord of the Flies*. Faber, 1964.
Grahame, Kenneth. *The Wind in the Willows*. Methuen, 1980.
Gregory, James. *Of Victorians and Vegetarians: The Vegetarian Movement in Nineteenth-Century Britain*. Bloomsbury, 2007.
Hardy, Thomas. *Collected Poems*. Wordsworth Editions, 1994.
—. *Jude the Obscure*. St Martin's Press, 1966.
Joyce, James. *Ulysses*. Minerva, 1992.
Lawrence, D. H. "Autobiographical Fragment." *Late Essays and Articles*, edited by James T. Boulton, Cambridge UP, 2014, pp. 49–68.
—. *The Poems, Volumes I and II*. Edited by Christopher Pollnitz, Cambridge UP, 2013.
—. *Reflections on the Death of a Porcupine and Other Essays*. Edited by Michael Herbert, Cambridge UP, 1988.
—. *Studies in Classic American Literature*. Edited by Ezra Greenspan et al., Cambridge UP, 2003.
London, Jack. *The Call of the Wild* and *White Fang*. Paul Hamlyn, 1967.
Mwangi, Evan Maina. *The Postcolonial Animal: African Literature and Posthuman Ethics*. U of Michigan P, 2019.
Norris, Margot. *Beasts of the Modern Imagination: Darwin, Nietzsche, Kafka, Ernst, and Lawrence*. Johns Hopkins UP, 1985.
Pacyga, Dominic A. "Chicago: Slaughterhouse to the World." *Meat, Modernity and the Rise of the Slaughterhouse*, edited by Paula Young Lee, UP of New England, 2008, pp. 153–66.
Rohman, Carrie. *Stalking the Subject: Modernism and the Animal*. Columbia UP, 2009.
Saki. *The Complete Saki*. Penguin, 1982.
Shakespeare, William. "Macbeth." *The Complete Works*. Clarendon Press, 1988, pp. 975–1000.
Sinclair, Upton. *The Jungle*. Penguin, 1986.
Soper, Kate. *What is Nature? Culture, Politics, and the Non-Human*. Blackwell, 1995.
Tolstoy, Leo. "The First Step." Translated by Aylmer Maude, *Essays and Letters*, H. Frowde, 1909.
Tromanhauser, Vicki. "'Inside the "Butcher's Shop"': Women's Great War Writing and Surgical Meat." *Literature and Meat Since 1900*, edited by Seán McCorry and John Miller. Palgrave Macmillan, 2019, pp. 19–34.
Wells, H. G. *The Time Machine*. 1895. Penguin Books, 2005.
Williams, Raymond. *Keywords: A Vocabulary of Culture and Society*. Fontana, 1988.
Williamson, Henry. *Tarka the Otter*. Penguin, 2009.

3

VEGANISM, UTOPIA, AND SCIENCE FICTION

Joshua Bulleid

Introduction

SCIENCE FICTION REQUIRES readers to consider the possibility of alternative realities and worldviews. And, as ecocritical scholar Joshua Schuster recognizes, "being a vegan means living in a partially alternate world that has a science fiction feel because it involves continual cognitive estrangement from social norms" (219). To embrace veganism, Schuster argues, is to "call for another world where one stands with animals while disrupting the current order of power, sovereignty, and authority that is built on the exploitations of animals and Earth's others" (211). Here, Schuster hits upon the core mechanics of science fiction, as influentially described by Darko Suvin, as a genre whose "necessary and sufficient conditions are the presence and interaction of estrangement and cognition, and whose main formal device is an imaginative framework alternative to the author's empirical environment" as "validated by cognitive logic" (20, 79; italics removed).

Science fiction is also, therefore, an inherently *utopian* genre, in the sense of "utopia" as a "meditation on radical difference" that "aims at imagining, and sometimes even at realizing a system radically different from this one" (Jameson xii).[1] Broad definitions of utopia such as this encompass both positive "(e)utopian" possibilities and negative "dystopian" ones that nevertheless encourage progression towards more "positive" futures by warning about potential behaviors that should be avoided. Indeed, Suvin himself argues that utopia is merely the "sociopolitical subgenre of science fiction" (76; italics removed). His arguments have been taken up by a number of other influential science fiction scholars – most notably Fredric Jameson, whose *Archaeologies of the Future* (2005) is often seen as the founding text of twenty-first-century utopian studies. Even those critics who reject science fiction and utopia as "identical" genres maintain a close relationship between the two, so that "there is little doubt that utopia and SF are cognate literary forms" (Milner 90).

As Jameson argues, science fiction and utopia (hereafter "sf") encourage positive social change by forcing readers to "think the break" with dominant paradigms and ideologies (232). One ideology that has frequently been brought into question throughout sf's literary history is the dominant Western ideology of "carnism," or "the belief system [by] which eating certain animals is considered ethical and appropriate" (Joy, *Why We Love Dogs* 29–30), to which sf authors have regularly represented veganism as a more positive ideological counterpoint. Indeed, purely utopian endorsements of veganism date back (at least) to Plato's *Republic* (c. 308 BCE; see Bulleid, "Better Societies" 51–53), with many influential modern sf authors, including Arthur

C. Clarke, Philip K. Dick, and Marge Piercy, continuing the tradition well into the twentieth century. As leading Critical Animal Studies (CAS) scholar John Sorenson observes: "In the context of global capitalism and the ideology of neoliberalism ... the proposal that the interests of other animals should be given equal consideration to those of humans is regarded as *unthinkable*," arguing that it is essential for radicals to "think the unthinkable by accepting the politics of animal liberation as fundamental to its approach" (xv, xvi; italics added). Emelia Quinn has also recognized that veganism is "intimately connected to utopian speculations," whereby "meat-eating and the question of the animal present a difficulty in the present that requires resolution in fantastical imaginings" (10). Sf is therefore an indispensable tool in combating carnism and promoting veganism.

An increased interest in animal studies within sf criticism has also been encouraged by *Science Fiction Studies* editor Sherryl Vint and her book *Animal Alterity: Science Fiction and the Question of the Animal* (2010), wherein she argues that sf, "more than any other literature," is able to challenge the supposed separation between humans and other animals "because its generic premises enable us to imagine the animal quite literally looking at and addressing us from a non-anthropocentric perspective" (6). Although Vint's book begins with a chapter examining the science-fictional construction of a "human-animal boundary" that distinguishes between edible and non-edible animals, Quinn has noted that an examination of "vegan identity and praxis in science fiction" is "conspicuous" by its absence (10). Increasing interest in sf among both vegan studies and CAS scholars, along with sf's increased popular and critical presence, has seen the concurrent development of three vegan-focused studies of sf literature, by three of this collection's contributors, across three continents, two hemispheres and multiple disciplines within the last few years: Jovian Parry's PhD dissertation *Edible Subjectivities* (2019), my own PhD dissertation *Vegetarianism and Science Fiction* (2020), and Quinn's *Reading Veganism: The Monstrous Vegan, 1818 to Present* (2021). These studies are each centered around Western, Anglo-American vegan and literary traditions, primarily focusing on the canonical sf works of Mary Shelley, H. G. Wells, and Margaret Atwood.[2] To my knowledge, there has so far been no equivalent investigations of veganism and meat-eating in non-Western sf, although the global increase in the genre's popularity (to which both the Chinese and Japanese box offices and book sales charts will attest) means it is likely only a matter of time until such studies appear or become accessible. This chapter, meanwhile, broadly traces the historical development of vegan themes throughout modern Western sf – from the early nineteenth to the early twenty-first century – providing examinations of major examples in order to form a foundation for future studies into veganism and sf in other cultures.

Early Nineteenth-Century Foundations

The modern sf tradition is widely recognized as having its origins in Mary Shelley's *Frankenstein, Or the Modern Prometheus* (1818; see Aldiss and Wingrove 25, 36–46). The novel was written during a time of extensive vegetarian activism, Shelley herself being surrounded by a number of prominent vegetarian influences. Shelley's husband, the radical poet Percy Bysshe Shelley, for instance, was perhaps the nineteenth century's most influential vegetarian voice. The Shelleys were proto-vegans, who only ever allowed eggs and butter into their cooking "under protest" (Hogg 2, 419). *Frankenstein*, therefore, exists at the origin of not only modern sf, but the modern vegetarian and animal ethics movement as well.

As Carol J. Adams argues, much early nineteenth-century vegan philosophy is embedded in the text of *Frankenstein*. The novel's famous creature is an innate herbivore, who is also partially constructed from nonhuman material taken from "the dissecting room and the slaughterhouse" (37), thereby "endangering the carnivorist [*sic*] social order" and notions of human subjectivity by occupying a "hybrid position that is neither wholly human nor wholly animal" (Petsche 98–100). Although the creature once experiments with eating roasted offal left behind in a campfire (M. Shelley, *Frankenstein* 82), as Adams recognizes, he also immediately "rejects [the] Promethean gift" of meat-eating (126), maintaining his vegetarianism in the face of the fire's corrupting influence and continuing to feed on "berries, nuts, and roots" (M. Shelley, *Frankenstein* 88). Here, Shelley gestures towards her husband's "A Vindication of Natural Diet" (1813), wherein he charges Prometheus and Satan with humanity's fall into crime and disease through the corrupting influence of carnism – meat having been made edible to humans through the Promethean gift of fire (5–6).[3] Nevertheless, when proposing the creation of a companion, the creature also offers Frankenstein a vision of a "peaceful and human" vegan utopia – inspired by his reading of John Milton's *Paradise Lost* (1667) – telling him:

> My food is not that of man; I do not destroy the lamb and the kid, to glut my appetite; acorns and berries afford me sufficient nourishment. My companion will be of the same nature as myself, and will be content with the same fare. (120)

Shelley thereby embeds a Romantic endorsement of vegetarianism into the very foundation of modern sf, representing veganism as a utopian state of innocence, from which humanity (and potentially posthumanity) have fallen through carnist and speciesist corruption.

Similar vegan sentiments are present in Shelley's other foundational sf novel, *The Last Man* (1826), which depicts a vegan future utopia, the inhabitants of which sustain their "delightful" existence by feeding only on the "fruits of the field" (59). Like Frankenstein's creature, the novel's eponymous last man, Lionel Verney, begins life as an "unlettered savage," a "poacher" and a "shepherd" (22), who is only able to achieve a more moral, vegan state of being through Adrian's Romantic tutelage. Rather than a Fall from vegan innocence, *The Last Man* implies an inherently violent and carnivorous nature that can only be overcome through Romantic education. *The Last Man's* romantic ideals are also largely employed ironically and ultimately undermined by the indiscriminate destruction of an apocalyptic plague. Yet, the novel's tone is remorseful, rather than gleeful – the vulnerability and impermanence of its vegan utopia not negating its value as an ideal to aspire towards.

Romantic notions of vegan innocence persist throughout many notable works of nineteenth-century sf such as Edward Bulwer-Lytton's *The Coming Race* (1870) and Edward Bellamy's *Equality* (1897). However, as the century progressed and "science fiction" itself was solidified as a literary genre, representations of veganism became more critical and ironic – Samuel Butler seeing fit to amend two chapters lampooning vegetarian and animal rights advocates to the 1901 edition of his seminal utopian satire *Erewhon* (1872).

Late Nineteenth- and Early Twentieth-Century Responses

Modern science fiction was formally codified as a genre towards the end of the nineteenth century, through the technologically detailed "extraordinary voyages" of French writer Jules Verne and the "scientific romances" of English author H. G. Wells and the early American "pulps." The exoticized Hindu–Muslim Jem Chip in Verne's *Robur the Conqueror* (1886, trans. *The Clipper of the Clouds* [1887]) appears to be the only vegetarian character in all of his oeuvre, which is otherwise replete with enthusiastic and often exotic displays of carnism. By contrast, Romantic veganism is a frequent feature of Wells's work, where it is often satirized as nonsensical and repressive. As Peter Kemp observes, Wells's works are "larded with gastronomic metaphor . . . from the qualmishly vegetarian to the most raveningly cannibal" (7). Wells was also "the first significant writer who started to write sf from within the world of science" (Suvin 245), having studied zoology under T. H. Huxley, and he often appealed to evolutionary theory in an attempt to destabilize utopian notions of human superiority and Romantic veganism.

Wells's earliest and most influential works are often revisions and inversions of Mary Shelley's earlier sf novels. *The Time Machine* (1895) – from which "all subsequent significant sf can be said to have sprung" (Suvin 246) – employs the future, post-catastrophe setting of *The Last Man* while satirizing the Romantic veganism of *Frankenstein* and other nineteenth-century utopias. The novel depicts a far future, when humanity has (d)evolved into two separate species: the frail and seemingly unintelligent Eloi, who are "strict vegetarians" (Wells, *Machine* 27), and the cannibalistic, subterranean Morlocks who farm the Eloi for their meat. Wells's characterization of the two species is typically ambiguous, his nineteenth-century Time Traveller, who demands a meal of mutton upon returning from the future (14–15), providing a supposedly sensible middle ground between the Morlocks' bestial cannibalism and the Eloi's irrational fruitarianism, which the narrator naively romanticizes in the novel's epilogue as evidence that "gratitude and mutual tenderness still lived on in the heart of man" (91).

The same is true of the Beast People of *The Island of Doctor Moreau* (1896). As Quinn explores in *Reading Veganism*, Wells inverts the vegan innocence of Frankenstein's creature by having his eponymous Doctor Moreau try to make humans out of nonhuman animals through horrific vivisections and an oppressive law, which forbids the eating of "Fish or Flesh" in contrast to the continued and seemingly impulsive carnism (and potential cannibalism) of the novel's human characters (Wells, *Moreau* 59). Traditional species hierarchies are explicitly inverted in *The War of the Worlds* (1897/1898), wherein Earth is invaded by anthropophagous Martians who possess intellects as "vast and cool and unsympathetic" as "ours are to those of the beasts that perish" (7). As the narrator reflects: "The bare idea of this is no doubt horribly repulsive to us, but at the same time I think that we should remember how repulsive our carnivorous habits would seem to an intelligent rabbit" (125).

Although Wells's intentions when writing these novels were likely more misanthropic than empathetic, they were widely remarked upon for their vegan sympathies, which continue to be perpetuated through later adaptations. *The War of the Worlds* was recommended in *The Vegetarian* as "a good story for vegetarians to get their friends to read" (Harpur) and praised in another animal rights periodical as "an effective way to partially realize the attitude which the lower animal may take towards the lords of creation" ("Man under Martian"). The same pages also praised George du Maurier's *The Martian* (1897) and Camille Flammarion's *Omega: The Last Days of the World* (1894), which each contain depictions of more ethical and technologically advanced alien or future vegan civilizations. Popular adaptations and continuations of *The Time Machine* – including Stephen Baxter's authorized continuation *The Time Ships* (1995), which rewrites the Morlocks as intelligent vegetarians – have also largely endorsed the narrator's romantic sympathies (see Bulleid, *Vegetarianism* 76–77). As Brian Aldiss observes, it is also Moreau's vegetarian Beast People with whom "our conscience is [most readily] involved" ("Introduction" xxxiv). Ironically, through his antagonistic ambiguity, Wells's works have largely come to support the Romantic veganism he initially sought to satirize.

Ironic inversions of vegetarianism remain a staple of Wells's later scientific romances, with him later labeling real-world vegetarian advocates as "impracticable and unconvincing people," in *The Shape of Things to Come* (1933; 276). Nevertheless, Wells's earliest and most influential utopian novel, *A Modern Utopia* (1910), contains a seemingly genuine endorsement of veganism. As a member of its idealized ruling class of "samurai" explains to the narrator:

> In all the round world of Utopia there is no meat . . . in a population that is all educated, and at about the same level of physical refinement, it is practically impossible to find anyone who will hew a dead ox or pig. (Wells, *Modern* 192)

The novel and the samurai were well received by the Fabian Society, leading to the establishment of many real-life and often vegetarian utopian communities in their image (Smith 101). It is possible the samurai's statement was intended more ironically than it was received. Yet, again, Wells's ambiguous sympathies have ironically rendered him the science fiction author who has had perhaps the most direct real-world impact on the spread of veganism.

Perhaps the most influential early twentieth-century science-fictional utopia outside of Wells's works is Charlotte Perkins Gilman's *Herland* (1915), which also encourages veganism as an essential aspect of its utopian society. Gilman's eponymous utopian enclave is completely devoid of cattle, its women living entirely off a forest cultivated to achieve maximum food-producing efficiency and environmental sustainability. The inferiority of the outside world to Herland is considered "nowhere better shown than in the matter of the food supply," the Herlanders horrified to discover how dairy farming "robs the cow of her calf, and the calf of its true food" (Gilman, *Herland* 79, 47). Zoos and hunting have also been eradicated in Gilman's earlier utopia *Moving the Mountain* (1911), wherein meat-eating is also said to be "decreasing every day" (144, 202). *Herland*'s sequel, *With Her in Our Land* (1916), however, foregoes concerns about animal ethics to promote a deeply troubling global implementation of racist eugenics.

Racist and vegan philosophies are also blended in Mary E. Bradley Lane's earlier feminist utopia *Mizora: A World of Women* (1880–1881/1890), which, as John Miller explores in his chapter in this volume, contains perhaps the earliest depiction of synthesized meat. The Mizorans are no animal-lovers, however, keeping "no cattle, nor animals of any kind for food or labor" (Lane 18). Moreover, while Lane's depiction of synthesized meats exemplifies "an upbeat sense of the radical possibilities of technology characteristic of both its time and genre," alternative meats quickly became "signifier[s] of hypercontrol, blandness and over-civilization" as sf itself became more dystopian (Parry, *Edible* 134).

Dystopian Developments

Unappetizing synthetic food and artificial meats have been staples of sf's dystopian sub-genre since its inception. The trend is traceable to the meat-like paste in Wells's 1899 novel *When the Sleeper Wakes*, continuing throughout archetypal works such as Yevgeny Zamyatin's *We* (1921/1924) and *Nineteen Eighty-Four* (1949) by George Orwell, the latter author considering vegetarians "out of touch with common humanity" (*Road* 206–7). Moreover, while Warren Belasco contends that "a strong dose of vegetarianism" is found among the heroic survivors and rebuilders of dystopian literature (100), he gives no specific examples, with reverences for "pure" and "natural" meat being far more apparent among dystopian rebels than any suggestion of vegetarianism. Survivors in Ray Bradbury's *Fahrenheit 451* (1954), for example, celebrate their escape over a campfire-cooked, bacon breakfast (208–09), while the utopian saviors in John Wyndham's *The Chrysalids* (1955) declare meat-eating "simply a part of the great revolving wheel of natural economy" and that "to pretend that one can live without doing so is self-deception" (195). As Kingsley Amis observed, the "volume and intensity" of rural nostalgia within sf is "tremendous" compared to other genres (73), particularly within the dystopian mode, where it is commonly paired with a reverence for pre-industrial carnism.

Sf depictions of synthetic and cultured meats increased significantly from the 1940s, becoming particularly prominent among the mid-twentieth-century's many "population dystopias" (Miller 95). Perhaps the most well-known population dystopia is Harry Harrison's *Make Room! Make Room!* (1966), which provides the basis for the cult 1973 film *Soylent Green*, which famously concludes with the cannibalistic revelation that "Soylent Green is people!" (Fleischer), despite nonhuman meat remaining available in Harrison's novel. The most important and influential population dystopia, however, is probably Frederik Pohl and C. M. Kornbluth's *Space Merchants* (1952/1953). The novel famously features Chicken Little: an "insensible," "greybrown, rubbery hemisphere" whose "pulsating flesh" consists of chunks of regenerating meat (Pohl and Kornbluth 92, 90), and which provides the foundation for similarly repulsive future depictions of cultured meat, such as the "ChickieNobs" in Margaret Atwood's *MaddAddam* trilogy (2003–2013) or the "Singers" of Elizabeth Dogherty's *The Blind Pig* (2010). Alternative meats are a frequent feature of Pohl's other writing. Yet, he only ever engages with vegan politics in his first solo novel, *Slave Ship* (1956), wherein American soldiers use remote-controlled nonhuman animals to fight against the Vietnamese "Caodai" army, whose vegetarian leader questions their "slaughterhouse" and slave-like treatment (Pohl 113). The novel nevertheless ends by suggesting that the individual bonds between the Americans and their animals are more genuine than the blanket reverence of their opponents. Again, it is "unnatural" and *industrialized* meat-production that is represented as the enemy, rather than carnism itself.

The only major exception to the dystopian denigration of vegan meat alternatives appears to be Arthur C. Clarke, who frequently endorsed vegan solutions to ethical, economic, and environmental issues throughout both his influential sf and non-fiction writing. Although some of Clarke's earlier stories, such as "Food of the Gods" (1964), perpetuated traditional dystopian associations with alternative meat, he regularly endorsed hydroponic plant-farming and matter synthesis as the most practical means of sustaining extra-terrestrial colonies – rendering them effectively vegan – in his popular space colonization novels and influential real-world speculations, while also frequently promoting the development of alternative meats as an essential aspect of terrestrial sustainability (Bulleid, "We're All Vegetarians").[4] Clarke's increased exposure to Buddhism, upon moving to Sri Lanka in 1956, also inspired explicit endorsements of vegetarianism's ethical benefits throughout his later novels. The expanded, 1957 novel version of his earlier short story "The Deep Range," for instance, "surprised many sf readers by ultimately arguing for vegetarianism," despite the original story's endorsement of whale farming (Shippey). Although Clarke gave sf perhaps its most iconic depiction of carnism in the opening "Dawn of Man" sequence in *2001: A Space Odyssey* (1968) – co-written with director Stanley Kubrick – which was directly inspired by the then popular and intensely carnist "hunting hypothesis" of human evolution, he nevertheless re-established the utopian vegetarian theme in his series of *Space Odyssey* sequels, which again depict a more technologically advanced, vegan humanity which associates carnism with other "atrocious" and "calmly accepted" twenty-first-century practices (*3001* 87–88). Clarke's persistent vegan utopianism is merely a significant exception, rather than the rule, however.

Richard D. Ryder – the originator of the term "speciesism" – has nevertheless recognized how the "popularity of science fiction . . . affected the thinking of those of us who were involved in the revival of the animal protection movement," by promoting "the view that the universe may contain other intelligences" (88). Indeed, one of the twentieth century's most influential sf novels, Philip K. Dick's *Do Androids Dream of Electric Sheep?* (1968), which shares many thematic similarities with *Frankenstein*, pre-empted many foundational aspects of Peter Singer's Animal Liberation and Tom Regan's Animal Rights philosophies, emphasizing the capacity to suffer as an essential aspect of ethical subjectivity while rejecting moral distinctions based on intelligence. The novel presents empathy as the defining feature of humanity, its protagonist Rick Deckard reasoning that empathy "must be limited to herbivores or anyhow omnivores who could depart from a meat diet," since carnivores would be impeded by being made "conscious of the desire to live on the part of [their] prey" (Dick 31). The novel's human characters are therefore necessarily vegan, Deckard and other bounty hunters testing for empathetic responses to animal cruelty to identify and exterminate allegedly unempathetic androids. Although *Androids*' "animal theme" is absent from its more influential cinematic adaptation, *Blade Runner* (1982), many notable critics have praised the novel's engagement with animal ethics.[5] As Schuster points out, however, the "extreme rarity of live animals" in the novel "makes veganism both inevitable and perhaps irrelevant" (204).

Nevertheless, Dick himself often judged people in real life based upon their treatment of nonhuman animals, writing to vegetarian manufacturer Morningstar Farms in 1976 to congratulate them on the taste of their mock meats and suggesting that they redirect their advertising campaign to stress that "animals are our companions and friends and not something or some-one to be eaten" (*Letters* 6: 304). Animal ethics formed a cornerstone of Dick's personal philosophy and politics, which was frequently reflected throughout his fiction. The titular Martian creature of his earliest published story, "Beyond Lies the Wub" (1952), for example, is a vegetarian who debates ethics with a spaceship captain set on eating him and who questions how "any lasting contact" can be established with humans if they continue such "barbaric" behavior (30). Dick never became a vegan himself and even participated directly in animal slaughter. However, he perhaps did more than any other sf author to promote more empathetic and ethical relationships with other animals (see Bulleid, "Empathy" for further analysis). Although the overwhelming twentieth-century sf trend was towards dystopian depictions of veganism, perhaps its two most popular and influential authors – Dick and Clarke – continued to use the form to critique and undermine entrenched carnist attitudes.

The Critical Carnist Turn

The 1970s gave rise to an influential mode of sf, which Tom Moylan dubbed "critical" utopianism, for its emphasis on utopian imperfection and continued progress, along with the need for a "critical" social mass to implement social change (*Demand* 40–45). Moylan's four major examples of the critical utopian form – Ursula K. Le Guin's *The Dispossessed* (1974), Joanna Russ's *The Female Man* (1970/75), Samuel R. Delany's *Triton* (1976), and Marge Piercy's *Woman on the Edge of Time* (1976) – have "become something like a canon for American SF studies" (Milner 100).

Although Russ uses animal hunting as a marker of utopian female independence in *The Female Man*, the other authors include veganism as part of their critical utopian visions: the protagonist of Le Guin's *Dispossessed* is a vegetarian (72); in *Triton* Delany associates carnism with masculine conservatism, in contrast with progressive, vegan femininity; and vegan endorsements are particularly prominent in *Woman on the Edge of Time*, wherein Piercy's utopians have developed the ability to communicate with other animals via sign language, leading them to adopt a largely vegetarian diet, while also recognizing animal farming as an "inefficient use of grains" (100).[6] Adams identifies the protagonist of Piercy's earlier realist novel *Small Changes* (1973) as the feminist-literary "character who most successfully rejects meat and marriage" (119), suggesting Piercy's ongoing preoccupation with veganism. Her later, definitive, "critical dystopia" *He, She and It* (1991; published as *Body of Glass* outside of the US), however, continues the traditional dystopian associations between chemically cultured food and reverence for genuine animal agriculture.[7] Nevertheless, other critical utopias, such as Dorothy Bryant's *The Kin of Ata are Waiting for You* (1971), continue to feature veganism as a central part of their utopianism, and utopian animal advocates in neo-pagan pioneer Starhawk's *Fifth Sacred Thing* (1993) make an explicitly vegan argument when pointing out that "you can't really raise animals for dairy without killing the males" – meat-eating being one of their "most long-standing debates" (268).

Yet while veganism remained prominent among the most influential critical utopias, the era also gave rise to a number of influential ambiguous and even pro-carnist examples. Indeed, rather than any ethical conviction, the veganism of *The Dispossessed*'s protagonist primarily stems from a lack of animal life on his home planet, as does the quasi-vegan pescatarianism of the Getheneans in Le Guin's 1969 landmark sf novel *The Left Hand of Darkness* (1969). Her protagonists are otherwise unwaveringly carnist and, although Le Guin criticized factory farming in her essay "Without Egg" (2011), she later lampooned vegetarians as idiotic and overly sensitive in her satirical essay "A Modest Proposal: Vegempathy" (2012).⁸ Similarly, although Octavia E. Butler allegedly became a vegetarian because she "could not stomach the torture of animals" (Due 276), the "hyperempathetic" protagonist of her *Parable* series (1993–1998) conflicts with Dick's earlier rationalization of vegan empathy, declaring the killing of nonhuman animals a necessity (Butler, *Sower* 36–37). It is also considered inherently "human" to kill fish "for reasons that don't have much to do with nutrition" in Butler's *Xenogenesis* trilogy (1987–1989), wherein humans are preserved from nuclear extinction by non-hierarchical, vegan aliens called Oankali (676, 90), interpretations of which vary from ecofeminist vegans to genocidal slavers, as Jovian Parry explores in his chapter of the present volume.

The late twentieth century also saw an influx of utopian depictions of "naturalistic" carnism, often inspired by Californian Native Americans. Le Guin's later novel *Always Coming Home* (1985), which was greatly influenced by her father – the influential anthropologist Alfred Louis Kroeber – and his studies of Indigenous Californian cultures, presents an ethnological investigation of a future-culture, for whom meat is allegedly of "very little real importance" (437), yet who still raise domestic animals for meat, while birds and mammals are "regularly hunted by adults for food" (414–21). Ernest Callenbach's *Ecotopia* (1975) also established a "primitivist" and hyper-masculinist eco-carnism that continues to inform prominent works of ecological sf to this day, despite its author acknowledging that "there is no earthly biological reason why you must eat meat at all" (*Ecotopian Encyclopedia* 83). Callenbach's prequel, *Ecotopia Emerging* (1981), also reveals that many Ecotopian founders "were either vegetarians or followed diets in which . . . meat and fish were used sparingly" while regularly emphasizing the economic and environmental advantages of a vegan diet (166). Callenbach nevertheless reverted to a primitivist celebration of carnism in his only other fictional effort, "Chocco" (1994). "Chocco" was published in Kim Stanley Robinson's collection *Future Primitive: The New Ecotopias* (1994) alongside Le Guin's "The New Atlantis" (1975) and several other sf stories that show a similar reverence for the carnism of Native American and other allegedly "primitive" cultures.

Twenty-First-Century sf and the Rise of Neocarnism

The move away from utopian veganism in post-1970s sf is indicative of a recent phenomenon Melanie Joy has identified as "neocarnism." Although neocarnists recognize the environmental impacts of animal culture, they continue to endorse animal products that are allegedly "sustainable," "nutritional," and "humane," contending that "the problem is not *animal* agriculture, but *industrial* agriculture" (Joy "Understanding Neocarnism"; Joy and Tuider xi; italics original). Similar naturalistic sentiments are evident among earlier vegan advocates, such as Mary and Percy Shelley, who sought a return to a "natural diet" during the industrial revolution. Yet as Nick Fiddes recognizes in his influential examination of meat's symbolic qualities, no truly "natural" human diet "can ever have existed," the quest for a more natural existence being "clearly developed in response to the highly processed products of the modern food industry" (193; see also Parry, "Oryx" 242). Nevertheless, developments in ecological thought since the 1970s have seen the notion of "natural" being widely realigned with carnism, rather than veganism, which has become marginalized within twenty-first-century sf.

A neocarnist ideology consistently informs Kim Stanley Robinson's writing. His critical utopian *Three Californias* trilogy (1984–1990) draws obvious inspiration from Native American cultures, while advocating less-industrialized though still technologically enabled carnist social (re)organizations. Robinson's celebrated *Mars* trilogy (1992–1996) and other space colonization novels also assume the continuation of animal farming in (often Native American-inspired) off-world colonies and during deep-space exploration, despite their open debt to Clarke (see Bulleid, "Better Societies" 65). Perhaps more significant from a real-world perspective is Robinson's neglect of veganism in his more recent climate fiction novels. Robinson advocates for sf's capacity to imagine alternative paradigms as a "necessary survival strategy" in combating climate change ("Remarks" 9). Yet, while organizations such as the United Nations (UN) and the Intergovernmental Panel on Climate Change (IPCC) have increasingly called for a "substantial worldwide diet change, away from animal products" (UNEP 82), Robinson has continually neglected veganism throughout his works in favor of primitivist carnism. Animal agriculture's contributions to climate change are only ever brought up once, before being quickly dismissed, in Robinson's *Science in the Capital* series (2004–2006), the protagonist of which later joins a group of "Paleolithic" "fregans" who hunt zoo animals that have been released in the parks of Washington D.C. (*Fifty Degrees* 138, 285–86). Robinson also later revised *Science in the Capital* as *Green Earth* (2015), removing his environmentalist president's vision of a future when humanity will "share the world with all the other creatures" in favor of a recipe for steak marinade (cf. *Sixty Days* 516; *Green Earth* 1046; italics removed). Veganism is further disparaged in *New York: 2140* (2017), wherein those who find it "easier to eat fake meat or become vegetarian" than to kill their own animals are belittled by proud carnists, for whom the "unavoidable anthropomorphizing" of their farm animal has "no restraining effect" (Robinson 132). Robinson's most recent novel, *The Ministry of the Future* (2020), features a sympathetic portrayal of an ecoterrorist group which infects vast numbers of cattle with bovine spongiform encephalopathy ("mad cow disease") so that meat-eating becomes simply "too dangerous to continue" (229, 369), as well as efforts by its protagonists to establish "mostly" vegetarian, environmentalist communities (197, 544). Yet, while this perhaps suggests a greater awareness and acknowledgment of carnism's significant contribution to climate change, Robinson's previous writing showcases a deep-seated carnist attitude, which remains shared by many of twenty-first-century sf's most influential voices.

Margaret Atwood, who is undoubtedly the most critically examined and influential author of twenty-first-century sf, expresses a similar reverence for carnism. Masculinized meat-eating is often analogous to the oppression of Atwood's female protagonists in her early, realist novels, which are frequent features among vegan literary criticism.[9] Yet as Parry has argued, Atwood also "always wryly undermines any vegetarian message that might be read into her work" ("Oryx" 253). Atwood's neocarnist undermining of vegan utopianism is most evident in her *MaddAddam* trilogy, which describes a post-apocalyptic future wherein humans have been all but exterminated by a synthetic virus. The trilogy's genetically engineered species of "Crakers" are intended as a more peaceful and sustainable posthuman species and are therefore rendered (herbivorous) "vegetarians," whose peaceful nature is also attributed to their being "neither hunters nor agriculturalists" (Atwood *Oryx*, 186). However, the Crakers are also frequently characterized as incomplete and "inhuman" through their lack of culture, only being properly recognized as people once they take on carnist rituals brought about by their exposure to human characters. The humans themselves are represented as *essentially* carnist, the protagonist of the first novel, Jimmy/Snowman, frequently stressing an apparently biological need for "animal protein" in contrast to the Crakers' herbivorism (*MaddAddam* 12; see also *Oryx* 116, 187).

The trilogy's other human survivors largely derive from the God's Gardeners, a vegan religious cult who are "strict vegetarians" and active animal rights protesters variously described as "crazed," "fundamentalist," "pyromaniac," "animal welfare freaks" (*Year* 54, 48; *Oryx* 221, 239, 254, 397, 238; italics removed). They quickly revert to carnism in the post-apocalyptic setting, however, greeting fellow survivors with "delicious" slices of "pork" and promises of "bacon" cut from intelligent, genetically engineered "pigoons" (*Year* 470–71), the later protagonist, Toby, noting how it "hadn't taken them long to backslide on the Gardener Vegivows" (*MaddAddam* 46). Although the humans and pigoons later agree to stop eating each other (328–29), the humans continue to farm other animals as "an acceptable source of animal protein" (458), the pigoons given special privilege due to their intelligence and semi-human DNA. Although veganism is recognized and even encouraged as a more peaceful and sustainable mode of existence in the *MaddAddam* trilogy, it is ultimately represented as an ineffectual and incoherent practice compared with patriarchal (neo)carnism.

Despite veganism's increasing uptake in contemporary Western culture, representations of veganism within twenty-first-century sf remain rare and largely unflattering. Ironically, the *MaddAddam* trilogy is one of few sf texts to contain explicitly "vegan" characters, even if the series itself is "palpably hostile to animal advocacy" (Parry, *Edible* 229). Besides Atwood's Gardeners, the only vegan characters to appear in Andrew Milner and J. R. Burgmann's extensive global climate fiction survey, *Climate Change and Science Fiction* (2020), are the Alsatians in German author Dirk C. Fleck's *MAEVA!* trilogy (2008–15), the "overwhelming majority" of whom have "become vegetarian" (Fleck 315; translated in Milner and Burgmann 164), and Mélanie in French author Jean-Marc Ligny's *Exodes* (2012), who establishes a farm "dedicated to the protection of the non-human" (Milner and Burgmann 95–96). A carnist attitude towards climate change can also be gleaned from N. K. Jemisin's triple-Hugo-Award-winning *Broken Earth* trilogy (2015–2017), wherein the carnism of its human characters only intensifies as their environmental situation worsens, while the aberrant carnivorousness of other species is regarded as a "slapdash, last-minute fix" (*Obelisk* 93).[10] The protagonist of Arkady Martine's 2020 Hugo Award-winning novel *A Memory Called Empire* (2019) also goes from being "horribly tempted" and "a little horrified" by genuine animal meat to enjoying how its juices "bloomed over her tongue," within the space of a few pages (314–18). Conversely, Charlie Jane Anders's Locus Award-winning *The City in the Middle of the Night* (2019) involves its human characters coming to terms with the carnist treatment of their planet's indigenous race of intelligent, crustacean-like "crocodiles," while frequenting "vegetarian restaurant[s]" (161).

Nevertheless, direct engagements with veganism among twenty-first-century sf are rare and often ambiguous. The eponymous, extra-terrestrial "peace-keepers" of Karen Traviss's *Wess'har Wars* series (2004–2008) are considered "like vegans," since they "make no use whatsoever of other species beyond food plants and they have no tolerance of anyone who does," derogatorily referring to humans as "carrion eaters" (*City* 121, 173). Yet, while the Wess'har preach universal tolerance, they also enforce their ideology through genocidal totalitarianism that only intensifies as the series progresses – Parry ultimately criticizing the series for its reinforcement of carnist dualisms (*Edible* 105). Other notable twenty-first-century, science-fictional engagements with animal ethics include Michel Faber's *Under The Skin* (2000), wherein an alien abducts and butchers hitchhikers to send back to her home planet; Kazuo Ishiguro's *Never Let Me Go*, wherein cloned humans are harvested for their organs, providing an analogy for farm animals and the cultural acceptance of carnism; and Don LePan's *Animals* (2009), wherein children with disabilities are farmed for their meat, following the mass extinction of nonhuman species. LePan hoped his novel would "provide fodder for philosophical debate on the wider arguments concerning whether or not humans should kill and eat non-human animals" (157), although it has not had any significant critical or cultural influence so far.[11]

The prominent idealization and fetishization of Native American and other Indigenous cultures within post-1970s, Anglo-American sf also shows the need for further investigations into the work of Indigenous SF authors. Highlighting similarities between colonial treatments of Indigenous cultures and nonhuman animals can be an effective method of exposing speciesist prejudices, since they each operate on similar philosophies of "dehumanisation."[12] However, the suffering of Indigenous people themselves is often minimized or overlooked, when their suffering is transferred onto other, non-Indigenous subjects. Although Callenbach, Le Guin, Robinson, and Atwood all adapt idealized versions of Native American traditions, they each also interpret these Indigenous traditions through their own non-Indigenous perspectives to assert a "primitivist" (and often masculinist) carnism. Greater engagement with Indigenous texts, traditions, and communities would both clarify their positions and overcome the reliance on "primitivist" impositions and idealizations by non-Indigenous authors and would allow greater insight into the motivations behind non-Western carnist and vegetarian ideologies, which would assist in combating speciesism on a global scale.

Towards a Vegan Future?

Despite its current, (neo)carnist paradigm, modern sf remains indebted to a set of foundational authors whose works repeatedly confront the carnist prejudices prevalent within Western culture. Yet, while sf's vegan themes had previously been altered to reflect developments in animal ethics philosophy and activism, the ethical and environmental benefits of veganism have been widely overlooked by contemporary sf authors and critics. Despite the direct influence of sf on the 1970s Animal Rights and Animal Liberation movements, animal and vegan activists have had virtually no positive representation within twenty-first-century sf. Although "ecoterrorists" are often glorified in Robinson's fiction, they are rarely vegan, with explicitly animal activists more often represented as irresponsible, ineffective, often violent and overwhelmingly naive in his and other influential sf works, such as Atwood's *MaddAddam* trilogy.

Science fiction nevertheless offers a fertile medium through which to "think the break" with speciesism and carnism, while exploring the methods and motivations necessary to achieve a post-carnist future. The critical vegan impulses frequently contained in, and inspired by, sf have been a considerable, perhaps *essential*, catalyst for real-world change. Cultivating an increased awareness of, and critical engagement with, the genre's prominent and influential vegan tradition will only help the process become more fruitful. As Sorenson observes, "many ideas that are now seen as fundamental to the concept of social justice were once considered absolutely unthinkable," arguing that "with abolitionist animal rights as the basis of renewed political struggle, we can truly *think the unthinkable* and *imagine* new forms of emancipated social life and inclusive justice" (xv, xvii; italics added).

Notes

1. For more on the relation between veganism and utopian texts, see John Miller's essay in this collection.
2. At her own insistence, Atwood's sf – and that of other "mainstream" authors – has become commonly regarded as "speculative," rather than "science," fiction. Here, both terms are combined under the broad banner of "sf," the influential sf writer Ursula K. Le Guin famously asserting that Atwood's "arbitrarily restrictive definition seems designed to protect her novels from being relegated to a genre still shunned by hidebound readers, reviewers and prize-awarders," with Atwood later conceding that what she meant by "speculative fiction" was identical to what Le Guin (and many others) had long called "science fiction" (see Atwood, *In Other Worlds* 5–7).
3. Frankenstein's creature is perhaps more accurately described as vegetarian than vegan, since he has no qualms eating cheese and milk (83). See, for example, Bulleid, *Vegetarianism* 48.
4. Clarke's direct influence on *Star Trek* also led to one of Western culture's most pervasive cultural depictions of vegan utopia (see Bulleid "Boldly Going").
5. See Bulleid, "Dick"; Schuster; Taylor; Toth; and Vint, "Speciesism."
6. For expanded analysis of veganism in the critical utopian canon, see Bulleid, "Better Societies" 61–64.
7. Regarding Piercy and "critical dystopia," see Sargent.
8. Vegetarianism and animal ethics were a frequent topic of debate between Dick and Le Guin (see Bulleid, "Dick" 57).
9. For further examination of the relationship between veganism and feminism in Atwood's realist novels, see Adams, *The Sexual Politics* 118–20, 172, 175; Borrell; Bulleid, *Vegetarianism* 193–98; and Parker.
10. Jemisin herself appears to have no vegan inclinations, responding "You don't fuck with our bacon!" during a 2019 Twitter thread encouraging a boycott, following the deregulation of the US pork industry (Jemisin, "pork industry").
11. For further examination of Ishiguro, see Linett, 117–46; of Faber, see Dunn, and Matthew Calarco; and of LePan, see Parry, *Edible*.
12. See Adams, "War on Compassion."

Works Cited

Adams, Carol J. *The Sexual Politics of Meat: A Feminist-Vegetarian Critical Theory*. Twenty-fifth anniversary edition, Bloomsbury Academic, 2015.

—. "The War on Compassion." *Critical Animal Studies*, edited by John Sorenson, Canadian Scholars' Press, 2014, pp. 18–28.

Aldiss, Brian. "Introduction." *The Island of Doctor Moreau*, by H. G. Wells, xxix–xxxvi, Orion, 1993.

Aldiss, Brian W., and David Wingrove. *Trillion Year Spree: The History of Science Fiction*. Victor Gollancz, 1986.

Amis, Kingsley. *New Maps of Hell: A Survey of Science Fiction*. Harcourt Brace, 1960.

Anders, Charlie Jane. *The City in the Middle of the Night*. Titan. E-book, 2019.

Atwood, Margaret. *The Blind Assassin*. Virago, 2001.
—. *In Other Worlds: SF and the Human Imagination*. Virago, 2011.
—. *MaddAddam*. Virago, 2014.
—. *Oryx and Crake*. Virago, 2009.
—. *The Year of the Flood*. Virago, 2010.
Belasco, Warren. *Meals to Come: A History of the Future of Food*. U of California P, 2006.
Borrell, Sally R. *Atwood's Animals: Triangular Identification in The Edible Woman, Surfacing and The Blind Assassin*. U of Canterbury, Master's thesis, 2005.
Bradbury, Ray. *Fahrenheight 451*. Harper Collins, 2008.
Bulleid, Joshua. "Better Societies for the Ethical Treatment of Animals." *Ethical Futures and Global Science Fiction*, edited by Zachary Kendal, Aisling Smith, Giulia Champion, and Andrew Milner, Palgrave Macmillan, 2020, pp. 49–73.
—. "Boldly Going Vegan? *Star Trek*, Alternative Meat and Animal Ethics." *Science Fiction Studies*, Food Futures Special Issue, 2021.
—. "Vegetarianism and Animal Empathy in the Life and Works of Philip K. Dick." *Foundation*, vol. 48, no. 133, 2019, pp. 47–59.
—. *Vegetarianism and Science Fiction*. Monash U, PhD thesis, 2020.
—. "'We're All Vegetarians Up Here': Arthur C. Clarke, Synthetic Meat and Space Exploration." *Foundation*, vol. 49, no. 135, 2020, pp. 5–18.
Butler, Octavia E. *Parable of the Sower*. The Women's Press, 1995.
—. *Xenogenesis*. Guild America, 1989.
Calarco, Matthew. "Belonging to This World: On Living Like an Animal in Michel Faber's *Under the Skin*." *Literature and Meat since 1900*, edited by Seán McCorry and John Miller, Palgrave Macmillan, 2019, pp. 97–211.
Callenbach, Ernest. *Ecotopia Emerging*. Bantam, 1982.
—. *The Ecotopian Encyclopedia for the 80s: A Survival Guide for the Age of Inflation*. And/Or Press, 1980.
Clarke, Arthur C. *3001: The Final Odyssey*. Voyager, 1997.
Dick, Philip K. "Beyond Lies the Wub." *Beyond Lies the Wub, The Collected Stories of Philip K. Dick*, vol. 1. Gollancz, 2002, pp. 27–34.
—. *Do Androids Dream of Electric Sheep?* Del Rey, 1996.
—. *The Selected Letters of Philip K. Dick*, edited by Don Herron, 6 vols, Underwood Books, 1991–2010.
Due, Tananarive. Afterword to *The Bloomsbury Handbook to Octavia E. Butler*, edited by Gregory J. Hampton and Kendra R. Parker, Bloomsbury, 2020, pp. 274–80.
Dunn, Kirsty. "'Do You Know Where the Light Is?' Factory Farming and Industrial Slaughter in Michel Faber's *Under the Skin*." *Meat Culture*, edited by Annie Potts, Brill, 2017, pp. 149–62.
FAO. *Livestock's Long Shadow: Environmental Issues and Options*. United Nations, 2006.
Fiddes, Nick. *Meat: A Natural Symbol*. Routledge, 1992.
Fleck, Dirk C. *Feuer am Fuss*. Machinery, 2015.
Fleischer, Richard, director. *Soylent Green*. Metro-Goldwyn-Mayer, 1973.
Gilman, Charlotte Perkins. *Herland*. Pantheon Books, 1979.
—. *Moving the Mountain*. Charlton Company, 1911.
Harpur, Caldwell. Letter to the editor. "Martians and Sportsmen." *The Vegetarian*, 2 October 1897, p. 540.
Harrison, Harry. *Make Room! Make Room!* Ace, 1980.
Hogg, Thomas Jefferson. *The Life of Percy Bysshe Shelley*. Edward Moxon, 1858.
Jameson, Fredric. *Archaeologies of the Future*. Verso, 2005.
Jemisin, N. K. @Nkjemisin. "I sincerely hope that for every dollar the pork industry spent on buying Trump's cooperation for this nightmare, they lose ten from people giving up pork." *Twitter*, 18 Sep 2019, 7:28 am, twitter.com/nkjemisin/status/1174434957923667969.
—. *The Obelisk Gate*. Orbit, 2016.

Joy, Melanie. "Understanding Neocarnism: How Vegan Advocates Can Appreciate and Respond to 'Happy Meat,' Locavorism, and 'Paleo Dieting.'" *One Green Planet*, 29 July, 2019. <www.onegreenplanet.org/lifestyle/understanding-neocarnism>

—. *Why We Love Dogs, Eat Pigs, and Wear Cows: An Introduction to Carnism*. Conari, 2011.

Joy, Melanie, and Jen Tuider. "Foreword." *Critical Perspectives on Veganism*, edited by Jodey Castricano and Rasmus R. Simonsen, Palgrave Macmillan, 2016, pp. v–xv.

Kemp, Peter. *H. G. Wells and the Culminating Ape: Biological Themes and Imaginative Obsessions*. Macmillan Press, 1982.

Lane, Mary E. Bradley. *Mizora: A World of Women*. U of Nebraska P, 1999.

Le Guin, Ursula K. *Always Coming Home*. Grafton, 1988.

—. *The Dispossessed*. Granada, 1981.

—. *The Left Hand of Darkness*. Ace, 2010.

LePan, Don. "Afterword." *Animals*. Soft Skull Press, 2010.

Linett, Maren Tova. *Literary Bioethics: Animality, Disability, and the Human*, New York UP, 2020.

"Man under Martian Rule." *Herald of the Golden Age*, 15 August 1898, p. 94.

Martine, Arkady. *A Memory Called Empire*. Tor, 2019.

Miller, John. "The Literary Invention of In Vitro Meat: Ontology, Nostalgia and Debt in Pohl and Kornbluth's *The Space Merchants*." *Literature and Meat since 1900*, edited by Seán McCorry and John Miller. Palgrave Macmillan, 2019, pp. 91–110.

Milner, Andrew. *Locating Science Fiction*. Liverpool UP, 2012.

Milner, Andrew, and J. R. Burgmann. *Science Fiction and Climate Change: A Sociological Approach*. Liverpool UP, 2020.

Moylan, Tom. "The Critical Dystopia." *Scraps of the Untainted Sky: Science Fiction, Utopia, Dystopia*. Westview Press, 2000, pp. 183–99.

—. *Demand The Impossible: Science Fiction and the Utopian Imagination*, 2nd ed, edited by Raffaella Baccolini, Peter Lang, 2014.

Orwell, George. *The Road to Wigan Pier*. Harcourt, Brace and Company, 1958.

Parker, Emma. "You are What You Eat: The Politics of Eating in the Novels of Margaret Atwood." *Twentieth Century Literature*, vol. 41, no. 3, 1995, pp. 349–68.

Parry, Jovian. *Edible Subjectivities: Meat in Science Fiction*. York University, PhD thesis, 2019.

—. "Oryx and Crake and the New Nostalgia for Meat." *Society and Animals*, vol. 17, no. 3, 2009, pp. 241–56.

Petsche, Jackson. "An Already Alienated Animality: *Frankenstein* as a Gothic Narrative of Carnovorism." *Gothic Studies*, vol. 16, no. 1, 2014, pp. 98–110.

Piercy, Marge. *Body of Glass* [*He, She and It*]. Penguin, 1992.

—. *Small Changes*. Fawcett Crest Book, 1972.

—. *Woman on the Edge of Time*. The Women's Press, 1979.

Pinsker, Sarah. *A Song for a New Day*. Berkley Books, 2019.

Pohl, Frederik. *Slave Ship*. Ballentine, 1957.

Pohl, Frederik, and C. M. Kornbluth. *The Space Merchants*. Gollancz, 2003.

Quinn, Emelia. *Reading Veganism: The Monstrous Vegan, 1818 to Present*. Oxford UP, 2021.

Robinson, Kim Stanley. *Fifty Degrees Below*. Bantam, 2007.

—. *Green Earth*. Del Rey, 2015.

—. *The Ministry for the Future*. Orbit, 2020.

—. *New York: 2140*. Orbit, 2017.

—. "Remarks on Utopia in the Age of Climate Change." *Utopian Studies*, vol. 27, no. 1, 2016, pp. 1–15.

—. *Sixty Days and Counting*. Bantam, 2007.

Ryder, Richard D. "Speciesism in the Laboratory." *In Defense of Animals: The Second Wave*, edited by Peter Singer, Blackwell, 2006, pp. 87–104.

Sargent, Lyman Tower. "The Three Faces of Utopianism Revisited." *Utopian Studies*, vol. 5, no. 1, 1994, pp. 7–9.

Schuster, Joshua. "The Vegan and the Sovereign." *Critical Perspectives on Veganism*, edited by Jodey Castricano and Rasmus R. Simonsen, Palgrave Macmillan, 2016, pp. 203–23.

Shelley, Mary. *Frankenstein, Or The Modern Prometheus: 1818 Text*. Oxford UP, 2008.

—. *The Last Man*. Wordsworth, 2004.

Shelley, Percy Bysshe. "A Vindication of Natural Diet." *The Complete Works of Percy Bysshe Shelley*, edited by Roger Ingpen and Walter Edwin Peck, vol. 6, Ernest Benn, 1965, pp. 3–22.

Shippey, Tom. "Iconoclasm." *The Encyclopedia of Science Fiction*. 3rd, online edition, edited by John Clute, David Langford, Peter Nichols and Graham Sleight. Updated 6 September 2019. <sf-encyclopedia.com/entry/iconoclasm>

Singer, Peter. *Animal Liberation*. 3rd ed., Ecco, 2002.

Smith, David C. *H. G. Wells: Desperately Mortal*. Yale UP, 1986.

Sorenson, John. "Thinking the Unthinkable." *Critical Animal Studies: Thinking the Unthinkable*. Canadian Scholars, 2014, pp. xi–xxxiv.

St Clair, William. *The Godwins and the Shelleys: The Biography of a Family*. Faber and Faber, 1989.

Starhawk. *The Fifth Sacred Thing*. Thorsons, 1997.

Suvin, Darko. *Metamorphoses of Science Fiction: On the Poetics and History of a Literary Genre*. 2nd ed., edited by Gerry Canavan, Peter Lang, 2016.

Taylor, Angus. "Electric Sheep and the New Argument from Nature." *Animal Subjects: An Ethical Reader in a Posthuman World*, edited by Jodey Castricano, Wilfrid Laurier UP, 2008, pp. 177–94.

Toth, Josh. "Do Androids Eat Electric Sheep?: Egotism, Empathy, and the Ethics of Eating in the Work of Philip K. Dick." *Lit: Literature Interpretation Theory*, vol. 24, no. 1, 2013, pp. 65–85.

Traviss, Karen. *City of Pearl*. Eos, 2004.

UNEP. *Assessing the Environmental Impacts of Consumption and Production: Priority Products and Materials*. United Nations Environment Programme, 2010.

Verne, Jules. *The Clipper in the Clouds*. Anonymous translation, S. Low, Marston, Searle & Rivington, 1887.

Vint, Sherryl. *Animal Alterity: Science Fiction and the Question of the Animal*. Liverpool UP, 2010.

—. "Speciesism and Species Being in *Do Androids Dream of Electric Sheep?*" *Mosaic*, vol. 40, no. 1, 2007, pp. 111–26.

Wells, H. G. *First Men in the Moon*. Penguin, 2005.

—. *The Island of Doctor Moreau*, Penguin, 2005.

—. *A Modern Utopia*. Penguin, 2005.

—. *The Shape of Things to Come*. Penguin, 2005.

—. *The Time Machine*. Penguin, 2005.

—. *The War of the Worlds*. London: Penguin, 2005.

—. *When the Sleeper Wakes*. George Bell and Sons, 1899.

Wyndham, John. *The Chrysalids*. Penguin, 1968.

4

Veganism and Animals

Sune Borkfelt

Introduction

What can a vegan literary studies approach do for nonhuman animals? What do vegan literary studies approaches to animals look like? How can vegan readings contribute to our experience of textual animals? It seems obvious that to approach reading nonhuman animals through a vegan lens is bound to lean on the work done in literary animal studies to reclaim nonhuman animals as serious subject matter for literary studies. Surely, a vegan reading will, as John Simons puts it in *Animal Rights and the Politics of Literary Representation* (2002), "stress the ways in which animals appear in texts, are represented and figured, in and for themselves and not as displaced metaphors for the human" (6). In other words, when it comes to animals (and, indeed, a number of other subjects), the overlap between vegan literary studies and literary animal studies is bound to be significant. Yet, as I argue in what follows, reading through a vegan lens also has something particular to offer.

There are surely a multitude of ways in which answers to the questions I pose above might be approached, not least depending on how one attempts to define veganism in the first place. Insofar as the essence of veganism is an ethical stance against the objectification and exploitation of animals, nonhuman animals and our relations to them will always be close to the center of any vegan reading in one way or another. Yet, as Emelia Quinn and Benjamin Westwood have suggested, veganism should not be reduced to a mere practice (such as, for instance, refusing to eat animals). As they argue, "Veganism is messier and further reaching than that; an entanglement of identity, practice, and ethics that refuses to sanction the carnivorous subject" (Quinn and Westwood 5). Quinn and Westwood instead suggest that there is a "useful ambiguity" to veganism (5), a resistance to being defined as an end goal or a concrete practice, which instead allows, in Quinn's words, for a veganism that remains always "fragmentary and hybrid" and which "is attended by contradictions and inconsistencies that keep the line between real and symbolic sacrifice open to scrutiny" (150, 151). In this chapter's attempt to provide potential answers to the kinds of questions above, I embrace this idea of "veganism" not being a stable signifier and think of it instead as a kind of mode or heuristic through which texts might be read, or which one can read into texts while reading the human–nonhuman animal relations therein.

In this vein, I here suggest three (somewhat interconnected) ways in which a vegan lens can help us read nonhuman animals. These should be seen as an attempt to start a conversation rather than as exhaustive or final answers. Both drawing on literary animal studies and attempting to draw attention to veganism's specific contributions,

I first start rather narrowly, by suggesting that a vegan reading might pay particular attention to, and critically analyze, the relations that veg*n characters are depicted as having with nonhuman animals. Secondly, I argue that one may read for a vegan sensibility towards nonhuman animals which does not necessarily need to be connected to vegan or vegetarian practice, and which is far more widespread than one might perhaps at first glance think. Thirdly, I argue that veganism, with its ties to an ethics of consumption, is well-positioned – perhaps uniquely so – to bring nonhuman animals in from the margins of texts in the sense that reading through a vegan heuristic would see animals where most other readings might see only dead material, in this case in the form of meat. In all of this, a unifying thought is that veganism should be viewed as a de-objectifying discourse that can be applied in literary texts and to literary analysis.

Animals and Veg*n Characters

It seems obvious for vegan literary studies to take as a starting point characters that – for one reason or another – eschew the consumption of other animals. As work in the field has demonstrated in a variety of ways, to be vegan or vegetarian can be to occupy different spaces than the majority in contemporary discourses about issues such as food, violence, and nature, while those very cultural discourses construct ideas of veg*n identities that – whether construed as positive or negative – rely heavily on ideas of vegan views or practices as aberrant (see, for example, Wright, *Vegan Studies*; Quinn; Stobie). Though I implicitly suggest in the next section that it need not be the case, one might argue that in its refusal "to sanction the carnivorous subject" (Quinn and Westwood 5), veganism makes itself an aberration insofar as eating the dead bodies of other animals is the norm in most contemporary societies. To alter one's diet away from animal products is to alter one's relation to nonhuman animals. This is true materially, but it is also true in other ways, depending on the degree to which one embraces the ideological complexities of veganism and the sometimes complicated ways in which these are connected to consumption and objectification. For instance, as ecofeminist theorists have long pointed out, changing one's diet can be seen as a threat to societal order and ideas of dominance in patriarchal societies (see, for example, Adams, *Neither* 87–108; Gruen, "Dismantling"). In other words, a change of diet away from embracing meat-eating can change one's relations with others – human and nonhuman – in profound ways.

What, then, do the changes in human–nonhuman relations effected by dietary change mean for the depiction of relations to other animals when such seemingly aberrant characters appear in literary narratives? Given that veganism (and, in many cases, vegetarianism as well) is not just a dietary practice, but a complex repositioning of the subject in relation to its surroundings – and, in particular, in relation to other animals – vegan literary studies needs to critically examine how and whether this repositioning appears and affects the depictions of nonhuman animals in narratives with vegan and vegetarian characters.

Kate Thompson's *An Act of Worship* (2000) starts with an instance of a character observing nonhuman animals. "I was about three years old when I first saw the games a cat plays with a mouse," the narrator informs us in the first line of the novel's short and initially somewhat puzzling prologue, before elaborating on the experience:

It was quite clear that the mouse was taking no pleasure from the game. My sympathies were with it throughout, especially when it stood on its hind legs and raised it [sic] paws to the cat, as though it were pleading for its life. When my mother came in and saw what was going on, she tried to distract me and lead me away, but I couldn't be persuaded to leave until the mouse died and the cat, realising there was no sport left in it, began to eat it.

I don't remember being particularly upset, but my mother wrapped me in her arms in a comforting kind of way. (Thompson 1)

The mother, Sarah, turns out to be the protagonist of the novel, and much of the story is focalized through her via the narration of her unnamed son, whose birth the novel's main events precede.[1] The novel tells the story of the events that bring the narrator's mother, a vegetarian with a past as an eco-activist, together with his father Malachy, a small-town butcher in the Irish countryside. While Sarah is portrayed sympathetically, her vegetarianism is generally depicted as somewhat naive and as inspired by her deceased eco-activist boyfriend, after the initial meeting with whom she would only go "near a supermarket ... to picket it, and she had never eaten meat since" (28). She also repeatedly refuses to have a dialogue with Malachy about how and why he raises and slaughters cattle. Her relationship to nonhuman animals is one largely of estrangement and abstraction. When she initially visits Malachy's house where he keeps a few bullocks, the narrator tells us how Sarah "was fond of telling people how much she loved cows. They were gentle creatures, she said. The BSE cull was the worst slaughter of innocents that Britain had ever seen. The karma of such an act would surely rebound upon its perpetrators" (35). In reality, however, she at first finds that "the bit about loving cows was now being put to the test. At this distance, they looked extremely large and pushy," and only after seeing how they shrink back from her presence does she gain the confidence to really approach, thinking that she needs to "tune into their gentle souls. They were sure to understand that she was an ally, not an enemy" (35). However, she finds herself "surprised to discover that they were a good deal more comfortable in the butcher's presence than they were in hers" (36). As in the episode with the cat and mouse, the text depicts her as sentimental in a way that prevents her from recognizing that death and killing are a fact of nature, which one need not be overly upset about (or protect one's children from observing), even if one does recognize animals' subjectivity, whether they are mice or bullocks.

What we see in Sarah is an iteration of the idea that vegan and vegetarian sentiment stems primarily from predominantly female urbanites who are out of touch with what actually happens in the countryside and hence over-sentimentalize nature. Sarah is, after all, just a visitor to the novel's small-town community. Malachy, by contrast, attempts to achieve a balance in which he only slaughters one animal at a time and goes to extra lengths to ensure the bullocks are not afraid. The unlikely duo are drawn together while investigating a number of violent attacks on bulls in the area, carried out by a young man who seeks to prove his manhood to himself while his regular job at an industrial slaughterhouse is on hold due to a strike. As such, it is implied that the industrial killing of nonhuman animals is harmful and that what is needed is the balance that the narrator – as the child of a vegetarian and a butcher – perhaps embodies. In the epilogue, the child offers to be the one who kills the chicks that might be in surplus if they were to have chickens to get eggs, but Sarah does not want chickens exactly because she does not want to face the problem of breeding. In her preference of simply buying "good organic eggs in the market" (262), she thus reveals herself to be a hypocrite who prefers not to face the killing that the novel implies is only natural.

As a vegetarian, Sarah comes to represent an idea of overly sentimental modern humans, who do not want to face slaughter but instead, in the words of the French cultural critic Georges Bataille, "exile themselves . . . to a flabby world in which nothing fearful remains and in which . . . they are reduced to eating cheese" (11), as well as John Berger's modern urbanite for whom animals have disappeared and become abstractions, psychologically and physically marginalized from human lives. Hence, the vegetarian is little more than an extreme example of that "urban stranger" who has difficulty understanding that the sentence where the "peasant becomes fond of his pig and is glad to salt away its pork" contains an "and," and not a "but" (Berger 5).

When the novel briefly broaches veganism, it serves less as an alternative that allows for a more consistent relationship to animals, and more as a means by which to point out the distance from nonhuman animals that the vegetarian supposedly represents. While eating "a sandwich of rennet-free cheese and stale bread," Sarah wonders "whether it wouldn't be more ethical to be vegan. After all, to get milk you had to get calves, and if no one wanted calves, or only wanted them to eat, wouldn't it be better not to use dairy products at all?" (Thompson 41–42). But, she reasons, "then there wouldn't be any cattle. No warm, doe-eyed creatures grazing the pastures of Ireland" (42). Being vegan in this logic, it seems, is to marginalize animals even further from human spheres than Sarah does in her vegetarian ways,[2] in which they are at least still there, though sentimentalized ("doe-eyed creatures") and aesthetically objectified from a distance as part of a particular national Irish aesthetic. It may seem silly to eat "rennet-free cheese" when calves die from dairy production anyway, but at least such a production allows for a relationship to actual animals, should one seek it out; veganism, by contrast, is depicted as the ultimate estrangement from a reality that involves animals, and in which animals are therefore also – as with the cat and the mouse – inevitably killed. Slaughter, on the other hand, can – if done right – be the eponymous "act of worship" of the book's title and helps keep open the possibility that, as the narrator relates in the epilogue, "there may still be a future for the bullock in Ireland" (262).

Somewhat astonishingly, the idea of vegans as removed from nature and nonhuman animals may be found even where the only meat around is that of other humans. In Joseph D'Lacey's dystopian horror novel *Meat* (2008), nonhuman animals are completely absent and industrialized meat production relies on groups of humans designated as, and appropriated (physically and conceptually) into, "cattle." As such, the refusal to eat meat is easily the ethically correct choice from the reader's perspective, as the choice seems to be one between the extremes of veganism and cannibalism. Yet the concept of veganism is complicated by many of the meat-abstainers in the novel – followers of underground prophet John Collins – eating "nothing at all" (D'Lacey 155), on which they seemingly survive excellently (for which no real explanation is given). As Collins tells his disciples, he sees it as "ironic that we who subsist on light and air are forced to live where the sun cannot penetrate and where the air could not be more lifeless. Everything we do is in the nature of a sacrifice" (156). As such, veganism is framed as an in reality unrealistic quest for purity that entails sacrificing one's relationship to the material world and estranges those practicing it even from the needs of their own animal bodies. There is an echo here of the kind of critique of veganism that sees it as more about the virtues of the vegan than about actually saving animals. As, for example, the ecocritic Harold Fromm asks rhetorically:

> As the "ethical vegan" constricts his diet, social life, and everything else, in a futile attempt to make his footprint smaller and smaller, will he soon be walking on his toes like a ballet dancer? And if so, what is the step after that – pure spirit (a euphemism for bodily death)? (181)

Granted, Collins's followers in *Meat* show ideological and physical opposition to the institutionalized cannibalism of the novel's society, and they also seem to achieve a certain strength and sense of spiritual purity from their subsistence "on light and air," but their way of existence invites reading them as engaged in what Fromm calls "the hopeless longing for innocence" of the ethical vegan (183). As such, their depiction shows vegans as a kind of cult seeking distance from all things earthly (including animals) and disavowing their own animality.[3]

Albeit in somewhat different ways, both Thompson's and D'Lacey's depictions exemplify how cultural representations of vegetarians and vegans can be reductive and in fact distance veganism from actual animals by making these representations seem like a jumble of lofty or sentimentalist ideas and ideals that ultimately skews or dissolves relationships to other animals as well as to human animality. As such, these novels not only misrepresent vegans and veganism, but also disparage far more common sensibilities about nonhuman lives (and deaths), and negate de-objectifying discourses that, I suggest below, are central to ways in which veganism manifests itself.

Animals and Vegan Sensibilities

> I know nothing more shocking, or horrid, than the prospect of one of their kitchens covered with blood, and filled with the cries of creatures expiring in tortures. It gives one an image of a giant's den in a romance, bestrow'd with the scattered heads and mangled limbs of those who were slain by his cruelty.
>
> Alexander Pope, 1713 (289)

In the spring of 2000, as a first-year BA student in English, I turned in an exam paper on the history of vegetarianism in Britain before the Vegetarian Society was founded in 1847, and included – among many other things – the above quote from Alexander Pope along with a few lines from his poetic *Essay on Man*. I received a good grade and the paper subsequently appeared, for a short period, on a vegetarian website I was managing at the time. Here my paper was found by Tristram Stuart, who chose to criticize it (alongside the work of more established "vegetarian" historians such as Timothy Morton and Colin Spencer), in his book *The Bloodless Revolution*, for reading in Pope's words a kind of endorsement of vegetarianism (Stuart 215, 218, 574n2, 575n16).

My approach at the time may have been somewhat amateurish, but what Stuart's critique seemed to miss was that the crux of my argument was less about Pope (and a number of his contemporaries) endorsing a particular diet than about expressions of the kind of sensibility that sees something terrible or at least disturbing in the killing (and eating) of animals, even if most people at the time did not see abstaining from meat as a practicable alternative. What Pope expresses in the quote above is, I argue, an *affective* sensibility rather than an appeal to any kind of supposed rational consideration of moral issues. The sight is "shocking, or horrid" and there is a sense of being overwhelmed by the sight of blood and the sounds of "cries," given that both come from "creatures expiring in tortures." As Pope further suggests through his comparison to "a giant's den in a romance," there is something about this affective experience that triggers the imagination, allowing for an implicit comparison between the suffering and deaths of nonhuman and human animals. What I want to suggest here is that this kind of sensibility is a *vegan* sensibility insofar as it reveals the kind of feelings surrounding the killing and eating of other animals, which one could argue vegans simply choose to act on by letting them inform our vegan ethics. Even if most humans who experience such feelings find (or attempt to find) other ways of reducing cognitive dissonance in relation to killing, such vegan sensibilities are – and have historically been – far more widespread than the mere number of practicing veg*ns would suggest. Reading literary texts about killing and eating animals through a vegan heuristic can help our understanding of that. It is perhaps not coincidental then, that Pope turns to a literary example to find his comparison for the bloody kitchen he describes. The literary imagination allows for exactly this kind of exploration of affects that are frequently overruled by practicability or systems of thought in real life. A vegan reading can emphasize such affective content and highlight the vegan sensibilities it is rooted in, as well as how such affect is often dismissed as insignificant by dominant cultural narratives.

There is, however, a need to address the ways in which the aestheticization of violence can, in and of itself, function as a kind of objectification that vegan approaches need to be wary of. This is, for example, a central concern in Josephine Donovan's work, where she argues for an "aesthetics of care" that "does not objectify animal subjects for aesthetic purposes nor . . . aestheticize[s] animal cruelty" (215). A vegan literary studies approach to animals can with great advantage draw on Donovan's work, as well as the work of other ecofeminists who have theorized an ethics – and an aesthetics – of care. In this light, it may seem counterintuitive to look for vegan sensibilities in texts that perhaps often *do* seem to aestheticize violence and animal cruelty; yet I propose that vegan sensibilities can in fact often (though by no means exclusively) be discerned in exactly such texts, by reading them through a vegan heuristic. It remains important, of course, to read texts about violence against nonhuman animals critically and to deconstruct the ideologies of oppression that they also contain. For instance, Donovan points out how depictions of killing animals may rely on, and strengthen, patriarchal ideas in which male identities are tied to exerting dominance over animals and women (167–82). I would certainly argue that even while finding ways to appreciate depictions of violence against nonhuman animals for what they reveal about vegan sensibilities, vegan literary studies needs to be aligned with de-objectifying discourses that remain aware of such connections and resist the objectification of all living beings, whether human or nonhuman. What I suggest is that a vegan critical mode that maintains this balance *is* possible, and therefore that it is possible to appreciate aspects of violent depictions while resisting the various kinds of killing, exploitation, and objectification such texts contain and employ for aesthetic purposes.

I propose, indeed, that vegan sensibilities are found in depictions of slaughter. While the slaughter of animals is perhaps the one practice that seems – aesthetically and ethically – most opposite to vegan ideals, it is also a practice that, partly because it is typically obscured in modern Western societies, can be viewed as both extreme and normative in Western hegemonic carnist culture. It happens as a consequence of cultural ideologies that veganism criticizes implicitly and explicitly, yet the very same cultures that promote these ideologies have also increasingly tended to hide the violence of slaughter from the average citizen (see, for example, Fitzgerald 60; Lee). Hence, some slaughter narratives reveal the negotiation of complex and often negative feelings in relation to killing animals for food, even in the midst of a society that deems the eating of parts of dead animals entirely normative. This reveals a sensitivity to animals being turned into meat *as* animals – that is, an arguably de-objectifying sensitivity based on a discomfort, or rather, a vegan sensibility – that killing often brings about.

D'Lacey's *Meat*, discussed earlier in this chapter, is in its own way a novel whose main idea plays on exactly this sensibility that recognizes violence done to animals as counter to what many humans feel – and recognizes the suffering and death of nonhumans as comparable to that of humans – not unlike what Alexander Pope expressed. Such feelings have historically sometimes been suppressed as supposedly less reliable indicators of morals contrasted with the arguments of humans' supposedly "rational" minds. A vegan studies approach drawing on the retrieval of the moral value of feelings carried out by much ecofeminist work undermines this constructed dualism (see, for example, Donovan; Gruen, *Entangled*). In such a reading of texts, what I have here called vegan sensibilities can be highlighted as part of the value of literature, whether the texts depict such sensibilities, evoke them, or both.

Scottish author Archie Hind's *The Dear Green Place* (1966) is an example of a novel that in some ways seeks to defend the slaughter of animals and portray it as an important craft that reconnects the protagonist, Mat Craig, to the materiality of the world. When Mat, who is otherwise a writer and comes from a job as an office clerk, starts working at Glasgow's central slaughterhouse, the craftsmanship of the work is described in great detail and Mat expresses contempt for the "horrified" and "squeamish" depictions of slaughter by other writers (Hind 109–13). As in Kate Thompson's *An Act of Worship*, there is the sense that the slaughterer is somehow closer than others are to the realities of life and death, and thus also to "the frisky wee bullocks, the quiet maternal cows, the placid indifferent bulls" who are slaughtered (106). Yet even Mat – and Hind, who had first-hand experience as a worker in Glasgow's slaughterhouse – reveals sensibilities that seem to run counter to the killing he carries out. Specifically, Mat has problems coming to terms with the very moments of killing, starting as "the gun, the bolt pistol, was fired into their heads between the eyes" (106). As the animal drops to the floor there is

> an odd sound combining the slap of soft flesh and the solid but dull crunch of the padded bone as the chin bounced loosely on the concrete floor. Then the shuddering sigh and the spasm of the muscles as the animal tensed them to grip at the soft elusive life which suspired from the tiny hole in its forehead. Mat found this difficult to get used to, and with every crack and thud of a beast dropping he would ponder on the fragility of bone. (106)

Even here, then, in the perspective of a slaughterer, the taking of life causes uneasy feelings in response to the sense that the animal attempts to hold on to "soft elusive life" and at the sounds that evoke the physicality that humans and other animals share, including "the fragility of bone." Even more so, Mat worries with "horror" that in kinds of slaughter where the bolt gun is not used, there might be moments "of a possible combination of consciousness and the irrevocable state of death," which he thinks of as "a kind of metaphysical horror . . . even worse than the ineluctable obliteration of the gun" (107). In the novel, such affective moments are eventually explained away with "a commonsense view" or the idea that the cows are "too stupid" to experience fear at slaughter (106, 150). Yet a reading that retains its focus on the affective affirmation of animals' subjectivities found in the very situations of slaughter allows for the argument that there is a sensibility to nonhuman lives and deaths even in moments of slaughter, which approaches vegan sentiment.

Nonhuman animals are at the center of vegan ethical considerations and affects, and thus of vegan ways of life, and yet one of the necessities of such a life is arguably finding ways not to let your feelings or thoughts be about animals all the time, or at least to handle such thoughts and feelings constructively. As Westwood writes, "the permeation throughout society of the animal-industrial complex is deep, and far-reaching – even unavoidable. But, if one were to keep this in focus *all the time*, you would, of course, go mad" (193; emphasis in original). I would suggest that literary depictions of our all-too-often violent relations with nonhuman animals might help readers with such vegan sentiments handle such relations. This is because literary narratives offer always slightly new, slightly altered perspectives and reconfigurations of our relations with nonhumans, but also because they reveal how the horror or sadness many vegans feel at slaughter is far from isolated in vegans; it is, in fact, a sentiment expressed at many points in literary history. It is a sentiment that, however briefly it occurs in situations when characters are faced with animal death, works against the objectification of animals in those moments and allows vegan sensibilities to shine through.

Retrieving Animals in Meat Narratives

Analyzing and critiquing contemporary political and cultural narratives through a vegan lens, Laura Wright has argued that what vegan theorists "must do is reconstitute animals, as best we can and without attempting to speak *for* them, as present within narratives . . . that have worked actively to omit them" ("Vegans" 28; emphasis in original). Paradoxically, given that meat is sourced from (nay, *is*) nonhuman animals, meat narratives are among the narratives that most insistently attempt to omit and erase animal presences. As Carol J. Adams's application of the concept of the "absent referent" has demonstrated (along with the work of countless others in her wake), nonhuman animals (and their deaths) are purposefully made to disappear in, and from, the discourses of meat (*Sexual Politics* 51–53). The absent referent, writes Adams, "permits us to forget about the animal as an independent entity; it also enables us to resist efforts to make animals present" (*Sexual Politics* 51). Reading (and writing) through a vegan heuristic, however, clearly resists such absence. For the meat-eater, as Adams notes, animals "are absent from the act of eating meat because they have been transformed into food" (*Sexual Politics* 51), yet for the vegan meat is *not* food and thus appears again as (body parts from dead) animals.

This perceived presence or absence of the dead animal will naturally also have a profound effect on how we read the appearance of meat in literary narratives.[4]

For instance, from a certain (non-vegan) perspective, slaughter narratives such as the ones mentioned above become about the mere processing of material when the animal has been killed and is no longer exhibiting agency (and given the objectification of animals possibly even before that), but from a vegan perspective the animal remains. A vegan reading thus retrieves animals and insists on meat being ontologically different from objects of non-animal origin. In addition, it remains conscious that, as different scholars have amply demonstrated, the objectification of animal bodies is deeply entangled with various forms of exploitation of human bodies (see, for example, Adams, *Sexual Politics*; Wright, *Vegan Studies*). Excellently demonstrating one way of doing this, Seán McCorry has shown how the presence of meat in Sarah Kane's *Blasted* (1995) can be read as central to the way in which the play problematizes the human subject when one takes into account meat's animal origins and connections to killing and death. Here, McCorry suggests that the "ethical sensibility" of the play's vegetarian character "grows from her attunement to the exposure of the animal body . . . to violence" (758). Hence, he argues, hers "is an ethics of materiality rather than subjectivity, oriented toward embodiment as a site of harm" and "not quite founded on her belief in the injustice of taking nonhuman life" (758). There is a risk here of reducing vegans' response to meat to a purely visceral disgust that is ultimately seated in our own bodies, and thus of marginalizing nonhuman bodies in the discussion as simply a material cause of disgust, helping little to work against the objectification of animals. Yet I would argue that even at the root of such a visceral response are ties to animals as living beings. The nonhuman animals' (former) subjectivity plays an important part in rendering their bodies inedible to the vegan (or vegetarian), just as human subjectivity helps render human bodies inedible to the non-cannibal. Hence, an insistence on making the absent referent seen by viewing meat as animal body parts remains part of a de-objectifying vegan discourse.

Consider, as an example, the evocative description of the meat market in Émile Zola's *The Belly of Paris* (1873):

> On the opposite pathway other drays were unloading freshly killed calves, wrapped in canvas, lying on their sides like children in big rectangular baskets, from which only the four bleeding stumps of their legs protruded. There were also whole sheep and sides and quarters of beef. Butchers in long white aprons marked the meat with a stamp, carried it off, weighed it, and hung it up on hooks in the auction enclosure. Florent, his face glued to the bars of the window, stared at the rows of suspended carcasses, at the red of beef and mutton, and the paler meat of the veal, all streaked with yellow fat and tendon, and with their bellies gaping open. Then he arrived at the counters in the tripe market and passed by the pale calves' feet and heads, the rolled tripe neatly packed in boxes, the brains delicately arranged on flat trays, the bleeding livers and purplish kidneys. He paused to look at the long two-wheeled carts, covered with tarpaulins, which brought sides of pork hung on racks on each side over a bed of straw. The open end of the carts seemed like some candlelit mortuary chapel, suggesting the deep recesses of a tabernacle, such was the glow of all the raw meat. On the straw beds were tin cans full of blood from the pigs. Florent was in the grip of a dull fever. The stale smell of the meat, the pungent odour of the offal, overwhelmed him. (29–30)

Although they concern meat as material object, Zola's descriptions also reflect a certain point in the gradual removal of slaughter from public sight, and thus describe reminders of meat's animal origins that have later often been invisible to the public. It is clear, though, that meat's materiality does not prevent the dead animals and their various parts from being used as images evocative of death and decay. The dead calves lie "on their sides like children," reminding us that they are in fact cows' children, and the carts with "sides of pork" are like a "mortuary chapel" (*chapelles ardentes*). In this way, the description becomes a symbol of life framed by its beginning and end, yet the image seems more ominous and troubled than simple or positive. The dead nonhuman animals described resist simple metaphorization through the detailed descriptions, making it relatively easy to retrieve them from the metaphor. Attention is drawn to the fact of dismemberment through descriptions of animal bodies with "their bellies gaping open" (*le ventre ouvert*) and meticulous mention of particular inner organs. As Adams observes in *The Sexual Politics of Meat*, "We don't want to know about fragmentation because that is the process through which the live referent disappears" (60). In Zola's description, the live referent becomes difficult to avoid, thus retaining a sense of the lives that were lived before the bodies depicted were made meat. In all, the scene impresses a sense of disorder on the reader, despite the apparent order of the rows of bodies and parts: what should be inside – the organs – is outside, and what should be a source of life – a food market – is a place of death. The scene thus opens up the possibility for comparisons of human and nonhuman bodies and deaths, but keeps the animals in a kind of suspension between metaphor and frank representation that draws attention to their objectification.

It is worth noting, too, that the market is seen through the eyes of the protagonist Florent, a political dissident who has escaped from prison. There is thus an irony to his face being "glued to the bars of the window" as he looks in, but also a subtle biopolitical comparison between the control of human bodies he has escaped and that of the nonhuman animal bodies he is looking at. He is starving, yet the sights and smells come across as less than appetizing; rather than a starving man looking at food, he is a victim of incarceration looking at other victims behind bars, and the situation seems to worsen his nausea and fever.

The description stands in contrast to earlier descriptions of the vegetable market, which, significantly, is seen through the eyes of an artist, Claude. Unlike the "glow of all the raw meat" that reminds Florent of a mortuary, the "piles of greenery" at the vegetable market in the morning assume "delicate, shadowy hues – pale violet, milky pink, and greenish yellow, all the soft, light hues that turn the sky into a canopy of shot silk as the sun rises" (25). As the "fires of dawn" rise the vegetables grow

> brighter and brighter, emerging more and more clearly from the bluish shadows of the ground. Lettuces, endives, chicory, open and with rich soil still clinging to their roots, exposed their swelling hearts; bunches of spinach, sorrel, and artichokes, piles of peas and beans, mounds of cos lettuces . . . sounded every note in the scale of greens . . . a continuous scale of rising and falling notes that died away in the mixed tones of the tufts of celery and the bundles of leeks. But the highest notes, at the very top of the scale, came from the bright carrots and snowy turnips, scattered in tremendous quantities throughout the market, which they lit up with their medley of colours. (25)

Unlike the meat market, the vegetable market is full of life. The musical imagery employed in the descriptions of different shades of green form a life-affirming and lively symphony to accompany the fresh light shed by the rising sun, itself a symbol of life and beginnings, as opposed to the ending signified by death. As in the meat market, the quantities are enormous, but here their enormity adds to the delight, rather than the gloom, of the scene. The description goes on to describe the artist's dream impressed by, for example, the "barricade of orange pumpkins in two rows, sprawling at their ease and swelling out their bellies," "the varnished golden-brown" of onions, the "blood-red" (*le rouge saignant*) of tomatoes, "the soft yellow of a display of cucumbers," "the deep mauve of aubergines," with black radishes forming the only "dark patches in the brilliance of the early morning" (26). The contrast is underscored by Claude's reaction: "He found something extravagant, mad, sublime in all these 'amazing vegetables'! He maintained that they were not dead ... He could see them moving, he declared, see their leaves stir and open as if their roots were still firmly embedded in rich soil" (26). The scene is thus positively artistic, and is used to impress a connection between life and art, in which the "swelling hearts" (*cœurs éclatants*) of lettuces, the "blood-red" of the tomatoes and the "swelling ... bellies" (élargissant ... ventres) of the pumpkins are signs of life and wholesomeness in contrast to the fragmentation displayed by the severed internal organs and open bellies described with many of the same words at the meat market. In this way, Zola's novel can be read as registering a discomfort with the origins and connotations of undisguised meat products. The animal referent, found early in the novel, seemingly insists on remaining present and the scene renders meat a troubled image that inevitably reappears often as much of the story takes place around the market and in a butcher's family.

Concluding Thoughts

In attempting to argue for what vegan literary studies can do for animals, I have focused significantly on physical violence in the form of slaughter and meat. Such violence is concrete and easily posed as an antithesis to vegan sentiment, but attending to physical violence and killing through a vegan heuristic is of course not the only way in which a vegan reading can pay attention to nonhuman animals. In concluding, I would like to suggest that what the three interconnected approaches above have in common, more than a focus on violence or meat, is a focus on veganism as a de-objectifying discourse, and that there are other kinds of (de-)objectification to which vegan literary studies can attend. Indeed, one might go a step further and suggest that the text that de-objectifies animals in one way or another is, in a sense, a vegan text – or at least one that lends itself to vegan analysis.

An example of such a text, which does not use violent depictions, is Ursula Le Guin's "She Unnames Them" (1985). In this short story, a female narrator – who turns out to be Eve (and allegorically represents all women) – unnames first all the animals and then herself, thus dissolving the subject–object relations defined by language and originally cemented when God allowed Adam to name the animals (and woman) in Genesis. In unnaming, she removes the basis for categorizing animals according to species and thus for defining their purposes specifically according to human needs or wants. As Marian Scholtmeijer has observed, the story is one in which "animal indifference to language shows a woman the way out of the stories culture tells about women and animals" (255). Without these stories, those previously objectified by them can now engage in new modes of relation. In the narrator's words, the animals "seemed far closer than when their names had stood between myself and them like a clear barrier: so close that my fear of them and their fear of me became the same fear" (Le Guin 195). Fear was previously based on hierarchies, but unnaming has undone the hierarchies and now relations are being redefined so that "attraction was now all one with the fear, and the hunter could not be told from the hunted, nor the eater from the food" (196). These images of consumption may initially seem difficult to reconcile with veganism, but as Scholtmeijer points out, it is notable that "aggression has no place in Le Guin's vision" and that the woman and animals "achieve a victimless insurrection" in their "overthrow of language as the agent of reality" (255). In addition, I would suggest that what is attempted in the story is a kind of challenge to ontological and epistemological categories similar to that posed by veganism. Having returned her name, the woman realizes that she has abandoned the stability of the categories that the names gave: "I could not chatter away as I used to do. My words now must be as slow, as new, as single, as tentative as the steps I took going down the path away from the house [where Adam resides]" (Le Guin 196). What is left after linguistic decolonization may be vague and fumbling, but it aligns well with the kind of messy, inconsistent, unstable, shifting, and fragmentary conception of veganism that Quinn and Westwood propose, and which – like Le Guin's unnaming – destabilizes the hierarchies and discourses that objectify both humans and nonhumans.

Through a string of examples, this chapter suggests ways in which applying a heuristic that pays attention to veganism, its sentiments and sensibilities, can enrich our understanding of nonhuman animals and human–nonhuman relations in literary texts. Though I have just suggested that veganism can be a de-objectifying lens in other ways as well, it is perhaps not coincidental that I have made my arguments primarily through topics connected to meat and slaughter. After all, meat-eating, and the complex ideologies attached to the practice, might be viewed as the ultimate objectification both physically and conceptually, and hence slaughter as both the physical manifestation of the power that makes such objectification possible, and its ultimate end. Reading through a vegan lens, by contrast, might teach us ways of retrieving the nonhuman animal subject.

Notes

1. While British-Irish writer Kate Thompson is probably best known for her fantasy fiction for younger readers, it is worth noting that *An Act of Worship* is, despite the yet-to-be-born child narrator, a mostly realist novel decidedly aimed at an adult audience and one that, indeed, contains episodes of animal cruelty that are arguably anything but child friendly.
2. While it somewhat conflates individual dietary choice with universal vision, the idea that a vegan stance would ultimately simply mean that certain animals would not exist is reflected in some contemporary critiques of veganism. Donna Haraway, for example, argues in *When Species Meet* that vegans' "work to avoid eating or wearing any animal products would consign most domestic animals to the status of curated heritage collections or to just plain extermination as kinds and as individuals" (80).
3. In his critique, Fromm doubles down on this sense that vegans disavow human animality when he argues we cannot escape the consumption of others through the example of how

"to have been born at all we must have been eating our mother during gestation, and after birth we need her milk, which is just another dairy product from animals" (183). Laura Wright provides a poignant response to some of Fromm's ideas about vegan purity in *The Vegan Studies Project* (19–21). See also Emelia Quinn's essay in this collection for a further discussion of Fromm's critique and its manifestation in literary texts.
4. For an excellent and diverse collection of meat-centred readings of texts, see Seán McCorry and John Miller (eds), *Literature and Meat since 1900* (2019).

Works Cited

Adams, Carol J. *Neither Man nor Beast: Feminism and the Defense of Animals*. Continuum, 1994.

—. *The Sexual Politics of Meat: A Feminist-Vegetarian Critical Theory*. Tenth anniversary edition, Continuum, 2000.

Bataille, Georges, and Annette Michelson. "Slaughterhouse." *October*, vol. 36, 1986, pp. 11–13.

Berger, John. "Why Look at Animals?" *About Looking*. Writers and Readers, 1980, pp. 1–26.

Borkfelt, Sune. "Cause and Effect: The Development of Ethical and Religious Arguments for Vegetarianism, in Great Britain before 1847." Unpublished research paper, Aarhus University, 2000.

D'Lacey, Joseph. *Meat*. Oak Tree Press, 2013.

Donovan, Josephine. *The Aesthetics of Care: On the Literary Treatment of Animals*. Bloomsbury, 2016.

Fitzgerald, Amy. "A Social History of the Slaughterhouse: From Inception to Contemporary Implications." *Human Ecology Review*, vol. 17, no. 1, 2010, pp. 58–69.

Fromm, Harold. "Vegans vs. Evolution." *The Evolutionary Review*, vol. 3, 2012, pp. 180–84.

Gruen, Lori. "Dismantling Oppression: An Analysis of the Connection Between Women and Animals." *Ecofeminism: Women, Animals, Nature*, edited by Greta Gaard. Temple UP, 1993, pp. 60–90.

—. *Entangled Empathy: An Alternative Ethic for Our Relations with Animals*. Lantern Books, 2015.

Haraway, Donna. *When Species Meet*. U of Minnesota P, 2008.

Hind, Archie. *The Dear Green Place & Fur Sadie*, edited by Alisdair Gray. Polygon, 2008.

Lee, Paula Young. "Siting the Slaughterhouse: From Shed to Factory." *Meat, Modernity, and the Rise of the Slaughterhouse*, edited by Paula Young Lee. U of New Hampshire P, 2008, pp. 46–70.

Le Guin, Ursula. "She Unnames Them." *Buffalo Gals and Other Animals Presences*. Victor Gollancz, 1990, pp. 194–96.

McCorry, Seán. "'This Disgusting Feast of Filth': Meat Eating, Hospitality, and Violence in Sarah Kane's *Blasted*." *ISLE: Interdisciplinary Studies in Literature and Environment*, vol. 24, no. 4, 2017, pp. 753–66.

McCorry, Seán, and John Miller (eds). *Literature and Meat since 1900*. Palgrave Macmillan, 2019.

Pope, Alexander. "An Article from *The Guardian*, 21st May 1713." Appendix A in Edith Sitwell, *Alexander Pope*, Faber and Faber, 1930, pp. 286–93.

Quinn, Emelia. "Monstrous Vegan Narratives: Margaret Atwood's Hideous Progeny." *Thinking Veganism in Literature and Culture: Towards a Vegan Theory*, edited by Emelia Quinn and Benjamin Westwood. Palgrave Macmillan, 2018, pp. 149–73.

Quinn, Emelia, and Benjamin Westwood. "Introduction: Thinking Through Veganism." *Thinking Veganism in Literature and Culture: Towards a Vegan Theory*, edited by Emelia Quinn and Benjamin Westwood. Palgrave Macmillan, 2018, pp. 1–24.

Scholtmeijer, Marian. "The Power of Otherness: Animals in Women's Fiction." *Women and Animals: Feminist Theoretical Explorations*, edited by Carol J. Adams and Josephine Donovan. Duke UP, 1995, pp. 231–62.
Simons, John. *Animal Rights and the Politics of Literary Representation*. Palgrave, 2002.
Stobie, Caitlin E. "The Good Wife? Sibling Species in Han Kang's *The Vegetarian*." *ISLE: Interdisciplinary Studies in Literature and Environment*, vol. 24, no. 4, 2017, pp. 787–802.
Stuart, Tristram. *The Bloodless Revolution: Radical Vegetarians and the Discovery of India*. HarperPress, 2006.
Thompson, Kate. *An Act of Worship*. Liminal Books, 2019.
Westwood, Benjamin. "On Refusal." *Thinking Veganism in Literature and Culture: Towards a Vegan Theory*, edited by Emelia Quinn and Benjamin Westwood. Palgrave Macmillan, 2018, pp. 175–98.
Wright, Laura. "Vegans in the Interregnum: The Cultural Moment of an Enmeshed Theory." *Thinking Veganism in Literature and Culture: Towards a Vegan Theory*, edited by Emelia Quinn and Benjamin Westwood, Palgrave Macmillan, 2018, pp. 27–54.
—. *The Vegan Studies Project: Food, Animals, and Gender in the Age of Terror*. U of Georgia P, 2015.
Zola, Émile. *The Belly of Paris*. Translated by Brian Nelson, Oxford UP, 2007.

5

Veganism and Race

"Me luv life": Benjamin Zephaniah's Poetic Solidarities

Ruth Ramsden-Karelse

> Well what happened was, the *Daily Mail* had a cartoon of me reading poems to students, and I've got marijuana coming out of my ears, out of my mouth, there's marijuana spliffs on the floor, and there's a professor whispering to the audience, "if you hear any rumblings, it's Shelley, Keats, and Byron turning in their graves." And I just thought, you know . . . First of all, I didn't smoke then – I don't smoke now. Shelley, Byron, and Keats? I thought, what were they like?
>
> Benjamin Zephaniah, qtd. in Ahmed

The cartoon described here by Benjamin Obadiah Iqbal Zephaniah, in a 2019 interview with the BBC journalist Samira Ahmed, appeared in 1987, the same year in which a headline in *The Sun* newspaper, accompanying a photograph of the celebrated poet, novelist, playwright, musician, and activist, asked the British public: "would you let this man near your daughter?" The controversy instigated by the two newspapers would soon culminate in the withdrawal of the offer of a would-be historic Visiting Fellow Commonership in the Creative Arts that had been made to Zephaniah by Trinity College, Cambridge. As the two publications were to discover, however, and to quote Zephaniah's 1985 poem of the same name, you "can't keep a good dread down" (*Dread Affair* 24–25). A riposte to the racist coverage, in the form of Zephaniah's television play, *Dread Poets' Society*, was aired by the BBC in 1992, replete with the characteristic wordplay with which Zephaniah has earned the accolade of "Great Britain's premier black oral poet" (Middleton, "Zephaniah"). The play, Zephaniah's first, saw an electric storm transport the Romantic poets John Keats, Lord Byron, and Percy Bysshe Shelley, as well as the lesser-known poet, better-known novelist Mary Shelley, from a seance at Villa Diodati to a Birmingham-New-Street-to-Cambridge train carriage occupied only by Zephaniah and a witless car parts salesman (Zephaniah and Stafford).

The etymology of "dread" is traversed backwards across the course of the thirty-minute encounter, embodied in the fact that, although the long-dead writers at first perceive Zephaniah with fear or apprehension, they come to regard him with awe or reverence. Of course, both meanings relate to the Rastafarian sense of dread to which the play's title alludes: "dread or fear of the Lord; also, more generally, a deep-rooted sense of alienation felt by Rastafarians towards contemporary society" (*OED*). Refusing his rather un-vegan offer of a white feather quill ("I make mine up in my head, that's what it's for"), this self-described vegan Rastafarian transforms Byron's "sonnet-writing competition" ("we'll soon see who are the poets around here!") into a rousing demonstration of what Zephaniah calls "the rub-a-dub style" ("so compelling," enthuses Mary Shelley, "what do you call that meter?!"). The four *dead* poets are thus juxtaposed with the *dread* poet, whose scripted counterpart rather charmingly champions the ethos in which much of his poetry has its basis. As Zephaniah put it in a recent interview: "Life is important. It sounds a bit wishy-washy, a bit hippy, but LIFE is important" (Clifford). As a young poet and activist, Zephaniah recalls, he "was always trying to make people aware" of the ways in which the "mentality that life is not important" threatens both "animal" and "human rights" (Clifford).

This chapter is concerned with the ways Zephaniah has used poetry to contest this mentality, establishing the interdependence of all life while critiquing the conditions in which certain forms of life are rendered less "important" or more exploitable than others – conditions attendant on racism, sexism, and speciesism, for example. By articulating various demands for more life in this context, I argue, Zephaniah sketches the basis for a liberatory politics to which veganism, in and of itself, can offer only partial entry. What is further needed are radical solidarities that both recognize and work across differences of race, gender, and species, for instance. This politics therefore centers on the radical solidarities that revaluing life would demand from all of us who benefit from, and are affected by, the devaluation of lives that Zephaniah describes as "animal" and "human" (Clifford).

This politics is undoubtedly crucial to the future of veganism, the mainstream version of which often seems perversely determined to reinforce any mode of oppression other than that which it claims to protest. Alarmingly, vegan activism has tended to form a single-issue movement that further entrenches white supremacy by prioritizing ending the oppression of animals over ending the oppression of people – as when foods and products are declared "cruelty free" without consideration of the welfare of those involved in their production.[1] A. Breeze Harper of *The Sistah Vegan Project* comments that "being racialized in the USA means that veganism will be practiced in a way that reflects this [racialization]" ("Return").[2] This of course applies to whatever context in which those who practice veganism are racialized, and goes some way to explaining why all "activists of color" interviewed for one US study, the first of its kind, cited "experiencing or witnessing racism within the [animal rights] movement" as a cause of "burnout" (Gorski, Goodman, and Rising 373).

These activists' demoralization "by the failure of movement leadership to reflect the racial composition of movement activists" should remind us that the white face of veganism belies the diversity of those who practice it (Gorski, Goodman, and Rising 373). As Marilisa C. Navarro puts it, "the dominant narrative in Western veganism has been to prioritize white bodies, histories, and experiences" (287). Yet figures from the US suggest that Black Americans are the fastest-growing demographic of vegans, with eight percent already having identified as such in the late 2010s compared to just three percent of the population as a whole (Reiley). As Amirah Mercer compellingly details, many point to veganism's pre-Vegan Society precedents in the "long, radical history" of "plant based eating" in "Black American culture" featuring the promotion of vegetarianism by religious sects founded in the 1800s, and the Ital diet of Rastafarianism, as well as anti-capitalist culinary guidelines laid out by the Nation of Islam.[3] Yet the histories and experiences of those who are racially minoritized within the global North-centric vegan movement are elided. Acts of erasure include the repackaging of millennia-old foods from the global South as novel and exotic, which in turn leads to the exacerbation of extractive and exploitative labor practices by explosive global North demand. Further, establishments marketing a lucrative brand of white(-washed) veganism fuel the aggressive gentrification of historically Black and otherwise racially minoritized global North neighborhoods. Meanwhile, veganism makes for a particularly toxic single-issue movement since the living beings it supposedly centers are only ever spoken for.

The issues sketched here merely hint at a deep-rooted problem that has been addressed by a number of interventions, which together form a body of scholarship on veganism and race that is multifaceted and diverse.[4] Aph and Syl Ko, for example, welcome a multiplicity of approaches to veganism, not all of them animal-centered, while arguing that challenging the category of the animal as a mechanism of oppression is vital to the ultimate success of all anti-oppression activism, and warning that the "model of compartmentalizing oppressions tracks the problematic Eurocentric compartmentalization of the world and its members in general" (71). Rather than offering a detailed overview of the important and relatively recent scholarship on veganism and race, however, this chapter focuses on work produced over several decades by a single author, Benjamin Zephaniah, to suggest that productive means of thinking through questions addressed by this scholarship can be found in literary works. The literary is foregrounded here as a space in which the ambiguities, entanglements, and contradictions of a politics of veganism and social justice can be articulated in creative and meaningful ways.

As one site from which the aforementioned liberatory politics might emerge, I argue, Zephaniah's poems highlight the problematics of forms of vegan activism that obscure and myopically entrench the very systems of oppression they ostensibly seek to oppose – as is exemplified by various campaigns run by People for the Ethical Treatment of Animals (PETA), to which I will turn towards the end of the chapter. While demonstrating what poetic forms can offer to a vegan activist agenda, then, Zephaniah is instructive to that agenda, offering a remarkably thorough analysis of systemic modes of oppression along with his calls to rally against them. He articulates solidarities that are poetic both in a formal sense and in a necessarily figurative sense, thereby prefiguring a politics that is currently impossible while exercising certain imaginative capacities that will help us make it less so.

An Emergent Liberatory Politics

The investment in the lives of animals made particularly explicit in Zephaniah's *The Little Book of Vegan Poems*, published in 2001, has informed much of his poetry. As any good vegan surely should, he has taken up the carrot rather than the stick to enjoin readers to the cause. "Join Turkeys United an dey'll be delighted / An yu will mek new friends 'FOR LIFE'" (Zephaniah, *Turkeys* 89) is a more enticing offer than any made by PETA's fictional organization "Kentucky Fried Cruelty," for example ("Kentucky"). In this manner, Zephaniah has mapped a route to veganism that is alluring if practically impossible. As Harper points out, "going vegan is primarily enacted through *objects of consumption*" ("Return," emphasis in original). The reality that we all become consumers and/or consumed within a context to which exploitation and inequality are integral limits the possibilities of whatever cross-species entanglements veganism might be imagined to entail. Global capitalism fosters and thrives on the rendering of certain forms of life less livable than others and, as Audre Lorde reminds us, "the master's tools will never dismantle the master's house" (112). As the basis for a liberatory politics, the act of "going vegan" in itself is therefore unreliable at best. In Zephaniah's poetry, on the other hand, veganism is enacted through what he uses "Turkey's United" to symbolize. As he writes in "Black Politics of Today": "I give it an I need it, it is Solidarity" (Zephaniah, *Psalms* 62–63).

Veganism can be understood as a form of solidarity, Zephaniah suggests, with animals who can be seen to communicate clearly and comprehensibly: "Animals vote with their feet / Or their wings / Or their fins"; "I've never seen liberated animals / Protest by going back to their place / Of captivity" (*Too Black* 61). In another sense, as I will later argue, he acknowledges that this comprehension is not so clear and nor should it be. Nonetheless, what is unmistakably clear in his poems is that all life is fundamentally interdependent – and this is why his advocacy for veganism is only ever ambivalently animal-centered. According to Zephaniah, "dere are many reasons fe diet like a vegan" (*Psalms* 47). While these final four words suggest that veganism is not merely a diet, the allusion to a singular vegan as someone who has a diet that should be copied highlights the limitations inherent in the reality to which Harper points: that veganism currently is primarily enacted through consumption. These limitations, which Zephaniah both nods to and disputes, are registered in Nik Taylor and Richard Twine's understanding of veganism as "only an ethico-political beginning to addressing the interconnected oppression of people and animals" that "needs to be moored to a broader political vision" (12).

Zephaniah's poetry is one site from which a broader political vision emerges, and from which we might therefore work towards a liberatory politics. Zephaniah's investment in the lives of animals is just one angle from which he challenges systemic modes of oppression producing the conditions in which it is necessary for such investments to be articulated. He locates the animal lives he champions in a world in which it is people who are the problem but – at risk of sounding like a hashtag – not all people. Specifically, the problem is rooted in sensed superiority: the ideology of white supremacy, for example, of which mass colonization and enslavement were manifestations. "My people were rich but robbed / An we were healthy" conceptualizes colonization in broad terms inclusive of health and interspecies relations while refuting capitalist measures of wealth, given that capitalism continues to feed and promise feelings of superiority by encouraging "Blind Consumerism" (Zephaniah, *Propaganda* 58). Such feelings result in "a form of illusion known as 'the God complex'" that impacts negatively (but unequally so) upon all forms of life (58) – hence the need for radical solidarities that both recognize and work across difference. Zephaniah's understanding of inequality's atomizing function is articulated by his *Dread Poets' Society* scripted counterpart, who leaps to the defense of an outraged commuter whom the fictionalized Byron would attack: "Leave him, I thought you were the friend of the oppressed" ("he's not oppressed," quips Byron) "he's just a misguided proletariat the same as me! A victim of the oppressor!" What oppressor, wonders a dismayed Percy Shelley: "1987 . . . surely the Tories can't still be in power!" (Zephaniah and Stafford).

In this context, those turning to superficial forms of veganism – those who do not struggle against its consumerist limitations – will get mocked: "An now dat yu dying / Yu start turn Green" (Zephaniah, *Psalms* 47–48). What is required is a political vision that goes far beyond this: "Babylon must burn, / Burn Babylon, burn" (Zephaniah, *Too Black* 25). Zephaniah explains that "we've got to find a way of not just living in harmony with animals, but living in harmony with the earth . . . Rasta man been talking about this for a long time" (Clifford).

"Having a Word," the poem from which the reference to Babylon is taken, indicates two reasons why poetry offers an ideal vehicle for the solidarities Zephaniah articulates (*Too Black* 25). The first is to do with the relative flexibility of the form. This affords greater freedom both to illuminate complexities and contradictions inherent in oppressive notions linguistically sedimented into "common sense" and to crystallize what these preconceived notions might obscure, and thereby challenge hegemony. The second reason is to do with the inherently democratic nature of poetry, without which its aforementioned uses would be meaningless.

"A Strong Connection between Poetry and Politics"

Poetry is inherently democratic, as Zephaniah opens his first *Dread Poets' Society* performance by announcing: "I think it is important to tell this to the people, poetry was stolen from us, and that was evil" (Zephaniah and Stafford). This chapter unfortunately runs the risk of standing with the second (bad) category of poetry he proceeds to outline: "Put upon the bookshelf by the type that like to analyse, discussed in classy journals by the type with reading eyes."[5] Although "there's nothing wrong with reading, we must read to liberation," Zephaniah insists that "readers must not put down this long oral tradition" (Zephaniah and Stafford). His favorite places to visit are those where this "oral tradition is alive" – where "there is [still] a strong connection between poetry and politics" (Saguisag, Rosen, and Zephaniah 22) – and he has been on a mission to reignite this tradition in Britain since his early rise to prominence as a performance poet at late-1970s political demonstrations. Zephaniah warns that writers "cannot just talk about women's rights, freedom, whatever issue. That's not good enough. You have to get up and do something" (24). Poetry could be the thing that is done, he seems to imply, but only if it moves others to further constructive action. His aforementioned *Dread Poets' Society* recitation thus concludes: "Some have taken up the gun, some have taken up the pen, oppressors are aware of this and they fear both of them. Lawmakers and media try holding rappers back, and it is no coincidence that most rappers are Black" (Zephaniah and Stafford).

For Zephaniah, who eschews any historically and geographically blinkered conception of poetry as something found in books, poems come in many forms, including the rhymes and Anansi stories passed on to him by his mother (Ahmed). Unfortunately, however, "people's, children's passion for poetry is being killed . . . It becomes academic and it's killed" (Saguisag, Rosen, and Zephaniah 26). Instead, Zephaniah explains, "poetry should be alive. You should be able to dance it" ("A Day"). His poems certainly fit this bill. These are poems that are made to move out through the world, to be mobile – poems that move you and that continue to move your body and your head. Even without musical accompaniment, Zephaniah's performances modulate tone and pace to produce irresistibly driving and lingering rhythms. He doesn't write with the page in mind. His playfully loose rhyme, accessible lexicon, and signature blend of quotidian and fantastical imagery are not supposed to be stuck on the page and so don't stay there. As those of us who read his 1994 collection *Talking Turkeys* from the page at a young age can attest: regardless of how they are encountered, these poems stay with you.

Zephaniah is concerned, furthermore, with whom his poems are able to reach and therefore with whom they stay. Throughout his career, he has sought to use poetry not only as a form of protest against various, related forms of structural injustice but as a vehicle of communication with the structurally disadvantaged. He stopped writing for the stage in 1990 because "most theatre did not reach" these communities (Birch). He uses poetry to convey concentrated messages to mass audiences rather than preach to the choir. As seen in his occasional use of terms such as "overstand" and "downpress" throughout his poetry across several decades, Zephaniah engages in the Rastafarian practice of using language to counter epistemological confusion resulting from colonization. He acknowledges such confusion when he writes, "I have learnt that equality / May not mean freedom, / And freedom / May not mean liberation, / You can vote my friend / And have no democracy" (*Too Black* 25). Indeed, he remembers "as a very young boy wanting to be a writer but feeling that Standard English just couldn't contain" him: "Rastafari liberated me" (Middleton, *Rastafari* 148). This enables him to critique one worldview while in the same breath offering an alternative: "Dis is me, standing under understanding, / getting up and over, overstanding the / corruption of our role models" (Zephaniah, *Too Black* 49).

One apparently not corrupt role model emerges in the teleplay in which the four writers I previously referred to as the dead poets are of course very much not dead. Zephaniah imaginatively liberates them from the graves in which the *Daily Mail* alleged they were turning to convey how bizarre it was to suggest that they would be, given they were variously anarchist, opium-smoking, and allegedly "mad, bad, and dangerous to know" (Ahmed). Moreover, Zephaniah conveys what he elsewhere calls Percy Shelley's "humanity, passion," and "rock and roll attitude" ("My Man"). Admittedly, Byron's poetry is dismissed as lifeless, "sound[ing] just like the stuff they tried to make [Zephaniah] read in school," which "made [him] stop going to school" (Zephaniah and Stafford). Zephaniah thought "all old poetry was dead," in fact, before discovering Percy Shelley "the person and his politics" ("Benjamin"). This is the Percy Shelley whose "poetry was being quoted on the streets and chanted at demonstrations," who knew "the power of poetry" and, "more importantly . . . the power of the people" ("My Man"). Via Zephaniah, we receive Percy "the 'Dub' poet of his time" ("My Man"). From the rousing on-screen co-citation of *The Masque of Anarchy*, aired approximately four years before "Ye are many – they are few" was first alluded to in the Labour Party constitution (P. B. Shelley, *Masque* 20), Zephaniah emerges as Percy's poetic heir. As Mary Shelley exclaims to Percy upon discovering that Zephaniah partakes in that longstanding vegan tradition of traveling with homemade sandwiches: "Vegetarian! He is of our minds!" In this moment, Zephaniah the scriptwriter playfully claims his place at the literary (and vegetarian) table, casting himself as the very creature who allegedly appeared during the Villa Diodati game to offer inspiration for Mary Shelley's famously man-animated (and vegetarian) creature.[6] As he elsewhere represents veganism as pre-colonial norm, Zephaniah locates the oral poet as inspiration and foundation for all that is more comfortably canonical. Simultaneously, he makes the case for a re-animation (a re-dreading) of otherwise dead poetry (Zephaniah and Stafford).

Likewise, "Bought and Sold" reverses the logic of the *Daily Mail* caricature, with which this chapter opened, to explain that in fact "smart big awards and prize money / is killing off big poetry" and that it is not Romantic poets but rather "the ancestors [who] would turn in graves" about whom we should worry (Zephaniah, *Too Black* 15–16). Poetry is in need of reclamation, at risk of ancestors turning in their graves, because it is essentially life-giving and therefore important for those who are oppressed: "only poetry gives me life / and nakedness gives me knowledge" (Zephaniah, *Too Black* 50). Zephaniah might gain knowledge from nakedness in various related senses: in the sense of being honest and direct, for example; in the sense of attempting to cast off material investments in the oppressive structures he critiques; or in the sense of writing from a place of vulnerability to these structures. Although Byron is initially adamant that Zephaniah cannot be a poet ("look at him, he's not even wearing a floppy collar!"), the significance of this quality of vulnerability is commented upon by Mary Shelley, who counters with "he does seem to be much abhorred and despised by his fellow man," and by Percy who rather opportunistically adds: "it's long been my view that the true poet should be an outcast" (Zephaniah and Stafford). Indeed, Zephaniah's "mission to save poetry from academia" was partly "sparked by his own troubled childhood and how poetry was a lifeline for him" (Birch). Whereas "in his view, empire sucks the life out of others," according to one critic, Zephaniah "craves black flourishing. And poetry facilitates such flourishing, for it helps to awaken conscience and raise awareness of the rigors and inequalities of lives lived under oppression" (Middleton, *Rastafari* 141, 139).

Writing Down Babylon

This conscience awakening and awareness-raising involves countering the epistemological confusion of the "poster on a / hot tin street in Jamaica," for example, "that told [Zephaniah's mother] / that Britain loves her" (*Too Black* 48). It also involves illuminating the interconnectedness of various modes of systemic oppression to which Zephaniah speaks, which these modes of oppression necessarily occlude. In Rastafari, "Babylon" names a world order in which the African diaspora remains dispersed and oppressed. Since it refers to the Biblical story of the tower of Babel, the term implicitly recognizes that systemic modes of oppression (and the occlusion of their intersections) function linguistically. Hence, they might be resisted through linguistic innovation – in other words, poetically. So, while using poetry to challenge "our thinking about non-human animals," which he says "is very confused" (EVOLVE Campaigns), Zephaniah locates this confusion within broader patterns.

In Rastafari, "Babylon" refers to a world organized by slavery and by the Atlantic slave trade in particular. Rallying against this order, Zephaniah's poems frequently evoke enslavement as a real and symbolic condition – as in his pro-animal rights "Anti-Slavery Movements" (*Too Black* 61) – without losing sight of the historical specificity of the enslavements through which the conception of sovereign human being, including the human faculty of reason and individual will in which freedom was located, was founded to the exclusion of blackness. These are the conditions producing a present in which, as Rinaldo Walcott puts it, "Black people die differently" (143). It is "the crossing of the Atlantic," Walcott contends, that makes "the conditions of black death seem to repeat across time, space, and location" by inaugurating an "intimate relation to death in a fashion that" is – crucially – "different from many human others" (147, 146).

Zephaniah's poems illustrate various ways in which life possibilities are skewed within what Saidiya Hartman terms "the afterlife of slavery" (6). This is a present in which Black people are still forced to defend the very mattering of Black lives; a present in which a seventeen-year-old Zephaniah survived being beaten in a police station by the same police force that would murder his unarmed, distressed, and vulnerable cousin Mikey Powell three decades later (Hattenstone). As Zephaniah suggests in his 1983 "Dis Policeman Keeps On Kicking Me To Death," it is a present marked by a failure of action but more so by the success of oppressive systems:

> I got me up and took me to de place fe human rights
> A notice on de door said "Sorry, we are closed tonight"
> So I turn round and took myself to see dis preacher guy
> Who told me 'bout some heaven
> Dat was in de bloody sky,
> Now I don't wa'to kid myself
> But I don't think I'm free
> If I'm free den why does he
> Keep fucking kicking me

By using poetry to articulate various demands for more life in this context, Zephaniah sketches the basis for a politics of solidarity.

In doing so, he offers an alternative to problematic forms of vegan activism exemplified by PETA's 2007 "The Animal Liberation Project" (ALP). This controversial campaign was replete with the sort of self-congratulatory references to "compassionate people" (who "understand" better) that obscure the systemic nature of oppression and the radical solidarity its resistance thus demands from all of us who are variously affected by and who benefit from the exploitation of others in different and arguably inescapable ways. Although it was launched fourteen years ago at the time of writing, I want to consider the ALP here because it exemplifies certain problematics of vegan activism to which I would suggest we should pay further attention, and because it features audio narration by and a video interview with Zephaniah himself. Arguing that these problematics are highlighted in Zephaniah's poetry and that these poems make available a more complex and powerful analysis, I seek to demonstrate the non-identarian understanding of veganism to be found in Zephaniah's poetics.

Working across Difference

Describing its juxtaposition of "images of human suffering and nonhuman animal suffering," Harper suggests that the ALP caused outrage because these "emotionally sensitive materials" were offered without "sociohistorical context" ("Introduction" 23). Without any such context, attempts such as PETA's 2020 one-minute Superbowl Ad (allegedly rejected by Fox) to appropriate for an anti-speciesist agenda the work of anti-racist activists sound as an either alarmingly tone-deaf or frankly callous "all lives matter" riposte. There is another problem with the ALP, however, that warrants further attention. Although I understand, as another *Sistah Vegan* contributor, Joi

Marie Probus, writes, that "PETA's intent is not to imply that Black, Jewish, or Native American people are viewed by PETA or *should be viewed by anyone* as subhuman," I am not convinced that these images aim, as Probus states, "to evoke compassion" or empathy (160, emphasis in original). Rather, they seem designed to evoke pity. Some of us were offended by the campaign not only because the comparison was made but because of the position from which it was articulated. Historical subjects depicted were constructed as voiceless others and the viewer addressed as witness to their suffering. By issuing a call to act on behalf of those it rendered unable to act themselves, the ALP reinforced dangerous stereotypes in a manner in which PETA apparently revels.

What the ALP fails to recognize (or perhaps care about) is what Indigenous activist and scholar Margaret Robinson explains, drawing on the work of Black feminists and feminists of color: "speciesism creates a hierarchy among humans based on our assumed similarity to, or distance from, other animals" (77). Although, as Jennifer Polish points out, speciesism does not enable but rather "intimately interacts with racism (and other institutional -isms) to promote itself" (377),[7] this hierarchy can only ever be reinforced by those who fail to contest its operations – including those whose advocacy relies on lazy stereotypes. The ALP relies on such stereotypes by engaging an interpretive frame in which blackness is aligned with the state of being oppressed, construed as passive and negative, and whiteness with saviorism, construed as active and positive. This is the very frame ridiculed in Zephaniah's "White Comedy," and it is one he sidesteps by using poetry to engage feelings other than pity – declaring "I am in luv wid a hedgehog" (*Turkeys* 83), for instance – while highlighting that pity is of likely limited use to a vegan activist agenda, given it hasn't aided any anti-racist agenda as much as PETA would apparently have us believe.

Perpetuating the dangerous myth of white saviors ("changes only came about because thoughtful people demanded justice and fought against oppression"), the ALP erases enslaved and colonized people's achievement of their own liberation (PETA, "Animal Liberation"). Furthermore, the trope of vegans *seeing* better (the common implication that we are the ones who don't need the slaughterhouse's walls to be glass, for example) here works to erase ongoing systemic oppression and exploitation. If one way in which animals are made absent is when they are used as "metaphors for describing people's experiences," as Carol J. Adams famously argues (21), then the use of people as metaphors for describing animals' experiences, as seen in the ALP, is surely enough cause for alarm. White vegans would do well to remember Zephaniah's "A Modern Slave Song": "When yu trying to sell me beans to me / Remember I exist" (*Psalms* 52).

Unfortunately, there is further cause for alarm. PETA goes so far as to claim that "Beatings, lynchings, and burnings take place today just as they did in the past – only the victims have changed" and that "the only difference is that today's victims – used and abused because they are 'different' and powerless – belong to different species" ("Animal Liberation"). Such descriptions of animal oppression and exploitation that erase the ongoing oppression and exploitation of people are myopic and ultimately self-defeating. They also utilize a common and dangerous tactic, defending the rights of the minoritized (in this instance, animals) on the basis that they are "just like" those who benefit from their subjugation (in this instance, people). This tactic must be contested since it ultimately maintains hegemony, fostering forms of identification that necessarily exclude all those who cannot be read as "just like" in the same way. This means, for example, that the successes this tactic has brought campaigns for so-called gay marriage (which are more than many of the campaigners themselves imagined) hinder the cause of campaigns for trans rights since the latter campaigns are less easily able to articulate appeals to respectable sameness, whether or not sameness is desired by those whose rights are in question. For a truly liberatory politics, then, what is required are imaginative capacities for working across difference rather than collapsing difference by allocating a minimum acceptable value.

Zephaniah cultivates such capacities, using poetry to critically work across difference without flattening it into a "just like" post-humanism akin to what David Theo Goldberg warns us about when he cites filmmaker Michael Oblowitz: "the post-racial ... is the most racial" (1). While animating said animals' lives, Zephaniah highlights the limits of our understanding. "A Day in the Life of Danny the Cat" begins, "Danny wakes up / Eats / Finds a private place in the garden, / He returns / Plays with the plants / And sleeps." Pausing at "eats" and "sleeps" evokes a familiarly lazy feline rhythm sharply structured by the curt privacy upon which cats insist. Similarly, with a nod to Marie Antoinette, Zephaniah playfully acknowledges the impossibility of oppressors understanding the oppressed: "Be nice to yu turkey dis christmas / Invite dem indoors fe sum greens / Let dem eat cake an let dem partake / In a plate of organic grown beans" (*Turkeys* 89). Anthropomorphism affords an illusory but scintillating escape from the mode of denegation enacted by veganism's claim to human exceptionalism: "Ask any veterinarian / I'm just a vegetarian / We cows are people too" (*Too Black* 58). These poetic and necessarily aspirational solidarities suggest that anthropocentrism is inescapable and follow the instinct to read otherness as "just like" to its limits and fantastic conclusions. On the one hand, this functions as a critique of what it says about humans that we feel the need to *know* animals in order to not eat them (or indeed to see other people as just like us in order to recognize their basic rights). On the other, it suggests that something distinctly human gets lost when we don't try to know the unknowable by projecting ourselves onto animal others, and instead view them as products for consumption. This offers an important complication to Jacques Derrida's famous injunction to respect the "irreducible otherness" of the animal (380).

This view of animals is one symptom of alienation to which Zephaniah's hero Angela Davis alludes when she suggests that "the lack of critical engagement with the food that we eat demonstrates the extent to which the commodity form has become the primary way in which we perceive the world." This means that "we don't go further than what Marx called the exchange value of the actual object," Davis explains; "we don't think about the relations that that object embodies and that were important to the production of that object." What "would really be revolutionary," she argues, is to develop "a habit of imagining" the "human" and "non-human relations behind all of the objects that constitute our environment" (Davis and Boggs). Zephaniah's poems foster imaginative capacities that would seem useful here. As he explains, "the reason [he] write[s] is to get people thinking – not to change their minds – it's not straightforward propaganda" ("Poetic").

These habits of imagining and practices of thinking are key to the non-identarian understanding captured by Zephaniah's various discussions of veganism as a necessarily continual practice of ethical interrogation such as his poetry facilitates. Upon finding out aged eleven where meat "comes from" (Clifford), Zephaniah recalls telling his mother: "I won't eat my friends" (Ahmed). Such accounts bring to mind Judith

Butler's theorization of the inherent precariousness of social life, which stresses the importance of recognition to becoming human. The human subject is constituted, Butler argues, through recognition as such. Zephaniah "was living in a place at the time" in which he was dehumanized by other people; "where, as a black man, [he] was being bullied and chased and hunted down" (Ahmed). Asking "which humans count as the human" and "what racist norms . . . operate to distinguish among those who can be recognized as human and those who cannot," Butler points out that these questions are "made all the more relevant when historically entrenched forms of racism rely on bestial constructions of blackness" (*Notes* 36). It is "only through a critical approach to the norms of recognition," Butler suggests, that we can "begin to dismantle those more vicious forms of logic that uphold forms of racism and anthropocentrism" (37).

Such an approach would think more critically about the interrelation of racism and anthropocentrism than the ALP's framing encourages. It must, I would argue, position the active recognition of all people as "human subjects" as primary to the active recognition of "nonhuman living beings" (Butler, *Notes* 35). Himself interrogating the norms of recognition, Zephaniah suggests a non-exploitative perception of animals based in an understanding of the co-constitutiveness of life, human and nonhuman. "The things that left me alone were animals," he remembers. "When people were eating the beings that were not hunting me down, it was very instinctive for me . . . I was just being true to myself" (Clifford). Whereas the ALP promotes a sense of saviorism, Zephaniah articulates an understanding of solidarity based in the acknowledgment of mutual implication within structures of power and interrogation of attendant positionality. The latter involves noting what is rendered possible and what is not, and troubling the limits of the impossible to question the oppressive basis of the notion, as Zephaniah signals by evoking the absurdity of trying to join "Turkeys United," a "cause" non-existent among turkeys themselves (*Turkeys* 89).

This process of interrogation is juxtaposed with the initially unfamiliar label "vegan," of which Zephaniah expresses his early suspicion. Zephaniah is "kind of proud," he says, that it was only "a couple of years" after deciding he "didn't want to have any animal product" that he heard the descriptor "vegan." In fact, he "jumped on" and "started to fight" the "kid" who first called him a vegan: "'cause I thought he was calling me a name, a really bad name . . . like the N word" (Ahmed). While foregrounding his own subject position as someone dehumanized with racist slurs, Zephaniah forewarns dangers inherent in imposing neat, apparently identarian descriptors onto something that he tells us he had thus far experienced as a process of ethical interrogation. Similarly, Emelia Quinn has suggested that "the political efficacy" of the identificatory term "vegan" requires (151), following Butler's work on terms such as "woman" and "queer," "open[ing] the category as a site of permanent political contest" (*Bodies* 222).

Elsewhere, Quinn and Benjamin Westwood offer four reasons for thinking through "veganism as an inherently queer mode of being in, and relating to, the world, rather than as a discursively fixed identity category," the third of which is the structural resemblance of "vegan" to "queer" "as an umbrella term for a diversity of subject positions, which nonetheless rejects the stultifying logic of identity politics" (3). This comparison should remind us to remain closely attentive to important arguments about *queer*'s potential erasure of Black and Indigenous people and those who are otherwise racially minoritized within global-North-centric scholarship and beyond.[8] The flattening and extractive function of the umbrella term "vegan" when yielded uncritically is disastrous,⁹ since erasure of difference works to reinforce the conditions that render certain forms of life exploitable and disposable. Dismantling these conditions must remain the ultimate goal of a liberatory politics to which veganism can only ever offer partial entry and that offers the only real hope for that "kernel of utopian desire that undergirds" veganism (Quinn and Westwood 8). While critiquing these conditions, Zephaniah nurtures this utopian desire and exercises imaginative capacities that will help bring it into the realm of possibility, articulating poetic solidarities that are often fantastical and always thought provoking. The solidarities he articulates remind us, as Aurora Levins Morales puts it, that

> Solidarity is not a matter of altruism. Solidarity comes from the inability to tolerate the affront to our own integrity of passive or active collaboration in the oppression of others, and from the deep recognition that, like it or not, our liberation is bound up with that of every other being on the planet, and that politically, spiritually, in our heart of hearts we know anything else is unaffordable. (215–16)

Conclusion: Veganism as an Aspirational Form of Solidarity

Of all literary forms, the poem is perhaps an ideal vehicle for activist agendas. Language is "poetic" when it is emotive, illuminating, or provocative in some way, while formal conventions typically render poems memorable and shareable. Equally, relative concision and economical phrasing makes poetry a perhaps unlikely site of rigorous political analysis. Since such analysis runs throughout his poetry, Zephaniah not only demonstrates what poetic forms can offer to a vegan activist agenda but is instructive to that agenda. If this outspoken, easily recognizable, and by now self-described vegan can use poetry to offer a remarkably thorough and consistently intersectional analysis, it should not be difficult for this to happen in any other format.

As Zephaniah's poems remind us, none of us can simply renounce the ways in which we benefit from and are impacted by the systemic exploitation and oppression of animals and of other people. Veganism can therefore only be understood as a form of solidarity that is aspirational, and only in so far as we remain cognizant and critical of our various and distinct positionalities as beneficiaries of the interrelated modes of systemic oppression against which Zephaniah calls on us to rally. In this context, Zephaniah offers a beacon of hope for those of us who feel a sense of ambivalence about claiming vegan as a subject position but who are nonetheless committed to the ethos he expresses when he writes: "Me luv being, me luv singing, me luv loving / Me luv life . . . / I give it an I need it, it is Solidarity" *(Psalms* 62–63).

Notes

1. Navarro offers a helpful overview of scholarship on the ways in which "the mainstream vegan movement maintains and reinforces whiteness" (287).
2. See Armin Langer's essay in this collection for an in-depth analysis of *The Sistah Vegan Project*.
3. Mercer explains that "[Elijah] Muhammad's call to plant-based eating was a direct response to the very factors that had disrupted the Indigenous Black diet in America more than 300 years prior: capitalism and racism."

4. As this overview suggests, much of this work is concerned with a US context specifically. Three notable edited collections are cited here: Harper's 2010 *Sistah Vegan: Black Female Vegans Speak on Food, Identity, Health and Society*; Julia Feliz Brueck's 2017 *Veganism in an Oppressive World: A Vegans of Colour Community Project*; and A. Ko and S. Ko's 2017 *Aphro-ism: Essays on Pop Culture, Feminism, and Black Veganism from Two Sisters*.
5. Martin Rowe's reflections on the nature of academic publishing, in his contribution to this volume, raise similar concerns about the limitations of the academic book market for a democratic veganism.
6. Carol J. Adams notes the vegetarianism of Mary Shelley's creature in *The Sexual Politics of Meat*.
7. Seeking to make visible and interrogate the inherent whiteness of mainstream veganism, Polish further elaborates on "a principal problem in a lot of animal rights activism and scholarship" alluded to in this chapter, which "resides in the assumption that humans are always already positioned above animals" (377).
8. See, for example, Cathy Cohen's seminal 1997 intervention on the manner in which "queer politics" has "in many instances . . . served to reinforce simple dichotomies," in which she "envision[s] a politics where one's relation to power, and not some homogenized identity, is privileged in determining one's political comrades" (438).
9. See, for example, Rama Ganesan on vegan misappropriation of Hinduism (61–68).

Works Cited

Adams, Carol J. 1990. *The Sexual Politics of Meat: A Feminist-Vegetarian Critical Theory*. Bloomsbury Academic, 2015.
Ahmed, Samira. "Benjamin Zephaniah." *How I Found My Voice*. 22 April 2019, podcast, MP3 audio, 44:00. <https://play.acast.com/s/howifoundmyvoice/benjaminzephaniah>
Birch, Dinah (ed.). *The Oxford Companion to English Literature*, 7th ed. Oxford UP, 2009.
Brueck, Julia Feliz (ed.). *Veganism in an Oppressive World: A Vegans of Colour Community Project*. Sanctuary Publishers, 2017.
Butler, Judith. 1993. *Bodies that Matter: On the Discursive Limits of "Sex."* Routledge, 2014.
—. *Notes Toward A Performative Theory of Assembly*. Harvard UP, 2015.
Clifford, Ali. "Meet the Creative: Benjamin Zephaniah, Talking Trainers and Veganism." Interview by Franklin Boateng. *Incredibusy*, 26 October 2020. <www.incredibusy.com/in-conversation-with-benjamin-zephaniah-talking-trainers-and-veganism>
Cohen, Cathy. "Punks, Bulldaggers, and Welfare Queens: The Radical Potential of Queer Politics?" *GLQ: A Journal of Lesbian & Gay Studies*, vol. 3, 1997, pp. 437–65.
Davis, Angela, and Grace Lee Boggs. "On Revolution: A Conversation Between Grace Lee Boggs and Angela Davis." Lecture, University of California, Berkeley, 2 March 2012.
Derrida, Jacques. "The Animal that Therefore I am (More to Follow)." *Critical Inquiry*, vol. 28, no. 2, 2002, pp. 369–418.
EVOLVE Campaigns. "Benjamin Zephaniah: Why Veganism is the Ultimate Protest Against Animal Exploitation." 1 June 2012, YouTube video, 5:21. <www.youtube.com/watch?v=PSbnQEw54nw>
Ganesan, Rama. "Vegan Misappropriations of Hinduism." *Veganism in an Oppressive World. A Vegans of Color Project*, edited by Julia Feliz Brueck, Sanctuary Publishers, 2017.
Goldberg, David Theo. *Are We All Postracial Yet?* Polity Press, 2015.
Gorski, Paul, Stacy Lopresti-Goodman, and Dallas Rising. "'Nobody's Paying me to Cry': The Causes of Activist Burnout in United Statues Animal Rights Activists." *Social Movement Studies*, no. 18, no. 3, 2019, pp. 364–80.

Harper, A. Breeze. "Introduction: The Birth of the Sistah Vegan Project." *Sistah Vegan: Black Female Vegans Speak on Food, Identity, Health and Society*, edited by A. Breeze Harper. Lantern Books, 2010, pp. 20–35.

—. "The Return of the N*gger Breakers: The [White Racist] Vegan Playbook." *The Sistah Vegan Project: A Critical Race Feminist's Journey through the 'Post-Racial' Ethical Foodscape*, 26 November 2017. <www.sistahvegan.com/2017/11/26/the-return-of-the-ngger-breakers-the-white-racist-vegan-playbook>

Hartman, Saidiya. *Lose Your Mother: A Journey Along the Atlantic Slave Route*. Serpent's Tail, 2021.

Hattenstone, Simon. "Benjamin Zephaniah: 'Coppers were Standing on my Back and I Thought, I'm Going to Die Here.'" *The Irish Times*, 13 July 2020. <www.irishtimes.com/culture/books/benjamin-zephaniah-coppers-were-standing-on-my-back-and-i-thought-i-m-going-to-die-here-1.4300078>

Ko, Aph, and Syl Ko. *Aphro-ism: Essays on Pop Culture, Feminism and Black Veganism from Two Sisters*. Lantern Books, 2017.

Lorde, Audre. 1984. *Sister Outsider: Essays & Speeches by Audre Lorde*. Crossing Press, 2007.

Mercer, Amirah. "A Homecoming." *Eater*, January 2021. <www.eater.com/22229322/black-veganism-history-black-panthers-dick-gregory-nation-of-islam-alvenia-fulton>

Middleton, Darren J. N. "Zephaniah, Benjamin." *The Oxford Encyclopedia of British Literature*, edited by David Scott Kastan. Oxford UP, 2006.

—. *Rastafari and the Arts: An Introduction*. Routledge, 2015.

Morales, Aurora Levins. 1998. *Medicine Stories: Essays for Radicals*. Duke UP, 2019.

Navarro, Marilisa C. "Radical Recipe: Veganism as Anti-Racism." *The Routledge Handbook of Vegan Studies*, edited by Laura Wright. Routledge, 2021, pp. 282–94.

PETA. "The Animal Liberation Project." July 2007, archived at <www.web.archive.org/web/20071015030802/http://peta.org.uk/animalliberation>

—. "The Award- Winning PETA Ad the NFL Squashed: 'Don't Stand for Injustice'." 31 January 2020, YouTube video, 1:00. <www.youtube.com/watch?v=2XbCoOIEJ7s&feature=emb_logo>

—. "Kentucky Fried Cruelty." January 2003. <www.kentuckyfriedcruelty.com>

—. "Veggie Love – PETA's Banned Super Bowl Ad." 27 January 2009, YouTube video, 00:31. <www.youtube.com/watch?v=wDE9XpmDHE&feature=emb_logo>

Polish, Jennifer. "Decolonising Veganism: On Resisting Vegan Whiteness and Racism." In *Critical Perspectives on Veganism*, edited by Jodey Castricano and Rasmus R. Simonsen. Palgrave Macmillan, 2016, pp. 373–91.

Probus, Joi Marie. "Young, Black and Vegan." In *Sistah Vegan: Black Female Vegans Speak on Food, Identity, Health and Society*, edited by A. Breeze Harper. Lantern Books, 2010, pp. 153–65.

Quinn, Emelia. "Monstrous Vegan Narratives: Margaret Atwood's Hideous Progeny." *Thinking Veganism in Literature and Culture: Towards a Vegan Theory*, edited by Quinn and Benjamin Westwood. Palgrave Macmillan, 2018, pp. 149–74.

Quinn, Emelia, and Benjamin Westwood. "Introduction: Thinking Through Veganism." *Thinking Veganism in Literature and Culture: Towards a Vegan Theory*, edited by Quinn and Westwood. Palgrave Macmillan, 2018, pp. 1–24.

Reiley, Laura. "Black and Vegan: Hip Hop has Led the Way to a Plant-based Diet." *The Washington Post*, January 2020. <www.washingtonpost.com/business/ 2020/01/24/fastest-growing-vegan-demographic-is-african-americans-wu-tang-clan-other-hip-hop-acts-paved-way>

Robinson, Margaret. "Intersectionality in Mi'kmaw and Settler Vegan Values." *Veganism in an Oppressive World: A Vegans of Colour Community Project*, edited by Julia Feliz Brueck, Sanctuary Publishers, 2017, pp. 71–88.

Saguisag, Lara, Michael Rosen, and Benjamin Zephaniah. "Performance, Politics, and Poetry for Children: Interviews with Michael Rosen and Benjamin Zephaniah." *Children's Literature Association Quarterly*, vol. 32, no. 1, 2007, 3–28.
Shelley, Percy Bysshe. *The Masque of Anarchy: A Poem*. Edward Moxon, 1832.
Taylor, Nik, and Richard Twine (eds). *The Rise of Critical Animal Studies: From the Margin to the Centre*. Routledge, 2014.
Walcott, Rinaldo. "Black Queer Studies, Freedom, and Other Human Possibilities." *Understanding Blackness through Performance: Contemporary Arts and the Representation of Identity*, edited by Anne Crémieux, Xavier Lemoine, and Jean-Paul Rocchi, Palgrave Macmillan, 2013, pp. 143–58.
"Would You Let this Man Near Your Daughter?" *The Sun*, 27 April 1987.
Zephaniah Benjamin. "Benjamin Zephaniah: The book that changed my life." *Prospect Magazine*, 9 May 2019. <www.prospectmagazine.co.uk/magazine/benjamin-zephaniah-the-book-that-changed-my-life>
—. *City Psalms*. Bloodaxe Books, 1995.
—. "A Day in the Life . . ." *Sunday Times Magazine*, 23 August 1987.
—. "A Day in the Life of Danny the Cat." 8 November 2014, YouTube video, 1:42. <www.youtube.com/watch?v=5NytMswmZag>
—. "Dis Policeman Keeps on Kicking Me to Death (Lord Scarman Dub)." *Rasta*. Upright Records, 1983, CD.
—. *The Dread Affair: Collected Poems*. Arena Books, 1985.
—. *The Little Book of Vegan Poems*. AK Press, 2001.
—. "My man Shelley." *Benjamin Zephaniah: Zephaniah Speaks*. 16 May 2012. <https://benjaminzephaniah.com/my-man-shelley>
—. "Poetic Thoughts." *Benjamin Zephaniah: Zephaniah Speaks*, 16 May 2012. <https://benjaminzephaniah.com/poetic-thoughts/?doing_wp_cron=1614524241.8089120388031005859375>
—. *Propa Propaganda*. Bloodaxe Books, 1996.
—. *Talking Turkeys*. Puffin Books, 1994.
—. *Too Black, Too Strong*. Bloodaxe Books, 2001.
Zephaniah, Benjamin, and David Stafford, writers. 1992. *Dread Poets Society*, directed by Andy Wilson, aired 23 September 1992, BBC2.

6

VEGANISM, GENDER, AND QUEERNESS

Exploring Trans-Veganism through Jeanette Winterson's *Frankissstein*

Rasmus R. Simonsen

Introduction

THIS CHAPTER TRANSLATES to a literary context the theoretical findings of my previous work on queer veganism. In my 2012 essay "A Queer Vegan Manifesto," I write that the fact that vegans concern themselves "with species other than the human directly expresses a desire to transverse not to say disrupt the boundaries that uphold and police the categories that separate the human from the nonhuman" (Simonsen 54). Carol J. Adams has noted that since ethical vegetarianism was embraced by the British Romantics in the late eighteenth century, abstaining from animal products has been considered deviant in the Western world (152). Building on Adams's seminal work, I define queer veganism as a concept that "institutes a gap in the communal bond inherent to sharing and feasting on the flesh of nonhuman animals" (Simonsen, "Manifesto" 57). As Benjamin Westwood points out, negating "pleasure, nature, sociability, responsibility, pragmatics, empirical science, or capitalism (the list could go on), vegans are cast [in contemporary Western culture] as killjoys, ascetics, and masochists" (176). C. Lou Hamilton echoes this sentiment in her book *Veganism, Sex, and Politics*, but – pushing back against "the neoliberal truism that links enjoyment to excess and instant gratification" (194–95) – she asserts that "veganism allows us to rethink what we understand by pleasure and to reshape our identities" (195).

Veganism is inherently relational, and it thus intersects with the etymological definition of "queer" that Eve Kosofsky Sedgwick famously calls attention to in the foreword to *Tendencies* (1994): "the word 'queer' means *across* – it comes from the Indo-European root *–twerkw*, which also yields the German *quer* (transverse), Latin *torquere* (to twist), English *athwart*" (viii). In this essay, I reignite the meaning of "queer" to activate the *trans* potentiality inherent to the word. In my previous work, I focus on the possibility of forming vegan community on the basis of deviancy; principally, I argue that, "It is by negating the idea of identity as teleology that we might learn how to share our 'selves' across species boundaries" (Simonsen, "Manifesto" 66). This line of inquiry can be extended to a trans sense of kinship that "crosses" multiple lines of belonging: biological, historical, sexual, ethical, dietary, and so on.

This essay employs Jeanette Winterson's 2019 *Frankissstein* as a literary case study that explicitly demonstrates the possibilities and potentialities of a trans queer reading of veganism. Winterson's attention to transhumanism, transgenderism, and vegetarianism within the intertextual framework of a single novel provides a formal occasion for expanding the scope of queer vegan theory to show just how entangled different identity discourses have become in contemporary fiction.[1] Veganism has often been cast in negative terms within the Western world; from the mainstream media to academic discourse, vegans have largely been represented as being "contradictory, elitist, ill-informed, and antisocial" (Wright 20). The very concept of veganism centers on excluding certain foodstuffs and clothing objects. However, as Westwood has pointed out,

> To refuse is not simply to invite the discretely experienced effects of restriction and denial, a withering away enacted only by the one who refuses. It is relational, with implications for how we think about our ethical lives more broadly; a communicative act that elicits reactions and responses. (177)

But subscribing to any perceived, deviant position is likely to produce negative feelings simply due to external responses. In *Frankissstein*, the two main characters occupy different, yet related, outsider positions: Victor Stein is a transhumanist who is a professor of artificial intelligence, yet he is more invested in his experiments with bringing dead body parts back to life. Ry Shelley is a transgendered doctor who, we learn at the beginning of the novel, is researching the effect that companion robots might have on people's physical and mental wellbeing (Winterson, *Frankissstein* 25). Ry also ends up supplying Victor with body parts from the terminal ward in the hospital where they work.[2] Victor needs the parts for his experiments, probing "the boundary of smart medicine and machine learning" (87).

Although they often challenge Victor's more extreme notions, Ry is also a transhuman enthusiast. Ry relates to the central tenet of transhumanism, as they "have felt that [they're] in the wrong body. [They] can understand the feeling that any-body is the wrong body" (104). Both Ry and Victor are associated with the Alcor Life Extension Foundation – which, in the novel as in real life, offers cryopreservation as a way to "pause" the dying process, as they put it on their website (Alcor) – and the CEO, and co-editor of *The Transhumanist Reader*, Max More, makes an appearance (105). In addition to their trans identity, Ry is a vegetarian, which further signals their outsider status. We first learn of their vegetarianism in conversation with a particularly crass character, Ron, an inventor and purveyor of sexbots. Following a lecture by Victor at the Royal Society, Ron wants to celebrate by going out to dinner: "I could murder a steak," he says. "Good job it's already dead," Ry replies. "Ron looks at me more in sorrow than in anger. Ryan, I am extending the hand, he says. Thanks, Ron, but I'm vegetarian. I knew you wasn't a bloke, says Ron" (94). Naturally, Ron hates almond milk: "God, almond milk. Why??" (45). The so-called alt-right movement in the US has embraced cow's milk as a symbol of white masculinity,[3] and Ron's vehemence towards plant-based alternatives lumps him in with reactionary forces. A foil to Ry's character, Ron is thus the voice of chauvinism in the novel. Vocalizing familiar phobic objections and anxieties, he has a hard time understanding Ry's liminal position, and when Ron learns they are attracted to men, he "takes a step back. His hand moves protectively towards his crotch" (86). At different points in the novel, he also deadnames Ry (240). I am sure many have met a "Ron" in their lives. In the novel,

Ron's reactions to Ry clearly exemplify how vegetarianism, if not veganism, can act as what Hamilton calls a "flashpoint" – a moment of "crisis in the present" (10) – when negativity towards other minority positions intersects with a particular brand of omnivorous chauvinism.

Often mixing food with sexuality (*Written on the Body* being the most obvious example), Winterson's oeuvre brims with characters who search for moments of shared deviancy. The protagonist of *Frankissstein* is both transgendered and vegetarian. Winterson's retelling of Mary Shelley's Gothic classic, itself an important text in the vegan canon (see, for example, Quinn and Adams), *Frankissstein* is ripe for a queer reading that considers how vegetarianism and veganism intersect with transgenderism and transhumanism. Michael Eberle-Sinatra has argued that "Shelley incorporates science and sexual orientation within her novel" (186) and points to the masturbatory language used in Shelley's novel to describe the act of creating the creature (187). In *Skin Shows: Gothic Horror and the Technology of Monsters*, Jack Halberstam encapsulates the queer relationship between creature and creator: "The endeavor of Frankenstein to first create life on his own and then to prevent his monster from mating suggests, if only by default, a homoerotic tension which underlies the incestuous bond" (42). I build on such queer readings of *Frankenstein* by examining how Winterson's work produces a new response to Dana Luciano and Mel Y. Chen's query as to whether "the queer [has] ever been human" (186).

As in Winterson's previous works, love is a central signifier in *Frankissstein*; however, as she explores this thematic through a transhumanist optic, it expands considerably. Victor Stein, the main proponent of transhumanism in the book and the protagonist's complicated love interest, considers what it will be like "when non-biological life forms, without hearts, seek to win ours. Will they? I believe so," says Victor. He continues, claiming that, "All life forms are capable of attachment. Based on what? Not reproduction. Not economic necessity. Not scarcity. Not patriarchy. Not gender. Not fear. It could be wonderful!" (159). In her latest novel, then, Winterson expands the dictum of her 2004 effort *Lighthousekeeping*, "only connect" – which of course is an intertexual nod to E. M. Forster's *Howard's End* – to include a greater spectrum of affective possibilities, as she realizes the queer potential of Shelley's classic.

Even if "Transhuman means different things to different people; smart implants, genetic modification, prosthetic enhancement, even the chance to live forever as a brain emulation" (Winterson, *Frankissstein* 104), many transhumanist theorists specifically link transhumanism with transgenderism, as "[f]reedom of gender" is considered to be "the gateway to a *freedom of form* and to an explosion of human potential," as Martine Rothblatt puts it (318). Embracing transgenderism means realizing "that we are not limited by our sexual anatomy. Then comes the awakening that we are not limited by our anatomy at all. The mind is the substance of humanity. Mind is deeper than matter" (Rothblatt 318). In the context of this essay, the question becomes: is veganism compatible with transhumanism? On the face of it, transhumanism reproduces the concept of Cartesian dualism, in which mind rules matter. Indeed, the enthusiasm for technological transcendence, as expressed by Rothblatt, for instance, might not seem to leave much room for the material concerns that lie at the root of veganism: the plight of animals in modern-day factory farming. Nevertheless, it is instructive at this juncture to note that the goal of transhumanism, and posthumanism (more on the distinction between the two later), is not so much to transcend the material realm of species as it is to displace "a certain hegemonic, taken-for-granted assumption of the human as normative" (Graham 68). "Transcendence," Elaine Graham suggests, is less a spatial than a temporal concept, and the idea is that by transcending traditional hierarchies we can reach "beyond the now and the given toward future, unrealized possibilities" (68). This vision of a transhumanist future, therefore, "acknowledges the affinities between the human, nonhuman, and more-than-human . . . in a more integrated and responsible celebration of life in all its fullness and diversity" (69). Graham's nuanced view of transcendence, in this way, allows for a discussion of veganism in relation to transhumanism that can accommodate equally Rothblatt's "freedom of form" and an awareness of the material circumstances that connect us to nonhuman others. In fact, I argue that once "[t]he ideological and ontological difference between humanity and animality" (Simonsen, "Eating" 179) becomes moot, trans/posthuman existence is vegan by default.

Towards a Theory of Trans-Veganism

In her essay "Mind is Deeper than Matter: Transgenderism, Transhumanism, and the Freedom of Form," Rothblatt makes the argument that all transhumans are transgendered by default, as the point of transhumanism is to accept and to embody many different forms, including gender: "Transhumans welcome 'one mind, many forms' the way transgenders welcome 'one mind, many genders'" (320). The dream is that "Consciousness will be as free to flow beyond the confines of one's flesh body as gender is free to flow beyond the confines of one's flesh genital" (322). An important aspect of transhumanism, then, is "the need for inclusivity, plurality, and continuous questioning of our knowledge, as we are a species and a society that is forever changing" (More and Vita-More 1). As it happens, the emphasis on inclusivity is perhaps what most clearly separates transhumanism from posthumanism (although they are often conflated in the literature), as the latter connotes "a radically individualist vision in which freedom is reimagined as the agency to radically transform – and thereby transcend – the body" (Tirosh-Samuelson and Hurlbut 8). It seems that posthumanism is often applied in a teleological sense, whereas transhumanism could be considered the attitude necessary to achieve a state of posthumanity: "Transhumanists typically look to expand the range of possible future environments for post-human life, including space colonization and the creation of rich virtual worlds" (More 4). Nevertheless, both -isms stress transcendence – in the sense of "unrealized possibilities," as we saw above – and it is the prefix "trans-" that I am interested in, as it becomes the means for imagining how gender and species boundaries are crossed in a discussion of veganism in relation to Winterson's fiction.

But would we even need to eat in a transhumanist utopia? Wouldn't we be able to disregard material nourishment altogether once we have uploaded our consciousness into a central neuro-digital platform? Lauren Beloff makes the argument that since, in Western societies, "staying alive or the basic biological survival of a human is mainly solved through man-made social infrastructures that offer the prerequisites for living . . . it is no longer necessary to consider the development of a human and his physiology from a traditional perspective of survival" (86). Victor Stein's character in *Frankissstein* echoes Beloff's sentiment. He argues that, "Once out of the body you will be able to choose any form you like, and change it as often as you like"

(Winterson 115). Although some transhumanists disavow, or wish to move beyond, any material or organic existence, in his thought experiment, Nick Bostrom supposes that the "good" posthuman life would include being

> involved in a large voluntary organization that works to reduce suffering of animals in their natural environment in ways that permit ecologies to continue to function in traditional ways; this involves political efforts combined with advanced science and information-processing service. (32)

The transhumanism of Winterson's novel, primarily vocalized through Victor (the modern and much more liberally minded counterpart to Shelley's Gothic Prometheus), similarly retains a link to biology: "Animal, vegetable, mineral. The gods appeared in human form and animal form, and they changed others into trees or birds. Those were stories about the future. We have always known that we are not limited to the shape we inhabit" (*Frankissstein* 115). When Victor discovers that Ry is transgender, he suggests that they should think of themselves as "future-early" (119). The link that transhumanist theorists have made to transgenderism thus clearly figures in Victor's philosophy. In a sense, trans individuals live in the future, as they inhabit bodies that are not yet widely accepted by society.[4] Furthermore, as will become apparent later in this chapter, transgendered vegans have connected the predicament of farm animals with their own experiences, and transgenderism and veganism can be seen to respond to a similar liberatory impulse.

Might that be the reason Winterson chose to make her protagonist, the transgendered transhumanist Ry, vegetarian? Winterson leaves the question open, and since vegetarianism doesn't figure as an overt thematic, readers are left to make their own connections in relation to the trans ethics of the novel. The author was vegetarian for a period of seven years but went back to eating meat "when Organic farming gave us a chance of clean, honest food," as she wrote in 2004 (Winterson, "Vegetarian"). The scope of this essay doesn't allow me to interrogate her claims to "cleanliness" and "honesty," neither will I tarry with her "provocative," not to say disingenuous or insensitive, tweets of 2014 ("Jeanette Winterson: a rabbit killer and proud of it"). Winterson tends to infuse her work with autobiographical elements, and Ry's vegetarianism thus creates a connection to her younger self. However, Ry's diet can perhaps better be explained by the fact that Shelley was herself a vegetarian. As Adams has argued, in writing *Frankenstein*, "Shelley allies herself with Romantic vegetarians who decoded all tales of the primeval fall with the interpretation that they were implicitly about the introduction of meat eating" (153). Intriguingly, Adams suggests that since Victor Frankenstein uses both human and animal parts to construct his creature, the result is a "herbivorous" hybrid (158). In a move towards biological essentialism, Shelley, to Adams's mind, renders the creature, at least partly, "anatomically vegetarian" (158). But the animal parts also establish the nonhuman status of Frankenstein's creation: "a Being who, like the animals eaten for meat, finds itself excluded from the moral circle of humanity" (158). In Winterson's novel, frequent allusions are made to Ry's "doubleness," and Ry's vegetarianism is thus linked both to Shelley's biography and to the fictional creature, who chiefly consumes nuts and berries but, like Ry, doesn't shun cheese or milk when available (Shelley 72–73). In *Frankissstein*, vegetarianism, as a trope, emphasizes the trans-narratological impetus of the novel, the blending of actual and fictional worlds. On this point, nevertheless, we should remember that since meat carries clear masculine connotations, the creature's vegetarianism is a condemnation of what Adams calls "the food of the fathers as well as their mores" (159); "the maternal principle," in this way, becomes something like the unthought of "Romantic vegetarianism" (159) – the main practitioners of which, after all, were firmly entrenched in patriarchal structures. The feminist and feminine traits of Romantic vegetarianism, as revealed by Adams, inheres in Ry's trans identity as well, then, through the narratological link to both Shelley and the creature. Disregarding Winterson's own ethics, I will push beyond the question of authorial intent to explore Ry's vegetarianism later in this chapter as an important component of the trans kinship model that her novel allows us to imagine.

Of course, transhuman fantasies are not a recent invention. Jayna Brown shows how, for instance, H. G. Wells, in his 1895 essay "The Limits of Individual Plasticity," mused about "the potential to stretch the limits of what we could think of as a discrete living being" (Brown 329). Later, in the middle of the twentieth century, Aldous Huxley coined "transhuman" as a term to connote a kind of "cosmic self-awareness," which is more metaphysical than biological and does not take us beyond the human species (Brown 332). As Brown demonstrates, the transhuman legacy of both Wells and Huxley are marred by their eugenic thinking (333). By queering transhumanism, Brown suggests, we will be able "to broaden our thoughts about biological life away from notions of ancestral descendancy to the possibility of ethical connections and political affiliations that do not rely on being related" (323). In a move similar to that of Rothblatt, Brown wants to "unsettle" the concept of life to show that kinship need not rest in "heterosexual reproduction" (323). In doing so, "thinking past the human life span is crucial" as it "lets in the strange and unrecognizable, which requires an entire new paradigm for life itself" (323–24).

To make room for a vegan critique that can contain both transhumanism and transgenderism, I draw on the work of Halberstam who applies an asterisk to the concept of "trans" as a way to put "pressure on all modes of gendered embodiment" (*Trans** xiii). Halberstam didn't invent this diacritical way of writing "trans"; the *OED* traces it to 1995, but it is not easy to pinpoint exactly when people started using it to cover a wide spectrum of gender fluidity. Nevertheless, as Halberstam explains, trans* connotes the refusal "to choose between the identitarian and the contingent forms of trans identity" (xiii). He goes on to unpack the use of this particular punctuation mark: "the asterisk modifies the meaning of transitivity by refusing to situate transition in relation to a destination, a final form, a specific shape, or an established configuration of desire and identity" (4). Without ignoring the important work of naming, studying, recognizing, and accounting for "historically situated differences . . . if only because they provide histories of legally sustained hate and antipathy" (10), Halberstam's playful use of the asterisk depends on seeing language

> as a shifting eco-system within which words might fly, fall, or fail to convey their message, but also one within which words might hover over the multiplicity to which they point, relieves us of the mundane task of simply getting the name right. (9)

The asterisk of trans* is particularly significant in regard to *Frankissstein*, as it allows for a discussion of how the transgender and transhuman elements of the book intersect. Henceforth, I will use "trans" with an asterisk when I want to capture a multiplicity of forms in Winterson's novel. As such, without losing sight of the context of Halberstam's account, the expanded form of trans* – which opens up to "unfolding categories of being organized around but not confined to forms of gender variance" (4) – can also refer to trans-historical and trans-fictional; after all, Winterson's novel flits between the early nineteenth and twenty-first centuries. The overarching aim of my chapter, then, is to show how the trans* ethos of *Frankissstein* creates a series of attachments that traverses space, time, gender, and – perhaps most crucially for an understanding of the literary relation between queer theory and veganism – diet.

Unpacking the Trans* Connections of *Frankissstein*

Frankissstein primarily focuses on the developing, yet sometimes fraught, bond between Ry and Victor. To Victor, the path to expanding one's thinking about life and what it means to have a self is to embrace one's deviancy, first of all. As he puts it, "we are freaks according to the behaviour of the world" (171). He elaborates by connecting both transhumanism and transgenderism with a fundamental loneliness:

> We're loners – that's an anti-evolutionary position. Homo sapiens needed the group. Humans are group animals. Families, clubs, societies, workplaces, schools, the military, institutions of every kind, including the church. We even manage illness in groups. It's called a hospital. You work in one. (171)

Veganism can be a lonely position as well, choosing to eat differently from the majority and claiming a different ethical position. Nonetheless, my aim here is not to conflate the exclusionary feel of veganism with the myriad experiences of trans individuals but, rather, to point out the productive intersections that can arise from placing positions of deviance in conversation with each other.

Several of the personal essays and critical reflections gathered in Feliz Brueck and McNeill's anthology *Queer + Trans Voices: Achieving Liberation through Consistent Anti-Oppression* connect veganism and animal rights activism with experiences related to being transgender. In her essay, "Tran-scending the 'Man' and the Meat-Eater," Doel Rakshit specifically compares "suffering in a closet" with "the sufferings of [nonhuman animals] in cages" (96). As a trans woman, her "identity became the driving force behind her participation in nonhuman animal rights activism" (Rakshit 97). Growing up in India, Rakshit's sense of invisibility as a closeted trans woman made her more empathetic towards the animals suffering in the agricultural system ignored or simply unnoticed by the world outside, and her trans identity has become inextricably entwined with her veganism as a result.

In the introduction to a special issue of *Transgender Studies Quarterly*, Eva Hayward and Jami Weinstein interrogate how "the prefixial nature of *trans* – across, into, and through: a prepositional force – further transfigure the 'animal turn'" in the humanities (196). As "the animal turn has enabled creatures to migrate from the margins to the center of theoretical interrogatives" (196), we can, in turn, consider what happens when "[t]rans* meets animals" (196) – in a discussion of veganism, for instance. In their provocative conceptualization, Hayward and Weinstein fuse trans* with animality to achieve the Frankensteinian concept of "tranimalities," which "is a double orientation: animalities are specificities but remain thresholds of emergence. Tranimalities is murmuration, schooling, and swarming" (200). A plural breeding ground, the concept of "tranimalities wishes to focus on trans-infused apprehensions and engagements with the expansive world of possibility opened up by non-anthropocentric perspectives" (201).

Transhumanism similarly emphasizes an expanded sense of empathy with others – including the nonhuman. More notes that "transhumanists typically adopt a universal standard based not on membership in the human species but on the qualities of each being" (13). In More's qualitative optic, then, "Creatures with similar levels of sapience, sentience, and personhood are accorded similar status no matter whether they are humans, animals, cyborgs, machine intelligences, or aliens" (13). In terms of identity, Steve Fuller notes, explicating Rothblatt, that transhumanism conceives of a "substratum-neutral conception of content ... that can be embodied as male, female, carbon, silicon, as well as mixtures of them, according to certain specified conventions" (114). It thus becomes clear that transhumanism intersects with veganism as the former acknowledges that "[t]he utterly unique status of human beings has been superseded by an understanding that we are part of a spectrum of biological organisms and possible non-biological species of the future" (More, "Transhumanism" 10). Veganism is inherently plural as well. As several contributors to Emelia Quinn and Benjamin Westwood's anthology *Thinking Veganism in Literature and Culture* acknowledge, veganism is "messy," and we should always ask how veganism is "thought and practiced together with other identities," as Allison Covey writes (226). In relation to animal rights, trans* thinking can help us move beyond issues like linguistic gendering, for instance. As Patti Nyman suggests, "As we move toward recognizing the personhood and moral standing of nonhumans through rescue and sanctuary, telling their stories, and talking about their relationships, we can also take a more consistently anti-oppressive stance by moving toward using 'they' and 'them'" (227).

Trans-veganism expands the fight against speciesism to include what Fuller calls "speciationism," which is "the meta-level equivalent of ... speciesism" (116). The main culprit of speciationism, as Fuller sees it, is Donna Haraway, whose attachment to the "wisdom of nature" means that she privileges the way in which "one becomes a species – namely, through the evolutionary process" (116). This means that, for Haraway and other evolutionists, wishing "to pursue diversity outside the evolutionary process, say, through xenotransplantation and prosthetics" becomes suspect as it goes against the teleology of nature (116). Speciationism is thus skeptical, if not hostile, to the notions of "species change" and "gender change" equally (116). Haraway is wary of veganism, as she suggests in *When Species Meet* that vegans do not wish to acknowledge that "there is no category or strategy that removes one from killing" (106); as she puts it, "there is no way of living that is not also a way of someone, not just something, else dying differentially" (80). However, as I remind myself and other vegans in "A Queer Vegan Manifesto," "Dead animal bodies daily pass by vegan 'lips' – understood as a figure for the threshold of the self – as it is by internalizing the loss of animal lives that a crucial component of vegan ethics and identity is established" (Simonsen 71). Vegans confront death head on, in fact, and Haraway's claim that choosing not to consume animal products means that one cannot appreciate or participate in the "mortal entanglements of human beings and other organisms" (106) ignores central tenets of veganism altogether. Haraway has a reductive, or retrograde humanist,[5] view of veganism, which she equates with other "exterminationist nonsolutions such as shutting down all stock ranching ... and working against the deliberate breeding of herding, pet, and show dogs" (105). When she claims that the logical outcome of veganism is consigning "most domestic animals to the status of curated heritage collections or to just plain extermination as kinds and as individuals" (80), she misses the posthuman potential of veganism, especially in its queer or trans form, that takes seriously the potential to transverse species boundaries. To be clear, veganism doesn't strive to end suffering by exterminating those domestic animals who languish in today's factory system. Rather than dispatching certain species to what Fuller calls sanctuary "comfort zones" (133), the idea is to keep rethinking our attachment to other species and what new kinship models might look like.

Aligned with vegan theory, the ethics of plurality promoted by both transhumanists and transgender theorists is in direct response to oppressive systems. Traditionally, progressive thinking and practices – not to mention the act of coming out – have often been met with hostility and sometimes outright violence. Halberstam notes how when transgender individuals are forced back into heterosexist alignment, "match[ing] up both sex and gender," the past and present are also made to converge: the perceived concealment of a person's past normative self is revealed to make sense of their present appearance – but only in an effort to brutalize them (*Queer Time* 82). Quoted above, Rakshit's comparison between the kinds of suffering trans people and nonhuman animals experience speaks to ideologically violent attempts to cleave gender and species norms to a normative destiny as defined by majoritarian concerns and desires. Arguably, the most uncomfortable, but also perhaps the most realistic in terms of trans histories, passage in *Frankissstein* is the sexual assault Ry endures in the bathroom of a Texan bar at night.

In the men's room, Ry's attacker takes offense at the fact that Ry uses the stall instead of the urinal. Screaming at Ry, he taunts them to urinate "LIKE A MAN" (Winterson, *Frankissstein* 241, all caps in original). He then lunges at Ry's crotch, finding "what I don't have" (242). Ry manages to escape and takes cover outside. The interior monologue that follows voices an all-too-common reality for trans people:

> This isn't the first time. It won't be the last. And I don't report it because I can't stand the leers and the jeers and fears of the police. And I can't stand the assumption that somehow I am the one at fault. And if I am not at fault, then why didn't I put up a fight? And I don't say, try working on the Accident and Emergency unit for a few nights and see where putting up a fight gets you. And I don't say the quickest way is to get it over with. And I don't say, is this the price I have to pay for ... ? For ... For what? To be who I am? Cry at night for what you can't understand in yourself or others. Cry at night. Don't you? The tears make my knees wet as I sit with my face on my legs as small as I can make myself. Make myself. This is who I am. (244)

Violence against trans individuals is common; this violence is systemic, and Ry's justified fear that reporting the incident will simply result in humiliation and another moment of injustice resonates with Halberstam's reading of *Boys Don't Cry*, the pivotal 1999 film by Kimberly Peirce, which also contains an atrocious rape scene. When

Brandon, the trans protagonist of the film, reports the crime committed against him, the police treat him "as a 'girl' who must have been 'pleased' by the attention of the young men, whom they consider normal, sexual subjects" (Halberstam, Trans* 104). In this way, "the rape scene damns the police, highlights the role of violence in the enforcement of normativity, and draws the audience's sympathies to Brandon in a way that makes transphobia morally reprehensible" (104). In a parallel to Boys Don't Cry, Ry's indeterminate gender identity impels the man's monstrous act against them. In Frankissstein, Ry's attacker screams at them, "YOU FUCKIN' FREAK!" (242), and the fact of their hybridity legitimizes the violence against them – not just in the mind of the reprehensible aggressor but also in relation to the system of normativity that has rendered trans lives precarious in the first place.

Aside from the violent reality thrust upon trans individuals, indeterminacy and the violence it breeds is a common trope in Gothic fiction: confusion as an excuse to dehumanize perceived "monsters." The threat of "destabilization," as Michael Grantham writes (14), is the catalyst for reacting violently towards monsters.[6] Grantham argues that there exists an "affinity between the monster and the transhuman" based on how – as they present "alternative modes of being" – they "challenge the very notion of what it means to be human" (18). This affinity, as I have noted, can be extended to transgenderism, since trans individuals challenge what it means to have a gender. Furthermore, the sexual violence that Ry suffers acts as a trans-narratological moment since the novel at this point shifts back to the point of view of Shelley. The transition hinges on the question, "What is your substance, whereof are you made?" (Winterson, Frankissstein 245). Adapted from the first line of Shakespeare's Sonnet 53, it becomes something of a refrain, or a trans-historical invocation, that triggers a shift in the narrative. It occurs at different points in the novel, but on page 245, it is displayed in a large bold font on a separate page to signal clearly how Ry's trauma in the present tense of the novel spills into the past circumstances of Shelley as re-imagined by Winterson. Winterson suggests that trauma is intergenerational, as she connects Ry's pain to Shelley's mourning over her husband and children on the pages that immediately follow.[7] Shelley's pain over losing her children, in particular her son, fondly dubbed "Willmouse," becomes an instance for discussing transhumanism as a means of avoiding violence and hurt, where an individual's integrity and safety can be guaranteed, finally. As Winterson writes, "We cannot hurt what is not there" (254). If the absence of male genitalia marks Ry as an object of abuse, the absence of a body altogether, Winterson suggests, is the promise of liberation. "What if," Winterson's Shelley wonders, "my Willmouse had been a spirit, able to put his body on and off as he pleased? No infection could have taken him. Our bodies could be like suits of clothes, while our minds run free" (254).

Once more, the theoretical proliferation of the concept of trans* in recent years proves helpful in terms of seeing it "not [as] a thing or being . . . [but] rather [as] the processes through which thingness and beingness are constituted" (Hayward and Weinstein 196). In their detailed and inventive explication of the asterisk, Hayward and Weinstein assert that this diminutive diacritical mark "repurposes, displaces, renames, replicates, and intensifies terms, adding yet more texture, increased vitalization" (198). In relation to Winterson's novel, the connections between past and present, fiction and reality, time and space intensify when conceptualized according to a trans* logic.

Vegetarianism and Cellular Kinship

Ry connects their trans subjectivity specifically to hybridity (Winterson, *Frankisssstein* 83); they avow doubleness: "I am a woman. And I am a man. That's how it is for me. I am in the body that I prefer. But the past, my past, isn't subject to surgery" (122). Ry's transitioning is ongoing – what Prosser refers to as "the movement in between a destination" (11) – and their scars "are beautiful," even a "mark of freedom" and comfort: "When I find them in the night, in the dark, I remember what I have done, and I go back to sleep" (Winterson, *Frankisssstein* 120). In Shelley's *Frankenstein*, the monster perceives himself to be "hideously deformed and loathsome": "I was not even of the same nature as man . . . Was I then a monster, a blot upon the earth, from which all men fled, and whom all men disowned?" (83). If the deformed body of the monster in Shelley's classic is a source of rejection, in Winterson's retelling, Victor is "not afraid of [Ry's] scars or their bumpy beauty" (120). Winterson thus creates a parallel between the monster's body and Ry's; for the former, his scars signify the violation he has suffered at the hands of his creator; for the latter, the liberation of creating a body that feels like home. Grantham points out that the monster's ostensibly unpleasant "aesthetic properties solidify its identity as other than human and serves to reinforce its ability to evoke sensations of fear and anxiety" (15). However, and more apropos of Winterson's fiction, as the trope of "monstrosity" has been reproduced across genres and centuries, it "has become a conspiracy of bodies rather than a singular form" (Halberstam, *Skin Shows* 27). If indeed monstrosity cuts through the human form, exposing it to trauma and otherness, "it does not necessarily follow that cuts sever or break things off, either spatially or temporally, producing absolute differences of this and that, there and there, now and then," as Karen Barad suggests (406). Barad is writing in dialogue with Susan Stryker's ground-breaking essay, "My Words to Victor Frankenstein," in which the author proclaims her affinity with all things creaturely as she deconstructs the anthropocentric notion of "superior personhood": "I find no shame . . . in acknowledging my egalitarian relationship with non-human material Being; everything emerges from the same matrix of possibilities" (240). Winterson's novel is one output of this "matrix," which engenders connections between and across bodies and their histories. In fact, *Frankisssstein* – the title itself is held together, however awkwardly, by the desiring force of "kiss" – engages in the process of what Barad has called "re-membering," which is "a matter of . . . tracing entanglements, responding to yearnings for connection, materialized into fields of longing/belonging, of regenerating what never was but might yet have been" (407). In this way, Ry's memory of their trans-becoming, their "queer self-birthing" (Barad 388), can be understood as a metaphor for how, intertextually, Winterson regenerates Shelley's classic to create a new field of desire, which allows for disparate monstrous parts to express their yearnings for one another.[8]

Although, as we have seen, Ry doesn't escape persecution, in many ways, they represent a different potential of monstrosity, in keeping with Stryker's invocation: Ry's transformation was voluntary; the monster's was not. Consequently, they have very different reactions to their own bodies. However, they are both vegetarian by choice, and even if Winterson doesn't elaborate on this connection,[9] this part of their respective ethics serves as a crucial attachment between the characters, whose ostensible monstrosity is multiplicitous. In addition to his monstrous form, it is noteworthy that part of what marks the creature as superior to humans in *Frankenstein* is his (primarily)[10] vegetarian diet: "I was more agile than [humans], and could subsist upon coarser diet" (Shelley 83); he later remarks that his food "is not that of man" (102–03). As Emelia Quinn has pointed out, vegetarianism at the time of the Romantics was associated with "prelapsarian ideas of a pacifist Golden Age and a Promethean fall from grace" (99). If the Romantics looked to a mythical past, transhumanists today have their eyes fixed upon a utopian future; what connects them is the sense that they exist apart from their present moment. They reach across temporal and ontological divisions to imagine a radical way of living otherwise.

The trans* ethics of *Frankissstein* affirms hybridization, and Winterson translates Brown's queering of biology into a speculative world where fictional characters are as ontologically significant as real-life persons. The greater point of Winterson's fiction, and trans* theory, is that life is fundamentally fluid. When Victor and Ry meet for the first time, he asks them, "have we met? And the strange, split-second other-world answer is *yes*" (107). In *Skin Shows*, Halberstam makes the claim that the Gothic is an "essentially consumptive genre which feeds parasitically upon other literary texts" (36), but I would argue that Winterson's boundless textual methodology rather seeks to establish a kinship with her progenitor. In *Frankissstein*, the words on the page become like cells in a biological framework that have the capacity to proliferate beyond a heterosexual matrix of reproduction. Within a trans* imaginary, Barad suggests that we should focus on regeneration instead of reproduction, as it is through the former trope that we can "empower and galvanize the disenfranchised and breathe life into new forms of queer agency and embodiment" (411). The way in which Winterson's novel is set up as a series of exchanges between the past and the present, reality and fiction, recalls Prosser's description of trans narratology that views the act of narration as "the link between locations: the transition itself" (9). In relation to *Frankissstein*, we can thus update Winterson's (borrowed) dictum "only connect" to "only transition."

If transhumanisn concerns the "continuity of life across substrates" and transgenderism the "continuity of gender across body-types" (Rothblatt 323), then transdiegeticism concerns the continuity of narrative across bodies of work. However, in each case, what is carried across from one domain to another will undergo some form of change. Just "like Frankenstein's creature," trans individuals are "monstrous" to the extent that "their (re)birth" marks them "as 'something more, and something other' than their medical service providers may have intended or imagined" (Hayward and Weinstein 199). Trans-narratives are monstrous as well; they are prepositional as the matter of the text forms connections based on the logic of *with* and *of* (see Hayward and Weinstein 199). The energy to connect transgender concerns with animality reflects the overarching anti-essentialist position of transhumanism. In this mix, veganism might almost seem like a foregone conclusion, especially if we view it as the expression of an alliance with oppressed others, with whom we share a cellular and affective kinship. Transhumanism should reject speciesism along with sexism and racism since adherence to any socially constructed hierarchy (however "natural" it may claim to be) is ultimately discordant with the radical thrust of its position.

In *Frankissstein*, Ry explains the t-shirt slogan "Give Up Meat" that some young men are wearing at the Tec-X-Po conference on robotics in the language of metaphor: "It's not that the future will be vegetarian – just that they believe that soon enough the human mind – our minds – will no longer be tied to a body that is a substrate made of meat" (35). But the one doesn't necessarily exclude the other: giving up the "meat" stratum we inhabit might naturally lead to giving up the one we eat. As I have suggested, eating meat (and other animal products) seems wholly out of place in a transhumanist ethics that stresses difference, diversity, and inclusion. In what constitutes something like the metatextual dénouement of *Frankissstein*, Shelley encounters her fictional creation, a distraught Victor Frankenstein, in an asylum. He pleads with her to "unmake" him (214), return him to the immaterial realm of the novel whence he came, so that he may escape his new "gross" body (215). The textual irony is almost too much to bear at this point, but the dialogue between Shelley and her creation is significant because, despite Frankenstein's accidental transcendence from one fictional realm to another, his regard for the human race (imperilled by the monster run rampant) does not depend on his ontological state:

> Mary Shelley said, If you are not of the human race, why should you care for it? For the love of it that you bear, he answered. Love that you have taught me. Shall I quote our book? *My heart was fashioned to be susceptible of love and sympathy.* She said, Those words are spoken not by Victor Frankenstein, but by his creature. We are the same, the same, answered Frankenstein. (215)

The refrain of sameness (are we not, in the end, made of the same "substance"?) accompanies the trans-vegan position that I have aimed to explicate in this chapter. As in Winterson's novel, love is at the crux of trans* – a love that transcends gender, sexuality, time, and species. In a heated moment, the present-day Victor voices his frustration: "Race, faith, gender, sexuality, those things make me impatient . . . We need to move forward, and faster. I want an end to it all, don't you see? An end to the human, I said. An end to human stupidity" (199).

"Human stupidity" covers everything from denying climate change and the kind of behavior that accelerates it to trans- and homophobia as well as omnivorous chauvinism, which, as we have seen, is represented by the entrepreneurial sexbot manufacturer, Ron, in the novel. Adopting a trans* ethics of care and inclusivity, in the future, our relationship to meat will be transformed. It might in fact no longer exist, either as nourishment or substance.

Notes

1. Lori Gruen has coined the concept of "entangled empathy" to suggest that we are always already "in relationships with others and are called upon to be responsive and responsible in these relationships by attending to another's needs, interests, desires, vulnerabilities, hopes, and sensitivities" (3). I would urge the reader to keep Gruen's concept in mind, as Winterson's novel exactly stages a series of different responses to trans identity that intersect with the vulnerabilities of what Derrida would call other others.
2. I use the plural pronoun to describe Ry since, although embodying a masculine form, they have chosen not to transition fully (in a biological sense, at least): "When I look in the mirror I see someone I recognise, or rather, I see at least two people I recognise. That is why I have chosen not to have lower surgery. I am what I am, but what I am is not one thing, not one gender. I live with doubleness" (89).
3. Vasile Stănescu writes that, "Meat and dairy consumption became articulated in the nineteenth-century as an example of 'white privilege' intended to differentiate white male

workers from the immigrant counterparts who were ... cast as 'effeminate rice eaters'" (106). In regard to anti-Chinese immigration in the US of the early twentieth century, lactose tolerance became a way for white Americans to claim racial superiority (107–08). Racism goes hand-in-glove with other forms of hate, and, responding to the "fears about diet, race, and citizenship" that are embedded in Trumpism, proponents of the alt-right frequently use "soy boy" as a homophobic slur towards their critics (113).
4. In his influential work *Second Skins: The Body Narratives of Transsexuality*, Jay Prosser emphasizes what he calls "body narratives" to carve out a space for "texts that engage with the feelings of embodiment; stories that not only represent but allow changes to somatic materiality" (16). Prosser thus wields a critique that takes on both normative medical practices and poststructuralist theorists, who tend to reduce bodies to a series of textual effects, which cannot account for the literal, or indeed essential, experience of transitioning.
5. Carol J. Adams coined "retrograde humanism" to define what "happens when people who are not vegan assert their own humanism in the face of what feels like an ethical confrontation" (Wright 21).
6. See Emelia Quinn's essay in this volume for more on the monstrous.
7. A note of caution is appropriate here: Winterson tends to frame capital-E emotions as universal concepts, and the movement from a specifically queer and trans experience of trauma to one rooted in a heterosexual matrix appears too smooth in *Frankissstein*. She loses sight of important distinctions, in turn, which is a narrative strategy that deserves to be critiqued in full.
8. I owe this particular phrasing to Barad's poetic description of how an electric field distributes energy (395).
9. Adams makes the point that due to "the compressed form of the Creature's vegetarian statement" in Shelley's novel, it is "elided from our collective memory" (161). The minority position of vegetarianism in Western societies, combined with Winterson's personal, and somewhat aggressive, omnivorous ethics, might explain why that particular link between the Creature and Ry does not come into focus in *Frankissstein*.
10. Early in the monster's development, as he is still figuring out how to feed himself, he chances upon a fire that had been left by some travelers. In addition to discovering that fire brings light and heat, he finds that "this element was useful to me in my food; for I found some of the offals that the travellers had left had been roasted, and tasted much more savoury than the berries I gathered from the trees" (Shelley 72). However, at this point in the story, he has yet to reach what we, in the context of the terminology of this essay, could call his transhumanist ethos, which includes a specifically vegetarian component: "I do not destroy the lamb and the kid, to glut my appetite" (103). Adams points out that in the original myth of Prometheus, the "discovery of fire is the story of the inception of meat eating" (154), since meat is not edible before being cooked. In turn, the Creature rejects the "Promethean gift" of fire (155).

Works Cited

Adams, Carol J. *The Sexual Politics of Meat: A Feminist-Vegetarian Critical Theory*. Continuum, 2010.
Alcor. *What is Cryonics?* 2020. 13 February 2021. <www.alcor.org/what-is-cryonics/>
Barad, Karen. "Transmaterialities: Trans*/Matter/realities and Queer Political imaginings." *GLQ: A Journal of Lesbian and Gay Studies*, vol. 21, no. 2–3, 2015, pp. 389–422.
Bardini, Thierry, and Dominique Lestel. *Journey to the End of the Species, 1: Guide to Singular Metamorphoses*. Dis Voir, 2010.
Beloff, Lauren. "The Hybronaut Affair A Ménage of Art, Technology, and Science." *The Transhumanist Reader: Classical and Contemporary Essays on the Science, Technology, and*

Philosophy of the Human Future, edited by Max More and Natasha Vita-More, Wiley-Blackwell, 2013, pp. 83–90.

Bostrom, Nick. "Why I Want to be a Posthuman When I Grow Up." *The Transhumanist Reader: Classical and Contemporary Essays on the Science, Technology, and Philosophy of the Human Future*, edited by Max More and Natasha Vita-More, Wiley-Blackwell, 2013, pp. 28–53.

Brown, Jayna. "Being Cellular: Race, the Inhuman, and the Plasticity of Life." *GLQ: A Journal of Lesbian and Gay Studies*, vol. 21, no. 2–3, 2015, pp. 321–41.

Covey, Allison. "Ethical Veganism as Protected Identity: Constructing a Creed under Human Rights Law." *Thinking Veganism in Literature and Culture: Towards a Vegan Theory*, edited by Emelia Quinn and Benjamin Westwood, Palgrave Macmillan, 2018, pp. 225–47.

Eberle-Sinatra, Michael. "Readings of Homosexuality in Mary Shelley's Frankenstein and Four Film Adaptations." *Gothic Studies*, vol. 7, no. 2, 2005, pp. 185–202.

Forster, E. M. *Howard's End*. Edited by Oliver Stallybrass, Penguin, 2000.

Fuller, Steve. *Nietzschean Meditations: Untimely Thoughts at the Dawn of the Transhuman Era*. Schwabe Verlag, 2020.

Graham, Elaine. "The Posthuman in the Postsecular Imagination." *Perfecting Human Futures: Transhuman Visions and Technological Imaginations*, edited by J. Benjamin Hurlbut and Hava Tirosh-Samuelson, Springer VS, 2016, pp. 51–72.

Grantham, Michael. *The Transhuman Antihero: Paradoxical Protagonists of Speculative Fiction from Mary Shelley to Richard Morgan*. McFarland & Company, 2015.

Gruen, Lori. *Entangled Empathy: An Alternative Ethic for Our Relationships with Animals*. Lantern Books, 2015.

Halberstam, Jack. *In a Queer Time and Place*. New York UP, 2005.

— . *Skin Shows: Gothic Horror and the Technology of Monsters*. Duke UP, 1995.

— . *Trans*: A Quick and Quirky Account of Gender Variability*. U of California P, 2018.

Hamilton, C. Lou. *Veganism, Sex and Politics: Tales of Danger and Pleasure*. Hammer/On, 2019.

Haraway, Donna. *When Species Meet*. U of Minnesota P, 2008.

Hayward, Eva, and Jami Weinstein. "Introduction: Tranimalities in the Age of Trans* Life." *TSQ: Transgender Studies Quarterly*, vol. 2, no. 2, 2015, pp. 195–208.

"Jeanette Winterson: a rabbit killer and proud of it." 18 June 2014. *The Guardian*, 17 February 2021. <www.theguardian.com/books/shortcuts/2014/jun/18/jeanette-winterson-rabbit-killer-twitter>

Luciano, Dana, and Mel Y. Chen. "Has the Queer ever Been Human?" *GLQ: A Journal of Lesbian and Gay Studies*, vol. 21, no. 2–3, 2015, pp. 183–207.

More, Max. "The Philosophy of Transhumanism." *The Transhumanist Reader: Classical and Contemporary Essays on the Science, Technology, and Philosophy of the Human Future*, edited by Max More and Natasha Vita-More, Wiley-Blackwell, 2013, pp. 3–17.

More, Max, and Natasha Vita-More. "Roots and Core Themes." *The Transhumanist Reader: Classical and Contemporary Essays on the Science, Technology, and Philosophy of the Human Future*, edited by Max More and Natasha Vita-More, Wiley-Blackwell, 2013, pp. 1–2.

Nyman, Patti. "Beyond Binaries: An Interspecies Case for They/Them Pronouns." *Queer + Trans Voices: Achieving Liberation Through Consistent Anti-Oppression*, edited by J. Feliz Brueck and Z. McNeill, Sanctuary Publishers, 2020, pp. 225–27.

Oxford English Dictionary. "Trans*." 2018. OED.com. 24 February 2021. <www.oed.com/view/Entry/63485327>

Prosser, Jay. *Second Skins: The Body Narratives of Transsexuality*. Columbia UP, 1998.

Quinn, Emelia. *Reading Veganism: The Monstrous Vegan, 1818 to Present*. Oxford UP, 2021.

Rakshit, Doel. "Tran-scending the 'Man' and the Meat-Eater." *Queer + Trans Voices: Achieving Liberation Through Consistent Anti-Oppression*, edited by J. Feliz Brueck and Z. McNeill, Sanctuary Publishers, 2020, pp. 95–98.

Rothblatt, Martine. "Mind is Deeper than Matter Transgenderism, Transhumanism, and the Freedom of Form." *The Transhumanist Reader: Classical and Contemporary Essays on the Science, Technology, and Philosophy of the Human Future*, edited by Max More and Natasha Vita-More, Wiley-Blackwell, 2013, pp. 317–26.

Sedgwick, Eve Kosofsky. *Tendencies*. Routledge, 1994.

Shelley, Mary. *Frankenstein*. Edited by J. Paul Hunter, 2nd Norton Critical Edition, W. W. Norton & Company, 2012.

Simonsen, Rasmus R. "Eating for the Future: Veganism and the Challenge of In Vitro Meat." *Biopolitics and Utopia: An Interdisciplinary Reader*, edited by Patricia Stapleton and Andrew Byers, Palgrave Macmillan, 2015, pp. 167–90.

—. "A Queer Vegan Manifesto." *Journal for Critical Animal Studies*, vol. 10, no. 3, 2012, pp. 51–80.

Stănescu, Vasile. "'White Power Milk': Milk, Dietary Racism, and the 'Alt-Right'." *Animal Studies Journal*, vol. 7, no. 2, 2018, pp. 103–28.

Stryker, Susan. "My Words to Victor Frankenstein above the Village of Chamounix: Performing Transgender Rage." *GLQ: A Journal of Lesbian and Gay Studies*, vol. 1, 1994, pp. 237–54.

Tirosh-Samuelson, Hava, and J. Benjamin Hurlbut. "Introduction: Technology, Utopianism and Eschatology." *Perfecting Human Futures: Transhuman Visions and Technological Imaginations*, edited by J. Benjamin Hurlbut and Hava Tirosh-Samuelson, Springer VS, 2016, pp. 1–32.

Westwood, Benjamin. "On Refusal." *Thinking Veganism in Literature and Culture: Towards a Vegan Theory*, edited by Emelia Quinn and Benjamin Westwood, Palgrave Macmillan, 2018, pp. 175–98.

Winterson, Jeanette. *Frankissstein*. Vintage, 2019.

—. *Lighthousekeeping*. Harper Perennial, 2004.

—. "Vegetarian." 10 March 2004. *Jeanette Winterson*, 17 February 2021. <https://www.jeanettewinterson.com/journalism/vegetarian/>

Wright, Laura. *The Vegan Studies Project: Food, Animals, and Gender in the Age of Terror*. U of Georgia P, 2015.

7

Veganism and Postcolonialism

Dogs without Masters: Astray with Akbar and in André Alexis's *Fifteen Dogs*

Alexandra Isfahani-Hammond

"Might does what might will do, whether it was humans beating you for pissing or Atticus insisting that dogs should not speak."

Benjy, in *Fifteen Dogs* (61)

Prefatory Note: On Genre
This essay pairs intimate reflections about my relationship with a dog named Akbar with a reading of Trinidadian-Canadian author André Alexis's novel, Fifteen Dogs (2015). My fusion of memoir with critical contemplation exemplifies autotheory, the interdisciplinary practice that foregrounds individual experience to shatter hierarchical knowledge-production. For Rea McNamara, autotheory "dismantles vertical pipelines of colonial thinking" and is "a way of thinking through 'high' cultural theory via our physical, embodied selves." bell hooks, a pioneering practitioner of autotheory, describes "the 'lived' experience of critical thinking" (2) wherein there is no gap between theory and practice. While self-reflective, hooks emphasizes that theorizing everyday life is ultimately a strategy for collective liberation, for it furnishes the production of a healing, revolutionary space enabling her to "imagine possible futures, a place where life could be lived differently" (2). Recent, notable examples of autotheory within critical animal studies scholarship include Chloë Taylor's conceptualization of transspecies disability. Taylor's inquiry into "crip time" is grounded in an analysis of Elisabeth Tova Bailey's care for a wild snail while bedridden with a neurological disorder as well as Taylor's own relationships with the abandoned cats she fosters during a period of acute depression. In another instance, blending personal and critical meditations, Kathryn Gillespie ponders her ministrations to an infirm hen and dog to conceptualize what she calls a multispecies doula approach to animal death ("Provocation"). Gillespie demonstrates that nurturing attendance to an animal in their transition, and public display of grief following their death – including the production of her article – speak to a life and death that matter, subverting our mainstay relation to other species.

Autotheory is ideally suited to critical animal studies perspectives since it allows for an exploration of veganism and animal liberation as embodied practices. It is uniquely generative for an exploration of postcolonialism because it is an inherently anticolonial methodology. In this essay, privileging caregiving and grieving for a dog is a strategy for rebuking the hierarchical human/animal relationship and the conceit of dominion that is foundational for postcolonial structures of domination. Piecing together Akbar's biography redresses nonhuman animals' erasure from imperial histories and serves specifically as a landing pad for the itinerance of the "stray." Whereas nonhuman animals have generally been omitted from decolonizing work, this essay contributes to correcting that omission, following Yamini Narayanan's observation that anthropocentrism undergirds colonialism and the state of exception based on the animal/human binary (476); Gillespie's approach to farmed animals as colonized subjects and to sanctuary as "rebuking the logic of capitalism and coloniality" ("Unthinkable" 2); and Maneesha Deckha's interrogation of interspecies justice as pivotal for decolonization. The decolonizing momentum of this methodological endeavor is redoubled when my reflections on Akbar lead intuitively to pondering my own sublimated non-European ancestry.

The hybrid quality of the essay that follows is also profoundly informed by what Brianne Donaldson describes as the disruptive and productive potential of being "host to creaturely ghosts who reorient (an author's) outlook and vocations through threads of affective feeling" (xviii). Thinking about dogs with and in honor of the individual dog who stole my heart, Akbar animates my foray into humans' totalitarian relationships towards canines and inspires radical alternatives to the ethos of mastery. As Donaldson puts it, he is a creature "whose living and dying was not a discreet moment with a beginning and end but, rather, persists into the present," sometimes a "steadfast companion" while at others "an unpredictable specter of memory" (xviii). Both the multilayered, non-linear format of this work as well as its appreciation of extra-rational being-in-the-world, including dreamt reality, speak to what Donaldson calls the world-changing experience of "loss, feeling and care" that erodes "barriers of species, individuality and dominant structures of meaning" (xxi). The ghosts of my forebears simultaneously speak through Akbar's narrative, a chorus that lends dimension to my excavation of his history and our kinship bond, steadfast companions and specters of memory who exceed and unsettle the bulwark of anthropocentrism and white supremacy, revealing intertwined genealogies of more-than-human, canine, and Persian affiliation.

Introduction

IN MY ESSAY, "Akbar Stole My Heart: Coming out as an Animalist" (2013), I describe how adopting an abandoned mongrel led me to veganism and critical animal studies. Living with Akbar, caring for him and being cared for by him, resulted in a process of transformation from the inside out. I clutched him in my arms as I watched Shaun Monson's *Earthlings* (2005) and made the connection between my companion and the pigs, chickens, lambs, and baboons in animal agriculture and laboratory experimentation, becoming instantly vegan. I also reoriented my academic research; whereas my early career focused on comparative race and slavery studies, I began centering the animal as a construct wielded to rationalize the domination of both nonhuman species as well as categories of homo sapiens constructed as less than human, and the entanglement of racialization with animalization in the exercise of power. My love for Akbar required this reorientation. Now, fourteen months since his passing, my life's work continues to be imbued with his presence. In the pages that follow, I bring the text of my friend's life in the urban sphere of Los Angeles into conversation with the free-roaming Torontonian dogs of André Alexis's *Fifteen Dogs*. Alexis's apologue addresses both the imperialist ethos of mastery and deleterious effects of canine/

human co-evolution as well as a singular canine/human love relationship in which species boundaries dissolve.

My approach to both Akbar's life and Alexis's apologue is informed by Narayanan's theorization of "an anthropocentric sense of (privileged) human imperialism over non-humans and poor humans" (475). Narayanan centers the postcolonial non-belonging of "free-ranging" dogs in Indian cities who, like the cows, monkeys, and other species who live in the streets, are criminalized and expendable. She observes that thinking about coloniality in relation to urban space "hitherto has been anthropocentric, assuming that questions of the right to city, or contentions over space are solely human concerns" (482). In addition to Narayanan's observations of free-roaming dogs' deterritorialization, I am in conversation with scholarship that conjures radical alternatives to humans' imperialism over animals. Moving between Akbar's life and Alexis's pack, I attend to the colonial conceit of mastery over dogs as well as heterotopian alternatives to the anthropocentric order, imagining pathways from placelessness to sites of belonging.[1]

The subversive spheres I foreground include the physical turf wherein I care for my dog friend – the cocoon of our apartment during his decline, the forest clearing where we spend our final hours together – as well as zones that resist definition: the threshold between the worlds, the domain of dreams, and the world within a world wherein I endeavor to abide with him following his passing. It is the cocoon of Akbar's cosmic energy that rescues me when, confounded by his absence, I teeter on the brink. Throughout, I play with the idea of bewilderment as a state of being that facilitates the dissolution of speciesist systems of knowledge. For Ibn 'Arabi, bewilderment, or "the disabling of rational faculties," is a prerequisite for an encounter with the Real (Almond 1). The state of confusion wherein previous knowledge is swept away is a gift, such that that the spirit becomes bewildered in the face of God. Pursuing this thread as a poetic opening to a future without animal exploitation, the old English of bewilder means to lure astray, into the wild, what we might think of as the shedding of the human facade. This conceptualization of a wild place speaks to my world-altering experience of grieving for Akbar. When he became ill, I started praying to the god of dogs, then to the dog of gods. I realized that the name I had chosen to give confidence to a traumatized stray – Akbar, which means "the great" – was portentous. "God is Great" (*Allahu Akbar*) but also, by extension, "Akbar is God." In the words of Sant Tukaram, "I couldn't lie anymore, so I started to call my dog God."

Akbar and Alexa

The first word I wrote upon receiving Akbar's cancer diagnosis was "Akbaralexa," fusing our names on paper to solidify our bond before he left his body. I whispered to him that I would always be with him, in this world and the next, for he was my forever dog and I, his forever primate. I captured Akbar's scent, breathing him in as I had my dying mother. I took in his liquids, tasting the blood that dripped from the incision on his knee following surgery to remove a mast cell tumor, licking the saliva from my fingers after inserting pills down his throat.

I had looked after Akbar from the age of two until he was white-muzzled and his ribs protruded, a youth transformed into an old man before my eyes. By turn, he had cared for me from the moment he jumped into my car, inducting me into rituals of play that would alter me, a rambunctious girl awakening in the body of a middle-aged woman. He instructed me in the art of protecting him from things that made him tremble – including cars, men, trash bins, and sudden noises. Akbar led me into the brush, sharing with me his exuberance about digging holes so that I could sense in my own body the delight of burying potato chips in the sand. He accompanied me when my parents died.

What would I do without him? I shook when Akbar's seizures began, wobbled when he was unsteady on his feet. I was on my knees as I maneuvered him through backwards walking and figure eights designed to nourish the weakening neurological links between his brain and extremities. Akbar patiently endured the manipulations, even prancing over cavaletti poles, hauling himself up to a standing position to snatch a treat from my hand, eyes gleaming with the desire to excel. When Akbar growled playfully at me to throw the ball, I chased after it with him to help him locate it, nudging it closer to his nose, his sense of smell not what it had been.

Akbar bounced back from cancer, IBD, liver and neurological disease, even surviving pneumonia at the age of sixteen, defying prognoses that he had days or weeks to live. The vet said he kept beating the odds because of his strong heart, free of the wear and tear appropriate to a sixteen or seventeen year old, the organ of a young adult, his heart's endurance like his indomitable zeal for fun despite a history of trauma. But eventually, time would betray us. I never again left his side after the day in mid-March when I returned home to find him, legs splayed and unable to stand, softly crying. From then on, I squatted behind him supporting his hips to keep him from tipping over as he ate and drank. When he wandered aimlessly, I swaddled him in my arms, where he fell instantly asleep, snoring, exhausted from his rounds. Still, I stuck to the idea that there was an escape route from the predicament we were in, if only I could make him very small so that death wouldn't find him. I dreamt that I tucked Akbar away in my purse. But even then, there was so little of him to hold onto. He was light as a feather, so that I continually reached inside to see if he was there.

Finally, Akbar spoke to me in human language, the only time he did so. In my dream, he was having a bad night, pacing compulsively. Swaddling didn't resolve his agitation, so I took him to the Museum of Modern Art, thinking an outing might break the spell. But Akbar kept slipping away from me, turning a corner into a never-ending series of gallery rooms. I realized my plan was a failure and we should return home. Our apartment wasn't far but, of course, I didn't have his leash or harness. Though he had lost a lot of weight, carrying him all the way would be difficult. Then it started pouring with rain. I considered taking an Uber despite the pandemic but I didn't have my mask. No matter what new scheme I thought up, I hit a wall. I held Akbar in my lap as we sat on a bench together, gazing out the floor-length windows at the rainy street, museum-goers milling around us, a portrait of despair. Then Akbar guided me. It was time to stop striving. No ingenious new plan would alter his pathway around the corner, into another gallery room or dimension where I could not follow him, at least not in the usual way. He did so by posing the question that resounded inside me in the few days that remained to us: "If you realized this museum outing was futile, would you admit it out loud?" It was time to help him out of his body, a gift I was unable to bestow upon my father when his own agony had become intolerable, despite piercing blue eyes that pleaded for release.

Fifteen Dogs

With its explorations of love, grief, prayer, and dreams as the vehicles for communication with the more-than-human, Alexis's *Fifteen Dogs* has been a generative interlocutor as I process Akbar's passing. An important narrative thread is the bond between the poodle, Majnoon, and the human, Nira, who commune together in a heterotopia that excludes Nira's husband, Miguel. Unlike humans, between whom miscommunication is the standard – as Hermes, the god of translators, puts it: "You'd swear they understood each other, though not one of them has any idea what their words actually mean to another" (Alexis 14) – Majnoon and Nira's paths to understanding are mutually taken, learning what is important to each. Nira plays her favorite music for Majnoon, shows him her favorite films, and reads her favorite novels to him aloud, while Majnoon recounts stories and composes poetry he recites for her. Nira takes in Majnoon to the extent that she "had the odd but fleeting sensation that Majnoon had entered her consciousness in some new way" (125). This echoes Majnoon's experience of the divine when Hermes visits him in a dream: the god, disguised as a poodle, "spoke no particular language. Its words were in Majnoon's mind, like a strange idea" (123).

The premise of *Fifteen Dogs* is that the gods, Apollo and Hermes, make a wager about whether or not other animals would be more or less happy if endowed with "so-called human intelligence" (169), an attribute Apollo calls "an occasionally useful plague" (15), arguing that if another species had it they would inevitably die unhappy. They conduct their experiment on fifteen dogs boarded in a veterinary hospital, the majority of whom unlock their cages and leave, minus three who reject the change and remain behind. What follows is a narrative about the pack's grappling with what they call "the new way of thinking" (17) as they live out their lives in the city streets and in the den they create in Toronto's Hyde Park. Grounded entirely in the dogs' perspectives, the narrative explores their reactions, which range from that of Prince, a mutt who relishes "the imposition of primate language" (17) and dedicates himself to composing poetry, to Atticus, a Neapolitan Mastiff who violently endeavors to return the pack to their prior condition of unadulterated caninity.

The dogs who remain in their cages in the veterinary hospital because they want to return to their "masters" fare badly. Agatha, an elderly Labradoodle, awakens the next morning to be ruthlessly slapped by veterinary technicians and administered a lethal injection. The mutt, Ronaldinho, lives with a condescending family and is bitter and disillusioned upon his death. The Whippet-Weimaraner cross, Lydia, suffers so deeply from being left alone that she becomes catatonic, whereupon the vet determines that the best course of action is to end her life. While returning "home" is not a good option, neither is roaming the streets. Of the travails of Benjy, a beagle, and Dougie, a Schnauzer, in the streets of Toronto, Alexis writes, "For as many kindnesses as they'd had from perky summoners, there had been bewildering cruelties: stones thrown, beatings with sticks" (65). Humans' behavior is perilously erratic: "While one might kneel down to scratch your beard, another who looked exactly like the first would kick you, throw stones, or even do you to death. It was, in general, best to avoid them" (26). Periodic invitations to come indoors generally end poorly as well, since humans' words are "unpredictably consequential ... Before you know it, they've taken up your plate of food, or the door sounds and an intruder comes in" (43). After being caged and subjected to testing, Majnoon reflects on humans' cruelty: "*This* was humanity, this unpredictability, this cruel behavior and bullying" (46, emphasis in original).

Taken in for six months by the human couple, Randy and Claire, Benjy mistakenly assumes that he is safe. For a time, the couple value him as an entertaining pet, yet when they move, they abandon him, whereupon Benjy subsists on toilet water and forages for food, eventually consuming a packet of mouse poison pellets and dying a slow and excruciating death. Just as the protections afforded by human status are historically and culturally contingent – with vast sectors of homo sapiens relegated to the status of killable beasts – so are those of pet. Whereas the expression, "die like a dog," refers to the irony of a human perishing in the undignified and acutely painful manner supposedly appropriate for a lowly canine, Benjy's death "like a mouse" points to the extreme vulnerability of the animalized in the anthropocentric order: a pet can at any moment be demoted to the status of expendable vermin.[2]

Akbar and Alexa

I have been eager to piece together Akbar's early biography since I first adopted him. At the outset, the only information I had was that he had been a "stray." Strayed from what? He was originarily placeless, "natally alienated" in the words of Orlando Patterson, the definition of Giorgio Agamben's "bare life": a sick dog abandoned in the streets, coughing up blood on a sidewalk. But once the shelter provided me with his medical records, I had a lead. The man who signed for Akbar's hospitalization was easy to find online. He told me that a group of houseless people had been trying to care for a dying Akbar, whom they called Brutus. The man, who worked with a cat rescue, took him to the emergency room, where he was diagnosed with parvovirus. The vet suggested euthanasia, but the cat rescue offered to pay for his treatment, including a full month's quarantine. Akbar's rescuer couldn't recall what part of town he had been in nor any additional details, for there had been so many animals. The numbers of unwanted dogs and cats in the streets of Los Angeles to whom he had attended overwhelmed his memory.

Akbar's life would not be taken. It would be preserved via the chance intervention of a cat rescuer. But the sort of life he would have remained to be determined. Following a month-long hospitalization, Akbar was sent to a shelter, where he was renamed Bennie and lived in a concrete stall for three months. At one point, he was adopted by a woman who returned him two weeks later because, as she later told me, "he soiled my entire house." The details of this episode required no detective work: within the first few days of our life together, a dogwalker at a West Los Angeles park recognized him, called out "Bennie!" and put me in touch with Akbar's previous, short-term guardian over the phone.

My own intervention in Akbar's life might not have panned out. One of thousands, I saw his headshot on Petfinder and was simultaneously intrigued and intimidated by the intensity of his gaze. I decided against pursuing him. Ironically – or belying my unconscious purpose – I drove to the shelter where he was located, a full hour away, to meet a dachshund named George. When I arrived, I was frozen in my tracks. Akbar was staring at me from atop a stack of cages arranged pyramid-style. A volunteer leashed him so that I could take him for a stroll in the yard, where he largely ignored me, growling at other dogs and desperately searching for dropped bits of kibble on the floor. I told the volunteer I liked him but wanted to meet George. Leaving Akbar in a pen with several other dogs, I walked in the direction of George's stall. When I looked over my shoulder, he was fixed to the spot where I had left him at the edge of the pen, up on hind legs, staring, determined to keep an eye on me. A woman who visited the shelter regularly to play with the dogs approached; like Akbar, there was urgency in the way she held my gaze: "Bennie seems to really like you. He's been here for a long time."

The precarity of a dog's life is exacerbated by being an "impure breed." Akbar was a deep mongrel who didn't get the attention of the more breed-distinct dogs at the shelter nor throughout his life. One trainer called him a "JYD" (junkyard dog). Akbar was not included when strangers invariably inquired about friends' dogs' pedigrees, at which point I would crouch down to pay him compliments. A human at the dog park asked if Akbar meant "little terrorist," just as my Iranian mother had been called "terrorist" by a passenger on the LA Rapid Transit. I didn't think fast enough to reply that Akbar was my great-grandfather's name, nor that I had chosen the name to embolden a terrified mutt. Akbar's named raced him, just as the Akbar tattoo I have on my forearm races me, making visible my Persian descent while simultaneously announcing my kinship with a dog.[3] My mother sung Akbar a makeshift tune in Persian about Akbar Khan, adding "khan" (*ruler*) in homage to both Akbars, one canine, the other human, whose grave in the holy city of Karbala was decimated by US bombs. Writing Akbar's narrative is a sojourn into my Iranian matrilineage, obscured by immigration and assimilation, leading to my Sufi grandfather, a disorganized landlord who allowed stray dogs and cats to live in his empty properties, and my grandmother, who fed yoghurt to stray dogs and cats to induce vomiting and rid them of the poison administered by animal control.

My ancestors' gestures laid the groundwork for his arrival, but unlike my grandfather, I had no idea how to even invite a dog into a car. On our first walk together, Akbar lay himself down, digging his nails into the sidewalk. The marks and scars of his life in the streets were visible on the surface of his body, in the neck wound that was either a cigarette burn or from being run over by a car. Worse, his trauma was embedded in his cells, causing him to tremble at the sight of trash bins, bus stop shelters, bicycles, shopping carts, skateboards, crowds of humans, and men. Bringing Akbar into my home meant that things would be different than I expected. I would not, as I'd fantasized, take him to cafes to sit calmly at my side while I worked, much less on research trips to Brazil, where he would surely have had a heart attack confronted with the throngs of pedestrians and street vendors, the densely packed humanity on the sidewalks of Copacabana, one of my favorite locales. I had adopted a dog thinking he would be my companion on urban adventures, locally and globally. The opposite occurred: I would need to cultivate safe spaces, including our domestic sphere, secluded parks and beaches. He wedged himself shoulder to shoulder between Cosmo and Arbor – my friend's tough, territorial dogs – to get through traffic to the park. Once there, I immediately unleashed him, whereupon he was a rambunctiously playful young adult. The Akbar who was untouched by trauma sprinted, leaped, and tumbled with his friends.

If, as Narayanan observes, dogs without masters do not belong in the city streets, they are also unwelcome indoors without having their behavior restructured to fit humans' likes and dislikes. Some of the ways in which I brought Akbar into my domestic sphere were gentle. House-training, for instance, is a defensible practice intended to make living together indoors sanitary. Akbar learned not to eliminate indoors within two weeks. Presented with an array of chew toys, he stopped ripping apart carpets and gnawing on electrical cables. The only holdout was the bedspread, which took a few more months and numerous trips to the fabric store together. There, the kind owner seemed to take pleasure in finding scraps matching the red and pink pattern of the bedspread, giving them to me for free so that I could sew up Akbar's holes, affectionately nodding to him and wishing us better luck this time around.

Yet I wish I had managed his fear better: the trips to the vet with his body spasming in my arms, the walks down the major thoroughfare outside our front door. Some of my actions were more of master than friend. The first of many unforgivable things I did to Akbar occurred early on, when a trainer had me address his separation anxiety by banging hard on the bedroom door until he stopped barking, scaring him into silent submission. The worst was holding Akbar in place to "desensitize" him to skateboards, a breach of trust that aggravated his fear. The result was that, on two occasions, he ran away from rather than towards me when skateboards came near. For the remaining nine years of his life, I could never again unleash him in areas where they might be present.

Fifteen Dogs

Dog/human relationships are often sugar-coated in the language of collaboration, mutual interdependence, and friendship. The reality is that obedience and the trope of mastery are core elements of humans' relations to dogs, sullying even my profound love story with Akbar. *Fifteen Dogs* calls forth a subversive, anti-hierarchical dog/human relationship, but it is also a profound indictment of the detrimental impact of coevolution.[4] The human, Miguel, embodies "Man's" aspiration to master his so-called "best friend." When Benjy speaks aloud to him, his immediate response is to determine whether he can roll over, play dead, sing, whisper, stand up, and beg. He teaches him to memorize the first page of Thackeray's *Vanity Fair*, which Benjy recites without understanding its meaning. Miguel thinks Benjy's ability to obey commands is more impressive than the potential to converse and reason with a dog. Majnoon is blown away by this irony: "It seemed to him that what humans called 'intelligence' (knowing the accepted names for things, performing feats that required a certain mental dexterity) was in every way inferior to the *knowing* he remembered from his previous life as a dog, the life before he was sideswiped by 'thinking'" (87).

Majnoon reflects on the grey areas in his relationship with his former "master." He had been proud of his ability to do what he asked, enjoyed getting treats and being petted, but resented the condescension and barely suppressed the impulse to run away (21). Prince describes the "behavior his presence elicited in humans: cooing, fur rubbing, rolling about on the ground with him, smugness, condescension, chirpily rendered orders" (158). Dougie recoils against the clinginess of a woman who briefly takes in Benjy and him. In his "back-cracking struggle" to evade her embraces, he wonders aloud to Benjy, "Do you think she could kill us when she squeezes?" (66). The problem with humans is not always, or only, violence, but the indignities to which they subject dogs, indignities that are themselves on a continuum with killability. Like Miguel, Randy is impressed by Benjy's tricks, but kicks him if he climbs on his lap and, as described, ultimately abandons him to an excruciating death. Benjy observes the relationship of mastering dogs to other forms of domination. Just as his own "tricks" are a manipulation designed to ingratiate himself with those he perceives as strong, he observes Randy and Clare's dominant/submissive role-playing and the performativity of their whiteness, noting their application of creams to make themselves paler than they already were: "Was there something about white that brought status?" (109).

The personalities of the fifteen dogs subjected to "primate mind" (19) are painfully distorted. The pack's self-conscious body language and vocalizations are "an imitation of an imitation of dogs" (73). Despite Atticus's prohibition against speaking – as he puts it, "our ancestors did very well without this language" (60) – they cannot recuperate authentic caninity:

> There were still growls, lowered eyes and exposed necks. But along with that there were strange movements of the head, there was a kind of muzzle-pointing that had nothing to do with indicating direction, there was a stuttered bark that sounded to Benjy like human imitations of barking. (73)

The imposition of human thinking not only robs the pack of authenticity but leads certain of them to a "might is right" mentality. Some of the dogs become totalitarians, as brutal as any human. Outlawing the new tongue, Atticus ruthlessly murders or banishes dissidents who persist in using it, aided by the Labrador brothers, Frick and Frack, and the mutt, Max. The irony is that Atticus's cruelty is borne of the new tongue; it "felt like instinct but was anger" (97). At Atticus's announcement of his leadership and the injunction against speaking out loud, Benjy reflects, "Might does what might will do, whether it was humans beating you for pissing or Atticus insisting that dogs should not speak" (61).

As a counterpoint to this ethos, Alexis posits the subversive domain of Nira and Majnoon. Their alternate reality is hard won. When Majnoon responds "yes" to the offer of a treat (46), Nira literally loses consciousness. As Majnoon observes, "It was evident that, for whatever reason, humans could not stand to be spoken to by dogs" (46). Faced with the fact that "they had brought an intelligent being into their home" (48), she has Miguel take him to the veterinarian, who cages, holds down, prods, and pokes Majnoon for three days to discover what is "wrong" with him. At another point, Nira pulls rank, insisting that she is second in order of command after Miguel, an "unspeakably rude" (121) offense which causes Majnoon to bear his teeth, growl, lower his tail, and, since he is unwilling to hurt her, leave the house. Nira ultimately relinquishes the conceit of higher status, overcoming her fear of contending with a thinking dog. The "divine intimacy" (144) that evolves between Majnoon and Nira disorders the master/dog paradigm. Nira refuses to allow anyone to refer to Majnoon as "her" dog: "I'm as much his as he's mine," she says (132). Majnoon reflects that Nira was "a being who completed him, made him more than he would otherwise have been" (142). As he puts it, ". . . this human is not a master. I do not know what Nira is, but I am not afraid" (71). Species classification erodes, such that Nira is initially destabilized and Majnoon feels "adrift between species" (47). Together, they are at once unmoored yet intimately bonded in a realm beyond anthropos, where the worn-out commands of the Masters – "sit, stay, roll over" – subside to a hush, then vanish just as Nira comes to hear and revere her Majnoon, relinquishing normative discourse: "the distance between (them) narrowed until each could anticipate what the other wanted . . . By degrees, they had less use for words or English" (132).

I want to note that Alexis names Majnoon after a poodle who passed away named Layla, to whom he was close, thereby not only situating the novel as a "headstone" (Alexis, "Zoo") but also conjuring the ancient Arabic tale of star-crossed lovers, "Layla and Majnun."[5] Majnun's longing for Layla is signified by his name, which means "mad" or possessed by spirits. Layla is simultaneously human and a reminder of the divine. Majnun gives himself over to her, burning in remembrance of his beloved, so that eventually the distinction between lover, beloved, and love itself dissolves. This is a transformative experience which is also a rewilding, for Majnun inhabits the wilderness and identifies with animals, freeing them from the snares of hunters. In Alexis's apologue, the mutual admiration of Majnoon and Nira leads also to the obliteration of the individuated self. They become so close that,

> One morning [Majnoon and Nira] discovered that they'd dreamed of the same field, the same clouds, the same house in the distance – wooden with a red-brick chimney. They had dreamed of the same squirrels and rabbits. They had drunk from the same clear stream. There was only one difference: when Nira, in her dream, looked into the water, she saw Majnoon's face reflected back at her, while Majnoon, in his, saw Nira's face where his should have been. (132)

Reading Akbar's narrative alongside that of *Fifteen Dogs* therefore leads to yet another unveiling of my non-European cultural heritage, revealing a story that prescribes discarding the human facade at the same time that it beckons me to examine the legacy of Islamic mysticism embedded in my cells.

Given that Majnoon and Nira are mortals, their love portends exquisite suffering. As Alexis puts it, "The veil that separates earthly beings is, at times, a tragic barrier, but it is also, at times, a great kindness" (127). Majnoon becomes elderly and it's time for his life to end, but the identities of Nira and Majnoon are so deeply entangled that when the Fate, Atropos, goes to clip the string of his life, she clips Nira's and her husband's threads instead (133). Flustered and spiteful, she then adds extra years to the remaining thread, that of the aged Majnoon, to make up for the difference (133).

Nira's and Miguel's lives are cut short when they go away for the weekend, leaving Majnoon waiting, incredulous as a day's tardiness becomes two: "If Monday was bewildering, Tuesday was strange beyond language" (137). Eventually, Miguel's family arrives to take possession of the house, whereupon Majnoon runs away, taking cover from dog catchers, keeping watch from a series of hiding places as the home he shared with Nira is emptied, renovated, and put up for sale. A new family moves in, but still Majnoon won't give up on her. Sometimes neighborhood dogs join him at whatever vantage point he has taken up, sitting at a slight remove, sharing his task as a mark of respect. His yearning for the world within a world wherein he and Nira resided informs his attachment to the physical locale of their house, a mere remnant of the sacred space that evades him:

> Majnoon looked over at the house he had been contemplating for five years: red brick, tall chimney, pyramid roof, a window with shutters on the third floor, a bay window on the second floor, front porch with its own roof, blue spruce in the front

yard. You might almost have said that he loved its bricks, aluminum and wood, but, of course, they were precious only because Nira had lived within. (145)

Eventually, Zeus takes pity that Majnoon's suffering is unnecessarily prolonged and sends Hermes to intervene. He comes to him as a poodle whom Majnoon immediately recognizes as a god. Majnoon asks him where Nira is, to which Hermes replies that he will take him to her but to do so, he must abandon his vigil. Majnoon refuses, still certain that Nira will return.

Waiting with Majnoon, Hermes asks if there is anything else he can do for him. Majnoon could ask anything, including the meaning of life, or why we die, but all he cares about is Nira. So he asks Hermes what Nira meant by love. To explain, Hermes leads Majnoon on a tour of every time Nira felt or said love in her life, revealing such a rich and deeply felt tapestry of her that his sorrow becomes intolerable and he agrees to give up his vigil:

> As Majnoon's understanding of Nira's "love" deepened, so did his distress. Nira was restored to him as if she were there with them, but she was far from him as well, and it was suddenly unbearable to be without her.
>
> Majnoon could not even keen, so overwhelmed was he by grief. All he could manage was a sigh. He lay down on the rust-colored pine needles and put his head on the crux made by his paws . . .
>
> At that moment, Majnoon would have done anything to see Nira again. And so, trusting in the god of thieves, he gave up his vigil. And his soul travelled through the evening with Hermes as its guide. (148)

Akbar and Alexa

One week after Akbar passes away, I return to our haunt in Franklin Canyon where I had taken him for a final sniff, retracing our steps, lying face down in the leaves and twigs to affix myself to the clearing where we had rested alongside each other. I embrace the forest floor, howling silently to avoid the attention of nearby hikers. I am bewildered by the memory of Akbar's body going slack in my arms, his head tumbling to the side. Unable even to keen, I would gladly have allowed myself to be led away by Hermes as he conveyed Majnoon from his bereft waiting spot. It isn't the end of our world, but a transformation of its topography requiring new skills to navigate. Without Hermes to scoop me up, I find other means to join him in a zone that resists definition. I keep up my prayers to the god of dogs and the dog of gods, steadfast like Atticus, who humbles himself before the entity he calls "Great Dog" (96). Akbar helps: he accompanies me in my dreams, appearing as a squirrel swimming in a stream, inviting me to follow him until the stream becomes a vast ocean. The first time Hermes leads Majnoon to Nira, he appears in a dream as a poodle "in a meadow bounded on four sides by darkness," with "grass so green it looked painted" (122). I am inseparable from Akbar in landscapes like Majnoon's too-green dream meadow that is also akin to Alexis's Olympus: "It cannot be captured in human language because it was created by the divine. The closest one could come . . . to defining it would be 'nowhere' and 'nothing,' though it is something and somewhere" (91). Shirin Neshat describes this presence in absence: "I . . . had hidden you in my eyes, And from that moment on,

I never saw you again . . . At last . . . you were safe with me" (Alipour). When Akbar came back from the hospital, I had transformed the apartment into an incubator infused with the scent of lavender, wrapping my body around his. Now Akbar is my incubator, like a kindly, canine trojan horse, his perimeters those of the stratosphere. I curl into a fetal position inside him. Sometimes I do handstands or dance.

Like our places that are nowhere but somewhere, the seasons since Akbar passed feel like a multitude of moments heaped into a pile. C. S. Lewis asks, "If the dead are not in time, or not in our sort of time, is there any clear difference, when we speak of them, between *was* and *is* and *will be*?" (24). Writing about Akbar keeps him present, such that our relationship is ever-evolving. Like a poem that lingers in the air: once uttered, forever in the eternal present, as Alexis notes of the verse composed by his beagle character, Prince. What might the future still hold for us? In a dream, I lose Akbar in the field where I had played as a child. He is elderly and wanders off in the direction of a thoroughfare, leaving me frantic. But then a band of rebels arrives and pries open a door, ushering me up several flights of stairs into their headquarters where, in a little room, Akbar soundly sleeps. Wakened by my arrival, Akbar stretches, yawns, and comes strolling out to greet me. These guerilla warriors are working behind the scenes, dismantling the existing order, including tender interventions like finding lost dogs.

To accompany a loved one in the interstitial space between life and death is an education in the dissolution of façades. I had already witnessed the undoing of the Human when I attended to my dying parents greeting the spirits of their own parents at their bedsides, then leaving their earthly incarnations. When my father took his last breaths in my arms, I told him, "I will never stop holding you. After you leave your body, I will continue to embrace you when I hold Akbar and Aziz (my other dog)." Like the god's "strange idea" in Majnoon's mind, the words surprised me. How had they gotten into my head? Six years later, I used the same bottle of rose oil to bathe Akbar's body that I had used on my father's corpse.

Writing about the passing of her dog, Nikita, Jessica Ullrich refers to "deaths (that) have left wounds that will not be healed but that can be soothed by dedicating something to them: an obituary, a film, a text, a theory, a life" (129) as well as the political value of animal obituary. With this tribute, I have sought to allay my sorrow while simultaneously encouraging an awareness of the gods, dogs, and other beings whose sacred nature is revealed through a process of transformation that is both personal and world-changing. Edwidge Danticat observes that "we look to death narratives, and to the people in our lives who are dying, for some previously unknowable insights, which we hope they will pass on to us" (29). Such narratives impart glimpses of transgressive spheres, on the other side of the species divide. Akbar's trajectory is a storyline within which I am bound to abide: to keep him with me, not so much as a phantom sleuthing at my side, but in a manner akin to that of an amateur astronomer reading constellations in the night sky, unsure of their meaning but with unwavering faith in the interpretive process, striving to connect the glimmers of light.

Notes

1. I am indebted to Paula Arcari's invitation in her call for papers, "Heterotopia, Radical Imagination, and Shattering Orders" (2021). Drawing upon Michel Foucault's "Of Other Spaces" (1967), *Order of Things* (1989), and "Space, Knowledge and Power" (2002),

Arcari engages with the concept of heterotopia as a means for subverting and dismantling our destructive orientations towards other animals. Thinking "otherwise" with Foucault, language is undermined and common names shattered, creating what Foucault calls a "simultaneously mythic and real contestation of the space in which we live."

2. At other times, the expression, "Die like a dog," is invoked vindictively, as when Donald Trump relished describing Abu Bakr al-Baghdadi's demise, "whimpering like a puppy." See Isfahani-Hammond, "When Trump Calls Someone a Dog."
3. I am inspired by Jessica Ullrich's comments regarding her tattoo of her dog's name, Nikita. In addition to reversing the dynamic of humans branding animalized beings to denote ownership, her tattoo speaks to her desire to keep Nikita under her skin: "to bury her – or what she was for me – in my body" (123).
4. *Fifteen Dogs* nonetheless reflects periodic anthropocentric bias. Alexis normalizes carnism and dogs' instrumentalization in harming and destroying other species. For instance, Prince yearns for the old days of duck and gopher hunting with his "master," Kim, fondly recalling the crack of the rifle (150).
5. There are countless renditions of the ancient Arabic story of Layla and Majnun, not only in Arabic but in Persian, Turkish, and Indian languages. The most famous version is the narrative poem composed by Nizami Ganjavi in 1188.

Works Cited

Agamben, Giorgio. *Homo Sacer: Sovereign Power and Bare Life*. Trans. Daniel Heller-Roazen, Stanford UP, 1998.
Alexis, André. *Fifteen Dogs*. Toronto: Coach House Books, 2015.
—. "Zoo: On the Animalistic Origins of a Novel." *Literary Hub*, 18 May 2015.
Alipour, Yasi. "Shirin Neshat, Facing History." *The Brooklyn Rail*, September 2015.
Almond, Ian. "The Honesty of the Perplexed: Derrida and Ibn 'Arabi on 'bewilderment.'" *Journal of the American Academy of Religion*, vol. 7. no. 3, 2002, pp. 515–37.
Arcari, Paula. Call for papers for the symposium, "Heterotopia, Radical Imagination, and Shattering Orders: Manifesting a Future of Liberated Animals." Biennial Meeting of the European Association of Critical Animal Studies, 21–25 June 2021, Edge Hill University, Ormskirk, Lancashire, England.
Danticat, Edwidge. *The Art of Death: Writing the Final Story*. Grey Wolf Press, 2017.
Deckha, Maneesha. "Unsettling Anthropocentric Legal Systems: Reconciliation, Indigenous Laws, and Animal Personhood." *Journal of Intercultural Studies*, vol. 41, no. 1, 2020, pp. 77–97.
Donaldson, Brianne. "Transformed by Ghosts: Towards Futures of Less Loss." *Feeling Animal Death: Being Host to Ghosts*, edited by Donaldson and Ashley King. Rowman and Littlefield, 2019, pp. xv–xxix.
Foucault, Michel. *Order of Things: An Archaeology of the Human Sciences*. Routledge, 1989.
—. "Of Other Spaces: Utopias and Heterotopias." *Architecture/Mouvement/Continuité*, Oct. 1967, pp. 1–9.
—. "Space, Knowledge, and Power," *Power: the Essential Works of Michel Foucault 1954–1984 V.3*, edited by James D. Faubion, Penguin Books, 2002, pp. 349–64.
Ganjavi, Nizami, *The Story of Layla and Majnun*. Shambala, 1978.
Gillespie, Kathryn. "Provocation from the Field: A Multispecies Doula Approach to Death and Dying." *Animal Studies Journal*, vol. 9, no.1, 2020, pp. 1–31.
—. "An Unthinkable Politics for Multispecies Flourishing within and beyond Colonial-Capitalist Ruins." *Annals of the American Association of Geographers*, 29 September 2021.
hooks, bell. "Theory as Liberatory Practice." *Yale Journal of Law and Feminism*, vol. 4, no. 1, 1991, pp. 1–12.

Isfahani-Hammond, Alexandra. "Akbar Stole My Heart: Coming Out As An Animalist." *e-misférica: Performance and Politics*, vol. 10, no. 1, Winter, 2013.

—. "When Trump Calls Someone a Dog, He's Tapping into Ugly History." *The Conversation*, 13 December 2019.

Lewis, C. S. *A Grief Observed*. HarperCollins, 1961.

McNamara, Rea. "A Deep Feminist Dive into Autotheory." *Hyperallergic*, 20 June 2021.

Monson, Shaun, director. *Earthlings*. 2005.

Narayanan, Yamini. "Street Dogs at the Intersection of Colonialism and Informality: 'Subaltern Animism' as a Posthuman Critique of Indian Cities." *Environment and Planning: Society and Space*, vol. 35, no. 3, 2017, pp. 475–94.

Patterson, Orlando. *Slavery and Social Death: a Comparative Study*. Harvard UP, 1982.

Taylor, Chloë, "Of Gimps, Gastropods and Grief: Feminist New Materialist Reflections on Elisabeth Tova Bailey's *The Sound of a Wild Snail Eating*." *Disability and Animality: Crip Perspectives in Critical Animal Studies*, edited by Stephanie Jenkens, Kelly Struthers Montford, and Chloë Taylor, Routledge, 2020, pp. 256–76.

Tukaram, Sant. "First He Looked Confused." *Love Poems from God: Twelve Sacred Voices from the East and West*, translated and edited by Daniel Ladinsky, Penguin, 2002, p. 333.

Ullrich, Jessica. "Every Love Story is a Ghost Story: The Transformative Power of Dog Dedication." *Feeling Animal Death: Being Host to Ghosts*, edited by Brianne Donaldson and Ashley King, Rowman and Littlefield, 2019, pp. 113–34.

8

Veganism and the Monstrous

"Not text, but texture": *Pale Fire* and Monstrous Vegan Literary Criticism

Emelia Quinn

Introduction

In his review of Carol J. Adams's 1990 *The Sexual Politics of Meat*, the conservative journalist and novelist Auberon Waugh speculated, facetiously, that the book might be

> a gigantic Nabokovian practical joke, written by some male academic, no doubt an émigré from Eastern Europe, whose misogyny is so enormous that it can find adequate expression only by posing as a madwoman trying to establish common cause between the two separate causes of radical feminism and evangelical vegetarianism.

Waugh here conflates Adams's iconic work of vegan literary studies with Vladimir Nabokov's 1962 novel *Pale Fire*. Vegan literary studies, in Waugh's reading, appears as the hideous progeny of identity-based criticism: an offshoot of postmodernism that, like the satirical commentary of the vegetarian Charles Kinbote in *Pale Fire*, subjects literary texts to monstrous distortion, drawing implausible connections in order to support the author's own agenda.

Vegan studies has attracted increasingly negative press over the past few years as a field that is seen to embody the worst,[1] most monstrous, excesses of the humanities, associated with a form of "identitarian madness" and so-called "grievance studies" (Lindsay et al.). Samantha Pergadia notes in her contribution to this volume that "As an interpretive strategy of how one should eat, vegan literary studies may seem like bad literary criticism, reducing complex or ambiguous meaning to a single political and ethical agenda" in contrast to "[g]ood literary criticism [which] has become synonymous with extending ambiguity, refusing political takeaway, and attending to questions of form or genre" (241). *Pale Fire* offers therefore a particularly prescient conflation of vegetarian moralism with acts of bad literary criticism. Formally resembling a scholarly edition of poetry, Kinbote's extensive commentary to the diegetic "Pale Fire" poem of the fictional poet John Shade reveals the former to be Charles the Beloved – vegetarian, homosexual, and deposed king – and his narrative works to satirize acts of literary criticism that impose the biography of the critic onto texts.

This essay considers the function of Kinbote as an embodiment of the monstrous excesses associated with vegan identity and a signifier of repellent vegan reading practices. In this way, I position Kinbote as a monstrous vegan figure, one who exemplifies veganism's resistance to delimitation as a consistent or stable subjectivity. Throughout this essay I define veganism as a complex coming together of utopianism and insufficiency: a mode of striving that acknowledges a sense of complicity and failure in its practice. Unlike vegetarianism's focus on the non-ingestion of meat, veganism's aspiration to exclude all forms of animal exploitation, and the practical impossibility of such an endeavor, means that veganism might best be defined as a monstrous assemblage of contradictions, failings, and utopian imaginings. Kinbote's vegetarianism betrays the slipperiness of identity categories, and the futile grasping towards an ethical life, which speaks directly to this sense of vegan monstrosity.

My conception of vegan monstrosity therefore posits veganism as a mode of life that embraces, rather than resists, difficulty and complexity. Counter therefore to the charge of "reducing complex or ambiguous meaning to a single political and ethical agenda," monstrous vegan reading practices require an embrace of the errant nature of language and meaning, reveling in a proliferation of textual possibilities. In what follows I use *Pale Fire* to unpack the seeming incompatibilities of veganism and literary criticism and argue that vegan literary studies needs to embrace, rather than resist, monstrous excesses of meaning.

The Monstrous Vegan

The monster is a seemingly inescapable social convention and source of fear, superstition, and awe throughout human history. Monsters are disruptive to human attempts to assert order and control over the world and frequently exist at the borders of human and non-human animal definition. *The Oxford English Dictionary* (*OED*) notes the origins of the monster as a creature who "is part animal and part human, or combines elements of two or more animal forms." In contemporary work on cinematic monsters, monsters represent "disorder, confusion of identity, social havoc" (Wolfe 108), figures that "always escape human comprehension; they demonstrate what we do not know, and remonstrate against our presumption to know" (Bohlmann and Moreland 18). For Jack Halberstam, writing on the Gothic novel, the monster offers an infinitely interpretable body, functioning as monster "when it is able to condense as many fear producing traits as possible into one body" (21). The production of fear is seen to emanate from "a vertiginous excess of meaning," where "multiple interpretations are embedded in the text and part of the experience of horror comes from the realization that meaning itself runs riot" (2).

Vegetarians and vegans frequently figure in modern Western culture as monstrous. In *Reading Veganism: The Monstrous Vegan, 1818 to Present* (2021), I trace the iteration of what I call "the monstrous vegan" as a literary trope that has recurred across the Anglophone literary canon over the past 200 years. A wide range of literary vegan monsters are also found across the present volume: from Jovian Parry's reading of the vegan Oankali in Octavia E. Butler's *Xenogenesis* trilogy (1987–1989) to Christopher Sebastian's diagnosis of the green-skinned Elphaba Thropp in Gregory Maguire's *Wicked* (1995) as a monstrous vegan figure. More recently, a plethora of news stories focusing on the death of children through neglect, depicting "veganism as a menacing danger inflicted by negligent, uninformed parents – primarily mothers – on their children" (Wright 92), and the vegetarian and vegan vampires popularized in Stephanie Meyer's *Twilight* saga and the American television series *True Blood*,[2] are exemplary of the ways in which the vegan haunts contemporary culture as a threatening and anxiety-inducing presence.

In the case of media portrayals of the filicidal vegan mother, the extension of ethical concern to nonhuman animals is made monstrous through the presumed prioritization of animal suffering over, and at the expense of, human suffering.[3] In other denigratory discourses, veganism is figured as monstrous for its challenge to heteronormative gender roles, disruptive of what Adams defines as the sexual politics of meat, through which "meat is a symbol of male dominance" (56). Veganism is also frequently made monstrous through its association with hypocrisy, inconsistency, and a misguided desire for purity. The ecocritic Harold Fromm, for instance, critiques the futility of veganism's ethical aspirations: "The real 'crime' is existence, not being or using animals." In addition, vegetarianism and veganism are entangled with fascistic and eugenicist purity discourses in the history of Nazi Germany. Adolf Hitler is a figure who demonstrates vividly that a vegan diet or ethics does not render one innocent of brutality and cruelty, and the historical detail of his vegetarianism is often used as a rebuke to delegitimize the work of animal rights activists or vegetarian proselytizers. Nazi vegetarianism was premised on the argument that "The human race . . . had become contaminated and impure through a mixing of the races and the eating of animal flesh" (Arluke and Sax 12–13). For James Stanescu the representation of vegetarian vampires is intimately connected to the monstrosity associated with the Nazi's promotion of vegetarianism as an ideal Aryan diet, with both desiring to be "innocent and pure" (42).

From a vegan studies perspective, veganism is often understood to be monstrous to omnivorous eaters due to the attention drawn, by a disruptive vegan dinner guest, to the instability of the lines drawn between the edible and inedible, or killable and non-killable. For Richard Twine, drawing on Sara Ahmed's concept of the "feminist killjoy," the *vegan* killjoy exposes a normative order of happiness as anthropocentric and "[i]n willfully speaking up . . . may engender anxiety, discomfort, guilt, and risks exclusion for doing so" (625). If, in Marie Mulvey-Roberts's terms, monstrosity "functions as a looking-glass, permitting us to see our own inner monster and revealing the extent to which monsters are us" (9), vegans are monstrous because they force an uncomfortable and unwelcome reflection on the instability of carnivorous appetites.

However, for the poststructuralist philosopher Jacques Derrida, the ascription of a vegetarian or vegan identity does not resolve such discomforting ambiguities. For Derrida, vegetarian identities, and, by extension, vegan identities, negate the possibility of ethical response. Derrida argues that the incalculable is central to ethics: "there is no responsibility, no ethico-political decision, that must not pass through the proofs of the incalculable or the undecideable. Otherwise everything would be reducible to calculation" ("Eating Well" 273). Vegetarianism is associated with "A limited, measured, calculable, rationally distributed responsibility." As in Fromm's critique, veganism is criticized by Derrida for granting only an illusion of "good conscience" (286).

Derrida's emphasis on the incalculable as the source of true ethical response can be read as an embrace of monstrous excesses of meaning and is mirrored in Nabokov's own reflections on literature, arguing that the reader must remain open to the ambiguity of texts. Nabokov expressed disdain for writers aiming for direct moral messages, with the resultant books deemed "topical trash" ("On a Book" 75). To write moral texts, for Nabokov, is to negate the value of art as an effect of style and the experience of "aesthetic bliss," defined as "a sense of being somehow, somewhere, connected with other states of being where art (curiosity, tenderness, kindness, ecstasy) is the norm" (75). By contrast, vegan reading practices, drawing on the influential work of Adams, have tended to prioritize the literal over the inexplicable, enacted through the recovery of the absent referent animal from its dismemberment through metaphor. Ethical veganism's concern with the lived reality of nonhuman animals, and the amelioration of their suffering, often therefore stands in opposition to literary abstraction.

This opposition embodies the seemingly irreconcilable tension between activism and academic study that has, in part, motivated the formation of Critical Animal Studies (CAS): a discipline that seeks to move away from the "inherent tensions, contradictions and conflicts" (Pederson and Stanescu 262) associated with conventional Animal Studies criticism. However, in its satire of acts of definitive literary interpretation, *Pale Fire* makes clear that the negation of "inherent tensions, contradictions and conflicts" is a problematic mission statement in a literary context. Mary Shelley's famous description of *Frankenstein* (1818; a book that, as Adams first noted, contains its own foundational monstrous vegan figure) as her "hideous progeny" is only one of innumerable occasions throughout literary history in which the novel form is equated with the monstrous. Kinbote himself fears his notes taking on "the monstrous semblance of a novel" (Nabokov, *Pale* 73). As vegan literary studies emerges as an academic discipline we are therefore required to ask how (if at all) we are to remain open to the myriad possibilities of texts and their monstrous mutations of meaning if we are seeking, in advance, to either remember the nonhuman animal – the literal behind the symbolic – or extract a distinct and pre-ordained vegan message or ethics. How, in other words, do we reconcile the desire to be a "good" literary scholar with the desire to be a "good" vegan?

This essay argues that reading *Pale Fire* through a vegan lens need not require a turn away from the monstrous. *Pale Fire* has been considered by critics both as an experimentation with language, rife with tensions and contradictions, and a deeply moral text. Morality, however, is not to be found on the surface of the work but precisely at sites of ambiguity. Vegan reading practices are seen to benefit from Shade's injunction in his "Pale Fire" poem to read not for text "but texture" (53). As I will show, vegan reading practices must turn away from CAS's pragmatic emphasis on consistency and resolution, and embrace instead the monstrous.

Nabokov's *Pale Fire*

Pale Fire takes an experimental form that mimics a scholarly edition of poetry, featuring a foreword, poem, line-by-line commentary, and index. The foreword introduces the first-person narration of Kinbote, a literary scholar living in self-imposed exile following the death of the fictional American poet John Shade. Kinbote is in possession of, and editing for publication, Shade's last written work. What follows is "a poem in heroic couplets, of nine hundred ninety-nine lines, divided into four cantos" (11) said to have been authored by Shade in the months preceding his death. Shade's poem is an autobiographical reflection on death and the afterlife and offers commentary on his near-death experience following a heart attack; the suicide of his daughter Hazel; and his relationship with his beloved wife Sybil. The real meat of *Pale Fire*, however, is in what follows Shade's poem: Kinbote's expansive commentary. Proposing itself as a serious scholarly exercise to provide the poem with a sense of "human reality" (23), Kinbote's notes degenerate into a narcissistic rendering of his experience as the last King of Zembla. Disappointed that the poem makes no explicit mention of the Zemblan narrative he had recounted to the poet before his death, Kinbote uses his notes to insist on his centrality to the work: presenting to the reader "all the many subliminal debts to me" (233).

Disguised as an émigré professor of English literature in the American town of New Wye, Kinbote's notes to Shade's poem trace alignments between the days in which Shade was composing his poem and the journey of the Zemblan assassin Gradus as he seeks out Kinbote. On arrival at Kinbote's rented home, Gradus's poor aim results in Shade becoming the accidental victim of his bullets. However, Kinbote also alludes to the official, and ostensibly more convincing, narrative of Shade's death. In this version, Gradus is in fact John Gray, an escapee from an asylum for the criminally insane who mistakes Shade for the judge who sentenced him. In the final note of his commentary, we find what appears to be Kinbote's confession: that he is simply "an old, happy, healthy, heterosexual Russian, a writer in exile," the alter ego of a Professor Botkin, a "lunatic who imagines himself to be [an imaginary king]" (235).

Kinbote's true identity nonetheless remains an enigma in the novel and debate rages among Nabokov scholars as to the true diegetic author of both the poem and its notes. The irresistible hint provided in Shade's poem – "*Man's life as commentary to abstruse / Unfinished poem.* Note for further use" (58) – has led many scholars to suggest that Kinbote is the fictional creation of Shade. Similarly, the autobiographical links with Nabokov's own life, including his own father's death as the unintended victim of an assassin's bullet, and his employment as a Russian émigré writer teaching literature at a US institution, make it difficult to neatly separate Kinbote's narrative from the constructive forces of the non-diegetic author. In such readings Kinbote is, like Frankenstein's monster, a being created by, and at the mercy of, male creative forces beyond his control. In "Kinbotean" readings, by contrast, Shade and his poem are the fictional creation of Kinbote, whose engaging commentary evidences his superior artistic gifts.

Kinbote is described by Shade's wife Sybil as "the monstrous parasite of a genius" (138). In addition, Douglas Fowler notes Kinbote's monstrosity in relation to his homosexuality, which is "always an aspect of sterility and monstrosity in Nabokov's world" (114). Kinbote's homosexuality is inextricably tied, in the homophobic undercurrent of the novel, with his desire for young boys and relationships with male students; obsessive stalking of Shade; and deep-seated misogyny as, for instance, when he dismisses Shade's emotional account of his daughter's death as "too labored and long" (Nabokov, *Pale* 157). For Steven Kellman, Kinbote's homosexuality is also tied to his vegetarianism, as just "one of his aberrations" (538). However, rather than simply a convenient device to signal his deviance, I argue that Kinbote's vegetarianism contributes in important ways to the narrative's concern with the ethical implications of reading, writing, and eating.

Eating Monstrously

In his essay "On the Eating of Flesh," the Ancient Greek philosopher Plutarch provides a now famous reproach against meat-eating:

> Can you really ask what reason Pythagoras had for abstaining from flesh? For my part I rather wonder both by what accident and in what state of soul or mind the first man who did so, touched his mouth to gore and brought his lips to the flesh of

a dead creature, he who set forth tables of dead, stale bodies and ventured to call food and nourishment the parts that had a little before bellowed and cried, moved and lived. How could his eyes endure the slaughter when throats were slit and hides flayed and limbs torn from limb? How could his nose endure the stench? How was it that the pollution did not turn away his taste, which made contact with the sores of others and sucked juices and serums from mortal wounds? (541)

Plutarch condemns the monstrous predilections of humankind, positioning meat-eating as an originary corruption that condones and supports needless violence. Plutarch's evocative depiction of meat-eating as a process of barbaric slaughter, and disgust-inducing consumption of sores and serums, renders it a monstrous and abject activity.

Kinbote's articulation of his vegetarianism offers a comic extension of Plutarch's disgust at the sores and serums of meat, with the logical endpoint of the Plutarchan argument presented as a disgust at the contaminating potential of *all* bodies. A symptom of what Gerard de Vries notes as Nabokov's disdain at the irrationality of mankind, it is Kinbote the "strict vegetarian" (Nabokov, *Pale* 17) who is presented as a monstrous eater. Recalling an occasion where Shade had suggested that he "try the pork" during a faculty lunch, for instance, Kinbote describes lecturing to his new colleagues that:

Consuming something that had been handled by a fellow creature was, I explained to the rubicund convives, as repulsive to me as eating any creature, and that would include – lowering my voice – the pulpous pony-tailed girl student who served us and licked her pencil. (17)

The comedy of Kinbote's disruptive misanthropic presence is reinforced here through his overt misreading of the outcome of this response as having "set everybody at ease" thanks to his "free and simple demeanor" (17).

In his reference to the unnamed "girl student," Kinbote invokes a discourse of monstrous femininity. The adjective "pulpous" renders her as pulp, that which the *OED* defines as "a soft, moist, formless substance or mass of material," associated with organic matter. Shade's daughter Hazel is also a pulpous figure in the novel, described as a "blurry shape" in Shade's verse before disappearing "[i]nto a crackling, gulping swamp" (Nabokov, *Pale* 43). Barbara Creed defines the "monstrous-feminine" as a figure who "draws attention to the 'frailty of the symbolic order' through her evocation of the natural, animal order and its terrifying associations with the passage all human beings must take from birth through life to death" (83). For Creed, woman is monstrous for the attention she draws to the instability of the subject's construction in the symbolic realm of language, undermining our understanding of ourselves as "whole and proper" (13). Kinbote's misogyny is, through his telling adjective, associated with his fears about the permeability of the organic body and its terrifying similarity to meat; mere pulpy flesh.

There is also an irresistible link to be drawn between "pulpous" and the pulp of pulp literature: that which is lurid, popular, or poor in quality. Pulp fiction is associated, in Halberstam's work, with the monstrous female body. In relation to *Frankenstein*, Halberstam writes that

The aborted female monster can be read as the ugly popular fiction . . . that is always debased in relation to some notion of high culture. She is the body of work that is always "half-finished," that inspires violence, and that literally is reduced to pulp. (31–32)

The female monster is, for Halberstam, the "fleshy center" that haunts the otherwise machinic and technological structure of *Frankenstein*, a pulp narrative that "is formless and endlessly repeatable" (52). As a result, "while the [male monster] becomes part of his author's identity, [the female monster] threatens her maker with his own dissolution" (50).

A similar dynamic is found at play in *Pale Fire*. In contrast to the female as formless pulp, Shade is associated with the "high" literary form of poetry. This high status, in contrast to the pulp, grants him solidity within the socio-symbolic. The pulpous is also starkly contrasted to the verbosity of Kinbote's use of language that is anything but "free and simple" (Nabokov, *Pale* 17). Marianna Torgovnick argues that while Kinbote sees himself, like Shade's daughter Hazel, as a "nomenclatorial agitator" and while his linguistic play offers a poststructuralist embrace of the infinite regress of language, his analytical methods insist on parallels that "resembles structuralism's passion for order" (33). Kinbote's reading practices are driven by a desire to assert a sense of overarching design and order that will immortalize him as part of Shade's verse, in contrast to Hazel's association with a "jumble of broken words and meaningless syllables" (Nabokov, *Pale* 151).

The distinction between the formlessness of the corporeal body and the security that Kinbote associates with poetic language is supported by the ironic juxtaposition between Kinbote's disgust at eating anything "handled by a fellow creature" and his enthusiastic *handling* of Shade's manuscript. The focus, throughout the novel, on the materiality of Shade's poem – written on "eighty medium-sized index cards," "held by a rubber band," and enclosed in a "manila envelope" (11–13) – considers poetry in relation to its physicality and original copy. The formlessness of the female figure, of pulp narratives that proliferate meanings in endlessly reproducible versions, is figured, by contrast, as an object of abjection for Kinbote. His desire to establish the *original* of Shade's poem, to cement the moment of generation of the words – ascribing precise dates, for instance, to each index card – bespeaks a desire to cement and secure the symbolic realm as a fixed and secure entity. However, the irony that Kinbote rules out twelve additional cards as only "first drafts" (13), acknowledges that several cards had been "recopied" (11), and admits, in one instance, to having fabricated their contents (180), demonstrates the slippery nature of language.

Of note for the purposes of this chapter are the ways in which insecurities about language and the body are explicitly tethered to the novel's satirical treatment of vegetarianism. In his refusal to consume anything "handled by another creature," Kinbote's vegetarianism is presented as an impossibly restrictive moral code. The conflation of the vegetarian and the literary critic is grounded in a shared desire to eliminate ambiguity and make abject the pulp form of the corporeal body. The characterization of Kinbote therefore satirizes the Plutarchan response to meat-eating as leading ultimately to a desire to absent oneself from physical reality altogether.

Writing Monstrously

There is a fascistic tinge to Kinbote's desire to avoid the contamination of other bodies, and vegetarianism is associated implicitly with the monstrosity of the Nazi party in

Pale Fire, with allusions to recent German history to be found throughout the novel. Kinbote's note to lines 433–434 begins "In 1933" and refers to Shade's wife Sybil as "dear S. S." (163), an implicit reference to the paramilitary group that accompanied the Nazis' rise to power in the same year. In his note to line 470, Kinbote notes Shade's hatred of racial prejudice in specific relation to Jewish identity (172). Kinbote also describes, in his foreword, that in a "skit performed by a group of drama students" at the university, he was depicted "as a pompous woman hater with a German accent, constantly quoting Housman and nibbling raw carrots" (20). That the presumed Russian exile in America, Botkin, is presented with a German accent tarnishes him with the stain of recent political history. This Germanic tinge and satiric portrayal of carrot-nibbling vegetarianism tethers him to Hitler's own vegetarianism, which played a significant function in Nazi propaganda (see Arluke and Sax).

Kinbote's discussion of the origins of his vegetarianism also explicitly raises the specter of political despotism, with his vegetarianism originating from reading the story of "an Italian despot" who was "tied, naked and howling, to a plank in the public square and killed piecemeal by the people who cut slices out, and [ate] them" (Nabokov, *Pale* 125). Kinbote's rejection of meat is here linked to the abject sight of the disintegration of the human form and cannibalistic fears of what it means to become an object of consumption. For Ann Anlin Cheng, "the specter of cannibalism always haunt[s] the omnivore" (73), and there is a transgressive delight in overcoming such anxieties, becoming the eater rather than the eaten. For Cheng, to engage in flesh-eating is to acknowledge the fragility of human exceptionalism and our own status as edible produce. In Kinbote's case, his refusal of meat comes to embody a fascistic failure to acknowledge and sympathize with the vulnerability of other bodies. Kinbote is, as Richard Rorty notes, a "particular sort of genius-monster – the monster of incuriosity" (161). As Brian Boyd argues,

> Kinbote thinks himself devoted to Shade and Shade's poem ... yet he cannot make the effort to understand the particulars of Shade's imaginative world (words, things, customs, allusions, intentions), so that his performance as editor becomes an exact image of all moral myopia, all failure to make the effort to respect the sheer difference of another individual. (180)

This distancing of himself from the vulnerability of the biological body is also evident in Kinbote's reiteration of the misanthropic retreat of Timon of Athens which aligns his vegetarianism not with the embodied response envisioned by Plutarch – a disgust response in the face of serums and sores – but with a discursive rehearsal of a prior textual referent. Kinbote's comparison of himself to "Timon in his cave" (68) – a reference to Shakespeare's *Timon of Athens*, a quote from which *Pale Fire* draws its name – positions him as a textual assemblage. Banishing himself to a cave, Shakespeare's Timon declares his hatred for, and spurns all contact with, humankind. Not only a textual referent for Kinbote's misanthropy, Timon also provides a literary antecedent through which to inscribe his vegetarianism. Shakespeare's Timon sustains himself in his exile on a vegetarian diet of roots. Marta Pellerdi stresses the "obvious" quality of Timon and Kinbote's parallelism, since "Kinbote is a vegetarian, like Timon, living in the woods and equally lonely in his voluntary exile" (110). The connections to *Timon* evoke also the anxiety of authorship explored in the novel, since scholars have suggested that "Shakespeare began to write an earlier play, that the manuscripts of both versions were somehow preserved together, and that a 'redactor', the real villain of the piece, conflated them and added further confusions of his own" (Maxwell ix–x). In this description we find an uncanny mirror to the villainous redactions of Kinbote in his conflation of his and Shade's writing.

As with his disgust at the treatment of the Italian despot, Kinbote's monstrous vegan identity, via Timon, is a Plutarchan disgust response that has been mediated through acts of reading. This mediation creates a discursive distance between Kinbote and the nonhuman animals his vegetarianism ostensibly serves. For Derrida, we must resist the homogenizing tendency of language – as with "animal" which lumps together innumerable species, from insects to cows – and encounter the singular animal being in all its irreducible otherness (*Animal*). Vegetarianism is for Derrida, as noted above, an opting out of the incalculable response and responsibility required in the face of suffering. Similarly, for Donna Haraway, as noted in the introduction to this volume, the complexity of our daily interactions with nonhuman others is irreducible to any preformed code or ethics. For Haraway, there is a need, as humans, to recognize and embrace the multispecies entanglements constituting our lives with animals. Veganism is positioned by Haraway as antithetical to the project of exploring and cultivating various networks of multispecies co-flourishing: a moral absolute that "would consign most domestic animals to the status of curated heritage collections or to just plain extermination as kinds and as individuals" (80). Veganism is, for both Derrida and Haraway, an act of linguistic violence, in its predetermined ethical response, that fails to recognize our embodied entanglement with nonhuman others. Similarly, as a poorly translated textual referent (with *Timon of Athens* carried on his person in Zemblan translation throughout Kinbote's account), Kinbote's vegetarianism functions to distance himself from the pulpy formlessness of the corporeal body and can be read, in Haraway's terms, as a failure to acknowledge his entanglement and co-constitution with other bodies.

Reading Monstrously

In his extensive nine-page note to lines 47–48 Kinbote's claim that "I have no desire to twist and batter an unambiguous *apparatus criticus* into the monstrous semblance of a novel" (73) stands in ironic contrast to the resultant novel that far surpasses the bounds of Shade's original poem. In contrast to the supposedly "unambiguous" realm of literary criticism, Kinbote's commentary becomes the monstrous novel *Pale Fire*, parodying attempts at scholarly objectivity.

However, Kinbote's commentary is often considered a work of art in its own right. As Torgovnick notes, "Kinbote manages to vindicate his claims to creative being . . . The tale of Zembla and Charles's development and flight have a wild vitality and a narrative appeal that justify Kinbote's eventual claim for his own story versus Shade's" (28). The re-reader of *Pale Fire* finds that what first appears on the surface as a willful misreading of Shade's poem on Kinbote's part is comprised of an intricate web of shadows and illusions, and of interplay between poem and criticism. With each re-reading, it therefore becomes less and less clear that we *are* meant to read Kinbote's narrative as pure farce, encouraging instead an embrace of the immaterial shadows to be found in his writing.

Nabokov's novel is itself not a static entity, but comes to be constituted by the reader and their willingness to engage actively with the text. The need to flip back and forth throughout *Pale Fire*, to participate in the jigsaw puzzle to assemble events, to follow and then retrace Nabokov's many red-herrings, is to resist the imposition of any authoritative meaning, insisting instead on the readerly role in creating and experiencing events. The novel's form therefore refuses to grant Kinbote the authorial control he seeks, as each reader encounters anew the radical ambiguity and unreliability of his text. Rather than a preordained design, we are encouraged, in Shade's terms, to read for "the contrapuntal theme; Just this: not text, but texture; not the dream / But topsy-turvical coincidence, / Not flimsy nonsense, but a web of sense" (Nabokov, *Pale* 53). These lines encourage a focus on the moral beauty in the texture of texts, resistant to attempts to capture a singular or definitive meaning.

The recurrence of dogs in the pages of *Pale Fire* provides an apt demonstration of what reading for texture might look like in practice. In his autobiography, *Speak, Memory*, the repeated appearance of dogs (30, 31, 48, 101, 102, 150, 152, 158) is tethered to Nabokov's claim that "The following of such thematic designs through one's life should be, I think, the true purpose of autobiography" (27). In Ole Nyegaard's analysis of dogs in Nabokov's earlier *Lolita*, "The dog is only one element within the fabric that makes up the universe of the novel – as the paranoid Humbert correctly surmises, someone outside the scope of his understanding, a synchronizing phantom, has combined these elements" (140). Nyegaard continues that the dog "is not employed as a motif because of any traditional symbolism pertaining to dogs ... The symbolism of the dog is effectuated through patterning: the dog becomes a symbolic presence inside the text through accumulation of meaning" (143). Here the dog lacks symbolic weight or literality, instead part of a patterning and accretion of meaning that exists within the textual world of the novel. Nyegaard refuses therefore to implement a definitive reading of the role of dogs in *Lolita* since "what we are offered in [Nabokov's] aesthetics and his fiction is not a final truth, but the reading process in itself as an ideal" (153). Similarly, in *Pale Fire*, from the "happy sheep-dog" (116) that appears during Kinbote's escape from Zembla, to the "fat little white dog" (221) that Gradus carefully steps over, and the sound of a "boxer dog who most of the neighbors disliked" (225), canines linger in the background of the narrative. Without a clear or definitive purpose, these dogs are coincidental traces. They can draw attention to Kinbote's and Nabokov's respective authorial control as much as they advance a specific form of attentiveness to animal presences: a refusal of overt symbolism that allows them to make meaning through attention to their accumulation. This is not a recovery of the absent referent animal behind the metaphor (à la Adams) but a reveling in the agency of the representational qualities of language itself.

What we find at the heart of *Pale Fire* is a directive to discern meaning through the coincidence and texture of language, a meaning that is felt only through participatory and attentive readerly engagement. Kinbote advances a mode of reading and interpreting that is monstrous in its narcissistic acts of projection and disembodiment. And yet, his monstrous projections congeal as a web of sense, an unexpected revelation of interconnection and entanglement in the world. It is this, I argue in the final section of this essay, that is perhaps the most helpful way of conceiving of and enacting vegan literary criticism.

Monstrous Vegan Literary Studies

While vegan studies has, to date, had relatively little influence within literary studies, or the humanities more broadly, it has attracted infamy in the British and North American press. In 2021, for instance, *The Sun* newspaper lambasted the work of two animal rights philosophers as "PC Poppycock" (Crowson); an article in *The Critic* warned that the label "vegan studies" would bring ridicule to historical monuments (Starkey); and *The Routledge Handbook of Vegan Studies* was reviewed by *Campus Reform* (Richardson), a national conservative student-run online paper that "exposes liberal bias" across US universities.

Within the academy there is also a move against the work of so-called "critical" projects. One high-profile hoax that came to light in 2018, orchestrated by tenured professors working at US institutions, critiqued such work as overly totalizing in its commitments and expressive of a form of naive dogmatism that fails to do justice to the complexity of entanglements and the need for ethical relationality. As noted in the introduction to this essay, treating veganism as an identity category, rather than dietary preference, is often perceived as a monstrous offshoot of the "identitarian madness" associated with so-called "grievance studies" (Lindsay et al.). Furthermore, Traci Warkentin critiques an all-or-nothing approach to veganism among Animal Studies scholars, promoted wholesale in a way that ignores long-standing ecofeminist work that has drawn attention to "its dislocated, universal application and potential for a Western ethnocentric and androcentric bias" (501).

In *Pale Fire*, vegetarianism is equated with an aspiration to live as pure text, aligned with Fromm's polemical critique of veganism as "an open-ended but futile metaphysic of virtue and self-blamelessness that pretends to escape from the conditions of life itself." What we might now call vegan reading practices are aligned in Nabokov's novel with the willful imposition of authorial biography on the text in an attempt to control the errancy of both the corporeal body and language. However, to argue that vegan criticism is a totalizing gesture that excludes complexity and responsivity is to simplify what it means to live a vegan life. Counter to the moral policing or purity discourses associated with veganism by critics such as Fromm, the practical impossibility of living a fully vegan life means that veganism requires continual negotiation and decision-making. In Gary Steiner's terms, veganism is not the aspiration of the "beautiful soul" but "a gnawing horror born of a recognition of what is being done to billions of animals *right now* and of the seeming futility of one's decision" (63). Veganism is, I argue, resistant to purity discourses, with monstrous vegan figures embodying the insufficiency, failure, and horror that frequently attend the experience of living a vegan life. Such monsters offer a way of thinking through the complex coming together of utopianism and insufficiency that inhere in vegan modes of being in the world.

In Matthew Cole and Kate Stewart's delimitation of "a hypothetical 'ideal' vegan" form of media (320), required to counteract what they see as veganism's widespread misrepresentation, Kinbote would require exorcising as a monstrous aberration of the ideal vegan type. However, I argue that Kinbote's monstrosity performs the difficulty of vegan identity in ways that are of crucial importance for vegan theoretical discourse. Firstly, Kinbote is presented as a textual assemblage, constructing himself through Shade's poem and articulating his vegetarianism through Shakespeare's *Timon of Athens*. In his desire to absent himself from physical entanglement with others, he becomes pure text. This is of particular interest for vegans: offering a purely textual form of the self that is distinct from bodily states of disgust or pleasure. Indeed, veganism *is* often an awkward fit on the corporeal body, creating a monstrous sense of self that is composed of a hybrid form of prior discursive referents that do not always match up neatly with individual alimentary or aesthetic pleasures. As Wright notes, veganism is "a delicate mixture of something both primal *and* social" (7, my emphasis).

Secondly, *Pale Fire* acknowledges a sense of complicity in violent and oppressive systems. *Pale Fire* engages with Nabokov's broader concern with the moral value of literature in the wake of the Holocaust, "questioning whether goodness of any kind, even artistic, is possible any more" (Brodsky 55). In related ways, vegan literary studies requires recognition of our complicity in violence against nonhuman animals and of the limitations of language as a medium through which to extend our sympathy and concern. Literature offers us only a limited and detached medium through which to consider the animal, one that inevitably privileges the vegan subject of language. Kinbote, in Rorty's terms, teaches readers how to "become less cruel" by drawing attention to the "blindness of a certain kind of person to the pain of another kind of person" (141). However, in order to recognize this lesson we must first acknowledge our implication in the same processes as Kinbote: monstrous readers projecting egoistic desires onto texts. We are not allowed to adopt a position of innocence or absolution as we, like Kinbote, physically handle *Pale Fire* the novel and search for meaning through our rampant consumption of the lives it contains.

Thirdly, Kinbote's narration is undeniably humorous. Akin to what I have elsewhere defined as "vegan camp," the humor associated with Kinbote's pedantic vegetarianism might offer itself to some vegan readers as a way of laughing back against the evident anxiety that veganism triggers in Nabokov as a writer. Such laughter has the ability to force an acknowledgment of vegan complicity in monstrous systems, a failure to be horrified by Kinbote's moral myopia, while simultaneously satirizing anthropocentric culture and enacting an "aspirational gesture that looks to a future in which ... exploitation will no longer have the power to wound" (Quinn, "Notes" 928).

The monstrous vegan thus shows us that vegan literary studies need not be about discerning and defining the "correct" representation of veganism. Nor need vegan literary studies be about constructing a canon of vegan texts that fulfil certain pre-established criteria. There is no correct or definitive vegan representation, nor a definable sense of what makes for a vegan novel, poem, or short story. Rather than seek to reconcile the myriad contradictions and inadequacies of monstrous vegan figures, I argue that we might pose as madwomen, to use Waugh's terms, and embrace the monstrous as a form that rehearses the key paradoxes involved in living a vegan life.

Conclusion

Veganism comes to attach itself to the figure of the monster because something about veganism itself *is* monstrous. Veganism disrupts existing boundary divisions between the human and nonhuman, by drawing the animal into the sphere of kinship and concern. It refuses to cohere into a fixed moral code, striving for a utopian end to animal suffering while, in its delimitation by that which is "possible and practicable" (Vegan Society), it dwells with darker questions of complicity and failure. As such, counter to Kinbote's ostensible desire to impose meaning, and to live in a world of impossible linguistic purity, vegan literary studies must embrace the monstrous as a mode of thinking. To live as a vegan monster is to exist in a state of complicity with violence, and to represent the radical disjuncture and often irreconcilability of the body, and its desires, with the subject, as it is articulated through language.

Vegan literary studies is not a niche canon of explicitly vegan texts. While it often involves the study of texts that explicitly engage with veganism, it also encompasses texts ostensibly unrelated to veganism: texts that offer new ways of thinking about the self, the nonhuman animal, and the relations between the two. As noted in the introduction to this volume, Evan Maina Mwangi's sense of the "vegan unconscious" provides a helpful rationale for reading with and for veganism in texts where it is not explicitly articulated. Mwangi is utopian in his definition of the vegan unconscious as an "affirmative expression of potential . . . a latent possibility that the societies portrayed in the text will embrace a future where animals will not be killed to satisfy human needs" (9). Looking for the "vegan unconscious" of ostensibly un-vegan texts risks willful misreadings of texts that mimic Kinbotean acts of narcissistic application of the critic's biography onto the text. However, in seeking the vegan potentialities of literary texts, we might also come closer to the texture of the text sought by Shade. Reading for the "contrapuntal theme" offers not the complete utopian vision of a cruelty-free novel but a web of connections and textures to be found as we look towards such a future.

Pale Fire makes clear that reading is a risky business. For Nabokov, there are certain modes of reading, metaphorically aligned with vegetarianism, that foreclose the possibility of curiosity about others and enact a retreat to the solely linguistic. There are others though that, through an openness to coincidence and connection, reveal the moral value of art. Even the latter is compromised, however. For Robert Merrill, "the paradox at the heart of *Pale Fire*" is that "art is the most precious human product, yet art makes nothing happen. Let us fight the utter degradation, ridicule, and horror of death, but let us not suppose that this fight will be 'won' in the sense that Shade and Kinbote suggest" (461–62). The experience of living a vegan life, and of seeking vegan meaning in literary texts, enacts a monstrous refusal to have a clear or overt vegan meaning cohere into definitive moral sense while not abandoning the hope that it might.

Reading for the vegan unconscious of texts, in the monstrous Kinbotean model, offers therefore an apt parallel to the experience of living a vegan life. It is a willful attempt to insist on possibilities that don't yet exist, or that might never exist. It is a desire to find solace in the promise of non-violence even if the articulation of such desires is often flawed, incomplete, or insufficient to the scale of violence being confronted. It requires therefore a careful mixture of the "curiosity, tenderness, kindness, ecstasy" ("On a Book" 75) that Nabokov associates with the aesthetic bliss of true art, attending to the nonhuman while embracing the unpredictability and inexplicability of the text.

In this essay I have enacted my own willful Kinbotean reading of *Pale Fire* to insist on its utility for vegan studies and the need for vegan reading practices that embrace a monstrous errancy of meaning. My reading of Nabokov extends only limited concern to nonhuman animals, thinking instead about the way in which veganism addresses anxieties about the self and other, the reader and the text. This speaks to the multitude of possibilities for vegan studies. Future vegan literary scholarship need not look for fixed meaning and concrete moral messages but the vegan potentialities of a text, seeking, in Shade's words, "not text, but texture; not the dream / But topsy-turvical coincidence, / Not flimsy nonsense, but a web of sense" (Nabokov, *Pale* 53).

Notes

1. See, for example, Crowson, Richardson, and Starkey, outlined in more detail below.
2. For more on vegan vampires see Stanescu and Wright. Ali Ryland's essay in this volume provides further examples of the vegan vampire trope as found in Young Adult fiction.
3. This is also a critique leveled at veganism from the perspective of critical race studies. As Ruth Ramsden-Karelse's contribution to this volume notes, "vegan activism has tended to form a single-issue movement that further entrenches white supremacy by prioritizing ending the oppression of animals over ending the oppression of people" (p. 109).

Works Cited

Adams, Carol J. *The Sexual Politics of Meat: A Feminist-Vegetarian Critical Theory*. Twenty-fifth anniversary edition, Bloomsbury Academic, 2015.

Arluke, Arnold, and Boria Sax. "Understanding Nazi Animal Protection and the Holocaust." *Anthrozoos*, vol. 5, no. 1, 1992, pp. 6–114.

Bohlmann, Markus, and Sean Moreland. *Monstrous Children and Childish Monsters: Essays on Cinema's Holy Terrors*. McFarland & Company, 2015.

Boyd, Brian. "Shape and Shade in *Pale Fire*." *Nabokov Studies*, vol. 4, no. 1, 1997, pp. 173–224.

Brodsky, Anna. "Nabokov's *Lolita* and the Postwar Emigre Consciousness." *Realisms of Exile: Nomadism, Diasporas, and Eastern European Voices*, edited by Domnica Radulescu, Lexington Books, 2002, pp. 49–66.

Cheng, Ann Anlin. "Sushi, Otters, Mermaids: Race at the Intersection of Food and Animal; or, David Wong Louie's Sushi Principle." *Resilience: A Journal of the Environmental Humanities*, vol. 2, no. 1, 2014, pp. 66–95.

Cole, Matthew, and Kate Stewart. "(Mis)representing Veganism in Film and Television." *The Routledge Handbook of Vegan Studies*, edited by Laura Wright, Routledge, 2021, pp. 319–32.

Creed, Barbara. *The Monstrous-Feminine: Film, Feminism, Psychoanalysis*. Routledge, 1993.

Crowson, Isaac. "Dr Doolally. 'Woke' University Doctors Call for New Laws to Protect Animals from HATE SPEECH." *The Sun*, 17 June 2021.

Derrida, Jacques. *The Animal That Therefore I Am*. Fordham UP, 2008.

— '"Eating Well," or the Calculation of the Subject: An Interview with Jacques Derrida.' *Points . . .: Interviews, 1974–1994*, edited by Elisabeth Weber, translated by Peggy Kamuf, Stanford UP, 1995, pp. 255–87.

Fowler, Douglas. *Reading Nabokov*. Cornell UP, 1972.

Fromm, Harold. "Vegans and the Quest for Purity." *The Chronicle of Higher Education*, 4 July 2010.

Halberstam, Jack. *Skin Shows: Gothic Horror and the Technology of Monsters*. Duke UP, 1995.

Haraway, Donna. *When Species Meet*. U of Minnesota P, 2008.

Kellman, Steven. "'The only fit food for a man is half a lemon': Kafka's Plea and Other Alimentary Aberrations." *Southwest Review*, vol. 95, no. 4, pp. 532–45.

Lindsay, James A., Peter Boghossian, and Helen Pluckrose. "Academic Grievance Studies and the Corruption of Scholarship." *Areo Magazine*, 2 October 2018.

Maxwell, J. C. "Introduction." *The Life of Timon of Athens*. Cambridge UP, 1968, pp. ix–xlii.

McCarthy, Mary. "Bolt from the Blue." *The New Republic*, 4 June 1962.

Mulvey-Roberts, Marie. *Dangerous Bodies: Historicising the Gothic Corporeal*. Manchester UP, 2016.

Mwangi, Evan Maina. *The Postcolonial Animal: African Literature and Posthuman Ethics*. U of Michigan P, 2019.

Nabokov, Vladimir. *Lolita*. Penguin Classics, 2015.

—. "On a Book Entitled 'Lolita.'" *Encounter*, 1959, pp. 73–76.

—. *Pale Fire*. Penguin Classics, 2016.

—. *Speak, Memory: An Autobiography Revisited*. Vintage, 1989.

Oxford English Dictionary. "monster n., adv., and adj." *OED Online*, Oxford University Press, Sept 2021.

—. "pulp n." *OED Online*, Oxford University Press, Sept 2021.

Pederson, Helena, and Vasile Stanescu. "Conclusion: Future Directions for Critical Animal Studies." *The Rise of Critical Animal Studies*, edited by Nik Taylor and Richard Twine, Routledge, 2014, pp. 262–76.

Pellerdi, Marta. "The Role of Biography and Literary Allusions in Vladimir Nabokov's 'Pale Fire.'" *Hungarian Journal of English and American Studies*, vol. 2, no. 1, 1996, pp. 103–16.

Plutarch. "The Eating of Flesh." *The Animals Reader: The Essential Classic and Contemporary Writings*, edited by Linda Kalof and Amy Fitzgerald, Bloomsbury, 2007, pp. 154–57.

Richardson, Katelynn. "Professors Publish $250 Book on Vegan Studies, its Links to 'Queer Theory,' 'Anti-Racism,' and 'Ecofeminism.'" *Campus Reform*, 14 June 2021.

Rorty, Richard. *Contingency, Irony, and Solidarity*. Cambridge UP, 1989.

Quinn, Emelia. "Notes on Vegan Camp." *PMLA*, vol. 135, no. 5, 2020, pp. 914–30.

—. *Reading Veganism: The Monstrous Vegan, 1818 to Present*. Oxford UP, 2021.

Shakespeare, William. *The Life of Timon of Athens*. Cambridge UP, 1968.

Stanescu, James. "Toward a Dark Animal Studies: On Vegetarian Vampires, Beautiful Souls and Becoming-Vegan." *Journal for Critical Animal Studies*, vol. 10, no. 3, 2012, pp. 26–50.

Starkey, David. "See, the conqu'ring hero comes – to be ridiculed by vegans." *The Critic*, January/February 2021.

Steiner, Gary. *Animals and the Limits of Postmodernism*. Columbia UP, 2013.

Torgovnick, Marianna. "Nabokov and his Successors: 'Pale Fire' as a Fable for Critics in Seventies and Eighties." *Style*, vol. 20, no. 1, 1986, pp. 22–41.

Twine, Richard. "Vegan Killjoys at the Table – Contesting Happiness and Negotiating Relationships with Food Practices." *Societies*, vol. 4, 2014, pp. 623–39.

de Vries, Gerard. "'Perplex'd in the Extreme': Moral Facets of Vladimir Nabokov's Work." *Nabokov Studies*, vol. 2, 1995, pp. 135–52.

Warkentin, Traci. "Must Every Animal Studies Scholar be Vegan?" *Hypatia*, vol. 27, no. 3, 2012, pp. 499–504.

Waugh, Auberon. "Dread sisters of the veggie cause." *The Sunday Telegraph*, 13 May 1990.

Wolfe, Cary. *Animal Rites: American Culture, the Discourse of Species, and Posthumanist Theory*. U of Chicago P, 2003.

Wright, Laura. *The Vegan Studies Project: Food, Animals, and Gender in the Age of Terror*. U of Georgia P, 2015.

9

VEGANISM AND DISORDERED EATING

The "Planned Cow" and "No end to Meat":
Veganism and Disordered Eating

Laura Wright

Introduction

SINCE ITS TRANSLATION into English in 2015, South Korean novelist Han Kang's *The Vegetarian* has garnered considerable attention for its exploration of feminism, veganism, and disordered eating.[1] As Amy-Leigh Gray and Dana Medoro note in their contribution to this volume, "*The Vegetarian* at first represents veganism in terms of relinquishment and withdrawal. The act of giving up meat is quickly followed by Yeong-hye's desire to strip herself of appetite, relationships, clothing, and existence as a human woman. It seems conventional and straightforward" (187). They then go on to show how the novel is anything but. The novel, originally published as three novellas, tells the story of Yeong-hye who, as a result of a dream, stops eating meat.

The first part of the novel is narrated by Yeong-hye's unnamed husband; the second and third parts are narrated in the third person but focalized through her brother-in-law and her sister In-hye, respectively. Yeong-hye's dreams are the only part of the novel narrated in her voice. In her dream, she sees

> *across the frozen ravine, a red barn-like building. Straw matting flapping limp across the door . . . a long long bamboo stick strung with great blood-red gashes of meat, blood still dripping down. Try to push past the meat, there's no end to the meat, and no exit. Blood in my mouth, blood-soaked clothes sucked onto my skin.* (Kang 19–20, italics in original)

But no-one in Yeong-hye's life will allow her not to eat meat. Her husband says, "Before my wife turned vegetarian, I'd always thought of her as completely unremarkable in every way" (11), noting that her "passive personality . . . suited [him] down to the ground" (11); after she becomes vegan, he sexually assaults her. At a family dinner during which she refuses to eat meat, Yeong-hye's father hits her and attempts to force feed her pork while her husband and brother-in-law restrain her. Ultimately, Yeong-hye is hospitalized and force fed, but the narrative ends with her sister In-hye demanding that the force-feeding stop. The narrative ends before Yeong-hye's death, at a point after which she has declared to her sister that she is, in fact, becoming a tree. Such an ending places Kang's narrative and Yeong-hye's potentially transformative veganism in a space of limbo – a moment of In-hye's life beginning after she leaves her husband and child and Yeong-hye's life ending, with neither potential fully actualized in the text.

Margarita Carretero-González argues that *The Vegetarian* is not about redemption or transformation but, rather, about a woman with a disease who finds herself, at the end, on the verge of death and that "the beautiful prose almost runs the risk of romanticizing a mental illness, a dangerous tendency," particularly in narratives about anorexia (176). While I understand this argument and the frustration with Yeong-hye's seeming powerlessness, I have argued elsewhere "that it is [her family's and culture's] refusal to accept her ethical veganism, and not the veganism itself that causes what should have been a positive and healing dietary and lifestyle decision to become disordered to the point of her probable starvation" (Wright, "Dangerous"). At the end of the novel, Yeong-hye's resistance to meat and patriarchy ultimately empower her sister to leave her family and seek an independent life on her own. That said, Kang's novel illustrates a broader theme that is prevalent in literary works that link vegetarianism and veganism to starvation: the line between veganism and insanity for women is impossible to navigate.

By contrast, for men in literary works, veganism and starvation are most often linked to a striving for artistic understanding and for a greater common good – even as the modus operandi behind both is the same: an ethical resistance to an established order of hierarchical othering and cruelty. In this chapter, I want to examine this paradox by looking at the ways in which literary representations of vegetarianism – and veganism more specifically – often treat such lifestyle choices as a form of pathologically disordered eating for women and an ethical pursuit for men, even as literary renderings of veganism also function as social critique, desperate entreaties for alternative modes of recognition, rites of passage, and acts of resistance in societies that exert gendered, cultural, racial, and religious norms that function to oppress human and nonhuman animals. I begin with Franz Kafka's 1922 short story "A Hunger Artist" and its alignment of starvation with art and aesthetics in its treatment of the hunger artist's waning appeal during a shift in the aesthetic zeitgeist of the story's present moment. The artist's inability to find the food that he likes and his insistence that the meaning of his starvation is misunderstood by his audience serve as an indictment of the public's inability to comprehend the creative vision of the artist.

In the remainder of the essay I consider three further texts. South African author J. M. Coetzee's 1983 Booker Prize-winning novel *Life & Times of Michael K* in many ways builds upon Kafka's story of starvation and misunderstanding, but the narrative places the starving man, the auspiciously named Michael K, within a more fraught political context, a fictional South African civil war during which Michael's starvation is more clearly aligned with a desire to escape codification in a society in which apartheid demands strict adherence to racial and gender-based classification. Canadian author Margaret Atwood's 1969 novel *The Edible Woman* depicts veganism as the precursor to insanity for Marian, the novel's female protagonist, who stops eating animals at a moment when she realizes, in the context of her ensuing marriage, their subjectivity as aligned with her own. Zimbabwean novelist Tsitsi Dangarembga's 1988 *Nervous Conditions*, the first novel published in English by a Black Zimbabwean woman, tells the story of Tambu, a teenage Shona girl who witnesses the bulimia and subsequent nervous breakdown of her cousin Nyasha. Veganism is never explicit in the novel, but Nyasha's "nervous condition" is very much a reaction to her unsuccessful attempts to resist "the Englishness" of her education and her meat-heavy diet, which alienates her from a more traditionally plant-based Shona diet. In Kafka's and Coetzee's work, men's starvation is associated with passion, with art, and with the plight of being misunderstood and mistranslated. For the women of Atwood's and Dangarembga's novels, on the other hand, veganism is the first step towards mental illness and possibly death for women who feel they have no other option but to starve to avoid inscription within patriarchy. But while Coetzee's and Dangarembga's works also underscore these associations, their texts nevertheless complicate and challenge such gendered stereotypes, offering a postcolonial vegan unconscious that offers new and potentially empowering ways of thinking about the revolutionary potential of non-standard diets.

Veganorexia or Veganism as Disorder

In my 2015 monograph *The Vegan Studies Project*, I explored in depth the ways in which veganism is often associated with disordered eating, particularly when practiced by women. In the fourth chapter of the book, "Death by Veganism, Veganorexia, and Vegaphobia: Women, Choice, and the Politics of 'Disordered' Eating," I examine the problematic policing of women's dietary choices broadly speaking, and the pervasive narrative of disorder and privation that is often associated with women's vegetarianism and veganism more specifically. In 2011 Matthew Cole and Karen Morgan noted that the few sociological studies of veganism that existed generally treated vegans problematically "as a subset of vegetarians and their veganism tends to be viewed as a form of dietary asceticism involving exceptional efforts of self-transformation" (135).[2] This association with "asceticism" continues to be seen in research that links vegetarianism and veganism to eating disorders, like anorexia nervosa and bulimia – which are classified in the *Diagnostic and Statistical Manual of Mental Disorders* (DSM-5) – or to "disordered eating," eating that deviates from the norm and can be harmful but does not rise to the level of diagnostic classification.[3] Chloë Taylor has argued that "alimentary appetites, like sexual appetites, continue to be sites of normalization, or that how we eat is a target of what Foucault calls disciplinary power" (132), which she demonstrates in terms of the recent medical codification of orthorexia nervosa, a "disorder" that specifically "pathologizes vegetarianism . . . [via] the power that medical diagnoses can have in shaping society" (134). Because many such studies rhetorically construct vegetarianism and veganism as *restrictive* and therefore necessarily link these diets with pathology, the often anti-speciesist reasons that many people become vegan are subsumed by societal narratives of disorder and privation that fail to recognize veganism as potentially transformative – and often as a form of feminist resistance against patriarchal control of women's bodily autonomy. I have argued that veganism in any form can easily be characterized as disordered eating in societies within which the consumption of animals and animal products is treated with primacy, as a necessity, and as an indicator of virility.

While studies about eating disorders like anorexia nervosa and bulimia began to demand attention in the 1980s, self-starvation practices have a much longer history, often associated with mysticism and the belief that such practices could provide extra-human power to practitioners. According to Arthur Crisp et al., "researchers have found case material in the historical literature suggestive of anorexia nervosa over many centuries" (147), and eating disorders have historically been more common in women than in men. In some sense, this prevalence in women is the case in large part because women themselves are treated as aberrant generally in cultures that hold men to be the norm. Joan Jacobs Brumberg's foundational study *Fasting Girls: The History of Anorexia Nervosa* (1988) discusses the medieval European phenomenon of *anorexia mirabilis*, prolonged female fasting that was considered miraculous (43). Further, anorexic women "are perceived (want to be perceived, and perceive themselves) as . . . special, superhuman, or even sub-human, animal-like beings" (Medeiros 13). More recently, since the 1970s or so, both women and men have practiced *inedia* or breatharianism, a belief loosely based in the Hindu concept that the vital life force *prana* is the sole form of sustenance necessary; those who practice *inedia* claim that they need neither to eat nor to drink in order to survive (Kerr).

I should note that ethical veganism, on the other hand, is marked by none of these assumptions associated with self-starvation or with a denial of sustenance or with mysticism, despite the rhetoric of privation and asceticism that is often employed by non-vegans to characterize it. Rather, veganism is pathologized because it serves as a confrontation to peoples and cultures in which the consumption of meat is the standard. In other words, vegans, specifically vegan women, who non-pathologically refuse to eat meat and animal products in meat-centric societies are policed differently from women who consume animal products – although it is certainly worth noting that women's dietary choices are frequently policed regardless of what they eat (Bates). Veganism is treated as pathological when practiced by women within social structures that do not accommodate veganism. One could argue that the pathology of capitalist patriarchal societies, not the women in them, underscores the often aggressive and punitive enforcement of "standardized" eating. That said, women's dietary practices – regardless of whether they are vegan – are scrutinized disproportionately to men's, and the policing of women's consumption of food in patriarchal societies is, according to Maxine Woolhouse et. al "based on historical constructions of women 'as body' . . . and ruled by their bodies, which are regarded as unstable, inherently weak . . . and unreliable . . . yet simultaneously voracious, threatening and therefore in need of control" (46).

In her 2021 *Feminist Philosophy Quarterly* piece, Megan Dean notes the pervasive phenomenon that she has termed the "Vegetarianism and Eating Disorder Hypothesis" that is typical in studies that examine eating disorders in girls, and she posits that vegetarianism practiced by girls and young women "should be understood as a potential risk, sign, or 'cover' for dangerous pathological eating" (2). However, in recent years, some studies have worked to problematize the idea that vegetarian and vegan diets are potentially masking eating disorders. A 2006 study looked at the plant-based diets of adult women and concluded that in considering the motives for their choices about what and how they ate, vegetarians and vegans "tend to avoid animal products for ethical and health reasons rather than as an excuse or cover for dietary restraint" (Fisak et al. 199). In her 2014 article in *Societies*, Dean argues that "veganism is, or can be, a Foucauldian ethical practice of freedom" (3), and she uses the respective work of Taylor, Sandra Bartky, and Susan Bordo to trace the ways in which, within patriarchal societies, women's bodies are policed and punished for their dietary choices, noting in particular Bartky's assessment of the pervasiveness of the policing of women's eating practices – both external and internalized – and the tacit punishment for non-conformity. Dean notes, "as contemporary patriarchy is largely unattached to an institution, there is no one particular person or group who act as disciplinarians for this normalizing dieting project" (131). In such a schema, Bartky recognizes that everyone functions as the disciplinarian and that the disciplinary role is also internalized: "this disciplinary power is peculiarly modern: it does not rely on violent or public sanctions, nor does it seek to restrain the freedom of the female body to move from place to place. For all that, its invasion of the female body is well-nigh total" (79–80)

Pushing back against the "Vegetarianism and Eating Disorder Hypothesis," Dean argues that:

> Drawing from feminist work on narrative agency and identity, I argue that wrongly accepting the hypothesis can damage the moral and epistemic agency of young women and girls. I then build on feminist critiques of weight-loss dieting and Foucauldian work on eating to suggest that the self-shaping effects of what I call "ethical vegetarianism" give us additional reasons to be cautious of discouraging it. (2)

There is good reason to push back against this long-held hypothesis as well as to consider *actual* disordered eating, particularly for women, as a symptom of patriarchal societies that deny women full individualization. For Kim Chernin, there is a clear connection between the act of eating and the "struggle for identity" (xviii) for women, and eating disorders function as unsuccessful rites of passage for women in societies that do not recognize or condone such transformative rites: "Much of the obsessive quality of an eating disorder arises precisely from the fact that food is being asked to serve a transformative function that it cannot carry *by itself*" (Chernin 167, my emphasis). Similarly, Brumberg characterizes food refusal as evidence of "*mentalities in transition*" (99, emphasis in original). Rites of passage mark the end of one phase of life and entry into another. They involve acceptance into communities of others who have similarly passed through the ritual to achieve membership within the new social order. In patriarchal societies, women's attempts to be recognized and celebrated for moving from one phase of life to another are restricted, as, in patriarchal cultures, women's traditions are de facto the traditions of men.

Kafka, Coetzee, and Starving Male Artists

Christopher Kocela discusses the way in which veganism is rendered as restrictive self-denial in Richard Powers's 2006 novel *The Echo Maker*, noting that the character of Daniel Reigel, American environmental activist and Buddhist convert, is characterized by this lover Karin Schulter as a "scarecrow vegan" (58) when she sees him naked for the first time. According to Kocela, in Powers's novel, Daniel is "a fervent Buddhist" who "meditates four times per day, refuses to let Karin eat meat, smoke, or even curse in his presence, and maintains such a high-minded view of conservation that he alienates those around him" (107). Daniel, whose very name constitutes an anagram for "denial," is depicted as misguided and repressed, denying himself pleasure and repressing his potential homosexuality. When Karin attempts to adopt his diet, she finds herself physically weakened and resentful. I mention this characterization to illustrate the ways that male veganism is often treated – both in life and in literature – as aberrant, queer, and emasculating. While not definitively designated as disorder in Powers's novel, Daniel's veganism is the vehicle via which the reader is introduced to a character whose animal rights activism and strict adherence to Buddhism are rendered too extreme, too alienating, and as a form of repression of pleasures, culinary and sexual.[4]

In its presentation of Daniel as an environmentalist who has taken his environmentalism to the extreme, Powers's contemporary novel echoes Franz Kafka's 1922 short story "A Hunger Artist," in which the protagonist, an unnamed hunger artist who fasts during an undesignated historical period during which the public's taste for public fasting has waned. In previous decades, the narrator tells us, "the whole town took a lively interest in the hunger artist; from day to day of his fast, excitement mounted; everybody wanted to see him at least once a day" (268). The story characterizes the artist's struggle to keep the public interested in his art and his displeasure with the fact that "he alone knew, what no other initiate knew, how easy it was to fast. It was the easiest thing in the world" (270). At the beginning of the story, the impresario allows the artist to starve for a period of forty days and no longer. Later, after the public loses interest, no-one bothers to ensure that the artist breaks his fast, and his cage is taken out of the spotlight and placed instead with the cages of the circus animals, whom he thanks, realizing that without them, he would have no audience at all.

The artist is ultimately forgotten until a supervisor sees his cage and, thinking it empty and of potential use for another circus animal, discovers the artist in the straw that lines the cage, still fasting. When the supervisor asks if he'll ever stop his fast, the artist replies that he cannot, "because I couldn't find a food which I liked. If had found it, believe me, I should have made no fuss and stuffed myself like you or anyone else" (277). And with these words, he dies. The connection between hunger and artistry and between hunger as establishing force that makes the artist fully aware of his – and in these cases, always "his" – existence and his struggle for a successful articulation of his vision in a world where his work is misunderstood and unappreciated is, of course, apparent in Kafka's story as well as, according to Moraru, before him in Knut Hamsun's "no less disturbing 1890 novel *Hunger: hunger is poiesis*, my hunger has a poetic force to it (from the Greek *poiein*)" (12). This hunger, "makes me ... by almost unmaking me as the overwhelming need furiously wells up in me and drags me on the brink of nonbeing as Auster observes in his [1993] essay 'The Art of Hunger'" (Moraru 12).

Kafka, of course, was a "strict vegetarian," who, according to Steven G. Kellman, when offered a sausage by a co-worker in Prague responded by saying, "the only fit food for a man is half a lemon" (532). Like Moraru, Kellman notes that in his creation of his hunger artist, "Kafka elevates refusing to eat into a principle of aesthetics" (532). Given Kafka's vegetarianism, which he practiced for ethical and health reasons, the hunger artist's declaration that he does not eat because he cannot find the food that he likes tacitly treats the artist's starvation as more than a merely aesthetic issue; the food that he would like, one might assume, is food that does not result from cruelty. The meager food that the artist is forced to eat at the end of his fast by "ladies who were apparently so friendly and in reality so cruel" (271) is never specified and only described as a "carefully chosen invalid's repast" (270). Kellman notes this tradition of "aberrant" eating as directly linked to vegetarianism in the works of more contemporary vegetarian artists as well,[5] and he mentions in particular South African author J. M. Coetzee, whose *Life & Times of Michael K* I have previously argued owes much to Kafka's "A Hunger Artist." Like Kafka, Coetzee is also a strict vegetarian, and in *Life & Times*, a vegan ethos infuses the resistance to eating that Michael K undertakes as he seeks to escape all forms of codification during a fictional civil war in South Africa, a society whose apartheid government was established and maintained through racial codification and strict policing of the boundaries between racial groups.

Michael K is not an artist, but rather a man who ultimately considers himself a gardener – and his obsession with growing a garden (an undertaking that is ultimately unsuccessful) and "living off the land" (Coetzee 116) becomes as much of a driver of his starvation as does the hunger artist's quest to perfect his art and Daniel's environmentalist zealotry. Michael is initially described as a man with a "disfigurement" whose "mind was not quick" (4). At the age thirty-one, Michael sets out from Cape Town to take his ailing mother to her childhood home in the countryside of Prince Albert. She dies on the journey, and after her death, Michael continues the journey and moves into the abandoned farm that he believes to be his mother's childhood home. There, "famished and exhausted" (53), he kills a goat, which he "eats without pleasure" (56). He eventually attempts to grow a garden, and according to David Attwell, Michael's cultivation of the land is an attempt to "protect a posthumanist, reconstructed ethics . . . But the condition for such ethical reconstruction is a recognition of the pervasive intrusiveness of totalitarian violence" (97) in South Africa. Michael grows pumpkins, caring for them as if they are his children. However, when the grandson of the farm's owners returns and assumes that Michael is the caretaker, Michael leaves the farm and begins "the great hunger" (67), with which he is consumed for the rest of the novel. Michael is captured and placed in a series of work and rehabilitation camps from which he unsuccessfully attempts to extricate himself: he is first conscripted into a labor gang, escapes again to the farm where he lives in a hole in the ground, and is later taken to the resettlement camp of Jakkalsdrif.

Michael's attempts to live off of the land fail, as he is taken from one camp to another, growing thinner and weaker with every move, until by the end of the novel he is nearly starved to death, imagining a future in which he can live on spoonfuls of water pulled from the wreckage of a ruined water pump. The narrative traces Michael's desire to "be out of all the camps at the same time" (182), and the notion of "camps" functions as a signifier of not only the labor and resettlement camps from which he escapes through various holes in fences, but also of the camps of race and gender, as well as the rehabilitation camp where he is taken after he collapses. But in his refusal to eat, Michael refuses to let his diet be policed and standardized, seeking, as the medical officer at the rehabilitation camp where he is taken after he collapses, "the bread of freedom" (146): food that is removed from the mechanizations of cruelty and suffering.

That food can only be, it seems, the plants that Michael grows for himself; when he eats one of his pumpkins, he notes that "for the first time since he had arrived in the country he found pleasure in eating" (113). The contrast between the lack of pleasure that he experiences when he kills and eats the goat and the pleasure that he feels while eating a vegetable that he has grown is of note, given that Coetzee's work often situates the slaughter of animals within the intersecting oppressions of South Africa's racist and gender-based oppressions.[6] In this way, Coetzee's novel both imitates and breaks from the tradition of the starving male artist and the alignment of hunger with aesthetic preference.[7] Unlike Kafka's artist who finds life in his cage a source of comfort, in Coetzee's novel, Michael pushes back against the various people who enter his life asking him to "tell them the story of a life lived in cages. They want to hear about all the cages I have lived in, as if I were a budgie or a white mouse or a monkey" (181). In both aligning himself with and distancing himself from nonhuman animals that are kept in cages, Michael's commentary indicates a recognition that life within a cage – or in a camp or via a racial classification – is confining and oppressive. In this case, hunger is not art or spectacle, but an ethical vegan quest that fails in the face of fascism and carnism.

Margaret Atwood and Pathological Vegan Victims

In Kafka's story and Powers's and Coetzee's novels, veganism is either literal or implicit as is an explicit recognition of, and affiliation with, the lives of nonhuman animals: the hunger artist is situated in a cage with other circus animals and thanks them for their presence; Daniel works at a crane refuge, recognizing that the destruction of their habitat will be complete during his lifetime: "a few more years, and we can say goodbye to something that has been around since the Eocene" (57); and Michael K shuns killing animals after killing a single goat, striving to live on the vegetables that he grows. In order to shift from these authors to an examination of eating disorders and veganism in works by, and about, women, I want to note Kafka's and Coetzee's lived vegetarianism and the fact that Coetzee's work in particular has always been hyper-aware of the limits of the empathetic imagination and respect for the alterity of various others, particularly when it comes to his position as a white male writer.

Canadian author Margaret Atwood is not a vegetarian. She did, however, "go partially vegetarian" ("Margaret Atwood Goes") on her book tour for *Year of the Flood*: "I've themed myself, though I shouldn't use the term vegetarian because I'm allowing myself gastropods, crustaceans and the occasional fish. Nothing with fur or feathers, though," and she is keenly aware of the arguments for a plant-based diet, which she respects, if not fully accepts. In an interview during which she was asked about her feelings about lab-grown meat, Atwood said, "if one of the arguments against eating meat is to do with cruelty and animal intelligence," then lab-produced meat is an option. Further, she says, "there's also the environmental argument for it. Are you going to eat meat and support ethical farming or turn your back on the whole thing? We know the arguments because our daughter is vegetarian." Many of Atwood's novels engage with vegetarianism and veganism, and contain vegetarian or vegan characters; that said, vegetarianism and veganism in Atwood's works are always fraught undertakings, either too utopian and hypocritical – as is the case with the novels in her *MaddAddam* trilogy, *Oryx and Crake* (2003), *The Year of the Flood* (2009), and *MaddAddam* (2013), all three of which satirize veganism. With regard to Atwood's vegetarian characters, Chloë Taylor notes:

> vegetarianism and compassion for nonhuman animals are . . . consistently represented by Atwood in her fiction as a self-defeating persecution-paranoia and a loss of touch with reality. In the semi-happy endings of her novels and short stories, from *The Edible Woman* and *Surfacing* to "Moral Disorder" and *The Year of the Flood*, Atwood has her female vegetarian characters overcome their mental turmoil and return to eating meat. (135)

In Atwood's first novel *The Edible Woman* (1969), vegetarianism and veganism are explicitly linked to the eating disorder of the protagonist Marian, a white middle-class Canadian woman who works as a consumer product tester. Marian ultimately overcomes an eating disorder that manifests as a means of trying to regain a sense of control over the loss of self she feels after she agrees to marry her fiancé, Peter. Marian's anorexia begins while she and Peter are dining out one evening, and Peter orders filet mignon for the two of them. Marian realizes that she is letting Peter make decisions for her about what she eats and drinks, which, she notes, "got rid of the vacillation she had found herself displaying when confronted with a menu" (Atwood, *Edible* 159). But when Peter cuts into his meat, Marian perceives him doing so as a "violent action" (162):

> watching him operating on the steak like that, carving a straight slice and then dividing it into neat cubes, made her think of the diagram of the planned cow at the front of one of her cookbooks: the cow with lines on it and labels to show you from which part of the cow all the different cuts were taken. (163)

In that moment, Marian finds herself unable to continue eating her own steak, even as she tries to convince herself to do so. When she looks back down at the meal in front of her, she suddenly becomes aware that the meat on her plate was once a living animal and recognizes the meat as "part of a real cow that once moved and ate and was killed, knocked on the head while it stood in a queue like someone waiting for a streetcar" (164). She realizes that "everyone knew that," but also concedes that "most of the time you never thought of it" (164). Afterwards, Marian finds herself unable to eat "anything that had an indication of bone or tendon or fiber" (165). This recognition of the vulnerability of the cow is clearly the result of her own ensuing helplessness as she feels her autonomy slipping away from her the closer she gets to marrying Peter. In her resistance to her own commodification, she becomes aware of the ways in which the bodies of animals are commodified and consumed, and she becomes physically unable to eat them, at least temporarily; her recognition that the meat on her plate was once a living cow restores what Carol J. Adams refers to as the "absent referent" (20) – the animal itself – to the discourse of meat, and she uses *The Edible Woman* to explicate the term (119–20).

After her inability to eat meat cut from what she refers to as the "planned cow," Marian realizes that "the Planned Pig and the Planned Sheep were similarly inedible" (165). But this recognition does not lead Marian to an awakening that would allow her to identify with the animal and embrace a vegan diet as a feminist form of resistance and an assertion of the self that she feels she is losing to Peter. Eventually, Marian's aversion to specific foods becomes more pronounced, becoming, by all critical estimations, anorexia nervosa: "she not only loses the ability to eat anything with a semblance of vitality but is also haunted by the idea that she herself is being consumed" (Hobgood 147). Marian longs "to become again a carnivore, to gnaw on a good bone" (Atwood, *Edible* 189). At the end of the novel, Marian is again carnivorous, her apparent recovery from anorexia comes as she bakes a cake in the image of a woman and eats it with her friend Duncan. She decides not to marry Peter, but the novel leaves the reader wondering what other options are available for a woman like Marian, confined as she is by Western conceptions of appropriate early 1960s-era femininity.

Marian's vegetarianism and subsequent veganism are the first steps towards Marian's full-blown eating disorder. Taylor notes that Atwood's characters often experience "various kinds of delusion" that lead them to become vegetarian, and from there, "vegetarianism is just a quick slide from insanity" (140). In the case of Marian, it seems clear that despite her initial recognition of meat as animal and animal as helpless victim, her decision not to eat animals is more about her inability to overcome her own sense of powerlessness. In other words, she feels for the cow insofar as the cow is an entity onto which she projects her own helplessness. Her empathy for the cow, therefore, is rather a displaced empathy for herself as she works to repress her uncertainty about marriage and motherhood; that empathy doesn't extend to actual cows and their vulnerability and suffering in the service of being rendered meat. And because genuine empathy for the other is not the motivating factor behind her dietary decision, she is unable to be empowered by opting out of eating animals and animal by-products. Instead, she abdicates control completely and stops eating everything. That she regains control at the end of the novel comes at the expense – not as a result – of her veganism. When she feels empowered by her decision not to marry Peter, her empathy for the cow (and for all animals that she once consumed for food) ends as she symbolically consumes herself, in the form of a cake she bakes in her likeness in what I would argue constitutes another act of repression and even symbolic self-harm.

Tsitsi Dangarembga: Postcolonial Eating Disorders and the Vegan Unconscious

The "slide from insanity" that Taylor discusses regarding Atwood's work is even more pronounced in Tsitsi Dangarembga's *Nervous Conditions*, which tacitly links the meat-laden British diet mimicked by the young Shona protagonist Tambu's Westernized cousin Nyasha to the eating disorder, bulimia, that Nyasha develops over the course of the novel. The novel opens with an epigraph from Jean-Paul Sartre's preface to Algerian psychiatrist Frantz Fanon's 1961 foundational study of the psychology of the colonized, *The Wretched of the Earth*: "the condition of native is a nervous condition." Fanon's study examines the nervous condition of the colonized man, and Dangarembga's novel presents, via a female *Bildungsroman* that follows the narrative trajectory of Charlotte Brontë's *Jane Eyre*,[8] the various nervous conditions of colonized Shona women in the 1960s. The novel opens with protagonist and narrator Tambu's jarring assertion: "I was not sorry when my brother died" (Dangarembga 11). It is the death of her brother Nhamo that allows Tambu to leave her impoverished rural family to attend the mission school where her uncle Babamukuru is headmaster. There, she obtains a Western education alongside her cousin Nyasha, who has lived abroad in England and chafes at the patriarchal politics of Shona culture. While Tambu initially finds the Western diet served by her aunt Maiguru too rich and unfamiliar, she eventually assimilates and enjoys eating at her uncle's table, recognizing

> its shape and size, had a lot to say about the amount, the calorie content, the complement of vitamins and minerals, the relative proportions of fat, carbohydrate and protein that would be consumed at it. No one who ate from such a table could fail to grow fat and healthy. (106)

Nyasha, on the other hand, sits at the dinner table reading a copy of D. H. Lawrence's *Lady Chatterley's Lover* in bold defiance of her parents' insistence that she eat dinner and as an affront to her father's fury at his daughter's adolescent and

Western-influenced sexuality. When her father insists that she eat, she does but then throws up everything, admitting to Tambu that she uses a toothbrush – a Western implement – to do so. At one point in the novel, Babamukuru threatens Nyasha over her refusal to obey traditional Shona norms with regard to feminine behavior. As she is getting ready to go out for the evening, he calls her a whore because of her outfit and make-up and threatens to kill her if she keeps defying him. Tambu realizes that

> The victimization . . . was universal. It didn't depend on poverty, on lack of education or on tradition. It didn't depend on any of the things I had thought it depended on. Men took it everywhere with them. Even heroes like Babamukuru did it. And that was the problem . . . all the conflicts came back to this question of femaleness. Femaleness as opposed and inferior to maleness. (116)

At the end of the novel, Nyasha, nearly starved to death, suffers a nervous breakdown, rips pages from her books with her teeth, and rails against "the Englishness," against her father, and also against the ways in which her father is the victim of colonization. She says finally, "I'm not one of them, but I'm not one of you" (201), indicating her hybrid status and displacement from both Western and Shona cultures. When her parents take her to see a psychiatrist, they are told that she cannot have an eating disorder, that Africans don't suffer from eating disorders, which the doctor views as a strictly Western phenomenon: "Maiguru's brother immediately made an appointment with a psychiatrist . . . But the psychiatrist said that Nyasha could not be ill, that Africans did not suffer in the way we had described. She was making a scene" (206).

As noted in the introduction to this volume, Evan Maina Mwangi's 2019 study *The Postcolonial Animal* calls for an examination of "the vegan unconscious" that places veganism in "African contexts to be useful to the study of African literature where the texts do not even openly espouse vegetarianism" (7). Mwangi notes that he is unable to find an African language equivalent to "vegan," and calls for caution in imposing veganism upon African texts. A vegan unconscious certainly exists within *Nervous Conditions*, as Nyasha is alienated from a more traditional plant-based Shona diet and forced to eat meat. When Tambu is accepted into a highly competitive convent school, her mother rages at Babamukuru and Maiguru for killing her son and taking her daughter. To Tambu she says, "You are so selfish you would betray your mother for meat" (208). Just as there is no African language equivalent to "vegan," there is seemingly no Shona equivalent to "bulimic," as the disorder, particularly in the 1960s, was thought to be entirely Western. Such a perception, of course, underscores a lack of recognition of the ways in which colonization impacted native Africans who were pulled between the poles of assimilation and resistance to Western norms. As Fanon notes,

> In the colonial context the settler only ends his work of breaking in the native when the latter admits loudly and intelligibly the supremacy of the white man's values. In the period of decolonization, the colonized masses mock at these very values, insult them, *and vomits them up*. (134, my emphasis)

In the case of Nyasha, the "vomiting up" of these values is linked not only to her failed resistance to colonization and patriarchy but also to her alienation from a more traditional plant-based Shona diet.

There is a considerable body of scholarship that has engaged with the impact of colonialization and Western dietary practices on indigenous foodways. Leela Gandhi notes that "equating beef with imperial virility" and plant-based diets with femininity and weakness was an "ideological tactic" (84) pushed back against by M. K. Gandhi's lived vegetarian ethic and his rhetorical aligning of the partition of India with the vivisection of the continent. Regarding postcolonial cultures, vegetarianism and veganism, when discussed at all, have tended to be associated with colonization and elitism. Maneesha Deckha argues against such a stance, noting that "perception that antimeat advocates are ignorant of and/or unresponsive toward non-Western cultures whose traditional diets are animal-based. This critique is often advanced through the example of subsistence hunting practices of indigenous peoples" (534).

Rather than uncritically accepting such assertions, Deckha suggests that such elitist arguments fail to consider "the enormous amounts of plant and land resources that are required to sustain current Western levels of flesh consumption . . . and ignore the richness of non-Western flesh-free food traditions and ideologies of nonviolence toward all living beings" (535). While *Nervous Conditions* does not address plant-based eating as a means of postcolonial resistance, the text does engage with this vegan unconscious to place the Western meat-centric diet embraced by the novel's Westernized characters in stark contrast to the predominantly plant-based traditional diet of the Shona. In the *Routledge Handbook of Vegan Studies*, Sarah Rhu and I argue that in *Nervous Conditions*, Tambu's family "lives on a homestead where their food is primarily plant-based. *Sadza*, a thick porridge made from grains, forms the staple of their diet." Further, Tambu's family also eats "rape, *covo*, tomatoes, *derere* and onions – which she grew on a plot that had been my grandmother's" (Dangarembga 8). *Covo* is a leafy green like kale, and *derere* is a mucilaginous vegetable, and "Dangarembga leaves many nouns, especially words for foods, untranslated in *Nervous Conditions*, suggesting that the book's audience may be Zimbabweans who are familiar with these vegetables and fruits from their traditional diet" (Rhu and Wright 275–76) including the wild monkey oranges and mangosteens that Tambu's brother Nhamo picks and eats on his walk home: "matamba and matunduru. Sweet and sour. Delicious" (Dangarembga 3). The inclusion of these foods and their status as untranslated for a Western audience forces the reader to confront the primacy with which the narrative presents indigenous Shona dietary norms.

Conclusion

With the exception of "A Hunger Artist," none of the other works discussed in this essay end with the death of the protagonist, and each narrative provides a different lens through which to view the connection between plant-based diets and pathological eating. In *The Edible Woman*, veganism is treated merely as a step towards anorexia nervosa as opposed to a fully realized empathetic response to the linked oppressions that impact Marian's life. Her return to carnism is a return to the established order in which she is a consumer of both animal bodies and patriarchy, a trajectory that is mirrored in many of Atwood's subsequent treatments of veganism as well. Conversely, in *The Vegetarian*, the bodies of the animals that Yeong-hye has eaten, and her refusal to consume animals further, function as an overt recognition of the suffering of animals, and unlike Marian, Yeong-hye does not return to her carnivorous ways but instead extends the circle of her empathy to include the natural world via the kinship she feels with trees. The novel ends with her sister's liberation – a freedom she has only been able to attain via a recognition of her sister's having "smashed through all the boundaries" (186) and after In-hye demands that the hospital staff stop force-feeding her sister.

In *Nervous Conditions* and to a lesser extent in *Life & Times of Michael K*, we see Mwangi's vegan unconscious placing plant-based eating within a broader patriarchal colonial frame. For a vegan reader, *Nervous Conditions* demonstrates the ways in which indigenous foods and foodways – like indigenous peoples – were colonized and often erased. The novel situates the traditional vegetable-centric Shona diet in stark contrast to the meat-centric European fare eaten by the assimilated Babamukuru and his family. Nyasha's refusal to digest such food results in a "nervous condition" insofar as her status as an African girl negates her from a diagnosis for anorexia nervosa, but more importantly because she is unable, at least by the end of the novel, to see her refusal of European food as having the potential to decolonize her diet. The vegan reader, however, might see in the narrative a postcolonial roadmap for such decolonization. While *The Vegetarian*, *Life & Times of Michael K*, and *Nervous Conditions* all end in a space of narrative uncertainty, that same uncertainty offers the potential for a productive shift from disordered to empowered vegan eating.

Notes

1. In addition to my previous work on Kang's novel, see also analyses by Caitlin E. Stobie, Margarita Carretero-González, and Liz Mayo.
2. In recent years, however, more positive sociological studies have emerged, as detailed in the annotated bibliography in this volume.
3. For example, in their 1986 study, Rao Kadambari, Simon Gowers, and Arthur Crisp characterize vegetarians as "one face of the ascetic stance" (539), and vegans as "severe" vegetarians and "abstainers" (541).
4. This trope is fairly pervasive. For other examples, see such films as Mike White's *Year of the Dog* (2007) and *Beatriz at Dinner* (2017) and Bong Joon-ho's *Okja* (2017), as well as novels such as Jonathan Franzen's *Purity* (2015) and Margaret Atwood's *MaddAddam* trilogy (2003, 2009, and 2013).
5. In addition to Coetzee, he mentions Percy Bysshe Shelley (but omits Mary Shelley), Leo Tolstoy, George Bernard Shaw, Ted Hughes, V. S. Naipaul, Margaret Atwood – who is not, nor has ever been vegetarian – and Alice Walker. He also makes passing reference to the aberrant presentation of vegetarianism in Vladimir Nabokov's *Pale Fire*, which is rehabilitated for a vegan reader by Emelia Quinn's essay in this collection.
6. See in particular Coetzee's most famous novel, *Disgrace* (1999), wherein, after his daughter is gang-raped on her farm, protagonist David Lurie engages the limits of the empathetic imagination in his attempts to recognize the interiority of various "others." Whatever empathy of which he is capable presents itself via his unexpected identification with the dogs for whom his daughter cares and with two sheep, tethered without water before slaughter.
7. When asked about Kafka's influence on *Life & Times of Michael K*, he responded, "I don't believe that Kafka has an exclusive right to the letter K. Nor is Prague the center of the universe" (qtd. in Morphet 457).
8. Dangarembga's novel does not end, as Brontë's does, with the marriage of her protagonist, but rather with Tambu's ultimate recognition that despite her acceptance into a

highly selective school for girls, she remains alienated as a Black colonial subject. The school places four girls in each dorm room, but the six African students are forced to room together, illustrating their segregation from the student body overall.

Works Cited

Adams, Carol J. *The Sexual Politics of Meat: A Feminist-Vegetarian Critical Theory*. Twenty-fifth anniversary edition, Bloomsbury Academic, 2015.

Attwell, David. *J. M. Coetzee: South Africa and the Politics of Writing*. U of California P, 1993.

Atwood, Margaret. *The Edible Woman*. Anchor, 1998.

—. *MaddAddam*. Anchor, 2014.

—. *Oryx and Crake*. Knopf Doubleday, 2004.

—. *The Year of the Flood*. Anchor, 2010.

Bartky, Sandra Lee. *Femininity and Domination: Studies in the Phenomenology of Oppression*. Routledge, 2015.

Bates, Laura. "'Are You Really Going to Eat That?' Yes, and It's Nobody Else's Business." *The Guardian*, 24 July 2014. <www.theguardian.com/lifeandstyle/womens-blog/2014/jul/24/women-meal-choices-control-female-bodies-food-policing>

Bordo, Susan. *Unbearable Weight: Feminism, Western Culture, and the Body*. U of California P, 2004.

Brontë, Charlotte. *Jane Eyre*. W.W. Norton, 2016.

Brumburg, Joan Jacobs. *Fasting Girls: The History of Anorexia Nervosa*. Vintage, 2000.

Carretero-González, Margarita. "Looking at the Vegetarian Body: Narrative Points of View and Blind Spots in Han Kang's *The Vegetarian*." *Through a Vegan Studies Lens: Textual Ethics and Lived Activism*, edited by Laura Wright, U of Nevada P, 2019, pp. 165–79.

Chernin, Kim. *The Hungry Self: Women, Eating, and Identity*. Harper, 1994.

Chiorando, Maria. "Young Women 'Driving Growth of the Vegan Movement' Say Analysts." *Plantbasednews.com*, 18 June 2018. <www.plantbasednews.org/culture/young-women-driving-growth-of-the-vegan-movement-say-analysts>

Coetzee, J. M. *Disgrace*. Penguin, 1999.

—. *Life & Times of Michael K*. Penguin, 1983.

Cole, Matthew, and Karen Morgan. "Vegaphobia: Derogatory Discourses of Veganism and the Reproduction of Species in UK National Newspapers." *British Journal of Sociology*, vol. 62, no. 1, 2011, pp. 135–53.

Crisp, Arthur et al. "The Enduring Nature of Anorexia Nervosa." *European Eating Disorders Review*, vol. 14, 2006, pp. 147–52.

Dangarembga, Tsitsi. *Nervous Conditions*. Ayebia Clarke Publishing, 2004.

Dean, Megan. "Eating as a Self-Shaping Activity: The Case of Young Women's Vegetarianism and Eating Disorders." *Feminist Philosophy Quarterly*, vol. 7, no. 3, 2021, article 2.

—. "You Are *How* You Eat? Femininity, Normalization, and Veganism as an Ethical Practice of Freedom." *Societies*, vol. 4, 2014, pp. 127–47.

Deckha, Maneesha. "Toward a Postcolonial, Posthumanist Feminist Theory: Centralizing Race and Culture in Feminist Work on Nonhuman Animals." *Hypatia*, vol. 27, no. 3, 2012, pp. 527–45.

Fanon, Frantz. *The Wretched of the Earth*. Grove Weidenfeld, 1961.

Fisak, Brian J. et al. "Challenges Previous Conceptions of Vegetarianism and Eating Disorders." *Eating and Weight Disorders: Studies in Anorexia, Bulimia and Obesity*, vol. 11, no. 4, pp. 195–201.

Gandhi, Leela. *Affective Communities: Anticolonial Thought, Fin-de-Siècle Radicalism, and the Politics of Friendship*. Duke UP, 2006.

Hobgood, Jennifer. "Anti-Edibles: Capitalism and Schizophrenia in Margaret Atwood's *The Edible Woman*." *Style*, vol. 3, no. 1, 2002, pp. 146–67.

Kadambari, Rao, Simon Gowers, and Arthur Crisp. "Some Correlates of Vegetarianism in Anorexia Nervosa." *International Journal of Eating Disorders*, vol. 5, no. 3, 1986, pp. 539–44.

Kafka, Franz. "A Hunger Artist." *Franz Kafka: The Complete Stories*, edited by Nahun N. Glatzer, translated by Willa and Edwin Muir, Schocken Books, 1971, pp. 268–77.

Kang, Han. *The Vegetarian*. Hogarth, 2015.

Kellman, Steven G. "'The Only fit Food for a Man is Half a Lemon': Kafka's Plea and Other Culinary Aberrations." *Southwest Review*, vol. 95, no. 4, 2010, pp. 532–45.

Kerr, Breena. "The People Who Think Air Is Food." *GQ*, 7 September 2017. <www.gq.com/story/breatharians-the-people-who-think-air-is-food>

Kocela, Christopher. "Scarecrow Veganism: The Straw Man of Buddhist Vegan Identity in Richard Powers's *The Echo Maker* and Jonathan Franzen's *Purity*." *Through a Vegan Studies Lens: Textual Ethics and Lived Activism*, edited by Laura Wright, U of Nevada P, pp. 107–27.

"Margaret Atwood Goes Partially Veg for *The Year of the Flood*." *Vegetarian Star*, 18 September 2009. <www.vegetarianstar.com/2009/09/18/margaret-atwood-goes-partially-veg-for-the-year-of-the-flood>

Mayo, Liz. "A Quiet Riot: Veganism as Anti-Capitalism and Ecofeminist Revolt in Han Kang's *The Vegetarian*." *The Routledge Handbook of Vegan Studies*, edited by Laura Wright, Routledge Press, 2021, pp. 101–10.

Medeiros, Paulo. "Cannibalism and Starvation: The Parameters of Eating Disorders." *Disorderly Eaters: Texts in Self-Empowerment*, edited by Lilian R. Furst and Peter W. Graham, Pennsylvania State UP, 1992, pp. 1–27.

Moraru, Christian. "'To Eat is to Compose': Theory, Identity, and Dietary Politics after Kafka." *Symploke*, vol. 19, nos. 1–2, 2011, pp. 11–16.

Morphet, Tony. "An Interview with J. M. Coetzee." *Social Dynamics*, vol. 10, no. 1, 1984, pp. 62–65.

Mwangi, Evan Maini. *The Postcolonial Animal: African Literature and Posthuman Ethics*. U of Michigan P, 2019.

Powers, Richard. *The Echo Maker*. Picador, 2007.

Rhu, Sarah, and Laura Wright. "'You Would Betray your Own Mother for Meat': A Postcolonial Vegan Reading of Tsitsi Dangarembga's *Nervous Conditions*." *The Routledge Handbook of Vegan Studies*, edited by Laura Wright, Routledge, 2021, pp. 272–81.

Stobie, Caitlin E. "The Good Wife? Sibling Species in Han Kang's *The Vegetarian*." *ISLE*, vol. 24, no. 4, 2017, pp. 787–802.

Sullivan, Victoria, and Sadhana Damani. "Vegetarianism and Eating Disorders – Partners in Crime?" *European Eating Disorders Review*, vol. 8, no. 4, 2000, pp. 263–66.

Taylor, Chloë. "Abnormal Appetites: Foucault, Atwood, and the Normalization of an Animal-Based Diet." *Journal for Critical Animal Studies*, vol. 10, no. 4, 2012, pp. 130–48.

Timko, C. Alix, Julia M. Hormes, and Janice Chubski. "Will the Real Vegetarian Please Stand Up? An Investigation of Dietary Restraint and Eating Disorder Symptoms in Vegetarians Versus Non-Vegetarians." *Appetite*, vol. 58, 2012, pp. 982–90.

Woolhouse, Maxine et al. "'Cos Girls aren't Supposed to Eat Like Pigs are They?' Young Women Negotiating Gendered Discursive Constructions of Food and Eating." *Journal of Health Psychology*, vol. 17, no. 1, 2011, pp. 46–56.

Wright, Laura. "The Dangerous Vegan: Han Kang's *The Vegetarian* and the Anti-Feminist Rhetoric of Disordered Eating." *(In)Digestion in Literature and Film*, edited by Niki Kiviat and Serena J. Rivera, Routledge Press, 2020, pp. 121–34.

—. "Minor Literature and 'The Skeleton of Sense': Anorexia, Franz Kafka's 'A Hunger Artist,' and J. M. Coetzee's *Life & Times of Michael K.*" *Journal of Commonwealth and Postcolonial Studies*, vol. 8, no. 1, 2001, pp. 109–23.

—. *The Vegan Studies Project: Food, Animals, and Gender in the Age of Terror*. U of Georgia P, 2015.

—. *Writing out of All the Camps: J. M. Coetzee's Narratives of Displacement*. New York: Routledge, 2006.

Part II
Genres and Forms

10

Prose

Dreaming Vegan: Han Kang's *The Vegetarian*

Amy-Leigh Gray and Dana Medoro

In the voice of a male narrator whose first sentence abruptly turns to the past, as if caught on a temporal fault-line, South Korean writer Han Kang opens her novel *The Vegetarian: A Novel* (2007): "Before my wife turned vegetarian, I'd always thought of her as completely unremarkable in every way" (3). Without introducing himself, Mr Cheong thus begins the section he narrates, his curt statement aiming to establish control over his sense of time and his newly vegan wife. Narrating in the first-person singular, he traces the end of his marriage to the beginning of his wife's transformation, angry that his life breaks into a before-time that he cannot reclaim. He looks backward – repeatedly recalling scenes of his wife in the kitchen and preparing meat – pressing the counterforce of his retrospective narrative against the vortex of her turning-vegan. He also insistently refers to her as "my wife," in a kind of lexical pinning that runs parallel with the physical pinning that takes place when he holds her down and assaults her. It is not until her mother asks after her and her father angrily shouts, "Yeong-hye, are you still not eating meat?" that she shifts out from under the possessive diction and into a name (28). But this naming becomes something she defies too, increasingly unable or unwilling to hear it, even when directly addressed.

As scholars of *The Vegetarian* have argued, Yeong-hye's radical disruption of carnivorous consumption threatens all manner of hierarchical ordering and power. Her veganism is read by other characters as distinctly pathological, as Laura Wright maintains, and declared a medical emergency; only as a sick and dangerous vegan is she rendered intelligible in the patriarchal structure of her world.[1] In this chapter, we follow a similarly vegan, feminist route into *The Vegetarian* but we shift it slightly, away from seeing Yeong-hye as a puzzling object of interpretation. We argue that while Kang introduces Yeong-hye as a kind of closed book – "always difficult to read," in the words of another character – she also casts her as a reader and writer herself, binding Yeong-hye's vegan dreaming to her intellectual openness (129).

Just before Yeong-hye materializes in the light of an open fridge – peering into it as if it were suddenly legible as a space filled with dead animals – she is introduced as someone who disappears into books. Interestingly, it is Mr Cheong who recalls Yeong-hye as an avid reader, something his narrative at once establishes and downplays. With characteristic disdain, he remarks:

> While I idled the afternoon away, TV remote in hand, she would shut herself up in her room. More than likely she would spend the time reading, which was

practically her hobby. For some unfathomable reason, reading was something she was able to really immerse herself in – reading books that looked so dull I couldn't even bring myself to so much as take a look inside the covers. Only at mealtimes would she open the door and silently emerge to prepare the food. (5)

This passage sets up Yeong-hye's rich, inaccessible, intellectual or mental life. The quiet seclusion of her room reflects the shape and mystery of her books, enclosing her in a space where she is immersed in words. Mr Cheong's indifference obscures the books that Yeong-hye reads but his memory of her "emerg[ing] to prepare the food" divides her pastime from his mealtime, producing a significant division between reading and eating meat.

It seems that Yeong-hye's awakening to the horror of meat is thus precipitated by her intimacy with books, even if Mr Cheong does not quite grasp the connection. Formed out of once-living trees, the paper she handles and the pages she reads command her attention and then widen it, into her comprehension of meat as once-living animals. To borrow Carol J. Adams's terminology, Yeong-hye recovers the absent referent. By immersing herself in words, she absorbs other worlds into her unconscious mind, which then surface in and as her dreaming. When the forest stares back at the human characters towards the end of the novel, it similarly surfaces as an entity to be reckoned with and it returns us to the beginning of the novel, where unnamed books are introduced alongside an initially unnamed wife. "I had a dream," Yeong-hye replies when asked why she repudiates meat. But the dreaming follows the reading, as a kind of narrative reordering of what seeps from paper and into her longing to become part of the forest.

Yeong-hye's connection with paper and ink widens further when Mr Cheong describes her occupation before her transformation: as a writer "subcontracted by a manhwa [comics] publisher to work on the words for their speech bubbles, which she could do from home" (4). It is easy to miss the potential significance of this recollection, diminished as it is by Mr Cheong's inclusion of the term "subcontracted" and the connotations of working from home. But against the grain of his arrogance, we are invited to visualize Yeong-hye's work – how she once engaged with illustrations of individuals split apart from their own words and separate from the thoughts that came to them. As a writer of speech-bubble content, Yeong-hye worked with language as material that arrived from the outside, linked belatedly to the outlines of bodies, and not as something generated from within. It follows, then, that the empty spaces perhaps presented Yeong-hye not only with a way of seeing her own relationship to thinking, able to detach herself from words that did not fit, but also with a sense of speech bubbles' openness to any linguistic and conceptual permutation or revolution.

When Yeong-hye announces towards the end of the novel that she is "not an animal anymore," her sister, In-hye, asks, "What are you talking about? Do you really think you've turned into a tree? How could a plant talk? How can you think those things?" (154). The mysterious look in Yeong-hye's shining eyes invites us to fill in the answers: that trees can talk, not only to one another while alive and through their network of roots, as Yeong-hye realizes when she takes to hand-standing, but also after their transformation into books.[2] Here, the novel itself comes to terms with its own violent history, as a product of a forest that resembles a "massive animal," ferociously protecting itself from death (183). And yet, in another conceptual turn, the transition that trees undergo in death, into paper and books, also conveys a form of rebirth. Their own painful metamorphosis potentially opens onto another, one that takes place deep within those who read, pushing us to reinvent what it means to be human and what it means to hold and bear knowledge in a world where lifeforms – plant, animal, human, atmospheric – impinge on each other, enmeshed in intimate webs of killing and creation.

When In-hye begins to see from Yeong-hye's point of view, she thinks of "the innumerable trees she's seen over the course of her life" and realizes that she does not know "what those trees . . . had been saying" (169). Enclosed within *The Vegetarian* is the vegetarian through whom trees attempt to speak, in a language that is at once untranslatable and familiar. Book and character share the same nomenclature and change places with one another, wrought through the same crises in knowability, form, and boundaries. As the first-person narration of Mr Cheong's section gives way to the free indirect discourse of the two sections that follow, Yeong-hye's vegan metamorphosis articulates itself in terms of a feral shift towards the wild forest ground and into a dreamscape where a different order of existence and understanding flickers.

The Vegetarian at first represents veganism in terms of relinquishment and withdrawal. The act of giving up meat is quickly followed by Yeong-hye's desire to strip herself of appetite, relationships, clothing, and existence as a human woman. It seems conventional and straightforward: Yeong-hye purges the fridge and freezer of meat; she gets rid of her leather shoes; and she clears her mind, explaining simply that "it wouldn't be right" not to become vegan (13). This emptying-out, however, turns into a filling-up: by nightmares and memories of slaughter; and by a world in which there appears to be *"no end to meat, and no exit"* (12, italics in original). Yeong-hye renounces everything connected to a formerly carnivorous self – including withdrawing her body from human reproduction – only to feel saturated and bloody.

Her first dream interrupts Mr Cheong's section with an italicized sequence that pushes into it, moving the nightmare space of a barn into that of the kitchen, along with the blood and "familiar and yet not" faces that force Yeong-hye's body into a fleshy reality of pain (12). Her voice makes its way into his narrative and shifts it into truncated sentences that do not conform to his past-tense account. Filled with gerunds, her phrases turn verbs into nouns in an unsettling urgency that reflects the persistent present of a nightmare with no end. Both timeless and situated firmly in time, disembodied yet undeniably rooted in the body, Yeong-hye's dream becomes a text within a text whose contents spill over and reconfigure her waking life.

As other dreams surface, they combine indeterminate fragments marked by viscous, seeping edges with very specific childhood memories of her father's torture of Yeong-hye's pet dog, which she then eats. Here, the novel's vegan politics come into sharper focus, in the convergence of memory and uncertainty and through the agony attendant upon Yeong-hye's transformation. What *The Vegetarian* communicates about veganism is that it is not so much a matter of choosing – of taking an ethical step and starting over, free of meat – as it is being overwhelmed by the evidence of human violence against other animals. In Yeong-hye's recollection of the dog, its eyes are what haunt her and follow her as the line between human and animal existence shatters.[3] To become vegan, the novel implies, is to be moved into sensory, inescapable confrontations with the stubborn fleshiness of meat, of animal lives ingested along with blood and tissue, where no easy divisions exist. Visual and tactile boundaries between self and other become difficult to discern and retain, and time begins to contract and expand. The sensation of being *"shut up behind a door without a handle"* (28, italics in original), as if frozen inside a meat-locker, alternates with the terror of being adrift in infinite darkness.

In her dreams, Yeong-hye slides into pools of blood that seep from unknown bodies as her decisive embrace of veganism, in turn, dissolves the outlines of a self she tries to recognize and escape. Her attempt to break from what might be called the time of meat, where predictable dynamics secure mindless consumption, is replaced by the disorientation that meat's routines leave in its wake. Her dream sequences project her inside a temporality unbound by the institutions that seek to categorize bodies and read their marks. For Mr Cheong, her veganism marks a painful rupture in the progression of time, and he recalls her decision to repudiate meat with vivid precision. Standing before the fridge, Yeong-hye materializes in his line of sight to slice his anticipated future from his comfortable present. Her upright stance is knife-like, and her edges are sharpened by the light of the fridge; she all but literally castrates him.

In fact, her motionless body obliterates the child he imagines "gurgling 'dada'" in the future and pairs veganism with an unbinding from heterosexual reproduction (6). It empties from the father's table the presence of children, whose futures are laid out in patriarchal forecasts alongside those of slaughtered animals, endlessly regenerated for consumption. Yeong-hye's bare breasts and the shadows of her nipples surface throughout Mr Cheong's narrative as reminders of this annihilation – of the milk she will not produce and the bodies she withdraws from his control. Ghostlike in the middle of the night, Yeong-hye terminates his chance at self-replication through her body, and just when he began to imagine himself as a father.

When Mr Cheong describes her as utterly incomprehensible and frightening to him, he communicates the extent to which her withdrawal from him threatens everything that secures him in place, including his own sense of differentiation from others. She refuses to consent to sex with him because he "smells of meat" and effectively turns him inside out; what he ingests, she implies, ends up leaking past his outlines, detaching him from the masculinity he takes as real and solid (17). When both husband and father attempt to reorient her towards the highly symbolic, meat-laden tables where patriarchal authority persists, Yeong-hye meets them there, but on her own terms, braless in translucent clothing and resolute in her veganism.

In another feminist turn, the novel depicts the men as profoundly rattled by the transformations set into motion by Yeong-hye's defiance. Where her brother-in-law becomes swept up by flowers that appear to command him to paint them into being on Yeong-hye's body, her husband finds himself groping for his shoes and trying to regain his metaphoric footing (41). Just as the blood in Yeong-hye's IV bag betrays its backward flow into the saline, mixing up the substances and the direction of their movement, so too does Mr Cheong's consciousness turn towards memory and then confuse itself in dreams. His nightmare of committing murder, for example, slips into the sensorial excess of Yeong-hye's italicized sections, at odds with his own narrative tone of precision and reason. Because he cannot specify whose intestines he digs into and wrenches out in his dream – whether human or other animal – he leaves the body's classification open and loses the ability to distinguish slaughter from murder. He also recounts the tactility of the flaying about which he dreams in a simile, so that his dream about pulling apart flesh with his hands is "like eating fish" but not confirmed as fish, confounding any sense of certainty and confusing touch with taste (50).

The section narrated by Mr Cheong closes shortly after this dream, when he recalls seeing Yeong-hye clutching a bird, unable to ascertain whether the marks on its bleeding body derive from her teeth or a predator's. He cannot tell if she saved the bird by crushing it in her grasp or if she found it that way. Everything that was once straightforward and distinct for him becomes imprecise and harrowing. When Yeong-hye asks, "'Have I done something wrong?" her self-division in this moment is at once frightening and heartbreaking; it is as if she takes flight from herself, only to venture back with a sense of bafflement (58).

Recalling the earlier allusion to comic-books, Yeong-hye seems to have shifted from one panel into another but not forward in time or with any memory of herself in the panel before. She holds a bird, but she does not know how it came to be in her hand. Indeed, the effect of the comic-book panels moving from the pages of Yeong-hye's work and into *The Vegetarian*'s reordering of time and space makes sense of this strange, still moment. The form of the comic-book also seems to account for the lag time that arises between the characters' utterances and the belated recognition of their own voices, such as when In-hye implores Yeong-hye's physician towards the end of the novel to help her sister, "unaware of the shrill scream coming from her own mouth," as if it were a speech bubble attached to her (175). The scripts of meat that play out across different dinner tables in conversations to which Yeong-hye is subjected seem likewise to float from those who recite them, suspended in predictability. The unwillingness, on the part of others, to contemplate the reasons for Yeong-hye's veganism allows them to guard the outlines of their identities and remain detached from what they eat. Those who do wonder what is "happening inside her" find themselves shifting into her dream world, drawn into its depths (89).

The story of Yeong-hye's veganism thus takes shape in relation to the comic-book's structure and lexicon, connecting her work as a writer to her enclosure in this novel.[4] Her transformation moves through three sections, each of which functions like a panel holding her within a particular time frame. The notion of the panel's bleed, moreover, accounts for the leaking of Yeong-hye's dreams across the borders of the sections and into the minds of the characters through whom the sections are focalized. The representation of blood splashing in different directions also appears to take its cue from "the splash" as the term for a panel without borders. As *The Vegetarian* nears its conclusion and brings the two sisters together, Yeong-hye and In-hye enter a sort of gutter space, the term for the spaces between panels in a comic, and face each other in this weird realm of between-ness. At once empty and full, where meaning is made in the movement through panels, the gutters hold interpretation open, suspending everything, even as a narrative unfolds across them.

As the last section dissolves bounds of time and distinctions between real and dream spaces, the sisters leak into each other, opening another way of being beyond the panels that seek to contain them. By the end of the novel, it becomes possible that Yeong-hye's experience does not precede In-hye's, but rather twists around and follows it, dreamt backward by In-hye into the plot's unfolding. As the one sister becomes the medium of the other's rescue – in agonizing deliveries from captivity as carnivorous human women – the storyline is submerged beneath the dreaming and bends to its temporality. Furthermore, when In-hye's son dreams of a white bird in the third section of the novel, it becomes possible in retrospect to see him dreaming both Yeong-hye and his mother into being, in a strange reversal of reproductive time and bodies. The question of who dreams whom into existence echoes across the novel, as one realm of consciousness breaks across boundaries and alters what humans assume is real.

Against her initial efforts to measure time and remain detached from Yeong-hye's ways of seeing, In-hye slowly moves into the attenuating line between dreaming and waking that accompanies Yeong-hye's veganism. She hears Yeong-hye's voice when she is suspended in that halfway realm, alert to Yeong-hye describing "*roots . . . sprouting out of my hands [and] flowers bloom[ing] from my crotch*" (127, italics in original), and she is filled with anger when her son's voice awakens her from this vision. As In-hye increasingly opens herself to Yeong-hye's point of view, she imagines forms of embodiment experienced as a fragile communion with trees, plants, animals, and the earth.

In-hye's body mirrors Yeong-hye's all along: the shared blood that runs through their veins also leaks into contestations of the familial and menstrual futurities that press on them throughout each of the novel's three sections. Where Yeong-hye bleeds from her wrists, hoping to release the animal lives inside of her own body and escape into a different way of being, In-hye bleeds uncontrollably from a "tongue-like polyp . . . stuck to the vaginal wall", as if a plant-like entity begins to take shape inside of her, birthing itself (162). These two modes of bleeding reflect one another, "gaping black wound[s] still sucking" (163). They recall slaughtered animals sticking to insides, lacerations from the outside, and female bodies that gush and splash against the walls that close in on them.

The novel approaches a tenuous conclusion, in which everything remains held open between the converging bodies of the two sisters. Reclined at the threshold between life and death, Yeong-hye becomes the mode of her sister's transformation; turned inward like a book of secrets, she seems to slip out of reach, but she also draws In-hye towards her. If in Yeong-hye's dreams "familiarity bleeds into strangeness," then it also reverses, strangeness bleeding into familiarity. In-hye looks deeply into Yeong-hye's eyes, where she is reflected back: herself and another. When In-hye speaks, she enters into an intimate proximity with Yeong-hye, moving "her mouth right up to Yeong-hye's ear." Her words are tentative, interrogative – "'Yeong-hye? [. . .] Perhaps this is all a kind of a dream [. . .] but surely the dream isn't all there is?'" before they break off into ellipses points: "'Because . . . because then . . .'" (182). It is her last utterance, faltering on its way towards an answer that never arrives, forever imminent.

As In-hye's thoughts hover, leaving the possibility of a dream world open and pressing, a black bird appears only to disappear in the dazzling summer sun. It marks the cusp between the real and the dream worlds and flickers into view as the soaring shadow of the captive white bird. The two women also remain in flight, at once safe and trapped inside the confined space of the ambulance, held still as they hurtle towards an uncertain horizon in a heavy atmosphere. In-hye lets go of her son in her mind, thinking about him as someone who can soon "read on his own," and then returns to her memory of her husband and sister, covered in flowers and willing to "stake everything and lose everything" (182). She remembers how he painted his and Yeong-hye's bodies and reframes her initial impression of their intimacy, letting go of it as betrayal or infidelity and seeing it instead as them relinquishing their human elements. She then turns towards another memory, this time of herself as plant-like, feeling rainwater crossing and leaching into her flesh, spreading into her veins.

In the last two paragraphs, words and whispers dissipate, and we are left with breath, quiet and steady, and eyes, like those of Yeong-hye's childhood dog who stares up at her from her bowl of soup, that invite us to follow the horizon line. The novel closes with In-hye's gaze as she tracks, almost predatorily, the forest that in turn tracks her. In-hye's eyes first look up with her raised head, then to the black bird, and then to the trees by the side of the road. With her gaze on the tree line, she apprehends the forest as it becomes both elemental and animal: "green fire undulating like the rippling flanks of a massive animal, wild and savage" (182). Her eyes call us back to Yeong-hye's own stare, which holds others in its unknowable depths, described throughout the novel as unnerving and steady. Folded together into "her," the two women become subject and object of that "dark and insistent" stare of the closing sentence (183). Kang summons In-hye's and Yeong-hye's eyes into quiet yet feral protestations that turn the tree line into a "wild and savage" horizon, unfixed.

On this horizon resides the anticipatory yet palpably present dream of veganism, another way of being in the world, devastating and ablaze. In a novel wherein text and body slip into each other – *The Vegetarian* referring internally to Yeong-hye and back to itself – Yeong-hye's vegan body becomes a leaky text attempting to write itself from within, struggling under the hands of men writing her, each of whom imagine her in a freeze-frame of words, paint, or video recordings. Yeong-hye's identity as a writer filling speech bubbles thus converges with her identity as a vegan, emptying herself of the patriarchal reality of meat to fill others with vegan dreaming, turning them towards a vegan being.

Notes

1. For further scholarship on Han Kang's novel, see Westwood on vegan speech-acts; Beeston on Yeong-hye and metamorphosis; Carretero-Gonzalez on the female vegan body and narrative point of view; Beeston and Mayo on veganism and anti-capitalism; and Stobie on veganism and species kinship.
2. In-hye's inquiry into how trees might feel and communicate points us towards Peter Wohlleben's research in *The Hidden Life of Trees*.
3. Many animal studies and vegan studies scholars, following the work of Jacques Derrida, have located the gaze as a pivotal space for encounter and transformation. While we believe that Yeong-hye's contact through the eyes, touch, sound, and through books all contribute to her transformation, it is worth pointing out the importance of the gaze.
4. See Hilary Chute's "Comics as Literature?: Reading Graphic Narrative" and Scott McCloud's *Understanding Comics* for thorough descriptions of comic-book terminology as they relate to narrative form and temporality. See also Glenn Willmott's essay in this volume for more on the intersections of veganism and comics.

Works Cited

Adams, Carol J. *The Sexual Politics of Meat: A Feminist-Vegetarian Critical Theory*. Continuum, 2011.

Beeston, Alix. "The Watch-Bitch Now: Reassessing the Natural Woman in Han Kang's *The Vegetarian* and Charlotte Wood's *The Natural Way of Things*." *Signs*, vol. 45, no. 3, 2020, pp. 679–702.

Carratero-Gonzalez, Margarita. "Looking at the Vegetarian Body: Narrative Points of View and Blind Spots in Han Kang's *The Vegetarian*." *Through a Vegan Studies Lens:*

Textual Ethics and Lived Activism, edited by Laura Wright, U of Nevada P, 2019, pp. 165–79.

Chute, Hilary. "Comics as Literature?: Reading Graphic Narrative." *PMLA*, vol. 123, no. 2, 2008, pp. 452–65.

Kang, Han. *The Vegetarian: A Novel*. 2007, translated by Deborah Smith, Granta, 2018.

Mayo, Liz. "A Quiet Riot: Veganism as Anti-capitalism and Ecofeminist Revolt in Han Kang's *The Vegetarian*." *The Routledge Handbook of Vegan Studies*, edited by Laura Wright, Routledge, 2021, pp. 101–10.

McCloud, Scott. *Understanding Comics*. Kitchen Sink Press, 1993.

Stobie, Caitlin E. "Good Wife? Sibling Species in Han Kang's *The Vegetarian*." *ISLE: Interdisciplinary Studies in Literature and the Environment*, vol. 24, no. 4, 2017, pp. 787–802.

Westwood, Benjamin. "On Refusal." *Thinking Veganism in Literature and Culture: Towards a Vegan Theory*, edited by Emelia Quinn and Benjamin Westwood, Palgrave Macmillan, 2018, pp. 175–98.

Wohlleben, Peter. *The Hidden Life of Trees: What They Feel, How They Communicate*. Greystone Books, 2016.

Wright, Laura. "The Dangerous Vegan: Han Kang's *The Vegetarian* and the Anti-Feminist Rhetoric of Disordered Eating." *(In)Digestion in Literature and Film: A Transcultural Approach*, edited by Niki Kiviat and Serena J. Rivera. Routledge, 2020, pp. 121–34.

11

POETRY

Stewart Cole

Introduction

THE BODIES OF critical work in both ecocriticism and animal studies offer productive approaches to poetry that alert us to how the artform's figurative and musical dimensions allow it to engage with nonhuman nature in ways that transcend mere depiction and powerfully convey our utter embeddedness in what we inadequately dub "the environment."[1] Such engagements thereby serve to undermine the anthropocentric discourses that authorize our continued exploitation and destruction of the other-than-human world. If a vegan approach to poetry is to distinguish itself from these critical ancestors, then, it must both draw upon the anti-anthropocentrism and empathetic attention to the nonhuman other that, at their best, they so successfully cultivate while also going beyond those considerable virtues to somehow embody, in its critical practice, the refusal at the root of veganism – namely, the radical abstinence from consuming or using the products of animal exploitation and execution. While recognizing this fundamental difficulty in staking out a specifically vegan reading practice, this chapter confronts that difficulty as a productive challenge, attempting to provisionally delineate a vegan mode of reading poetry in the teeth of the apparent discreteness of the realms of criticism and consumer choice. In the first section, I turn to one of the touchstone works of literary animal studies, J. M. Coetzee's *The Lives of Animals* (1999), drawing from that text's engagement with animal poems four potential parameters for the vegan critic of poetry. In the second section, I undertake an experiment within those parameters, taking as a test object D. H. Lawrence's poem "Fish" – a text that, I argue, evokes meat-eating as a means of gesturing ethically beyond it, to a world in which the human consumption of animal flesh is seen as a paltry squandering of our relational potential vis-à-vis the nonhuman other, a world in which veganism's sliver of utopian promise has blossomed into fulfillment.

Towards a Vegan Approach to Poetry: Elizabeth Costello's Poetics of Corporeality

The second of *The Lives of Animals*' two sections, entitled "The Poets and the Animals," offers a rare instance of poetry being approached in illuminating ways from what might be construed as a vegan perspective, as the fictional novelist-critic Elizabeth Costello compares the poetry of Rainer Maria Rilke to that of Ted Hughes in terms of their portrayals of nonhuman animals, specifically big cats. In Rilke's "The Panther," claims Costello, "the panther is there as a stand-in for something else" – that is, he is a symbol, "dissolv[ing] into a dance of energy around a center . . . a vital embodiment of the kind of force that is released in an atomic explosion" (Coetzee 50). Abstracted into a typification of "elementary particle physics," Rilke's panther is voided of its bodily animality, becoming a mere vehicle of the poet's ideational scaffolding, a high concept in a panther suit (50). Conversely, in Costello's reading of Hughes's poems "The Jaguar" and "Second Glance at a Jaguar," "we know the jaguar not from the way he seems but from the way he moves" (51):

> By bodying forth the jaguar, Hughes shows us that we too can embody animals – by the process called poetic invention that mingles breath and sense in a way that no one has explained and no one ever will. He shows us how to bring the living body into being within ourselves. When we read the jaguar poem, when we recollect it afterwards in tranquility, we are for a brief while the jaguar. He ripples within us, he takes over our body, he is us. (53)

In Costello's estimation, then, Hughes's jaguar poems epitomize poetry's capacity to effect a sense of embodiment so complete as to transcend representational distance and allow for something akin to possession or even metamorphosis, a kind of being-with that is the apotheosis of empathy.

For Costello – who by this point in the narrative has set herself at odds with her university hosts by asserting her ethical vegetarianism, broaching the dreaded comparison between factory farming and the Holocaust, and ridiculing Western man's hubristic exaltation of reason as decisively lifting us into an ontological sphere above that occupied by our nonhuman animal brethren – the ability that poetry affords us to virtually become the embodied other can serve as an ethical bulwark against Cartesian conceptions of nonhuman animals as mechanistic, impenetrably alien, and therefore by implication categorically less worthy of moral concern than the eminently relatable beings of our own species. Poetry is thus a window into what elsewhere in the text Costello terms the "fullness of being" of human and nonhuman animals alike, "the sensation – a heavily affective sensation – of being a body with limbs that have extension in space, of being alive to the world" (33). Claiming, in response to the titular question of Thomas Nagel's classic essay "What Is It Like to Be a Bat?", that "being fully a bat is like being fully human, which is also to be full of being" (33), Costello stakes out fullness of being as the core ontological state shared among all animals, quashing the idea of the inscrutable other as an ethically hollow pose, and asserting that "there is no limit to the extent to which we can think ourselves into the being of another" (35). Within the framework of Costello's thinking throughout *The Lives of Animals*, then, poetry is singled out as the most immediate means of achieving the kind of radical empathy that she clearly sees as a precondition to animal liberation, enabling us as it does to go beyond "think[ing] ourselves into the being of another" (35) to reach the point of "bring[ing] the living body into being within ourselves" (53).

Though I am both more hopeful about the ethical usefulness of recognitions of alterity and more skeptical of poetry's capacity to collapse representational distance in opening us up to habitation by the body of the other, I see in Costello's poetics of corporeality four key emphases through which one might map out the contours – speculative, provisional, contingent, but a germane starting point nonetheless – of a specifically vegan mode of reading poetry. First, Costello's insistence on the flat ontology of fullness of being as a bodily state universal to animality places her in generative dialogue with key ideas in animal and vegan studies – most productively for this chapter's purposes Matthew Calarco's concept of *indistinction*, the "shared space of exposed embodiment" (423), occupied by human and nonhuman animals alike, the explicit recognition of which is foundational to any ethical veganism. A vegan mode of reading poetry would be alert both to poetic figurations of this zone of indistinction and to the way that, as we can derive from Costello's analysis, poems are capable of enforcing in their readers an embodied awareness of this zone.

Second, in her emphasis on how poetry "mingles breath and sense in a way that no one has explained and no one ever will" (53), Costello signals an intense awareness of *poetic form*, and particularly of how poetry's music is integral not only to its capacity to embody the fullness of human and nonhuman animal being but also, therefore, to its ethical affect. A vegan mode of reading poetry would thus be sensitive to the rhythms of poetic form in both their ephemeral and technical aspects – an appropriately dual orientation given that, as Emelia Quinn and Benjamin Westwood note, veganism itself can be seen "as a shifting, perhaps unfixable, mix of affect and rationality, a confusion between reasoned, willed response and emotional, instinctive reaction" (12) – and to the ways in which the rhythms of form serve to figure, on the one hand, states of exposure and vulnerability that harbor the very ethical imperatives that give rise to veganism, and on the other, patterns of music and silence that speak to the tensions between verbal mastery and its relinquishment. For if, as Joshua Schuster maintains, "[t]he vegan decision not to devour . . . turns on a sovereign refusal of sovereignty" (215), then a vegan mode of reading poetry might productively regard the oscillations of poetic form in analogous terms, as embodying an ethically cogent interplay of exertions and refusals of verbal sovereignty.

Third, Costello's choice to single out the work of omnivore and one-time sheep farmer Hughes as ethically and affectively exemplary points to a crucial imperative for a vegan mode of reading poetry: if it aspires to relevance beyond the estimated less than one percent of the world's population that identifies as vegan – and it should, not least in the interest of swelling that number to the benefit of the planet and the beings who inhabit it – *it cannot limit itself to engaging only with vegan authors or texts with explicitly vegan content.*[2] Instead, a vegan mode of reading poetry with any likelihood of attaining a broad critical relevance would need to be rooted in the recognition that while ethical veganism entails radically abstaining from forms of consumption – in diet, clothing, entertainment, and beyond – that accede to and thereby sustain the exploitation and slaughter of nonhuman animals, the vegan ethos is at root a response to the anthropocentric attitudes that make such abuses not just possible but utterly central to the functioning of global economies. Vegan critics of poetry, then, should find themselves taking up not only texts that embody alternative, anti-anthropocentric frameworks but also those that espouse the very attitudes that veganism finds its origins in opposing. In other words (and to adapt terms from Carol J. Adams's *The Sexual Politics of Meat*), a vegan mode of reading poetry will attend not only to "vegan words" but also to "texts of meat"; for, as Costello asserts in defending her particular attention to the masculinist, primitivist, omnivorous Hughes: "writers teach us more than they are aware of" (53). This verity should serve to remind vegan critics that encounters with scenes of carnivorism, for example, might ultimately advance the project of animal liberation by helping us to know the adversary (so to speak) in a way that confining one's engagement to a vegans-only echo chamber certainly cannot.

This brings me to the fourth and final emphasis inherent in Costello's poetics of corporeality that we might adopt in shaping the contours of a vegan approach to poetry, and that is its *utopianism*. Costello's insistence that in the readerly transfixion of our encounter with Hughes's poetic jaguar, "*he is us*" speaks to an extraordinary faith both in the capacity of verbal artifacts to register in powerfully embodied terms, and further, in the way that such poetically occasioned bodily overwhelmings might reverberate as positive alterations in awareness, in behavior, and ultimately in the fates and lives of animals (53, emphasis added). In other words, Costello displays the unabashed conviction that poetry can be a force for what the utopian theorist Ruth Levitas terms "the education of desire" – that is, for aspirationally orienting its audience towards better ways of living and being. This dovetails with a salutary emphasis in recent work in vegan studies on veganism itself as a utopian dispensation. For example, Quinn and Westwood refer to "the end of the exploitative use of nonhuman animals for human benefit" as "the kernel of utopian desire" that animates "vegan praxis" (8), while Quinn herself asserts that "[t]he utopianism of veganism . . . is premised on the knowledge of an inevitable failure" (165), and Schuster avers that "[t]he vegan does not think that power and violence will go away in a fully vegan world – but there is no reason to relent on a desire for utopian ways of living together either" (216). This utopian motif doubtless emerges from the motive admixture of realism and hope summed up by Tristram McPherson in his deft taxonomizing of the ethical basis for veganism: "In a slogan: it is vanishingly unlikely that one will make a difference by being vegan, but if one does, it will be a correspondingly massive difference" (222). In other words (and this is the essence of the utopianism informing all of the above formulations), despite the seeming inevitability of veganism's failure to bring about a world in which nonhuman animals are no longer exploited, the prospect of such a world – shimmering in that state of potentiality that the West's preeminent philosopher of utopia, Ernst Bloch, names the "Not Yet" – is veganism's core source of sustenance. A vegan mode of reading poetry, then, will be attuned both to those moments in poems at which we might glimpse the lineaments of a world beyond exploitation and to the propensity of poetry itself – in its mingling of sense and breath, word and music, the articulate and the as-yet inarticulable – to gesture beyond what is, to evoke new configurations of reality through the "ferrying across" of metaphor, and therefore to harbor utopian possibilities through its very nature as a figurative artform.

Vegan Reading in Practice: D. H. Lawrence's "Fish"

D. H. Lawrence's poem "Fish," from his 1923 collection *Birds, Beasts, and Flowers*, serves as an apt artifact upon which to practice the vegan mode of reading poetry provisionally delineated above. Like Hughes, Lawrence was far from vegan (the word having been coined twenty-one years after the publication of *Birds* and fourteen years after his death).[3] Also like Hughes, he was an inveterate omnivore, an occasional farmer of animals, and often espoused a masculinist primitivism that, from the ecofeminist perspective that inheres in the fabric of vegan studies, can rightly be described as retrograde (see, for example, Adams, "Why Feminist-Vegan"). In his 1925 essay "Reflections on the Death of a Porcupine," for example, Lawrence seeks to naturalize oppression and exploitation, pronouncing that "every man, in the struggle of conquest towards his own consummation, must master the inferior cycles of life, and never relinquish his mastery" (363) and offering among the examples of "inferior cycles of life" the butterfly's less "vivid" life in relation to that of the snake, the ostrich's in relation to the cat's, and the Mexican's in relation to his own. In the same essay, however – an essay built around his remorse at killing a porcupine that he felt pressured by cultural mores to kill, despite his aversion to doing so ("It is a duty to kill the things. But the dislike of killing him was greater than the dislike of him" [349]) – Lawrence elaborates a strange distinction between *existence*, the population or species-level plane on which "inferior cycles of life" must be "master[ed]," and *being*, the plane on which individuals of all species attain an "incomparable and unique" ontological exaltation (358). Anticipating Elizabeth Costello's terminology, Lawrence sets out the following as an "inexorable law of life": "Any creature that attains to its own *fullness of being*, its own *living* self, becomes unique, a nonpareil. It has its place in the fourth dimension, the heaven of existence, and there it is perfect, it is beyond comparison" (358, first emphasis added). Having used the concept of existence to affirm anthropocentric and racialist hierarchies, then, Lawrence uses the concept of being to posit a flat ontology in "the fourth dimension, the heaven of existence" – and the signal example he chooses of this fullness of being ("[t]he dandelion in full flower, a little sun bristling with sun-rays on the green earth" [358]) makes it clear that this dimension is not, as it may sound, a Platonic otherworld, but is rather a mode of embodied existing in the present closely akin to Costello's "heavily affective sensation ... of being alive in the world" (Coetzee 33). And as with Costello, Lawrence's vision of fullness of being can be seen to dovetail with his conception of poetry's capacity to figure the embodied vitality of human and nonhuman animal alike. In his most direct statement of poetics, the 1919 essay "Poetry of the Present," Lawrence sets himself off against the past- and future-oriented poetry of his English Romantic forebears Keats and Shelley to call for a Whitmanesque "poetry of this immediate present" (or, further down, "[t]he seething poetry of the incarnate now"): a *vers libre* capable of embodying the "quivering momentaneity" that is "the quality of life itself" (79). Unsurprisingly, he takes recourse to the other-than-human for his most elaborate figuration of this poetry's aspirations:

> For such utterance any externally applied law would be mere shackles and death. The law must come new each time from within. The bird is on the wing in the winds, flexible to every breath, a living spark in the storm, its very flickering depending on its supreme mutability and power of change. Whence such a bird came: whither it goes: from what solid earth it rose up, and upon what solid earth it will close its wings and settle: this is not the question. This is a question of before and after. Now, *now*, the bird is on the wing in the winds. (82)

What we see in Lawrence, then, is a poet who, on the one hand, accedes to the anthropocentric logic against which veganism defines itself while, on the other hand, repeatedly paying tribute to the nonhuman world not as a source of symbols – for this is what he objects to in Keats's nightingale and Shelley's skylark: that they become emblematic of their poetry's past- and future-orientations, its avoidance of present-tense vitality – but rather as a world of co-existents equivalent to the human in their "living spark," their "supreme mutability and power of change," their sheer being in the *now*. Similarly, while Lawrence routinely fixates on the inscrutable alterity of the nonhuman, he does so in a way that communicates a respect and even reverence that leads him to question the power we humans bestow upon ourselves to hurt, kill, and consume our fellow beings by virtue of their membership of a species other than our own.

"Fish" is perhaps the most lucid illustration of these characteristic ambivalences in Lawrence's work, a poem spoken by a self-hating omnivore whose persistence in seeing the titular creature as "meat" despite his intense awareness of the fish's vibrantly embodied capacities for fear, joy, pain, and beyond, raises crucial questions for the vegan critic in terms of why knowledge of nonhuman animals' fullness of being translates for so few of us into a strong-enough conviction of their intrinsic worth that we refuse to be complicit in their exploitation, suffering, or death. What are the barriers that prevent such knowledge from issuing in that refusal, and in surveying such barriers, can we glimpse the contours of a future world in which they have fallen away – a multispecies utopia of nonviolent coexistence?

From its opening lines, "Fish" suggests that humanity's sense of its unique capacity for anguish is a chief obstacle to achieving such a vision:

> Fish, oh Fish,
> So little matters!
>
> Whether the waters rise and cover the earth
> Or whether the waters wilt in the hollow places,
> All one to you.
>
> Aqueous, subaqueous,
> Submerged
> And wave-thrilled.
>
> As the waters roll
> Roll you.
> The waters wash,
> You wash in oneness
> And never emerge.
>
> Never know.
> Never grasp. (76)

"So little matters" sets out a clear contrast to the human speaker, encumbered by a species status that means that nothing is ever "All one to [him]," for to be human is to bear the burden of pastness and futurity, to abide in segmented time, unable as the fish is to "wash in oneness," condemned to always "know" and "grasp." While this might be taken as a straightforward tribute to the fish's transcendent capacity to live in pure unity with what elsewhere in the poem is rhapsodized as "the naked element," it also tacitly aggrandizes humanity for the ostensible complexities of our relationship to time, our spectrum of emotional responses, and our knowledge and comprehension – potentially turning what seems like a tributary testament to what fish can do that we cannot into a set of grounds upon which to justify subjecting them to anything that our prehensile grasp affords.

This ambivalence is compounded as the poem continues, proffering its most vivid depiction of the fish's embodiment:

> Your life a sluice of sensation along your sides,
> A flush at the flails of your fins, down the whorl of your tail.
> And water wetly on fire in the grates of your gills;
> Fixed water-eyes.
> . . .
> No fingers, no hands and feet, no lips;
> No tender muzzles,
> No wistful bellies,
> No loins of desire,
> None.

The first of these stanzas wonderfully exemplifies Costello's poetics of corporeality, as the pervasive alliteration combined with the long, fluid free-verse lines serve to figure the fish's kinetic embodiment, the poem's music enforcing a "sluice of sensation" upon us as we read, urging a rhythmic giving-over to the body of the other. At moments like these (and despite its virtuosity), the poem seems a relinquishment of mastery, transcending, to the extent that such a thing is possible, the anthropocentric limits of human language – a feat aptly condensed in the metaphor of "water wetly on fire" in the fish's gills, an image that collapses opposing elements into each other as if to evaporate the conceptual-linguistic order of things. In the second of these stanzas, however, the fish as such disappears, becoming the numinous object of an anaphoric negative theology, disembodied by being defined only by what it is not. Just as Costello concedes of Hughes's work that "despite the vividness and earthiness of the poetry, there remains something Platonic about it" (53), one frequently sees in Lawrence's animal poems, for all their presencing of the nonhuman body, this tendency to abstract the being in question into an emblematic singularity – as when several stanzas later, he deems the fish "Himself all silvery himself / In the element / No more."

To his credit, however, the speaker of "Fish" repeatedly signals his recognition of this emblematizing tendency and pulls back from it to more fleshly ground. Indeed, while critics usually conceive of the poem in halves – with Carrie Rohman's deft characterization of the first half as attempting "to inhabit fish ontology through the poetic imagination" and the second as "insist[ing] upon the radical alterity of the fish and elaborat[ing] the narrator's profound inability to comprehend its experience" standing at the apogee of this tendency (97) – "Fish" can also be seen as effecting a tidal interplay of assertions and corrections. After asserting that the fish is "No more" than "himself / In the element," for example, he recalls himself to its bodily substance and vulnerability ("Food of course! . . . Fear also! / He knows fear!"), which then leads into one of the poem's most overt instances of self-correction:

> Food, and fear, and joie de vivre,
> Without love.

> The other way about:
> Joie de vivre, and fear, and food,
> All without love.

As though realizing that listing "Food" first risks consigning the fish to a realm of biological utility, he repositions "Joie de vivre" to grant it primacy, thus emphasizing the nonhuman capacity for emotion (with the shift to French signaling that the fish's emotional spectrum can translate only imperfectly into human terms). This is a pattern throughout the poem: having emphasized the fish's solitude, the speaker pulls back to acknowledge his sociality ("Admitted, they swarm in companies"); having personified a fish ("A slim young pike with smart fins / And grey-striped suit"), he pulls back to avow the falseness of the anthropomorphizing gesture ("I had made a mistake, I didn't know him. / . . . I didn't know his God"); having caught a fish and "Unhooked his gorping, water-horny mouth," he condemns the hubris of ordaining himself a taker of life ("And my heart accused itself / Thinking: I am not the measure of creation."). This string of ambivalent vacillations issues, towards the end of the poem, in what from the vegan critic's perspective must be seen as its climax:

> He outstarts me.
> And I, a many-fingered horror of daylight to him,
> Have made him die.
>
> Fishes,
> With their gold, red eyes, and green-pure gleam, and under-gold,
> And their pre-world loneliness,
> And more-than-lovelessness,
> And white meat;
> They move in other circles.

The fish "outstarts" the speaker because, as the latter has acknowledged in the previous lines, "He was born in front of my sunrise, / Before my day." The fact of the fish's temporal priority reproves the speaker as an upstart, reducing the human and his exalted capacity to grasp to a grotesque smudge of appendages, "a many-fingered horror of daylight." The speaker's body is not just exposed but overexposed, his blurry corporeality meager in comparison to the rainbowed vividness of the fish's. This discrepancy in stature is nicely figured by "made him die," a formulation that emphasizes the culpability of the act both through its passivity as compared to the obvious alternative, "killed him," and in the way it casts the vaunted human power of making as a blunt tool for petty de-creation. And yet even as the speaker stands in rapt tribute to the fish's beauty, contrite at his possessive violations of the animal's alterity, he cannot help thinking of "white meat."

That the poem's first reference to fish as human food comes in its coda might seem to tacitly posit a kind of carnivorous teleology – as though it is inevitable that "meat" is the fish's ultimate destination – yet, in keeping with the poem's structural rhythm, the speaker strongly hints that he has no taste for fish, at least not now, as he displaces the "Thirst for fish" onto "Cats, and the Neapolitans," with "their oversulphureous lusts," withdrawing once again into a reverential agnosticism: "But I,

I only wonder / And don't know. / I don't know fishes." While on the one hand the poem's final stanza – "In the beginning / Jesus was called The Fish . . . . / And in the end" – might be read as literally apotheosizing the speaker's and Lawrence's abstracting, emblematizing, Platonic tendencies, on the other hand it affirms the sanctity of the fish's bodily existence by linking its death to sacrifice. That this also raises the specter of communion – thus ennobling the prospect of taking the body of the fish into one's mouth – is typical of this poem's tormented confrontation with the feckless violence of human efforts to apprehend, possess, and consume nonhuman others. Given the push and pull of assertion and correction that constitutes the poem's more than 160 lines – with each correction inclining to compassion, respect, and a refusal of the exploitative dynamics of dominion – the vegan critic of "Fish" might be led to speculate that if the poem had been allowed to continue indefinitely in this corrective rhythm, it would eventually have arrived at a vegan ethos, so vividly does it evoke the utopian prospect of a distant future in which humanity has at long last corrected itself free of thoughtless anthropocentrism and the violences it authorizes.

Notes

1. See, for example, Jonathan Bate's *The Song of the Earth*, Onno Oerlemans's *Poetry and Animals*, Cary Wolfe's *Ecological Poetics*, the readings of T. S. Eliot and D. H. Lawrence in Carrie Rohman's *Stalking the Subject*, and the readings of W. H. Auden in Kelly Sultzbach's *Ecocriticism in the Modernist Imagination*.
2. See also Sune Borkfelt's and Emelia Quinn's chapters in this volume for further arguments against too rigid a definition of what counts as a "vegan text."
3. For more on Lawrence's complex relationship to nonhuman animals, see Catherine Brown's contribution to this volume.

Works Cited

Adams, Carol J. *The Sexual Politics of Meat: A Feminist-Vegetarian Critical Theory*. Bloomsbury, 2017.
—. "Why Feminist-Vegan Now?" *Feminism & Psychology*, vol. 20, no. 3, 2010, pp. 302–17.
Bate, Jonathan. *The Song of the Earth*. Harvard UP, 2000.
Calarco, Matthew. "Being Toward Meat: Anthropocentrism, Indistinction, and Veganism." *Dialectical Anthropology*, vol. 38, no. 4, 2014, pp. 415–29.
Coetzee, J. M. *The Lives of Animals*, edited by Amy Gutmann, Princeton UP, 1999.
Lawrence, D. H. *Birds, Beasts, and Flowers*. 1923. Black Sparrow, 2008.
—. "Poetry of the Present." *The Bad Side of Books: Selected Essays*, edited by Geoff Dyer, New York Review Books, 2019, pp. 77–82.
—. *Reflections on the Death of a Porcupine and Other Essays*, edited by Michael Herbert, Cambridge UP, 1988.
Levitas, Ruth. *The Concept of Utopia*. Syracuse UP, 1990.
McPherson, Tristram. "The Ethical Basis for Veganism." *The Oxford Handbook of Food Ethics*, edited by Anne Barnhill, Mark Budolfson, and Tyler Doggett, Oxford UP, 2018, pp. 209–40.
Oerlemans, Onno. *Poetry and Animals: Blurring the Boundaries with the Human*. Columbia UP, 2018.
Quinn, Emelia. "Monstrous Vegan Narratives: Margaret Atwood's Hideous Progeny." *Thinking Veganism in Literature and Culture*, edited by Emelia Quinn and Benjamin Westwood, Palgrave Macmillan, 2018, pp. 149–73.

Quinn, Emelia, and Benjamin Westwood. "Introduction: Thinking through Veganism." *Thinking Veganism in Literature and Culture*, edited by Quinn and Westwood, Palgrave Macmillan, 2018, pp. 1–24.

Rohman, Carrie. *Stalking the Subject: Modernism and the Animal*. Columbia UP, 2009.

Schuster, Joshua. "The Vegan and the Sovereign." *Critical Perspectives on Veganism*, edited by Jodey Castricano and Rasmus R. Simonsen, Palgrave Macmillan, 2016, pp. 203–23.

Sultzbach, Kelly. *Ecocriticism in the Modernist Imagination: Forster, Woolf, and Auden*. Cambridge UP, 2016.

Wolfe, Cary. *Ecological Poetics; or, Wallace Stevens's Birds*. U of Chicago P, 2020.

12

The Graphic Novel

Understanding Comics in a Crisis of Entanglement

Glenn Willmott

This chapter has two aims: to present a basic semiotics of comics relevant to a vegan reading practice and to demonstrate its critical value in a reading of a widely available and celebrated trade comics serial, *Monstress* (published from 2015), by Marjorie Liu and Sana Takeda.

As the various chapters within this section of the present volume attest, many literary forms and genres invite vegan reading practices. One might naturally think that comics, just like other literary forms and visual art practices, is merely susceptible to vegan critique. But this would miss something curious about comics that goes beyond its openness to critical alternatives. No matter the creator, the style, or the content, strange as it may sound, comics *calls* for vegan reading. Like other arts, it is true, we see in it a capacious, adaptable tradition of mimesis and imagination, able to represent multifarious aspects of our world and ourselves.[1] But we may notice something else: it is an entire tradition of art – of formal creative practices and generic reading habits – built on a unique approach to expressing lives and their environments. Thus human-animal discourses and ecocritical interests, as I will sketch out below, are central to the making of comics as an aesthetic form and as a historical genre.[2] Coming from this perspective, *vegan reading* sets a particular challenge. I take the challenge to be to expose the panoply of power relations evoked in representations of the appropriation of nonhuman by human lives. Such a task can have no final horizon of knowledge; it is totalizing, as extensive as the entanglements of its world or worlds extend, never certain and complete.[3] Comics, which displays a lively world-building on its sleeve, invites this task of reading in a unique and provocative way.

The visual language of comics develops a long tradition of the grotesque in art, which depicts deformed or hybridized human, animal, and plant figures in ornamentation and design. This tradition enters comics through its origins in nineteenth-century caricature, from whose generic purposes the modern comics figure of the plastic, stylized person – human, animal, in-between or other – has been freed.[4] The many kinds of animalized and other nonhuman characters in *Monstress* are descendants of the grotesque tradition. But the modern cartoon is no longer limited to signifying satirical exaggeration or social *typage* and so does not need to ask the twentieth-century reader to complete it with some mimetic referent. Of course, it may do. In the most realist of comics, like in Hal Foster's 1929 *Tarzan* adventure strip or the mid-century Classics Illustrated comic books, overt stylization is suppressed and the possibilities of the grotesque are muted. However, such naturalistic realism is relatively rare and risks rigidity, looking and scanning indeed more like illustration than comics. The likes of Mickey Mouse, Charlie Brown, or Wonder Woman are more representative. Such grotesques may be beautiful or ugly, but not *conventionally* unified. They will be composed of some recognizable traits and features, but they are their own imaginary species, *sui generis* posthuman creatures. Their physical coherence and subjective rationale is something new that their creator has imagined for them. And they do not exist in isolation. Cartoon figures are always seen embedded in worlds whose relationships to them cannot be tacitly omitted as is possible in verbal narrative, because the space of the page always surrounds them, both constituting and supplementing them. The substance of this space is normally filled in with setting, although occasional *découpage* for close-ups may offer only empty space. If characters are not consistently embedded in a represented environment, the absence of environment is overt. A visual narrative medium such as film will have a similar environmental conditionality; comics is unique in presenting this environmental space both linearly (in a sequence of panels) and holistically (across panels and page compositions).

In this sense, world-building is essential not only to the narrative imagination of comics, but to its very aesthetic form. What holds the artificial species and environments of any particular comic together is its style. In the popular strip *Calvin and Hobbes*, the tiger, Hobbes, is a weird, artificial amalgam of human, animal, and abstract elements, but these are held fluidly together by Bill Watterson's drawing style for the character; moreover, this figure belongs coherently with the graphic style of Calvin and of all the other objects that normally make up the strip's storyworld. Style in comics allows what might seem like conflicted or disparate elements to appear mysteriously unified, becoming the subliminal, non-mimetic sign of a fantasy personhood or ecology.

The modernist art historian Wilhelm Worringer saw the impulse to abstraction in figural stylization as a way of simplifying and imposing order and unity upon the actual complexity and entanglement in the welter of life (16). The evolution of style in comics may be understood in these terms, as the emergence of diverse ways that comics creators represent, via the artifice of cartooning abstraction, the ontological entanglement of actual lives and things.[5] This stylistic drive towards abstract entanglements may be thought of as effecting a kind of material dialogism among the many pictorial and verbal signs that make up comics. However, because some of these elements are simply expressive forms rather than signs (are, in common parlance, abstract rather than figural or verbal), I prefer to refer to the cognitive and semiotic work of comics more broadly and completely as a *diaphany* – a showing across and showing through – of stylistically entangled beings and spaces.

A vegan reading of comics, in my view, will look for how entangled lives are thus hidden or revealed, and also for how they are caught up in power relations that determine their appropriation or consumption by other lives. The impact of comics calls forth, in both signification and style, a material drama of inside and outside, of assertive personhood and mere substance, in which power relations are always plotted. To illustrate this, I will discuss the gorgeous and troubling storyworld of *Monstress*, in which the protagonist must struggle with an internal *daimon* whose hunger turns her into a violent predator, while she herself is prey to the appropriative machinations – not only digestive – of others. The art of *Monstress* suggestively integrates this plot conflict with a profuse, multilayered graphic design and a fantasy world-building that explores matriarchal power, alternative race and species relations, and queer sexualities.

Let's enter this world the way a comics reader does – not word by word, but image by image. We notice something upon entry right away, because where we enter, where we start immersing ourselves in the storyworld, is not fixed in advance: a peculiarity of comics is the indistinct borderline between story and paratext. The story hardly begins, and our eyes must perform a dance, partly guided but largely improvised, between looking and reading. We find ourselves in a densely layered aesthetic and semiotic world via the comics conventions of (firstly) extra-diegetic splash pages,[6] which are free to combine elements from across the narrative into their own, dream-like logic, and (secondly) diegetic *mise-en-scène*, which even in isolated narrative moments offer a welter of images and signs – words merely among them – all unified by style.

Readers of the original first issue, of the collection of early issues into the first volume, and of the collection of early volumes into the first book, will all see different illustrations for covers, flyleaves, title pages, and frontmatter, none of which are insignificant to how we read the story to come. But the first thing all readers will see, following this, are two full-page illustrations facing each other (4–5). On the left, headed "Chapter One," is an image of a young woman with flowing black hair. Seen from behind, turning towards us, what stands out are the back and sleeves of her long white garment, ornately patterned with stylized bronze flowers and leaves. Her left arm, below the elbow, seems to be in shadow but on closer inspection reveals a prosthesis of dark, grained wood, embossed with the same bronze foliage pattern as her dress. We find her startled, confronting a towering, ornate Art Deco bronze assemblage that echoes motifs from her dress and arm.

This assemblage has other features as well: wing and feather motifs, steampunk machinery motifs, and in the center of its mandala summit, the hint of a human face shrouded in headgear and cloak recalling Egyptian animal-god icons – perhaps Horus or Anubis. If we linger on the page, we notice the cyborgian assemblage is itself built on or against a murky tangle of weird organic elements – skeletal fragments of unidentifiable species, giant bird talons, twisted ligaments of vegetation or flesh – that emerge from a background of furious, fine-lined hatchwork and blotty, dark cloud. It is as if background and foreground are stitched together, never distinctly separable.

On the right, facing page, the dark background is recalled, but here the young woman faces us naked, her prosthesis gone, against a wall of abstract murk covered in hatchwork. She wears a metal collar and chain ornamented in the style of the facing page. A riding crop gestures towards her, its owner out of view. On her chest is a red tattoo or brand in the shape of a human eye, turned vertical. The eye mirrors an identical ornamental pattern in the center of the assemblage that we might otherwise have overlooked. The pattern evokes the mystical third eye of transcendental or enlightened vision. Placed on the woman's chest rather than forehead, and echoing the pinched form of her navel – and similarly in the midriff of the goddess-like assemblage – this icon of true vision seems more than usually grounded in the body. This entire page is the first panel of the narrative, and it contains both captions, for the slave's thoughts, and also speech bubbles, for the dialogue of the slaver. The woman's thoughts reveal that she is "here" in search of an elusive person. The slaver's dialogue identifies the slave only as "lot eight-one-nine," and describes her as seventeen, a virgin, and "Arcanic, but with a *fully* human appearance."

So, as readers, what do we know so far? We know there are slaves and owners in this world, that there is a familiar ideology to justify slavery based on human-nonhuman distinctions, and that these distinctions are animalized (by the riding crop and lack of clothes). We know that the body is important here, either as mere property or as more profound sign, a borderline between inside and outside, the seen and the unseen, and also as a figural hybrid or grotesque that is not self-evidently distinguished from whatever is non-body (prosthesis, assemblage, murky biofacts). What do we not know? We do not yet know that the monstrous eye is a sign of a creature within her, and thus that even her nakedness is a kind of veil or clothing, obscuring complexity, like the masked goddess of the assemblage. We do not yet know, but will know soon, that along with animals and a variety of life forms, there are five "races," or creatures who exhibit personhood and who use language, in this world: a grotesque character menagerie of humans, talking Cats, Ancients (immortal anthropomorphic animals with magical powers), Arcanics (animalized mixtures of humans and Ancients), and Old Gods (fantastically powerful, archaic monsters with grotesque non-humanoid forms that seem to be assemblages of internal anatomy).

Among the humans are witches, the Cumaea, who gradually eat and eventually kill the Arcanics in order to digest their magic. Without yet having access to the taxonomy of this unique world, we likely identify the protagonist as a type: she is an underdog, the young victim of an oppressive society in which various groups identify themselves as justified in consuming or otherwise appropriating as resource, and to this end animalizing, other groups. We do not yet know that the cyborgian woman figure is the young woman's foremother, though we may sense from the illustration that she represents some kind of intricate entangling of human, animal, artificial, and supernatural agencies – an entangling with which the protagonist is visually involved and included. Nearly everything in this story belies the discourse of in-group purity with which the slavers (and other humans, and other "races") justify their appropriations of others' lives. We can guess that the plot might follow the struggle of our heroine to refuse those discourses, and in a diversely hybridized world, to respect the value of entanglement against anthropocentric (or any species-centric) violence and exploitation. But there is a disturbing twist. We do not yet but soon will know that the heroine's special power, which comes from her symbiosis with another creature within, is precisely one of violent consumption. The creature, an Old God, emerges as an extension of her body when it is driven – so that she too is driven – by a fantastic, indiscriminately destructive hunger to survive. In this world of fluid animal-human-other kinds of creatures and needs, what kind of heroine can she be?

The central image of *Monstress*, around which nearly everything turns, is hunger. A drive to consume others is at the existential core of its protagonist and also, as a synecdoche for violent appropriations across competing lives, it is embedded in the social and historical fabric of its storyworld. Thus the opening pages of *Monstress* offer a complex microcosm, gradually to be unfolded, of a storyworld that is defined by multiple conflicting in-group regimes of appropriation and justification. In this way, the comic raises into sharp relief an intersection of conditions, presented as either natural or historical, that animate vegan ethics. Hunger is represented as both *internal* to characters (literally in the case of the appetites of Maika or the Cumaea; figuratively in the case of imperialists or slavers) and *primal* to the world (since of the Old Gods, older than any humanoid in the world, "we know next to nothing . . . except that they are creatures of immense and destructive power, who the poets believe once threatened nearly all existence" [173]). This interiority and archaism of hunger paints the picture of an ecological world in which all life is sustained not only by a biophysical entanglement with, but also consumption of, other lives and their artifacts. This is what makes symbiotic and predatory Maika, an uncanny allegory of ourselves, monstrous. Yet we are encouraged to side with Maika because she is deeply troubled by her hunger, practices restraint, and attempts to draw a line between life that may be eaten (for example, wild hyenas) and may not be eaten (personified, social characters who may or may not be animalized).[7]

Maika's practices of consumption do not represent a vegan ethics or worldview. But I propose that she does represent a vegan crisis in her storyworld. For a start, where she draws her moral line is represented in far more ambivalent terms in her world than in the reader's. The distinction between "mere" animals and personified animals – the basis of the justice of her appropriation of other lives – is hopelessly muddied by the textual and visual ambiguity of the range of personified hybrid human-animal creatures, and even by the existence of personified Cats who are not visually distinct from "mere" animals at all, until they speak. The diaphany of animalized figures in the storyworld makes it impossible to draw the convenient lines between person and animal that are conventional to the reader's dominantly omnivorous societies. Why not consider those hyenas (indeed, surely not accidentally, another species of cat) as persons too?

The implicit confusion of the "animal" does not seem lost on Maika. She herself reflects with dissatisfaction on the lines she draws, as seen in Plate 1. In dialogic overlay with the images of her eating the hyena, her thoughts dwell on another, failed drawing of that line: "When we were slaves and starving, we once ate the contents of a dead boy's stomach. We said it wasn't like eating the boy. But now I know the truth. It *was*" (26). Why? The boy has consumed other lives, vegetable or animal. We must infer that for Maika, the boy is made of those other, outside lives, and in a sense, *is* those other lives, brought inside him. To eat that entanglement is to eat the boy. This revelation, linked to the eating of the hyena and punctuated by tears in her eye, tells us that she cannot be sure to which side of the line the hyena belongs, or of her own appropriative justice. The challenge of this uncertainty, for Maika and for her reader, invites a disposition towards a continual questioning and provisional representation of justifiable violence that Emelia Quinn and Benjamin Westwood argue define vegan positionality (4).[8]

The imagery and style of these pages reinforce the story's deconstruction of human versus animal identity. When the hunt begins, Maika's eyes go blank, lacking irises or pupils, just like those of the animals – a depersonalization effect that for the reader is powerfully cognitive as well as semiotic. The animals seem like selfless things or forces, but so does Maika. Predator and prey are flattened into one, eerily opaque agency. We do not see Maika's eyes again during this episode. Yet the last image of the animal before its death is a close-up of its fearful, open eye, this time with its staring pupil, and this increased realism suddenly personifies the creature as one capable of knowledge and suffering. Who are we looking at, looking at Maika, looking at us? Curiously, in that hyena's slit-pupil eye, we see an image of Maika's chest brand, the third eye. But this third-eye motif is white, not red, so it is unclear whether it is literally a reflection of Maika's brand or if it is some kind of magical or symbolic vision. In either case the superposition of the two vertical eye patterns – feline and iconic – suggests that the hyena's subjectivity mirrors the inner vision of Maika; they are more kindred, and similarly entitled to sympathy and justice, than might appear.

This crisis in justice, the uncertainty in how to draw a line between mere prey and personified victim, between what may be violently appropriated and what may not, is communicated to us in graphic features that are, therefore, both dialogic and diaphanic, showing as well as telling. The diaphany of symbols (like the third eye) and figures (like the realist eyes) is extended by elements of Takeda's abstract, non-figural style, like line and color. The most remarkable abstract effect is the hatchwork, which gives texture to figures and grounds here and throughout the narrative. This hatchwork consists of criss-crossing groups of about three to seven short, fine, black parallel lines. In the opening pages discussed earlier, this hatchwork fills up about half of the area of the right-hand page. There, before turning the page to discover the ornate setting for the episode, we might mistake the hatchwork for the mimetic texture of a wall against which Maika stands. Instead, we realize that here, as elsewhere, it is ornamental and expressive, an abstract motif that visually grounds the criss-crossing interests and spatial plenitude of a world whose foundation is not empty, Euclidean space but rather crowded and everywhere gestural, alive.

The left-hand page draws this motif out into longer, flowing filaments of interlocking lines that could be either abstract or figural, a dark mesh that belongs to the living assemblage and doubles Maika's flowing, dark hair. In short, hatchwork is an abstract motif that we see, rather than read, as a principle of construction and connection in the storyworld itself, of ontological entanglement. Returning to the final scene of the hunt described above, we see how powerful this motif may be. Two narrow middle panels create a Rorschach symmetry unfolding from the center of the page. In the upper of the two, the black silhouettes of Maika, the hyena, and the land leak flowing, black streaks that merge with hatchwork that fills the surrounding space. This in turn mirrors the mixture of criss-crossed flows of linework that emanate from the silhouette of Maika in the large top panel, enmeshing her in her surroundings. In the lower middle panel, a close-up of Maika's bloody hand reaches for something against a reddish background of which the hatchwork and flowing filament motifs are again the expressive fabric.

Here, significantly, the hatchwork is drawn right across the outlines of the hand, as if this abstract element permeated it. In the bottom image, the hatchwork crosses again from background into the figure, in the close-up of Maika's profile and eye. This dissolution of boundaries is also evident in the flowing linework that crosses over from background into the parts of the bloody hand and hyena organ, and echoed in the profuse, flowing linework of her hair. Even in these elements of pure style, then, the separation of background and figure, self and other, is refused: everything is entangled. Not only human and animal, but living and nonliving things – the entire environment. This effect is reinforced in the panel and page compositions, by a similarly figural, abstract, and boundary-defying use of color, a blood red.

If what I have called a vegan crisis in Maika's character and storyworld were grounded only in an ecology of ontological hunger, then we might read the story as an apology for violence, as a reification of appropriation and injustice in the inevitability of nature. But as the ambivalence of Maika's hunt shows us, the justifying lines she draws, and we ourselves draw, are presented as conventional rather than natural, and

Plate

Plate 1 Page 26 of Marjorie Liu and Sana Takeda's *Monstress* (2015).

for her, open to question and circumstance. The reader must already suspect this discursiveness of hunger – a discourse that reaches beyond eating to appropriations for sex and labor – from the complex social contexts of slavery and racism announced at the story's opening, ones that explicitly exploit a self-serving language of human versus nonhuman justice. This context is directly evoked as Maika consumes her prey.

The final panel closes with speech captions that return us to the prison in which Maika and other "nonhuman" humanoid creatures are enslaved, waiting to be killed to feed the Cumaea. "Open," she says aloud, "Come on . . . *open*" (26) – referring to the lock on her dungeon cell. She is now prey, the appropriated. She will soon magically succeed in opening the lock and liberating herself and her fellow prisoners, which makes her a sympathetic, idealized figure, heroic. Paradoxically, then, she here comes to represent not some essential violence and appropriation in the primal hunger of the world, but the need to counter forms of socially justified violence and appropriation with a more egalitarian practice of respect for others' flourishing and care. It is this paradox in her figuration that I have described as a vegan crisis. The story works towards solving it by exploring the nature of hunger in terms of both symbiotic and social entanglements. Ultimately, it is a narrative about the unfixedness of animal life, and about the social shaping, and the need for a difficult reshaping, of its hungers.

Readers who are familiar with *Monstress* will know that I have left aside some remarkable features of its storyworld. The commonplace prejudices of our own world do not exist in it. It is tacitly matriarchal: all characters of greater status and authority are women and the men are almost exclusively subordinates. There are also nonbinary characters, reflecting a move away from rigidly defined gender categorizations. Skin color seems irrelevant: it is explicitly diverse, nobody comments on it, and it says nothing about social status, power, or ethnicity. Sexuality too seems queerly free of social regulation. If it weren't for the violent, denigrating aims of nearly all the "races" – here meaning humans and other creatures – to ruthlessly control and exploit each other, it would be a utopia. In these ways, the comic overtly represents what we inevitably read as intersectional figures of species, race, gender, and sexuality. But by presenting figures that signify as intersectional, such as characters who are women of color, in a context in which familiar significations of racist and sexist experience are overturned, the narrative presents at once a liberating social imagination and one insistently unfree of systemic injustice. In the logic of the storyworld itself, there is no intersectional experience: denigrated or exploited groups do not overlap. It is as if the storyworld were intentionally designed for a contradictory structure of feeling, combining hope – "there's nothing natural to exploiting this group, it doesn't have to be this way" – with pessimism – "nevertheless, must we always construct another to exploit?"

The point of this is less philosophical, I think, than emotional. We do not brush aside the consuming problems of *Monstress* as homogeneous and dystopian. What I have called a vegan crisis in the figure of a consuming heroine and her entanglements, social and symbiotic, is both attached to intersectional experiences and detached from them, reminding us simultaneously of the way injustices may stick together ideologically in familiar attitudes of oppression and appropriation and of the way, when those attitudes are defamiliarized, they may fall apart. Not only signs, but images and abstractions, shape how we understand this crisis. *Monstress* asks us to see ourselves in the mirror of its entangling style. We are drawn deep into its utopian vision of compassion, even of freedom, while forced to struggle with Maika at the shifting, discursive limits of what we are as biophysical consumers.

My vegan reading practice here has concerned itself both with how entangled lives are hidden or revealed, and also with how they are inevitably caught up in appropriative and consuming power relations that draw borderlines between inside and outside, self and other, violence and care. Comics make those borderlines visible. Its foundation in style renders them imaginary but also re-imaginable.

Notes

1. Comics and comics studies normally refer to a field narrower than graphic narrative, yet broader than the graphic novel. Graphic narrative is a formalist term that describes any fixed sequential image art, from Egyptian tomb murals to the Bayeux tapestry, to Wonder Woman comics. Comics refers to the industrial and artist traditions of graphic storytelling that evolved from the turn of the twentieth century to the present, encompassing mass media newspaper and magazine comic strips, trade serial comic books, varieties of underground comix, and graphic novels published as stand-alone books. Sustained scholarly engagement with comics, and comics studies as a generally recognized field of research, in English-speaking North America was sparked by the impact of Art Spiegelman's graphic novel, *Maus*, in two volumes in 1986 and 1991, which coincided with the flourishing of trauma studies, and of Scott McCloud's accessible guide to comics as a form in *Understanding Comics* in 1993. This period saw an explosion of public and scholarly interest in the graphic novel, which is to say, book-length stories typically written and drawn by a single comics creator, with bookstore shelf space next to literature. As a result, some serial trade comics for adults also gained wider attention (and are sometimes called graphic novels), such as Neil Gaiman's *Sandman* and Alan Moore's *Watchmen*. These sophisticated trade comics publications, along with independent works such as *Ghost World*, *One! Hundred! Demons!*, *Persepolis*, and *Fun Home*, became common additions to university syllabuses. Comics scholarship has grown into a recognized field in North America, with academic associations, conferences, and professional journals. The comic discussed here, *Monstress*, grows out of the adult trade comics industry. This tradition and the independent artist tradition of the graphic novel and zine – although the latter invites more freedom of expression and creative experimentation – are not easily distinguished by any but institutional definitions. *Monstress* has been recognized by multiple awards for its writing and art. I am aware of only one scholarly study of *Monstress*, by Dany Prince, which I highly recommend for a reading of this work's iconoclastic role in the misogynist tradition of modern genre fantasy, and more generally for a further introduction to comics as a form.
2. Full arguments for these claims, more general than the immediate interests of this case study, are found in my essays on comics environments, "Worldmaking," and on comics figures, "Animalized Character."
3. The political questions of inter-species entanglement and consumption that arise in this essay find more extensive development across the work of Donna Haraway. While her particular arguments are not directly discussed in this essay, her work in *When Species Meet* and *Staying with the Trouble* has highlighted the essentially digestive foundation of ecologically related lives and offered controversial critical engagements with its justice and representation.
4. For further discussion of the grotesque in comics, see my "Animalized Character."
5. I believe that Worringer's notion of entanglement, though rooted more in existential than in scientific ideas, is consistent with Karen Barad's ecocritical usage.

6. Splash pages are comics pages in which a large portion of the page is a single illustration, as on a title page.
7. Maika may be a version of the postmodern, ethically troubled vampire popularized by Anne Rice, Stephenie Meyer, and others. This figure is considered in relation to vegan concerns by Stanescu and by Wright as well as in Ali Ryland's contribution to this volume.
8. The figure of vegan crisis in Maika seems to me analogous to the vegan condition discussed by Quinn and Westwood in the comparable context of vegetarian versus vegan discourses of violent appropriation or "sacrifice": "If, as Matthew Calarco suggests, the distinction between vegetarianism and veganism comes down to a 'contestation of where one draws the line between "symbolic" and "real" sacrifice,' in Derridean terms, then the vegan condition would be one in which this line in provisional, and continually subject to scrutiny" (Quinn and Westwood, 4).

Works Cited

Barad, Karen. *Meeting the Universe Halfway: Quantum Physics and the Entanglement of Matter and Meaning*. Duke UP, 2007.
Barry, Lynda. *One! Hundred! Demons!* Sasquatch, 2002.
Bechdel, Alison. *Fun Home*. Houghton Mifflin, 2006.
Clowes, Daniel. *Ghost World*. 1993–1997, Fantagraphics, 1997.
Foster, Hal. *Tarzan*. Metropolitan Newspaper Service, 1929.
Gaiman, Neil, et al. *The Sandman*. DC Comics, 1989–1996.
Haraway, Donna. *Staying with the Trouble: Making Kin in the Chthulucene*. Duke UP, 2016.
—. *When Species Meet*. U of Minnesota P, 2007.
Liu, Marjorie, and Sana Takeda. *Monstress: Book One*. Image Comics, 2019.
McCloud, Scott. *Understanding Comics*. Kitchen Sink, 1993.
Moore, Alan, and Dave Gibbons. *Watchmen*. DC Comics, 1986–1987.
Prince, Dany. "'No One Made Me; I Was Always Like This': The *Monstress* in Us." *Journal of Popular Culture*, vol. 54, no. 1, 2021, pp. 67–86.
Quinn, Emelia, and Benjamin Westwood. "Introduction: Thinking Through Veganism." *Thinking Veganism in Literature and Culture: Towards a Vegan Theory*, edited by Quinn and Westwood, Palgrave Macmillan, 2018, pp. 1–24.
Satrapi, Marjane. *Persepolis*. 2000–2004, English translation Pantheon, 2003–2005.
Spiegelman, Art. *Maus*. 1980–1991, Pantheon, 1991.
Stanescu, James. "Towards a Dark Animal Studies: On Vegetarian Vampires, Beautiful Souls, and Becoming-Vegan." *Journal of Critical Animal Studies*, vol. 10, no. 3, 2012, pp. 26–50.
Watterson, Bill. *Calvin and Hobbes*. Universal Press Syndicate, 1985–1995.
Willmott, Glenn. "The Animalized Character and Style." *Animal Comics: Multispecies Storyworlds in Graphic Narratives*, edited by David Herman, Bloomsbury Academic, 2017, pp. 53–77.
—. "Comics: Worldmaking in the Anthropocene." *Modernism and the Anthropocene*, edited by John McIntyre and Jon Hegglund, Lexington Books, 2021, pp. 153–72.
Worringer, Wilhelm. *Abstraction and Empathy: A Contribution to the Psychology of Style*. Translated by Hilton Kramer, 1908, Ivan R. Dee, Publisher, 1997.
Wright, Laura. *The Vegan Studies Project: Food, Animals, and Gender in the Age of Terror*. U of Georgia P, 2015.

13

Adaptation

No one mourns the *Wicked*, but we should

Christopher Sebastian

Introduction

Various interpretations, from the political to the psychoanalytic, of L. Frank Baum's 1900 novel *The Wonderful Wizard of Oz* have existed almost since the moment the novel was published. The endless interpretive possibilities of the text are one of the lasting gifts bestowed by Baum. Historian Quentin Taylor, for instance, offers an analysis of the characters in the original story, in which the Scarecrow represents the troubles of American farmers in the late nineteenth century, the Tin Man represents workers during the rise of the Industrial Revolution, and the Cowardly Lion functions as a metaphor for former US Secretary of State William Jennings Bryan.

Of course, each new adaptation or interpretation of the novel is a product of its time. The film critic Nicholas Barber describes the 1939 MGM film *The Wizard of Oz* as more of an anti-fairy tale than a fairy tale, one that revealed the dangers of following a popular but incompetent politician and reinforced the belief that success comes to those who work hard. The 1975 Broadway musical *The Wiz* provided a provocative, soul-stirring interpretation inspired by Motown and the movement for Black liberation (Smalls). In 1985, the film *Return to Oz* offered a grim, haunting fever dream that reflected the nature of high-concept, atmospheric films of the early 1980s (Murch).

Literary adaptations of Oz were, by contrast, in limited supply until Gregory Maguire's explosive 1995 novel *Wicked: The Life and Times of the Wicked Witch of the West*. Maguire's work merges elements of Baum's original novel with ones from the 1939 film. For instance, Baum's witch is not green, but Maguire employs the iconic green hue of her skin from her MGM iteration. Maguire does though keep much of Baum's Oz geography intact, which is necessary because the geopolitical landscape is key to his story, a story of good and evil.

While veganism is never addressed directly in *Wicked*, perhaps a step too far for a work that treats vegetarianism as a gray area, a vegan reading is critical to understanding the novel's complex portrait of human relationships with other animals. This short essay draws on Evan Maina Mwangi's conception of the "vegan unconscious" of African literary texts to demonstrate the unconscious vegan sentiments of *Wicked*. I demonstrate the possibilities and potentialities for this literary adaptation as a form through which to express the trope of the monstrous vegan, first elaborated by Emelia

Quinn, in order to explore how speciesism is practically expressed in the novel and to understand veganism as one of a multiplicity of approaches in achieving animal liberation. In order to carry out such an analysis, we must first understand what a monstrous vegan is. According to Quinn, the monstrous vegan can be recognized by four defining characteristics, each of which will be examined in this analysis of *Wicked*:

> First, monstrous vegans do not eat animals, an abstinence that generates a seemingly inexplicable anxiety in those who encounter them. Second, they are hybrid assemblages of human and nonhuman animal parts, destabilizing species boundaries. Third, monstrous vegans are sired outside of heterosexual reproduction, the product of male acts of creation. And finally, monstrous vegans are intimately connected to acts of writing and literary creation. (3)

The Green Revolution

Wicked follows the life of Elphaba Thropp from before her birth to her grisly death and offers an entirely different,[1] sympathetic perspective to that found in the death of Baum's Wicked Witch of the West. Born an outcast because of her off-putting green skin to a formerly upper-class mother and a religious fundamentalist minister father, Elphaba was raised as a missionary and then sent off to study at Shiz University.

A Munchkinlander by birth, Elphaba is raised in Quadling Country, which is described as wet, marshy swampland, the Quadling people described in ways that reflect settler colonial attitudes about Native Americans. Elphaba's father muses to himself that "a Quadling ranked about as low on the social ladder as it was possible to get and still be human" (Maguire 45). To her university friends, Elphaba recalls the pillaging of that land and the extraction of resources at the behest of the tyrannical wizard, who, over the ensuing years, drained the rich swampland to uncover ruby deposits. Also like Native Americans, the Quadling people were chased, killed, and rounded up in settlement camps and then starved "for their own protection" (134). This resettlement resulted in ecological devastation, including a scarcity of fresh water and widespread drought. Clearly, the history of these events informed Elphaba's understanding of racial capitalism, the need for environmentalism, the brutality of the state in the ongoing extraction of natural resources, and the need for Indigenous resistance. Speaking to her college friend, she makes clear that "It's the systemic marginalizing of populations … that's what the wizard is all about" (135).

Elphaba is also described repeatedly throughout the novel as dressing very shabbily, but not solely because of her poverty. She is proud of scoring secondhand boots and gloves that she gets very cheaply because they were formerly owned by a mortician (122). These details also speak to Elphaba as an early proponent of sustainable clothes and thrifting culture, hallmarks of environmental activism.

Because veganism is often understood as firmly intersecting with environmentalism, this re-occurring theme of ecology acts as signposting for the person Elphaba will become – a fierce advocate for Animal Rights and political dissident. Even the green hue of her skin gently foretells of her green philosophy. But using the second trait in Quinn's monstrous vegan, hybridization, Elphaba's physical presentation can be understood on a deeper level.

Elphaba's green skin positions her as an eternal outcast, someone who is not considered entirely of human origin by those around her. Although she is not physically composed of "human and animal assemblages" (Quinn 3), she represents an abstraction of the human and the animal. When describing Elphaba to the nanny shortly after the child's birth, her father could not bring himself to call the baby "her," instead using "it," the pronoun usually reserved for nonhumans as living objects. He also animalizes her by explaining that the baby could not nurse because she has the teeth of a shark (Maguire 22). Eventually those baby teeth fall out and are replaced by more human-looking ones, but this othering follows Elphaba throughout her life as people continually shun her for her appearance. But it is also this othering that can be observed as the genesis for her kinship with nonhumans – and shared oppression is a key entry point into liberation politics.

Regarding the third trait through which Elphaba can be understood as a monstrous vegan, creation outside of heterosexual reproduction, she still neatly fits. Although she is introduced as the child of human parents, the pigmentation of her skin is a mystery that causes widespread speculation. Her mother, not known for her fidelity, fears that the child could have been fathered by someone else and that Elphaba's skin is a punishment for her adultery. Her father fears that Elphaba is cursed with green skin for his own lack of religious conviction. Either way, there is agreement among everyone in the family that Elphaba is the product of a spiritual or otherworldly intervention.

Of Animals and animals

Baum was never a very consistent world-builder for the Oz universe. Over the course of several novels, he vetoed his own rules as quickly as he introduced them. In *The Wonderful Wizard of Oz*, it is established that Toto cannot speak. However, in the sequel *TikTok of Oz*, Baum engaged retroactive continuity so that all animals speak, whether they are in Oz by birth or just visiting. By modern standards, this alteration would be an unforgivable sin to fandoms. However, this reworking of the narrative gave future writers the freedom to experiment with the canon.

Maguire takes talking animals to a daring new frontier by establishing that Oz is inhabited by both Animals (with a capital "A") and animals (lowercase). Animals with a capital "A" speak, wear clothes, and even hold jobs, while animals (lowercase) are domesticated, exploited as livestock, used for experimentation, or live in the wild. But far from the whimsical talking animals reminiscent of a Disney film, Maguire's Animals face systemic disenfranchisement.

Under the matrilineal ruling monarchy of Oz, Animals live quite well. When monarch Ozma the Bilious dies, her husband Pastorius becomes the Ozma Regent until their daughter is old enough to take the throne. But after the Wizard's unexpected overthrow of the monarchy in a coup d'état, he gradually strips away the rights of Animals through piecemeal legislation. He places bans on their movement, restrictions on what jobs they can hold, where they can live, and whether or not they are able to study. All these things happen over time, never fast enough for the human population to collectively notice or care, and each new ban shifts the status of Animals ever closer to their animal counterparts.

Doctor Dillamond, a Goat who teaches life sciences at Shiz University, is the first Animal central character that the reader encounters. He is introduced during a train journey in which he shares a berth with recently accepted student Galinda (who later shortens her name to Glinda and becomes the future Good Witch of the North). Galinda, described as a social climber, is clearly prejudiced against Animals and has no trouble treating Dillamond poorly, as does the conductor who requests their tickets. During their tense exchange, Dillamond speaks passionately about the worsening situation of Animals in Oz. Accommodation for those who have hooves instead of hands presents as a type of ableism, the conductor calls him a beast (a term that he likens to a slur), and he has to pay double the fare that a human has to pay for his first-class ticket (Maguire 65).

Dillamond focuses his academic research on finding evidence to support his hypothesis that there is no inherent difference between Animals and humans. This academic focus is ironic because it reveals that hidden within the pages of Maguire's work is a damning indictment of white supremacy. Dillamond is so dedicated over the course of his entire career to trying to parse the inherent similarities shared between Animals and humans that he never really looks at the similarities between Animals and *animals*, or for that matter, humans and animals. Even in Maguire's fictional universe where Animal Rights is a central theme, the status of animals remains unchanged. Here animals (lowercase) are still objects.

Only the rights of Animals are found to be under moral, ethical, and legal consideration by all parties, and these rights are based on their proximity to humans. But ownership of "human" as a political identity has always been seen almost exclusively through the white gaze. Animals, including the doctor, wrap themselves up in the trappings of civilization, attempting to reproduce the things valued by a white supremacist system: education, economic status, fine clothes. By centering his work around the human, Dillamond hopes for Animals to be delivered by the politics of respectability. He does not seek to abolish the hierarchy so much as he seeks a better position in it. Instead of choosing solidarity with the animal, Dillamond looks for protection through strategic alignment with the human. This shortsightedness proves to be his undoing when he is brutally murdered by an agent of the State, his throat having "been slit as thoroughly as if he had wandered into an abattoir" (Maguire 128).

After Dr Dillamond's murder, he is replaced by Dr Nikidik (a human) as the Life Sciences professor. In a pivotal scene during a lecture, Dr Nikidik presents to the class a frightened lion cub (who would later become the Cowardly Lion) on a wheeled trolley, asking the class, "Who can tell me if this is an Animal or an animal?" (144). Without hesitation, Elphaba stands up and immediately delivers the most decisively vegan response: "It seems to me the answer is that its mother can. Where is the mother?" Nikidik rephrases the question.

> Will someone here venture a hypothesis as to the nature of this specimen? And give reason for such an assessment? We see before us a beast at a tender age, long before any such beast could command language if language were a part of its makeup. Before language – assuming language – is this still an Animal? (144)

Not backing down, Elphaba again enquires about the mother. In reply, Nikidik offers, very cryptically, that the mother had died in an explosion, but he also takes this as an opportunity to belittle Elphaba. He declares her questions impertinent and calls her a bleeding heart. He then asks, "Now do you think that if we could cauterize that part of the brain that develops language, we could eliminate pain and thus its existence? Early tests on this little tom lion show interesting results" (145). Bolstered by Elphaba's resistance, other students come to reject Dr Nikidik's experimentation and help the lion cub to escape. Angered by their refusal to participate, Nikidik exclaims, "I will not preside over such shocking refusal to learn! . . . You are leaping to hare-brained conclusions based on sentiment and no observation" (145).

This exchange is crucial for several reasons. First, it is important to the continued development of Elphaba into Quinn's monstrous vegan. She "exemplifies the role of the monstrous vegan . . . confronting those around them with violence, inconsistency, and the intangible nature of human desires" (Quinn 179). She stands alone at first among her classmates in objecting to the exercise in the lecture hall, establishing her as the outsider and the lone rebel who disrupts the other students' learning experience, even if they are equally uncomfortable with the subject matter. Second, Dr Nikidik diminishes her reasonable outrage at using a sentient person, irrespective of species, as an experimental subject by calling her a bleeding heart, as if this emotional response is devoid of logic and reason. It's a form of gaslighting that is frequently employed to undermine advocates for any type of justice by framing their protest as irrational and hysterical, and deploying this tactic also holds deeply misogynistic undertones. Paired with accusing her of leaping to "hare-brained" conclusions, Nikidik dismisses Elphaba as both an irrational woman and as someone with the intellectual capacity of a rabbit.

Third, and perhaps most importantly, Nikidik proposes cauterizing the part of the brain that develops language. This mandate comes across as almost cartoonishly insidious because it doesn't remove consciousness or sentience (which would be equally objectionable). The only thing such an action accomplishes is to eliminate the ability for humans to differentiate between Animals and animals, making them incapable of expressing themselves in human language and effectively silencing them.

Scholars frequently interpret Animal Rights in Maguire's work to be a stand-in for the rights of some other marginalized group (see, for example, Kheirbek), and they're not wrong to do so. *Wicked* encourages readers to make this interpretation because Maguire provides such rich insight into racial, ethnic, and class divisions. But it's equally important to interrogate why Animal Rights should necessarily be a stand-in for anything at all. The reason why allegories about Animal Rights are effective is because the treatment of animals can be easily recognized as morally reprehensible in and of itself for a myriad of reasons, not least of which being that *humans are animals ourselves*. This fact seems to be overlooked by literally everyone except Elphaba, who internally muses to herself about the nature of human animals:

> She went to the Grimmerie and hauled open its massive cover – leather ornamented with golden hasps and pins, and tooled with silver leaf – and pored through the tome to find what makes people thirst for such authority and muscle. Is it the sheer nature of the beast within, the human animal inside the Human Being? (Maguire 293)

Elphaba recognizes the Human Being as socially constructed, while the human animal is real. She also unwittingly observes that bigotry has no basis in biology. It is purely ideological. Nonetheless, bigots argue endlessly that bigotry is necessitated because of a perceived biological imperative. This is not to say that species is a social construct.

Physical differences between all animal species, including humans, are very real. However, speciesism as a fundamental belief in the exceptionalism of humans is as contrived as racism, sexism, or homophobia. There are no characteristics that universally persist in all humans or are universally absent in other animals that make humans more special. Yet the myth of human exceptionalism, animated by the myth of white supremacy, is absolute.

The Grimmerie itself also should not be overlooked because it represents the fourth trait of a vegan monster. The Grimmerie is a magical spell book, or grimoire, of which Elphaba can only read parts because the text originates from another world (ostensibly Earth). The book bears examination because, through it, a reader can easily observe Elphaba's passion for and intimate relation with literary creations and pursuits. As the only person in Oz other than the Wizard who is able to read and comprehend any parts of the Grimmerie at all, and as the most dedicated custodian of the book, Maguire could not have followed a stricter roadmap to establishing a vegan monster. She even relies (unsuccessfully) on it as a tool of resistance by seeking to use it to depose the Wizard's regime (293).

Vegetarian, Vegan, or Neither

Of course, the most important trait that distinguishes Elphaba as a vegan monster in Quinn's framework is food. The first time Elphaba talks explicitly about diet, she is in her dorm room studying the sermons of the early unionist ministers. These texts, which focus on evil, address the morality of eating Animals. Describing the texts to her roommate Galinda, Elphaba says,

> I'm not *interested* in it. It's just what the early sermons are all on about. So I'm thinking about what they're thinking about, that's all. Sometimes they talk about diet and not eating Animals, and then I think of that. I just like to think about what I'm reading. Don't you? (80)

As a result of these sentiments, a reader might discern that Elphaba undergoes a vegan or vegetarian awakening. By insisting she is not personally interested, Elphaba carefully carves out distance between herself and other people who don't eat meat. Yet she clearly understands the potency of such abstention. The positionality of animal consumption as overtly evil within a religious context would be something that the child of a minister considered.

Curiously enough, Elphaba never identifies definitively as vegetarian, although in her early years, she might have been. As a toddler, she turns away from fish that her mother tries to feed her. She repeatedly rejects it, throwing it on the ground, saying, "Breakfast. Breakfast in the dirt. Breakfast for the bugs" (33). Her food is frequently described as meatless, as, for instance when, "Glinda concentrated very hard and tried to make Elphaba's leftover sandwich elevate outward over the canal. She only succeeded in exploding the thing in a small combustion of mayonnaise and shredded carrot and chopped olives" (138). And Maguire includes enough vivid descriptions of her eating apples for a leitmotif to be established. However, in her late thirties, towards the close of her abruptly ended life, Elphaba does eat fish.[2] Furthermore, the birth of the winged monkeys, a hallmark of the Wicked Witch in most Oz incarnations, is a direct result of her animal/Animal experimentation during her exile. This latter is, of course, a bizarre juxtaposition when placed next to the anti-vivisectionist that Elphaba is while studying at Shiz.

So if she does choose to be exclusively vegetarian at any point, she is not so during her entire lifetime. Elphaba does, however, have a vegetarian affectation. Her former classmate and one-time lover Fiyero takes note of her anger when he eats a pork roll:

> "I wouldn't be surprised if the pork roll you're devouring in such perfect mindless affluence, is cut from a Pig," she snapped at him once.
> "Just because you've already eaten, you don't need to ruin my appetite," he protested mildly. Free-living Animals were not much in evidence in his home territory, and the few sentient creatures he'd known at Shiz had, except at the Philosophy Club that night, made little impression. The plight of the Animals had not much touched him. (197)

Judging by this passage, Elphaba's avoidance of animal products is rooted in a fear of accidentally eating an *Animal* when consuming an *animal*. She also becomes, in the process, the "vegan killjoy" theorized by Richard Twine, with Fiyero appearing defensive in response to implicit questioning about his animal consumption.

A clearer *vegan* ethic is indirectly introduced when Elphaba holds a conversation with a Cow and two Sheep after freeing them. Having grown bitter after a lifetime of human maltreatment, the Cow recalls in graphic detail the violence she experienced:

> Sweetheart, my udder is sore from their daily yanking. I am tapped for milk morning and night. I won't even go into what it's like to be mounted by a – well, just never mind. But worst, my children have been fattened on milk and slaughtered for veal. I could hear their cries from the abattoir, they didn't even bother to move me out of hearing range!" Here she turned her head to the wall, and the Sheep came up on either side of her, pressing like a living pair of warm bookends against her lower sides and underbelly. (316)

This passage lays bare the sexual, physical, and emotional violence of dairy. The Cow speaks unapologetically, and the implication is clear: the theft of bodily autonomy, the use of animals as chattel slaves, and the taking of animal lives is abhorrent. The only observable difference between doing these things to an Animal or an animal lies in their ability to express themselves in human words and thought.

In this way, *Wicked* falls short in fully advocating for animals with a lowercase "a" by only engaging the reader's empathy for Animals (capital). However, it still presents a kind of vegan unconscious that may achieve that engagement more discreetly. For Mwangi, the vegan unconscious is an "affirmative expression of potential . . . a latent possibility that the societies portrayed in the text will embrace a future where animals will not be killed to satisfy human needs" (9). Mwangi argues, in the context of African literature, that while his source texts do not directly engage with vegan ethics, "African authors grapple with the possibilities of alternatives to meat eating and encourage us to minimize animal suffering as much as possible" (7).

Although eating animals (or Animals) is a common theme throughout *Wicked*, vegism is never the conscious imperative of the narrative.[3] Vegetarian or vegan, it does not matter. Individual consumer choices, while important, are essentially an irrelevancy to the project of animal liberation. Maguire's depiction of it in Oz, as in real life, underlines the fact that socio-political movements are not straight lines that start or end with the choices that individual consumers make.

In terms of the real-world vegan movement, this can be a deeply unpopular position. While many vegans want simple solutions to enormously intricate social problems, their familiar chant of just "Go Vegan" can be reductive because it doesn't necessarily confront speciesism as the underlying bigotry that informs those consumer choices or the ways in which Animal exploitation and identity politics play a role in human relationships. It also can ignore the reality that people are not perfect, that people may perform veg-ism at different times and for a variety of reasons, and that they may cease to perform it for even more reasons.

The reader will never know precisely how much veg-ism is a part of Elphaba's journey, and that should be okay. Navigating one's ethics within liberation struggles is a lifelong process. Whether or not Elphaba adheres to a strict plant-based diet does not change the fact that she is labeled an extremist by some and a revolutionary by others, depending on their social location relative to the subjugation of Animals. And as with so many dissidents, she passes into history in her death-by-water as a violent insurgent.

The Death of Culture, the Death of a Witch

As a document, *Wicked* is a reminder that historical texts are often incomplete. Nigerian author Chinua Achebe said in a 1994 interview with the *Paris Review*, "There is that great proverb – that until the lions have their own historians, the history of the hunt will always glorify the hunter" (Brooks).

If *The Wonderful Wizard of Oz* documented the original version of a nation's living history, the retelling of events in *Wicked* provides a more complete story. It reminds readers that no history book should be regarded as a definitive work. Multiple perspectives are needed to understand that people and movements are organic, messy, and complex. In this way Maguire's work is elevated from the status of homage to pastiche.

History is written by the victors. The wizard documents his coup as a peaceful transition of power. So too is Elphaba's tale rewritten in such a way that she fully becomes a terrorist and, therefore, an enemy of the state. In the end she dies alone, tormented, and reviled by most.

By contrast, the excitement around the controversial novel died quietly and peacefully. No more great adaptations of the Oz universe would be seen on the horizon until after the turn of the century. And then on 10 June 2003, like a phoenix, it roared back to life. The musical *Wicked* premiered on Broadway as a blockbuster hit. Much of the subversive politics remained intact; nonetheless, some would argue that the heart of the story was ripped out.

How? Bluntly put, whitewashing, or the ongoing Disney-fication of mass-produced culture. Not only does Elphaba fake her death so that she may live free from persecution, animals are erased entirely, more so even than in Maguire's novel. As told by Adorno and Horkheimer, Maguire's animals may be casualties of the culture industry, that being little more than the achievement of standardization and mass production created for the sole purpose of making people feel good and complacent. The warped, grotesque beauty of the novel was replaced by glitter, high-energy singing, and a happy ending where nobody, especially the witch, dies. It is the cheap copy of a novel that was itself a reinterpretation of a previous work. And like a photocopy of a photograph of a painting of a person, each new iteration is an order of magnitude removed so far from the original that it is not recognizable to the first artist.

However, a less cynical interpretation of the musical adaptation of *Wicked* is that it too is a product of its time. In a post-9/11 United States, *Wicked* stormed the stage to remind viewers that one person's terrorist is another person's freedom fighter. The stage production's happier ending is a salve for a population still experiencing a collective trauma, particularly a young nation that was itself birthed in the grip of white supremacy and imperialism. These competing identities of terrorist and freedom fighter also are parsed out on stage in a way that is palatable to audiences who otherwise likely cannot tolerate animal representation that does not frame them as exploitable resources. Laura Wright describes the post-9/11 moment as a defining cultural shift when a vegan studies project could emerge. She writes, "in the post-9/11 moment, the choice to be vegan meant to step outside of the confines of what constituted an agreed-upon 'American' identity" (31). Wright explains that veganism is a threat to this American identity.

But a theatrical production with a happy ending does not pose the same threat. It preserves the audience's emotional wellbeing by allowing Elphaba to go off into the sunset with her lover instead of die a martyr for the cause of Animal liberation. By shifting the focus from the political struggle to a romantic interest, the vegan unconscious is no longer foregrounded, and the musical absolves audiences of having to reconcile the treatment of Animals in Oz with our collective treatment of animals in real life. This revision is in stark contrast to the ending of the novel. In *Wicked* the novel, the reader is forced to sit in their discomfort, to reckon directly with the entanglements of human and Animal oppression. And so too perhaps the enduring takeaway of *Wicked* the novel is absolution denied – denied Elphaba and denied humans for our unconscionable acts against the inhabitants of the natural world.

Notes

1. Maguire derived the name Elphaba from L. Frank Baum's initials L-F-B.
2. Because multiple interpretations of vegetarianism have diminished the meaning of it to exclude all animal flesh, fish may not be entirely excluded from a vegetarian diet depending on the reader's social and cultural experience.
3. Veg-ism is used here as a stand-in for both veganism and/or vegetarianism.

Works Cited

Adorno, Theodor, and Max Horkheimer. "The Culture Industry: Enlightenment as Mass Deception." *Dialectic of Enlightenment*. Stanford UP, 2020, pp. 94–136.
Barber, Nicholas. "The Subversive Messages Hidden in The Wizard of Oz." *BBC*, 12 August 2019.
Baum, L. Frank. *TikTok of Oz*. Reilly & Britton, 1914.
—. *The Wonderful Wizard of Oz*. G. M. Hill Co., 1900.
Brooks, Jerome. "Chinua Achebe, The Art of Fiction No. 139." *The Paris Review*, no. 133, 1994.

Kheirbek, Taymaa Hussein, and Roza Awat Ezzat. "The Use and Symbolism of Animals in The Wonderful Wizard of Oz." *Language Literacy: Journal of Linguistics, Literature and Language Teaching*, vol. 4, no. 2, 2020, pp. 203–11.

Maguire, Gregory. *Wicked: The Life and Times of the Wicked Witch of the West*. HarperCollins, 1995.

Mwangi, Evan Maina. *The Postcolonial Animal: African Literature and Posthuman Ethics*. U of Michigan P, 2019.

Quinn, Emelia. *Reading Veganism: The Monstrous Vegan, 1818 to Present*. Oxford UP, 2021.

Return to Oz. By Walter and Gill Dennis Murch. Directed by Walter Murch, produced by Paul Maslansky, Walt Disney Pictures, 1985.

Smalls, Charlie. "The Wiz: the Super Soul Musical Wonderful Wizard of Oz." Atlantic, 1975.

Taylor, Quentin. "Money and Politics in the Land of Oz." *The Independent Review*, vol. 9, 2005, pp. 413–26.

The Wizard of Oz. Directed by Victor Fleming, George Cukor, Richard Thorpe, Norman Taurog, Mervyn LeRoy Vidor et al., MGM, 1939.

Twine, Richard. "Vegan Killjoys at the Table – Contesting Happiness and Negotiating Relationships with Food Practices." *Societies*, vol. 4, no. 4, 2014, pp. 623–39.

Wright, Laura. *The Vegan Studies Project: Food, Animals, and Gender in the Age of Terror*. U of Georgia P, 2015.

14

The Philosophical Essay

Josh Milburn

Introduction

IN HER CONTRIBUTION to the 2018 collection *Thinking Veganism in Literature and Culture*, Sara Salih recounts the challenges of teaching animal studies in a literature department. She began a class with a work of philosophy and, in her chapter, asks:

> What was a bunch of literature and creative writing students supposed to make of Peter Singer's *Animal Liberation*, the first book on our reading list? Instead of engaging with the book's uncompromising moral message, the students focused on Singer's rhetorical strategies, which some of them dismissed as polemic. I now understood I had unconsciously wished to shock, perhaps even convert the students taking my course, and I felt disappointed and stupid when I saw how they responded to the text as any other text – a literary artefact to be analysed and assessed. (Salih 63)

The vegan students had heard it all before, recounts Salih, while the non-vegans became instantly defensive (63). Salih "thought of withdrawing from" her own class, and drafted an email to Singer – but this was never sent. "[T]he class," she reports, "quietened down when we got onto the more familiar territory of literary texts" (64).

Philosophical exploration of the ethics of human–animal relationships – what we can call *animal ethics* – forms part of the prehistory of vegan (literary) studies (see Wright, "Doing" xv; *Vegan* 11), and remains an important touchstone for scholars of veganism in literature (Quinn and Westwood 16; Milburn). It is thus not surprising that Salih included animal ethics in her course. But the response of her students, and her consequent frustration, is understandable, too. To what extent does it make sense to group philosophical essays within or alongside more conventional literary texts? Should scholars of vegan literature respond to philosophical essays "as any other text" (Salih 63)? This chapter interrogates – without necessarily *answering* – these questions.

It is first worth saying that there are multiple traditions of philosophy that may be of interest to vegan literary scholars. We can first distinguish between the so-called "continental" and "analytic" traditions of philosophy. Continental philosophy has its origins in French and German thought, and is at the foundation of much contemporary literary theory. The philosopher Jacques Derrida is a recognizably continental philosopher who is a frequent source of engagement for vegan literary scholars (see, for example, Schuster).

Analytic philosophy, on the other hand, takes its lead from the sciences, especially mathematics, aiming to answer philosophical questions with scientific rigor. Within analytic philosophy, we can identify two approaches to animal ethics: "traditional" and "non-traditional" (Crary). The traditional approaches are more familiar: the animal welfare philosophy of Peter Singer and the animal rights philosophy of Tom Regan are paradigmatic examples. The non-traditional approaches are worth mentioning in this chapter, however, as this non-traditional work sometimes involves close engagement with literature. Cora Diamond (without using this language) establishes the differences between the traditional and non-traditional approaches to animals in an early criticism of Singer. In doing so, she engages closely with literature and poetry to understand human relationships to animals ("Eating Meat"). In more recent work ("Difficulty"), she looks to J. M. Coetzee's *The Lives of Animals* – a book that, incidentally, includes an ironic piece of short fiction by Singer, in which a fictionalized Singer criticizes the use of fiction to think about animal ethics: he (the fictional version, at least) prefers "to keep truth and fiction clearly separate" ("Reflections" 86).

However, for better or worse, the work of "traditional" analytic animal ethicists – especially Singer – remains both influential and widely read. Salih's choice to start her course with his work is not, I think, atypical. For students across multiple disciplines, Singer's work may be some of the only philosophy they read – and, indeed, for many students, his work may be some of the only animal protectionist scholarship with which they engage. For many vegan theorists, meanwhile, Singer's work has been formative.[1] And, indeed, his influence and readership stretches well *beyond* the academy, to animal activists and members of the public. As such, this chapter advances by way of conversation with Singer's 1974 essay "All Animals Are Equal," a version of which appears as the first chapter of his *Animal Liberation*, taking this as representative of a certain kind of philosophical essay. I begin by placing the essay in context. I then use the essay to reflect on the goals and tools of analytic philosophy, contrasting these with the goals and tools of literary work and literary analysis. I conclude by returning to reflect on the role of work like Singer's in vegan literary studies.

Singer in Context

Singer, an Australian, became a vegetarian in Oxford (UK), where he was undertaking graduate studies in philosophy. After attending a lecture in autumn 1970, Singer met the philosopher Richard Keshen, also a graduate student, and the pair ate together. Keshen's meal was vegetarian, and he introduced Singer to the moral case against meat. Over the next few months, Singer was introduced to some of Keshen's friends, becoming a part of (what became known as) the "Oxford Vegetarians" (Garner and Okuyleye 15–31).

Particularly important for Singer's developing thought was Ros Godlovitch, another Oxford philosopher. Godlovitch had moved to Oxford from Canada with her husband Stan, who was reading for a graduate degree in philosophy. She began, but did not complete, a graduate degree herself. Godlovitch and Singer formed a close friendship, and influenced one another considerably (Garner and Okuleye 53–66). Importantly, though, Godlovitch's arguments leant on rights theory – while Singer was (and remains) part of the utilitarian tradition of moral philosophy. Singer's supervisor was R. M. Hare, a noted utilitarian philosopher, but the former was already a utilitarian by the time he arrived in Oxford. Singer was also significantly influenced by Richard Ryder, another of the Oxford Vegetarians. Ryder, a clinical psychologist who lived in Oxford but was not attached to the university, coined the term "speciesism," which Singer significantly popularized.

In 1971, *Animals, Men and Morals*, a collection edited by Stan Godlovitch, Ros Godlovitch, and John Harris, was published by Victor Gollancz. This book was "the first substantial work on animal ethics since Henry Salt's work at the turn of the century" (Garner and Okuleye 93), and contained contributions from several of the Oxford Vegetarians (though not Singer, who joined the group too late), as well as a range of other figures, including the novelist and animal activist Brigid Brophy.

In 1973, Singer reviewed the American release of *Animals, Men and Morals* for the *New York Review of Books*. In response to his article – entitled "Animal Liberation" – the publisher Simon & Schuster invited him to write a book. Thus, *Animal Liberation*, first published in 1975, was born. An early version of its first chapter – "All Animals Are Equal" – was published in 1974 in the journal *Philosophic Exchange*, and versions of the chapter have been widely anthologized since.[2] Singer's early work played a major role in placing animal ethics in the philosophical mainstream – and animal ethics provided scaffolds for the emergence of *other* animal-friendly academic disciplines, including animal studies and vegan studies. But the influence was not solely academic. *Animal Liberation* "is probably the best-selling academic book of all time" (Garner and Okuleye 133), and has led to Singer being called (somewhat problematically) the "father" of the "animal rights" movement.[3]

No contextualization of Singer is complete without mention of controversies. Naturally enough, any defense of animals attracts criticism, both from those committed to animal use and from those preferring alternative approaches to animal protectionism. Despite criticism, the core of Singer's views on animals has remained relatively constant. Significant controversy has also been attracted by Singer's *other* work, however. His views on infanticide, for example – in short, the idea that the parents of certain severely disabled infants should be free to choose to have their child euthanized if they wish – have led to him being accused of being a eugenicist. Incidentally, these views are alluded to in *Animal Liberation* (18–20). For some in animal studies, concerns about Singer's views (as well as a desire to decenter traditionally dominant positions) justify questioning the prominence offered to Singer's work.[4]

Goals

Animal ethics, as I am here using the term, refers to the philosophical analysis, defense, or exploration of normative claims about animals and human–animal relationships. *Normative* claims are simply claims about what we should do, including about what is valuable. The central claim for which Singer argues in "All Animals Are Equal" is that we should extend the basic principle of equality that we extend to other humans to members of other species. What this means is *not* that animals (including humans) should all be *treated* the same, but that equal consideration should be granted to their interests. For Singer, our refusal to do this, and the fact that we count trivial human interests as weightier than even very strong interests of nonhuman animals, ultimately rests upon *speciesism*, in direct analogy to racism or sexism. *Like* interests, Singer says, should be treated alike (whether they belong to humans or animals) and *unlike* interests should be treated *unalike*. Humans and animals who can suffer – who are *sentient* – both have strong interests in not suffering; these strong interests should both be taken account of in our reasoning about what to do.

Singer does not take these conclusions to be a matter of opinion. He is not concerned with explicating his own view so much as understanding "the point of view . . . of the Universe" (Sidgwick, qtd. in Singer, *Animal Liberation* 5). If a philosophical essay like Singer's is read primarily as creative writing, rhetoric, or a statement of the author's views, its aim is missed. Indeed, insofar as Singer's work does contain the rhetoric identified by Salih's students, it is arguably failing: Singer's arguments should stand or fall on their own strength. This is not to say that Singer's work is devoid of rhetoric or (despite Singer's own hopes, perhaps) emotion. Animal ethicists, and Singer especially, care about these issues, and are frequently motivated to influence their readers (see Garland 124–25). Frustratingly, perhaps, dispassionate argument – even, by philosophical standards, excellent argument – is not always very good at convincing.[5]

Even when rhetoric is present, however, philosophical essays are primarily works of academic analysis or enquiry. While the essay may *serve* as a work of literature, it is the arguments (which may take many forms) that the author offers for analysis.

Analysis

Philosophy and literature are domains of words. Central to analytic philosophy is the tool of conceptual analysis. Concepts are the building blocks of statements and arguments, and conceptual analysis is simply the study of said building blocks. Conceptual analysis can involve a range of different exercises (Olsthoorn 153–54).

First, it could involve breaking a tricky concept into parts, either to simplify things (offering "bite-size" pieces of a concept) or to complicate them (revealing that matters have been over-simplified). Take Singer's talk of *equality*; his argument rests upon a splitting of equality into its empirical component (for example, equality of IQ) and its moral component, the latter of which is his primary concern (*Animal Liberation* 3–5).

Second, we can get to the bottom of the *correct* understanding of a particular concept. The best example of this comes from something Singer – in my view – gets wrong. He conceptualizes speciesism as "a prejudice or attitude of bias in favor of the interests of members of one's own species and against those of members of other species" (*Animal Liberation* 6). This conceptualization fails to capture (what are sensibly called) speciesist attitudes favoring the interests of dogs over those of pigs. Analysis of the concept *speciesism*, of which there has been much since Singer's early work, reveals the imprecision of his conceptualization.

Third, philosophers work through the relationships between different concepts. Singer, for example, is very clear that sentience is a more suitable basis for equal consideration than (say) intelligence precisely because of the particular relationship that sentience has to interests – it is a *prerequisite* for the possession of interests.

Through his use of conceptual analysis, Singer aims to leave little ambiguity in his use of language. Indeed, ambiguity is typically seen as a flaw in analytic philosophy. This is in sharp contrast to works of literature, in which creative and careful use of ambiguity can be central to works' appeal. This difference speaks to the different goals of philosophical and literary works – it is Singer's aim to lay bare, not to court ambiguity.

Argument

Philosophers love to argue, in that they love crafting arguments. The reason for this is that good arguments can get us somewhere new – something we believed is shown false, something we did not believe is shown true.

Arguments have premises (claims taken as a starting point) and conclusions (claims derived from those starting points). Ideally, the conclusion will follow from the premises: because of the logical relationship between them, if the premises are true, then the conclusion is true. An argument with this kind of relationship is called a *valid* argument. The gold standard is a *sound* argument: a valid argument with true premises. The conclusion of a sound argument, even if surprising, must be true.

There are two ways we can challenge an argument. We can argue that one or more of the premises are not true, and so that, even if it is valid, the argument is not sound. We are thus not obliged to accept the conclusion as true. It may be true, of course, but this argument does not demonstrate that. Or we can argue that one or more of the argumentative moves – the presented relationships between the statements – is/are illegitimate, and so the conclusion does not follow from the premises. Again, the conclusion may still be true – this is just not shown by the argument.

Playing around with arguments – either by crafting them, or challenging those crafted by others – makes up a great deal of the substance of philosophical essays. Consider the following simple argument, inspired by Singer. I have laid it out formally (as opposed to in prose). This is mostly a style matter; prose arguments are generally easier to read, but formulaic arguments are generally easier to analyze. Singer's arguments in *Animal Liberation* are in prose, no doubt reflecting his desire to speak to a wide audience.

> Premise 1: If pigs are sentient, then they have interests.
> Premise 2: Pigs are sentient.
> Conclusion: Pigs have interests.

This is a valid argument, meaning that if someone seeks to challenge it, they must challenge the truth of the premises. For example, they might challenge premise 2. Singer gives over a great deal of space in "All Animals Are Equal" to engaging with these kinds of empirical questions (*Animal Liberation* 9–15). Interestingly, among philosophers, Singer is particularly willing to spend time engaged with the empirics, believing that applied and practical philosophy is possible only with an understanding of empirical facts.

Philosophers, of course, need not be particularly qualified to explore empirical facts; when reading Singer's summary of biological evidence of animal sentience, we must remember that we are not reading the work of a biologist. That philosophers need not be experts in empirical matters is one reason that their considerations are sometimes far removed from the real world. Another is simply because concern about empirical facts can obstruct philosophical exploration. Singer does not need to settle debates about race and IQ, or point to a real-world movement campaigning for IQ-based rights, to make the points he wishes to make about IQ. There is a potential relationship between the philosophical essay and works of (vegan) literature, here. Both step away from empirical reality (to a minor or very great extent) in order to expose something of interest.

While philosophers need not be good at spotting when premises of arguments are true or false, they are (or should be) good at spotting when arguments are fallacious – that is, when they employ a form of argument that does not lead where it purports to lead. In addition to making his own case, Singer is quick to point out the fallacies in the cases of his opponents. For example, he explains how claims that animals cannot have rights are "irrelevant" when it comes to refuting the arguments of *Animal Liberation* (8). This is because no argument in his book depends upon the claim that animals have rights. Though Singer is quick to dismiss challenges to him, he does so by explicitly identifying argumentative flaws. Sometimes, philosophers spend a great deal of time (re)constructing (possible) challenges to their position to expose argumentative missteps. Consider Singer's analysis of arguments that animals are non-sentient (10–15). For those not invested in the arguments, such passages can be uninteresting. Indeed, in recognition of this fact, Singer invites readers to skip them if already convinced (10).

Experiments

Animal ethicists also frequently utilize arguments known as "thought experiments" – hypothetical scenarios we are inclined to view one way rather than another. Thought experiments are often baroque, outlandish, or shocking. Indeed, it is the starkness of some of Singer's words that prompt the defensive reactions mentioned by Salih at the start of this chapter: they might seem alarming, crass, or provocative. But they serve a particular argumentative role, drawing out our intuitions about morality.

Take Singer's talk of a split society in which those with a greater-than-100 IQ are seen as morally superior, while those with a lower-than-100 IQ are seen as morally inferior (*Animal Liberation* 3).[6] How would we feel about this (fictional) society? It is abhorrent. But Singer's point is not the simplistic claim that both *this* hierarchical society and *our* hierarchical society are abhorrent. Rather, he is revealing that the argument "Such-and-such a hierarchy is based upon IQ difference, and therefore justified" is flawed. If it were not flawed, this fictional society would contain a justified hierarchy. But we feel quite sure that it does not.

Where does this leave us? We could reject our intuitions about this case, accepting that the hierarchy is justified. Or we could adapt our moral theory, concluding that something other than IQ difference is required for a hierarchy to be justified – including for human–animal hierarchies. In this case, Singer wants us to adapt our theory, meaning that we should reject any claim that human–animal hierarchy is justified because of IQ differences. However, he will be the first to say that some of our intuitions should be rejected. Indeed, *Animal Liberation* is essentially a plea that we reject our intuitions about the obvious superiority of humans over animals.

Animal ethicists deploy these thought experiments, then, as part of a scholarly method of balancing. Sometimes our intuitions must be rejected, and we must accept some things that, initially, sound surprising, or even unpleasant. Sometimes we must adjust our theoretical understanding, because thought experiments have shown us that our previous understanding goes wrong in some way. This balancing act is the method of *reflective equilibrium*. It is the most common method of contemporary analytic moral/political philosophy, and, indeed, it may be its *only* (defensible) method (Knight 46).

Perhaps some works of literature – including, say, speculative fiction – can be seen as offering or involving thought experiments. They, too, can test our intuitions, to help us see that our beliefs, justifications, or rationalizations may not hold up under scrutiny. But works of literature are inevitably richer, and more open to interpretation, than even the most vivid thought experiments of philosophers. Indeed, it is possible that contemporary literary work on animals *deliberately* seeks to complicate Singer-inspired arguments. After all, thought experiments (as I am here using the term) are moves in an argument, rather than creative works. On the other hand, there is space for animal ethicists to *draw from* works of fiction to explicate their thought experiments. This is not something that Singer does in "All Animals Are Equal," but it is something one sees elsewhere – indeed, some of philosophy's most famous thought experiments borrow directly from fiction. For example, in *The Republic* (itself a work of fiction, insofar as it is presented in dialogue form), Plato's character of Socrates invokes the Ring of Gyges, an artifact that makes its wearer invisible. But drawing thought experiments from literature will (almost) inevitably strip scenarios from their fictional contexts: the whole point of a thought experiment is that variables are narrowed, complexities are ironed out, choices are limited.

Concluding Thoughts

An exploration of "All Animals Are Equal" – taken as representative of an essay in analytic animal ethics – has shown us some of the challenges that arise when trying to read it as, in Salih's words, "a literary artefact to be analysed and assessed" (63). Philosophical essays are not written for analysis of this sort, and, given the essay's particular aims and methods, such analysis may well be a frustrating experience for the literary scholar.

But none of this is to say that the vegan literary theorist should not be reading philosophical work – far from it. Vegan scholarship and vegan lifestyles are ethically motivated, and philosophical analysis offers some of the best tools at our disposal to interrogate, understand, justify, and explain ethical beliefs. Without engagement with normative work – including, but not necessarily limited to, philosophical essays – vegan literary theory will rest solely upon conviction or faith. This need not always be a negative, but it is not going to leave the theorist well-equipped to understand the arguments underpinning veganism. Vegan literary scholarship must not be reduced to activism – but scholars cannot be wholly detached from their subject matter. They must (at least) reflect on their work's relation to moral and political action, progress, and critique.

Whether philosophers effectively deploy literary devices or not – and whether philosophical argument makes for effective activism or not – it is undeniable that philosophical essays have the power to move and to change minds. Dozens of people have told me that they have changed their dietary habits through their engagement with philosophical texts. Many have told me of the deep emotions stirred in them by philosophical essays: anger, elation, hope ... And, more, for many engaging with animal ethics for the first (or hundredth) time, something just *clicks*, everything falls into place, they *get it*.

Singer's *Animal Liberation* is certainly one text that can do this. But it is far from alone. I vividly recall one postgraduate student who – so far as I know – had never encountered animal ethics before, who told me that she had been literally moved to tears by the (in her words) *beauty* of Sue Donaldson and Will Kymlicka's *Zoopolis*. I would be the first to describe *Zoopolis* as inspiring, paradigm-shifting, a must-read – but I confess that I had not previously thought of it as *beautiful*.[7] These responses, both emotional and aesthetic, I hope, give further reason to encourage vegan literary scholars to look to philosophy and animal ethics.

All the while, however, they should remember Salih's words. It is the "moral message" that is key. Though the vegan literary scholar should of course bring her expertise to bear on the language of the philosophical essay, she should be prepared, too, to engage with philosophical essays on their own terms.

Notes

1. The long-running podcast *Knowing Animals* (which I presently host) quizzes animal studies scholars; Singer's is one of a short list of names, along with Carol J. Adams, that appears repeatedly in answer to the question of the first piece of "pro-animal scholarship" read.
2. The version referred to in this chapter is from *Animal Liberation*'s 1995 edition.
3. Concern with animal rights' patrimony has contributed to significant female voices being overlooked (compare Fraiman, on a similar trend with Derrida), and Singer does not support animal *rights* anyway (Singer, "Animal Liberation").
4. This chapter did not originally focus on Singer's writing, as I hope to champion the diversity of positions and figures in my discipline. The chapter's ultimate focus reflects the fact that it *is* Singer being read. I do not think this necessarily a bad thing. Despite philosophical disagreements with Singer, I recognize that his work is engaging, accessible, and rich. People seeking an entry into animal ethics – or even philosophy as a whole – could do far worse.
5. This is not unique to philosophy. The best scientific studies of vaccine safety and efficacy, for instance, are unlikely to challenge vaccine hesitancy.
6. This is not presented as a thought experiment in the typical sense, but it is easy to reframe it as one.
7. I should say that Donaldson and Kymlicka's words in a different essay certainly stirred my own emotions. For better or worse, I am hardened to the horrible things that we do to animals, but reading the following lines gave me feelings of sickness, sadness, and anger:

   > [We need] reforms in our understanding of animal freedom and flourishing. We noted earlier that [farmed animal sanctuary] mission statements typically define animal freedom and flourishing in terms of species-typical behaviors. According to this view, in order to know how an individual animal wants to live, we need to know the behaviors and activities typical of her species, and ensure that she can engage in them. Pigs like to root and build nests. Chickens like to scratch and take dust baths. Stimpy, a rabbit rescued from a lab, was lucky enough to end up in Margo DeMello's sanctuary where he "was able, before he died, to run and jump, to groom another rabbit and be groomed, to taste grass and dig in the dirt, to feel the sun and sniff the breeze, to do rabbit things and feel rabbit pleasures." ("Farmed Animal Sanctuaries" 67, quoting DeMello 87)

   Incidentally, I am not personally drawn to ideas about "species-typical behaviour." I also note that DeMello is not philosopher.

Works Cited

Crary, Alice. "Ethics." *Critical Terms for Animal Studies*, edited by Lori Gruen, U of Chicago P, 2018.
Diamond, Cora. "The Difficulty of Reality and the Difficulty of Philosophy." *Partial Answers*, vol. 1, no. 2, 2003, pp. 1–26.
—. "Eating Meat and Eating People." *Philosophy*, vol. 53, no. 206, 1978, pp. 465–79.
DeMello, Margo. "Rabbits in Captivity." *The Ethics of Captivity*, edited by Lori Gruen, Oxford UP, 2014.
Donaldson, Sue, and Will Kymlicka. "Farmed Animal Sanctuaries: The Heart of the Movement?" *Politics and Animals*, vol. 1, 2015, pp. 50–74.
Fraiman, Susan. "Pussy Panic versus Liking Animals: Tracking Gender in Animal Studies." *Critical Enquiry*, vol. 39, no. 1, 2012, pp. 89–115.
Garland, Christopher. "By Any Means of Persuasion Necessary: The Rhetoric of Veganism." *The Routledge Companion to Vegan Studies*, edited by Laura Wright, Routledge, 2021.
Garner, Robert, and Yewande Okuleye. *The Oxford Group and the Emergence of Animal Rights*. Oxford UP, 2021.
Knight, Carl. "Reflective Equilibrium." *Methods in Analytical Political Theory*, edited by Adrian Blau, Cambridge UP, 2017.
Milburn, Josh. "The Analytic Philosophers: Peter Singer and Tom Regan." *The Routledge Companion to Vegan Studies*, edited by Laura Wright, Routledge, 2021.
Olsthoorn, Johan. "Conceptual Analysis." *Methods in Analytical Political Theory*, edited by Adrian Blau, Cambridge UP, 2017.
Quinn, Emelia, and Benjamin Westwood. "Introduction: Thinking Through Veganism." *Thinking Veganism in Literature and Culture*, edited by Quinn and Westwood, Palgrave Macmillan, 2018, pp. 1–24.
Schuster, Joshua. "The Vegan and the Sovereign." *Critical Perspectives on Veganism*, edited by Jodey Castricano and Rasmus R. Simonsen, Palgrave Macmillan, 2016.
Salih, Sara. "Remnants: The Witness and the Animal." *Thinking Veganism in Literature and Culture*, edited by Emelia Quinn and Benjamin Westwood, Palgrave Macmillan, 2018, pp. 57–77.
Sidgwick, Henry. *The Methods of Ethics* (7th ed., reprint). Macmillan, 1963.
Singer, Peter. "All animals are equal." *Philosophic Exchange*, vol. 5, no. 1, 1974, pp. 103–16.
—. *Animal Liberation* (2nd ed.). Pimlico, 1995.
—. "Animal Liberation or Animal Rights?" *The Monist*, vol. 70, no. 1, 1987, pp. 3–14.
—. "Reflections." *The Lives of Animals*, by J. M. Coetzee, edited by Amy Gutmann, Princeton UP, 1999.
Wright, Laura. "Doing Vegan Studies: An Introduction." *Through a Vegan Studies Lens*, edited by Wright, U of Nevada P, 2019, pp. vii–xxv.
—. *The Vegan Studies Project*. U of Georgia P, 2015.

15

The Exposé

Through a Vegan Lens: The Challenges and Ethics of Exposé

Sangamithra Iyer

We cannot pretend that we do not know this. We are not ostriches, and cannot believe that if we refuse to look at what we do not wish to see, it will not exist. This is especially the case when what we do not wish to see is what we wish to eat.

Leo Tolstoy, "The First Step," (45)

The world runs ... on the fuel of this endless fathomless misery. People know it, but they don't mind what they don't see. Make them look and they mind, but you're the one they hate, because you're the one that made them look.

Karen Joy Fowler (232)

Introduction

THE PURPOSE OF the exposé form is to expose, to bare, to bring to light, to disclose, display, uncover, unmask. Exposé is often an attempt to reveal truths deliberately kept hidden. In the case of exposé related to the impacts associated with human consumption of billions of nonhuman animals each year, exposé has the challenge of exposing violence to a human populace pretending not to know; or to expose the systems of power that hide violence and lull society to complacency. Musician Sir Paul McCartney is often quoted as saying, "If slaughterhouses had glass walls, everyone would go vegetarian." But what happens when the exposé writer who encounters those glass walls refuses to fully see through them, or sees but does not go vegetarian?

This chapter looks at the form of exposé through a vegan literary lens that is inclusive of multiple perspectives including those of animals, labor, immigration, feminism, and the environment. By looking closely at four texts, this chapter shows how the vegan literary exposé seeks to wake a population pretending to be sleeping. Two of the popular literary exposés written by omnivores – Michael Pollan's *The Omnivore's Dilemma* (2006) and Jonathan Safran Foer's *Eating Animals* (2009) – will be in conversation with two academic exposés by vegan writers who explore the ethical challenges of the form and of bearing witness – Timothy Pachirat's *Every Twelve Seconds: Industrialized Slaughter and the Politics of Sight* (2011) and Kathryn Gillespie's *The Cow with Ear Tag #1389* (2018). This essay is also itself a form of exposé, exposing the fictions and omissions made in Pollan's and Foer's texts and the ways in which they reinforce strategies of concealment.

The Meat Exposé

Over the past two decades, there has been a growing popular literary canon exposing the modern realities behind the consumption of animal bodies written by omnivores, from Eric Schlosser's *Fast Food Nation* (2001) to Michael Pollan's *The Omnivore's Dilemma: A Natural History of Four Meals* (2006) and Jonathan Safran Foer's *Eating Animals* (2009). A larger vegetarian literary history precedes these works. Consider the anthology *The Ethics of Diet: A Catena of Authorities Deprecatory of the Practice of Flesh Eating* edited by Howard Williams in the late 1890s, which anthologized writers from Pythagoras to Thoreau and acknowledged the foundation of Jain and Buddhist philosophies. The case against eating animals has been articulated and rearticulated over centuries, well before these recent omnivorous writings exposing the evils of factory farming.

Many of the texts within this new literary canon are fraught exposés torn between a desire to share and process the truth about what is done to animals and a desire to justify that continued treatment. The authors refuse to fully look at that which they do not wish to see. What causes such a disconnect? To expose the practices involved in meat, dairy, and egg production is to recognize that carnivorous cultures are founded on violence to all beings on this planet. To expose this reality is to also expose our complicity in these systems. This truth often puts the writer and reader in a defensive, vulnerable, and uncomfortable place, unable to accept inconvenient truths. And the privileged writer or reader may be unable to imagine a world other than the one that has served them so well.

In his treatise *What Then Must We Do?*, Tolstoy offers this advice when confronting uncomfortable truths regarding his own privilege: "First: not to lie to myself; and – however far my path of life may be from the true path disclosed by my reason – not to fear the truth" (157). Exposé written with a vegan lens does not fear the truth and aims to relieve not only the discomfort of the writer and reader but also the animals. It is writing that is in service of the animal and not the story a writer pretends to be true. Literary exposé with a vegan lens and ethics attempts to do what vegan visual artists such as Sue Coe and photographer JoAnne MacArthur do when witnessing animal injustice: pay attention and not look away.

Denial of Hidden Horrors

The difficulty of exposing and challenging deeply protected societal norms around eating animals has a long history. Consider animal rights advocate and social reformer Henry Salt in his *A Plea for Vegetarianism*, written near the end of the nineteenth century:

> It is a mournful fact that when people have no wish to understand a thing, they can generally contrive to misunderstand it; and the hopelessness of pleading with those who will not or cannot comprehend is one of the first lessons learnt by Food Reformers, as indeed, by reformers of all kinds. (19)[1]

In the opening chapter of her book *The Cow with Ear Tag #1389* Gillespie discusses this mournful fact. When Gillespie tells people that she studies and teaches the lives of animals in the food system, she is interrupted with "'Don't tell me, I don't want to know!'. . . Or they know enough to know that they don't want to know more" (13). Pachirat's *Every Twelve Seconds* also wrestles with what is "hidden in plain sight," providing a close account of "what it means to participate in the massive routinized, slaughter of animals for consumption by a larger society from which that work is hidden" (6). Both vegan authors, Gillespie and Pachirat expose uncomfortable violences and silences that are ubiquitous in our food system, with the aim that the reader will not turn away. For Pachirat, the intent is to "provoke reflection on how distance and concealment operate as mechanism of power in modern society" (3). For Gillespie, the purpose of her book is "to combat the act of forgetting and looking away" (14).

And then there have been other texts of troubled omnivores, which have shaped popular discussion, particularly in the US, around the consumption of meat, which go far enough to expose the horrors, but avoid fully challenging them. In these texts, it is not the reader who turns away, but the writer. In *The Omnivore's Dilemma*, Pollan investigates industrial animal agriculture, big and small organic farms, and hunting and writes passionately about the abuses of factory farming and how "it offers a nightmarish glimpse of what capitalism is capable of in the absence of any moral or regulatory constraint whatsoever" (318). He further notes, "Vegetarianism doesn't seem an unreasonable response to the existence of such an evil" (319). It is, however, an unreasonable response for Pollan. Compared to other chapters of in-depth investigative research and practical experience, Pollan's reluctant journey into vegetarianism is mostly a brief mental debate with and dismissal of Peter Singer's *Animal Liberation*. While Pollan invests significant time in the company of Joel Salatin and Angelo Garro, a smaller-scale raiser and slaughterer of animals, and a hunter, respectively, who serve as his guides to these practices, he chooses no real-life encounter with a vegan mentor to show him the ropes of plant-based eating, share a meal, or reveal other perspectives of the lives of animals raised for food. Instead of spending time on a farm animal sanctuary to consider the perspectives of vegans and the rescued animals in their care, Pollan chooses distance from the subject of veganism: "[N]owadays it seems we either look away or become vegetarians. For my own part, neither option seemed especially appetizing; certainly, looking away was now completely off the table" (Pollan 307); nonetheless, he still looks away.

Pollan hides behind statements like "to think of domestication as a form of slavery or even exploitation is to misconstrue that whole relationship – to project a human idea of power onto what is in fact a symbiosis between the species" (320). Gillespie, on the other hand, acknowledges the etymological roots of the word "cattle," which comes from "chattel, meaning property, and calls up references to chattel slavery" (8). She chooses not to use the word cattle, because she wants to reimagine a different relationship with cows. Gillespie focuses on dairy, because there is the public perception that the industry is benign and often associated with bucolic images. What her book does that is rarely acknowledged in most food exposés is fully reveal the reproductive manipulation and emotional harm done to animal bodies in the dairy industry. "You know, it's kind of sad. Even when we remove the calves so quickly, the cows'll bellow for the calves – like they're looking for them – for a couple of weeks a lot of time," one dairy worker told Gillespie (56).

Pollan, on the other hand, ignores dairy in his dilemma. Had he explored the full lives of animals raised for milk and cheese, perhaps he would not have readily equated domestication with symbiosis. In contrast, Gillespie uses the word "violence" to describe what is routinely done to animals used for food, even though her critics may view her language as hyperbolic. She hopes to illuminate "the ways that violence against certain lives and bodies has become so normalized that it is not viewed as violence at all" (Gillespie21). Gillespie notes, for instance, that

> The connection between dairy and slaughter is one that is under-recognized in public consciousness just as the many facets of routine dairy production – artificial insemination, semen production, feeding, tail docking, castration, dehorning, birthing, milking, transport, sale, slaughter, and rendering – are largely absent from the popular image of dairy production. (17)

Even in his short foray into vegetarianism, Pollan established convenient exceptions for himself. In the Young Readers edition of his book, Pollan writes: "I decided that eggs and milk can be gotten from animals without hurting or killing them – or so, at least, I thought" (Chevat and Pollan 252). Remember, Pollan's vegetarian experiment begins *after* he has read *Animal Liberation*, and he has already forgotten and looked away from dairy and eggs, pretending not to know what he has already learned. Ultimately, Pollan dismisses abstaining from animal products, without investigating those products with the same level of rigor as his research into other kinds of eating, admitting that

> I have to say there is part of me that envies the moral clarity of the vegetarian, the blamelessness of the tofu eater. Yet part of me pities him too. Dreams of innocence are just that; they usually depend on a denial of reality that can be its own form of hubris. (362)

Yet, it is Pollan who denies reality and refuses to fully process his experiences so he may forget and look away. While bearing witness to industrial animal factories, Pollan's discomfort is clear:

> Standing there in the pen alongside my steer, I couldn't imagine ever wanting to eat the flesh of one of these protein machines. Hungry was the last thing I felt. Yet, I'm sure that after enough time goes by, and the stink of this place is gone from my nostrils, I will eat feedlot beef again. (84)

The discomfort is still present at Joel Salatin's smaller-scale grass-fed animal farm: "Was I going to be able to enjoy eating chicken so soon after my stint in the processing shed and gut-composting pile?" (264). It remains after Pollan's experiments with hunting too: "Just then I could have made myself vomit simply by picturing myself putting a fork to a bite of this pig. How was I ever going to get past this?" (357).

Denial is at the heart of *The Omnivore's Dilemma* and comes to mirror Tolstoy's exclamation of "This is dreadful!" in his essay "The First Step." Tolstoy investigates the slaughterhouses of Moscow and talks to butchers conflicted with pity for the animals: "[T]hat man suppresses in himself, unnecessarily, the highest spiritual capacity – that of sympathy and pity toward living creatures like himself – and by violating his own feelings becomes cruel" (39). Pollan acknowledges his discomfort, examines it, but ultimately suppresses it in order to continue killing and eating animals. Many other omnivorous writers have narratives with similar trajectories. The writer learns some truth about food, and wrestles with it. There is tension between the belly, the brain, and the heart. The belly ultimately wins. "But it tastes so good," the writer laments. The writer and reader get past their discomfort.

But exposé through a vegan literary lens does not aim to "get past" uncomfortable truths, but rather sits with them. Often, writers like Pollan get past them by believing there is a better way to raise and kill animals, and that is the conclusion of their investigations. Gillespie posits that the conversation should be "less about *how* humans in the United States kill animals for food and more about *whether* they should raise them and kill them for food at all" (112). Pollan instead glorifies Joel Salatin, as a means or a model to excuse his own meat-eating. I interviewed Pollan in 2006 for *Satya* magazine. I remember asking how a book about food could be centered around conversations with a few white men. How were there no women in this discussion? He said it was a fair point and perhaps in his venture into sustainable agriculture, there may have been someone else he could have chosen, but that no one was as compelling a character as Joel Salatin to him.

In the years since Pollan made Salatin famous, critiques of Salatin have emerged. Farmer Chris Newman challenged the economic viability of Salatin's model and was met with racist hostility. "Salatin penned an appallingly racist screed about me in response to one of my essays on small farming back in November, and has a storied history of hostile, racialized rhetoric toward people of color in both public and private," Newman wrote in a Medium post. Newman further notes that "most people haven't read his books or his blog, which are full of racist dogwhistles, poor-shaming, homophobic screeds, full-throttle misogyny, science denial, and naked appeals to White ethnocentrism." While developing his moral justification for raising and killing animals, Pollan did not notice or scrutinize the agricultural icon he created to make his case.

Visibility and the Ethics of Witness

Pachirat's first chapter begins with the animals – an account of six cows escaping the holding pen of a Nebraska slaughterhouse. Most were recaptured and transported back to the slaughterhouse, but one cream-colored cow ran loose and was shot by the police. "They shot it, like ten times" (2) one slaughterhouse worker recounted and made comparisons to a similar incident of how the police shot an unarmed Mexican man. Pachirat notes "how the work of killing is hidden even from those who participate directly in it. The workers who reacted with outrage and disgust to the shooting of a single cow by the Omaha police participate in the killing of more than 2,400 cattle on a daily basis" (9).

The exposé, and its logic of exposure, could be equated with Pachirat's term "politics of sight," which he defines as an "organized, concerted attempt to make visible what is hidden and to breach, literarily or figuratively, zones of confinement in order to bring about social and political transformation" (15). Throughout the book Pachirat makes visible the invisible labors of slaughterhouse work. The appendix on "Division of Labor on the Kill Floor" lists 121 different job titles corresponding to figures and maps of slaughterhouse floor plans presented earlier in the book. The job titles alone, from tail ripper and belly ripper to ear/nose cutters, graphically reveal that this hidden work is about dismembering bodies. Pachirat invokes slaughterhouse labor conditions reminiscent of Upton Sinclair's muckraking novel, *The Jungle*, published a century earlier.

Pachirat also shows differences between the inside and the outside of the slaughterhouse, between supervisors and production workers, and the most jarring are the sensory differences between workers on the kill floor and those in fabrication areas. The former wear their own clothing, in a steamy area filled with "leaking liquids – from blood to urine to feces to vomit to bits of brain matter to bile" (40), compared with the latter, in chilled temperature-controlled areas dealing with solids of animals and with more sanitary measures and protections in place. What Pachirat also learns is that each worker is distanced from other aspects of the slaughterhouse: "There are 121 job functions, 121 perspectives, 121 experiences of industrialized killing" (47). Pachirat's exposé is based on his experience gaining employment inside a slaughterhouse and working on the kill floor. He resigned "finding ethical dilemmas involved with my quality-control work untenable" (17) and continued conducting interviews with slaughterhouse workers and community groups.

Pachirat does not name the slaughterhouse in his book and changes the names of most of the individuals. He states upfront that "I entered the kill floor to provide an account of contemporary industrialized slaughter, not to expose a specific place," and he was ethically committed to not "implicate specific individuals or places" (17). Here, Pachirat hides certain details about a specific place, to expose larger truths about systemic violence.

Gillespie also shares her ethical dilemmas in doing this kind of research. The title of her book comes from a cow with ear tag 1389 at an auction that she attended. Understanding that this investigative work is emotionally intense, Gillespie employs what she calls "buddy system research " (95). She notes she and her buddy serve as companions who "accompany each other into field and analysis research processes that are emotionally taxing, potentially physically unsafe, or otherwise troubling to encounter alone" (Gillespie 95). Gillespie advocates for "embodied practices that honor the deeply emotional and often traumatizing nature of research dedicated to uncovering injustice and structural violence" (95).

The auction is filled with internal conflict for Gillespie who witnesses the cow in question collapse on the floor. She documents her mental anguish:

> Should I have bid? Was it too late to buy her? What would happen to her because she didn't sell? How would I transport her if I did buy her? Would she fit in my station wagon if I put the seats down? . . . What ethical questions were involved with financially contributing to the auction and were these outweighed by the good it might do to buy her and give her a different life? Why this cow and the dozens of others I had watched pass through the ring? (97)

Gillespie notes that "witnessing can also be an ethically fraught and emotionally traumatic process precisely because it is dedicated to witnessing – watching, documenting – and not centered on doing something to change the conditions for those who are the subjects of violence" (99).

In her statement that "I was already struggling with the fuzzy ethical gray line between witnessing and voyeurism when watching animals suffering in the auction yard" (102) Gillespie brings a vegan literary lens to the form of exposé by acknowledging these ethical dilemmas and searching for alternative ways of knowing and learning. "I came to understand that there are many ways of building knowledge about dairy production that do not involve such overt complicity in harming animals," (102–03), she writes. She also centers knowledge learned from animals and caregivers at sanctuaries, recalling that "the lasting emotional trauma some animals experience from their pasts is visible at every sanctuary I have visited" (130).

In recounting the ethical conflict at the auction, Gillespie ponders her role as researcher versus activist. She notes how other activists may have acted more quickly: "There are many animal activists that would have bought the cow with ear tag #1389 or intervened on her behalf after the auction was over" (99), thus further questioning bearing witness alone without acting. But by writing what she observes and posing the ethical questions that this witness work raises, Gillespie creates a "buddy system" approach with her readers as well, offering a space to think through and process these concerns on the page.

Exposé Fictions

The question of what to do when witnessing animal suffering also comes up in Jonathan Safran Foer's book *Eating Animals* (2009). In a section called "Hiding/Seeking," Foer provides multiple first-person accounts from named and unnamed contributors. He begins with his own narration of a section called "I'm Not the Kind of Person Who Finds Himself on a Stranger's Farm in the Middle of the Night," and describes a visit to a turkey factory farm with an animal activist named "C" (Foer 81).

"C" is prepared to document conditions and is equipped with a bag to make a rescue that night, but Foer is uncomfortable about the idea of participating in a rescue. "I had no idea what she was referring to, and I didn't like it" (82), he admits. This visit occurred in the backdrop of increasing ag-gag legislation and the criminalization of animal exposés and activism. As a writer, Foer was worried about getting caught and carried with him a copy of the California Penal Code 597e, which permits entry to care for a domestic animal in need.

Foer witnesses the following: "a chick is trembling on its side, legs splayed, eyes crusted over. Scabs protrude from bald patches. Its beak is slightly open, and its head is shaking back and forth" (89). Foer doesn't know what to do. "C will know what to do," he writes. "And she does. She opens her bag and removes a knife. Holding one hand over the chick's head – Is she keeping it still or covering its eyes? – she slices its neck, rescuing it" (89). To this vegan reader, this act is surprising, as many animal activists who do this kind of documentation work usually participate in an "open rescue" where they try to carry out a few individuals who are sick, get them veterinary care to euthanize or rehabilitate them, and relocate them to sanctuaries if they recover. Rescue has a particular meaning in animal rights circles and isn't equated with the act of mercy killing.

I am not aware of any animal activist who breaks into a factory farm to slice animal necks, and "C" doesn't do this either; it is here that we find the fictions Foer employed in his non-fiction work of exposé. If you go to the notes section buried at the end of *Eating Animals*, you will find this note about this visit with "C": "The identifying characteristics of a character, and the timing and location of and participants in some of the events, in this chapter have been changed" (288). I understood the intent to protect activists like "C" for legal reasons, by masking her identity. But Foer does more than just change "identifying characteristics of a character, and the timing and location of and participants in some of the events." He changes the events themselves.

I know the person behind Foer's character of "C," and I do not wish to disclose her identity to expose Foer. But I do wish to set the record straight. "C" did not slice a turkey's neck open to rescue them. "C" wanted to bring live turkeys out of the farm that night to rescue them, but Foer was reluctant to break the law. He could have saved lives that night, but instead he invented a character named "C" who mercy kills them on the page. This scenario fits the narrative contradictions of the other voices in the book – like the vegetarian rancher, Nicolette Niman, and the vegan who builds slaughterhouses, Aaron Gross, who each narrates a section of *Eating Animals* and allows for Foer's own contradictions in continuing to eat meat.

The only other anonymous figure besides "C" is in the section called "I am a Factory Farmer" (94). The notes at the end of the book reveal this about the "I" of the factory farmer: "This monologue is derived from the statements of more than one factory farmer I interviewed for this book" (289). Unless readers consult the narrative's notes, they would not know that the factory farmer is not a real person, but a composite. Is "C" also a fictional composite? Foer doesn't say so explicitly in the notes section.

Early in the book Foer states,

> While this book is the product of an enormous amount of research, and is as objective as any work of journalism can be – I used the most conservative statistics available (almost always from government, and peer-reviewed academic and industry sources) and hired two outside fact checkers to corroborate them – I think of this as a story. (14)

Foer chooses "story" over "facts" when presenting the voices of the animal activist "C" and the factory farmer – people who would not be in a position to challenge him without exposing themselves in the process.

In addition to changing the events in which Foer participated, he narrates a section by "C," entitled "I am the kind of person who finds herself on a Stranger's Farm in the Middle of the Night" (90). To support a fictional event, Foer has to invent a back story for "C." "That turkey chick I euthanized on our rescue, that was hard. One of my jobs, many years ago, was at a poultry plant. I was a backup killer, which meant it was my responsibility to slit the throats of the chickens that survived the automated throat slitter," his character "C" confesses (90). "So because of my work on the kill line, I knew the anatomy of the neck and how to kill the chick instantly" (90), Foer has "C" explain. But here Foer shows some sloppiness in creating the "C" voice: "and every part of me knew that it was the right thing to put *it* out of *its* misery. But it was hard, because that chick wasn't in a line of thousands of bids to be slaughtered. *It* was an individual. Everything about this is hard" (90; my emphasis). Most animal activists would not call a turkey chick an "it." We might therefore infer that this section is voiced by Foer the novelist and not the animal activist.

Foer takes care to give himself permission to take these liberties in the text. He writes a character "C" who says to him:

> That's why I agreed to help you. I don't know you. I don't know what kind of book you're going to write. But if any part of it is bringing what happens inside those farms to the outside world, that can only be a good thing. The truth is so powerful in this case it doesn't even matter what your angle is. (92)

Consider switching truth and angle in that last sentence: The angle is so powerful in this case it doesn't even matter what your truth is.

Foer knows that the situation he invented in which an animal activist breaks into a farm to kill animals is an anomaly and spends much of the "C" narrated section trying to make it believable, with "C" asserting that

> I wanted to be sure that when you write your book you don't make it seem like I kill animals all the time. I've done it four times, only when it couldn't be avoided. Usually I take the sickest animals to a vet. But that chick was too sick to be moved. (92)

Again, Foer at the time of the turkey farm visit had the opportunity to participate in a rescue of these turkeys but chose not to and instead later invents a dramatic ending he did not witness for the benefit of his story, taking advantage of how the marginalized animal activists cannot afford the visibility to challenge him and hiding behind a legal disclaimer to protect identities.

For years, I knew the truth of what really happened and felt conflicted speaking publicly about it. I was a student at Hunter College MFA program when Foer came to visit in 2009, and at that time, I tried to confront him about these liberties he took. I asked him how many people comprised the factory farmer monologue. He told my class that the factory farmer was created from conversations he had with two farmers. I asked about the notes on the "C" chapter. I did not reveal that I knew her or her version of the story. He said he changed details for legal purposes. I asked him at his book signing afterwards about the use of composite characters in non-fiction and he said he did not composite "C." I did not tell him I knew that he asked the person who inspired "C" a series of hypothetical questions after his visit, such as if she or anyone she knew participated in killing an animal during an investigation and, if so, how would they do it. She did not, nor did she know that he would speculate the answers to these questions to create the character "C" as a novelist would, instead of reporting on what he actually witnessed.

At the time, I did not feel that I had the power to expose this truth. *Eating Animals* was doing well, was being read at many colleges, and had the possibility of steering readers away from eating animals. If it came out that Foer had fictionalized parts, would that fact discount all the other truths about the realities of eating animals documented in the book? But ethically, I was troubled by the liberties Foer took in writing about actions he did not witness, which were never committed by his character "C" in real life, and how he used his power and privilege as a writer to distort the truth about an activist to serve his narrative.

Despite his investment in this subject matter, Foer, like Pollan, doesn't land in a vegan place. The film *Eating Animals*, based on Foer's work, ends with a clear message to support eating animals from smaller farms as the solution. Years after writing *Eating Animals*, Foer confesses in an article in *The Guardian*, "I ate meat a number of times. Usually burgers. Often at airports. Which is to say, meat from precisely the kinds of farms I argued most strongly against." This reckoning with his own hypocrisy and with climate denial becomes the subject of his next non-fiction project *We Are the Weather*, in which, ultimately, Foer settles on abstaining from meat two-thirds of the time, essentially recycling Mark Bittman's idea of "Vegan Before Six." Foer continues to forget and look away part-time to continue eating animals.

Vegan activists like the person behind "C" are deeply entrenched not only in animal rights but in food justice and labor rights. Their work is intersectional, and it was a missed opportunity by Foer not to further explore those intersections and create a more accurate portrait of an animal rights activist and how they live choosing to not look away. By inventing a character, Foer spends too much space on the page explaining how an event that didn't happen happened, instead of giving voice to the emotionally complex work of witness and rescue.

I share this now, because I think the work of exposé through a vegan literary lens, like the works of Gillespie and Pachirat, means not looking away and no longer pretending to still be sleeping. Having more literature to accurately capture the vegan activists who do this work of witness, rescue, and rehabilitation, while not looking away, will help expose what Tolstoy called "the highest spiritual capacity – that of sympathy and pity toward living creatures" (39) so that the writer, reader, and animal can be relieved of their discomfort.

Note

1. For more on the extended history of vegetarian and vegan thought in the nineteenth century, see James Gregory's chapter in this volume.

Works Cited

Chevat, Richie, and Michael Pollan. *The Omnivore's Dilemma: The Secrets Behind What You Eat*. Young Readers edition, Dial Books for Young Readers, 2015.
Foer, Jonathan Safran. *Eating Animals*. Little Brown and Company, 2009.
—. "Jonathan Safran Foer: why we must cut out meat and dairy before dinner to save the planet." The Guardian, 28 September2019. <https://www.theguardian.com/books/2019/sep/28/meat-of-the-matter-the-inconvenient-truth-about-what-we-eat>
Fowler, Karen Joy. *We are all Completely Besides Ourselves*. Putnam's Sons, 2013.
Gillespie, Kathryn. *The Cow with Ear Tag #1389*. U of Chicago P, 2018.
Newman, Chris. "Everything I Want to Do Is Racist." Medium Post, 4 September 2020. <https://sylvanaqua.medium.com/everything-i-want-to-do-is-racist-3ff6a6bb5e01>
Pachirat, Timothy. *Every Twelve Seconds: Industrialized Slaughter and the Politics of Sight*. Yale UP, 2011.
Pollan, Michael. *The Omnivore's Dilemma: A Natural History of Four Meals*. Penguin Press, 2006.
Salt, Henry. *A Plea for Vegetarianism and other Essays*. Manchester Vegetarian Society, 1886.
Tolstoy, Leo. "The First Step." *The Ethics of Diet: An Anthology of Vegetarian Thought*, edited by Howard Williams, William Crow Books, 2009.
Tolstoy, Leo. *What Then Must We Do?* Translated by Aylmer Maude. <http://www.vidyaonline.net/dl/whatthenmustwedo.pdf>

16

Realism

Samantha Pergadia

> What is it that frightens us about a "novel of causes," and conversely, does fiction have to exist in some suspended, apolitical landscape in order to be literary? Can it not be politically and temporally specific and still be in good literary taste? We are leery of literature that smacks of the polemic, instructional, or prescriptive, and I guess rightly so—it's a drag to be lectured to—but what does that imply about the attitudes toward intellectual inquiry? ... I see our lives as being a part of an enormous web of interconnected spheres, where the workings of the larger social, political, and corporate machinery impact something as private and intimate as the descent of an egg through a woman's fallopian tube.
>
> Ruth Ozeki, "A Conversation with Ruth Ozeki"

Introduction

THERE IS NO missing the political message of Ruth Ozeki's 1998 novel *My Year of Meats*. As protest literature, the novel lodges a vigorous critique of the meat industry: from its abuse of workers, to its treatment of animals, chemical and hormonal poisoning of consumers and residents near sites of industrial farming, and work as an extension of US imperialism. The epigraph above comes from an interview with Ozeki appended to the novel. She responds to the unnamed interviewer's question about whether she worried that *My Year of Meats* would turn into a "novel of causes," a pejorative label attached to literature that reeks of the political, the didactic, the prescriptive. The division between aesthetic and political literature summons Ozeki's recitation of "literary taste," a metaphor that, beginning with David Hume, equates gustatory appetite with aesthetic appetite (Hume 231–58). Yet to politicize the appetite is considered poor literary form. As an interpretive strategy prescriptive of how one should eat, vegan literary studies may seem like bad literary criticism, reducing complex or ambiguous meaning to a single political and ethical agenda. Good literary criticism has become synonymous with extending ambiguity, refusing political takeaway, and attending to questions of form or genre.[1] Ozeki reworks this division between the aesthetic and the political to envision a continuous interconnection of the private with the political, of gustatory appetite and aesthetic appetite, of conditioning that folds questions of aesthetic taste onto political conditioning. In *My Year of Meats*, the political seeps into the biopolitical, creating an indistinguishability between the politics and art that shape consumers.

My Year of Meats is concerned with the relationship between fiction and reality, with the role fiction plays in contouring reality, and with the fictional feel of realism itself. It can be read as a novel of protest that carries forward Upton Sinclair's realist mode for protest literature against slaughterhouse practices, as found in his 1906 social realist novel *The Jungle*. The political uptake of realist fiction has always been its most unpredictable and uncontrollable outcome. In perhaps the most quoted and mythologized line from Sinclair's writing, he laments the political misfires of *The Jungle*: "I aimed at the public's heart, and by accident I hit it in the stomach" ("What Life" 594). In Sinclair's *Autobiography*, he disavows *The Jungle* as registering a sympathy for pigs on the slaughterhouse line, insisting that "For 56 years I have been ridiculed for a passage in *The Jungle* that deals with the moral claims of dying hogs – which passage was intended as hilarious farce" (164). As Sinclair retrospectively recounts it, the intended socialist and working-class politics of *The Jungle* were dwarfed by the public's fixation on the pigs themselves and on food safety. Sinclair advocated for the working-class immigrants represented by his character Jurgis rather than for the animals who were a "metaphor for exploited workers" (Lundblad 109). Yet the metaphor exceeded its intended aim, as the animals elicited their own sympathy. Instead of protections for workers, President Roosevelt passed the Meat Inspection Act and the Pure Food and Drug Act of 1906, a legislative response Sinclair condemned as a boost to the monopolistic meatpacking industry. Carol J. Adams has argued that butchering failed as a metaphor for the worker in Sinclair's novel, because the passage contained "too much information on how the animal was violently killed" (78–79).

Realist slaughterhouse fiction extending from *The Jungle* to *My Year of Meats* illustrates a connection between realism and the exposure of slaughterhouse and meatpacking practices that prompts us to consider the work of metaphoric similitude itself. While some may assume a direct relationship between realist protest literature and its political uptake, the specific nature of this relationship is uncertain. This essay considers what happens when we read Ozeki's *My Year of Meats* for its vegan politics, a readily available takeaway that often remains muted through a scholarly hermeneutic that attends instead to the ecocritical resonances of the novel or that treats the animals as mere metaphors for the treatment of women. Included in a 2017 list by Mercy For Animals of "12 Incredible Books that Every Vegan Should Read this Summer," *My Year of Meats* was adopted within animal rights circles as supportive of a vegan ethics. Such a reading seems in line with the novel's plotline, as the two central characters refuse to consume meat by the novel's end. Despite the novel's explicit statements on boycotting meat, other political takeaways emerge as the dominant concerns of Ozeki's novel. This essay ultimately asks, what are the political demands that realist fiction makes on readers, in particular the politics of what one should consume?

My Year of Meats as Realist Fiction

As a genre, realism aims to represent its subject matter through the aura of the possible or empirical. In contrast to speculative, fantastical, utopian, or satirical fiction, realist fiction creates a simulacrum of things as they are, a metonymic splicing of the world. It is, therefore, the genre of the mundane, the everyday, the proximate. In Ozeki's novel about the meat industry, multiple styles of documentation create the sense of realism. The story centers a Japanese-American documentarian, Jane Takagi-Little, who lands a job producing *My American Wife!*, a Japanese television show sponsored by an American meat-exporting company, BEEF-EX. The documentary show within the novel consolidates ideals of American femininity, whiteness, and beef consumption, packaging this trio through episodes that depict American households and the wives who put dinner on the table. Their recipes are included to propel the purchase of American beef by Japanese housewives. Each episode features a typical American housewife, preparing dinner that incorporates American beef, advertising American values and products to Japanese viewers. Across the world, Akiko, a Japanese housewife married to Jane's boss, consumes these episodes and follows along preparing the show's recipes. The climax of the novel interweaves Jane's and Akiko's reproductive stories: Akiko turns up at Jane's apartment pregnant from her husband's assault, just as Jane mourns a miscarriage that possibly resulted from an accident filming at a slaughterhouse. Both, incidentally, have forsaken meat.

At the start of the novel, Jane has defaulted to a meager vegetarian diet "of cabbage and rice" because she cannot find a job to provide her more (Ozeki, *Meats* 7). As she films the show, Jane delights in and partakes of the meat products marketed to Japanese consumers. As Jane produces and undertakes research for these episodes, she discovers the history of a synthetic hormone, *Diethylstilbestrol* (DES), used as a growth hormone for cows and as a pregnancy drug for women. Jane becomes increasingly averse to promoting meat. In her most subversive act, Jane casts a "biracial vegetarian lesbian couple" as the stars of *My American Wife!* (177). Unknowingly cast in a show to sell beef, the couple explain their ethical vegetarianism – a diet practiced as protest to a product that is, they explain, "unhealthy. Not to mention corrupt, inhumane, and out of control" (177).[2] By the novel's end, Jane has adopted vegetarianism as a refusal of the meat industry.

What relationship does Jane's abstention from meat have to the novel's ethics of meat consumption? How does a vegan hermeneutic create a strategy of reading that refuses to relegate fiction to the realm of the apolitical? Ozeki creates a protocol of interpretation in which the literary is compatible with a political takeaway. Through a parodic relationship to realism, the novel aims at a verisimilitude that indicts meat consumption. It incorporates documents that appear to be mundane transcriptions: memos between Jane and John about the production of *My American Wife!*, excerpts from a geography textbook, and ingredient lists for recipes from the show. At the level of form, Ozeki illustrates the author as woven into and produced through her fictional persona. Bookended with two mirrored author's notes, *My Year of Meats* cleaves its author-figure between Ozeki and Jane. The opening "Author's note" comes from Ozeki, while the closing "Author's note" bears Jane's signature. In the first note, Ozeki declaratively warns "This is a work of fiction," a statement with consequence beyond classification. Ozeki's continual references to actual events, people, or locales serve the mere purpose of providing the novel "a sense of reality and authenticity." This paratextual framing denies the novel as a documentation or catalog of the real, while elevating the "sense of reality," which could denote either the *sensation* or the *meaning* of reality. Ozeki marshals real people, places, and events to induce the perception of authenticity, yet she also hints that reality might be discerned or achieved through fiction. Ozeki continues with the disclaimer usually preceding films, that other names, characters, places, and incidents are "the product of the author's imagination" and "their resemblance, if any, to real-life counterparts is entirely coincidental." Instead of suggesting an accident of chance that relates fiction to reality, Ozeki connects fiction to realism through *coincidence*, the simultaneous occupation of place and time. Rather than disclaim the realism of the novel, Ozeki's paratextual note primes its reader to see fiction cleaved to reality. The reader's task becomes discerning whether the novel is fictional realism or realist fiction.

Fiction pries open a realism unavailable to styles of documentation. This realist novel concludes with a fictional bibliography, a seemingly paratextual addendum that is contained within the fiction itself. This bibliography tracks Ozeki's research process, and contains entries of mostly non-fictional sources about DES and factory farming.[3] Presented through the fictional persona of Jane, the "Author's note" preceding the bibliographic entry (a mirror of the "Author's note" that precedes the entire novel), reads: "Although this book is a novel, and therefore purely a work of my imagination, as a lapsed documentarian I feel compelled to include a bibliography of the sources I have relied on to provoke these fictions –J. T. –L." (363). The author's note could be seen as issuing from either Ozeki or Jane, as both share these biographical details and both have just presented a novel. Not until the signature do we discover the addenda as a note from Jane Takagi-Little and not Ruth Lounsbury Ozeki. Here the relationship between factual and fictional material is one of provocation, the non-fiction catalog of sources on slaughterhouses and hormonal poisoning provoking, inciting, giving rise to the fiction. Within the novel, Jane envisions truth as a layered and fabulist entity: "Truth lies in layers, each of them thin and barely opaque, like skin" (175). The oxymoronic phrase, "truth lies" captures the fabulist nature of truth genres and the realist revelations of fictional genres. Jane continues that "truth was like race and could be measured only in ever-diminishing approximations" (176). In an interview following the novel's release, Ozeki remarked, "I don't like to be lied to. I don't like to be fooled. And I certainly don't like to be poisoned" (quoted in West). Through literary realism, Ozeki's docu-novel makes available the factual poisoning illegible to readers of the history of DES. Fiction uncovers a connective truth that lies latent in newspaper clippings or history books about industrial farming.

Ozeki draws attention to the strategies of composition that propel the texture of realism. In miniature, the novel dramatizes in its plot this relationship between fiction and reality. Jane's documentary distorts and fictionalizes reality, which in turn alters reality. The novel announces this process most explicitly through Suzie Flowers, the documentary's first housewife, who discovers her husband's infidelity during filming. The film crew edits the family's story, representing a reconciliation between the couple by distorting the sequence of scenes. But when Suzie and her husband watch the fictionalized version of their marriage, it leads to an actual reconciliation between them, an aspiration to the fictional ideal. Jane remarks:

> . . . I take a Japanese television crew out to Iowa to film a documentary about this American wife, we make a total fiction of the facts of her life, and now, a year later, she tells me that those facts have turned right around and aligned themselves with our fiction. So go figure . . . There's no denying, I thought. In the Year of Meats, truth wasn't stranger than fiction, it *was* fiction . . . Maybe sometimes you have to make things up, to tell truths that alter outcome. (Ozeki 360)

This statement doubles as a testament to Ozeki's novel, which makes available a relationship between fiction and realism that regards fiction's interventionist relationship to the real.

Realism and Multispecies Politics

If Ozeki's realist novel aims to intervene in real historical events, what is the content of that intervention? Among its many critiques of industrial meat-farming, the novel presents American meat as an extension of US imperialism. *My Year of Meats* belongs to a canon of contemporary texts – Jessica Hagedorn's *Dogeaters* (1990), Han Kang's *The Vegetarian* (2007, translated 2015),[4] Larissa Lai's *Salt Fish Girl* (2008), Bong Joon-ho's *Okja* (2017) – that consider the simultaneous export of American culture and food through Asian foodways.[5] Published ten years after the 1988 US-Japan Agreement on Beef Imports, which ended Japan's quotas on imported beef, Ozeki's novel emerged at the end of a decade that saw an increase in the Japanese import and consumption of American beef. The 1988 bilateral negotiations did not emerge through a mutually beneficent process, but through strong-armed multilateral coercion that followed Japan's continued rejection of trade agreements. The United States, Australia, and New Zealand complained to the General Agreement on Tariffs and Trade (GATT) about Japan's restrictions on beef imports, finding the quotas to be in violation of GATT Article XI:1. International pressure compelled Japan to revise the terms of its trade agreement, resulting in the ultimate bilateral easing of the quota system. *My Year of Meats* was published the same year as the USDA's publication of a ten-year assessment of the 1988 Negotiation, which found that the agreement resulted in a 90 per cent increase in the value of US beef imports in Japan, an increase in volume by over 50 per cent, and a rise of beef imports by $1 billion (Dyck 103). The US controlled 61 per cent of the total Japanese beef import value (Dyck 104). By 1998, the American slaughterhouse had become a global industry, producing the meat that composed and constituted bodies around the world.

Ozeki's novel connects disparate events, rendering perceptible continuities between the Japanese beef quota system, American ideals of race and gender, and the violence against animals perpetrated by the meat industry. Ozeki explains the connection between realist fiction and metaphor, saying that the novel originated with a literary conceit in which farm animals and meat functioned as metaphor, with "women as cows; wives as chattel (a word related to cattle); and the body as meat, fleshy, sexual, the irreducible element of human identity ... television as a meat market" ("Conversation" 6). As Ozeki's research into the meat industry unfolded, dramatized in Jane's corresponding research in the novel, this metaphor turns into a material connection. Ozeki learns of the history in which both women and cattle were subjected to DES, and she turns her character Jane into the offspring of these women, known as "DES daughters," who suffer reproductive impairment from these embryonic intrusions. In Ozeki's novel, Jane's research process connects the dots that turn metaphor into a material relationship.[6] An association between cows and women emerges through descriptions of mechanical Japanese housewives. Jane comes across an article about Japanese meat-vending machines that stereotypes the Japanese housewife as "cut off from contact with the world" so that she "prefers to interact with machines" (Ozeki, *Meats* 87). This potential consumer of American beef "finds the human interaction necessary to purchase meat distasteful," so the challenge for meat marketers is to "'de-humanize' meat," a challenge addressed with vending machines that distribute meat absent of a human mediator or its connection to a once-living nonhuman animal (87–88). Jane reads this article and tries to piece together, as a detective, the historical elisions compressed in this market strategy to dehumanize meat. Ozeki pairs this fictional article with the actual 1992 shooting of Yoshihiro Hattori, a sixteen-year-old Japanese exchange student killed by a butcher when he asked for directions. Jane draws a line of connection between these two episodes and the cross-cultural exchange between Japan and America as mediated by cultures of meat. After the butcher was acquitted of manslaughter, the story became a source of shock for Japanese audiences, to whom it was an unambiguous murder warranting criminal sentencing. Jane explains how Japanese media sought to explain the American propensity for violence and attachment to guns, how violence is synonymous with American culture, "what's left of local color" (89). Jane connects the American appetite for hunting with this act of homicide: "And while I'm not saying that [Rodney] Peairs pulled the trigger because he was a butcher, his occupation didn't surprise me. Guns, race, meat, and Manifest Destiny all collided in a single explosion of violent, dehumanized activity" (88–89).

Ozeki's novel reaches for a mode of connecting disparate episodes and events through an institution that has concealed its history. The remnants of the Union Stock Yard era of meat production emerge in similes that describe urban spaces, including the Chicago apartment of Sloan, Jane's boyfriend and father of her unborn child: "Like an abattoir, it could be hosed down without too much difficulty if anything unsightly, like an attachment or a sentiment, happened to splatter the walls" (220). Jane describes the difference between the Midwest and New York: "The city slams you. Middle America is all about drift and suspension. It's the pervasiveness of the mall-culture mentality, all of life becomes an aimless wafting on currents of synthesized sound, through the well-conditioned air." And with a simile that disanimates and dehumanizes meat (162), "In New York, you walk down the streets like that, you're dead meat." By contrast, Akiko's body perceives a highly figurative reanimation of meat, when, after consuming American beef, "she'd start to feel the meat. It began in her stomach, like an animal alive, and would climb its way back up her gullet, until it burst from the back of her throat" (37). The simile "like an animal alive" does not just describe affinity or likeness, but an actual bodily reanimation of vital animals in Akiko's digestive process.

At the slaughterhouse, this relationship between metaphor and materialism turns into a nearly farcical connection between violence against women and violence against the animals of meat production. If the visual realm is the preferred tactic of animal liberationist material – exposing scenes of extraordinary violence that occur behind concealed factory farm and slaughterhouse doors – Ozeki's novel creates a different optic. Her description of the slaughterhouse line enters into the psyche of the cows who move along it:

> Down below, a cow was herded into the pen by a worker wielding an electric prod. The cow balked, minced, then slammed her bulk against the sides of the pen. She had just watched the cow before her being killed, and the cow before that, and she was terrified. Her eyes rolled back into her head and a frothy white foam poured from her mouth as the steel door slammed down on her hindquarters, forcing her all the way in. The worker next to us leaned over and, using a compression stunner, fired a five-inch retractable bolt to her brain. He pressed a button and the metal side of the pen rose up, to reveal the stunned cow, collapsed and twitching on the floor. But the stun was incomplete. (283)

While Sinclair's description of the Chicago stockyards captured the squeals of the pigs, Ozeki translates these yelps and cries into an emotional and affective domain that permits interior animal life. The bovine is gendered female, a marking often omitted from descriptions of beef cattle. Jane imagines the cow's anticipatory anxiety, having witnessed the cow that preceded her. The cow's balking, mincing, and jerking is not the movement of an unfeeling automaton. Ozeki translates this movement into an affective register that touches the cow's interior life, the imagination of herself in the future and her fear of death.

Jane experiences a sensory overload reminiscent of Sinclair's description of the overwhelming sounds and smells of the abattoir: "Stepping into the slaughterhouse was like walking through an invisible wall into hell. Sight, sound, smell – every sense I thought I owned, that was mine, the slaughterhouse stripped from me, overpowered and assaulted" (281). In a scene that borders on camp, the slaughterhouse depicts a literalist association between women and cattle, as a misstep of the cameraman sends Jane "sprawling into the path of a thousand pounds of oncoming carcass," lifting her up off her feet as she becomes a part of the assembly line itself (284).[7] The line between subject and object, observer and observed, fiction and reality dissolves in this moment that conjoins Jane to the cattle she documents, ultimately leading to the discovery of her miscarriage.

After her miscarriage, Jane sits in her home watching footage of the slaughterhouse, prompting a neighbor to file a noise complaint, saying that "it sounded like there was animals being slaughtered down here or something" (326). The scene offers an uncanny verisimilitude – the documentary footage of animals slaughtered is likened to the sound of animals being slaughtered, which, in fact, are the sounds captured by the documentary footage. The captured representation seeps too readily into the thing itself. The police officer who arrives in Jane's apartment sees the footage and asks "How can you watch that stuff?" to which Jane quips "How can you eat it?" (326). In this retort, Jane connects vision to a gustatory politics. The visual register demands an ethical recentering, one that refuses meat consumption.

This is not to say that the novel endorses a simple claim that individual consumer choices are the means to ethical and equitable utopian foodways. One of the final scenes depicts Akiko riding on an Amtrak train through the Deep South, as she realizes "that the people who lived here were poor" (336). A fellow passenger introduces her to what is known as "the Chicken Bone Special" food option. He explains,

> It's called the Chicken Bone, Miss A-KEE-kow, because all these poor black folks, they too poor to pay out good money for them frozen cardboard sandwiches that Amtrak serves up in what they call the *Lounge Car*, so these poor colored folk, they gotta make do with lugging along some home-cooked fried children instead. (338)

This encounter draws attention to the racialized and class politics of access, of how systems and structures shape who gets to choose. A vegan hermeneutic would attend to this takeaway of Ozeki's novel without reinscribing individual consumer choice as an unencumbered political program. Such a reading practice demands a move from the metaphors that connect the characters and events of the novel to a materialist reading practice that envisions underlying relations. To *see* the slaughterhouse footage is to know the connections between DES poisoning of cattle and women, to know the global internationalist politics of meat exportation and its racialized politics in the US, and to feel a mutual sympathy with the sensation of animals on the slaughterhouse line. Realist fiction opens up these sensations that make available a multispecies politics.

Notes

1. See Emre for a historical account of the "bad readers" who contrast good literary critics.
2. For an account of the connection between veganism and lesbianism, see McKay.
3. Included in this bibliography is a 1996 non-fiction detective story about various endocrine disrupters (including DES), *Our Stolen Future: Are We Threatening Our Fertility, Intelligence, and Survival? – A Scientific Detective Story* (Colborn, Dumanoski, and Myers). Prefaced with a note from Al Gore, then Vice President to Bill Clinton, this book finds its way into Ozeki's fictional bibliography and its aesthetic form bears resemblances to the realist and detective blend of *My Year of Meats*.
4. For a close reading of Kang's *The Vegetarian*, see Amy-Leigh Gray and Dana Medoro's contribution to this volume.
5. Several scholars of Asian American literary studies have considered the significance of food and consumption to race and ethnicity. See Xu, *Eating Identities*, Chiu, *Filthy Fictions*, and Ku et al.'s edited collection *Eating Asian America*.
6. For more on the way meat activates a peculiar relationship between metaphor and materialism, see Adams (45–47).
7. For more on camp as a mode of working through the horrors of the slaughterhouse, see Quinn.

Works Cited

Adams, Carol. 1990. *The Sexual Politics of Meat: A Feminist-Vegetarian Critical Theory*. Continuum, 2010.

Chiu, Monica. *Filthy Fictions: Asian American Literature by Women*. Altamira Press, 2004.

Colborn, Theo, Dianne Dumanowski, and John Peterson Myers. *Our Stolen Future: Are We Threatening Our Fertility, Intelligence, and Survival? – A Scientific Detective Story*. Dutton, 1996.

Dyck, John. "U.S.-Japan Agreements on Beef Imports: A Case of Successful Bilateral Negotiations," ed. U.S. Department of Agriculture. 1998.

Emre, Merve. *Paraliterary: The Making of Bad Readers in Postwar American Fiction*. U of Chicago P, 2017.

Hume, David. "Of the Standard of Taste." *Essays: Moral, Political, and Literary*. Cosmo Classics, 2006, pp. 231–58.

Ku, Robert Ji-Song, Martin F. Manalansan, and Anita Mannur. *Eating Asian America: A Food Studies Reader*. New York UP, 2013.

Lundblad, Michael. *Birth of the Jungle: Animality in Progressive-Era U.S. Literature and Culture*. Oxford UP, 2015.

McKay, Robert. "A Vegan Form of Life." *Thinking Veganism in Literature and Culture: Towards a Vegan Theory*, edited by Emelia Quinn and Benjamin Westwood, Palgrave, 2018, pp. 249–71.

Ozeki, Ruth. "A Conversation with Ruth Ozeki." *My Year of Meats*, by Ozeki. Penguin, 1998, pp. 6–14.

—. *My Year of Meats*. Penguin, 1998.

Quinn, Emelia. "Notes on Vegan Camp." *PMLA*, vol. 135, no. 5, 2020, pp. 914–30.

Sinclair, Upton. *The Jungle*. 1906. Oxford UP, 2010.

—. "What Life Means to Me." *Cosmopolitan*, vol. 41, no. 6, October 1906, pp. 591–95.

—. *The Autobiography of Upton Sinclair*. Harcourt, Brace and World, 1962.

Von Alt, Sarah. "12 Incredible Books That Every Vegan Should Read This Summer." *ChooseVeg*, Mercy for Animals, 7 June 2017, chooseveg.com/blog/12-incredible-books-that-every-vegan-should/.

Xu, Wenying. *Eating Identities: Reading Food in Asian American Literature*. U of Hawai'i P, 2008.

West, Cassandra. "She Found a Metaphor to Sink Her Teeth Into." *Chicago Tribune*, 23 June 1999.

17

The Memoir

Black Female Vegans on Decolonizing the Body and Mind: A. Breeze Harper's *Sistah Vegan* Project

Armin Langer

Introduction

According to 2019 Gallup data, people of color in the United States are three times as likely to adopt plant-based diets than white Americans. Nine per cent of Americans of color professed not to eat meat, while only three per cent of white Americans claimed the same. Besides health, environmental awareness was the key motivator for eschewing meat (Hrynowski). Animal agriculture is a leading contributor to the ongoing climate crisis, impacting communities of color more than white ones. Black and Indigenous communities and other communities of color experience greater negative consequences from pollution and environmental degradation, and industrialized animal farms and runoff are often in working-class, non-white neighborhoods (Harper 51). As public opinion surveys prove, Americans of color are more concerned about environmental issues than white Americans (Ballew et al.; Leiserowitz and Akerlof; Mohai; Pearson et al.).

Even though people of color in the US are more likely than white people to choose a meatless diet, veganism is generally associated with whiteness. This association is true not only for the wider public but also for communities of color themselves (Greenebaum; Wallach 155). Jessica Greenebaum suggests that this association is due to the over-representation of white people in vegan marketing and some prominent vegan groups' seeming prioritization of animal rights over human rights (1). Animal rights and vegan non-profits like People for the Ethical Treatment of Animals (PETA) have repeatedly antagonized marginalized communities (Pellow 261; Wrenn 197). PETA campaigns have compared the suffering of Jews in the Holocaust and enslaved Black Americans to that of animals without also acknowledging the lived suffering of humans during these historical instances.[1] Human rights organizations like the Anti-Defamation League (ADL) and the National Association for the Advancement of Colored People (NAACP) have criticized this comparison, arguing that defaming Jews and Black people as animals has a long history in "Western" societies (Balleck 14; Davis 479).[2] While being called an "animal" is not necessarily offensive in itself,[3] it can be offensive in the context of racism and antisemitism (Haslam, Loughnan, and Sun). White Americans and Europeans have likened members of marginalized outgroups like Black and Indigenous people or Jews to "inferior" animals. Such metaphors have been used to justify violence against them (Jahoda; Livingstone Smith).

The work of critical race feminist scholar A. Breeze Harper notices these developments, observing "that mainstream rhetoric around veganism was very 'postracial' – it didn't consider things like socioeconomic class or geographic privilege" ("Defined Plate" 49). Harper, a Black woman who grew up in a working-class family, recalled that initially, she too felt that ethical consumption was for privileged white people. She was a "fervent literary activist when it [came] to antiracism, anticlassism, and antisexism" ("Social Justice" 81) but did not recognize "how eco-sustainability, animal rights, and plant-based diets could be integral" to her work. She thought that "these issues were the domain of the privileged, white, middle- and upper-class people of America" since "[r]ace and class struggle is not a reality for them, so they can 'waste' their time on saving dolphins" (116).

Harper's work deals with misconceptions about the purported incompatibility of veganism and pro-Black politics by reclaiming veganism from systematic racism and other "isms" negatively affecting Black Americans. Under the influence of Black Marxism, decolonial world systems theory, Black feminism, and critical race studies, in 2005, Harper launched the *Sistah Vegan Project*. *Sistah Vegan* started as an online community of Black female vegans discussing how veganism can help decolonize their bodies and minds. The "sistah vegans" imagined a vegan model that challenges racism, environmental degradation and the high rates of disease plaguing the Black community. The online discussions eventually led Harper to the publication of an anthology with the same name ("Doing Veganism" 138–39).

Harper's 2010 anthology *Sistah Vegan: Black Female Vegans Speak on Food, Identity, Health, and Society* presents a series of autobiographical essays and poems on nutrition and health, ecological sustainability, animal rights, and distributive and racial justice from a diverse community of North American Black female vegans. In *Sistah Vegan*, veganism is much more than what one consumes: the anthology demonstrates how the space accorded to Black female vegan voices is vital to enacting decolonization of the body, the mind, and vegan spaces. Instead of prescribing a universal set of vegan principles, *Sistah Vegan* presents a wide range of individual voices promoting veganism as a personal narrative rooted in the authors' personal practices and experiences. In the memoir form of the volume, veganism becomes an active practice of writing the self, a writing that constructs a new script outside of colonial legacies. The genre of memoir is especially appropriate to demonstrate these individual circumstances. Autobiography has historically served as a genre for marginalized communities who used this genre to counter stigmatization (Couser 31). The memoirs in *Sistah Vegan* make marginalized voices available to a broader readership and have the power to express vegan thought. This essay demonstrates, through a close reading of *Sistah Vegan*, the power of memoir in deconstructing racialized ideas of veganism.

Decolonizing the Body

Sistah Vegan was the first book to centralize the Black female vegan experience in the US ("Defined Plate" 50). In his essay in this volume, Martin Rowe, lead editor at Lantern Books, notes that *Sistah Vegan*'s diverse expression and multi-dimensional narrative reinforced Lantern's operating notion that when we talk *about* veganism, we're really talking *through* veganism: that is, veganism is a lens by which we can discern more keenly the realities of our and others' lives; and, conversely, that its insights are themselves refracted through ours and others' experiences." (353)

Sistah Vegan tells how and why the Black female vegan authors made their dietary and lifestyle choices. They also report on the hurdles faced on their way, often linked to hegemonic whiteness and hegemonic masculinity in "Western" civilization. The contributors confront the belief that veganism is a "white thing" and illustrate their arguments with personal stories (*Sistah Vegan* 26; "Social Justice" 116, 120). Author Tara Sophia Bahna-James encapsulates the ambition of the volume as a whole when she states that "I owe it to others like me to stand up and declare that I exist" (386).

Sistah Vegan aims to decolonize the Black female self. This process begins with realizing the hegemonic whiteness embedded in US society's view of the body: Native Americans, Asian Americans, Mexican Americans, and African Americans are more lactose intolerant than white Americans. According to a 2005 Cornell study, it is primarily people whose ancestors came from places where dairy herds could be raised safely and economically, such as in Europe, who have developed the ability to digest milk. On the other hand, people whose ancestors lived in climates that could not support dairy herding, such as large parts of Africa and Asia, cannot digest milk after infancy (Lang). Harper recalls how at Dartmouth College, her white, environmentalist fellow students told her to be "environmentally conscious" and to eat "healthy" – but in a way that was healthy only for white people:

> I remembered that cow's milk has been constructed in America as "healthy for everyone"—despite that myself as well as most Native Americans, Asians, and African-Americans are more lactose intolerant than white people. I thought these kids at Dartmouth were preaching yet another ethnocentric message about health and food that assumed everyone was from a Euro-Anglocentric ancestry, could digest the same things as them, and had monetary stability to make it happen. ("Social Justice" 116)

Physician Milton Mills called the phenomenon that Harper describes "dietary racism." Dietary racism stands for institutionalized racism implicit, for instance, in USDA dietary guidelines that recommend daily dairy consumption, although most Black Americans are lactose intolerant (Muwakkil). Mills co-authored a two-part article, published in 1999 in the *Journal of the National Medical Association*, an organization of 20,000 Black American physicians, and urged the federal government to develop guidelines "for all Americans" (Berton, Barnard, and Mills 206). Dietary racism can be observed in the distribution of agricultural subsidies, too: the US government subsidizes fruits and vegetables at significantly lower levels than meat and dairy. Fruits and vegetables are neither on the menu at the fast-food outlets nor on the shelves of the convenience stores that may be the only sources of nutrition in low-income communities of color (Treuhaft and Karpyn 7–8). Dietary racism is also a tool of the American far right whose claims about milk, lactose tolerance, race, and masculinity can be connected to similar arguments during the nineteenth century, when European colonizers labelled colonized populations of color as "effeminate corn and rice eaters" because of their real or alleged lack of consumption of meat and dairy (Gambert and Linné; Stănescu).

Food justice is a reoccurring topic in *Sistah Vegan*. Robin Lee's chapter describes a cycling event sponsored by a local hospital in the Bronx. First, Lee chronicles her experience with sizeism when another participant implied that she could not compete because of her size. She then observes that the hospital was giving away junk food, the very snacks which contribute to the illnesses that the hospital treats. Rampant diabetes in the Bronx community makes this action especially problematic. Lee addressed the volunteers at the tables: "How dare they hand out these items, which clearly are counterproductive to the very information they are trying to convey" (185). This story points to the weaknesses of neoliberalism: companies keep people sick for profit. But prior to that, they judge the Black woman for not conforming to "Western" beauty norms, although she was able to do the bike-a-thon. "Western" sizeism and ableism are issues for Harper too: "If you look at what is considered a moral, healthy body, at least in the past 40 or 50 years, it's a thin, able-bodied, white, middle-class person," claims Harper, "and for a long time, the fat black woman was used as the epitome of the unhealthy, immoral body. What does it mean to pathologize particular body types?" ("Defined Plate" 51).

"I naively thought that as long as I exercised four times a week I could load up on as many sweets as I wanted," Harper remembers ("Social Justice" 86–88). However, at the age of twenty-seven, Harper was diagnosed with a uterine tumor. After the diagnosis, she began researching how the tumor could have developed. She found help in the work of holistic health practitioners, such as Queen Afua, who pointed to "hormones and antibiotics in meat and dairy, refined sugar and wheat flour, nonorganic produce consumption, and environmental pollution" as the potential source of Harper's reproductive ailments ("Social Justice" 109). Harper came to believe that US mainstream food practices "manifested as disease" in her womb, which led her to veganism. Instead of getting into a medical-scientific analysis, Harper expresses her felt experience. A memoir is an apt genre for self-narration, since it does not simply list facts or data, but privileges personal experiences. Although the genre of memoir comes with risks of being (further) invalidated as less serious, ecofeminists such as Carol J. Adams have identified the need to regard emotional responses to suffering as appropriate sources of knowledge. Arguably, Harper is also doing this feminist work of re-investing in the power of the personal.

Decolonizing the Mind

Sistah Vegan is more than a guide on avoiding certain diseases by becoming vegan. Harper even asserts that "*Sistah Vegan* is not about veganism," but "about using veganism as a platform to explore the intersections of structural racism, sexism, classism, and capitalism" ("Defined Plate" 49). Besides the body, the mind too must be decolonized. Harper brings up Queen Afua who suggested that African American women's bodies did not only suffer from "the toxicity of the standard American diet, but also from four hundred years of trauma induced by slavery" (Harper, "Social Justice" 109–10).

Indeed, several contributors to *Sistah Vegan* understand veganism as a tool of Black liberation. Harper writes that Americans, particularly Black Americans, cannot obtain social justice without challenging post-industrial dietary practices and food beliefs ("Social Justice" 84). This idea is also expressed in the chapter "The Fulfilment of the Movement," where Adama Maweja draws a connection between the Civil Rights movement and veganism. She describes how in college she realized that Black Americans are "sick, diseased, imprisoned, dysfunctional, obese, and dying" at disproportionate rates. When she confronted her instructors with this information, they claimed ignorance as the cause and admitted having no solutions (316). Maweja began to see in veganism the Black community's liberation and the fulfilment of the Civil Rights movement.

Maweja and others argue that this recognition means rejecting food that originated in the enslavement of Black Americans – such as soul food culture – and resisting the temptation to enjoy US consumer society, as one's enslaved ancestors could not. Soul food, Harper states, is part of the "cycle of addiction," even if it is widely regarded as an essential part of Black American culture. Quoting author Derrick Jensen, Harper writes that "to be addicted is to be a slave. To be a slave is to be addicted." She warns that "those who were originally enslaved to harvest sugar cane (Africans and indigenous Americans) are now enslaved in multiple ways: as consumers of sucrose, hormone-injected processed meat and dairy products, and junk food" ("Social Justice" 100–01). Therefore, environmentally sustainable nutritional practices must be part of an antiracist and antipoverty praxis. To confront fast food and soul food culture, Harper refers to Black and Indigenous collective memories and encourages people of color to follow their ancestors' dietary practices from pre-colonial times:

> There are thriving communities of color throughout America that . . . have adapted their ethnic identity to more plant-based diets from their people's indigenous philosophy before colonization, while simultaneously practicing eco-sustainability, decolonization, and respect for nonhuman animals. These communities wholeheartedly know that "the master's tools will not dismantle the master's house," nor will his concept of food production or abuse of natural resources and nonhuman animals. (100–01)

Food can be a weapon to control groups of people and used for greed, profit, and power. But food can also be a source of healing, cultural identity, and life. What one consumes has profound effects not only on one's own health but on that of the whole world. Black Americans engaging in mass consumption do not only harm their own health, Harper argues, but are also supporting companies that frequently exploit workers and disrespect human rights in the US and beyond. Consumers of products which are not fair-trade and certified organic risk financing the "cultural genocide of those whose land and people we have enslaved and/or exploited for meat as well as sucrose, coffee, black tea, and chocolate" (99–100). Harper warns that "racially and socioeconomically oppressed minorities in America, who continue to experience institutionalized and overt classism and racism, are collectively complicit – and usually unknowingly – in being oppressors to" people of color and lower-class people in low- and lower-middle-income countries (102–04). Decolonizing the Black mind affects not only the lives of Americans of color but also communities of color around the world. The memoir form matters for making this argument: in this context, the act of writing itself can be a means of decolonizing the mind. I argue that Black female vegans writing *as* Black female vegans challenges hegemonic whiteness and masculinity. The genre of memoir can have further benefits in the realm of political transformation. Intertwining personal and collective politics lends the memoir a certain accessibility to readers on political and philosophical issues that is often missing in political and philosophical writing. For this reason, postcolonial authors – for instance, Ngũgĩ wa Thiong'o – often make use of autobiographical impulses.

Decolonizing Vegan Spaces

The process of decolonization of Black female bodies and minds leads to decolonizing vegan spaces since many Black vegan struggles occur within hegemonic white vegan spaces. In the chapter "Being a Sistah at PETA," Ain Drew addresses a blind spot within the white-dominated mainstream vegan community. She describes her excitement to start a job at PETA, with the hope of doing outreach to the Black community. However, she tells of how she became more skeptical when she felt that the leadership was not interested in reaching people where they were. Drew's impression was that "PETA wasn't as concerned with helping Black folks overcome our health issues as they were about getting us to stop wearing mink coats or promoting dog-fighting" (178). Drew is not alone with her critique: PETA has been accused of being insensitive to racism, for instance, when they recommended the football team Washington Redskins to change their mascot but not their name, although the name is offensive to Native Americans, or when PETA activists demonstrated in KKK robes against breeders' efforts to create a dog "master race" (Pellow 261; Wrenn 197). Considering such PETA actions, David N. Pellow has stated that PETA failed to build alliances with people of color and other marginalized communities (261). I would characterize PETA's behavior as "color-blind." In societies heavily influenced by racism, such as North America and Europe, race defines one's position in the social hierarchy. Ignoring this context is a form of color-blind behavior (Delgado and Stefancic 7, 144). PETA might wish to raise awareness of speciesism in the various ethnic and racial groups, but by not acknowledging race and the role it plays in contemporary human societies, they show a color-blind behavior. In contrast to PETA, Drew suggests a vegan strategy that is not color-blind. Drew argues that even though it is valid to criticize mink coats and dog-fighting, many vegans miss the bigger picture when talking about these things instead of focusing on change that can improve the lives of marginalized communities *and* also reduce the suffering of animals.

Drew is not the only author in the anthology to maintain that veganism should not "merely" be about animal rights. To some contributors, animal rights are a crucial part of the fight against systemic oppression, while for others, animal rights are less relevant. This position might seem unusual for a vegan volume, but this diversity of personal experiences is one of the strengths of Harper's work and point to the significance of memoir in destabilizing monolithic ideas of what vegan identity is or does, therefore enacting the work of extending and multiplying our definitions or understandings of veganism.

In the chapter "Journey toward Compassionate Choice," Tara Sophia Bahna-James too emphasizes the importance of multivalence – and of reaching people where they are. She draws stories from her life and emphasizes that becoming vegan was a gradual process for her. Vegan groups and individuals should not assume that one size fits all.

The traditional white middle-class approach does not speak to all people in all situations. She recommends refraining from judgment of the people vegans are trying to reach, as not everyone is able to see things as vegans see them, or to make the changes that vegans have already made (387). Bahna-James writes:

> I think it's so important that Black women be included in the vegan dialogue, not only because we are so frequently left out of it, and not only because falling victim to blind consumerism can be considered another form of allowing ourselves to remain oppressed and suppressed, but also because the vegan cause will not be wholly effective until it addresses the diverse spectrum of circumstances and psychologies that contribute to the practices it is trying to overcome. (415)

Decolonizing vegan spaces is an ongoing process. Following the publication of her anthology, Harper has seen "a tremendous rise in food-justice organizations, critical food studies scholarship, and social media – blogs, Facebook groups – that directly question how white-supremacist systems create inequality and oppression – from food access to food ethics to the food commodity chain" ("Defined Plate" 52). Building on the book's favorable reception, Harper created *The Sistah Vegan Project* website, an online memoir where she writes about her "journey through the 'post-racial' ethical foodscape . . . and beyond." Her blog collects stories about her life as a vegan Black woman in the United States. Harper continues to engage with issues such as healthcare, motherhood, education, systemic racism, and privilege, to name a few. She has developed online classes, seminars, conferences, and other materials to support the community. In 2015, she organized the conference "Vegan Praxis of Black Lives Matter." A year later, she ran as the Humane Party – "a vegan political party dedicated to the rights of both human and nonhuman animals" – Vice Presidential nominee for the 2016 US presidential election (Bowie).

Black, Female, and Vegan

Being Black, female, and vegan can be a marginalizing experience in "Western" societies laden with white hegemonic masculinity and the cultural hegemony of meat. But being Black, female, and vegan can also open doors and strengthen one's commitment to live in line with one's values. A. Breeze Harper's *Sistah Vegan* provides living examples of just how they do this. *Sistah Vegan* addresses dietary racism, which results in a disproportionate number of Black people and people of color having diabetes, hypertension, high blood pressure, and obesity. *Sistah Vegan* introduces possibilities for longer, stronger, and healthier lives by kicking junk-food habits. The project encourages Black women to "[f]ight ignorance, fight deception, fight self-loathing, fight fear of the other, be a witness to the truth as you have experienced it – reject the inevitability of that unspoken social contract – and in doing such, empower people to make compassionate choices for themselves" (Bahna-James 405). Harper's goal is not for everyone to become vegan. Rather, it is to understand veganism as a way to challenge institutionalized racism, ecological devastation, health disparities, and other forms of distributive injustice in US society. *Sistah Vegan* emboldens readers to reflect on hegemonic whiteness and racism in food. The memoir form here is a means of revelation to readers – but also a powerful mode of reclamation of identity for the writers themselves.

Notes

1. For more on PETA's controversial campaign tactics concerning questions of race, see Ruth Ramsden Karelse's essay in this volume.
2. By putting the term "Western" in inverted commas throughout the essay, I wish to express my discomfort with this term. Edward W. Said showed how the idea of a "Western civilization" created a binary between "the West" ("the Occident") and "the East" ("the Orient") and justified colonialism and imperialism by depicting "the West" as superior to "the East."
3. On the contrary, such comparisons can foster positive attitudes towards both animalistic and human outgroups: Kimberly Costello and Gordon Hodson suggest that by highlighting animal-to-human similarities, one can make the animalistic outgroup worthy of moral concern. Focusing on these shared qualities has positive implications for the concern towards marginalized human groups as well (Bastian et al.).

Works Cited

Adams, Carol J. "Caring about Suffering: A Feminist Exploration." *The Feminist Care Tradition in Animal Ethics*, edited by Josephine Donovan and Carol J. Adams, Columbia UP, 2007, pp. 198–226.

Bahna-James, Tara Sophia. "Journey toward Compassionate Choice: Integrating Vegan and Sistah Experience." *Sistah Vegan: Food, Identity, Health, and Society*, edited by Breeze A. Harper, Lantern Books, 2010, pp. 384–417.

Balleck, Barry J. *Modern American Extremism and Domestic Terrorism: An Encyclopedia of Extremists and Extremist Groups*. ABC-CLIO, 2018.

Ballew, Matthew, Edward Maibach, John Kotcher, Parrish Bergquist, Seth Rosenthal, Jennifer Marlon, and Anthony Leiserowitz. *Which Racial/Ethnic Groups Care Most about Climate Change?* Yale Program on Climate Change Communication, 2020.

Bastian, Brock, Kimberly Costello, Steve Loughnan, and Gordon Hodson. "When Closing the Human-Animal Divide Expands Moral Concern: The Importance of Framing." *Social Psychological and Personality Science*, vol. 3, no. 4, 2012, pp. 421–29.

Berton, Patricia, Neal D. Barnard, and Milton Mills. "Racial Bias in Federal Nutrition Policy, Part II: Weak Guidelines Take a Disproportionate Toll." *Journal of the National Medical Association*, vol. 91, no. 4, 1999, pp. 201–08.

Bowie, Richard. "Vegan Political Party Names Dr. Breeze Harper as VP pick." *VegNews*, 10 June 2016. <https://vegnews.com/2016/6/vegan-political-party-names-dr-breeze-harper-as-vp-pick>

Costello, Kimberly, and Gordon Hodson. "Exploring the Roots of Dehumanization: The Role of Animal Human Similarity in Promoting Immigrant Humanization." *Group Processes & Intergroup Relations*, vol. 13, no. 1, 2010, pp. 3–22.

Couser, G. Thomas. *Signifying Bodies: Disability in Contemporary Life Writing*. U of Michigan P, 2009.

Davis, Janet M. "The History of Animal Activism: Intersectional Advocacy and the American Humane Movement." *The Routledge Handbook of Animal Ethics*, edited by Bob Fischer, Routledge, 2020, pp. 479–91.

Delgado, Richard, and Jean Stefancic. *Critical Race Theory: An Introduction*. New York UP, 2001.

Drew, Ain. "Being a Sistah at PETA." *Sistah Vegan*, by Harper, 2010, pp. 172–80.

Gambert, Iselin, and Tobias Linné. "From Rice Eaters to Soy Boys: Race, Gender, and Tropes of 'Plant Food Masculinity.'" *Animal Studies Journal*, vol. 7, no. 2, 2018, pp. 129–79.

Greenebaum, Jessica. "Vegans of Color: Managing Visible and Invisible Stigmas." *Food, Culture & Society*, vol. 21, no. 5, 2018, pp. 1–18.

Harper, A. Breeze. "Defined Plate: Sistah Vegan Project's Breeze Harper Dishes On Mindful Eating." Interview by Vera Chang, *Bitch: Feminist Response to Pop Culture*, Winter 2014, pp. 49–52.

—. "Doing Veganism Differently: Racialized Trauma and the Personal Journey towards Vegan Healing." *Doing Nutrition Differently: Critical Approaches to Diet and Dietary*, edited by Allison Hayes-Conroy and Jessica Hayes-Conroy, Routledge, 2016, pp. 133–50.

—, (ed.). *Sistah Vegan: Food, Identity, Health, and Society*. Lantern Books, 2010.

—. "Social Justice Beliefs and Addiction to Uncompassionate Consumption." In *Sistah Vegan*, by Harper, 2010, pp. 81–128.

Haslam, Nick, Steve Loughnan, and Pamela Sun. "Beastly: What Makes Animal Metaphors Offensive?." *Journal of Language and Social Psychology*, vol. 30, no. 3, 2011, pp. 311–25.

Hrynowski, Zach. *What Percentage of Americans Are Vegetarian?* Gallup Poll Social Series. Gallup, 2019.

Jahoda, Gustav. *Images of Savages: Ancient Roots of Modern Prejudice in Western Culture*. Routledge, 1999.

Lang, Susan S. "Lactose Intolerance Seems Linked to Ancestral Struggles with Harsh Climate and Cattle Diseases, Cornell Study Finds." *Cornell Chronicle*, 1 June 2005. <https://news.cornell.edu/stories/2005/06/lactose-intolerance-linked-ancestral-struggles-climate-diseases>

Lee, Robin. "Hospital-Sponsored Junk Food at 'Healthy' Bike-Riding Event?" *Sistah Vegan*, by Harper, 2010, pp. 181–87.

Leiserowitz, Anthony, and Karen Akerlof. *Race, Ethnicity and Public Responses to Climate Change*. Yale Project on Climate Change, 2010.

Livingstone Smith, David. *Less Than Human: Why We Demean, Enslave, and Exterminate Others*. St Martin's Press, 2011.

Maweja, Adama. "The Fulfillment of the Movement." *Sistah Vegan*, by Harper, 2010, pp. 309–47.

Mohai, Paul. "Dispelling Old Myths: African American Concern for the Environment." *Environment: Science and Policy for Sustainable Development*, vol. 45, no. 5, 2003, pp. 10–26.

Muwakkil, Salim. "Many Who 'Got Milk' Get Sick." *Chicago Tribune*, 26 June 2000. <https://www.chicagotribune.com/news/ct-xpm-2000-06-26-0006260022-story.html>

Ngũgĩ wa Thiong'o. *Decolonising the Mind: The Politics of Language in African Literature*. James Currey, 1986.

Pearson, Adam R., Jonathon P. Schuldt, Rainer Romero-Canyas, Matthew T. Ballew, and Dylan Larson-Konar. "Diverse Segments of the US Public Underestimate the Environmental Concerns of Minority and Low-Income Americans." *Proceedings of the National Academy of Sciences of the United States of America*, vol. 115, no. 49, 2018, pp. 12429–34.

Pellow, David N. "Teaching Anti-Racism through Environmental Justice Studies." *Teaching Race and Anti-Racism in Contemporary America: Adding Context to Colorblindness*, edited by Kristin Haltinner, Springer, 2014, pp. 257–64.

Said, Edward W. *Orientalism*. Vintage Books, 1979.

Stănescu, Vasile. "'White Power Milk': Milk, Dietary Racism, and the 'Alt-Right'". *Animal Studies Journal*, vol. 7, no. 2, 2018, pp. 103–28.

Treuhaft, Sarah, and Allison Karpyn. *The Grocery Gap: Who Has Access to Healthy Food and Why It Matters*. PolicyLink, 2010.

Wallach, Jennifer Jensen. *Getting What We Need Ourselves: How Food Has Shaped African American Life*. Rowman & Littlefield, 2019.

Wrenn, Corey Lee. *Piecemeal Protest: Animal Rights in the Age of Nonprofits*. U of Michigan P, 2019.

18

Young Adult Fiction

Ali Ryland

Introduction

Adolescents occupy a liminal space in Western societies; their quest for identity, their pushing of boundaries, and their struggle to become "masters of their domain" (Halberstam 47) can lead to creative breaks with cultural traditions imposed on them by an aging populace. Similarly, veganism also departs from institutionalized customs; from novel food practices to questioning long-held conceptions of species difference, new ways of thinking are embedded in veganism's philosophy. Moreover, it is younger generations who are driving veganism's increasing popularity in the West.[1] It is timely, then, that young adult (YA) fiction – defined as "genre books that . . . [are] written about and for adolescents" (Garcia 5) – is brought to the attention of vegan literary studies, with both YA and vegan literature reflecting, and queered by, these sentiments of revolt.

Emelia Quinn and Benjamin Westwood, noting the propensity for queer readings of vegan literature, have argued that veganism acts as a challenge to "normative gendered and sexual identities" by expanding "the scope of queer ideas of alternative affiliation to include relations with nonhuman animals"; indeed, veganism could be defined as "an inherently queer mode of being in, and relating to, the world" (3). Similarly, James Stanescu has argued that vegan literary studies must be "queer . . . to break down the dualism between human and animal" as queer theory forces us to "accept the irreducible difference of the other" (33, 27).

Equally, YA fiction has recently benefited from centering queer youths – creating the new sub-genre "Queer YA" (Mason 4, 16) – and from modern analyses that argue that queer theoretical concepts are well-established in the genre. For example, in *Queer Anxieties of Young Adult Literature and Culture*, Derritt Mason follows Kathryn Bond Stockton's argument that "the child from the standpoint of 'normal' adults is always queer" as the child "can only be 'not-yet-straight,' since it, too, is not allowed to be sexual" (Stockton 7). Indeed, Stockton continues, "children grow sideways as well as up . . . because they cannot, according to our concepts, advance to adulthood until we say it's time" (6).

It is this conception of "growing sideways" that Mason adapts to demonstrate how Queer YA is consumed by an anxiety that is a result of attempts to mold the "queer child" into a young person expected to adhere to the disciplinary heteronormative structures of adulthood (Mason xvi, 15). And while Mason argues that Queer YA has its "roots in the anxious emergence of adolescence" (16) – what he calls a "sideways queerness" (6) – arguably all YA fiction continually comes into tension with fixed societal conceptions of "growing up" into the heterosexual order. Similarly, maturity is associated with removing one's emotional affinity with animals; while children are seen to treat animals as "partners in their environment" (Huggan and Tiffin 194), both their "queer temporalities" and "blatant animalities" (Stockton 123) are expected to be expunged with the ushering in of adult heterosexual society. As such, this pro-animal queerness inherent to veganism and adolescence can allow for the radical challenging of traditional norms in YA and vegan literature.

However, due to YA literature's liminal position between children's and adult fiction, it can also reproduce the world of the latter – a world with predetermined notions of gender, sexuality, and humanity. This essay offers a close reading of Blair Richmond's *Lithia* Trilogy (2011–2014) to demonstrate that the generic mainstays of YA, particularly when it comes to the popularity of vampire novels, are aligned with conservative politics that see even ostensibly vegan novels reinforce heteronormative carnism. I conclude with a consideration of Peter Dickinson's *Eva* (1988) to argue that the YA form nonetheless has the potential to promote radical queer possibilities by playing on its ability to reject the rationalism of "grown-up" adult fiction.

Sap-Suckers and Soy-Boys

Blair Richmond's *Lithia* Trilogy (2011–2014), composed of *Out of Breath* (2011), *The Ghost Runner* (2012), and *The Last Mile* (2014), is printed by Ashland Creek, a vegan press.[2] Its themes of displacement and rebellion are characteristic of YA literature; nineteen-year-old vegan Kat escapes her violent past by hitchhiking to the fictional town of Lithia in the Pacific Northwest of the United States and falls in love with Roman, an attractive actor. When he is revealed to be a vampire, Kat leaves him for a vegan environmentalist named Alex, a vampire who survives on tree sap, not blood. The phenomenon of "vegetarian vampires" – vampires who eschew human blood – has become a prominent feature of Western popular culture over the past few decades, as noted by scholars such as Stanescu and Laura Wright. *Lithia* can be read as a response to Stephenie Meyer's *Twilight* (2005); the plot of the latter likewise involves a virginal young woman (Bella) falling in love with a male vampire (Edward Cullen). But while *Twilight*'s Cullen family "consider themselves akin to vegetarians" because they consume animal blood (Stanescu 28), Richmond's "good" vampires have a plant-based diet.

Lithia continually exposes the ethical inconsistency of *Twilight*'s "vegetarian vampires," particularly when portraying Alex's transition to veganism; his first attempts to swap human for deer blood are reminiscent of the film adaptation of *Twilight* (2008) which begins with a deer fleeing, only to be caught by Edward (Wright 56). But Alex, unlike Edward, feels intense "guilt," choosing to starve himself (before finding sap) rather than continue preying on animals (Richmond, *Breath* 160). As Kat notes, vampires who consider their human victims as "just food" are akin to "people" who "don't see cows and chickens and pigs as living, breathing creatures but only as food" (Richmond, *Ghost* 111). However, there are similarities between Alex and Edward; they are both "fundamentally brooding creatures, racked by guilt and shame" (Stanescu 30), even if the latter's remorse is only for his human victims. As Stanescu elaborates, "in this way vegetarianism enters into an economy of the sacred and the profane, the innocent and the guilty, and the pure and the polluted," and "vampires who are shown to be able to overcome The Hunger are seen as being somehow more human and less animal" (29–30).

This "desire to distance the human – read in terms of rationality, control, individualism, an escape from the body – from the animal" (Stanescu 33) is part of what ecofeminists have documented as both a "flight from the feminine" (Bordo 441) and from the animal, due to the historical associations of women and animals as irrational beings. While *Lithia* reproduces the binaries of human/animal, rational/irrational that vegan theorists often attempt to challenge, it does acknowledge the gendered complications of veganism. When Roman suggests that Kat "take a break" and "try the steak" (Richmond, *Breath* 71) on their first date, the ensuing conversation represents the reality of male hostility to women's vegan diets. For example, after the term "vegansexuality" ("veg*n women" who "might reject sex with meat eaters") drew international media attention online, Annie Potts and Jovian Parry compiled "the forceful – and sometimes violent – responses 'vegansexuality' evoked from those positioned as heterosexual omnivorous men in particular" (59, 54). Tellingly, the reason behind Roman's insistence that Kat eat meat is similarly violent when Alex reveals that "to a vampire, the blood of a human vegan is no different than that of a deer. The blood will keep you alive, sure, but it won't taste the same, and it won't offer the same energy" (Richmond, *Breath* 207).

While Kat's predicament parallels the dark undercurrent of a society that commits violence against women, Alex's comment reifies notions of hyper-masculinity by suggesting that only omnivorous humans give vampires "energy." The traditional classification of meat as both "masculine" and "virile" is rooted in the mythology that one gains strength through eating muscle, hence why meat-eating has traditionally symbolized masculinity (Adams 4, 11). But the corollary to this myth is that vegans are figured as unhealthy, an argument that Roman uses against Kat: "runners need protein." Kat counters this assertion by stating that "I get it from tempeh, tofu, nuts . . . all sorts of foods" (Richmond, *Breath* 72). However, the suggestion that vegan blood is unsatisfying intimates that vegans receive little vitality from their diet, reinforcing stereotypes that assign feminine-coded weakness to the vegan body.

There are other signs that the series follows more in Meyer's conservative footsteps than in radical representations of vampirism. The primary narrative arc, for instance, centers around a romantic choice between two male characters: the bland vegan, Alex, or Roman, the carnivorous "gorgeous man, with dark hair and a slender build, and tall" that she cannot take her "eyes off" (Richmond, *Breath* 36). While Kat is immediately attracted to Roman, her interest in Alex is, at first, platonic only; though she later describes Alex as "cute" (43), he cannot compete with Roman's "darkly handsome presence" (*Ghost* 5). As she elaborates:

> Roman is exciting and romantic, but as much as I like being with him, something about it feels dangerous. Alex is sweet and a good friend, but as much as I think he's not the one I want to be with, something about him makes me feel safe. (*Breath* 158)

Here, Roman is the thrilling choice precisely because he is the erotic embodiment of male threat. He, unlike Alex, wants to "devour" her (201). Penetrative consumption (blood-sucking) may be anti-vegan violence against women, but it is simultaneously stimulating.

Alex is constantly emasculated at the hands of Roman, who derisively calls him a "sapsucker" (157), linking him to the yellow-bellied woodpecker with the same name – a cowardly (hence the yellow belly) and weak animal. "Sapsucker" also calls to mind the modern term of offense, "soy-boy," a slur used to emasculate men through the idea that soy contains phytoestrogens which are (erroneously) thought to feminize men, while linking men to the so-called effeminate practice of dietary veganism (Gambert and Linné 132). But Alex is instantly eroticized once he is shown to be a sexual threat; he bares his "stalactite-like" fangs (Richmond, *Breath* 196) and hauls Kat against her will to the top of a tree in Lithia's redwoods *before* explaining that he only uses them to pierce plant-life. Despite Kat's initial horror, this confrontation leads to them sharing their first kiss. Kat's abduction by a dangerous (if reformed) predator is both exhilarating and romantic, aligning carnivorism again with masculine vitality and sexual vigor, while implicitly tying veganism to feminized lethargy. While Alex still has feminine "sapsucker" traits, the exposure of his deadly physiology, combined with the capture of Kat, are the actions of a manly, rampaging vampire.

Lithia's refusal to queer or destabilize traditional conventions of sexuality and gender is made more explicit in the sequels. In *The Ghost Runner*, Kat leaves Alex and reunites with a newly vegan Roman, provoking the anger of his creator, arch-vampire Victor, who exacts his revenge on Kat and her friends. Yet when Kat tries to warn her friend Lucy about Victor, the latter assumes Kat wants to talk for a different reason: "It's Roman isn't it? . . . What is it, is he gay? A transvestite? I always thought there was something a little feminine about him" (*Ghost* 71). This comment is peculiar, as no earlier descriptions of Roman have suggested that he fits outside of gendered norms – although Sue-Ellen Case has argued that vampires are "always already" queer figures. "From the heterosexist perspective," she says, "queer sexual practice . . . impels one out of the generational production of what has been called 'life' and history, and ultimately out of the category of the living" (4). If "the organic is the natural" while "the queer has been historically constituted as the unnatural" and "queer desire, as unnatural, breaks with this life/death binary of Being through same-sex desire" (3), then vampires, in a particularly pernicious form of homophobic rhetoric, are queer in that they cannot give life; they take life from others.

Yet a reading of Roman as always having been queer cannot be the answer when *Lithia*'s vampires, like *Twilight*'s, have not before offered any alternative to the manufactured heteronormativity of teen girl desire. If Roman is only now being positioned as an effeminate homosexual, perhaps it is veganism that has queered him, just as domineering masculinity sexualized Alex.[3] While *Lithia*'s vegan vampires are emasculated when they transition, they challenge Case's analysis that vampires are queer by refusing to kill; Alex ensures he feeds on various trees and only "as little as necessary" (Richmond, *Breath* 205). Even vampiric sterility can be dealt with when Kat, newly affianced to Roman, argues that parenthood is not limited to one species:

> I think of Alex and his four dogs, and how he seems like a dad when he's with them, even though his "kids" have four legs instead of two—and I think I'll be happy starting with a few rescued dogs, or cats, or bunnies, and Roman and I can just see how it goes from there. (*Mile* 104)

Vegan vampires are day-walkers, integrating into heterosexist society through marriage and dog-children.

But while Roman aspires to adapt to these customs and make the "vampire myth" (103) of human-vampire marriage a reality, this fragile fantasy rests on Roman continually domesticating his "bloodthirsty" (*Ghost* 187) instincts. However, his conversion is both recent and fraught; before going vegan, Roman laments Kat "asking me to give up who I am" (*Breath* 212), only then doing so to prevent himself from "losing" her (*Mile* 85). While Alex is vegan through and through, Roman's fortitude rests entirely on Kat; hence why, when Roman falsely believes her to be dead from poison, he tumbles Victor – her supposed killer – into a volcano, returning the mountain that had previously threatened to overwhelm the town "to its slumber" (220). Unable to survive as a vegan vampire without Kat, Roman takes his life – before he can revert to his old ways.

Though Kat is initially distraught, the deaths of Roman and Victor allow for her to later hear "the sounds of nature at one with itself, again. The sounds of peace" (*Mile* 231). While "peace" also refers to the fact that in *The Ghost Runner*, a greedy developer's plans to ruin the landscape were halted by a forest fire, the tranquility that settles over the volcanic landscape is directly related to the fiery deaths of the unnatural carnivores. The conclusion of the trilogy then sees Kat and Alex reunite at Alex's animal sanctuary next to the now harmonious forest. However, this ending is disquieting because it recalls how nature can also be used as a "rationalization for injustice" against marginalized humans (Seymour 32). Lithia's environs are calmed because the aberrant (even queer) vampires who are unable to – or struggle the most with – conforming to society's norms, are dead. Those able to integrate reap heteronormativity's rewards: a relationship, a house, and dependents. In Lithia, what is "natural" is obeying the status quo – minus the meat-eating.

Lithia is written to be a teen fantasy corollary to *Twilight*, and this led to it reproducing the prejudices of a novel written by noted arch-conservative author Stephenie Meyer. For example, Wright notes how Meyer replicated "a narrative of abuse" towards women (52–53), which is mirrored in *Lithia*, with Kat's abduction by Alex, and his sexualized threatening of her before revealing he paid for her shoplifted sandwich – "'what's that in your pocket? And don't say you're just happy to see me'" (Richmond, *Breath* 16) – being just two examples. Consequently, while *Lithia* could be the first series to initiate a vegan YA literary canon, its mimicking of the most successful vampire series in that genre allows for narratives that reproduce matrices of oppression that are inconsistent with both veganism's philosophy and its freaky queernesses. The remainder of this essay argues that it is YA novels that are not specifically about veganism, such as Peter Dickinson's *Eva* (1988), that can open more queer vegan possibilities than those tied to the *Twilight* format. *Eva*'s prestigious standing (such as there is one) in the field of YA literature, and its troubling of the human–animal binary, demonstrates how YA fiction is ripe for queer vegan readings.[4]

Hybrid Worlds

Eva begins by depicting a future world where a dying thirteen-year-old girl named Eva has her mind mapped onto the brain of Kelly, one of the lab chimpanzees that she has grown up around – a costly procedure paid for by a broadcast company in return for interviews with her new hybrid self. Her parents try to raise Eva as if she has not fundamentally changed, aspiring to dress her in "human" clothes – which would conveniently cover any "sexual swellings" (Dickinson 47) she may have on her now chimp-rump – while hoping that she can still aspire to human heteronormative customs. As Eva surmises, her parents furtively want her to "choose a dishy male" at the chimp enclosure, while her dad "finds some boy with an IQ of a hundred and eighty who's just walked under a bus" to create a new chimp-human hybrid so that they can "have a lovely wedding and live happily ever after" (89–90). But Eva understands the logical inconsistencies in her parents' revulsion towards her animal self, telling her parents: "our babies would just be chimps . . . they'd be Kelly's, really" (90).

The implication that Eva's parents wish to postpone her mating with a chimp until they can manufacture another hybrid recalls Stockton's theory that delay is central to children's "supposed gradual growth, their suggested slow unfolding . . . figured as vertical movement upward (hence, 'growing up') toward full stature, marriage, work, reproduction, and the loss of childishness" (4). Instead, Eva's advancement into adulthood is not delayed, but shattered; her advancement as a chimp engaging with the species' polygynous culture is accelerated once the new hybrid experiments fail, and Eva chooses to mate with multiple chimps. The novel ends with an elderly Eva on her new chimp island (having managed to escape from both her parents and the television cameras, saving the chimp colony from extinction) considering that "few of the humans who'd visited over the years had really come to terms with the idea of Eva having children . . . Once when someone had asked about her newest baby who the father was Eva had laughed and said she didn't know" (Dickinson 240). Notions of fatherhood and monogamy do not exist in her queer chimp world.

Indeed, the only way for Eva to find happiness outside of these received human norms is to understand the fragile nature of human–animal alterity, and to embrace her new embodied reality: "the only way to become whole was to pull the wall down, to let the other side back in . . . a new pattern, not Eva, not Kelly – both but one" (41). Her success lies in being young enough to have not spurned her childhood kinship with animals and because, thanks to her early exposure to chimps, she can conceive of herself as being "a chimpanzee as well as a human" (150). Thus, *Eva* could be described as engaging in what Jack Halberstam has called a "creative anthropomorphism" that links "animals to new forms of being and offer us different ways of thinking about being, relation, reproduction, and ideology" (42). Instead of depicting "ordinary and banal forms of anthropomorphism" (51), Eva's chimp friends are "bright" (Dickinson 193) in their own way and have their own motivations; one male chimp carries Eva to safety during an escape attempt not due to, as the humans infer, glossy ideals of "comradeship" (233), but because she was "coming into oestrus" (223). Consequently, *Eva* can be read as a posthuman queer vegan tale because it refutes ossified notions of the human while challenging dominant heteronormative narratives; Eva is unique from the adults around her in that she still retains her childlike empathy with nonhumans, refusing to "grow up" into the anti-animal heterosexual order.

As the chimps win their fight to live and mate free of their enclosure and the overbearing media presence, this creative anthropomorphism additionally marshals queer and anti-capitalist strategies of resistance "against human exceptionalism" (Halberstam 51). Indeed, given YA fiction's tendency to be a site of revolt – both children and young adults "are in a constant state of rebellion against their parents" (47) – vegan literary studies would do well to further investigate this genre for instances of vegan narratives that upend the human–animal binary and figure animals as beings worthy of respect. As "maturity is associated with the control of emotion/affect, with masculinity, and with the objectifying gaze of 'science'" (Cole and Stewart 39–40), YA fiction that queerly refuses to embrace said maturity, and instead rejects all that is "serious and the rational" in adult fiction, allows for greater empathy and identification with nonhumans.

Conclusion

YA fiction can be a radical genre, breaking down the borders of species, sexuality, class, and more, and is well-placed to reject the convention that maturity requires severing emotional ties with animals. While vampire fiction is an over-explored medium, *Lithia* does expose the inconsistencies behind one of the most successful vampire series of all time, *Twilight*, if at the same time replicating the text's traditionalist intolerances. Thus, the limitations of YA literature are revealed when it relies on normative tropes rather than embracing, like *Eva*, a queer "creative anthropomorphism" (Halberstam 42) that can lead to a revolutionary upheaval of all imaginative fiction – not just YA. Only by welcoming the freaky queerness inherent in veganism can there be real refusal "to sanction the carnivorous human subject" (Quinn and Westwood 5) – a concept central to vegan literature.

Notes

1. The Vegan Society reported in their 2016 study that 41% of vegans were aged 15–34.
2. For more on Ashland Creek Press see Martin Rowe's chapter in this volume which includes a first-person account of the publishing experiences of John Yunker, Ashland Creek's co-founder.
3. This loss of masculinity through a refusal to suck blood is also paralleled in the TV show *Buffy the Vampire Slayer*. As Wright notes, "In the case of both Angel and Spike, drinking the blood of an animal and not a human is indicative of impotence: Angel, the 'most sexualized and eroticized of all the characters' . . . cannot have sex or he will become Angelus" (49).
4. *Eva* was "highly commended" for the annual Carnegie medal, the British literary award for children and young adult books.

Works Cited

Adams, Carol J. 1990. *The Sexual Politics of Meat: A Feminist-Vegetarian Critical Theory*. Twenty-fifth anniversary edition, Bloomsbury Academic, 2015.
Bordo, Susan. "The Cartesian Masculinization of Thought." *Signs: Journal of Women in Culture and Society*, vol. 11, no. 3, 1986, pp. 439–56.
Case, Sue-Ellen. "Tracking the Vampire." *Differences: A Journal of Feminist Cultural Studies*, vol. 3, no. 2, 1991, pp. 1–20.
Cole, Matthew, and Kate Stewart. *Our Children and Other Animals: The Cultural Construction of Human-Animal Relations in Childhood*. Taylor & Francis Group, 2014.
Dickinson, Peter. 1988. *Eva*. Macmillan, 2001.
Gambert, Iselin, and Tobias Linné. "From Rice Eaters to Soy Boys: Race, Gender, and Tropes of 'Plant Food Masculinity.'" *Animal Studies Journal*, vol. 7, no. 2, 2018, pp. 129–79.

Garcia, Antero. *Critical Foundations in Young Adult Literature: Challenging Genres.* Sense Publishers, 2013.

Halberstam, Jack. *The Queer Art of Failure.* Duke UP, 2011.

Hayn, Judith, Jeffrey Kaplan, and Amanda Nolan. "Young Adult Literature Research in the 21st Century." *Theory into Practice*, vol. 50, no. 3, 2011, pp. 176–81.

Huggan, Graham, and Helen Tiffin. *Postcolonial Ecocriticism: Literature, Animals, Environment.* Taylor and Francis, 2010.

Mason, Derritt. *Queer Anxieties of Young Adult Literature and Culture.* U of Mississippi P, 2021.

Potts, Annie, and Jovian Parry. "Vegan Sexuality: Challenging Heteronormative Masculinity through Meat-free Sex." *Feminism & Psychology*, vol. 20, no. 1, 2010, pp. 53–72.

Quinn, Emelia, and Benjamin Westwood. "Introduction: Thinking Through Veganism." *Thinking Veganism in Literature and Culture*, edited by Emelia Quinn and Benjamin Westwood, Palgrave Macmillan, 2018, pp. 1–24.

Richmond, Blair. *The Ghost Runner.* Ashland Creek Press, 2012.

—. *The Last Mile.* Ashland Creek Press, 2014.

—. *Out of Breath.* Ashland Creek Press, 2011.

Seymour, Nicole. *Strange Natures: Futurity, Empathy, and the Queer Ecological Imagination.* U of Illinois P, 2013.

Stanescu, James. "Toward a Dark Animal Studies: On Vegetarian Vampires, Beautiful Souls, and Becoming-Vegan." *Journal for Critical Animal Studies*, vol. 10, no. 3, 2012, pp. 26–50.

Stockton, Kathryn Bond. *The Queer Child, or Growing Sideways in the Twentieth Century.* Duke UP, 2009.

Vegan Society. "There are three and half times as many vegans as there were in 2006, making it the fastest growing lifestyle movement." *Vegansociety.com*, 16 May 2016.

Wright, Laura. *The Vegan Studies Project: Food, Animals, and Gender in the Age of Terror.* U of Georgia P, 2015.

19

SATIRE

The (Im)possibilities of Vegan Satire

Nicole Seymour

Introduction

IN 2011, CANADIAN ACTOR Elliot Page tweeted, "Why are vegans made fun of while the inhumane factory farming process regards animals and the natural world merely as commodities to be exploited for profit?" In its alignment of ridicule and exploitation, Page's question seems purely rhetorical. However, this essay begins, perhaps facetiously, by offering a series of answers to this question. The remainder of the essay then considers how vegans[1] from the Global North have responded, sometimes preemptively, to their status as the butt of cultural jokes by satirizing both non-vegan culture and themselves. I begin with popular paraliterary texts, including comics, cookbooks, and stand-up comedy. I then turn to Nobel Prize-winning author Olga Tokarczuk's novel *Drive Your Plow over the Bones of the Dead* (2009, translated into English in 2018), which both engages in satire, humor, and irony and offers philosophical reflections on those modes, including their pitfalls and possibilities, from a distinctly feminist perspective.

Throughout, I work with the *Oxford English Dictionary*'s (OED) definition of satire as a literary or artistic work "which uses humour, irony, exaggeration, or ridicule to expose and criticize prevailing immorality or foolishness, esp. as a form of social or political commentary." I should note, though, that any discussion of satire, humor, irony, or other rhetorical-political forms is subjective. For example, at times I will describe some things as "funny" or "unfunny," when they are so perhaps only to me. And, of course, those aforementioned forms are always contingent. The question posed by my queer theory professor Kathryn Schwarz in a seminar back in 2004 continues to reverberate: "Is it satire if no one gets it?"

Vegan Killjoys and Cranks

As perhaps exemplified by Page's Tweet, vegans often appear as awkward, humorless killjoys, ruining dinner parties the world over with their "sincerity and despair" (Quinn 919). Vegan activist Carol J. Adams explains that "vegetarians of decades past were seen as isolated individuals holding odd (nondominant) cultural positions ... There's a reason one of the early 1960s popular natural health food restaurants in London called themselves 'Cranks'" (90) – meaning, a kind of fussy or grumpy eccentric.

Statistically speaking, vegans *are* odd; a recent Gallup poll found that only three per cent of Americans identify as such (Reinhart). As memoirist Eric Lindstrom, author of *The Skeptical Vegan: My Journey from Notorious Meat Eater to Tofu-Munching Vegan—A Survival Guide* (2017) sums it up in a notable deadpan, "Vegans will complain. They don't mean to, but the world is against them" (xiv).

Another widespread perception of veganism that renders it subject to ridicule is its "dependen[ce] upon restriction and privation" (Wright 121). This perception obviously has some basis in reality, as vegans eschew animal-derived foods and products, from cheese and honey to leather and silk. Further, veganism has been historically associated with other forms of prohibition such as alcohol and tobacco temperance (Adams 92). Restriction and privation seem to oppose values such as playfulness, indulgence, and lack of restraint – which are the hallmarks of humor, based on Henri Bergson's classic idea that "rigidity is the comic, and laughter is its corrective" (18). In sum, vegans are perceived as themselves unfunny, while provoking laughter in others.

Like many who strictly adhere to a particular worldview or practice, vegans are often perceived as both smugly moralistic and lacking in self-awareness – and, thus, in need of comeuppance via mockery. Recall *The Simpsons*' humorous depiction of Lisa Simpson's "level-5 vegan" boyfriend – who scoffs at her mere vegetarianism and brags that he "won't eat anything that casts a shadow." Or consider how often vegans insist that they see what non-vegans do not – as with Lindstrom's focus on the latter's "cognitive dissonance" (145) or Adams's work on "the normally absent referent status of the cow within the hamburger" (69). "*You* don't know you're eating a cow," so the move seems to go, "but *I* know you're eating a cow." Or, perhaps: "You think you're eating a hamburger, but it turns out you're eating a cow!" In my book *Bad Environmentalism*, I draw on Bronislaw Szerskynski's argument that environmentalists typically employ "corrective" rather than "thoroughgoing" irony (350); their deployments are typically outwardly directed rather than self-directed, claiming the "moral high ground" (347). Thus, we could say that much vegan discourse trains its eye on everyone but itself.[2] Bergson proves invaluable yet again here: "a comic character is generally comic in proportion to his ignorance of himself . . . He becomes invisible to himself while remaining visible to all the world" (16–17). Thus, comedy might emerge *simply from the existence* of the vegan's (supposed) "self-invisibility."

Finally, veganism is sometimes associated with fundamentalist identitarianism – another kind of rigidity – and a concomitant lack of intersectionality. "Being vegan is a *lifestyle* and not a *diet*" (x), Lindstrom insists, continuing, "veganism is compatible [with] any range of religious and political beliefs . . . You can believe in Second Amendment [gun] Rights . . . while still supporting animal sanctuaries. You can be pro-life and be, well, pro-life" (119). The privileging of veganism as a dietary identity over any other religious or political affiliation makes veganism look like a narrow-minded, single-issue politic. (In Lindstrom's scenario, human reproductive rights take a back seat to animal rights.) Politically conscious observers *including* vegans might find that the aforementioned positions warrant some mocking.

While some of the aforementioned accounts come from vegan sources, they seek to capture non-vegans' impulse to ridicule. But some vegans have offered alternative explanations of their own. Richard Twine observes that "[v]eganism constitutes a direct challenge to the dominant affective community that celebrates the pleasure of consuming animals"; he notes, generously, that "[i]t is unsurprising that omnivores indulge in a defensive discourse" (628–29). A less generous version of this claim might be: veganism provokes various anxieties in non-vegans – over their possible immorality, the fragile masculinity that they may be attempting to prop up through meat-eating, or some other shortcoming – and the latter swat these anxieties away by cracking jokes. Ironically, though, such explanations may simply reinforce the mainstream perception of vegans' sense of superiority: calm, moral, secure. Indeed, animal philosopher Cora Diamond suggests that some non-vegans *simply do not experience* those anxieties in the first place – and that that might be the most alienating and disturbing thing of all, to a vegan (46). But in any case, it would be inaccurate to suggest that only meat-and-dairy eaters "celebrat[e] . . . pleasure" or, more specifically, engage in satire around veganism – as we will see below.

Satirizing the Other, Satirizing the Self

Satirization of non-vegan culture can be found just about anywhere, from stand-up comedy to cookbooks, enacting Emelia Quinn's idea that "humor and parody can diffuse the seeming triumph of an anthropocentric culture over the nonhuman animal" (915). Consider, for example, what I have elsewhere called the "[vegan] speculative comedy" (Seymour 225) of confessional stand-up artist Simon Amstell, who, in his special *Do Nothing* (2010), observes: "people talk about the past, history, like that was all ridiculous . . . I would like to be in the future . . . so I can look back at this time and say . . . *Do you remember when people got upset when their pets died, but then when other animals died, they ate them??*" Amstell playfully defamiliarizes what remains, as noted above, a vast statistical norm. We see a slightly different approach with a popular article from US satirical media outlet *The Onion*, "written" by fictional farmer Hank T. Norman and headlined, "We Raise All Our Beef Humanely On Open Pasture And Then We Hang Them Upside Down And Slash Their Throats." Here, the duplicity of animal farming is highlighted through a deadpan approach that suggests the self-invisibility of *non-vegans*.

Similarly grim-yet-hilarious moments of satire can also be found in Richard Watts's web-and-print comic series *Vegan Sidekick* (2013–), typically rendered with crude stick-figure images and typed dialogue that recalls the fonts of early word-processing programs. In one panel from *Vegan Sidekick vol. 3*, we see a poster on that wall that reads, "Real men eat corpses," a take-off of the supposed cultural truism "Real men eat meat" that mimics the latter's exaggerated bluntness. In another *Vegan Sidekick vol. 3* panel, one stick figure introduces another as, "this is my friend Chloe. The VEEEGAN." The comic thus subtly, and humorously, suggests that it is *non-vegans* who are obsessed with, and therefore stigmatize, other people's diets. As I discuss below, however, the series is also often notably *un*humorous.

Some vegan literary texts straddle the line between other- and self-satire, as with Lindstrom's mock-report that he became vegan with the help of Omnivores Anonymous (OA):

> We learned we were powerless over [meat, dairy, and eggs] . . . We came to believe that a power greater than ourselves could restore us to sanity. His name was Joaquin Phoenix, and his lifetime commitment to veganism was legendary . . . We cleared our closets of wool, silk, and leather, even though we loved our Limited

Edition Tommy Bahamas [*sic*] Pool Ball silk shirt, and . . . we cleared our arteries of gunk and goo and our guts of fat and poo. (57)

Lindstrom subtly critiques non-vegan behavior by playfully framing it as an addiction and a health threat. At the same time, his references to "goo" and "poo" rescue veganism from the realm of the sentimental and strait-laced. And for good measure, he seems to undercut himself with a detailed reference to questionable fashion sense ("Tommy Bahamas Pool Ball silk shirt"). At such moments, Lindstrom parallels Amstell, whose pro-vegan takes are accompanied by self-ridicule about his neuroticism and other failings. In one bit from *Do Nothing*, for example, Amstell recalls the moment that he caught his own reflection and realized he was too old to wear hoodies.

Lindstrom also engages more extensively in self-satire, such as when he riffs good-naturedly on the old joke, "Q: How do you know if someone's vegan? A: Don't worry, they'll tell you!", with an exaggerated account: "[J]ust by approaching a vegan and starting a conversation about anything, they will begin to shake . . . holding back with all their might . . . prepared to strike at any moment . . . poised . . . ready to let you know: They. Are. Vegan" (xii, ellipses in original).

Vegan food and cooking, in addition to vegan affect and behavior, provide targets for literary self-satire. Amanda Cohen and Grady Hendrix's *Dirt Candy: A Cookbook* (2012) – also a memoir of Cohen's struggles in the restaurant industry – states, "People have a lot of preconceived notions about vegetarian food and most of them aren't very flattering. This is not entirely unfair." This statement is accompanied by one of Ryan Dunlavey's comic illustrations: the cover of a fake cookbook that reads, "*The New Harvest Flavorless, Self-Righteous, Holier than Thou, Health-Obsessed, Over-Cooked Vegetable and Gloopy Brown Sauce Cookbook*" (93). Maybe we could also understand the New York vegetarian/vegan restaurant that calls itself not Superior Burger but *Superiority* Burger as similarly engaging in self-satire. (Or not.)

Sometimes the self-satire or humor of vegan literature is more subtle, as with the title of Annie Nichols's lifestyle guide/cookbook *How to Be Vegan and Keep Your Friends* (2019). A bit from vegan stand-up comedian Julio Torres makes the same point more explicitly: "I don't miss cheese, but I do miss getting asked to do things. I miss my friends, and I miss my family." These works acknowledge the challenges that veganism poses to interpersonal relationships, for better or worse.

Nichols's *How to Be Vegan* also admits that, even linguistically, veganism entails restraint: "[t]he Vegan Society in England established the term 'vegan' in 1944 by amalgamating the first and last letters of the word 'vegetarian' and deleting the bits in between (*how apt*)" (2, emphasis added). As we will see below, though, other vegan literary texts insist that veganism is, instead, a matter of indulgence. Sarah Conrique and Graham I. Haynes's *The Vegan Stoner Cookbook* (2013) is, like Nichols's book, gently humorous, featuring silly illustrations of the predominantly pre-packaged ingredients, such as a box of "Awful Falafel Mix" and "'Old Grapes' Raisins." In this way, *The Vegan Stoner* subtly violates any ideal of vegan purity imagined outside of consumerism or processed foods. Meanwhile, the very notion of a "vegan stoner" complicates the stereotype of an uptight pedant.

While their outwardly-directed satire offers trenchant cultural critiques, the self-satire and humor found in these texts has several potential benefits, or at least ideals. Those elements can challenge the aforementioned killjoy stereotype and also prove welcoming to neophyte audiences intimidated by the prospect of vegan transition, or at least vegan cooking. Second, and on a more philosophical level, these texts invoke Kenneth Burke's definition of "true irony": what James W. Fernandez and Mary Taylor Huber, drawing on James A. Boon, have explained as being "humble, not superior to the enemy, but based upon a fundamental kinship with the enemy" (cited in Seymour 57). In this scenario, veganism is free to flourish, relieved of the burden of agonistic struggle.

Try-Hards: Some Failures of Vegan Satire

Not all satirical, humorous, or playful attempts to (re)articulate veganism succeed, and here I will consider a few kinds of arguable failures. For one, Lane Gold's cookbook *Vegan Junk Food* (2018), rendered in bright red and yellow vintage Americana style, stresses the idea that, despite their killjoy reputation, "[w]ithin the safe bubble of the vegan community its practitioners are noticeably joyous, especially about food" (Twine 637). We can also see the book as attempting to position veganism *against* restraint and deprivation – and, therefore, implicitly and ideally, not subject to ridicule. But *Vegan Junk Food* goes so overboard with its claims about pleasure, indulgence, and "badness" that it sometimes reads as laughably defensive, like the dorky high schooler who brags about doing loads of drugs to impress the cool kids. For a "Lentil Walnut Pâté," Gold insists, "[t]his recipe . . . [is] about decadence. Splurge on . . . a plate of high-quality olives, and revel in the indulgence of it all!" (156). She also promises that "these moist muffins emit the most sinful banana-vanilla aroma while they're cooking" (25). Such diction – "sinful," "rich," "decadence," and "indulgence" – recurs constantly throughout the cookbook.

At other times, though, *Vegan Junk Food* wags a finger. For example, a S'mores cake recipe instructs, "[m]ake sure to seek out vegan marshmallow cream; traditional marshmallow contains gelatin – no good" (177). My point is not that vegan discourse must somehow be more consistent than non-vegan discourse – although it must be said that vegan cultural producers such as Watts frequently attack non-vegans on the basis of logical inconsistency, as we will see below. Rather, I mean to say that such moments remind us that the "sinfulness" or "badness" of *Vegan Junk Food* is largely performative, insofar as it ultimately observes very clear limits.

While *Vegan Junk Food* concentrates on food as a source of "bad(ass)ness," Michelle Davis and Matt Holloway have attempted to create a "bad(ass)" culinary persona under the moniker Thug Kitchen. Their *Thug Kitchen: The Official Cookbook* (2014) attempts to swerve around the perception of vegans as sanctimonious as well as wimpy by promising, "No lectures and no bullshit – just some plant-based recipes with a fuckton of swearing and a dash of health advice for good measure" (xii). But the strange thing is that, first, the cookbook absolutely comes off as lecturing, and, second, that it does so much more abrasively than any vegan lecture you might imagine. To wit: the book tells us early on that "The first rule of *Thug Kitchen* is: Read the recipe. Second rule of *Thug Kitchen*? READ THE GODDAMN RECIPE" (xiv). This cocksure swaggering veers into unintentional self-parody or camp in its over-the-top incessancy, as when a "Breakfast Greens" recipe a few pages later declares, "This goes great with Biscuits and Gravy (18) if you've got some fucking time" (7).

Further, Thug Kitchen's attempts at "badness" or "hardness" are appropriative and even racist, as with a section on snacks that inexplicably features a photograph of a low-income Mexican-American neighborhood. Davis and Holloway, who are both white, have long been critiqued for partaking in "digital blackface" (Jackson) – or brownface, as it were – considering that they launched their brand in 2012 with an anonymous blog and have relied on the perception that the figures behind it were low-income people of color. (The aforementioned cookbook does not include their names or images.) Black vegan chef Bryant Terry captures the humor*less*ness of Thug Kitchen's attempts at humor in sarcastically imagining a (white?) reader's response: "'*Those* kind of people,' the [Thug Kitchen] gag suggests, 'intimidating you into . . . preparing arugula or tempeh? How absurd, how shocking, how hilarious!'" (emphasis added).[3]

Other attempts at vegan satire fail, in my view, due to their rigid insistence on logic and that aforementioned lack of self-awareness. Consider one comic strip on the Vegan Sidekick Instagram account. In the first and third panels, a smiling human figure tells another, "I gave my dog an electric shock so hard that he was paralyzed LOL . . . [T]hen . . . I slit his throat." The other figure is aghast, scowling and asking, "OMG WHAT THE FUCK IS WRONG WITH YOU??" In the fourth and final panel, the first figure says, "Dog? I meant to say pig." The other responds, "Oh rite. Yeh, that's humane . . . lolbacon" (Watts, "Electric Shock"). To both love dogs and eat pigs is illogical, goes the claim. As Watts explains on the Vegan Sidekick Facebook page,

> Primarily I use logic to analyze the various arguments . . . defending exploitation of, or harm to, animals. Part of what I do also involves ridiculing these arguments . . . I am essentially calling everybody out and showing that veganism is the logical choice to make.

But many if not most humans are deeply *il*logical and *ir*rational, as evidenced by, well, the history of human civilization (see Goldhill).

I would also add here that while humor is not, generically speaking, a required outcome of satire, *Vegan Sidekick* frequently reinforces the negative stereotype of the humorless killjoy vegan. For example, one comic from *Vegan Sidekick vol. 3* addresses the aforementioned joke about knowing whether someone is vegan with the text, "HOW DO YOU KNOW IF SOMEONE IS VEGAN, DON'T WORRY THEY'LL FUCKING TELL YOU LOLOLOLOL." While the original joke is actually funny – don't take my word for it, but that of Lindstrom, a genuine vegan! – this response to it is mirthlessly mocking. Looking back at the "lolbacon" bit above, we see that (non-vegan) laughter seems to be more the *topic* than the *product* of the *Vegan Sidekick* repertoire. In fact, it would be worth briefly comparing this comic to Amstell's bit, considering that they seemingly bear the same premise: people who love dogs will gladly eat pigs. Couched within Amstell's self-aware neuroticism and awkward stage presence, the bit is indeed quite hilarious and thought-provoking. In *Vegan Sidekick*, we instead find a grim insistence on "superior[ity] to [an] enemy" that can boast its own superiority, or at least dominance; a seemingly endless cycle of ridiculing those who would ridicule you. Below, we will see how "self-visibility" and a deeply comic worldview offer relief from that cycle.

"Remaining Visible": *Drive Your Plow* and Self-Aware (Anti-?)Irony

Tokarczuk's *Drive Your Plow over the Bones of the Dead* has been described as "an astonishing amalgam of murder mystery [and] dark feminist comedy" (Perry). The Booker Prize-listed novel is narrated by an older woman, Janina Duszejko, who lives in a remote Polish village near the Czech border. Duszejko is vegetarian, finds animal products such as leather and fur repulsive, and often eats vegan in deference to her friend (Tokarczuk 68). The plot begins with the death of her detested neighbor, a poacher who chokes on a bone after having killed and eaten a deer. Several strange deaths of local men follow – a police commander, the owner of a fox-fur farm, a club president, a priest who blesses hunters – with Duszejko soon insisting, despite others' opinion that her claim is "absurd," that "it's Animals taking revenge on people" (209, 75).[4]

Droll and deadpan commentary from our narrator is sprinkled throughout, taking aim at gender and social norms in addition to cultures of animal use and abuse. Tokarczuk's novel thus implies, contra Lindstrom, that veganism cannot be so easily linked to dominant or anti-progressive standpoints. Duszejko makes cracks, for instance, about men's tendency to develop obsessions with World War II once they hit middle age (24) and the absurdity of romantic relationships: "How do people manage to spend decades living together in a small space? . . . I'm not saying it hasn't happened to me too. For some time I shared my bed with a Catholic, and nothing good came of it" (157). But what I am most interested in is how the novel focuses on Duszejko's status within her society, and perhaps among some readers, as an unbearably pitiful figure of pathos. Much like J. M. Coetzee's well-known literary character Elizabeth Costello, Duszejko is "haunted by the horror of what we do to animals. [She is] wounded by this knowledge . . . and by the knowledge of how unhaunted others are. The wound marks her and isolates her" (Diamond 46).[5] We hear, for example, about the morbid and maudlin private graveyard she maintains for dead animals she finds in the forest. And in one scene, she comes upon a boar that has been shot by hunters. "Sorrow, I felt great sorrow, an endless sense of mourning for every dead Animal. One period of grief is followed by another, so I am in constant mourning" (Tokarczuk 101), she reports to us.

While Duszejko's self-introspection is therefore evident, it is matched by her deep awareness of how she appears to others. Thus, she contrasts those referenced above who are "invisible to [the]msel[ves]." A persistent irritant, the consummate crank, Duszejko regularly writes letters of complaint about other citizens' behaviors and makes repeated visits to the police; when she first reports her neighbor's poaching to the police commander, she "could almost hear his thoughts – to his mind I was definitely a 'little old lady,' and once my accusatory speech was gathering strength, a 'silly old bag,' 'crazy old crone,' or 'madwoman'" (26). Elsewhere she acknowledges that she is "a little infantile" (113). And when she goes to report that the aforementioned boar has been unlawfully killed out of hunting season, she delivers a long graphic treatise on animal suffering and then considers the unmoved police guard standing in the room. "He was one of those ironists who don't like pathos, so they button their lip to avoid being infected by it. They fear pathos more than hell" (107), she surmises.

I find this particular passage quite stunning, not just because of its incisive wisdom – many people do indeed prefer irony to pathos, whether out of fear, embarrassment, beliefs about rhetorical efficacy, or some other reason – but also because I find myself directly interpellated by it. That is, I suspect that I myself am one of those ironists. Interestingly, though, Duszejko associates irony primarily with the patriarchy. When she shouts at the male police officers and other local men that she finds shooting pheasants, one of them relates, "with a note of irony in his voice," "'it's just the old lady from Luftzug. She wants to call the Police'" (63). Here, irony is on the side of the Man, literally and figuratively. Later, she offers one of her many internal monologues to the reader, a tendency that may indeed evoke that lecturing-vegan stereotype:

> That's what I dislike most of all in people – cold irony. It's a very cowardly attitude to mock or belittle everything, never be committed to anything . . . Like an impotent man who can't experience pleasure himself, but will do all he can to ruin it for others . . . At the same time the ironists always have a world outlook that they proclaim triumphantly. (89)

We could understand Duszejko's concern as a pragmatic one. Proceeding from the point that irony is one of the most common modes of expressing satire, Dannagal Goldthwaite Young observes that, "because satire requires staying in [a] state of play, downplaying its own moral certainty," this mode is "difficult to employ purposefully" (209–10).[6] Those in direct pursuit of a specific goal, such as the cessation of animal killing, might not want to reach for irony and satire first. And they might even see those modes as *complicit* in the system that includes animal killing.

But considering her previously established self-awareness, we could assume that the, well, irony, of the aforementioned internal monologue is not lost on Duszejko: she herself spends most of her own waking hours "proclaim[ing]" her "world outlook" (89).[7] Further, she herself is often impotent, in the non-sexual sense of the term: unable to move others with her emotional pleas. But perhaps more to the point: many readers will, along with our narrator's fellow citizens, find Duszejko quite insufferable for much of the narrative. It is a relief to those readers, then, to see how she answers in the later part of the novel a probing question that she posed earlier, a question not unlike Page's: "Are [people's] minds incapable of reaching beyond petty, selfish pleasures? The whole, complex human psyche has evolved to prevent Man from understanding what he is really seeing" (106). Here, she sounds like those noted above who ascribe cognitive dissonance or repression to non-vegans. Ultimately, though, she finds that "the psyche is our defense system . . . For it would be impossible to carry the weight of this knowledge [that] every tiny particle of the world is made of suffering" (225). Maybe, then, there is a place for blissful ignorance or playful distraction after all, or even for something like a "warm irony." Those modes might provide respite from what Diamond calls "wound[ing] knowledge" (46).

Conclusion: Spoiler Alert

Near the end of *Drive Your Plow*, we learn that it is Duszejko, in fact, who has murdered the men in question and planted the seeds of the animal-revenge theory. For example, she took a deer hoof from her dead neighbor's house and made prints in the snow around the body of the police commander. She later insists to the reader that the deer she saw outside the neighbor's house "chose me from among others – maybe because I don't eat meat and they can sense it – to . . . act in their Name" (255). For some readers, this twist will feel a bit cheap, and the critical-fairy-tale feel of the novel heretofore will have lost some of its magic. While, as Matthew Calarco observes, "[a]nimals are always more than what our categories allow us to say or think about them" (39), this twist at least partially chickens out on the novel's tantalizing suggestion of nonhuman revenge.

But the twist opens up interesting questions about genre, and about satire and comedy in particular. I am struck by an early moment in the novel in which Duszejko reflects on the phenomenon of "natural death": "something new is bound to follow, as it always has – isn't that a comical paradox?" (57). Whether you find the capture and killing of hunters, furriers, and meat-eaters – humans responsible for capturing and killing animals – to be in any sense "natural" might determine whether you find the novel ultimately comic. Or even if you don't, perhaps you will find "comical paradox" in the tale of a vegan so concerned with animal death that she causes human deaths, or in the subtler subplot of the novel, in which Duszejko slowly warms to humans, forming a friend group with other local misfits – all while moonlighting as a misanthropic murderer. Deliciously, just before Duszejko escapes with a scientist friend to Białowieża Forest at the novel's close,[8] we learn that the misogyny and ageism she endured from local men was precisely what allowed her to get away with their murders. Explaining that she brained her victims with blocks of ice carried in used grocery bags, she winks to the reader, "Old girls like me always go about with plastic bags, don't they?" (261). Surely there's a pun to be found there about "old bags." But as always, whether or not you "get it" is up to you.

Acknowledgments

Thank you to Chris Balaschak, Alice Bell, Annie Castro, and Jacob J. Erickson for suggesting some of the texts covered here. I am also grateful to the Rachel Carson Center for an Alumni Fellowship that allowed me to work on this essay, and for conversations with Alfonso Donoso there.

Notes

1. Some of the figures I discuss may fall at different points along the spectrum of vegetarianism to strict veganism. I therefore use "vegan" as an expansive term.
2. See also Quinn on vegan "condescension" and Eve Kosofsky Sedgwick's notion of "paranoid criticism."
3. Seemingly repentant after nearly a decade as "Thug Kitchen," Davis and Holloway finally changed their brand name to "Bad Manners" as of two months before this writing (Alam).
4. For more on the patriarchal status of these occupations in Polish society, see Marianna Szczygielska's 2018 conference paper on the film adaptation of the novel, "Wildlife Revenge: Human-Animal Drama in *Spoor* (2017)."
5. See Coetzee's *The Lives of Animals* (1999) and *Elizabeth Costello* (2003).
6. Young's empirically based research finds satire "especially fruitful as a forum *not* for mobilization but for exploration and rumination" (210). It is certainly not useless, then.

7. Further, as I demonstrate in *Bad Environmentalism*, political "commit[ment]" is in no way incompatible with irony, humor, or other similar modes.
8. For the sociopolitical importance of this space, see Eunice Blavascunas's book *Foresters, Borders, and Bark Beetles: The Future of Europe's Last Primeval Forest* (2020).

Works Cited

Adams, Carol J. *Hamburger*. Bloomsbury Academic, 2018.

Alam, Anam. "Thug Kitchen Has Changed its Name After Years of Backlash." *The Vegan Review*, 13 July 2020.

Amstell, Simon. *Do Nothing: Live*. Universal Pictures UK, 2010.

Bergson, Henri. "Laughter: An Essay on the Meaning of the Comic." Trans. Cloudesley Brereton and Fred Rothwell, Macmillan, 1911.

Blavascunas, Eunice. *Foresters, Borders, and Bark Beetles: The Future of Europe's Last Primeval Forest*. Indiana UP, 2020.

Calarco, Matthew. *Thinking through Animals: Identity, Difference, Indistinction*. Stanford UP, 2015.

Cohen, Amanda, Ryan Dunlavey, and Grady Hendrix. *Dirt Candy: A Cookbook: Flavor-Forward Food from the Upstart New York City Vegetarian Restaurant*. Clarkson Potter, 2012.

Conrique, Sarah, and Graham I. Haynes. *The Vegan Stoner Cookbook: 100 Easy Vegan Recipes to Munch*. Ten Speed Press, 2013.

Diamond, Cora. "The Difficulty of Reality and the Difficulty of Philosophy." *Philosophy and Animal Life*. Columbia UP, 2008.

Gold, Lane. *Vegan Junk Food, Expanded Edition: 200+ Vegan Recipes for the Foods You Crave – Minus the Ingredients You Don't*. Adams Media, 2018.

Goldhill, Olivia. "Humans are born irrational, and that has made us better decision-makers." *Quartz*, 4 March 2017.

"Hank T. Norman." "We Raise All Our Beef Humanely on Open Pasture and then Hang Them Upside Down and Slash Their Throats." *The Onion*, 22 January 2013.

Jackson, Laur M. "Memes and Misogynoir." *The Awl*, 28 August 2014.

Lindstrom, Eric. *The Skeptical Vegan: My Journey from Notorious Meat Eater to Tofu-Munching Vegan – A Survival Guide*. Skyhorse Publishing, 2017.

"Lisa the Treehugger." *The Simpsons*. Fox, 19 November 2000.

Nichols, Annie. *How to Be Vegan and Keep Your Friends: Recipes and Tips*. Reprint edition, Quadrille Publishing, 2019.

Perry, Sarah. "Drive Your Plow over the Bones of the Dead by Olga Tokarczuk – The Entire Comic Catastrophe." *The Guardian*, 11 September 2018.

Quinn, Emelia. "Notes on Vegan Camp." *PMLA*, vol. 135, no. 5, 2020, pp. 914–30.

Reinhart, RJ. "Snapshot: Few Americans Vegetarian or Vegan." *Gallup*, 1 August 2018.

"Satire." *Oxford English Dictionary*, Oxford University Press.

Seymour, Nicole. *Bad Environmentalism: Irony and Irreverence in the Ecological Age*. U of Minnesota P, 2018.

Szerszynski, Bronislaw. "The Post-ecologist Condition: Irony as Symptom and Cure." *Environmental Politics*, vol. 16, no. 2, 2007, pp. 337–55.

Terry, Bryant. "The Problem with 'Thug Cuisine.'" *CNN*, 10 October 2014.

Tokarczuk, Olga. *Drive Your Plow over the Bones of the Dead*. Trans. Antonia Lloyd-Jones, Fitzcarraldo Editions, 2018.

Torres, Julio. "Comedy Central Stand-Up Presents: Julio Torres – The Hardest Part of Being Vegan." 5 October 2017. <https://www.youtube.com/watch?v=vIrwSxYHIKE>

Thug Kitchen, LLC. *Thug Kitchen: The Official Cookbook: Eat Like You Give a Fuck*. Rodale, Inc., 2014.

Twine, Richard. "Vegan Killjoys at the Table – Contesting Happiness and Negotiating Relationships with Food Practices." *Societies*, vol. 4, 2014, pp. 623–39.

Watts, Richard. "I Gave My Dog An Electric Shock." Instagram post, 26 February 2016. <https://www.instagram.com/p/BCQ7zGoRXB9/?taken-by=vegansidekick>

—. *Vegan Sidekick vol. 3 Adult Edition*. Lulu Press, Inc., 2015.

Wright, Laura. *The Vegan Studies Project: Food, Animals, and Gender in the Age of Terror*. U of Georgia P, 2015.

Young, Dannagal Goldthwaite. *Irony and Outrage: The Polarized Landscape of Rage, Fear, and Laughter in the United States*. Oxford UP, 2019.

20

Utopian Fiction

John Miller

Introduction

In *The Faber Book of Utopias*, John Carey notes that "Not many writers have tried to imagine utopias for other creatures besides humans" (380). Undoubtedly, *Homo sapiens* is the center point of the utopian tradition, but there are exceptions. The example Carey gives of an animal utopia is Rupert Brooke's poem "Heaven," in which fish imagine the appealing prospect (to them) of a world with "no more land" (380). Moreover, many texts which focus restrictedly on the human good also contain significant reflections on human–animal relations. While Thomas More's foundational *Utopia* (1515) is concerned primarily with human interests, at many points it illustrates the connection of human and nonhuman animal lives in a way that is critical of species violence. The Utopians, for example, "look on the desire of the bloodshed, even of beasts, as a mark of a mind that is already corrupted with cruelty" (108). Earlier in the text in the section which focuses on the failures of European societies, More provides an extended critique of the social impacts of sheep farming and specifically the practice of enclosure through which "the owners, as well as tenants, are turned out of their possessions" (44). The focus on animal agriculture here anticipates the significant number of utopian texts that, even if they do not say much about what the future lives of animals might be like, do imagine vegetarian and vegan societies. In Samuel Butler's *Erewhon* (1872), for instance, the inhabitants abstain from eggs on the basis that "to eat a fresh egg was to destroy a potential chicken" and from milk "as it could not be obtained without robbing some calf of its natural sustenance" (230), though the Erewhonians' vegan culture emerges as part of a satirical structure that makes it hard to take their pro-animal orientations at face value. A more recent, and more straightforwardly committed, vegan utopia is Simon Amstell's mockumentary *Carnage* (2017) in which the carnist present is seen through the lens of a vegan future. A third example – and one with a particular claim to literary historical significance – is Mary Bradley Lane's feminist utopia *Mizora: A Prophecy*, serialized in *The Cincinnati Commercial* in 1880–1881 and subsequently published in book form in 1890.

Lane's novel is notable as perhaps the earliest literary representation of cultured meat (CM), that is to say meat produced in a laboratory cell culture without direct need for animal death. As a substance that promises sustainable meat without animal suffering, CM has a clear link to the idea of utopia, but a complex relationship, as we shall see, to vegan ethics. My aim in this chapter is not to make a simplistic claim about whether CM is a good idea or not, but to offer a critical archaeology of CM's utopian promise that goes back to its (possibly) originary moment in *Mizora*. CM is widely heralded for its aura of futurity. With its challenge to traditional ideas of nature and authenticity, CM is postmodernism on a plate. But it is also a substance with a long history. As a field that concerns food politics in combination with the politics and ethics of human–animal relations, vegan studies is particularly well placed to interrogate the complex network of distinct ideological positions and discursive and material histories in which CM is marinated. Doing so contributes to the aims of a specifically vegan utopian studies concerned with two interlinked tasks: firstly, to critique an anthropocentric utopian tradition by exploring the ways in which animals function in imaginings of human futures; and secondly, to establish an alternative literary history of utopian imaginings that foregrounds animals and posits the idea of a zootopia as the image of a future world premised on a lesser violence towards other creatures.

(Post) Meat Futures

In their foundational work for both the manufacture and the critical analysis of CM, the artists Oron Catts and Ionat Zurr are clear about the product's utopian potential. Catts and Zurr began producing CM in 2000 with *Semi-living Steak*, an installation in which meat was cultivated from ovine muscle cells "in a 3D tissue culture bioreactor" ("Semi-living"). It was, they claim, "the first known proof-of-concept for using tissue culture exclusively for food," and, on the surface at least, very good news for animals. Here is how Catts and Zurr conceptualize the implications of the process for creatures who under usual circumstances would be destined for the abattoir: meat is cultivated "from a biopsy taken from an animal, which is left in the paddock alive and healthy"; as the cells proliferate, the steak grows, but the animal heals ("Disembodied" 106). Consequently, Catts and Zurr speculate that humanity is poised to move towards "a utopian future" in which not only "the killing and suffering of animals destined for food consumption," but also "the ecological and economic problems associated with the food industry, would be reduced dramatically" ("Disembodied" 106).

Since Catts and Zurr's early installations, this "victimless utopia," as they name it ("Disembodied" 110), has moved significantly closer to technical and commercial realization. Given the amount of investment CM has attracted since the start of the millennium, there seems every chance that agriculture may be about to arrive at what the research institute New Harvest have called a "post-animal bioeconomy." December 2020 saw a significant step towards that goal when Restaurant 1880 in Singapore became the first venue to sell a meal made from CM to the paying public. The occasion was marked by suitably utopian rhetoric. The first table to receive their meal of cultured chicken nuggets "included a group of inspiring young people committed to building a better planet." One twelve-year-old diner noted that "It's definitely made me see how small things, like just changing the way we eat, can literally change our entire lives" (AP News). By this reckoning, CM is more than just food; it becomes the embodiment of the hope that technological advances will forge a viable future from the wreckage of a damaged planet.

Not everyone is delighted. Sections of the meat industry have moved to address what appears to be an existential threat to the idea of meat as much as an economic challenge for conventional animal agriculture. From its inception, CM has been plagued by uncertainty about the most apt nomenclature to describe and market it. Names proliferate like cells: in vitro meat, clean meat, good meat, lab-grown meat, cell-based meat, fake meat, immaculate meat, meat 2.0. While those involved in its production are clear that, whatever you call it, it definitely *is* meat (in that it is essentially the same substance as conventional meat), the meat industry insists that it most definitely is not. Lawsuits have been filed by meat producers in the US anxious to formally restrict the meaning of the word "meat" to matter derived from a killed animal. The National Cattlemen's Beef Association has identified one of their key priorities as "protecting the industry and consumers from fake meat and misleading labels on products that do not contain real beef" (Abbott). To take control of the emerging new language of animal protein is to keep hold of the meanings of meat. If CM embodies a wider spirit of techno-optimism, it also involves a broader interrogation of the philosophy and semiotics of meat. In this way CM exemplifies a striking tension between tradition and innovation.

Such renegotiations of the meanings and material processes of meat production inevitably impinge on the territory of vegan studies, inflecting debates around the parameters of plant-based diets and adding a new dimension to debates around food ethics and the politics of human–animal relations. Accordingly, there is a significant and growing body of pro-animal scholarship that wrestles with the emerging questions CM provokes. Josh Milburn is perhaps the most prominent supporter of cultured meat from within vegan studies. For Milburn, "animal ethicists and vegans should be willing to cautiously embrace the production of in vitro flesh" (249) primarily because of its potential to "to end the suffering and death" (259) of conventional meat production. Against Milburn's view, numerous objections have been raised. Clean Meat Hoax, an "informal group of animal rights scholars and activists" list fifteen reasons for suspicion, including, contra the views of the National Cattlemen's Beef Association, the supposition that CM helps "the Meat Industry fold cellular meat into its wider strategy *of preserving animal agriculture*" (emphasis in original). Moreover, despite having a significant influence on the development of CM, Catts and Zurr remain playfully wary of its utopian promises, highlighting the possibility that their category of the "Semi-Living" might become "a new class for exploitation" and pointing out the multiple ways in which CM still relies on the objectification of animals, such as in the use of fetal bovine serum (produced from the blood of unborn calves) as the growth medium ("Disembodied" 106). Intriguingly then, the utopian aura that surrounds the development of CM is contested both by (some of) those who want to kill animals for food and (some of) those who wish to keep animals from harm.

Among the most crucial, and in some ways the most obvious, insights into CM is one that has a strong connection to vegan perspectives: ultimately, CM is haunted by purposelessness, notwithstanding the undoubted seriousness of the issues it is slated to address (from global heating to global pandemics). As Erica Fudge notes in one of the earliest engagements with CM in literary studies, there is an easier and cheaper solution to meat's manifold harms: just eat plants (161). Part of CM's function therefore is, as the Clean Meat Hoax group suggest, to reinforce "the myth that meat is something we all need" and to hammer home the contention that a widespread adoption of veganism is unimaginable. Beyond this we might recall Fredric Jameson's observation that capitalism "requires a frontier, and perpetual expansion, in order to sustain its inner dynamic." Biotechnology relocates this frontier from geography to genetics so that CM functions as part of capitalism's incorporation of ecological emergency into its underlying structures as something like a get-out clause. These points are only the beginning of a larger task to comprehend the phantasmagoric quality of CM's appearance of necessity.

As CM has become increasingly established in public debates around meat, it has attracted a considerable body of popular and academic writing, though this tends to get historically stuck at Winston Churchill's brief allusion to lab meat in a 1932 essay in *Popular Mechanics*, partly because as a white, male, upper-class, straight, meat-lover Churchill adds an all-encompassing hegemonic endorsement to what can seem an outré idea. Meanwhile the literary critical attention CM has attracted has been concentrated mainly on Margaret Atwood's dystopian depiction of engineered meat in the *Maddaddam* trilogy (2003–2012) and elsewhere (see McHugh, Nye, Parry). There are in fact a significant number – certainly more than seventy – works of fiction that include representations of CM (or something like it), mainly, and unsurprisingly, in the genres of science or utopian fiction.[1] Such speculations do not constitute a script for the material development of CM (though there are numerous uncanny examples of history acting out fiction), but they do allow a deepening of critical engagements with its meanings, which (as with conventional meat) are constituted in part historically. To recognize CM's history is to understand how its development expresses and inflects underlying social and cultural factors at the intersection of species, technology, ecology, and economics; history allows us to trace the fluctuating patterns of desire and anxiety that are acted out in the dream of utopian protein. Accordingly, the rest of this chapter moves towards a deceptively simple question: what does cultured meat mean in its (possibly) foundational moment in *Mizora*? This question, in turn, leads to a broader, concluding reflection on the directions a vegan utopian studies might take.

Mizora's Post-Animal Bioeconomy

The 1880s were heady days for utopian imaginings. As Jean Pfaelzer summarizes, there were over one hundred utopian novels published in the US in the period 1886–1896 (3). Although Lane is a little known figure, an Ohio schoolmistress who wrote only two books (the other *Escanaba* from 1895 is now lost), she can claim a certain literary historical significance. *Mizora* was among the earliest texts of the *fin-de-siècle* utopia boom; more specifically, the novel is, as Pfaelzer claims, the "first significant, all-female utopia written in the United States" (xi). The narrative concerns the travels of a Russian noblewoman Vera Zarovitch who, sentenced to exile in Siberia for her revolutionary views, "attempts a journey no other of my sex has ever attempted" (Lane 8): escaping from her captors across the Arctic Ocean towards the North Pole, where, rowing alone over the "undulating waters" (13), she is swept into a whirlpool. She fears the worst, but finds herself with "bewildered delight" transported to "a land of enchantment" (14). This is Mizora, a secret world in which "not a man nor the suggestion of one, was to be seen" (16) and in which an egalitarian feminist commune flourishes. Utopian fiction played a significant role in the feminist agitation of the late nineteenth and early twentieth centuries in the work of writers like Elizabeth Burgoyne Corbett and Charlotte Perkins Gilman, for example. Lane's gynocentric, post-capitalist society of universal education and freedom from poverty and servitude represents a trenchant antidote to the hidebound patriarchal attitudes of small-town America, even if the novel remains tied, as Pfaelzer argues, to "stereotypes of women: most notably through the lingering presence of the 'angel of the house' motif" (147–48).

At the heart of the idealized society Vera discovers are intimate connections between diet, health, and social equality that derive primarily from biotechnology. Vera explains that

> Agriculture in this wonderful land, was a lost art. No one that I questioned had any knowledge of it. It had vanished in the dim past of their barbarism. With the exception of vegetables and fruit, which were raised in luscious perfection, their food came from the elements. A famine among such enlightened people was impossible, and scarcity was unknown. Food for the body and food for the mind were without price. It was owing to this that poverty was unknown to them, as well as disease. The absolute purity of all that they ate preserved an activity of vital power long exceeding our span of life. (Lane 26)

The Mizoran promise of food's "absolute purity" evokes widespread concerns about food adulteration at the *fin-de-siècle* and broader anxieties about physical and cultural degeneration, while also suggesting a more general achievement of social perfection that is key to Lane's social vision.

How this purity is realised is imagined in some detail by Lane.

> The Mizorans took certain chemicals and converted them into milk, and cream, and cheese, and butter, and every variety of meat, in a vessel that admitted neither air nor light. They claimed that the elements of air and light exercised a material influence upon the chemical production of foods, that they could not be made successfully by artificial processes when exposed to those two agents. Their earliest efforts had been unsuccessful of exact imitation, and a perfect result had only been obtained by closely counterfeiting the processes of nature.
>
> The cream prepared artificially that I had tasted in London, was the same color and consistency as natural cream, but it lacked its relish. The cream manufactured in Mizora was a perfect imitation of the finest dairy product.
>
> It was the same with meats; they combined the elements, and the article produced possessed no detrimental flavor. It was a more economical way of obtaining meat than by fattening animals. (56)

Evidently, there are some notable points of difference between Mizoran biotechnology and the development of CM today. Rather than beginning with animal cells, Mizorans begin the process in the chemical constituents of life; perhaps the most straightforward technical gloss would be to think of Mizorans synthesizing meat and dairy products from amino acids. Because of this process, there is significantly less doubt about the vegan credentials of Mizoran CM than there is about our own version, given the ongoing use of fetal bovine serum in its manufacture. No animal is needed in Mizora, and yet this is no meat substitute of the Quorn or Tofurkey variety (made from mycoprotein in the first case and wheat and soya in the second), but a "perfect imitation" of the material substance of meat and dairy products produced by "counterfeiting the processes of nature," a conceptualization of food technology at the heart of the novel's social organization.

Lane's engagement with the idea of Nature provides a notable echo of the ur-text of literary biotech, Mary Shelley's *Frankenstein* (1818). While Victor Frankenstein's "fervent longing to penetrate the secrets of nature" (Shelley 38) is the basis for one of literature's most enduring cautionary tales, Lane adapts Shelley's language to offer a more upbeat view of the ethical implications of biotechnology. In Mizora, the whole of society "might be called a great school of Nature, whose pupils studied her every phase, and pried into her secrets with persistent activity, and obeyed her instructions as an imperative duty" (Lane 64). For Lane, the trope of the secret allows for technology to appear not as the violation of some natural law, but as a fulfilment or expression of the deep structures of nature which unsettles the conventional opposition between the natural and the artificial. It is the same philosophy of science that underpins the novel's other great technological advance: the development of a form of in vitro fertilization that enables the extinction of males and which is likewise based on the ability to "control Nature's processes of development" (104). The Mizorans harness rather than violate nature (and it is worth noting in passing, as further evidence of this pattern, that there are some prescient descriptions of renewable energy in the novel too). If *Frankenstein* pivots on the creature's violent revenge on the over-reaching scientist who created him, *Mizora* is all about harmony, a point emphasized through the luxuriant feast that greets Vera on her arrival in this wonderful new land.

After enjoying a "chemically prepared" beefsteak "of a very fine quality," Vera is presented with a cup "that looked like the half of a soap bubble with all its iridescent beauty sparkling and glancing in the light" (18). The beverage it contains resembles a chocolate "whose flavor could not have been surpassed by the fabled nectar of the gods" (18). Such purple prose adds a conventionally Romantic ambience to Mizora that extends to the depiction of landscape with its "languorous atmosphere, the beauty of the heavens, the inviting shores," veiled "behind a haze of purple and gold" (14). These landscape aesthetics have a significant, albeit only implicit, role in the novel's depiction of its post-animal bioeconomy. With livestock farming taking up 30 per cent of the planet's land surface today, CM promises to free up a huge amount of space. Accordingly, Lane emphasizes the ample, uncrowded habitations of Mizora. Each family enjoys ground that is "ornamented like a private park" with "cascades, fountains, rustic arbors, rockeries, aquariums, tiny lakes, and every variety of landscape ornamenting" (41). Although Lane never makes the connection explicitly, Mizora's remarkable synthetic food production is part of what makes this kind of landscape imaginatively tenable. Released from the burden of productivity, the land becomes a place of leisure rather than labor.

This utopian geography is a theme that runs through CM's speculative pre-history. Churchill noted how synthetic food production would produce a new landscape in which "Parks and gardens will cover our pastures and plowed fields." Spinning out from the specific vision of *Mizora* to the twenty-first century's social and ecological dilemmas, the promise of repurposed grazing land for rewilding or other forms of global heating mitigation is an attractive one, and an idea in which environmental politics and aesthetics are brought into conjunction. The Mizoran wildlife captures something of this as Vera notes how "Birds of bright plumage flitted among the branches, anon breaking forth into wild and exultant melody" (14). But if the bird is gauged to function metonymically as a sign of social harmony and ecological flourishing, *Mizora* is no zootopia. There is little for pro-animal scholars and activists to cling on to in Lane's utopia.

Eugenics, Utopia, and Vegan Studies

So far, CM's utopian appeal in Lane's novel has revolved around its connection to human wellbeing with a specific emphasis on social justice, physical health, and an idealized geography. Although the Mizoran diet is "vegetarian" (Jacobs 195), Mizora does not fit with the pro-animal ethical coordinates that modern formulations of vegetarian or vegan diets for the most part entail. In fact, the ideal state of Mizora is represented as emerging through the deliberate exclusion of animals. When Vera first arrives in this "enchanted country" (Lane 15), among her first observations is that "No animals were visible, nor sound of any. No hum of life. All nature lay asleep in voluptuous beauty, veiled in a glorious atmosphere" (15). The transition from the realization of the absence of animals to an appreciation of the Romantic landscape subordinates ethics to aesthetics. Where animals do appear in the text they feature purely as aesthetic effects, as in the birds that flit so merrily among the branches and whose presence is recognized in their songs rather than in their physical forms. Animal life to the Mizorans appears vaguely disgusting; domestic creatures connote a "state of barbarism" and have "long been extinct" (54).

Nor is the extinction of the majority of animals the only uncomfortable element of Lane's utopia. *Mizora* displays a good deal of enthusiasm for a policy of eugenics which has resulted in the production of complete racial homogeneity. When Vera is shown a portrait gallery including many paintings of pre-revolutionary Mizora, she notes casually that while all the Mizorans she has met have had blonde hair, many of the pictures represent people of "dark complexions" (92). After questioning one of the Mizoran matriarchs, Vera learns that these people have been "eliminated" (92). Vera experiences some unease at the discovery but moves on quickly and the novel does little to question the chilling racist agenda at the heart of Mizoran culture. Elimination, moreover, is a term that recurs throughout the text: "the coarser nature of men was eliminated from the present race" (104); the Mizorans "have eliminated hereditary diseases, and developed into a healthy and moral people" (108). The same language underpins Mizora's food revolution too: "To eliminate from our food the deleterious earthy matter is our constant aim" (45). The extinction of animals and the production of beastless meat are part, therefore, of a network of eliminations in which undesirable bodies are cleared out to make way for a world of sterile perfection. This motif – of the insular land severed from the rest of the world and shorn of unwanted elements – is a recurrent element of utopian imaginings from More onwards. What it means in the context of *Mizora* is that cultured meat is not so much utopian protein as eugenic protein; its "absolute purity" testifies to an authoritarian biopolitics that is the ultimate consequence of the Mizorans' ability to reach into the secrets of nature. In *Mizora*, CM represents the materialization of a fascist principle of hygiene.

We might therefore identify three key components of CM's meaning in *Mizora*. Firstly, in familiarly utopian mode, it represents the overcoming of *social* problems via technological innovation so that the widespread perils of late nineteenth-century life (poverty, sickness, injustice) can be vanquished as part of what seems (at some moments of the novel at any rate) a radical socialist vision of universal equality. Secondly, CM facilitates an *aesthetic* utopianism, through the perfection of bodies and landscapes so that the blight of ugliness, work, slaughter, and mess can be removed from life in the service of an idealized culture. Thirdly, it expresses the perfection of various forms of *political* violence through which the possibility of life, for humans or animals, is based on the techno-ideological maneuvers of a genteel but merciless elite. If there is any message we might (albeit hesitantly) extrapolate from Mizora to our own times it is to be wary of the ways in which cultured meat forms part of the wider operations of economic and political power. It is not the substance itself that sounds a jarring note, but rather its cohesion with the violence of the overarching system, a point which emphasizes the need for debates to continue to situate CM in the wider context of our carno-capitalism.

It is possible to imagine a carnivorous reading of *Mizora* that posits a return to meat as the antidote to the bleak purity of Lane's utopia. Certainly this fits with a strand in the literary history of cultured meat in which its representation results in a sentimental hankering after traditional forms of animal agriculture, as in Frederik Pohl and Cyril Kornbluth's classic novel of cultured meat *The Space Merchants* (1953). Such a position, however, involves a movement back to *Mizora*'s other setting, "the refuge for oppression" (147) of the late nineteenth-century US that Vera returns to at the novel's despondent denouement. Any carnivorous reading would also serve to emphasize concern that CM is not a way out of meat culture but a diversification of it. Clearly, there are more alternatives available to politics, and indeed to literary criticism, than a straightforward either/or between carnist nostalgia and eugenic fantasy, positions which are in any case intimately bound up with one another as the twin domains that *Mizora* moves between. Both of these positions are in any case premised on animal death, either through the slaughter of conventional animal agriculture or the eliminations behind Mizora's quiet, lush landscapes.

A vegan critical perspective, however, necessarily focuses on pathways beyond these forms of violence. In this context, a vegan utopian studies offers an expansion of the range of interests at play in the imagining of better worlds to come. As such, vegan studies forms part of an alliance with decolonial, ecological, queer, and feminist perspectives in the wider task of critiquing and reclaiming utopian imaginings by addressing the question of to whom the future might be thought to belong. From an animal-centered perspective this involves the literary historical task of assembling an alternate literary history of the utopia, seeking zootopias which cross with and diverge from anthropocentric utopian traditions. Part of this project is to examine the ways in which the ethical demands animals place on us are refused in utopian fictions. CM in *Mizora* is part of this refusal. This begs a larger question to energize the literary historical task of a vegan utopian studies: from what discourses and social practices might a zootopia be made? It appears, moreover, that in the literary history of cultured meat there may be relatively little interest in animal futures, but a great deal of interest in the development of science. The relationship between vegan literary studies and the history of meat technology seems likely to remain an informatively awkward one which helps us understand CM as a new set of challenges rather than as a magic bullet for the ever deepening perils of anthropocentric cultures.

Note

1. See Joshua Bulleid's essay in this collection for further examples of CM in these genres.

Works Cited

Abbott, Chuck. "Lab-grown Meat is not Beef, Say Ranchers." *agriculture.com*. 27 March 2018.
AP News. "Eat Just Makes History (Again) with Restaurant Debut of Cultured Meat." *apnews.com*, 21 December 2020.
Butler, Samuel. *Erewhon*. 1872. Penguin, 1970.
Carey, John (ed.). *The Faber Book of Utopias*. Faber and Faber, 1999.
Catts, Oron, and Ionat Zurr. "Disembodied Livestock: The Promise of a Semi-living Utopia." *Parallax*, vol. 19, no. 1, 2013, pp. 101–13.
—. "Semi-living Steak." *Tissue Culture and Art Project*, tcaproject.net, n.d.
Churchill, Winston. "Fifty Years Hence." *Popular Mechanics*, vol. 57, no. 3, 1932, pp. 390–97.
Clean Meat Hoax. *cleanmeat-hoax.com*, n.d.
Fudge, Erica. "Why It's Easy Being a Vegetarian." *Textual Practice*, vol. 24, no. 1, 2010, pp. 149–66.
Jacobs, Naomi. "The Frozen Landscape in Women's Utopian and Science Fiction." *Utopian and Science Fiction by Women: Worlds of Difference*, edited by Jane L. Donawerth and Carol A. Kolmerton, Liverpool UP, 1994, pp. 190–202.
Jameson, Fredric. "The Politics of Utopia." *New Left Review*, vol. 25, 2004.
Lane, Mary Bradley. 1881. *Mizora: A Prophecy*. Syracuse UP, 2007.
McHugh, Susan. "Real artificial: Tissue-cultured Meat, Genetically Modified Farm Animals, and Fictions." *Configurations*, vol. 18, no. 1, 2010, 181–97.
Milburn, Josh. "Chewing Over In Vitro Meat: Animal Ethics, Cannibalism and Social Progress." *Res Publica*, vol. 22, no. 3, 2016, pp. 249–65.
More, Thomas. 1515. *Utopia*. Verso, 2015.
New Harvest. "Mission & Vision." *new-harvest.org*, n.d.
Nye, Coleman. "The Matter of In-Vitro Meat: Speculative Genres of Future Life." *The Palgrave Handbook of Twentieth and Twenty-First Century Literature and Science*, edited by Neel Ahuja et al., Palgrave Macmillan, Cham, 2020, pp. 375–95.
Parry, Jovian. "Oryx and Crake and the New Nostalgia for Meat." *Society & Animals*, vol. 17, no. 3, 2009, 241–56.
Pfaelzer, Jean. "Introduction." *Mizora: A Prophecy*. Syracuse UP, 2007, pp. xi–xl.
—. *The Utopian Novel in America, 1886–1896: The Politics of Form*. U of Pittsburgh P, 1985.
Shelley, Mary. *Frankenstein: The Modern Prometheus*. Colburn and Bentley, 1831.

21

Speculative Fiction

Vegan Cannibals from Outer Space: Octavia Butler's *Xenogenesis* trilogy

Jovian Parry

Introduction

IF YOU ARE what you eat, it stands to reason that it must be impossible to eat and remain unchanged. Routine exchanges of regulatory signals and genetic material between eater and eaten threaten the skin-encapsulated human self with contamination and corruption by the other from within. However, that same "persistence of others in the flesh" (Landecker, "Exposure" 169) also highlights how any subject, human or otherwise, can only emerge via relationships of corporeal intimacy with other species and other selves. To these ends, Donna Haraway engages the evolutionary theory of symbiogenesis – literally, "becoming by living together" – as an alternative origin story engendering new insights into the origins, dynamism, and diversity of Earthly life. A secular creation myth hinging not on "cooperation" or "competition" but rather "indigestion" (Haraway, "Symbiogenesis"), symbiogenesis unsettles atomistic understandings of the self, instead understanding subjectivity as fundamentally dynamic, entangled, and always-already multiple.

Speculative fiction has a long history of direct engagement with the theory of symbiogenesis (see, for example, Simak). One such work is Octavia E. Butler's groundbreaking *Xenogenesis* trilogy (1987–1989),[1] a sf story centrally concerned with the power dynamics of eating.[2] In *Xenogenesis*, symbiogenesis informs an ethic of non-violence that eschews hierarchy and mandates dietary veganism yet remains embedded in deeply uneven power relations of coercion and instrumentalization. This confluence of utopian impulses and the acknowledgment of the inevitable insufficiency of such impulses is a constitutive feature not only of Butler's sf, but of veganism itself (Quinn and Westwood 1). Both sf and veganism share a quality of estrangement from social norms (Schuster 219); symbiogenesis has likewise been deployed as a stratagem of imagining otherwise. As such, *Xenogenesis* thickens and complicates configurations of species and subjectivities, acknowledging selves as protean multispecies assemblages while affirming the differential accountability of such selves to others, human and otherwise.

Symbiogenesis

Symbiosis describes the long-lasting corporeal intimacy – obligate or optional, parasitic or pathogenic – of differently-named organisms. Symbiotic relationships express their liveliest potentialities in the phenomenon of symbiogenesis, or "long term stable symbiosis that leads to evolutionary change" (Margulis and Sagan, *Genomes* 12). In symbiogenesis, separate species "form a symbiotic consortium which becomes the target of selection as a single entity" (Mayr xiii), leading to "the appearance of a new phenotype, trait, tissue, organelle, organ, or organism formed through a symbiotic relationship" (Hird 58). The paradigmatic example is the mitochondria living inside nearly all eukaryotic cells (ours included), "descendants of ancient, oxygen-using bacteria that were either engulfed as prey or invaded as predators" (Margulis, "Power" 31). Once in a while, the result is not digestion but symbiosis and from there, symbiogenesis: the emergence of a completely novel intra-cellular organelle still nestled within the cells of all Earthly animals and which (among other things) enables us "to survive the ravages of the poisonous gas oxygen" (Hird 29). From a symbiogenic perspective, the individual actor-organism is really a holobiont, a consortia of macro- and microscopic creatures living in corporeal intimacy, revealing the autonomous individual subject as a biologically untenable construction: "the evolution of our 'selves' is already polluted by histories of encounter" (Tsing 29). As Rosi Braidotti argues, the living subject, human or otherwise, does not precede the relational encounter with alterity but emerges through it as an intra-active assemblage of multiple and differentially converging materialities, species, and allegiances.[3]

The robust body of feminist sf criticism on symbiogenesis (see, for example, Alonso; Bollinger; Dowdall; Ferreira; Magnone; Pak; Schell) has largely elided what for Haraway and Margulis is too compelling to be ignored: that symbiogenesis proceeds through a kind of "abortive cannibalism" (Margulis and Sagan, *Genomes* 13), wherein one party is "eaten but not digested" by another (Hird 82), an alimentary "truce rather than war" that gathers self and non-self together in a "tense proximity" (Crist and Tauber, "Selfhood" 524). Developments in nutritional epigenetics support this interpretation, understanding metabolism and gene expression as intra-active rather than discrete processes: DNA is not a static set of instructions for building a body, but a dynamic poem that is constantly being edited and rewritten through the nutritive intra-action of eater and eaten. Bodies are not bunsen burners converting food to fuel, but instead can be seen as chimerical "whirlpools" in which genetic and chemical material from the eaten persist in the flesh (Landecker, "Metabolism" 8). As Haraway puts it, "Getting hungry, eating, and partially digesting, partially assimilating, and partially transforming . . . are the actions of companion species" (*Staying* 65).

Haraway's enthusiasm for symbiogenesis as a paradigm for thinking through subjectivity-as-consortium is equaled by her apparent disdain for subjectivities informed by veganism: in *When Species Meet* (2008), for example, Haraway shrugs off "the demands individual animals might make as ventriloquized in rights idioms" (28), pointedly asserting that "eating and killing cannot be hygienically separated" and chastising those who weaponize their dietary choices as a "way to pretend innocence or transcendence or a final peace" (295). Haraway's straw figure of the ecologically alienated vegan pretending innocence of killing and dreaming of freedom from the shackles of the food chain has been deployed in broader food activism discourses to delegitimize plant-based diets as one end of an untenable "extreme," with the unfettered atrocities of the animal industrial complex on the other – this despite a robust body of theoretical and ethnographic literature demonstrating that contemporary vegans are perfectly aware of their own alimentary "non-innocence" (see, for example,

Giraud). Rather than a purity-based injunction against zoophagy, vegan praxis can instead operate as a "worldly mode of engagement that acknowledges the realities of violence" and the insufficiency of individual consumer responsibility without letting such insufficiencies preclude action (Pick 68). This messy and fluctuating zone of entanglement is the territory vegan literary criticism seeks to explore (Quinn and Westwood). My own vegan reading of *Xenogenesis* foregrounds the ways in which Butler deploys the trope of the vegan alien to interrogate the ethics of symbiogenic indigestion, soundly rejecting a politics of purity while remaining deeply committed to a multispecies utopianism that is always-already insufficient, always-already in flux.

Xenogenesis and Vegan Cannibals

A Black feminist writer of sf in the late twentieth-century US, Butler is renowned for her relentless interrogation of the dynamics of domination, acquiescence, and resistance (Melzer 54–56), as well as her exploration of the fluidity of the boundaries between self and other (Idema; Wolmark 29), themes central to her magnum opus *Xenogenesis*. In the trilogy, nuclear holocaust has decimated life on Earth, nearly obliterating the human population and devastating ecosystems and species worldwide. Protagonist Lilith Iyapo (a Black anthropologist from the US) and other human survivors awaken on an alien spaceship 250 years later, cured of their radiation poisoning, and are given the chance to return to a restored Earth. The catch? Their alien rescuers/captors, who call themselves the Oankali, have sterilized all surviving humans to ensure that they can only reproduce via genetic hybridization with the Oankali (achieved via interspecies copulation). Their children will be human–alien hybrids sharing and exceeding the capacities of both species. The Oankali – a term loosely translating to "gene traders" (Butler, *Lilith's* 41) – incorporate genetic material from other species they encounter in a process of conscious evolution, hybridizing themselves with each successive "trade" of genes:

> We're not hierarchical, you see. We never were. But we are powerfully acquisitive. We acquire new life – seek it, investigate it, manipulate it, sort it, use it. We carry the drive to do this in a minuscule cell within a cell – a tiny organelle within every cell of our bodies. (41)

This organelle – "the essence of ourselves, the origin of ourselves," as the Oankali put it – enables the aliens to "perceive DNA and manipulate it precisely" without resorting to technical mediation, allowing hybridization "with life-forms so completely dissimilar that they were unable to even perceive one another as alive" (41). Across millions of years and multiple "trades" and transformations, the Oankali are "always changing in every way but one – that one organelle" that constitutes the core of their identity and the engine of their evolutionary process (41).

Butler acknowledges her debt to the theory of symbiogenesis within the text. As Laurel Bollinger argues, the trilogy "describ[es] mitochondria's incorporation with human cells in an overt reference to the then-speculative endosymbiotic theory" ("Symbiogenesis" 42).[4] "They could not exist without symbiotic relationships with other creatures," an Oankali character muses, "Yet such relationships frighten them" (Butler, *Lilith's* 427). By acknowledging the symbiotic dependencies of human life and crafting a speculative narrative of consciously orchestrated xeno-symbiogenesis between humans and an alien species of consummate symbionts, Butler actively contests this anthropocentric fear of symbiosis, and the narratives of human exceptionalism and organismal atomism that inform and enable it. However, as Haraway reminds us, symbiosis is not a synonym for "mutually beneficial" (*Staying* 60); symbionts can be parasites, enemies, or profoundly unequal partners (Margulis, "Power"). Perhaps this ambiguity explains why, in *Xenogenesis*, Oankali aliens provoke such varied and discordant readings: from non-violent vegans embodying an ecofeminist ethic of anti-hierarchical inter-relationality to anthropophagic slave-masters and interstellar bio-pirates executing a eugenic pogrom of forced miscegenation to effect the genocide of the human species.

Critics who skew towards a positive evaluation of the Oankali point out the resonance between the corporeal, empathic epistemology of the tentacled aliens and a feminist ethic of embodiment and shared vulnerability (Alaimo; Harper). The hungry gene traders experience eating as a "legitimate mode of intellectual, emotional knowledge" (Parasecoli 81)[5] – they "read" genetic information through taste, and even share in the sensations of the critters they nibble, rendering outright butchery and meat-eating "as unacceptable as slicing off their own healthy limbs" (Butler, *Lilith's* 564). In this sense, the Oankali are vegans from outer space come to show humankind the error of its eco-cidal and carnist ways by espousing "an ecological worldview of situated connectedness and constitutive interrelations" (Alaimo 147) and providing a "paradigm for feminism and anti-racism" (Harper 111).

However, as Haraway points out, for the Oankali, "hierarchy is not power's only shape" (*Primate* 380): the gene traders' claim to have avoided hierarchies does not necessarily mean "they have eschewed power" (Bonner 56). While they inflict no physical violence upon other motile species, the Oankali have no qualms about genetically "assembling" other creatures to serve their needs willingly (Butler, *Lilith's* 446). The Oankali sterilization program is part of this pattern of supposedly non-violent instrumentalization: the only way humans can reproduce – or even experience sexual pleasure – is through Oankali mediation.[6] And reproduce they must: "Oankali-human families are expected to produce children upon children," hybrid offspring of the gene trade whose human genetic heritage will invigorate the next generation of Oankali explorers (Slonczewski). Lilith is not exaggerating when she describes herself as "part of a captive breeding program" (*Lilith's* 60), like a creature in a zoo: "we used to treat animals that way," she observes bitterly, recalling not only modernity's practices of human–animal relations, but also, as Chandra Martini notes, the sexual power dynamics of American chattel slavery (63); like so much of Butler's oeuvre, *Xenogenesis* is haunted by "the spectre of coerced miscegenation" (Peppers 50). Christa Grewe-Volpp argues that despite their egalitarian social structure and preference for coercion rather than violence, the Oankali are not as anti-hierarchical as they would have the humans believe; they relate to humans "like slave-masters . . . exercis[ing] power over them [and] forc[ing] them to submit to their own needs and desires" (163). While their haptic epistemology might indeed be antithetical to dualisms, it certainly does not stop the aliens from operating in domineering ways. They employ a strategy of "erotic colonization" (Stein 214) whereby they manipulate other creatures into serving their needs by neurally stimulating intensely gratifying sensations; the Oankali thus coerce humans into "forms of interspecies sex that brutally, yet pleasurably, incorporate humanity into an interspecies future" (Ahuja 380). Their "tasting" of genetic material from unsuspecting bodies raises uncomfortable questions of consent: in the case of Lilith, the Oankali "expropriat[e] her genetic/reproductive materials without consent and . . . combin[e] them into a mix that suits their needs for the 'trade'" (Stein 215). The Oankali consume Lilith's tissue, remix it with DNA from her dead lover and genetic material from three other Oankali "parents," and re-implant it in her body without her knowledge; rather inauspiciously, this "coerced pregnancy" is, as Stein notes, the first occurrence of xeno-symbiogenesis between the two species.

The Oankali's taste-based epistemology, intuitive from birth, also raises the uncomfortable possibility that these supposedly non-violent vegan explorers from outer space might in fact be considered people-eaters. The hybrid character Akin recounts how, while being breastfed by his human mother, he began to sample and analyze – to "taste," in the Oankali sense – "her flesh as well as her milk" (Butler, *Lilith's* 256). Consider the following exchange between Lilith and the Oankali Nikanj:

> "It's a good thing your people don't eat meat. If you did, the way you talk about us, our flavors and your hunger and your need to taste us, I think you would eat us instead of fiddling with our genes." And after a moment of silence, "That might even be better. It would be something we could understand and fight against."
>
> Nikanj had not said a word. It might have been feeding on her even then – sharing bits of her most recent meal, taking in dead or malformed cells from her flesh, even harvesting a ripe egg before it could begin its journey down her fallopian tubes. It stored some eggs and consumed the rest . . . (689)

According to Hammer, this "revelation" that the Oankali actually eat the humans they come into contact with "constitutes the true climax of the story" (93). For Hammer, the Oankali "need human mates because they literally consume their cellular structures whenever they touch them" (93) – it is through this alimentary encounter, this near-parasitic relation of commensality, that the xeno-symbiogenesis of Butler's trilogy is enacted. By tasting and consuming other creatures' bodily tissues in order to know and understand them in the "certainty of the flesh" (Butler, *Lilith's* 476), the Oankali literalize Margaret St Clair's assertion that "[i]ncorporation is the ultimate intimacy"; the Oankali would surely agree with her sentiment that "[t]here is no form of carnal knowledge so complete as that of knowing how someone tastes" (1).

The Oankali predilection for surreptitiously nibbling on human flesh is but part of a wider pattern of anthropophagic tropes in Butler's work. From the Clayarks' ravenous hunger for human meat in *Clay's Ark* (1996), to Doro's hunger for fresh bodies to wear and discard in *Wild Seed* (1980) and *Mind of My Mind* (1978), to the vampires of *Fledgling* (2005), and the Oankali themselves, anthropophagy occupies a position of "prominence and narrative significance in her major fiction" (Sands 2). Butler consistently deploys these "cannibal tropes in the service of narratives that emphasize the permeability of the skin boundary and the mutability of the self" (11) – narratives that emphasize the transcorporeality of bodies, the incessant exchange of matter than sustains and characterizes embodied life. This Oankali predilection to hybridize with rather than repudiate "the other" needs to be approached critically; while it is true that concerns of purity and self–other hyper-separation are alien to them, this anti-dualism does not sanction their unfettered drive to "collect" (Butler, *Lilith's* 239) biomaterial from other lifeforms.

When Butler describes the Oankali as an "acquisitive" rather than competitive species, she is surely not deaf to the term's more mundane meaning of "greedy" or "rapacious." The Oankali seek and consume difference because "they need it to keep themselves from stagnation and overspecialization" (239), and, crucially, because they have the power to do so with relative impunity, reaping the biodiversity of each planet they encounter "to fuel new iterations of themselves" (Dowdall 512) in a colonialist enterprise of interplanetary bio-piracy and genetic consumerism. As Slonczewski points out, "the closer one looks, the Oankali are not our opposites, but rather an extension of some of humanity's most extreme tendencies." The xeno-symbiogenesis effected by the Oankali is not innocent, but coerced and profoundly unequal; the Oankali cannot be beatified as epitomizing ecofeminist ideals of embracing difference and living ecologically and nonhierarchically. Even though human genetic material is present in the hybrid children of the two species, "it will be an Oankali species" (Butler, *Lilith's* 433), and "[it] will grow and divide as Oankali always have, and it will call itself Oankali ... and the Humans will be extinct, just as they believe ... They will only be ... something we consumed" (422–23; ellipses in original).

Oankali remain Oankali, even when utterly transfigured – as when so-called "trade partner" species are devoured. Indeed, the Oankali are in fact slowly cannibalizing not just humanity but the entire planet to build another living starship, at which point (some three hundred years in the trilogy's future) they will leave Earth a lifeless debris field as they set off in search of new "trade partners":

> It was not only the descendants of humans and Oankali who would eventually travel through space, in newly mature ships. It was also much of the substance of Earth. And what was left behind would be less than the corpse of a world. It would be small, cold, and as lifeless as the moon ... The salvaged Earth would finally die. (365)

The next generation of Oankali will no doubt tote a well-stocked gene bank of Earth species with them on their journey, and their own bodies will carry human genetic material to the stars, but they will ultimately remain Oankali, remain self, remain one. Slonczewski is surely correct in her assessment that the Oankali do not oppose but rather intensify humanity's most extreme "acquisitive" behaviors: "[h]umans disturb and pollute our ecosystem; the Oankali will literally consume every organic molecule of it."

If Oankali extend humanity's rapacious appetites to Brobdingnagian proportions, it is no less true that they also intensify to the point of estrangement "the very qualities that have at various times been held up as the basis for human identity and superiority," namely language, knowledge, emotion, and reason (Martini 55). This is part of the brilliance of Butler's trilogy – the Oankali "other" is at once radically different from, and uncomfortably similar to, hegemonic cultural notions of the human subject. Fluctuating between difference and similitude, alien and human, villain and benefactor, the Oankali elude taxonomic capture. When a hybrid character articulates this apparent contradiction by asking, "What are we that we can do this to whole peoples! Not predators? Not symbionts? What then?" (Butler, *Lilith's* 443), the answer must surely be that the Oankali are both, neither, and much else besides. Captors, saviors, vegans, cannibals, ecofeminists, ecophages, peaceniks, slave-masters: the Oankali occupy multiple and conflicting positions, resisting easy interpolation into any schemata of moral absolutism.

While my analysis has skewed towards a negative appraisal of the Oankali, I agree with Hammer that Butler's aliens encourage us "to think beyond the dichotomy of eating or being eaten, and further still, to contemplate new, heretofore unimaginable kinds of pleasure and fulfilment" (95). The bargain that the Oankali make with humans – hybridize or become extinct – may not be such a bad exchange after all. Their social structure is generally peaceful, they possess unparalleled intellectual and sensory capacities and are "essentially invulnerable to physical threats" (Martini 54). Humans who agree to reproduce with Oankali share in these benefits, enjoying total freedom from disease and injury, radically extended lifespans, and, as Slonczewski puts it, having easy access to "super-orgasmic" tentacle sex. Of course, these boons come at the cost not only of relinquishing any claim (however illusory) to a distinctly human subjectivity, but ultimately of extinguishing all planetary life. That the devoured Earth "would live on as single-celled animals lived on after dividing" might do little to mitigate the loss of untold billions of extinguished Earthly lives, but at least it offers the possibility of multispecies reworlding (Butler, *Lilith's* 365).

Refraining from idealizing either the phenomena of symbiosis/symbiogenesis or the Oankali themselves, *Xenogenesis* stresses that "tendencies towards subject boundary dissolution are never symmetrical and therefore cannot be innocent" (Pedersen 72), attending to Oankali–human relations in all their coercive specificity to explore the pleasures and possibilities of deconstructing boundaries between subjects while insisting that the subject "matters" as a figure to whom to hold oneself accountable. Butler's trilogy reimagines the well-worn science fiction trope of human–alien "first contact" to emphasize that subjects emerge intra-actively within the non-innocent space of the contact zone, where species entangle and "redo one another molecule by molecule" (Haraway, *Species* 217). These contact zones, as Haraway reminds us, "are difficult places of violence, injustice, and power differentials and it is precisely for that reason that sociality and responsibility are inextricably linked to them" (cited in Grebowicz and Merrick 107). *Xenogenesis*'s human and more-than-human subjects emerge in just such a zone; as Haraway argues, Lilith "fights for survival, agency, and choice on the shifting boundaries that shape the possibility of meaning" (*Primate* 379), enmeshed in a zone of "abject disempowerment, rape, and an overall lack of consent in establishing the terms of the interspecies encounter" (Martini 58). In this way Butler's narrative "forces us to face the subject – that overdetermined and ever-changing entity, structured by cultural inscription – while it refuses to allow us the solace of belief in a stable self" defined in juxtaposition to the other (Vint 76).

Xenogenesis's ambivalent narrative of interspecies entanglement articulates a subject that is always-already multiple, always-already in flux, emerging not autopoetically but only ever in sympoesis with a host of other lives and materialities. Ethics emerges in this interaction with alterity: by refusing to either erase the subject as an ethico-political entity or romanticize symbiogenesis as a synonym for the good, Butler's narrative remains committed to an always-already insufficient utopianism that reminds us that vegan subjectivities, like any other, are necessarily messy, contradictory, and avowedly non-innocent, whatever Haraway might have us believe. The challenge is to negotiate, in shared corporeal vulnerability, our relations with various, differentially entangled and excluded subjects as we imagine otherwise and move towards more sustainable and ethical relationships with Earth others.

Notes

1. Although originally published as *Dawn* (1987), *Adulthood Rites* (1988), and *Imago* (1989), this trilogy was conceived as a single narrative and my references use the sequentially paginated omnibus edition, published as *Lilith's Brood* (2000). Like most critics, I use the trilogy's original name, *Xenogenesis*.
2. Throughout this chapter I use "sf" as an umbrella term to signal that Butler's work contains elements of both speculative fiction and science fiction.
3. "Intra-action," a neologism coined by Barad, complicates "interaction's" presumption of the prior existence of independent entities, emphasizing instead that phenomena emerge and become determinate only through the process of relating (815).
4. Bollinger argues that the action of the *Xenogenesis* trilogy "depends upon symbiosis, not symbiogenesis, with the novels centring on the power dynamics between humans and the more-advanced Oankali rather than on the act of incorporating the organelle as a separate lifeform" (42). While the narrative does not center on the act of incorporating the intracellular organelle and the first novel indeed focuses on humans and Oankali as discrete entities, the following two thirds of the trilogy tell the story of the hybrid offspring of the first's main characters. That the bulk of *Xenogenesis*'s narrative is related by hybrid characters who are the first generation of new species born of symbiogenesis to me suggests that symbiogenesis does in fact play a significant role in the trilogy.
5. Parasecoli is not referring to Butler's work here, but is discussing Samuel Delany's *Stars in My Pocket Like Grains of Sand*, another sf text written by a Black author and published just prior to *Xenogenesis*; however, the insight is just as salient to Butler's Oankali as it is to Delany's many-tongued Evelmi. Taste-based epistemologies crop up in several different species in Delany's *Stars*: in another scene a being resembling a giant sentient jellyfish offers some of "its" own flesh to the novel's human protagonist, "if you're hungry, I'd be highly complimented if you'd eat some of me. Indeed, if there's any of you you can spare, body, hair, nail parings, dried skin..?" (69). For Parasecoli, Delany's narrative understands "cannibalism as a sort of gift exchange between races" (81).
6. Haraway argues that "Octavia Butler is a very frustrating writer in some ways, because she constantly reproduces heterosexuality even in her poly-gendered species" (cited in Grebowicz and Merrick 171 n8). Like all of Butler's novels, *Xenogenesis* presents a relentlessly heterosexual future. As Haraway points out, "heterosexuality remains unquestioned, if more complexly mediated. The different social subjects, the different genders that could emerge from another embodiment of resistance to compulsory heterosexual reproductive politics, do not inhabit this *Dawn*" (*Simians* 229). Slonczewski elaborates, "Nowhere is there a role for non-procreative forms of sexuality, such as gay or lesbian relationships. While Butler's characters occasionally take a critical view of homophobia, it is interesting that the Oankali "third sex," the ooloi, always takes a male form to seduce a female human, but a female form to seduce a male human" (Slonczewski). The utter lack of LGBT characters in *Xenogenesis* might even be understood as a kind of queer genocide: perhaps the Oankali have simply opted not to resuscitate any gay, lesbian, or trans humans as part of their project of erasing any kind of sexual partnership that is not at least potentially reproductive.

Works Cited

Ahuja, Neel. "Intimate Atmospheres: Queer Theory in a Time of Extinctions." *GLQ: A Journal of Lesbian and Gay Studies*, vol. 21, no. 2–3, 2015, pp. 365–85.

Alaimo, Stacy. *Bodily Natures: Science, Environment, and the Material Self*. Indiana UP, 2010.

—. "'Skin Dreaming': The Bodily Transgressions of Fielding Burke, Octavia Butler, and Linda Hogan." *Ecofeminist Literary Criticism: Theory, Interpretation, Pedagogy*, edited by Greta Gaard and Patrick Murphy, U of Illinois P, 1998, pp. 123–38.

Alonso, Irene Sanz. "Redefining Humanity in Science Fiction: The Alien from an Ecofeminist Perspective." Unpublished PhD Dissertation, Universidad de Alcalá, Madrid, 2013.

Barad, Karen. "Posthumanist Performativity: Toward an Understanding of How Matter Comes to Matter." *Signs: Journal of Women in Culture and Society*, vol. 28, no. 33, 2003 pp. 801–31.

Bollinger, Lauren. "Containing Multitudes: Revisiting the Infection Metaphor in Science Fiction." *Extrapolation*, vol. 50, no. 3, 2009, pp. 377–99.

—. "Symbiogenesis, Selfhood, and Science Fiction." *Science Fiction Studies*, vol. 3, no.1, 2010, pp. 34–53.

Bonner, Frances. "Desire and Difference, Slavery and Seduction: Octavia Butler's *Xenogenesis*." *Foundation*, vol. 48, no. 1, 1990, pp. 50–62.

Braidotti, Rosi. *The Posthuman*. Polity Press, 2013.

Butler, Octavia. *Clay's Ark*. Warner, 1996.

—. *Fledgling*. Seven Stories, 2005.

—. *Lilith's Brood*. 1987–1989. Hachette, 2000.

—. *Mind of My Mind*. Avon, 1978.

—. *Wild Seed*. Timescape, 1980.

Crist, Elaine, and Alfred Tauber. "Selfhood, Immunity, and the Biological Imagination: The Thought of Frank Macfarlane Burnet." *Biology and Philosophy*, vol. 15, no. 4, 2000, pp. 510–20.

Delany, Samuel. *Stars in My Pockets Like Grains of Sand*. Bantam, 1984.

van Dooren, Thom, and Deborah Bird Rose. "Lively Ethnography: Storying Animist Worlds." *Environmental Humanities, Voices from the Anthropocene*, edited by Serpil Oppermann and Serenella Iovino, Rowman and Littlefield, 2017, pp. 255–71.

Dowdall, Lisa. "Treasured Strangers: Race, Biopolitics, and the Human in Octavia E. Butler's *Xenogenesis*." *Science Fiction Studies*, vol. 44, no. 3, 2017, pp. 506–25.

Ferreira, Maria Aline. "Symbiotic Bodies and Evolutionary Tropes in the Work of Octavia Butler." *Science Fiction Studies*, vol. 37, no. 3, 2010, pp. 401–15.

Giraud, Eva. "Veganism as Affirmative Biopolitics: Moving Towards A Posthumanist Ethics?" *PhaenEx*, vol. 8, no, 2, 2013, pp. 47–79.

Grebowicz, Margret, and Helen Merrick. *Beyond the Cyborg: Adventures with Donna Haraway*. Columbia UP, 2013.

Grewe-Volpp, Christa. "Octavia Butler and the Nature/Culture Divide, An Ecofeminist Approach to the *Xenogenesis* Trilogy." *Restoring the Connection to the Natural World: Essays on the African American Environmental Imagination*, edited by Sylvia Mayer, LIT Press, 2003, pp. 149–74.

Hammer, Stephanie. "Watching the Forbidden Feast, Monstrous Appetites, Secret Meals and Spectorial Pleasures in Cocteau, Rice and Butler." *Food of the Gods: Eating and the Eaten in Science Fiction and Fantasy*, edited by George Slusser, U of Georgia P, 1996, pp. 86–96.

Haraway, Donna. *Primate Visions*. Routledge, 1989.

—. *Simians, Cyborgs, and Women: The Reinvention of Nature*. Routledge, 1991.

—. *Staying with the Trouble: Making Kin in the Chthulucene*. Duke UP, 2016.

— "Symbiogenesis, Sympoesis, and Art Science Activisms for Staying With the Trouble." *Arts of Living on a Damaged Planet: Ghosts and Monsters of the Anthropocene*, edited by Anna Tsing, Heather Swanson, Elaine Gan, and Nils Bubandt, U of Minnesota P, 2017, pp. 25–50.
—. *When Species Meet*. Minnesota UP, 2008.
Harper, A. Breeze. "The Absence of Meat in Oankali Dietary Philosophy, An Eco-Feminist Vegan Analysis of Octavia Butler's *Dawn*." *The Black Imagination, Science Fiction and Futurism*, edited by S. Jackson and J. Moody-Freeman, Peter Lang Press, 2011, pp. 111-29.
Hird, M. J. *The Origins of Sociable Life: Evolution after Science Studies*. Palgrave Macmillan, 2009.
Idema, Tom. "Species Encounters: O. Butler Meets Haraway Meets Deleuze and Guattari." *Narrating Life – Experiments with Human and Animal Bodies in Literature, Science and Art*, edited by Stefan Herbrechter and Elisabeth Friis, Brill, Rodopi, 2016, pp. 55–72.
Landecker, Hannah. "Food as Exposure: Nutritional Epigenetics and the New Metabolism." *BioSocieties*, vol. 6, no. 2, 2011, pp. 167–94.
—. "Metabolism, Reproduction, and the Aftermath of Categories." *Scholar & Feminist Online*, vol. 11, no. 3, 2013, pp. 1–10.
Magnone, Sophia. "Microbial Zoopoetics in Octavia Butler's *Clay's Ark*." *Humanimalia*, vol. 7, no. 2, 2016, pp. 109–30.
Margulis, Lynn. "The Origin of Mitosing Cells." *Journal of Theoretical Biology*, vol. 14, no. 3, 1967, pp. 225–74.
—. "Power to the Protoctists." *Dazzle Gradually, Reflections on the Nature of Nature*, edited by Lynn Margulis and Dorian Sagan, Chelsea Green Publishing, 2007, pp. 29–36.
—. "Symbiogenesis and Symbionticism." *Symbiosis as a Source of Evolutionary Innovation, Speciation and Morphogenesis*, edited by Lynn Margulis and Rene Fester, MIT Press, 1991, pp. 1–14.
Margulis, Lynn, and Dorian Sagan. *Acquiring Genomes: A Theory of the Origins of Species*. Basic Books, 2002.
Martini, Chandra. "Alien Others, Speculative Hybrids in Imaginary Worlds." Unpublished MA Thesis, McGill University, Canada, 2009.
Mayr, Ernst. "Introduction." *Acquiring Genomes: A Theory of the Origins of Species*, edited by Lynn Margulis and Dorian Sagan, Basic Books, 2002.
Melzer, Patricia. *Alien Constructions: Science Fiction and Feminist Thought*. U of Texas P, 2006.
Peppers, Cathy. "Dialogic Origins and Alien Identities in Butler's *Xenogenesis*." *Science Fiction Studies*, vol. 22 no. 1, 1995, pp. 47–62.
Pak, Chris. "'Then Came Pantropy': Grotesque Bodies, Multispecies Flourishing, and Human-Animal Relationships in Joan Slonczewski's *A Door Into Ocean*." *Science Fiction Studies*, vol. 44, no. 1, 2017, pp. 122–36.
Parasecoli, Fabio. *Bite Me: Food in Popular Culture*. Berg, 2008.
Pedersen, Helena. "Release the Moths: Critical Animal Studies and the Posthumanist Impulse." *Culture, Theory and Critique*, vol. 52, no. 1, 2011, pp. 65–81.
Pick, Anat. "Turning to Animals Between Love and Law." *New Formations*, vol. 76, 2012, pp. 68–85.
Quinn, Emelia, and Benjamin Westwood. "Introduction: Thinking Through Veganism." *Thinking Veganism in Literature and Culture: Towards a Vegan Theory*, edited by Emelia Quinn and Benjamin Westwood, Palgrave Macmillan, 2018, pp. 1–24.
Sands, Peter. "Octavia Butler's Chiastic Cannibalistics." *Utopian Studies*, vol. 14, no.1, 2003, pp. 1–14.
Schell, Heather. "Outburst! A Chilling True Story About Emerging-Virus Narratives and Pandemic Social Change." *Configurations*, vol. 5, no. 1, 1997, pp. 93–133.
Schuster, Joshua. "The Vegan and the Sovereign." *Critical Perspectives on Veganism*, edited by Jodey Castricano and Rasmus R. Simonsen, Palgrave Macmillan 2016, pp. 203–23.

Simak, Clifford. "Drop Dead." *Galaxy Science Fiction*, vol. 7, no. 1, 1956, pp. 5–35.

Slonczewski, Joan. "Octavia Butler's *Xenogenesis* Trilogy: a Biologist's Response." Paper presented at *31st Annual Science Fiction Researchers' Association Conference: Science Fiction Today*, Cleveland State University, 30 June. Kenyon College Department of Biology, 2000. <http://biology.kenyon.edu/slonc/books/butler1.html>

St Clair, Margaret. "Foreword." *To Serve Man: A Cookbook for People*, by K. Würf. Wildside Press, 1999, pp. 1–14.

Stein, Rachel. "Gene Trading and Organ Theft." *New Perspectives on Environmental Justice*, edited by Rachel Stein, Rutgers UP, 2004, pp. 209–24.

Tsing, Anna. *The Mushroom at the End of the World: On the Possibility of Life in Capitalist Ruins*. Princeton UP, 2015.

Vint, Sherryl. *Bodies of Tomorrow: Technology, Subjectivity, Science Fiction*. U of Toronto P, 2007.

Wolmark, Jenny. *Aliens and Others*. Harvester Wheatsheaf, 1993.

Part III

Textual Histories and Contexts

22

ANCIENT SCRIPTURE

Ancient Sacred Writings and Anymal Liberation

Lisa Kemmerer

Introduction

SACRED BOOKS ARE not only the oldest writings known to humanity but also among the most translated and well-read texts in the world – their importance must never be overlooked in the world of literature, particularly where ethics are concerned. This is no less true of anymal ethics,[1] including the ethics of diet. While one can certainly find scriptures that justify the exploitation of anymals, the sacred texts of the five largest world religions – two that emerged in what is now India (Hindu and Buddhist traditions) and three that began in the Middle East (Judaism, Christianity, and Islam) – reveal remarkably strong moral teachings against anymal exploitation and slaughter, requiring overt kindness, service, and caretaking of/respect for anymals and the Earth.[2] This chapter provides a survey of the core anymal ethics found in these five traditions in order to demonstrate the ancient literary antecedents pre-dating contemporary vegan philosophies and identities.

Hindu Traditions

For thousands of years, worship in India's Indus Valley revolved around nature, as recorded in the Vedas, which were "composed and handed down orally over a period of about 10 centuries" (roughly the fifteenth to fifth centuries BCE ["Vedic"]).[3] The earliest surviving hymns from these sacred texts of the Hindu religious tradition, contained in the *Rig Veda* (in their current form sometime before 1000 BCE), "express a sense of the vastness and brilliance of nature" (Embree, *Sources* 7). These writings require that the faithful protect both the "two legged and four legged," providing water and food for any creatures in need (Subramuniyaswami 204). The later *Yajur Veda* also speaks on behalf of "God's creatures, whether they are human [or] animal," warning that no life is expendable (204). In light of the environmental implications of modern anymal agriculture, those who hold nature sacred and live in a place where they are able to choose vegan must do so given that there is no industry – no force of any kind – as destructive to the natural world (and anymals) as the anymal food industries, including fish, dairy, and eggs (see Kemmerer, *Eating* 54–2, 51–83).

The *Upanishads* (700–500 BCE), the final and much-revered philosophical texts that close the Vedas, "speculate on the nature of the universe and humanity's relation to it" ("Vedic"). Reincarnation is first indicated in the *Upanishads*, carrying with it a sense of oneness through endless rebirths. Across incalculable ages, each *atman* (soul) has moved from birth to birth, from body to body, dwelling in innumerable individuals of every species. In this view, our present existence is "an infinitesimal part of a much larger picture that encompasses all of life" (Kinsley 64).

The *Upanishads* also teach that each being shares a common source and therefore carries "something of the divine" (Coomaraswamy and Nivedita 15–16). As a goldsmith fashions many ornaments from gold, the Great Goldsmith "makes many ornaments – different souls – out of the one Universal Spirit" (Subramuniyaswami 89). As all rivers join one great sea, which again rises into the atmosphere to become individual drops, so all living beings – whatever form they might take – are united through this shared source or "subtle essence" (Müller, *Chandogya* 102). The *Upanishads* honor all that exists as indistinct from Brahman, the Eternal, the All, "God." And so the *Svetasvatara Upanishad* praises Brahman, the Source, the ALL as indwelling on Earth: "Thou art the dark-blue bee, thou art the green parrot with red eyes, thou art the thunder-cloud, the seasons, the seas" (Müller, "Fourth Adhyana"). As with reincarnation, indwelling Brahman/*atman* links each creature to every other creature. Each being *is* none other than "the One that lies behind all" (Zaehner 7) so that all others are indwelling and each exists also "in the heart of all beings" (Mascaro, *Bhagavad* 71–72). In the *Bhagavad Gita*, the most famous portion of the *Mahabharata* (a sacred Hindu epic composed between 400 BCE and CE 400), the divine asserts, "I am the life of all living beings," "All beings have their rest in me" and "In all living beings I am the light of consciousness" (Mascaro, *Bhagavad* 74, 80, 86). The *Bhagavad Gita* indicates that an advanced spiritual practitioner "treats a cow, an elephant, a dog, and an outcaste" with the same high regard because *God is all*, and *true* devotees find "in all creation the presence of God" (Dwivedi 5). Those who respect Brahman must have "love for all creation" (Mascaro, *Bhagavad* 30). This is no less true for those shunned as outcastes than it is for cows mistreated in the dairy industry.

In the Hindu spiritual understanding, reincarnation is determined by karma. *Karma* means "action," and actions determine the next life: we create our future lives through how we behave in this life (Curtin, "Making" 71). Karma is a force of justice whereby every act carries "an inevitable result" (Embree, *Hindu* 51). Karma is as sure as gravity, and we reap precisely what we sow.

Further, *Ahimsa* or "not to harm" carries an injunction for "non-injury toward all living beings" (Jacobsen 287), demands "compassion for all living beings" (Long 99), and is "the first and foremost ethical principle of every Hindu" (Subramuniyaswami 195). *Ahimsa* is usually translated as "non-violence," but *ahimsa* is much more than this, it "is the absence of even a desire to do harm to any living being, in thought, word, or deed" (Long 97). The Hindu *Shastras* (texts that expound on Hindu philosophy and practice) explain that *ahimsa* requires doing what "is good for all creatures" (O'Flaherty 124). *Ahimsa* requires that we avoid even the accidental killing of other entities (Basham 59).

Even if other species are not recognized as kin, Indian texts note that choosing to consume flesh is cruel. The *Manu Smriti* (*Laws of Manu*, Shastra texts dated at about 100 BCE), one of the oldest and most important Hindu law texts, warns that one "who kills an animal for meat will die of a violent death as many times as there are hairs on that killed animal" (Dwivedi 7). In the *Mahabharata*, the deity Brhaspati encourages devotees to recognize all beings as like ourselves and treat them accordingly (Chapple, "Ahimsa" 113). Instructing the great warrior-sage Bhishma about karma, *ahimsa*, and abstaining from flesh, the divine states:

> 26. Meat is not born of grass, wood, or rock.
> Meat arises from killing a living being.
> Thus, in the enjoyment of meat there is fault . . .
> 29. If there were no meat-eaters,
> there would be no killers.
> A meat-eating man is a killer indeed,
> causing death for the purpose of food.
> 30. If meat were considered not to be food,
> there would be no violence.
> Violence is done to animals
> for the sake of the meat-eater only.
> 31. Because the life of violent ones
> is shortened as well (due to their deeds),
> the one who wishes long life for himself
> should refuse meat. (Chapple, "Ahimsa" 118–19)

Importantly, this passage implicates not only those who kill, but those who cause others to kill. In Hindu ethics, the consumer who orders, buys, or eats flesh is no less guilty than the butcher:

> The purchaser of flesh performs *himsa* (violence) by his wealth; he who eats flesh does so by enjoying its taste; the killer does *himsa* by actually tying and killing the animal. Thus, there are three forms of killing: he who brings flesh or sends for it, he who cuts off the limbs of an animal, and he who purchases, sells or cooks flesh and eats it – all of these are to be considered meat-eaters. (Subramuniyaswami 205)

Indeed, the "act of the butcher begins with the desire of the consumer," and avoiding flesh is "a way to live with a minimum of hurt to other beings" – a core moral requirement of *ahimsa*. Consuming mammals, "fish, fowl, or eggs is to participate indirectly in acts of cruelty and violence" (201).

While Hindus have rejected eggs and flesh for centuries, they have traditionally consumed dairy products. This makes sense in traditional communities, where milk was shared without harm to mother or calf. But contemporary dairy industries are among the cruelest of anymal industries. Dairy producers repeatedly impregnate cows, usually for up to five years, to cause cows to lactate, and then take newborns (from the womb to the slaughterhouse) so the mothers can be milked. The mothers are also sent to slaughter in their youth after about five years of exploitation (though cows at sanctuaries live for up to twenty-five years). Because of the cruelty of contemporary dairy production, the practice of *ahimsa* – not to harm – now requires abstinence from dairy products, as evidenced by the many Hindus who are vegans.[4]

Rooted in ancient still-sacred texts that teach of Brahman, reincarnation, karma, and *ahimsa*, Hindu religious traditions teach compassion for *all* fellow beings (Nelson 67), that "wanton killing of animals is little better than murder, and meat eating is little better than cannibalism" (Basham 58). Extending this line of reasoning, consuming dairy and eggs would be little better than forcefully acquiring and consuming human lactations and reproductive eggs. In light of reincarnation, eating anymals is "like eating the flesh of one's own son" (Chapple "Ahimsa" 114), and refusing flesh "is considered both appropriate conduct and one's *dharma*," or sacred duty (Dwivedi 7), and again, this is no less true of dairy and eggs. The "wise ones, who regard the life of [anymals] as their own breath," abstain from all anymal products (Chapple, "Ahimsa" 117).

Buddhist Traditions

Buddhism, commonly divided into Theravada and Mahayana branches, emerged in what is now Northern India. At least some Buddhist texts were composed soon after the Buddha's death (which was in the fifth century BCE), and were written starting around the first century BCE. The earliest Buddhist canon, the *Tripitaka*, was not established until the fifth century CE (Veidlinger).

Buddhism assumed much of the dominant philosophy of the region, including reverence for nature, reincarnation, karma, oneness, and the core moral ideal of *ahimsa*. Both ancient and modern Buddhist literature reveals "delight in the wooded and mountain heights" and in the wild anymals who share these secluded dwellings (Burtt 73). The Pali Canon (Theragata and Therigata) contains a series of poems called "Psalms of the Brethren and Sisters" (or Hymns of the Elders), composed by monks and nuns in the first century BCE, many of which celebrate the beauty of nature, and the spiritual strength of remote regions:

> Free from the crowds of citizens below,
> But thronged with flocks of many winged things,
> The home of herding creatures of the wild . . .
> Crags where clear waters lie, a rocky world,
> Haunted by black-faced apes and timid deer,
> Where 'neath bright blossoms run the silver streams:
> Such are the braes wherein my soul delights. (Burtt 75–76)

For centuries Buddhist practitioners tended to live far from bustling population centers (Fung 65), choosing a simple and more nature-centered life along the path of spiritual growth. A Chinese Buddhist poem, perhaps written by the poet Hanshan, whose name means "Cold Mountain" and who lived sometime before the ninth century, offers a vision of nature as providing a path beyond the material into the spiritual:

> I climb up the Way to Cold Mountain,
> But the Cold Mountain road is endless:
> Long valleys of boulders stacked stone upon stone,
> Broad streams thick with dense undergrowth.
> The mosses are slippery, though there's been no rain;
> Pines cry out, but it's not the wind.
> Who can get beyond worldly attachments
> And sit with me among the white clouds? (Sommer 167)

The great Japanese Zen Buddhist, Dogen (1200–1253), found in nature the *essence* of enlightenment, and that spiritual ideas themselves are "the entire universe, mountains and rivers, and the great wide earth, plants and trees" (Curtin, "Dogen" 198; Swearer 15). Reverence for nature provides a point of alignment between a vegan diet and Buddhist teachings, given that anymal industries and industrialized fishing are the number one causes of the most serious environmental concerns we now face.[5]

The regional philosophies of reincarnation and karma shape Buddhist ethics, which is to say, there is no hard line between human beings and other beings. *Jataka* tales (or "birth stories") teach ethics by recalling the previous lives of the Buddha, usually in anymal form, whether jackal, snake, swan, quail, horse, goose, tortoise, boar, cuckoo, pigeon, woodpecker, chameleon, chicken, human, mongoose, mosquito, otter, shrew, beetle, or osprey – seventy different species (Chapple, "Animals" 134, 145–46). These pre-Buddha anymals exhibit "compassionate and often heroic self-giving" for "the benefit of all living beings" (Martin 97, 98) and in each case "set an example" for human ethics (Chapple, "Animals" 135, 144). Just after his final birth, the Buddha announced: "For enlightenment I was born, for the good of all that lives" (Conze 36). Afterwards, he is asked to teach – not just for the sake of humanity, but in order to "rescue also the other living beings who have sunk so deep into suffering" (52). The *Abhidharmakosha* (fourth or fifth century, written by the monk Vasubandhu) tells of an enlightened practitioner, begging for food, who visited a home where he finds a mother holding a small child on her lap and eating fish curry, pausing to beat an unfortunate dog. Through his "power of intuitive knowledge," he is able to see "the relationship between all four of them in their previous lives," and laments that, in her ignorance, she is "Eating the flesh of her father, / Beating her mother's back,/ And nursing her enemy on her lap" (Tashi).

The highest spiritual goal (nirvana) can only be gained by avoiding harm to living beings (Mascaro, *Dhammapada* 68) and *ahimsa* "is an ethical goal" for every Buddhist (Shinn 219) – no creature lies beyond the scope of human ethics (Martin 99; Waldau, *Specter* 123). The *Dhammapada* (part of the canon attributed to the Buddha, and therefore of utmost importance) states:

> All beings tremble before danger, all fear death. When a man considers this, he does not kill or cause to kill.
> All beings fear before danger, life is dear to all. When a man considers this, he does not kill or cause to kill. (Mascaro, *Dhammapada* 54)

The canonical *Dhammika* instructs, "Let him not kill, nor cause to be killed any living being, nor let him approve of others killing" (Fausböll 66).

Bodhisattvas (Mahayana traditions) gain enlightenment, but instead of moving into nirvana, they return to be born again (and again and again), taking on an embodied existence to help save all creatures from the suffering that is inherent in the process of life, death, and rebirth. *Bodhisattavas* exemplify *ahimsa* (de Bary 81–82; Conze 30):

> A Bodhisattva resolves: . . . At all costs I must bear the burdens of all beings . . . I have made the vow to save all beings. All beings I must set free. The whole world of living beings I must rescue from the terrors of birth, of old age, of sickness, of death and rebirth, of all kinds of moral offence, of all states of woe, of the whole

cycle of birth and-death . . . from all these terrors I must rescue all beings . . . I must rescue all these beings from the stream of Samsara, which is so difficult to cross; I must pull them back from the great precipice, I must free them from all calamities, I must ferry them across the stream of Samsara. I myself must grapple with the whole mass of suffering of all beings. (Burtt 133)

Bodhisattvas, "desirous of cultivating the virtue of love, should not eat meat" (*Lankavatara Sutra*, de Bary 92). Moreover, the fourth-century *Lankavatara Sutra* (Mahayana) indicates that among his disciples, the Buddha forbade flesh altogether, and as with the Hindu tradition, those who eat flesh are as guilty of killing as those who wield the knife:

It is not true . . . that meat is right and proper for the disciple when the animal was not killed by himself or by his orders, and when it was not killed specially for him . . . Pressed by a desire for the taste of meat people may string together their sophistries in defense of meat-eating . . . and declare that the Lord permitted meat as legitimate food, that it occurs in the list of permitted foods, and that he himself ate it. But . . . it is nowhere allowed in the sutras as a . . . legitimate food . . . All meat-eating in any form or manner and in any circumstance is prohibited, unconditionally and once and for all. (*Lankavatara Sutra*, qtd. in de Bary 92)

If compassion is what motivates abstinence from flesh, then abstinence from dairy and eggs purchased in industrialized societies is now just as important given that these industries have been exposed for brazen indifference to the wellbeing and lives of anymals.

Jewish Traditions

The Tanakh, or Hebrew Bible,[6] was established in the first century CE, with at least some portions composed more than a thousand years earlier (Lim). These writings provide core Jewish ethics and philosophy and are also important to Christian and Islamic traditions: "Christianity inherits from Judaism, and Islam inherits from both Judaism and Christianity," such that the three "form one linked textual tradition" ("Faith Books").

The Tanakh teaches Jews to worship a single deity who created all that exists, is the sole proprietor, and remains invested in all that has been made: The "heavens to their uttermost reaches belong to the LORD your God, the earth and all that is on it!" (Deut. 10:14). In Psalms 50, God declares:

For every animal of the forest is mine,
the cattle on a thousand hills.
I know every bird of the hills,
the creatures of the field are mine. (10–11)

According to Genesis, the first book of the Hebrew Bible, God declares creation to be "good" six times before humans are created (Gen. 1: 4, 10, 12, 18, 21, and 25) and scriptures instruct the faithful to find "God in and through" nature (Cobb 506–07) – the

Jewish deity manifests in a burning bush and a whirlwind (Exod. 3:2; Job 38:1, 40:6), and speaks through a laboring burro (Num. 22:28).

The Tanakh depicts a God who remains personally invested in creation and who indicates that anymals are "to be respected, loved, and helped to attain their purpose according to God's will" (Hirsch). Rabbi Sherira Gaon of the tenth century wrote that anymals were created so that "good should be done to them" (Kalechofsky 95) and *Midrash Tehillim* (eleventh century or earlier), in the words of Rabbi Tanhum b. Hiyya, indicates that the "falling of rain is greater than the giving of the Law, for the giving of the Law was a joy only to Israel, while the falling of rain is a rejoicing for all the world, including the cattle and the wild beasts and the birds" (Schochet 146).

The covenant of Genesis 9 expresses God's concern for anymals and their habitat. Seven times scriptures note that the divine covenant is between God and "all the living creatures which are with you for all future generations" – between the Creator "and the earth" (Gen. 9:13). Jewish compositions such as this one repeatedly remind humanity that we are "not distinguished from other forms of life but [are] identified with them" (Hiebert 139). Ecclesiastes (Tanakh) also tells humans to "face the fact" that we "are beasts" (Eccles. 3:18). If we see animals as lowly and lesser, so much the worse for us.

Chapters 1 and 2 of Genesis are particularly important with regard to human relations with the rest of creation because they provide the only account of what God intended for creation before it was sullied by disobedience (the fall of Genesis 3) and ensuing human violence (Gen. 6:11–13). We are given a vegan dominion which "does not include the right to kill animals for food" (Allen 1:132) in God's stead. If we are to rule in the image of God – for and on behalf of God – then compassion and mercy ought to guide us.

> The LORD is gracious and compassionate,
> slow to anger and abounding in kindness.
> The LORD is good to all,
> and his mercy is on all his works. (Ps. 145:8–9)

Humans are *expected* to be compassionate, to work to secure the wellbeing of anymals (Schochet 144): "As God is compassionate . . . so you should be compassionate" (Schwartz 16). Critically, God gives all living creatures a vegan diet:

> God said, "See, I give you every seed-bearing plant that is upon the face of all the earth, and every tree that has seed-bearing fruit. They will be yours for food. And to all the beasts of the earth, all the birds of the air, and all the creatures that creep on earth – everything that has the breath of life – I give all the green plant for food." And it was so. And God saw all that he had made, and it was very good. (Gen. 1:29–31)

Genesis 1 shows a divine preference for a world without bloodshed, without fear and suffering, without predators and prey. Jewish sacred literature indicates that a vegan diet represents "the high ideal of God . . . an ultimate goal toward which all people should strive" (Schwartz 13).

This is supported by an ethic of compassion. The creatures of the earth are God's, they are good, and they are due human kindness –"compassion toward animals is an important theme of the Hebrew Bible" (Berman 3) and mercy towards anymals is central to the Jewish moral life (Cohn-Sherbok 83). Leviticus states simply, "Love your fellow as yourself " (19:18) and "fellow" has been an expanding concept for centuries such that this once narrow term (referring largely to one's religious community) has moved from fellow/neighbor Jew to fellow/neighbor race or nation, to fellow/neighbor human beings, and now expands to anymals – fellow living creatures.

Additionally, "*tsa'ar ba'alei chayim*," a biblical mandate not to cause "pain to any living creature" (Schwartz 15), also protect anymals. The *Shulchan Aruch* (*Code of Jewish Law*) states: "It is forbidden, according to the law of the Torah, to inflict pain upon any living creature" (Cohn-Sherbok 83; Ganzfried 84; Schwartz 19). Moreover, how we treat anymals is important – "punishment and absolution are clearly contingent upon compassion toward animals" (Schochet 165) – and God not only created a peaceful world, but scriptures describe the ideal future, the peaceful, vegan world that lies ahead, where

> The wolf shall dwell with the lamb,
> the leopard shall lie down with the kid,
> the calf and the lion and the fatling together, and a little child will herd them.
> The cow and the bear shall graze,
> their young will lie down together,
> and the lion, like the ox, shall eat straw.
> The nursing child shall play
> over the hole of the cobra,
> and the weaned child shall put his hand
> into the viper's nest.
> They will not hurt or destroy
> on all my holy mountain
> for all the earth shall be filled with the knowledge of YHWH [God]
> as the waters cover the sea. (Isa. 11:6–9)

Christian Traditions

Christians refer to the Hebrew Bible as the Old Testament. While Christian versions are different in a few important ways (sometimes including additional books, placed in a different order with different emphasis and punctuation, and frequently translated and interpreted in ways that diverge from Jewish tradition ["Bible Basics"]), the Christian text is the same where core philosophy and ethics are concerned. For example, the Hebrew Bible carries over teachings of nature as the sacred creation of a fully invested Creator who established a non-violent, vegan world in which "no creature was to feed on another" (Hyland 21). Furthermore, as with the Jewish traditions, humans are placed on the planet to respect and care-take creation (Genesis 2), which is expected to return to a Peaceable Kingdom – "on earth as it is in heaven" (Matt. 6:10).

The Christian tradition added the New Testament,[7] of which the first four books, collectively referred to as the Gospels, are particularly important, with stories of the life of Jesus and teachings attributed to Jesus. These books were composed in the first century CE, but were written and rewritten across time; only a few of many gospels were chosen for the New Testament. The canon of the New Testament was not set until sometime late in the first half of the first millennium ("History of The Bible").

Consistent with Genesis 3, the Gospels teach human beings to love God by living a humble life of service amid creation. In the Gospels, words attributed to Jesus teach of self-sacrificing service and humility: "Whoever wants to be first must be last of all and servant of all" (Mark 9:35) and "Whoever wishes to become great among you must be your servant, and whoever wishes to be first among you must be slave of all. For the Son of Man came not to be served but to serve, and to give his life a ransom for many" (Mark 9:35, 10:42–45). Christians are called to protect and serve creation, especially the downtrodden – "the least of these" (Matt. 25:40).

In light of climate change, vivisection, deforestation, species extinction, and factory farming, theologians such as Sallie McFague have argued that the imperative to assist the downtrodden must be "extended to nature: nature is the 'new poor'" (30). Professor of New Testament Studies at Temple Baptist Seminary, Richard Alan Young, argues that the "God who led the Israelites out of oppression and bondage in Egypt is the Creator God who is concerned with leading all creatures out of oppression, injustice, and bondage" (143). Not just furry, large-eyed anymals – the charismatic megafauna of contemporary environmentalism – but all who are endangered, distraught, exploited, or neglected, including chickens and fishes.

Jesus taught, "Blessed are the meek, for they shall inherit the earth" (Matt. 5:5). Ancient Christian texts teach that the Christian life should stand as "witness to Christ's love, compassion, and peace" (Kaufman and Braun 48). Jesus also teaches, "Be merciful just as your Father is merciful" (Luke 6:36) and "Blessed are the merciful, for they will receive mercy" (Matt. 5:7). As we require God's mercy, so anymals require our mercy.[8]

Christian traditions promote peace with *all* creatures and ask that we work our way back to the peaceful paradise created by God (Murti 31, 100). The gospels quote Jesus as saying "Blessed are the peacemakers" (Matt. 5:9) and scriptures teach that a "harvest of righteousness is sown in peace for those who make peace" (James 3:17–18). *The Lord's Prayer* (Gospels), believed to be spoken by Jesus, instructs the faithful to pray, "Your kingdom come. / Your will be done, on earth as it is in heaven" (Matt. 6:10), anticipating God's promised return of peace (Tanakh/Hebrew Bible) to Earth. Importantly, Christians are obligated to help bring about the Peaceable Kingdom (Buttrick 7:312), to participate in the "final triumph of God's will" (Allen 8:115): The fulfillment of God's plan can and will happen on this very earth through the "work of all who believe in Jesus Christ and his kingdom" (Buttrick 5:250–51).

Perhaps most important to Christian traditions, the "fruit of the Spirit is love" (Gal. 5:22–23). Scriptures reveal Jesus as exemplifying love and calling Christians to do the same. In 1 John 4:8 and 1 John 4:16 it is simply stated: "God is love." Here love is not merely an attribute, but love defines God's nature where "God's nature is not exhausted by the quality of love, but love governs all its aspects and expressions" (Buttrick 12:280). Love is "the paramount scripture . . . essential to the Christian way of life" (Allen 12:214). Sensitivity to suffering is often understood to indicate fidelity to a compassionate Creator and is understood to originate in the munificence of divine love that connects each of us with God (Allen 12:214). Echoing Genesis 2, Christian scripture encourages followers to sacrificial, Christ-like love that originates in the munificence of God's love and connects Christians back to the Creator (Allen 12:214). The *Catechism of the Catholic Church* states, "It is contrary to human dignity to cause animals to suffer or die needlessly" (2418) and we "owe" anymals "kindness" (2416).

Islamic Traditions

Islamic traditions accepted much of the Jewish and Christian canons, and added the Qur'an,[9] believed to be recited as a direct revelation from God through Muhammed, placed in a completed canon in the late seventh or eighth centuries (Qur'an). The Qur'an frequently refers to and rephrases ideas and passages from the Tanakh/Hebrew Bible and the New Testament, showing a continued tradition across Judaism, Christianity, and Islam.

Islam shares the Judeo-Christian belief that the universe is here by virtue of divine power and is "the personal creation" of Allah (Marshall 128). According to the Qur'an, "in the heavens and the earth there are signs for the faithful; in your own creation, and in the beasts that are scattered far and near, signs for true believers . . . signs for men of understanding" (45:1–8) – "Whichever way you turn there is the face of Allah" (Qur'an 2:115). Creation is inseparable from the Creator (Stoddart 42), has "intrinsic value," and is infused both with religious meaning and moral obligations (Ozdemir 21). The divine created the universe with the "breath of compassion" (Bakhtiar 16–17) and the Qur'an beseeches, "Do not defile the good earth, hallowed as it has been" (Qur'an 7:55–56). Because creation points back to Allah, it is due "watchfulness, gratefulness, and respect" (Ozdemir 21).

According to the Qur'an, Allah placed people "in dominion on the earth" (Qur'an 7:10), but being human requires "commensurate humility and sensitivity, predicated upon respect and reverence for the divine purpose in every created thing" (Said 164). The word *Islam* literally means submission – "surrender to God's law" (Esposito 69) – and humans are fundamentally "an instrument of Allah's Will" (Zaid 46–47), servants charged with vice-regency, "accountable before God" (Haq 129–30). The created world is an avenue of both sacred experience and sacred duties such that any privileges "follow and do not precede responsibilities" (Nasr 97). The relationship between humanity and Allah "is that of slaves to master"; "humankind has no rights, only duties" (Denny 8).

The Qur'an indicates that Allah is "Lord of All creatures" (Qur'an 69:28–52) and that the earth is "for all living beings" (55:10). Muhammad is the "first and surest guide for the understanding of the Qur'an" (Nasr 97) and how we ought to live: Muslims have a "beautiful model (*uswa hasana*)" in the Prophet (Foltz, *Animals* 18). *Hadith* ("Tradition"; eighth and ninth centuries CE) are the most authoritative Muslim texts after the Qur'an, and are believed to preserve stories from the life of Muhammad and his words. These texts demonstrate that Muhammad is "one of history's most influential social reformers," compassionate not only towards suffering and downtrodden people, but also towards suffering and downtrodden anymals (Berry 244–45). Muhammad "loved animals and displayed great kindness to them, and encouraged other Muslims to do likewise" (Nasr 97).

Hadith emphasize "compassion toward animals" as a religious requirement (Foltz, "Islamic" 254) and indicate that one with a heart filled with compassion and tenderness is likely to be spared on the day of judgment (Schuon 9). It is recorded that, when Muhammad was asked whether there was a heavenly reward for good deeds done for anymals, he replied that how we treat anymals is of moral and spiritual concern (Haq 150). In the *Mishkat* (a secondary source of *hadith*), the Prophet states, "If anyone wrongfully kills [even] a sparrow . . . he will face God's interrogation" (Haq 149) and that a good deed done for an anymal "is as good as doing good to a human being; while an act of cruelty to a beast is as bad as an act of cruelty to a human being" (*Mishkat al-Masabih* bk. 6, ch. 7, 8:178). *Hadith* teach that killing anymals without justification is "one of the major sins and that acts of kindness and charity to anymals will be rewarded by Allah" (Masri 46).

Al-Hafiz Basheer Ahmad Masri argues that "Islamic teachings have gone to great lengths to instill a sense of love, respect and compassion for animals" (45) such that any "act of cruelty toward animals is strongly forbidden" (Siddiq 455). The Qur'an reminds of those lost: "It is not their eyes that are blind, but their hearts" (22:46). In this way scriptures support the idea that "a true Muslim is one who honors, sustains, and protects the lives of creatures of God and does not kill them" (Foltz, *Animals* 111).

Our attitude towards anymals, and any measure of compassion we might have, ought to be expressed in our daily actions, and few daily actions are as important where compassion is concerned as our dietary choices. Moreover, killing is a grave sin for Muslims, one that can only be justified if one is in great danger (Foltz, *Animals* 93). In addition, the Qur'an forbids the consumption of blood. For all of these reasons, a vegan diet aligns directly with Islamic teachings, and of course vegan bounty was provided when Allah "laid the earth for all living creatures, with its fruits, palmtrees, and their fruiting dates, the grain in the blade and herbs of fragrance" (Qur'an 55:1–17): "We have spread out the earth and set upon it immovable mountains. We have planted it with every seasonal fruit, thus providing sustenance for man and beast" (Qur'an 15:19)

For those who choose to eat flesh, *halal* ("permissible") flesh is taken from an anymal who has been kept, tended, killed, and prepared according to strict requirements of Islamic law (Foltz, *Animals* 126). Importantly, *halal* flesh comes from an anymal that has been killed humanely (Llewellyn 233). However, in modern times undercover footage has repeatedly demonstrated that "humane" does not apply either to life or death for anymal products purchased in nations that have large factory farms, large transport trucks, or large slaughterhouses, even when ostensibly conforming to basic *halal* requirements. Contemporary Muslim scholar Tariq Ramadan writes: "Islamic teachings on respect for animal life are clear" and the way that anymals are treated in contemporary food industries "is unacceptable" (qtd. in Foltz, *Animals* 118). For Masri, the Prophet, in light of "His overwhelming concern for animal rights and their general welfare"

> would certainly have condemned (*La 'ana*) those who practice such methods, in the same way as he condemned similar other cruelties in his day. He would have declared that there is no grace or blessing (*Barakah*) – neither in the consumption of such food nor in the profits from such trades. (44)

Muslims must also eat only foods that are tayyib – wholesome, pure, nutritious and safe. But, a diet of flesh is associated with heart disease and cancers. Moreover, while "20 percent of the world's human population" – many of whom are Muslims – suffer from chronic hunger, due to the consumption of flesh, eggs, and dairy "more than half of all land under cultivation is given over to crops destined for livestock consumption" (Foltz, *Animals* 120). A diet of anymal products is inefficient and unsustainable, and "for the vast majority of Muslims . . . is not only unnecessary but is also directly responsible for causing grave ecological and social harm, as well as being less healthful" (Foltz, "Is Vegetarianism" 11). In contemporary times, out of respect for the creator, and imitating the compassion of the prophet, for those who are able, the written ethics of Islam point to a vegan diet.

Conclusion

If one asks an omnivore of faith what scriptures have to say on the topic of diet, they will likely point to certain short passages that justify their current food habits. Nonetheless, the world's largest religions provide a strong and consistent ethic of anymal protection, complete with a vegan diet, that amount to nothing short of a call for anymal liberation. Scriptures across traditions require humanity to cease the breeding of cattle, hens, turkeys, and hogs and rather than waste precious foods by cycling them through anymals, channel grains to hungry humans (Kemmerer, *Eating Earth* 9–13). Scriptures teach that the human body is "a temple of the Holy Spirit" (1 Cor. 6:19), yet a diet based on anymal products is linked with "a variety of human diseases, such as atherosclerosis, heart disease, stroke, adult-onset diabetes, various forms of cancer, and a host of other ailments, including kidney stones, osteoporosis, and obesity" (Young 105). Yet another problem, according to the Union of Concerned Scientists, is that "[s]eventy percent of all antibiotics in the United States go to healthy livestock," which contributes to "the rise of pathogens that defy antibiotics" (Kristof). Of particular relevance right now, "three out of every four new or emerging infectious diseases in people come from animals" ("Zoonotic Diseases"), including COVID-19, bird flu, swine flu, SARS, AIDS, and many other deadly viruses ("COVID-19 and Animals").

In contrast, a vegan diet takes "care of animals, the earth, and our bodies" and will also better feed those who are malnourished (Braun ix). Ancient sacred texts, so many centuries after they were composed, guide us to a better way of living – a more compassionate and sustainable path than the one most of us, particularly in wealthier nations, have grown accustomed to. This is often a surprising revelation, particularly for those living in the Western world. But on reflection, would it not be much more surprising if sacred writings justified enslaving and killing anymals for no better reason than that we prefer to eat eggs and bacon or dairy ice cream?

Notes

1. Anymal is a contraction of "any" and "animal," pronounced as "any" and "mal." "Anymal indicates all individuals who are of a species other than that of the speaker/author. In other words, if a human being uses this term, all species except *Homo sapiens* are indicated, but if a chimpanzee signs "anymal," they reference all species (including human beings) except chimpanzees. Using the term "anymal" avoids the use of: "animal" as if human beings were not animals; dualistic and alienating references such as "non" and "other"; and cumbersome terms such as nonhuman animals and other-than-human animals.
2. This chapter is indebted to my research and writing published in *Animals and World Religions*. For more on the topic at hand, including information on Chinese and indigenous traditions, please see *Animals and World Religions* (Kemmerer, 2012). Due to space constraints, this chapter is confined largely to texts from dominant branches of each religious tradition.

3. BCE and ACE (or CE) refer to before and after the common era and are synonymous with BCE and AD, but do not make reference to birth or death of Jesus out of respect for the world's diversity of faiths (and calendars).
4. See Kemmerer, *Animals and World Religions* (83–89).
5. See Kemmerer, *Eating Earth*.
6. Translations in this chapter are from the *Tanakh: The Holy Scriptures: Torah, Nevi'im, Kethuvim, The New JPS Translation* (Jewish Publication Society, 1985).
7. Translations in this chapter are from the *Holy Bible: New Revised Standard Version* (American Bible Society, 1989).
8. Anyone interested in learning more about modern anymal agriculture might wish to view undercover footage revealing what actually happens in anymal agriculture at websites like A Well-fed World <https://awellfedworld.org/factory-farms>, or simply search for any undercover clips. Only when we are blissfully ignorant of the truths of modern-day anymal agriculture is it easy to overlook the importance of compassion and mercy for anymals.
9. Translations in this chapter are from N. J. Dawood's *Qur'an*.

Works Cited

Allen, Clifton J. *Broadman Bible Commentary*. 12 vols. Broadman Press, 1971.
Bakhtiar, Laleh. *Sufi: Expressions of the Mystic Quest*. Thames and Hudson, 1987.
de Bary, William Theodore (ed.). *The Buddhist Tradition in India, China, and Japan*. Vintage, 1972.
Basham, A. L. *The Origins and Development of Classical Hinduism*. Oxford UP, 1989.
Berman, Louis A. *Vegetarianism and the Jewish Tradition*. KTAV, 1982.
Berry, Rynn. *Food for the Gods: Vegetarianism and the World's Religions*. Pythagorean, 1998.
"Bible Basics." *Bible Odyssey*. n.d. <https://www.bibleodyssey.org/en/tools/bible-basics>
Braun, Nathan. "Preface: Nathan Braun." *Good News for All Creation: Vegetarianism as Christian Stewardship*, by Stephen R Kaufman and Nathan Braun, Vegetarian Advocates Press, 2002.
Burtt, E. A. (ed.). *The Teachings of the Compassionate Buddha: Early Discourses, the Dhammapada, and Later Basic Writings*. New American Library, 1955.
Buttrick, George Arthur (ed. and trans.). *The Interpreter's Bible*. 12 vols. Abingdon, 1956.
Chapple, Christopher Key. "Ahimsa in the *Mahabharata*: A Story, a Philosophical Perspective, and an Admonishment." *Journal of Vaishnava Studies*, vol. 4, no. 3, 1996, pp. 109–25.
—. "Animals and Environment in the Buddhist Birth Stories." *Buddhism and Ecology: The Interconnection of Dharma and Deeds*, edited by Mary Evelyn Tucker and Duncan Ryuken Williams, Harvard UP, 1997, pp. 131–48.
Cobb, John B., Jr. "Christianity, Economics, and Ecology." *Christianity and Ecology: Seeking the Well-Being of Earth and Humans*, edited by Dieter T. Hessel and Rosemary Radford Ruether, Harvard UP, 2000, pp. 497–511.
Cohn-Sherbok, Dan. "Hope for the Animal Kingdom." *A Communion of Subjects: Animals in Religion, Science, and Ethics*, edited by Paul Waldau and Kimberley Patton, Columbia UP, 2006, pp. 81–90.
Conze, Edward (trans.). *Buddhist Scriptures*. Penguin, 1959.
Coomaraswamy, Ananda K., and Sister Nivedita. *Myths of the Hindus and Buddhists*. Dover, 1967.
"COVID-19 and Animals." *Centers for Disease Control and Prevention: Your Health*, updated 10 February 2021.
Curtin, Deane. "Dogen, Deep Ecology, and the Ecological Self." *Environmental Ethics*, vol. 16, 1994, pp. 195–213.

—. "Making Peace with the Earth: Indigenous Agriculture and the Green Revolution." *Environmental Ethics*, vol. 17, 1995, pp. 59–73.
Dawood, N. J. (trans.). *Qur'an*. Penguin, 1956.
Denny, Frederick M. *Islam and the Muslim Community*. HarperSanFrancisco, 1987.
Dwivedi, O. P. "Dharmic Ecology." In *Hinduism and Ecology: The Intersection of Earth, Sky, and Water*, edited by Christopher Key Chapple and Mary Evelyn Tucker, Harvard UP, 2000, pp. 3–22.
Embree, Ainslie T. (ed.). *The Hindu Tradition: Readings in Oriental Thought*. Vintage, 1972.
—. *Sources of Indian Tradition: From the Beginning to 1800*. Columbia UP, 1988.
Esposito, John L. *Islam: The Straight Path*. Oxford UP, 1988.
"Faith Books." *British Library*. n.d.
Fausböll, V. (trans.). "MettaSutta" and "Uragasutta" in "Urugavagga." *The Sutta-Nipâta, The Sacred Books of the East, Vol. 10*, translated by V. Fausböll, Clarendon Press, 1881.
Foltz, Richard C. *Animals in Islamic Tradition and Muslim Cultures*. Oneworld, 2005.
—. "Islamic Environmentalism: A Matter of Interpretation." *Islam and Ecology: A Bestowed Trust*, edited by Richard C. Foltz et al., Harvard UP, 2003, pp. 249–80.
—. "Is Vegetarianism Un-Islamic?" *Food for Thought: The Debate on Vegetarianism*, edited by Steven Sapontzis, Prometheus, 2004, pp. 209–22.
Fung, Yu-lan. *A Short History of Chinese Philosophy*. Free Press, 1948.
Ganzfried, Rabbi Solomon. *Code of Jewish Law*, bk. 4, ch. 191. Hebrew Publishing, 1961.
Haq, S. Nomanul. "Islam and Ecology: Toward Retrieval and Reconstruction." *Islam and Ecology: A Bestowed Trust*, edited by Richard C. Foltz et al., Harvard UP, 2003, pp. 121–54.
Hiebert, Theodore. "The Human Vocation: Origins and Transformations in Christian Traditions." *Christianity and Ecology: Seeking the Well-Being of Earth and Humans*, edited by Dieter T. Hessel and Rosemary Radford Ruether, Harvard UP, 2000, pp. 135–54.
Hirsch, Rabbi Samson Rafael. "Letter 4." *Nineteen Letters*. Feldheim (Elias edition), 1969.
"History of The Bible – New Testament." *History World*. n.d.
Holy Bible: New Revised Standard Version. New York: American Bible Society, 1989.
Hyland, J. R. *The Slaughter of Terrified Beasts: A Biblical Basis for the Humane Treatment of Animals*. Viatoris Ministries, 1988.
"Islamic Canon." *Abrahamic Study Hall*, n.d. <http://www.historyworld.net/wrldhis/plaintexthistories.asp?historyid=aa11>
Jacobsen, Knut. "The Institutionalization of the Ethics of 'Non-Injury' toward All 'Beings' in Ancient India." *Environmental Ethics*, vol. 16, 1994, pp. 287–301.
Kalechofsky, Roberta. "Hierarchy, Kinship, and Responsibility." *A Communion of Subjects: Animals in Religion, Science, and Ethics*, edited by Paul Waldau and Kimberley Patton, Columbia UP, 2006, pp. 91–99.
Kaufman, Stephen R., and Nathan Braun. *Good News for All Creation: Vegetarianism as Christian Stewardship*. Vegetarian Advocates Press, 2004.
Kemmerer, Lisa. *Animals and World Religions*. Oxford UP, 2012.
—. *Eating Earth: Environmental Ethics and Dietary Choice*. Oxford UP, 2014.
Kinsley, David. *Ecology and Religion: Ecological Spirituality in Cross-Cultural Perspective*. Prentice-Hall, 1995.
Kristof, Nicholas B. "Pathogens in Our Pork." *New York Times*, 14 March 2009.
Lim, Timothy. "Understanding the Emergence of the Jewish Canon." *Ancient Jew Review: Articles*. 2 December 2015.
Llewellyn, Othman Abd-ar-Rahman. "The Basis for a Discipline of Islamic Environmental Law." *Islam and Ecology: A Bestowed Trust*, edited by Richard C. Foltz et al., Harvard UP, 2003, pp. 185–248.
Long, Jeffery D. *Jainism: An Introduction*. I. B. Tauris, 2009.

McFague, Sallie. "An Ecological Christology: Does Christianity Have It?" In *Christianity and Ecology: Seeking the Well-Being of Earth and Humans*, edited by Dieter T. Hessel and Rosemary Radford Ruether, Harvard UP, 2000, pp. 29–45.

Marshall, Peter. *Nature's Web: Rethinking Our Place on Earth.* Cassell, 1992.

Martin, Rafe. "Thoughts on the Jatakas." *The Path of Compassion: Writings on Socially Engaged Buddhism*, edited by Fred Eppsteiner, Parallax, 1985, pp. 97–102.

Mascaro, Juan (trans.). *Bhagavad Gita.* Penguin, 1965.

—. *The Dhammapada: The Path of Perfection.* Penguin, 1973.

Masri, Al-Hafiz Basheer Ahmad. *Animal Welfare in Islam.* Islamic Foundation, 2007.

Müller, F. Max (trans.). *Chandogya Upanishad.* In *The Upanishads, Part I.* Dover, 1962, pp. 1–144.

—. trans. "Fourth Adhyana." *Svetâsvatara Upanishad. The Upanishads, Part II: The Sacred Books of the East*, vol. 15, 1884, Internet Sacred Texts Archive.

Murti, Vasu. "The Writings of Vasu Murti: They Shall Not Hurt or Destroy: Animal Rights and Vegetarianism in the Western Religious Traditions." *All-Creatures.org*, n.d.

Nasr, Seyyed Hossein. "Islam, the Contemporary Islamic World, and the Environmental Crisis." *Islam and Ecology: A Bestowed Trust*, edited by Richard C. Foltz et al., Harvard UP, 2003, pp. 85–106.

Nelson, Lance E. "Reading the Bhagavadgita from an Ecological Perspective." *Hinduism and Ecology: The Intersection of Earth, Sky, and Water*, edited by Christopher Key Chapple and Mary Evelyn Tucker, Harvard UP, 2000, pp. 127–64.

O'Flaherty, Wendy Doniger (ed.). *Textual Sources for the Study of Hinduism.* U of Chicago P, 1988.

Ozdemir, Ibrahim. "Toward an Understanding of Environmental Ethics from a Qur'anic Perspective." *Islam and Ecology: A Bestowed Trust*, edited by Richard C. Foltz et al., Harvard UP, 2003, pp. 3–38.

"Qur'ān." *Britannica*, n.d.

Regenstein, Lewis G. *Replenish the Earth.* Crossroad, 1991.

Said, Abdul Aziz, and Nathan C. Funk. "Peace in Islam: An Ecology of the Spirit." In *Islam and Ecology: A Bestowed Trust*, edited by Richard C. Foltz et al., Harvard UP, 2003, pp. 155–84.

Schochet, Elijah Judah. *Animal Life in Jewish Tradition: Attitudes and Relationships.* KTAV, 1984.

Schuon, Frithjof. *Sufism: Veil and Quintessence.* World Wisdom Books, 1979.

Schwartz, Richard H. *Judaism and Vegetarianism.* Lantern, 2001.

Shinn, Larry D. "The Inner Logic of Gandhian Ecology." *Hinduism and Ecology: The Intersection of Earth, Sky, and Water*, edited by Christopher Key Chapple and Mary Evelyn Tucker, Harvard UP, 2000, pp. 213–41.

Siddiq, Mohammad Yusuf. "An Ecological Journey in Muslim Bengal." *Islam and Ecology: A Bestowed Trust*, edited by Richard C. Foltz et al., Harvard UP, 2003, pp. 451–62.

Sommer, Deborah (ed.). *Chinese Religion: An Anthology of Sources.* Oxford UP, 1995.

Stoddart, William. *Sufism: The Mystical Doctrines and Methods of Islam.* Paragon Press, 1985.

Subramuniyaswami, Satguru Sivaya. *Dancing with Siva: Hinduism's Contemporary Catechism.* Himalayan Academy, 1993.

Swearer, Donald K. "The Moral Case for Saving Species: Thirteen Prominent Thinkers Explain Why Society Should Give High Priority to the Purpose of the Endangered Species Act." *Defenders*, Summer 1998, p. 15.

Tanakh: The Holy Scriptures: Torah, Nevi'im, Kethuvim: The New JPS Translation. Jewish Publication Society, 1985.

Tashi, Khenpo Phuntsok. "Importance of Life Protection: A Tibetan Buddhist View." *The Government of Tibet in Exile*, n.d.

"Vedic religion." *Britannica*, n.d.
Veidlinger, Daniel. "History of the Buddhist Canon." *Oxford Bibliographies*, 13 September 2010.
Waldau, Paul. *The Specter of Speciesism: Buddhist and Christian Views of Animals*. Oxford UP, 2001.
Webb, Stephen H. *Good Eating*. Brazos, 2001.
Young, Richard Alan. *Is God a Vegetarian? Christianity, Vegetarianism, and Animal Rights*. Open Court, 1999.
Zaehner, R. C. *Hinduism*. Oxford UP, 1962.
Zaid, Iqtidar H. "On the Ethics of Man's Interaction with the Environment: An Islamic Approach." *Environmental Ethics*, vol. 3, 1981, pp. 35–47.
"Zoonotic Diseases." *Centers for Disease Control and Prevention: One Health*. n.d.

23

Long Nineteenth Century Ephemera

James Gregory

Introduction

THIS CHAPTER EXAMINES the writings of vegetarians and those now called vegans, produced in the period known by modern scholars as the "long nineteenth century," *c.*1789–1914. This analysis is done principally through study of British and American texts and with an emphasis on works produced from the 1840s onwards. Technological, political, and educational changes led to an explosion in affordable print by the mid-nineteenth century, which was also a formative period for vegetarian societies organized in Britain and America. The vegetarian "movement," which was identified by outsiders as among radical or extreme social reform causes of the era (beyond more mainstream Anglo-American temperance and animal welfare, for instance), relied on oral communication through the public platform of lectures and discussion groups. There was also the performance of healthy and sociable living through such activities as banquets and vegetarian restaurants, and especially towards the end of the nineteenth century, in vegetarian athletic, cycling, and other physical activities. Literature played a critical role since actions gained wider value in nurturing the infant vegetarian cause and sustaining and winning converts, through the reporting and commentary in texts by vegetarian organizations or individuals. These ranged from pamphlets and periodicals, to books that included recipe collections, extracts from historic authorities, and poetry.

Vegan literary scholarship has largely focused on the traces of vegetarianism and veganism in the Novel or short story (see, for example Wright, and Quinn). Work has also been done on the pamphlet and periodical emanations of the early Vegetarian and Vegan Societies (see Wrenn, this volume). However, vegan literary scholarship must also take into account vegetarian-penned correspondence and essays published in the mainstream press, and the representation, satirical or otherwise, in newspapers and periodicals that were so important for the cultural life of a period before modern social media. Material objects beyond texts, of course, had critical roles in advancing individual and collective success in vegetarian reform. The British and American vegetarian movements sustained, with an increasing sophistication in advertising in the vegetarian press, a range of commodities sold by entrepreneurs providing foods or, for those espousing veganism *avant la lettre*, non-edible items such as clothing.

The textual development of vegan ideals and identities occurred in vegetarian and mainstream press through coverage of public lectures where one criticism levelled by opponents of vegetarianism was that to be vegetarian on ethical or animal-welfare grounds and continue to wear animal-derived materials was inconsistent. In response to this critique of "consistency," printed words in the form of news about pioneer vegans, fictional accounts of vegetarians in novels, short stories, and humorous sketches in the mainstream press, helped disseminate awareness of the possibilities of what became veganism.

Vegetarian thought from this period comes down to us through a variety of polemical texts, unsurprising for a movement that drew on the enthusiasms of literary men and women, including among its Victorian pioneers temperance publishers and booksellers like William Horsell. Tracts, "wafers," and envelopes, monthly periodicals, annuals, and almanacs – standard elements of the printed propaganda of reforming and philanthropic organizations in this period – expressed vegetarians' commitment to the printed word as a way of promoting the cause through material disseminated via the postal service; advancing the cause through rational discussion and sustained explanation in print media. But there was also a desire to promote news of activities, whether they be public talks, attractive feasts, sporting prowess, or the diverse achievements of vegetarian celebrities.

Carol J. Adams's *The Sexual Politics of Meat*, published in 1990, with its attention to "bearing the vegetarian word," especially by women writers, from the 1790s onwards (143), stimulated literary scholars to consider the roles of literary texts in the history of modern Western vegetarianism. Adams and others have explored how vegetarian ideas are found in literature from the Romantic era (from the late eighteenth century) onwards, while other work has identified the limited body of vegetarian-penned literary evocations of vegetarianism in novels, poetry, and short stories, and examined the uses of vegetarian characters in mainstream Victorian literary fiction in defining cultural norms through satire (Gregory, "Vegetable Fictions"). Canonical texts from this period by authors such as Mary Shelley and H. G. Wells have been re-read for their potential as texts for veganism (Quinn). This chapter concentrates less on conventional forms of literature like the novel or poem because veganism, as opposed to vegetarianism, rarely figured in fictional texts in this period. As Liam Young has explored, the periodical press was a significant aspect of vegetarian advocacy even before an established movement, through its "open-endedness ... the way in which each issue anticipates future issues and contributions" (xv), with promoters establishing a "print-based community and invit[ing] readers into the creation of vegetarianism" (xxvi; for an overview of the vegetarian press, see Gregory, *Of Victorians and Vegetarians* [141–50]). Instead, this chapter draws on the disciplinary insights of history to paint a broad picture of veganism's position in nineteenth-century print culture. Rather than attempting to read for the kind of "vegan unconscious" to be found in ostensibly non-vegan literary texts, as promoted by scholars such as Evan Maina Mwangi, I focus here on the *conscious* written traces of explicitly vegan thought. This provides the concrete textual history required for modes of reading such as Mwangi's and demonstrates the value of looking beyond the established literary canon to explore the significance of more ephemeral textual productions.

This chapter first establishes the descriptions or labels applied to those who took a vegan position in this period; then outlines key textual sites for vegetarians and vegans; looks at the texts on vegan diet in the form of recipe books; delineates debates on veganism reported and elaborated in the vegetarian and mainstream press in terms of substitutes for such basic items as shoe leather and wool; and, finally, argues for the significance of anti-vegetarian satire in the developing literary construction of the vegan in commentary outside the movement.

Veganism before the Vegan Society

Western vegetarianism and veganism appeared in the course of the long nineteenth century in texts explicitly promoting the vegetarian diet or espousing a lifestyle rejecting animal products as foodstuffs, material for clothing, and other items. Before the twentieth-century term "veganism" appeared, some proponents of vegetarianism argued that dietary change did not complete the reform required to achieve the "perfect way" (to use the phrase used by the mystic and vegetarian Anna Kingsford, on whom more, below). This position would be called (by commentators and promoters) variously "ultra vegetarian" (F. W. 63; *Good Health* 309), the "extreme school of vegetarians" (Oswald 72), or "ultramontane" (*Lucifer* 426). The English freethinker Francis Newman, instrumental in late-Victorian Britain in widening the appeal of food reform beyond rigid adherence to vegetarianism, characterized the London vegetarian George Dornbusch (who died in 1873) as one of the "few vegetarians rigid in the extreme" who eschewed not only all animal foods, but also vegetable oils and condiments (66). But Newman wrote also that it was a "matter of conscience not to increase his use of eggs and milk – of milk especially" (77).

In the early days of organized British vegetarianism, in discussing the problem of dairy foods, vegetarians considered pragmatically the need to be patient with "popular taste." In the words of "H. S." published in the "Vegetarian Controversialist" section of the *Vegetarian Messenger* in August 1851, it was "better to begin the change by abstaining from the flesh of animals first; and then if people choose, they can carry out the vegetarian principle in its more complete sense or not" (16). One early vegetarian on the public vegetarian platform, Williams of Coventry, abandoned animal-derived materials such as leather to be a "thorough going" and consistent vegetarian but did not think, in his speech at the third annual meeting of the Vegetarian Society in Salford's town hall, as reported in the *Vegetarian Messenger*'s first volume in 1849, that this was a reasonable demand of those who supported the Society (156).

Critics of the vegetarian diet pointed to the vegetarian label's inaccuracy since it included eggs and dairy foods. "Physical Puritanism," an anonymous essay by the scientist Samuel Brown in the leading progressive journal of the era, the *Westminster Review* in April 1852, alongside noting the inevitable link between "pseudo-vegetarian" demands for milk and killing "whole hecatombs of calves" and calling them "vegetarian trimmers" asked

> Why, they should deny us leather for our sandals, shoes, gloves, and other accoutrements; they should refuse us wool, for it is a morbid and a monstrous growth, and the clipping of it from the sheep's back must assuredly expose it to danger as well as wretched discomfort, they should allow us no horses to ride or drive ... they should invade a hundred usages, and provide a hundred substitutes, in order to comply with all the exactions of their theory: but it were neither pleasant nor profitable to follow them any further, until the grand experiment, to which they have just been called, be leisurely performed. The twenty-second century awaits the results with patience. (231)

The movement's name continued to be problematic, with critics describing ovo- and lacto-vegetarianism as "pseudo-vegetarian" (Dutton 69; Thompson 780) and rejoinders from vegetarians who admitted that the term was not one they particularly liked but that it was the generally accepted one (Salt, "Sir Henry Thompson" 57–58).

In *The Science of Cooking Vegetarian Food* (1856), the hydropathist and early vegetarian-temperance publisher William Horsell spoke to those who preferred to "adopt a diet consisting of the corns and fruits of the earth, exclusively" (ii). His text included answers to the problem of what to do with animals, being content to "leave the balance of creation with its Author," and argue for the superiority of machinery, hand labor by humans, and non-animal manures (88).

Nineteenth-Century Vegetarian and Vegan Texts

The "vegetable system" was promoted in the epic poem *Queen Mab*, published by the twenty-one-year-old Percy Bysshe Shelley, through a detailed note on the diet of vegetables and pure water in relation to health, economy, and morality appended to the poem on its publication in 1813 (see the lengthy note to the line "No longer now / He slays the lamb that looks him in the face," appended at 211–38) and printed separately that year as *Vindication of a Natural Diet*. Shelley's note cited the physician William Lambe's experience and quoted John Frank Newton's "luminous and eloquent essay" (228), *The Return to Nature, or Defence of a Vegetable Regimen* (1811). Shelley's work has been studied in the context of British vegetarianism within literary circles in the Romantic era (see, for example, Morton). As Shelley did not refer to animal foods such as milk or eggs, the essay might be deemed to promote a vegan diet, though not alternatives to other animal products (or animal labor). The essay was reprinted in several editions in the nineteenth century including in editions of Shelley's works and in an American medical work (Salt and Axon, "Prefatory notes" i). Shelley referred to the vegetarian diet in several other published works of poetry: *Alastor; or, The Spirit of Solitude* (1816); *Laon and Cythna; or, The Revolution of the Golden City: A Vision of the Nineteenth Century; In the Stanza of Spenser* (1817); and in the essay *Refutation of Deism* (published anonymously 1814), which quoted from Plutarch on the Pythagorean diet (Axon 8). For the more poetically or philosophically minded vegetarian convert, Shelley provided an important exemplar, as, for instance, for the Chartist poet James Elmslie Duncan, whose *Flowers and Fruits, or Poetry, Philosophy, and Science*, first published in 1843, included an essay on vegetarian diet that cited Shelley (see Gregory, *The Poetry and the Politics*).

Vegetarianism was subsequently espoused in cookery books, in pamphlets geared to a variety of different audiences and defending or promoting it on animal welfare, hygienic, aesthetic, and economic grounds. Dietary reform was advocated in periodicals of organized vegetarianism in Britain, North America, and other places, beginning before the pioneering British Vegetarian Society was formed in 1847, with the publications of the Concordium at Ham Common in Surrey (*The Healthian*; *The New Age*). The Concordium, founded by the mystic James Pierrepont Greaves, drew inspiration from the American transcendentalist Bronson Alcott, and in the era of Owenite socialism was viewed as a "sacred socialist" communitarian alternative to Owenism, in which dietary reform figured strongly (Latham). Titles such as Horsell's pioneering *Vegetarian Advocate*; its rival and successor emanating from northern England, the *Vegetarian Messenger* (later *Dietetic Reformer*); and the late-Victorian *Vegetarian* produced in London, promoted the cause to an indifferent or hostile public and sustained a sense of community among the hundreds who joined the societies in Britain. In the US, pioneer journals included the *American Vegetarian and Health Journal* which, as it stated in the first number of the first volume in 1850, emulated the *Advocate* in "diffusing these principles through our nation" (3).

Vegetarianism appeared in works of literature such as novels and short stories. A few of these appeared in British and American vegetarian periodicals: the British-born Henry Clubb's "Margaret Woodrow" in the Philadelphia-published *American Vegetarian and Health Journal* in January 1854 about the conversion of a tailor's family through the agency of mother and daughter reading the first number of the *Vegetarian Advocate*; or Mary Ann Whitaker's "Coals of Fire. A Tale," also appearing in the *American Vegetarian* from March 1854, with its tale of social advancement in working-class and industrial England, through vegetarian economies. But otherwise the literary representation came from hostile outsiders like the obscure hack writer and anti-Catholic polemicist G. M. Viner's *Aunt Eliza's Garret* (1854), satirizing Horsell as Screwberry Morsall and including the standard question intended to derail vegetarianism on the grounds of inconsistency, as discussed further below, on the wearing of leather and wool (100).

Weighty non-fiction vegetarian tomes also appeared, such as the Englishman John Smith of Malton's *Fruits and Farinacea the Proper Food of Man* (1845). Tellingly, the stereotyped American edition, produced by the unorthodox medical publishers Fowler and Wells and edited by Russell Thacher Trall in 1854, was embellished with illustrations, and, as described by the *American Vegetarian* in August 1854, a "beautiful lithographic frontispiece, and woodcuts which have lightened the appearance of the work, and increased its utility and attractiveness to the American reader" (165).

Being a recognized subject of the day, vegetarianism surfaced in sources outside the organized movement, whether in satirical or serious-minded magazines, learned periodicals, or sympathetic journals of progressive reform such as hydropathic (water cure) and phrenological journals. The *Water-Cure Journal* had a vegetarian department when the American Vegetarian Society could no longer support a journal in 1855. The vegetarians were adept at spotting signs of sympathy in works of physiology and anatomy and reprinting extracts from these works in their periodicals, as for example in the March 1854 edition of the *American Vegetarian and Health Journal* (62).

The veganism that existed in vegetarian texts varied from advertisements that promoted substitutes for leather and ivory, to recipes in periodicals and books that removed eggs and dairy products from culinary repertoires and substituted olive oil and baking powder. *The Science of Cooking Vegetarian Food*, William Horsell's work of 1856 which combined vegetarian cooking, domestic directory, and a history of the British Vegetarian Society, asserted the demand for substitutes for animal products (such as shoe leather, fats for soaps and candles) was "already" being met by the inventive (89). It is to this literary form of cookery book for the promotion of vegetarianism (and for confronting or sidestepping the extension into veganism) that the chapter now turns. Problematic foodstuffs such as dairy products, eggs, and honey were written about in ways that varied from the side glance to the head-on discussion of substitutes.

The Vegan Dietary in Nineteenth-Century Texts

Qualms about ignoring the logic of vegetarianism in terms of incomplete exclusion of animal foods surfaced in early-nineteenth-century British texts. The antiquary and literary scholar Joseph Ritson's *Abstinence from Animal Food a Moral Duty* (1802) expressed its writer's anxiety to defend the eating of eggs, which "deprives no animal of life, although it may prevent some from coming into the world to be murdered and devoured by others." Ritson said he became vegetarian after reading, in 1772, a passage from the Anglo-Dutch Bernard de Mandeville's philosophical work *The Fable of the Bees* (1714) on the unnaturalness of meat-eating (201). John Frank Newton's *The Return to Nature*, dedicated to William Lambe (published in 1811 and subsequently serialized in London in two numbers of *The Pamphleteer* in 1821–1822), while avoiding offering bill of fare or recipes, stressed avoidance of animal foods: the "very small quantity" of butter on toast, the pudding with "as few eggs in it as possible" (114).

One influential early recipe collection was Martha Brotherton's *Vegetable Cookery*. She was a member of a vegetarian Christian sect based in the Salford–Manchester region of northern England and founded by William Cowherd (and known as Bible Christians or Cowherdites). In its early nineteenth-century editions from serialization as "The System of Vegetable Cookery" in 1812 this had no concern about the use of eggs, butter, and milk. But later editions of the work, which Brotherton had first published anonymously, divided up the diet into three "styles," with the eggless and dairy-free as the "first style" (xlvi).

The Concordists, members of a small community established for "re-modelling society on a basis in which all shall be secured from the want and destitution in which thousands are now perishing" (*A Brief Account* 1) and based at Ham Common in Richmond outside London in the early 1840s, did not publish a recipe book but their tracts and serial publications give details of their vegetarian meals (*The New Age* 288). *A Brief Account of the First Concordium* did include Martha Brotherton's cookery book (though credited to the Cowherdite James Scholefield) among the works available from their London publisher, the radical John Cleave (8). It is clear that in their most spartan period diet was part of the Concordist process of simplification of lifestyles and pursuit of mankind's higher nature that was anthropocentric rather than concerned about animal cruelty (Gregory, *Of Victorians* 99; Latham). The influence of American health reformers such as Sylvester Graham can be discerned too. While the aristocratic Sophia Chichester as the "matron" of the Concordists might offer tea with milk and sugar in her private parlor to a guest, the public meals of the community involved unfermented bread from flour hand-milled on site, cold potatoes and raw peas, with cold coarse porridge, in the recollection of a visitor, who quoted one leading figure in the Concordist experiment, the Dorchester banker and Owenite socialist William Galpin, admitting that "we have to work to true naturalness and pure simplicity" (as later recalled by another, in "Quorum Pars Fui": 191). The published discussion of their vegan philosophy, in relation to diet, includes this passage from *A Brief Account of the First Concordium*:

> Man infringes the prerogative of divinity when he interposes between life and its sentient forms. Here the ingenious speculator may reply, "Then must we stay our hand from attacks even upon vegetable life, and never cut a cabbage or dig a potatoe:" and to this we do not object. It is probable, that in his more elevated state, man will never do either; the food conditions of his purer life will be found in those fruits of trees, shrubs, and plants which give off their produce periodically, without interfering in any manner with life. Thus man, in his simple and god-like

state, will be spontaneously supplied with his daily bread, or food, from the free gifts of Heaven, by the fruit-bearing creation, and nothing will be found to hurt or destroy in all God's holy mountain. (7)

The consequence of this fruitarianism would be "harmony established with the animal world – man associated with Goodness – crime, misery, and pain almost abolished in our land" (7). It was a diet motivated by "Love" and "Wisdom."

The American Asenath Nicholson's *Nature's Own Book*, a Grahamite work first published in 1835 (typographical and grammatical errors were the result of haste because of "the demands for receipts" which the second edition published that year corrected, see preface to this enlarged volume) avoided any "deleterious substances, either butter, eggs, or deadening spices" (iv), having described butter as a "questionable article" (16). Nicholson's work was reprinted in Glasgow in 1846, shortly before the Vegetarian Society was founded at Ramsgate on the south coast of England in 1847.

Much early Victorian vegetarian discourse was concerned with vegetarianism simply as diet. Yet products such as honey seem rarely to have been discussed, or viewed as problematic. The Anglo-Indian Captain Goode, a character in a tale in the non-vegetarian *Youth's Magazine, or Evangelical Miscellany*, published a few years after the Vegetarian Society appeared, asserted "undoubtedly" that honey is a "vegetarian diet ... as much as eggs and our large savoury omelets" – the cutlery used in the meal is made with "vegetable ivory" (H. R. E. 202–10). There was also approval of honey from the *Vegetarian Messenger* in November 1851 in its "Vegetarian Treasury" section (20), although the *Vegetarian Advocate*'s editor, the horticulturalist James Shirley Hibberd, in a translation of *Porphyry on Abstinence from Animal Food* (and published by William Horsell in 1851), gave the arguments of opponents in classical times against milk, wool, and honey and Porphyry's response (26). The question of honey's status also interested Americans, such as Carl Lindorme, writing briefly on "Honey and vegetarianism" in *The Phrenological Journal* in July 1885 (44).

A Few Recipes of Vegetarian Diet, an anonymous cookery tract from Great Malvern and penned by the Cowherdite James Simpson, was intended in 1847 to be followed up by a second part for those rejecting milk, butter, and eggs, or "Vegetarianism in this last acceptation of the term" (5). There was also John Smith of Malton's *The Principles and Practice of Vegetarian Cookery* (1860), which among its many accounts of "articles used in vegetarian diet," such as roots, tubers, and fruits, found the space to discuss clotted cream and other dairy products without condemnation. William Horsell's *The Science of Cooking Vegetarian Food* (1856), mentioned above, included substitutes for egg and butter and Horsell asserted that the presence of "considerable proportions of animal products and condiments" was incompatible with the "highest condition of man" (ii). His wife Elizabeth's cookery book, *Domestic Assistant and Guide to Vegetarian Cookery*, was designed as an improvement on the cookery books of the Cowherdites, "our Manchester friends ... without *animal products*, &c" as William Horsell's letter printed in the first number of *American Vegetarian* in 1850 stated (4).

Later works made efforts to exclude animal foods such as cheese and eggs (*The Best* 92), though the American-born Thomas Low Nichols's *Penny Vegetarian Cookery* argued in 1888 that the egg was made of "matter derived from vegetables," with the germ of animal life being microscopic (14). American vegetarian cookery books asserted that "pure diet" required no animal products, though as the second edition of Edward Howe's *The Vegetarian Cook Book* accepted in 1887, these products might "be used moderately by persons who imagine they need them" (52). The Bostonian Maude Sharpe's *Golden Rule Cook Book*, first published in 1907, also discussed non-dietary vegetarianism as true vegetarianism, rejecting fur and feathers as the "reapings from a dead body" (24).

The *British and Foreign Medico-chirurgical Review*, in a review of vegetarian texts in 1851, was not the last external critic, in its comparison of vegetarian statements of dietary principle against the egg-laden recipes of vegetarian cookery, to point out the contrast and claim that the "so-called vegetarian positively consumes, according to his own diet-scale, *as much animal food* as the avowed flesh eater" (79). For the reviewer, "oophagy" and "galactophagi" were really "kreatophagi," and what was happening with the vegetarian agitation was "the substitution of one form of Animal food for another" (80).

Others, outside the vegetarian movement, showed awareness of the role that soya might have in offering artificial milk and other dairy substitutes (Dujardin-Beaumetz 28). On milk, the Vegetarian Society's president Francis Newman's *Essays on Diet*, while noting that "substitutes from oleaginous nuts" had not yet been achieved, asserted that "We are in a state of transition. A future age will look back on this as barbarism; yet we are moving towards the higher and nobler development in becoming even thus partial vegetarians" (44; see also Young 256–57 on Newman's treatment of the contemporary expense of alternatives to animal fats). The prominent British sanitary authority Benjamin Richardson flagged up the Chinese substitute for animal foods as lentils, and that there was no doubt there would be a way to make non-dairy milk, on as large a scale as beer in breweries. The vegetarian press itself discussed plant-milks such as the sap of the *palo de vaca* or "cow-trees" of Venezuela and an article on these plants was directed for the attention of vegetarians in the horticultural magazine, *The American Garden* of New York (Sturtevant 30). Vegetarians sent testimony about substitutes for butter and milk – whether milk-less porridge or lentil and bean-based pastes as in the case of one correspondent to the *Dietetic Reformer* in February 1884 ("J. G. C. B.").

Vegetarianism and the Non-dietary Use of Animal Products

The charges of incompleteness or inconsistency were levelled against followers of a "vegetable diet" in British texts decades before organized reformers adopted the label of vegetarianism. The political radical William Cobbett's *A Year's Residence in the United States* (1818) pointed out the animal products that the vegetarian and radical publisher Sir Richard Phillips had not abstained from, in his personal clothing and in his publishing career (366). One reviewer of the vegetarian Charles Lane's *Dietetics*, riled by his argument in 1849, identified the republican and democratic tendency in the abstinence, but also, the threat to such manufacturers as leather-dealers, bristle merchants, violin-string makers, and woolen drapers (*Literary Gazette* 136). In Fruitlands, the American colony established by the Englishman Lane with Bronson Alcott, vegetarianism was extended to clothing: "The garments must be of linen, because those made from wool were the result of the use of cruel shears to rob the sheep of their wool" (Porter 9).

Pioneer British vegetarians of the Concordium community in the 1840s were advocates of linen instead of woolen clothes, alongside their vegetable diet, though this was related to a mysticism which promoted the "cold clothing" among the millenarian followers of John Wroe the Southcottian, according to the journalist and religious writer James Elimalet Smith's note on vegetarianism in his widely circulated penny working-class periodical *Family Herald* in November 1850 (444). Smith penned an anonymous critique of animal-derived products still used at the Concordium – horse-hair-stuffed sofas, ivory paper knives, and other animal derived items – which was published in the Concordists' *The New Age and Concordium Gazette* in December 1843 (139–40).

The problem of leather, wool, and other animal products often surfaced in anti-vegetarian texts into the late-Victorian period, when the movement was gaining more public attention in Britain (Byrne 429–30), just as it was verbally raised by opponents at the end of public lectures to advocate the cause. The late nineteenth-century vegetarian Henry Salt referred to it as the "consistency trick" in *The Logic of Vegetarianism: Essays and Dialogues* (1906) designed to undermine the credibility of vegetarian propaganda (41–46).

There was ingenious reasoning from vegetarian defenders, including the argument that leather was a comparatively modern material for shoes and boots, not used "except by soldiers and ploughmen," according to the *Vegetarian Almanac* in 1884 (qtd. in *Dietetic Reformer*, February 61). Apologists and polemicists corrected doubters by pointing to their successful substitutes: "I have my boots made of most excellent vegetable leather by Messrs Bond and Son, of Bridgwater, and no one can tell the difference," reported one such correspondent in *Dietetic Reformer* in March 1884 (69). Correspondence was an important way in which the readers who constituted the vegetarian movement raised questions and gave answers that helped develop vegetarian – and indeed vegan – practice (see Young 260–61); vegetarian periodical columns also offered advice on experiments in substitutes (Young 329–30).

James Simpson, the first president of the British Vegetarian Society, combated the argument against shoe leather by noting "felt, gutta percha, and panuscorium, or leather cloth," and mineral oil from coal rather than whale oil (*American Vegetarian* 4: 6 June 1854, 124) could be used. The early *Vegetarian Messenger* in its "Vegetarian Treasury" section in February 1851 reprinted the educational writer Charles Knight's eloquence on the recent spread of India rubber to England under the title "vegetable substances superseding animal productions" (3). The same journal also carried the manufacturer Halls's advertisements for Pannus Corium Boots and Shoes, "Leather superseded . . . admirably suited to meet the desires of all who practice Vegetarian principles," as "free from all animal substances" (e.g. December 1851). The firm advertised its products to vegetarians into the early twentieth century. Some other unlikely substitutes were promoted. The vegetarian *Food, Home and Garden*, published in Philadelphia, reviewed asbestos as a substitute in November 1899 (156). Even then, critics within the movement, as in the *Dietetic Reformer* in May 1885, might point to the problems when leather substitutes required animal gelatine and glue (131).

Thomas Wilson Richardson, a life-long vegetarian who became president of the London Dietetic Reform Society, wore canvas shoes and galoshes. His father explained this "full vegetarian costume," in a letter to the New York *Tribune* in 1877, that this was "not because he held it to be unlawful to shear a living animal . . . but simply as a practical and visible reply to the taunts of the inveterate, unreasoning beefeaters," on the leather question (reprinted *Phrenological Journal*, June 1877, 2). Richardson's striking presence on the public platform publicized vegan clothing through newspaper paragraphs; and in a more sustained way through the *Danielite Star* and in a few tracts

Richardson's own vegetarian organization, referred to below, promoted his own version of vegetarian reform. A more famous late-Victorian who produced diverse texts on vivisection, vegetarianism, and mysticism, was the medically trained Anna Kingsford. She discussed the leather question in a pamphlet on *The Perfect Way in Diet* first published in 1881 (5th ed., 107–08). As the *Dietetic Reformer* reported in September 1885, Kingsford wore underclothes and overclothes made from black pine fiber (274), while non-vegetarian magazines, such as *Bow Bells Weekly*, also reported on her rejection of furs and feathers and wearing of silk gloves (169). On the British vegetarian platform, at the leading venue for philanthropy in the metropolis at Exeter Hall during an International Health Exhibition, she made the point of wearing vegetarian boots, having "climbed the hills of Switzerland" in this footwear (Kingsford, *Addresses* 117).

In the early *Vegetarian Messenger*, the "slaughter of animals for their skins, oil, etc." was debated: the vegetarian should not sanction these, it was argued (*Vegetarian Messenger*, February 1853, "Controversialist and Correspondent" 4). The *Vegetarian Messenger's* "Vegetarian Treasury" for October 1852 informed readers of vegetable wool made from pine leaves in a factory near Breslau in Silesia (18). Later the *Dietetic Reformer* carried snippets of news about plant materials, for instance in 1883 readers learned about kapok as a "new vegetable wool" (363).

In what became a common answer to the problem of animal-derived materials, it was "one of demand and supply and when articles are required by a sufficient number to make them matters of commercial enterprise, the supply will readily be found" as February 1853's "Controversialist and Correspondent" section to *Vegetarian Messenger* asserted (4). "Invention is not stopped, but encouraged by the adoption of Vegetarian diet," another claimed (Bramley appendix, i). The vegetarian pamphlet of the Cambridge classical professor John Eyton Bickersteth Mayor boasted, "Our action is providing substitutes for all animal substances," with vegetable clothing, vegetable oils and fats, vegetable milk and vegetable cheeses (5). Henry Salt addressed the challenge by arguing that vegetarians used animal products such as bone and leather, "not because they have any preference or desire for these articles, but because under the present dietetic system substitutes are as yet either expensive or unattainable." The fault lay not with vegetarian "inconsistency" or the lack of substitutes from the vegetable kingdom but with the "unpleasant dietetic habits of other people" (Salt, "Food reform" 496.) Octavius Shrubsole (a vegetarian bank clerk from Reading) was optimistic, trusting to Nature and the "resources of civilisation," to provide vegetarian clothing (320). Members of the late-Victorian Women's Vegetarian Union were reported in the mainstream press to be praising:

> vegetarian clothing and stationery. Gloves of vegetable fibre, boots of the same delicate material and even vegetarian parchment, were all numbered among the articles that ought to be used exclusively by those who would follow the perfect way. Fell, no less than the flesh, is evidently an abomination . . . (*Glasgow Herald* 6)

Satirizing the Ultra-Vegetarian

As that passing comment from a Scottish newspaper indicated, news of vegan vagaries had a ready place in the late-Victorian press. Vegetarians were the common butt of comic paragraphs and asides in serious texts: an enthusiastic article on the substance gutta percha began by saying vegetarians had realized it was "good for their 'soles.'" (*Christian Repository* 76).[1] A continuation volume by Thomas Miller of that bestselling and notorious work of fiction for the working classes, *Mysteries of London*, parodied the early vegetarians in the metropolis through the invention of a Vegetable Volunteers Association, with two street entertainers hired as lecturers for the organization discussing their extreme beliefs: "If a member only burns a tallow candle he's expelled; as to shoes, they must all wear wooden ones, for to use leather is to encourage murder, slaughter, flaying, and tanning – all, as they say, tending to brutalise the human mind" (93). It was easy to ridicule a rejection of all animal products, as in the pages of Harry Furniss's comic periodical *Lika Joko*, in 1895, where a letter is imagined from one naive vegetarian, Lily Pears:

> I cannot tell you how *truly* shocked and *horrified* I was to learn from LIKA JOKO that our boots are made of *animal* substance. I always thought they came from shops, and grew on boot-trees or somewhere. I can honestly say I have not been so much *upset* since I did penance with hot mustard and water after swallowing a small slug in my salad two summers ago. I have *at once* resolved to give up *everything* of the nature of animal substance, even Juggins' all-wool clothing, and, what is *worse*, my silk petticoats and things which are manufactured by *silk-worms*, which, as we all know, are animals. I am wearing *nothing* but linen and cotton, and am now sitting wrapped in Turkish *towels* (which I only *hope* are not made from Turks), for the sake of warmth, as during the Christmas holidays it has been *impossible* to find anyone to make me clothes of linen quilted with cotton wool, which, as I understand, and fervently hope, is not wool at all. It is very cold at night, as I had to do away with all our *blankets*, and Rose Mary grumbles very much, but with several thicknesses of *brown paper* over the sheets I trust we shall hold on until proper *vegetarian blankets* can be made for us. It is most unfortunate that this should have been discovered at Christmas time, but, after all, we should not hesitate to shiver for the *Cause*. It is truly *dreadful* to find how many things are made from animals besides meat, and, I suppose, spirituous liquors, which, as we know, are quite as *unwholesome*. (*Lika Joko* 234)

Furniss, a leading cartoonist of the era, had been an artist for the preeminent satirical magazine for the middle classes, *Punch*, whose late-Victorian comment on veganism was a trio dressed in vegetable clothes, with the extract of a report from the meeting of the Vegetarian Federal Union in February 1898, about the "facility with which vegetarians might, if they pressed their demands upon their tradesmen, obtain vegetarian boots and vegetarian gloves" (72). In another sally in October 1897, "Botanical Boots" imagined the hungry vegetarians boiling down shoes of cabbage and roots though *Fun* had already exploited the comic potential of apparently edible footwear with its verse, after noting Kingsford's success in "eliminating from her clothing all animal products," in the verse "The Vegetable Boot" (263). The journalist Harry Jeffs disconcerted an advocate of such clothing at one vegetarian exhibition by inventing a story of sheep nibbling the shoes of one enthusiast asleep on Clapham Common (166). Unsurprisingly the journalist and prolific author Harold Begbie, in his satire on faddism published in 1902 (written with inside knowledge of the London vegetarian scene as erstwhile editor of Arnold Frank Hills's *Vegetarian*), has a Vegetarian Universal League at Martyrs Hall with stalls showing "specimens of vegetarian cloth, piles of vegetarian boots" (113). For wealthy Edwardian humanitarians there were fur substitutes, "humanitarian boots," and imitation leather ladies' bags advertised by suppliers such as the smart London department store Debenham and Freebody in the vegetarian *Herald of the Golden Age* (April 1912).

The pages of the popular press, newspapers, and periodicals, were sites for vegetarians to defend themselves against correspondents bringing up the question of leather and other materials, such as W. K. Parkis of Birmingham who responded to the prominent vegetarian and bread reformer Thomas Allinson by characterizing vegetable substitutes as "makeshifts," and suggesting the problem was to invent materials working "equally as well as leather" (224). Western vegetarians gestured towards vegan practices outside the West. One Indian vegetarian, Keshav Lal, optimistically punned that mankind was not so "literally hidebound" as to let its progress depend on skins, bones, and guts (qtd in Ramaiah 67).

Conclusion

Vegetarianism tended, despite the detractors or enthusiasts arguing for "consistency," to be seen in dietary terms rather than as something embracing the ethics of footwear. The identifiably vegan was a small part of vegetarian literature in the nineteenth century. It would hardly constitute a significant body of nineteenth-century thought in the sense of extensive and profound writing about complete avoidance of animal material and animal exploitation. Even less so would it figure in extensive literary form in works of fiction, though by the end of our period the vegetarian diet, made more prominent by the proliferation of vegetarian restaurants, had fleeting appearance in mainstream fiction of the modern city (Richardson). However, the wider vegetarian movement had to address the question of consistency in a way that propelled forward spoken and literary debates about animal products as diet and other forms of human consumption. There were those, for instance, who might balk at the necessity to use animal labor, such as the British Jewish promoter of animal rights in the first half of the nineteenth century, Lewis Gompertz (85–86). In addition, on the outer fringes of vegetarianism, there were some, such as the late-Victorian British reformer William Allan Macdonald, who combined vegetarianism of a strict form (raw foods comprising roots, nuts, fruits and vegetables) with clothing reform (326). For Macdonald, the question of dairy foods related to land and human population, the "reformed dietarian wards off this calamity by taking his butter in the form of nuts" (66).

"Extreme advocates" stood on the vegetarian platform at public banquets in gutta percha-soled and black canvas shoes (lawn tennis shoes), cotton-velveteen coats, dark linen drill waistcoats, and cotton cord (corduroy) trousers. Such outlandish appearances would be picked up in the mainstream press in sources as varied as the *Journal of Horticulture and Cottage Gardener* (356) and *Punch* in October 1884 (192). Lieutenant-Colonel Thomas Richardson, the man who wore this "vegetarian or non-animal" suit, and whose canvas footwear was mentioned above, led a group of "Danielites" who might be seen as proto-vegans carrying "their convictions and practices beyond all other vegetarians, even clothing themselves on vegetarian principles" ("Vegetarianism and Hygiene" 48) but Richardson denied membership required abstinence from milk or eggs.

Nevertheless, the argument for vegetarian boots could be taken as a symbol of the late nineteenth-century humane propagandist's exaggeration, as in George W. E. Russell's essay "The Faddist," published in his *Social Silhouettes* in 1906 (99), or grotesque and appalling character as Charles Frederick Kenyon (who wrote as Gerald Cumberland) recounted of theosophists he met in the entourage of the prominent freethinker, vegetarian, and theosophist Annie Besant, in *Set Down in Malice, a Book of Reminiscences* in 1919 (23) and in his novel, *A Lover at Forty*, in 1922 (103).

Whenever there was a character presented as independent-minded, vegetarianism might figure among their enthusiasms, as in the sympathetic "Sketch of a Character" in the *Metropolitan Magazine* in 1846, with its early use of the word "vegetarian" to describe an attractive bearded and un-English seeming painter and his household (423–28); the general reformer Laurence Temple, in a novel *The Story of a Marriage* (first published 1889) by the mother of the future prime minister Stanley Baldwin; and in a less judgmental fashion the prolific popular novelist Adeline Sergeant's *No Saint: A Study* in 1886, where the kindly Mrs Crockett is a teetotaler, homeopathist, antivaccinationist, and vegetarian, "naturally subversive of all ordinary rules of conduct" (44). American authors also brought vegetarianism into their stories, as in Harriet Prescott Spofford's *A Scarlet Poppy: And Other Stories* in 1894, where the comic story of the unhealthy consequences of the diet, "Best-Laid Schemes," features a vegetarian advocate, Emily Pearmain, who claims only to touch an egg "once in a while" (37).

Outside the vegetarian world, it was left to those speculative writers predicting the future to imagine a world of vegetarian clothes reflecting the practice of "extreme vegetarians already, carrying consistency to its limits," to quote the Englishman Thomas Baron Russell from 1905 in *A Hundred Years Hence: The Expectations of an Optimist* (299). The scientist and author Frank Hill Perry-Coste's *Towards Utopia: being Speculations in Social Evolution* of 1894 referred to the "lion" of the leather question in the pathway of vegetarianism (228). It is this passing and disparate commentary that constituted the literary engagement with actual, latent, and aspirational veganism in this period.

Acknowledgments

My thanks to Emelia Quinn and Laura Wright for advice and meticulous editing.

Note

1. See Nicole Seymour's chapter in this volume for an evaluation of the contemporary enmeshment of vegan identity and satire.

Works Cited

[Brotherton, Martha.] *Vegetable Cookery; with an introduction, recommending abstinence from animal food and intoxicating liquors. By a Lady. The fourth edition.* Effingham Wilson, 1833.
[Brown, Samuel.] "Physical Puritanism." *Westminster Review*. April 1852, pp. 217–36.
[Kenyon, Charles Frederick.] *A Lover at Forty*. Grant Richards, 1922.
[Kenyon, Charles Frederick.] *Set Down in Malice, a Book of Reminiscences*. Grant Richards, 1919.

[Simpson, James.] *A Few Recipes of Vegetarian Diet; with suggestions for the formation of a dietary, from which the flesh of animals is excluded; accompanied by scientific facts showing that vegetable food is more nutritive and digestible than the flesh of animals*. Whitaker, 1847.
[Smith, James E.] *The New Age and Concordium Gazette*. December 1843, pp. 139–40.
[Smith, James E.] "Vegetarianism." *Family Herald*. 9 November 1850, p. 444.
"Botanical Boots." *Punch*. 30 October 1897, p. 195.
A Brief Account of the First Concordium, or Harmonious Industrial College. Concordium, 1843.
"Fruit eater." "Then and Now." *Dietetic Reformer*. July 1861, pp. 70–71.
"J. G. C. B." "Experience." *Dietetic Reformer*. 1 February 1884, p. 47.
"Quorum Pars Fui." *Light*. 22 April 1882, p. 191.
"Sketch of a Character." *Metropolitan Magazine*. 45 (January to April 1846), pp. 423–28.
"The Vegetable Boot." *Fun*. 28 June 1882, p. 263.
"A vegetarian banquet." *Journal of Horticulture and Cottage Gardener*. 16 October 1884, p. 356.
"Vegetarian Vagaries." *Punch*. 18 October 1884, p. 192.
"Vegetarianism and Hygiene." *The Esoteric*, vol. 4, no. 2, 1890, p. 48.
Adams, Carol J. *The Sexual Politics of Meat*. Continuum, 2010.
American Vegetarian and Health Journal (1850–1854).
Axon, William E. A. *Shelley's Vegetarianism. Read at a Meeting of the Shelley Society*, University College, Gower Street, London, 12 November 1891.
Baldwin, Louisa. *The Story of a Marriage*. Dent, 1895.
Begbie, Harold. *The Curious and Diverting Adventures of Sir John Sparrow, Bart.; or, The Progress of an Open Mind*. Methuen, 1902.
Bow Bells Weekly, 16 March 1888, p. 169.
Bramley, J. F. *Vegetarian Messenger*, vol. 1, 1849, appendix: i.
British and Foreign Medico-chirurgical Review. July 1850, p. 79.
Byrne, William P. *Among the Faculty*. 1892.
Christian Repository. January 1860, p. 76.
Clubb, Henry S. "Margaret Woodrow." *American Vegetarian & Health Journal*, vol. 4, no. 1, January 1854, pp. 1–3.
Cobbett, William. *A Year's Residence in the United States*. Part II. 2nd ed. Sherwood, Neely and Jones, 1819.
Dietetic Reformer. 1 May 1885, p. 131.
Dietetic Reformer. 1 September 1885, p. 274.
Dietetic Reformer. 1883, p. 363.
Dietetic Reformer. 1884, p. 61.
Dietetic Reformer. July 1866, p. 92.
Dujardin-Beaumetz, George. "Vegetarianism from a Therapeutic Point of View." *The Dietetic Gazette*. April 1890, p. 28.
Duncan, James E. *Flowers and Fruits, or Poetry, Philosophy, and Science*. Printed for the author, 1843.
Dutton, Thomas. *Food – and – Drink Rationally Discussed*. Hirschfeld, 1898.
F. W., "Der Vegetarianismus." *Atlantis*, vol. 2, no. 3, 1854, p. 63.
Food, Home and Garden. Philadelphia. November 1899, p. 156.
Glasgow Herald. 3 April 1897, p. 6.
Gompertz, Lewis. *Fragments in Defence of Animals, and Essays on Morals, Soul, and Future State*. Horsell, 1852.
Good Health, vol. 28, no. 10, October 1893, p. 309.
Gregory, James. *The Poetry and the Politics: Radical Reform in Victorian England.*: I.B. Tauris, 2014.

—. "Vegetable Fictions in the Kingdom of Roast Beef: Representing the Vegetarian in Victorian Literature." *Consuming Culture in the Long Nineteenth Century: Narratives of Consumption, 1700–1900*, edited by Tamara S. Wagner and Narin Hassan, Lexington, 2007.

—. *Of Victorians and Vegetarians: The Vegetarian Movement in Nineteenth-century Britain.* Tauris Academic Studies, 2007.

H. R. E., "The Way to the Gift." *The Youth's Magazine or Evangelical Miscellany.* May 1849, pp. 202–10.

The Healthian. London. 1842–1843.

Herald of the Golden Age. April 1912.

Hibberd, James S. (ed.). *Porphyry on Abstinence from Animal Food, Translated from the Greek; Being a Carefully Revised and Amended Text with Copious Illustrative Notes and Comments.* Horsell, 1851.

Horsell, Elizabeth. *Domestic Assistant and Guide to Vegetarian Cookery.* Horsell, 1850.

Horsell, William. Letter published in *American Vegetarian*, vol. 1, no. 1, 1850, p. 4.

—. *The Science of Cooking Vegetarian Food; To Which are Added A Brief Sketch of the Rise & Progress of the Vegetarian Society; Reasons for Abstinence from Eating Flesh; Answers to the Chief Objections to a Vegetarian Diet; General Remarks on Food and Diet; and a Domestic Directory.* Vegetarian Depot, 1856.

Howe, Edward. *The Vegetarian Cook Book.* 2nd ed. New York, 1887.

Jeffs, H. *Press Preachers and Politicians: Reminiscences.* Independent Press, 1933.

Kingsford, Anna. *Addresses and Essays on Vegetarianism.* Watkins, 1912.

—. *The Perfect Way in Diet.* 5th ed. Kegan Paul, Trench, Trübner, 1892.

Latham, Jackie E. M. *Search for a New Eden. James Pierrepont Greaves (1777–1842): The Sacred Socialist and His Followers.* Associated University Presses, 1999.

Lika Joko. 5 January 1895, p. 234.

Lindorme, Carl A. F. "Honey and vegetarianism." *The Phrenological Journal.* July 1885, p. 44.

Literary Gazette: A weekly journal of literature, science, and the fine arts 1675, 24 February 1849, pp. 134–36.

Lucifer. 15 January 1890, p. 426.

Macdonald, William A. *Humanitism, the Scientific Solution of the Social Problem.* Trübner, 1890.

Macdonald, William A. *Science and Ethics: Being a Series of Six Lectures Delivered Under the Auspices of the Natural Law Research League.* Swan Sonnenschein, 1895.

Mayor, John E. B. *What is Vegetarianism?* Vegetarian Society, 1898.

Miller, Thomas. *Mysteries of London.* 3rd series, vol. 1, Vickers, 1849.

Morton, Timothy. "Joseph Ritson, Percy Shelley and the Making of Romantic Vegetarianism." *Romanticism*, vol. 12, no. 1, 2006, pp. 52–61.

Mwangi, Evan Maina. *The Postcolonial Animal: African Literature and Posthuman Ethics.* U of Michigan P, 2019.

The New Age, and Concordium Gazette. A Journal of Human Physiology, Education and Association. 1 September 1844, p. 288.

Newman, Francis W. *Essays on Diet.* Kegan Paul, 1883.

Newton, John F. *The Return to Nature, or, A Defence of the Vegetable Regimen: With Some Account of An Experiment Made during the Last Three or Four Years in the Author's Family.* Cadell and Davies, 1811.

Nichols, Thomas L. *Penny Vegetarian Cookery.* Franks, 1888.

Nicholson, Asenath. *Nature's Own Book: or Practical Results of A Vegetable Diet, Illustrated by Facts and Experiments of Many Years' Practice.* Brown, 1846.

—. *Nature's Own Book.* New York: corrected and enlarged ed. Wilbur and Whipple, 1835.

Oswald, Felix L. *The Bible of Nature; Or, The Principles of Secularism.* Truth Seeker, 1888.

Parkis, W. K. *Health.* 13 July 1883, p. 224.

Perry-Coste, Frank H. *Towards Utopia: being Speculations in Social Evolution*. Appleton, 1894.
Phrenological Journal. June 1877, p. 2.
Porter, Maria S. "Recollections of Louisa May Alcott." *New England Magazine*. March 1892, pp. 3–19.
Punch. 12 February 1898, p. 72.
Quinn, Emelia. *Reading Veganism: The Monstrous Vegan, 1818 to Present*. Oxford UP, 2021.
Ramaiah, Karupalli S. *Jeeva Kaarunyamu*. 1914.
Richardson, Elsa. "Cranks, Clerks, and Suffragettes: The Vegetarian Restaurant in British Culture and Fiction 1880–1914." *Literature and Medicine*, vol. 39, no. 1, 2021, pp. 133–53.
Ritson, Joseph. *Abstinence from Animal Food a Moral Duty*. London, for Richard Phillips, 1802.
Russell, George W. E. *Social Silhouettes*. Smith, Elder, 1906.
Russell, Thomas B. *A Hundred Years Hence: The Expectations of an Optimist*. Fisher Unwin, 1905.
Salt, Henry S. "Food reform." *Westminster Review*, vol. 126, no. 252, October 1886, pp. 483–99.
—. *The Logic of Vegetarianism: Essays and Dialogues*. 2nd ed., Bell, 1906.
—. "Sir Henry Thompson on 'Diet.'" Reprinted in *A Plea for Vegetarianism and Other Essays*. Vegetarian Society, 1886, pp. 57–58.
Salt, Henry S., and W. E. A. Axon. "Prefatory notes." P. B. Shelley, *A Vindication of Natural Diet*. Pitman, 1884.
Sergeant, Adeline. *No Saint: A Study*. Holt, 1886.
Sharpe, Maude R. L. *The Golden Rule Cook Book*. University Press, 1908.
Shelley, Percy B. S. *Queen Mab; A Philosophical Poem; With Notes*. Shelley, 1813.
Shrubsole, Octavius A. "The Practicability of Vegetarianism." *Westminster Review*, vol. 145, January 1896, pp. 312–20.
Smith, John. *Fruits and Farinacea the Proper Food of Man*. Churchill, 1845.
—. ed. Robert T. Trall. *Fruits and Farinacea the Proper Food of Man*. Fowler and Wells, 1854.
—. *The Principles and Practice of Vegetarian Cookery*. Simpkin, Marshall, 1860.
Spofford, Harriet. E. P. *A Scarlet Poppy: And Other Stories*. Harper and Brothers, 1894.
Sturtevant, Edward L. "Cow Trees. Attention of Vegetarians is Especially Requested." *The American Garden*, vol. 11, no. 1, January 1890, p. 30.
Thompson, Henry. "Diet in Relation to Age and Activity." *The Nineteenth Century*, vol. 17, no. 99, May 1885, pp. 777–99.
Vegetarian Messenger 1. 1849, p. 156.
Vegetarian Messenger. August 1851. 'H. S.': "Vegetarian Controversialist," p. 16.
Vegetarian Messenger. February 1853. "Controversialist and Correspondent," p. 4.
Vegetarian Messenger. November 1851. "Vegetarian Treasury," p. 20.
Vegetarian Messenger. October 1852. "Vegetarian Treasury," p. 18.
Viner, George M. *Aunt Eliza's Garret*. London, Elliott, 1854.
Water-Cure Journal and Herald of Reforms; devoted to Physiology, Hydropathy, and the Laws of Life. 1855.
Whitaker, Mary A. "Coals of Fire. A Tale." *American Vegetarian and Health Journal*, vol. 4, no. 3, March 1854, pp. 41–46; vol. 4, no. 4, April 1854, pp. 65–68.
Young, Liam. "Eating Serials: Pastoral Power, Print Media, and the Vegetarian Society in England, 1847–1897." Ph.D. Department of English and Film Studies, University of Alberta, 2017.

24

SOCIETY WRITINGS

Corey Wrenn

Introduction

WESTERN VEGANISM AND vegetarianism originated in nineteenth-century modern Britain. Early societies faced a diffused activist base and a generally ignorant public. Editorial teams were key movement leaders responsible for defining a path for social change, conceptualizing concepts and philosophies, and generally manifesting social movement ideas in a tangible way.[1] Magazines, journals, newsletters, cookbooks, and other print items served as important artifacts that immediately tied the reader to ideas and collectives that were often well beyond their immediate communities. Indeed, readerships became their *own* communities, often stretching across entire nations or across oceans.

There are far too many society publications to summarize here. Instead, this chapter highlights the early works of the Vegetarian Society in Britain, its offshoot, The Vegan Society (TVS), and their American reverberations. These organizations funneled most (if not all) of their meager funds into printing, recognizing their multifunctional role in carving out a movement and achieving desired goals. Their commitment to the literary face of the movement and their influence over movement dynamics mark them as suitable case studies. The discussion herein reflects a convenience sample of early issues of *The Vegan* (TVS) and *Food, Home and Garden* (Vegetarian Society of America [VSA]) supplemented by celebratory chronicles such as that of the American Vegan Society (Dinshah and Dinshah) and insight from movement historians, namely Adam Shprintzen, Colin Spencer, and Joanne Stepaniak. Although vegetarian history is relevant to the chronicle of vegan literary studies, I lend my attention most heavily to the efforts of TVS for obvious reasons.

The aforementioned scholars take interest in the materials produced by organizations and collectives given their function in defining problems, outlining solutions, and shaping activist identity. Yet movements are not the only shapers of identity (Gamson 242). Outside players including media influencers, government institutions, industries and advertising, and the public can also advance resonant characterizations. For Nonhuman Animal rights activists (Einwohner 258) and vegans (Cole and Morgan 134), the influence of so many external actors has entailed a diminishment of their ethical impetuses and spurred a general stigmatization. Defining vegan identity and resisting pejorative outsider-imposed depictions was key to sustaining the movement. The society was founded in 1944 by a group of disaffected members of the Vegetarian Society. At this time, nutritional science was just coming into its own with the discovery of vitamins and the consequences of their deficiencies (Carpenter

3023). Sound nutritional knowledge for even the standard animal-based Western diet was still under development; very little was scientifically known about the complete abstinence of animal products. Anecdotal evidence of the feasibility of a vegan diet did exist, aided by the West's encounters with new colonies where plant-based eating dominated and wartime rationing which made animal products scant for many. Yet a vegetable diet's association with poverty and crises such as war was not necessarily a strong selling point. From its beginning, TVS was committed to principles of rationality and scientific integrity to assuage the public's doubt. *The Vegan* and other publications like it were key to the normalization of vegan living and the advancement of vegan knowledge.

Cementing the Modern Usage of the Terms

TVS released the first issue of its homespun newsletter *The Vegan* in November of 1944 (Figure 24.1). Many of the first issues were typed, copied, and delivered by co-founder Donald Watson in what amounted to an intensely laborious exercise. Production also constituted a considerable expense, usurping the majority of the fledgling organization's meager coffers (G. Allan Henderson 5). Nonetheless, its writings were essential to the organization's operations. The society's founders suspected that the first issue of *The Vegan* would be "widely read" given its emphasis on addressing the ongoing debate between vegans and vegetarians which had encouraged the formation of the society. Writes Watson in the first issue: "The work of the Group at first will be confined to the propaganda contained in the bulletin" (1944, 2).

The newsletter was itself an act of resistance. TVS emerged from a debate that had transpired in the pages of the Vegetarian Society's own newsletter, and, while the idea of maintaining a vegan presence had been considered, it was ultimately blocked. Thirty readers of *The Vegetarian Messenger* subsequently donated to Watson in order to fund the publication of *The Vegan* (Stepaniak 3). "This is real pioneer work," contemplated Watson (1944, 2) as the fruit of his group's effort ripened into a bona-fide organization with a journal all its own. The inaugural issue encouraged future submissions and features related to philosophy and debate, gardening, childrearing, nutrition, media coverage, and advertising. Watson explicitly invited letters of disagreement as a measure of preventing the same stonewalling that vegans had experienced with the Vegetarian Society. The society, in other words, not only saw *The Vegan* as the leading voice of veganism, but the presider over the movement's larger discourse. The second issue claims that hundreds of letters had been received, thus demonstrating "that the formation of this Society is quite due" (Watson 1945, 2). As the society passed its twenty-year anniversary, the importance of *The Vegan* continued to be touted:

> The Society serves as a rallying point, and through its journal keeps members informed of the growing implications of veganism, keeps them in touch with trends and practices and through recipes and commodity lists is of great help to all those finding their way. (Sanderson 2)

For much of the organization's early decades, its literary efforts were its primary emphasis for the purposes of conceptualizing and advancing veganism.

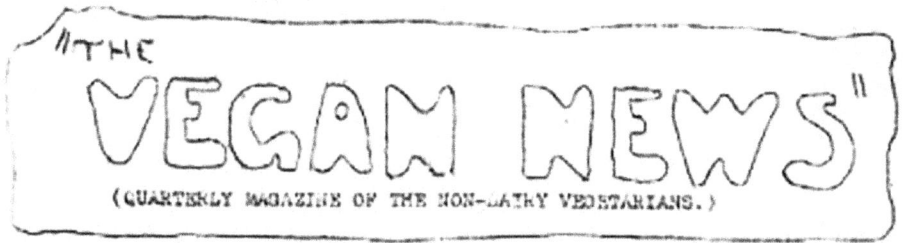

"THE VEGAN NEWS"

(QUARTERLY MAGAZINE OF THE NON-DAIRY VEGETARIANS.)

Price 2d. (post free 3d.) Yearly Subscription 1/-

NO. 1. NOVEMBER 1944.

The recent articles and letters in "The Vegetarian Messenger" on the question of the use of dairy produce have revealed very strong evidence to show that the production of these foods involves much cruel exploitation and slaughter of highly sentient life. The excuse that it is not necessary to kill in order to obtain dairy produce is untenable for those with a knowledge of livestock farming methods and of the competition which even humanitarian farmers must face if they are to remain in business.

For years many of us accepted, as lacto-vegetarians, that the flesh-food industry and the dairy produce industry were related, and that in some ways they subsidised one another. We accepted, therefore, that the case on ethical grounds for the disuse of these foods was exceptionally strong, and we hoped that sooner or later a crisis in our consciences would set us free.

That freedom has now come to us. Having followed a diet free from all animal food for periods varying from a few weeks in some cases, to many years in others, we believe our ideas and experiences are sufficiently mature to be recorded. The unquestionable cruelty associated with the production of dairy produce has made it clear that lacto-vegetarianism is but a half-way house between flesh-eating and a truly humane, civilised diet, and we think, therefore, that during our life on earth we should try to evolve sufficiently to make the 'full journey'.

We can see quite plainly that our present civilisation is built on the exploitation of animals, just as past civilisations were built on the exploitation of slaves, and we believe the spiritual destiny of man is such that in time he will view with abhorrence the idea that men once fed on the products of animals' bodies. Even though the scientific evidence may be lacking, we shrewdly suspect that the great impediment to man's moral development may be that he is a parasite of lower forms of animal life. Investigation into the non-material (vibrational) properties of foods has yet barely begun, and it is not likely that the usual materialistic methods of research will be able to help much with it. But is it not possible that as a result of eliminating all animal vibrations from our diet we may discover the way not only to really healthy cell construction but also to a degree of intuition and psychic awareness unknown at present?

A common criticism is that the time is not yet ripe for our reform. Can time ever be ripe for any reform unless it is ripened by human determination? Did Wilberforce wait for the 'ripening' of time before he commenced his fight against slavery? Did Edwin Chadwick, Lord Shaftesbury, and Charles Kingsley wait for such a non-existent moment before trying to convince the great dead weight of public opinion that clean water and bathrooms would be an improvement? If they had declared their intention to poison everybody the opposition they met could hardly have been greater. There is an obvious danger in leaving the fulfilment of our ideals to posterity, for posterity may not have our ideals. Evolution can be retrogressive as well as progressive. Indeed there seems always to be a strong gravitation the wrong way unless existing standards are guarded and new visions honoured. For this reason we have formed our Group, the first of its kind, we believe, in this or any other country.

Figure 24.1 Cover page for the first issue of the Vegan Society's newsletter (1944).

The second issue of *The Vegan* also uncovers the deliberation around the term "vegan" and, consequently, the organization's name. Alternatives included "allveg," "allvegist," "true vegetarian," "neo-vegetarian," "Benevore," "Sanivore," "Bellevore," "vitan," and "Dairybans" ("Dare to be a Dairyban, dare to stand alone!") (Watson 1945, 3). Ultimately, these names were rejected given their potential to solicit "derisive jibes," their similarity in tonality to sanitary products, or by virtue of poor grammar. Watson and his colleagues took care to deliberate this terminology as they recognized the literary legacy it would leave. "This opportunity to further enrich the English language is still open," Watson offers. "In the meantime we shall remain Vegans, our practice will be Veganism, and our magazine the 'Vegan News'" (3). Of course, the society's founders were not the first to consider terminology. A French researcher coined the word "végétalien" in 1920 to differentiate vegans from other vegetarians in his survey of plant-based practitioners (Fay Henderson 11). It competed with the society's carefully selected term, but the society also recognized that non-English languages would necessarily adopt variants of "vegan" to suit their cultural and grammatical requirements.

The term "vegetarian" was itself a recent addition to the English language; having been coined a century prior (Spencer xi), it competed with other labels such as Pythagorean, hygeian, and Grahamite in addition to a variety of food reform initiatives presenting their own alternative dietary schemes. "Vegetarian" became the official term with the launch of the Vegetarian Society in 1847 at a meeting in Ramsgate, a beachside town in southeastern England (Spencer 252). According to the International Vegetarian Union, the locution had already been in use in 1842, but with the abeyance of the organization not long after its 1847 founding, it was all but forgotten in the written records until re-emerging in the 1870s (Davis 55). The term "vegetarian" reflects the political history of the practice as key to the vegetarians' interest in health reform, teetotalism, and spiritual betterment, but it is not, as some have conjectured, based on the Latin term "vegetus" (meaning fresh and vital). Rather, it simply refers to a person who eats vegetables.

As with the emergence of veganism, vegetarianism was also a concept born of discord. By the 1870s, various British societies were in competition as to how it should be defined (Grummett 259). In fact, various British societies competed with each other in general, not coming under a shared umbrella until the formation of the International Vegetarian Union in 1908 and eventually merging (their journals included) into the Vegetarian Society of the United Kingdom in 1969. The early journals of the British vegetarian societies were influential in developing many concepts beyond vegetarianism's religious and nutritional heritage. Henry Salt, famed leader in Nonhuman Animal rights theory and mobilization,[2] claims to have developed many of his early essays from publications featured in *The Vegetarian* (iii).

There is speculation that early vegetarianism was actually intended to be vegan in practice, particularly as it was so frequently associated with religious purity and asceticism. This practice was sometimes referred to as "strict vegetarianism." For instance, Frank Aker, a member of the VSA, wrote a letter to the society's journal describing his interpretation: "[I have] been a strict vegetarian two years and five months, using the past year or more not even milk and its products, or eggs, as food." Like the vegans who formed TVS, he furthered that the strict vegetarianism he and his brother ascribed to was characterized by its ethical impetus: "a diet free from flesh is absolutely and entirely beneficial, but we became vegetarians from a sense of justice" (Aker 120).

According to historian John Davis, the first print appearance of "vegetarian" was in a journal produced by the Alcott homesteading experiment in the United States, and their interpretation of vegetarianism was also of the strictest kind (they even refused to employ animal manure, hair, or labor) (32). The Alcotts were themselves aware of previous such dietary practices among indigenous Americans, orphanages, religious faiths, and fad health regimens, using these examples as support for their own endeavors (Alcott 223).

In any case, if vegetarianism had been intended to entail a complete eschewing of animal products, this interpretation had gone by the wayside for most vegetarians in the twentieth century as the founding of TVS indicates. In the third issue of *The Vegan*, veganism is clearly defined as "the practice of living on fruits, nuts, vegetables, grains, and other wholesome non-animal products" (Watson 1945, 1). Joanne Stepaniak records the inclusion of the term "vegan" in the *Oxford English Dictionary* in 1962 where it is essentially defined as a stricter vegetarian. After various alterations, the dictionary finally settled on: "A person who does not eat or use animal products," a definition that persists today (*Oxford English Dictionary* [*OED*], "Vegan"). Interestingly, vegans are defined independently of vegetarians, but in a depoliticized manner. Vegetarians are defined according to their convictions: "a person who does not eat meat or fish, and sometimes other animal products, especially for moral, religious, or health reasons" (*OED*, "Vegetarian"). Yet across several variations in the late twentieth century, the definitive record of veganism provided by the *OED* and other prominent reference works has not included a recognition of its ethical component.[3]

American Interpretations

Although professional organizations first materialized in Britain, American collaborators and British expats quickly established American variations. The AVS was founded in 1850 by British immigrant William Metcalfe, who had studied under famous vegetarian advocate and champion of Britain's working poor Reverend William Cowherd (who had died many years prior) (Spencer 258). A journalist for Boston's *Daily Evening Transcript* reported on the society's first meeting and commented on the new concept of vegetarianism:

> At first I supposed this must be a gathering of enterprising agriculturalists for the improvement of the breed of pumpkins, cabbages and turnips. But it seems a "vegetarian" is one who confines himself [*sic*] to vegetable diet, and denounces all meat-eaters in the same terms of frantic denunciation that Garrison & Co employ towards the slaveholders. (Rowe)

Although this reporter seems to understand the core meaning of vegetarianism, his facetiousness is palpable. Indeed, this dismissiveness plagued the early society, and in tandem with the factionalism brought on by varying degrees of support for concurrent social movements (particularly the abolitionism mentioned by the reporter) would send the organization into abeyance.

By the late 1850s, the AVS had been subsumed under the British Vegetarian Society (BVS), and members received issues of the British *Vegetarian Messenger*. Facing financial difficulties, the BVS began to require BVS membership for access to the *Messenger*.

This ultimately drove many members of the American society to switch to the BVS to retain their access to the journal, demonstrating how valuable nineteenth-century vegetarians considered the movement's literary publications to be. Hemorrhaging members, the AVS ultimately dissolved in the midst of the US Civil War (Shprintzen 90–92). Thus the literary efforts of these vegetarian societies were not only vital in promoting information about vegetarianism, they were vital in maintaining group solidarity. Time again throughout the course of vegetarian and vegan advocacy in the West, publications proved to be lynchpins. There is an Irish proverb that muses: "Tír gan teanga, tír gan anam" ("A country without a language is a country without a soul"). It appears the same can be said of these early societies as their publications constituted the very core of their essence and survivability.

When another national organization, the Vegetarian Society of America (VSA), was established in 1886 in Philadelphia, it reflected new interpretations of vegetarianism based in modern advancements in food science, nutrition, technology, and industry. Established by Henry Clubb (who had worked with the earlier American national group in the 1850s and the British Vegetarian Society), the VSA promoted its message through its publication, *Food, Home and Garden*. Until the publication could be reliably produced, society president John Walter Scott produced his own monthly, *The Vegetarian*, which the society notes had "served a very useful purpose in keeping the sacred flame alive" (Vegetarian Society of America 3).

Literature as Activism

Not unlike *The Vegan*, issues of *Food, Home and Garden* were homespun, produced in a Philadelphia residence with a humble printer procured through member donations. Scott clearly recognized the value of such a publication, noting in the editorial of the first issue that the society had issued only a limited pressing in order to maximize its collectability as a "relic of great value" (Vegetarian Society of America 4). Like *The Vegan*, *Food, Home and Garden* also faced financial struggles (Clubb, No Title 10), but the society was acutely aware of its propaganda value. Consider, for instance, editor Henry Clubb's response to a woman who purchased several copies to share with like-minded friends who might be recruited to subscribe: "F., H. & G. is published not so much to *gather* the harvest as to sow the seed" ("Sowing the Seed" 43). The journal, he insists, is key to vegetarianism's success: "the object of the publication is to extend a knowledge of vegetarian principles and practice" ("Shall We Succeed?" 89). He besieges readers to donate ("Help friends help!") in order to "send a copy to every newspaper and magazine in the country" ("Sowing the Seed" 43) and "every [public institution] where the English language is read" ("For Public Libraries" 89).

The VSA's British counterpart had the luxury of aristocratic support to sustain publication commitments, but American vegetarians were left to repeated public appeals. Chides Clubb:

> Every one who neglects to send $1.00 for four copies of F., H. and G. is depriving him or herself of altruistic satisfaction of aiding the best cause on earth, in the most effective and cheapest manner ... the success of the cause depends on *your* doing it. ("Shall We Succeed?" 90)

The organization did its best under these constraints, distributing issues among YMCA clubs and public libraries. For members, the journal provided an array of advantages including correspondence, friendship, and even marriage ("Shall We Succeed?" 75). Readers were kept abreast of critical news, events upcoming and past, new products, new publications, recipes, personal anecdotes, and hard-hitting philosophical and scientific essays – all vital to sustaining far-flung vegetable eaters in an overwhelmingly speciesist society. However, repeated pleas to readers to both donate and spread the journal (a practice also seen in issues of *The Vegan*) demonstrates that, in addition to its ability to build solidarity and maintain networks, movement literature became an object of activism in and of itself. Readers could champion the cause by supporting the journal monetarily or by sharing copies with the uninitiated.

New Recipes for Veganism

Recall that Clubb describes his journal's production as a "sacred flame" to be preserved by whatever means. This "sacred" element of vegetarian efforts would come to challenge the meaning of veganism to include an element of religiosity. Early issues of *The Vegan* made little mention of spirituality and, in fact, regularly touted the importance of scientific thinking as a means of validating the movement (Wrenn, "Atheism" 6). One means by which early vegans differentiated themselves was through the denunciation of vegetarianism's legacy of occultism. Although vegetarianism had always had a heavy spiritual leaning, by the time of TVS's founding, vegetarian journals were reportedly printing astrological advice. Confounded by this fact, one scientist writes to *The Vegan*:

> The vegan's best friend is the chemist. Round the corner of economic recovery, our friend is waiting to flood the market with synthetic plastics to replace leather, fur, skins, bristles, catgut, bone and ivory. Here is the way, and it would be a poor compliment to the Scientist if the vegan were to accept his [sic] goods gladly and at the same time adopt unscientific beliefs, naïve dogmas or a superstitious outlook. Veganism has everything to gain by a wholehearted scientific attitude, and everything to lose by an unscientific approach. Do we want veganism to become another cult or sect of vegetarianism, or do we want it to be the main driving force of the whole progressive movement? (James 7)

The author commends *The Vegan* on maintaining its commitment to science, but it would only be a few years before the publication started to abandon its rational focus to mimic the spiritual emphasis of vegetarianism.

As postwar conservatism settled into the West, TVS began to reflect these wider value changes in its claims-making. Earlier issues of *The Vegan* focused on rebuilding Britain, revolutionizing nutrition, and raising happy, healthy children (Wrenn "The Vegan Society" 7). It also prioritized veganism as a matter of anti-speciesism. By the mid-twentieth century, its rhetoric focused more on improved welfare for farmed animals rather than liberation, and, likewise, improved welfare in the family home. The tone of the magazine became considerably more religious, a trend which persisted until the organization professionalized and likely hoped to appeal to a wider range of funding sources.

In the United States, where religiosity is arguably more resonant with the wider culture, spirituality was intertwined with the American interpretation of veganism and faced less pushback from members. With the encouragement of the British organization, Dr Catherine Nimmo established in 1948 the first vegan group in the United States, in Oceano, California (Stepaniak 6–7). She and her partner distributed issues of *The Vegan*. Later, the American Vegan Society (AVS) formed in New Jersey in 1960 and began publishing its own magazine, *Ahimsa*, which rebranded to a quarterly publication *American Vegan* in 2001 (AVS *History*).[4] The AVS founder, Jay Dinshah, produced an anthology four years later called *Here's Harmlessness*, which advanced veganism as a means of non-violence. Dinshah, who was an Indian-Persian American, based his interpretation of veganism in Asian spirituality (AVS *Ahimsa*). Veganism, he explained, was foundational to the "Pillars of Ahimsa":

Abstinence from animal products.
Harmlessness with reverence for life.
Integrity of thought, word, and deed.
Mastery over oneself.
Service to humanity, nature, and creation.
Advancement of understanding and truth.

While spirituality had come to redefine veganism by the middle of the twentieth century (a trend which persisted throughout much of the century), this trend was certainly supplemented by more secular claims-making. Dinshah's veganism was, more broadly, an extension of his ethical commitment to social justice for other animals (he was motivated to become an activist after visiting a Philadelphia slaughterhouse) (Dinshah and Dinshah 25).

Like the founders of TVS, Dinshah invested considerable time and resources in the literary advancement of veganism. He worked tirelessly in writing, publishing, editing, and lecturing on behalf of the AVS, the British Vegetarian Youth Movement, and other like organizations. He maintained a rigorous commitment to speaking. He is remembered as regularly taking up menial jobs only to put in his notice before lecturing tours. A year after marrying his partner Freya, they embarked on a countrywide trip to speak at various meetings and collectives relating to vegetarianism, health, gardening, and so on (Dinshah and Dinshah 59).

Freya took a supportive role with regard to Jay's frontline advocacy and his work on the *Ahimsa* magazine, but she did engage in her own motivational efforts through her food writings and cookbooks. The AVS claims her 1965 vegan cookbook is the first American cookbook to employ the term "vegan" in its title (Figure 24.2). *The Vegan Kitchen* was an outgrowth of the society's collaboration with the North American Vegetarian Society (NAVS) and their work in feeding conference-goers (Stepaniak 12). It was not the first vegan cookbook, however. That honor might go to Rupert Wheldon who published *No Animal Food* just 100 miles up the road from the Dinshahs in 1910. Although Wheldon acknowledges the welfare grounds for a totally vegetarian diet, his efforts were firmly grounded in his conviction that plant-based consumption is optimal for human health (11). Even earlier, Russel Thacher published *The Hygeian Home Cook-book* in 1874, which was vegan at least as far as ingredients (no mention of ethical commitment to other animals was made). In 1946, the Leicester

Figure 24.2 Cover of Freya Dinshah's 1965 cookbook, *The Vegan Kitchen*.

Vegetarian Society published *Vegetarian Recipes without Dairy Products*, and that same year, TVS published Fay Henderson's *Vegan Recipes* (Stepaniak 5). Henderson's book was promoted by the society as a "book of ideas" for "amplifying the non-dairy diet" (TVS, "Literature Available" 20). Prior to the 1970s, vegan (and even vegetarian) cookbooks were quite scarce (Spencer 359), such that the humble offerings provided by various societies were essential manuals in *doing* veganism.

Staking the Vegan Claim

By the 1970s, the AVS had begun collaborating heavily with the NAVS. When the NAVS hosted the World Vegetarian Congress, it launched *Vegetarian Voice* for promotional purposes. The newsletter would take on a life of its own. Continuing beyond the conference, it eventually printed 300,000 copies each run and catered to a mailing list of 20,000 (Stepaniak 10–11). Perhaps its most impactful contribution to the movement was its 1975 publication of a detailed instructional guide on how to start a society. Two years later, the number of societies in North America had increased tenfold. As the NAVS grew in movement presence, the amount of energy this growth entailed had begun to starve the AVS. The AVS's own publication, *Ahimsa*, had dwindled to just one small issue per year. After the AVS team returned to its own project, *Ahimsa* expanded and became an influential publication into the twenty-first century (Stepaniak 17). The AVS certainly had an influence over the NAVS, as *Vegetarian Voice* soon decided to cease any mention of Nonhuman Animal products in its content. The NAVS even required the World Vegetarian Conference (operated by the International Vegetarian Union) to adopt veganism in 1996 (Stepaniak 13). The NAVS and IVU are today primarily only vegetarian in name, applying vegan principles in all facets of their organizing and publications. The Vegetarian Society in Britain, by comparison, continues to publish recipes with animal ingredients in its e-newsletter.

Unlike TVS, the AVS remains a family operation and failed to expand in authority as did its British counterpart. Movement historians credit Dr John Robbins's *Diet for a New America*, not published until the late 1980s, as the true catalyst for veganism in the United States (Davis and Melina 3). Robbins was the heir to the Baskin Robbins ice-cream fortune and had come to veganism as a result of his medical training and personal tragedy (his uncle Burt Baskin died of a heart attack at age 54, which Robbins attributed to his high-cholesterol career path). *Diet for a New America* continued in the tradition of American veganism's spiritual interpretation, what Robbins described as "living in accord with the laws of Creation" (xiii). It became a bestseller and inspired a documentary of the same name for the Public Broadcasting Station (PBS).[5] The wide-reaching cultural impact of his book was an indication that society publications could no longer claim full authority over movement discourse.

Similarly, the power and jurisdiction of TVS in Britain was also being challenged. The counterculture of the 1960s and 1970s increased public interest in plant-based consumption, harmonious coexistence with nature, and resistance to violent state agendas. Television coverage, notably a 1976 episode of the BBC's *Open Door* program spotlighting vegans and 1982's *The Animals Film* on Channel 4, were especially mobilizing. These developments brought unprecedented attention to TVS, forcing it to reconsider its small, grassroots organizational style (Wrenn, "Vegan Society" 8–11). By the next decade, the society was also feeling the pressure of the wider anti-speciesist movement which was falling in line with prevailing neoliberal values of the late twentieth century that viewed free economic enterprise as the solution to social ills (this view led to an explosion in non-profits across the globe) (Wrenn, *Piecemeal* 212–13). The society also felt the pressure of its own members, some of whom had been involved in revitalizing other organizations in the movement. Because of its democratic organizational style, TVS was less able to resist "infiltration" from more powerful peer organizations which hoped to rationalize the movement writ large.

In 1980, TVS became a registered charity, and from thereon, editorials regularly featured pleas for donations to support this rather expensive bureaucratic move (Wrenn, "Vegan Society" 9). Prior to this, organizational publications called for donations primarily for the purposes of printing and distributing more publications. Now, they called for funds to support the organization itself. This shift indicated that the organization had become autonomous from the journal; it no longer depended on the journal in order to exist in the movement arena. Furthermore, pleas for donations to support the formalized organization might have become more regular, but the journal was by no means a major source for revenue. After professionalizing, grassroots fundraising becomes insufficient to sustain bureaucratic operations. Most charities accrue the majority of their wealth through grant-issuing foundations, state funding, and large gifts from affluent individuals (Wrenn, *Piecemeal* 119–29).

New Challengers

Early issues of *The Vegan* were deeply political and well into the 1990s featured reader and member contributions which challenged the prevailing vegan doctrines. As the society settled into its new professionalized identity, however, this spiritedness was noticeably dampened (Wrenn, "Vegan Society" 11–12). Longitudinal research in the Nonhuman Animal rights movement indicates that, as organizations professionalize and their message compromises, radical contenders emerge (Wrenn, *Piecemeal* 81–97). Although TVS has not significantly changed its definition of veganism over the years, the tempering of the society's activities overall has encouraged discussions about the meaning of veganism beyond the confines of *The Vegan*. TVS member and founder of the Animal Liberation Front (a radical direct action collective which emerged in the 1970s) Ronnie Lee, for instance, now suggests that the definition of veganism should include more than consumptive behaviors and explicitly recognize a moral duty to educate others (Chiorando). Indeed, this interpretation of veganism as a political identity rather than a simple diet or lifestyle is commonplace in the radical flanks of the Nonhuman Animal rights movement (Thomas et al. 836).

Others, however, have supported a depoliticization of veganism, shying away from the term itself as potentially alienating to would-be dabblers or converts (Wrenn, *Piecemeal* 110–11). Although veganism has become culturally resonant in the twenty-first century, "vegetarianism" as a catch-all term is seeing a resurgence in the movement. As with activists a century prior, today's activists continue to promote "vegetarianism" as a supposedly more welcoming term (as with "veg*nism," which is designed to more explicitly refer to both vegetarians and vegans). "Plant-based" is another challenge to TVS's carefully crafted terminology, and, like "vegetarian" and "veg*n," *can* refer to vegan individuals and products, but still makes room for the use of Nonhuman Animal products given the ambiguousness of what "based" ultimately entails.[6]

The AVS is an important hold-out in this trend. It has been increasingly bold in its use of the term "vegan." Following *Here's Harmlessness*, Dinshah published *Out of the Jungle* to develop his philosophy on vegan *ahimsa*. In the sixth edition, his daughter Anne adjusts the title to *Powerful Vegan Messages*, citing greater cultural familiarity with the term: "The title change to *Powerful Vegan Messages* recognizes the huge advances in veganism. Vegan is now a household word and is even considered cool or sexy in many circles. In 1967 most people had never heard of vegan" (Dinshah and Dinshah 11). This is not to suggest that the AVS had previously shied from the term. Quite the opposite, Dinshah's contemporaries remark on his adamant use of the label "vegan" at conferences and networking events, often to the confusion of long-time vegetarians who were unfamiliar with the concept (Dinshah and Dinshah 56).

In any case, *The Vegan* and *American Vegan* are no longer the authority on vegan discourse in the movement. In addition to the countless magazines and newsletters produced by Nonhuman Animal rights and dietary organizations, a variety of independent lifestyle vegan magazines are now readily available in supermarkets. In fact, the new millennium was a turning point in the movement's dissemination of information and networking. By this point, internet access had become commonplace in Britain, America, and elsewhere, reducing production costs and speeding transmission considerably. TVS responded by shifting to an online presence, operating a blog, podcast, and the expected social media accounts on Facebook, Twitter, YouTube, and Instagram. It, like other anti-speciesist organizations, continues to produce physical copies of its longstanding literary productions, but environmental concerns are pushing back on this tradition. *The Vegan*, for instance, is available in print for members at a slightly higher cost than its "eco" (read: digital) membership. While going digital may have been more consistent with the environmental claims-making associated with plant-based eating, it has the obvious disadvantage of undermining the organization's recruitment capability through traditional channels. Issues might be shared online (indeed, TVS maintains its entire back catalog on issu.com), but it is not clear that such sharing would have the same impact as a print issue with an attractive cover and physical substance. The society switched to a glossy, conventional magazine style after professionalizing for just this reason, restarting with vol. 1, issue 1 in 1985 (Howlett 3). Social media recruitment has now moved to websites and blogs, emails, podcasts, tweets, and posts. Whether or not online advocacy of this kind is superior in efficacy is hotly debated by social movement scholars (Fenton 154–57).

This critique presumes that the journal is still intended for advocacy purposes, which may not be the case as its content has changed more dramatically than its preferred channels. *The Vegan* lacks its once substantive character, reading more like a collection of blogs and social media posts. Spotlights of new vegan products for sale and assorted advertisements now dominate the pages. Astonishingly, the current issue as of this writing (2020, vol. 1) makes no mention whatsoever of Nonhuman Animals, nor does it even feature an image of a Nonhuman Animal. The vegan lifestyle has overshadowed ethical veganism, such that *The Vegan* is now better conceptualized as a product catalog than an activism tool. This shift might reflect the society's attempt to offset production costs, but it also reflects a movement now sidetracked by consumption politics.

On one hand, veganism has now become a dominant frame for the Nonhuman Animal rights movement (Bertuzzi 8), indicating the ultimate success of early organizations at least in their aim to mobilize activists. On the other, the growing consolidation of power in these organizations (evidenced in part by the gradual elimination of member submissions to publications by way of essays, critical letters to the editor, and so on) likely fueled individualization of activism by folks who recognized digital platforms as a means to have their opinions heard and to share their expertise (Wrenn, "Building" 5). At the very least, it offers a means of engagement beyond generic official membership characterized primarily by an annual donation. Bertuzzi observes that modern anti-speciesism is now characterized by its lifestyle politics and online mobilization (10). Although the digital era may have undermined the potency of many social movement newsletters and magazines, their earlier importance in granting legitimacy to a burgeoning idea should be appreciated. Explains TVS as it gears up for another transformation in journal style, "Over the years our magazine has been an essential point of contact for vegans worldwide, providing tips, information and updates on the vital work of the society" (TVS, "New Style!" 2020).

Keeping the Sacred Flame

The early publications of various vegetarian and vegan societies in the United States and United Kingdom illustrate the importance of published work in establishing an organization, lending weight to a philosophy, determining definitions, and nourishing group identity. These organizations, the VSA and TVS in particular, invested considerable efforts into producing regular journals for these purposes. These publications offered a key space where a small leadership cohort exerted its authority over a new movement while also providing space for members to participate, if not from direct contributions in article submissions or letters to the editor, then by simply supporting the organizations through subscription.

The literary productions of early vegan and vegetarian organizations served a number of critical purposes for a fledgling movement desperate to establish itself in a generally hostile, speciesist world. First and foremost, these publications were tangible evidence of *existence*. TVS, for instance, did not simply emerge as an organization independently: it emerged from discord in the *Vegetarian Messenger* and the resultant publication of *The Vegan*. People, of course, met off-the-page in planning the future of veganism, but the society truly became *real* through disagreements and innovations recorded in print. Although many of these publications were compiled by a small team (sometimes even by one person), they created a veneer of legitimacy for establishing groups. This was especially true as the journals and newsletters professionalized with crisp typesetting, photographs, pleasing illustrations, and consistent formatting. A small core of activists could ignite and sustain a movement from their writing pad or typewriter.

Similarly, these publications were vital in establishing movement goals, recruitment, and goal attainment. *The Vegan*, for instance, dedicated considerable space in its early issues to determining the meaning of veganism, the philosophy of veganism, and the aims of the society. These early publications also tended to be quite democratic. Although the editorial team obviously had the power to curate essay submissions, letters to the editor, and general reader feedback, they were remarkably open to disagreement and new ideas. This democratic movement behavior was typical of grassroots activism in the early waves of the movement, but has largely disappeared from today's organizations. TVS, for instance, deflated its "postbag" section in the 1990s, not long after having professionalized (Wrenn, "Vegan Society" 14). The internet would emerge as an important substitute for this lost accessibility, such that the newsletters, magazines, and other publications still operated by vegan and vegetarian organizations now find themselves *responding* to popular and contentious issues transpiring online rather than initiating or facilitating the movement's discourse as they once did.

That said, these publications were also useful in their ability to build group identity. More than giving vegans and vegetarians a platform to voice their ideas and concerns, they provided crucial networking services. Readership learned about important movement leaders and their philosophies, plant-based businesses, conferences, meet-ups, and (through classified ads) like-minded folks in their area. Many formed lasting friendships and marriages through these publications. Even those who never met another subscriber could feel connected. Simply receiving and reading these journals validated their vegan or vegetarian identity. Societies hoped to support these emerging identities as well. Many of the early issues spotlighted biographies, personal stories, anecdotes, and images of healthy, thriving herbivorous hominids. Every issue of *Food, Home and Garden*, for instance, began with a full-length account of a successful vegetarian.

These literary contributions were thus aimed at two audiences: movement members whom they hoped to sustain and would-be members of the public they hoped to recruit. To that end, editors regularly petitioned readers to donate to the production costs, as these tended to usurp the organization's coffers (sometimes to the point of disrupted publication). The publications became critical objects of activism, as they were, in these early years, the gospel of vegan and vegetarian philosophy. Little other media was available to compete before the commercialization of printing in the mid-twentieth century and widespread access to the internet at the turn of the twenty-first century. *Ahimsa, Food, Home and Garden, Vegetarian Messenger, Vegetarian Voice, The Vegan*, and others were projects that not only established the meaning of vegetarianism and veganism; they were key activism tools that lent credibility and spreadability to the cause.

Notes

1. I have written previously on the role of editorial teams in the development of the vegan movement in *Piecemeal Protest*.
2. The term Nonhuman Animal is capitalized here as a political measure to recognize the personhood of other animals.
3. Stepaniak does find two exceptions to this in variations utilized in 1986 and 1989 (3).
4. Nimmo was the first paying member and frequently wrote for *American Vegan* (American Vegan Society "Dr. Catherine Nimmo").
5. Information about the cultural impact of the book can be found on the author's website, <http://www.johnrobbins.info>
6. The launch of the Plant-based Whopper by Burger King is an excellent example. Although it could be presumed vegan, it was quickly revealed that the product was cooked on the main grill amid the fluids of animal bodies used in regular menu items. The restaurant later launched the Vegan Royale which was explicitly vegan. It continues (as of this writing) to coexist on the menu with the non-vegan Plant-based Whopper. Emerging consumer research, it is worth noting, does not support the efficacy of using "plant-based" language to better appeal to non-vegans. Average consumers are drawn to products labeled "vegan" more than those labeled "plant-based" (Anderson 4).

Works Cited

Aker, Frank. "From a Sense of Justice." *Food, Home and Garden*, June, 1897, p. 120.

Alcott, William. Vegetable Diet: *As Sanctioned by Medical Men, and By Experience in All Ages*. Fowlers and Wells Publishers, 1853.

Anderson, Jo. "What to Call Meat Alternatives: A Labeling Study." *Faunalytics*, 2019. <https://faunalytics.org/what-to-call-plant-based-meat-alternatives-a-labelling-study>

American Vegan Society. *Ahimsa*, 2020. <https://americanvegan.org/ahimsa>

—. *History*, 2020. <https://americanvegan.org/AVS-history>

—. "Throwback Thursday: Dr. Catherine Nimmo, Vegan Pioneer," 2020. <https://americanvegan.org/throwback-thursday-dr-catherine-nimmo-vegan-pioneer>

Bertuzzi, Niccolò. "The Individualization of Political Activism: A Reflection on Social Movements and Modernization, Starting from the Italian Animal Advocacy." *International Journal of Sociology and Social Policy*, online first, 2020, pp. 1–22.

Carpenter, Kenneth. "A Short History of Nutritional Science: Part 3 (1912–1944)." *The Journal of Nutrition*, vol. 133, no. 10, 2003, pp. 3023–32.

Chiorando, Maria. "Animal Liberation Front Founder Proposes New Definition of Veganism." *Plant Based News*, 20 August 2018. <https://www.plantbasednews.org/news/animal-liberation-front-founder-proposes-new-definition-veganism>

Clubb, Henry. No title. *Food, Home and Garden*, May, 1896, p. 10.

—. "Advantages of Organization." *Food, Home and Garden*, March, 1897, p. 75.

—. "For Public Libraries." *Food, Home and Garden*, April, 1897, p. 89.

—. "Shall We Succeed?" *Food, Home and Garden*, April, 1897, pp. 89–90.

—. "Sowing the Seed." *Food, Home and Garden*, June, 1896, p. 43.

Cole, Matthew, and Karen Morgan. "Veganphobia: Derogatory Discourses of Veganism and the Reproduction of Speciesism in UK National Newspapers." *The British Journal of Sociology*, vol. 62, no. 1, 2011, pp. 134–53.

Davis, Brenda, and Vesanto Melina. *Becoming Vegan*. Book Publishing Company, 2014.

Davis, John. *World Veganism: Past, Present, and Future*. John Davis, 2012.

Dinshah, Freya. *The Vegan Kitchen*. American Vegan Society, 1965.

Dinshah, Jay. *Here's Harmlessness: An Anthology of Ahimsa*. American Vegan Society, 1964.

Dinshah, Jay, and Anne Dinshah. *Powerful Vegan Messages: Out of the Jungle for the Next Generation*. American Vegan Society, 2014.

Einwohner, Rachel. "Bringing the Outsiders In: Opponents' Claims and the Construction of Animal Rights Activists' Identity." *Mobilization*, vol. 7, no. 3, 2002, pp. 253–68.

Fenton, Natalie. "The Internet and Radical Politics." *Misunderstanding the Internet*, edited by Natalie Fenton and Des Freedman. Routledge, 2012, pp. 149–76.

Gamson, William. "Bystanders, Public Opinion, and the Media." *The Blackwell Companion to Social Movements*, edited by David Snow, Sarah Soule, and Hanspeter Kriesi, Blackwell Publishing, pp. 242–61.

Grumett, David. "Vegetarian Society of the United Kingdom." *Cultural Encyclopedia of Vegetarianism*, edited by Margaret Puskar-Pasewicz, ABC-CLIO, LLC, 2010, pp. 208–10.

Henderson, Fay. "What's In a Name?" *The Vegan*, 1948, vol. 4, no. 2, p. 11.

Henderson, G. Allan. "Report by the Treasurer." *The Vegan*, vol. 3, no. 1, 1947, p. 5.

Howlett, Colin. "On the Move." *The Vegan*, vol. 1, no. 1, 1985, p. 3.

James, W. "Veganism and Science – and a Warning." *The Vegan*, vol. 4, no. 1, 1948, pp. 6–7.

Robbins, John. *Diet for a New America*. H. J. Kramer, 1987.

Rowe, Martin. "American Vegetarian Society 1850 & Remembering Rynn Berry." *HappyCow*. <https://www.happycow.net/blog/amvegsoc1850>

Salt, Henry. *The Logic of Vegetarianism*. The Ideal Publishing Union, 1899.

Sanderson, Jack. "Editorial." *The Vegan*, Autumn, 1965, pp. 1–3.

Scott, John. "The New Series." *Food, Home and Garden*, vol. 1, no. 1, 1896, pp. 4–5.

Shprintzen, Adam. *The Vegetarian Crusade: The Rise of an American Reform Movement, 1817–1921*. U of North Carolina P, 2013.

Spencer, Colin. *The Heretic's Feast: A History of Vegetarianism*. Fourth Estate, 1993.

Stepaniak, Joanne. *The Vegan Sourcebook*. Lowell House, 1998.

Thacher, Russel. *The Hygeian Home Cook-book*. S. R. Wells, 1874.

Thomas, Emma, Simon Bury, Winnifred Louis, Catherine Amiot, Pascal Molenberghs, Monique Crane, and Jean Decety. "Vegetarian, Vegan, Activist, Radical: Using Latent Profile Analysis to Examine Different Forms of Support for Animal Welfare." *Group Processes & Intergroup Relations*, vol. 22, no. 6, 2019, pp. 836–57.

"Vegan." *Oxford Dictionary of English*, 3rd ed. Oxford, 2015.

The Vegan Society. "Literature Available through The Vegan Society", vol. 2, no. 1, 1946, p. 20.

—. "*The Vegan* Magazine has a New Style!" *Blog*, 17 April 2020. <https://www.vegansociety.com/whats-new/blog/vegan-magazine-has-new-style>

"Vegetarian." *Oxford Dictionary of English*, 3rd ed., Oxford, 2015.

Vegetarian Society of America. "John Walter Scott." *Food, Home and Garden*, vol. 1, no. 1, 1896, p. 3.

Watson, Donald. *The Vegan News*. The Vegan Society, 1944, vol. 1, no. 2.

—. *The Vegan News*, vol. 1, no. 3, 1945, p. 1.

Wheldon, Rupert. *No Animal Food and Nutrition and Diet with Vegetable Recipes*. Health Culture Co., 1910.

Wrenn, Corey. "Atheism in the American Animal Rights Movement: An Invisible Majority." *Environmental Values*, vol. 28, no. 6, 2019, pp. 715–39.

—. "Building a Vegan Feminist Network in the Professionalized Digital Age of Third Wave Animal Activism." American Sociological Association Annual Meeting, 12 August 2019, New York, pp. 1–19.

—. *Piecemeal Protest: Animal Rights in the Age of Nonprofits*. U of Michigan P, 2019.

—. "The Vegan Society and Social Movement Professionalization, 1944–2017." *Food and Foodways*, vol. 27, no. 3, 2019, pp. 190–210.

25

MODERN LITERARY PRODUCTION

Veganism and the Contemporary Book Industry

Martin Rowe

Introduction

FOR THIRTY YEARS, I was fortunate to be able to pursue twin vocations professionally: book publishing and the cause of animal rights and veganism. This essay provides a personal account of these histories in order to reflect on the specificity of publishing texts that describe and advocate for veganism, and to consider the various market imperatives that have shaped, and continue to shape, the publication, dissemination, and reception of books that espouse veganism. I consider my own experiences forming Lantern Books, a publisher specializing in veganism, animal advocacy, religion, social justice, and psychology, before exploring the role of BISAC codes (the subject categories and subcategories used by bookstores and libraries to catalog books) to provide an example of the limitations the current publishing industry presents for niche publishers – using *Sistah Vegan*, a book that Lantern published in 2010, as an example. I conclude with reflections from other independent publishers of books on veganism, who speak to the various challenges and rewards of publishing pro-animal books in the current social, politic, and economic publishing climate.

***

It was perhaps foreordained that I'd work with books. I read avidly as a child, and studied English Literature and Language at university. My first job was in a bookshop in my hometown in England, which stirred in me a love of the business of writing and selling books. After university, I was hired as a research assistant to the biographer of T. E. Lawrence (of Arabia). I also compiled catalogs for another bookshop and became the mail-order director for a book distributor in London. In 1991, I moved to New York City and completed a master's degree. During that time, I volunteered at a bookstore, and after graduation I developed marketing material for a publisher. In 1995, Continuum Publishing Company hired me as promotion manager. Four years later, a colleague, Gene Gollogly, and I left to found Lantern.

My second calling was unexpected. I became a vegetarian on something of a whim in 1991 and a vegan when I moved in with my life-partner two years later. In 1994, I co-founded *Satya: A Magazine of Vegetarianism, Environmentalism, Animal Advocacy, and Social Justice*, a free monthly I edited until I started Lantern. I carried *Satya*'s subject interests over to Lantern, and over the course of twenty years published over two hundred titles on these subjects.

Experience suggests to me that issues cannot be understood in isolation. As a result, Lantern's books have tended to cross subject borders: animals and religion, veganism and spirituality, religion and social justice, non-violence to animals, and coping with trauma. Because veganism for me is an expression of values and orientations rather than "foodism" or lifestyle, I've published relatively few cookbooks. I'm skeptical about the expansive claims and miraculous cures that some assign to a vegan diet, and have (mostly) steered clear of such panaceas.

When Gene and I began Lantern, we knew that veganism and animal rights were niche markets. Fortunately, for the first ten years of our existence we also hosted and developed websites, as profitable a venture as book publishing is capital intensive and marginal. We published in other categories: contemplative prayer, interreligious dialogue, responding to violence, and policing. These books also served niche markets, but the authors were often attached to organizations or institutions that purchased books in bulk for their members. This was also true of some of our animal advocacy authors (we produced a number of titles by Ingrid Newkirk of PETA and three by Michael Greger of the HSUS). However, it's fair to say we'd have found it difficult to survive our first decade without revenue from our web business or sales from books not on veganism or animal rights.

That's not to say we remained any less committed, nor that readers of our vegan and animal advocacy books weren't enthusiastic. They were, and they expressed their gratitude often. Nor were we perfect as a publisher. Undoubtedly, some of our titles could have been better written, more sharply edited, and more attractively packaged. We almost certainly could have done more to market and promote them (a common authors' lament of their publishers). However, the fact remains that book publishing has always been, as marketing guru Seth Godin once acerbically put it, "an organized hobby, not a business." Until the advent of crowdfunding platforms, those issuing a book rarely conducted research to find out who, if anyone, might want their product before they delivered it. Until the arrival of print-on-demand technologies, how many copies publishers printed depended on bookstore managers (swayed by sales forces) guessing how many units they could move. Even today, publishers sell to retail outlets not knowing whether consumers will actually purchase those copies, or how many of those copies will occupy shelf space in a warehouse or a store for a few months before being returned. These known unknowns make budgeting difficult and forecasting almost impossible. The elusive bestseller we publishers search for (and sometimes land) is meant to compensate us for the many "surefire" hits that lose money. The odds on this gamble have lengthened as the number of books published each year in the US has exploded – a result of the emergence of self-publishing platforms like Amazon's CreateSpace, Ingram Spark, Xlibris, and others (see Piersanti).

In spite of that exponential increase in production, the number of readers in the US remains relatively flat (Watson), although this statistic, too, may be misleading. Surveys of reading habits rarely ask people to be honest about how much they actually read, let alone whether they read books, or buy books, or buy new books, or new nonfiction books, or books on subjects they don't already have strong feelings about (see, for example, Hess). Moreover, when you read articles that proclaim the return of the independent bookstore or that book sales are holding their own (American Booksellers

Association), it can be easy to assume that bookstores are doing well. But bookstores constitute a small segment of where books are sold, and the copies in those stores constitute an almost vanishingly small fragment of a market that extends from Amazon to Walmart, Target to Costco, SheWrites to Wattpad (see Peterson, and Streitfield).

Nor does volume equal success. In 2018, 675 million individual printed books were sold in the US (Watson), which is an impressive figure until you discover that, in the same year, the number of self-published books rose by 400,000 over the previous year, to 1.6 million (Bowker). That's the sum of the International Standard Book Numbers (ISBNs) issued, and not actual copies printed, which would be significant orders of magnitude greater. Leaving aside the sales of the hundreds of thousands of titles brought to the market by Lantern and other independent third-party publishers; and not including blockbusters such as Michelle Obama's *Becoming*, which sold 1.4 million copies *in its first week* (CBS), and by March 2019 was on track to be the bestselling memoir of all time (Merry); and disregarding the vast output of e-book singles and other content generated on online platforms, this means that the average sale of a book that year was 435 copies at the very most. With the former First Lady at the head of this very, very long tail, it's evident that hundreds of thousands of authors each year sell a mere handful of copies.

These realities are not unique to book producers or authors. Any independent filmmaker or musician will recognize the challenges of navigating a market where a vast amount is being produced by tens of thousands of individuals in the shadow of continued industry consolidation. (The Big Five trade publishers – Penguin/Random House, Hachette, Harper Collins, Simon & Schuster, and Macmillan – whose books crowd the shelves of chain and independent bookstore alike and who constitute somewhere around four-fifths of the book market, are owned by Bertelsmann/Pearson, Lagardère, News Corp, ViacomCBS, and Holtzbrinck, respectively. In November 2020, Penguin/Random House bought Simon & Schuster for $2 billion – further consolidating the industry.)

Academic presses don't have it any easier. In 2019, Stanford University announced it was stopping funding its own press, which led to considerable angst among academics about whether university presses should be expected to make a profit (Somin). Although reports of university presses' imminent demise may be premature, as Andrew Albanese and Annie Coreno have argued, they remain minnows in the field of education publishing. That market is dominated by another Big Five (McGraw-Hill, Houghton Mifflin Harcourt, Pearson, Scholastic, and Cengage), who likewise control about 80 per cent of it (Echevarria and Bowman). Even though these five aren't directly subsidized, they, like the trade, are often buttressed by multimedia ownership. They also exert a stranglehold over the extensive examination, textbook, and digital learning apparatuses in a system that is open to potential abuse (see, for example, Reingold).

The irony is that, in spite of dominating their relative markets; being synonymous in the public's mind with what it means to be a published author; and for many authors, representing the pinnacle of achievement, the profit margins of these corporations' book publishing divisions may be as narrow as Lantern's (see Greenfield) – if the book retails for a price that most mortals or students can afford. Committed to selling in advance of publication into bookstores, locked into multi-year publishing programs, competing for top authors through six- or even seven-figure advances, and dealing with significant overheads, trade behemoths sometimes struggle as much as the small fry does.

Whether big or small, all publishers depend on author "platforms." They aim to satisfy the author's core market first, and then hope for that strange serendipity that occurs when an author or topic, or both, catches the public's imagination and the book takes off. That no amount of pre-production preparation or post-publication promotion can guarantee that success is our collective frustration. It's also why we keep going, tossing book after book into the marketplace and hoping that one or two of them find an enthusiastic audience ready to spread the word.

Lantern and other small independents cannot compete for media or shelf space with multiply consolidated publishing houses, such as Random House. Nonetheless, we've survived. Lantern has surfed the tsunami that crashed over independent bookstores: first, through the expansion of Barnes & Noble and Borders, and then on the arrival and market domination of Amazon, which decimated the megastores themselves (Wahba). We've watched as book review pages have vanished from newspapers, followed by the disappearance of the newspapers themselves.

Wise heads at dot-com companies told us when we began that the printed word was dead; and we've charted the rapid ascent, plateauing, and gentle decline of e-books (Grady), as well as the collapse of numerous dot-com start-ups who prophesied we'd be gone by 2010. We've negotiated our way through 9/11, the global recession, and now a pandemic. We've accompanied the rise of crowdfunding and self-publishing; the spread of affordable typesetting and production software; and the blossoming of huge amounts of informative, entertaining, and sophisticated content online – all of it either free or readily accessible for less than the cost of a paperback.

Lantern has survived by not veering too far from our publishing biome, staying within genres, keeping costs low, outsourcing our work to freelancers, and trusting that our authors will maximize the utility of their books in a way that will benefit us. We've asked them to measure success not simply in terms of sales, but in how the book has helped them to achieve their goals: gaining tenure or a Ph.D., landing a speaking gig or addressing larger audiences, crowning a life or starting a career, branding an organization, or beginning anew. Traditionally published books rarely generate enough sales and royalties for an author to make a living from them. But they furnish third-party credibility, offer a sense of accomplishment, and function as a calling card for someone to announce themselves.

Sistah Vegan

A further challenge Lantern faces is a function of its interdisciplinarity and the relative structural rigidity of publishing. One way of illustrating this is through an examination of the BISAC codes (which I'll get to shortly) and *Sistah Vegan: Black Women Speak on Food, Identity, Health, and Society*, an anthology of two-dozen pieces edited by A. Breeze Harper, which we re-issued in a tenth anniversary edition in 2020.[1] The manuscript for *Sistah Vegan* came to Lantern via one of our authors, pattrice jones. She recommended to Breeze – who'd put out a call for black women vegans to submit their thoughts to her as part of the Sistah Vegan Project (<http://sistahvegan.com>) – that she send the manuscript to Lantern.

The manuscript was a revelation for me. Not only was it diverse in its means of expression – poetry, confessions, essays, conversations, and reflections – but "veganism" was a strand in a multidimensional narrative that encompassed (in part): colonialism, racism, personal and public health, body size and image, gender, sexuality, environmental awareness, food justice, slavery, the whiteness (perceptually, intellectually, and demographically) of veganism and the animal rights movement, Afrocentrism, intergenerational solidarity or conflict, feminism, self-care, class, and spirituality. *Sistah Vegan* reinforced Lantern's operating notion that when we talk *about* veganism, we're really talking *through* veganism: that is, veganism is a lens by which we can discern more keenly the realities of our and others' lives; and, conversely, that its insights are themselves refracted through ours and others' experiences.

The diversity of *Sistah Vegan*'s means of expression and the subject matter it covered laid bare the presumptuousness of someone like me, who is so privileged by economic status, whiteness, gender, and sexual orientation that we assume that wherever I might be is where a *movement* is centered, *the* conversation is occurring, and what constitutes truth or strategic thinking is being generated and shared. Because the publishing industry is still filled with gatekeepers who look and sound like me,[2] we assume that only the conversations *we* are part of, or read, or are sent, or that have already been published by people like us are what embody a set of ideas that are appropriate for the public sphere.

By extension, what *Sistah Vegan* made abundantly clear to me, a vegan, was that black women weren't just vitally engaged with veganism now, but they'd been talking, sharing, cooking, and mobilizing for years. They didn't need to be told there were problems with the food system, that the Standard American Diet was killing them and their families, and that there were better ways to live in community with one another, the planet, and the animals. What they needed was to be listened to. *Sistah Vegan* demonstrated that if the so-called vegan or animal rights "movements" hadn't heard from these women, it was because we [sic] hadn't bothered to pay attention or remove ourselves from our silos. That absence was not only a sad reflection of the failure of the "movements" to "reach out" but an unwelcome reminder that these "movements" weren't even movements: they were clubs with certain requirements for membership that inherently excluded those who talked through veganism in a different way than "we" did.

It was logical to assume that not only were these multifarious conversations happening among African American women in communities across the United States, but there was no reason to assume they weren't continuing among communities of every color and stripe. Not only that, but it was a good bet that these conversations were more interesting, more dynamic, and more grounded in lived experience than those taking place in the university lecture halls, conference centers, or hotel ballrooms where the movements' "leaders" gathered to speak about what veganism and animal rights were or meant or signified. *Sistah Vegan*'s richly interlaced chapters – many inherently in dialogue with one another – further suggested that how veganism and animal rights were discussed and published (the philosophical treatise, the recipe book, the screed against killing animals) limited the possible entry points to, the communities that could be formed from, and the scope and reach of, an infinitely rich universe of veganisms.

BISAC Blues

So, how might one categorize *Sistah Vegan* to be able to find it in a bookstore, library, or online? Before any book is published for sale to the public or an institution, it needs to receive an ISBN and all its relevant bibliographic details (metadata) organized and presented to the wholesalers and retailers, nowadays through the ONIX system.[3] In the last couple of decades, the Book Industry Study Group (BISG), founded forty years ago to conduct research on markets and the state of the industry, has developed BISAC codes to organize subject areas for the ever-increasing number of books published each year.[4] The codes, of which there are more than three thousand, are reviewed annually, and as of March 2020, fit into fifty-three different categories (from Antiques & Collectibles to Young Adult Nonfiction), with each category divided into subcategories and sub-subcategories. So, for instance, the Design category also has a Graphic Arts subcategory, which itself has an Advertising sub-subcategory. If your book, therefore, is an introduction to the use of graphic arts in advertising, you would assign it the primary BISAC code of DES007010. Because they are relatively frequently updated, BISAC codes offer a useful guide to emerging trends. However, because the taxonomies of categories and subcategories must remain relatively rigid to create an organizational structure worthy of the term, they can be Procrustean. Such is the case with *Sistah Vegan*.

So, to ask again, how might one categorize *Sistah Vegan*? The most obvious BISAC identification would be Vegan. However, the only place where the word appears is under Cooking, where it is its own subcategory, distinct from Vegetarian. Such a distinction shows that the concept of veganism, as well as the word, has gained currency and an acceptance and identity many of us in the 1990s could not have imagined. Back then, *Satya* and Lantern's titles (and authors) weren't confident enough to use the shorter "v" word for fear we'd alienate too many.

That progress, however, is shadowed by the fact that *Sistah Vegan* isn't a cookbook. Indeed, this categorization demonstrates the fact that the great majority of books published in the United States with the word *vegan* in them are about cooking and lifestyle. This veganism is usually depoliticized and deracialized, unless it self-consciously draws attention to veganism as an act of resistance.[5] It would be an almost perverse misreading of the book, therefore, to assign it to BISAC category CKB125000.

Another obvious category would be within African American Studies, and SOC001000 would allow me to place *Sistah Vegan* under Ethnic Studies/American/African American Studies, and SOC010000 would center *Sistah Vegan* within Feminism & Feminist Theory. However, this would in turn erase veganism as well as environmental and animal advocacy from the book's identity.

You will search in vain for a standalone Animal Rights category among the BISAC codes. Instead, it is a subcategory of Nature (NAT039000), as, indeed, are Animals. These in turn are subcategorized by species: bears, big cats, birds, butterflies and moths, all the way through to wildlife and wolves. Absent from the menagerie are cows, pigs, chickens, and other animals we raise for food. You will find them categorized under Juvenile Fiction/Animals (along with Dragons, Unicorns & Mythical) or Juvenile Nonfiction (accompanied by Dinosaurs & Prehistoric Creatures).

That Animal Rights is part of the Nature category is, like the standalone Vegan cooking subcategory, a mark of progress: at least, one might say, the BISAC codes hint at a rapprochement between animal rights and environmental ethics, when once writers such as J. Baird Callicott among others argued that the former had no place within the latter.[6] It's also gratifying that Ethology (Animal Behavior) is found as a subcategory of Science/Life Sciences/Zoology. It suggests increasing recognition that animal sentience and cognitive capacity not only form proper academic study, but that animals themselves may possess them.

Nonetheless, it's instructive that the animals with whom most of us interact most intimately (on our plate) don't even qualify as animals at all *within* Nature. It's hard not to see this absence as a perpetuation of the long-standing division between animal advocates and everybody else, with the latter considering farmed domesticated animals somehow de-natured and de-animalized, not only *because* they "allow" themselves to be slaughtered, but *in order* that they may be turned into meat.

It is, of course, a further signification of farmed animals' erasure as, in philosopher Tom Regan's formulation, "subjects of a life," that their "appropriate" role is as subjects of children's imagination and literature. That children respond deeply to animals is a truism. However, the publishing industry's assigning of books in this way implies that interest in the lives and experiences of individual animals who are not wild or charismatic megafauna is a childish concern, and that adult and/or rational engagement with such animals as subjects is impossible and inappropriate.[7]

Of Possibilities and Failure

It's possible that the BISAC codes will shift to reflect new understandings, and that the sheer volume of new titles on veganism and our relationship with other animals will open up new categories and subcategories. In this task, Lantern has been joined by, among others, Ashland Creek Press, Vegan Publishers, Sanctuary Publishers, and Faunary Press (the founders of which talk about their work at the end of this chapter).

Certainly, interest is booming. In the two decades since I co-founded Lantern, scholarship under the rubric of Animal Studies has blossomed. University presses at Georgia, Columbia, Illinois, Chicago, New York, Minnesota, and elsewhere have started and expanded publishing programs on animals across the disciplines.[8] Presses not affiliated with a university, such as Reaktion, Routledge, Lexington, Brill, and Palgrave Macmillan, have enabled scholars to collaborate to create anthologies from their research and turn Ph.D. theses into books.[9]

As much as the landscape for books about animals and veganism may have changed with the advent of Animal Studies – or is reflected by the volume you're reading this chapter in – much remains the same. That, all too often, four of the publishers above sell their titles for over one hundred dollars (print) and almost as much in e-book form, with each chapter being downloadable for twenty or thirty dollars (or euros or pounds), is a reflection of how saturated the market is with readily reproducible content. The high price points are both a cause and an effect of the continuing niche within which serious discussion about veganism and animals outside of cooking and children's books nests. These price points also, frankly, represent a shameful (if accidental) collaboration between academics and publishers to silo knowledge in unaffordable volumes that allow the former to add a line to their résumé and the latter to extract the most amount of money for labor that is essentially free (most academics don't receive a royalty advance for their books).[10] If you can publish monograph after monograph (or abstruse journal for that matter) at minimal cost to you and sell a hundred copies of each to a few libraries around the nation, then in aggregate you stand to make enough money to justify your existence.

That *Sistah Vegan* (price-point £18.99 in the UK, $22 in the US) refuses to slot neatly into any publishing category is an illustration of how hard such a book and the voices within it must struggle to demonstrate the scope, range, and depth of the subjects they cover – whether they end up in a bookstore or not. More uncomfortably, the continued stratification of BISAC categories also signals how we vegans and/or animal advocates have failed to present enough literature, or enough *persuasive* literature, to shift perceptions that veganism is more than cuisine and diet, or a lifestyle choice, and that farmed animals are, actually, animals, beyond their utility to farmers (Technology & Engineering/Agriculture/Animal Husbandry) or would-be cowboys (Juvenile Nonfiction/Farm Life *see* Lifestyles/Farm & Ranch Life). We've also failed in the academy and in the marketplace of ideas. You still won't find Animal Rights under Philosophy, Political Science, Social Science, or Religion in BISAC codes – a testament to how, in spite of our best efforts and *pace* Claude Lévi-Strauss, for most people animals do not appear good to think with, at least not in the English-language market of the United States. One ray of light might be adult fiction about animals (FIC067000). As this volume testifies, some of us don't leave behind a fascination with the world of other creatures when we grow up, and fiction offers a valuable and vital pathway to changing hearts and minds.

It's a sign of books' resilience as a repository of literal authority and cultural value that we still return to them for the first and last word on a subject, and vest them (and the people who write them) with an expertise that we do not possess. After all, that's why you're reading this. But then I would say that, wouldn't I? Like so many independent publishers, I have a romantic and self-righteously high-minded commitment to a calling that, in truth, has always been on the verge of collapse, dependent on unconventional accounting methods, and more reliant for its survival on penny dreadfuls, pulp fiction, and everything from *Valley of the Dolls* to *Captain Underpants* (90 million copies sold as of 2019) to *50 Shades of Gray* (the best-selling book of the decade) than any number of *Sistah Vegan*s.

As for books being an essential disseminator of the world's great ideas, this essay and the tome in which it is published won't likely see the light of day until spring 2022, at the earliest. By that time, COVID-19 may be forgotten, the publishing industry assailed by another crisis, and this essay out of date: a captured moment in a time. So, you might as well take to heart Seth Godin's advice for would-be authors from 2006, as true then as when you read these words:

> Understand that a non-fiction book is a souvenir, just a vessel for the ideas themselves. You don't want the ideas to get stuck in the book . . . you want them to spread. Which means that you shouldn't hoard the idea. The more you give away, the better you will do.

Publishers Speak

For this essay, I contacted six other independent publishers of books on veganism in spring 2020 and asked them to reflect on their experience as vegan publishers. Although we come from different backgrounds, we're all small and mission-driven and our sales are based in the US market. As you'll learn from their first-person accounts, these publishers confront many of the challenges outlined in this essay: how to reach beyond their niche, core markets; how to work within *and* yet counteract the consolidated dominance of large publishers and distributors; how to earn a living; how to adapt to the changing technologies and delivery of information within and beyond publishing; and shifting perceptions of how veganism is perceived and received in the marketplace.

Julia Feliz, Founder, Sanctuary Press (founded 2017): <sanctuarypublishers.com>

Sanctuary Publishers is not a traditional book publisher. It is resource activism. In an industry in which Black and Indigenous people are the least represented and given a platform, Sanctuary Publishers is purposefully carving a space in a world that denies people like me opportunities. It is a simple platform from which to reach our own on topics that are important to those of us with intersecting identities, which inform our everyday lives, experiences, perceptions, and basically, everything, while ensuring that nonhumans are also given a platform through those very experiences and our history, which are intertwined with their oppression and existence.

My original goal with Sanctuary Publishers was as an anti-capitalistic, self-sustaining book publishing system. I built up Sanctuary Publishers during nap times and between mealtimes, playtime, bath-time, and school drop-off and picks ups while isolated in a foreign country. Now a single parent and having moved back to the US, one of the biggest challenges in running a publisher is being able to afford to do this work while studying and working to make sure my children are taken care of. It's gotten more stressful now with the pandemic and having to also keep up with virtual school on top of everything else. I do worry about the ability to remain open, but even then, we are getting closer and closer to publishing our tenth book.

While Sanctuary Publishers has achieved so much in such a short time and hopes to do more, it has not made a profit because of the self-going system I committed to, in which my own authored books would pay for more books by others to help keep it all going. Funding-wise, I knew I wouldn't have as many opportunities for grants and funding because of the systemic inequality in the non-profit sector. It was important to me not to depend on white institutions that don't tend to support us and, when they do, may not do so for the right reasons. I had already felt used, silenced, and tokenized by the industry, and I wanted to keep other Black, Brown, and Indigenous people from that. There tends to be this idea that if we are given something, the donors then own us for as long as they need us or end up tokenizing us and our work; so, in the end, our voices are still drowned out. Sadly, it's not uncommon to also face inappropriate editing of our writing by those who do not share our cultures and perspectives, or to be rejected since those few published tend to be those who white communities can identify with and are kept comfortable by.

In essence, Sanctuary Publishers is as grassroots as it gets. The money raised from sales of the books is used to pay royalties to the authors and illustrators for their labor, donate to projects or efforts by marginalized vegans, pay for the basics of running a "business," pay for the publication of new books, and creating new resources, such as websites and booklets. We have even hosted two conferences for vegans of color. Through Sanctuary Publishers, I have been able to work with people all over the world in an effort to raise the voices of nonhuman animals through conversations about interconnections: not only with People of Color but also with vegans of all races that are also part of the LGBTQIA+ community.

Sanctuary Publishers is a commitment to justice and to advancing conversations by ensuring as many people as possible have a platform to speak about issues and how these affects them. Sanctuary Publishers has also been helpful for those of us not from the white mainstream majority to start to form bridges to reach our own communities and extend the conversation in ways that make sense to us, for us. It's a start – but there's still much left to do, including translations and audiobooks so that Spanish speakers and neuro-divergent people, for example, can also access our content. I still have hope that we will continue to exist, and welcome the support and help from those that understand our unusual, non-traditional values and goals.

Awareness and action across issues is part of my praxis: Consistent Anti-Oppression. This is why Sanctuary Publishers was started, why we are still going, and why we hope to do more, because there will be no liberation for all without a consistent commitment to anti-oppression across communities and movements. This is what I'm trying to work on within my little corner of the world.

A. Marie Houser, Founder, Faunary Press (founded 2016): <faunarypress.com>

I established Faunary Press in anticipation of other publishers having little idea what to do with my volume of short fiction, *After Coetzee: An Anthology of Animal Fictions*. The anthology features contributions that stage resistances by other animals to their conceptual and material captivity. This focus has a specific ethical spin, one generally absent from projects that aim(ed) to depict other animals or our lives with and among them. The tagline for Faunary Press – literature for and about animals – gestures towards an ethical motivation, though aesthetic concerns of course had equal focus.

In choosing to publish *After Coetzee*, the press took on the marketing challenges other publishers would have had. I approached these challenges with the same twee-punk spirit that went into crafting the book as a made object. I chose not to go down the generic route of sending the book to typical review outlets. Instead, I focused on my contacts and their contacts. The book's scholarly provenance meant that these contacts, many of whom are either academics or writers of conscience, would "get" what the book meant to do. In this way, our marketing flowed from the book's conception.

Additional challenges inhered in starting a press from scratch. Though I had worked in publishing, I served mainly as a copy and developmental editor. I had not been prepared for the myriad other decisions related to making and selling a book. It didn't help that, because the book represented a long, at times personal journey, I wanted my hand in *everything*, from press branding to cover design. (The book's foundational ideas took shape over twenty years ago, when I encountered anthropocentrism as an undergraduate student in philosophy and then as a graduate student in English.) Thankfully, collaborators came on board to provide administrative assistance and copyediting.

The primary challenge arose when it came time to distribute the book internationally as well as domestically. Yet I knew my audience, and I knew the book would have greatest longevity overseas (it has). I devised to craft-print the book on US shores but release it overseas by means of local, on-demand printing and distribution. This plan solved a number of problems but unknowingly introduced a couple of others. Namely, it relied on Amazon, a devil's bargain I would not make again.

I find that following up on *After Coetzee* is now our greatest conundrum. I've had a number of ideas, but difficulties that surrounded and overlapped the founding of the press and the publication of the book have in some ways induced silence and indecision in me. Small publishers need either time or money, resources we lack.

Several vegan publishers now exist; I am gratified to see that they do. Writing communities and activist communities can be disastrously competitive, but there's room at the veganic table for all. My hope is for collegiality and communality to characterize vegan publishing.

My final observation moves more in the direction of a wish. The imminent collapse of systems that sustain life on Earth must shape the next iteration of vegan publishing. When Faunary Press becomes active again, it will either forgo printing altogether or offer better digital options. But by "next iteration," I mean something more than just alternative methods of delivering the same content. Vegans already think capaciously and systemically; after a long period of hostility between environmentalism and veganism/animal rights/animal liberation, a period now largely passing, vegans have and must continue to make manifest the connections between destruction and consumption of animal bodies and the detonation of life-sustaining systems. I would like for vegan publishers to find creative ways to help them do so.

Casey Taft, Vegan Publishers (founded 2013): *<veganpublishers.com>*

We started Vegan Publishers because we perceived a need for more literature in this area, especially for children, and were looking for an additional source of income with our first child arriving. We are happy we did so because of reason number one, and not so much for reason number two. Our biggest challenge has always been distribution and meeting our sales targets, especially during difficult economic times where the average vegan may not have much disposable income. This has led to a greater shift towards children's books, since most households still buy books for their children, even if not for themselves.

We've learned a great deal about veganism since we started and have grown to be much stronger in our ethical convictions. We've expanded our understanding to interconnected forms of injustice and become more activist in our intentions and actions. We did not consider ourselves "activists" when we began, but do now, as we see literature as an important component of social movements, and have collaborated with other activists in different areas of vegan education.

It's a challenging time for all niche publishers. Areas of vegan publishing, such as cookbooks, have been absorbed by large mainstream publishers; other areas less so. From our experience, we realize that it's important to find different sources of income to continue to function, either by going the non-profit route, or expanding to other areas such as research consulting. Nobody should go into this area with the intention of making a large profit. We would be content to more or less break even, while engaging in this rewarding work.

John Yunker, Co-founder, Ashland Creek Press (founded 2011): <ashlandcreekpress.com>

I started Ashland Creek as an author. In 2008, I wrote a novel, *The Tourist Trail*, which tells the story of a vegan penguin researcher and her love affair with an anti-whaling activist (also vegan) on the run from the law. Though I had an agent, she was unable to find a mainstream publisher for the book. The animal rights themes were a challenge, but there was also the larger question of how to market the book – amid the Great Recession, no less.

My partner, Midge Raymond, and I have backgrounds in publishing, and we realized there might be other books out there facing similar obstacles. This led to Ashland Creek Press. By 2012, we'd published *The Tourist Trail* as well as an additional five books by other authors, four of which were debut novels. We continue to publish between two and four books a year, all of which have themes related to animals and environmental protection.[11]

The challenges we face are similar to that of all publishers – finding readers for the books you publish. Every year sees hundreds of thousands of new books published, with fewer and fewer book reviews and other channels for promoting books. And, as an indie press, it can be challenging to find shelf space within the dwindling number of bricks-and-mortar bookstores.

As a vegan press, we face challenges in educating audiences – including vegans. Vegans are well accustomed to reading the labels of the food they purchase to see if it's vegan, and we'd love to see them bring a similar awareness of the books they read, to support vegan and vegetarian authors (and not only the ones who write cookbooks!). We started EcoLit books, a site for readers and writers of environmental fiction, to bring more awareness to these issues. Although EcoLit Books is not specifically vegan, it's a great way for vegan readers to discover books by similarly minded authors.

Ultimately, though, our mission has always been to publish books for all readers along the full spectrum of animal rights and environmental issues. Not all of our authors are vegan (though we're thrilled that many of them are), and certainly not all of our books' readers are vegan. But because our goal is to open readers' hearts and minds to the issues of animal rights and the environment – and especially the connection between the two – our books are aimed at all audiences. What matters most to us is publishing great stories: books that have something to say and will improve the world for animals and human animals alike.

Recently, we've noticed more environmental fiction emerging from mainstream publishers, which is exciting to see. However, these novels generally fall into the category of "cli-fi" and tend to be dystopian. Very rarely do we see novels that tackle animal rights, animal rescue, or veganism in authentic ways, and these are the kinds of books we still hope to discover and publish. We also want to see literature that isn't set in the future but in the here and now – fiction that offers a glimpse of our current society and inspires hope for change, rather than a grim, apocalyptic worldview.

Although we publish non-fiction such as David Brook's *The Grass Library*, Roger Thompson's *No Word for Wilderness*, and Jacki Stole's *Dogland*, we love to publish fiction because it can be subversive; it can go places non-fiction cannot. As publishers –

and as authors – it's heartening to know how effectively books can inspire change. When I hear from readers who have enjoyed *The Tourist Trail* and have given up eating seafood due to what they learned through the story, it means the world to me. And we feel the same way about our books and our ACP authors.

Charles Stahler, Co-founder, Vegetarian Resource Group (founded 1982): <vrg.org>

When my partner, Debra Wasserman, and I moved to Baltimore in 1982, we started a new group, which since Debra and I were vegan, was always vegan-oriented. Our main purpose was educational with a belief in science and practical information. My mom was a science teacher and Debra's dad was a scientist, so we probably had more of a belief in traditional science than many people in the movement.

In the beginning, we did many outreach booths/presentations and received the traditional questions about veg diets being too hard and complicated. Many veg cookbooks at that time were good, but too complex and the preparation and cooking took too long. So in 1983 we created *Vegetarianism for the Working Person*, with quick recipes. It was given a two-sentence mention in *Changing Times* magazine, and we received 300 orders. That launched us as a book publisher. Established publishers told us no one was interested in quick-and-easy recipes, so we did an expanded book ourselves. *Vegetarian Times* magazine bought 10,000 in a perfect-bound format, and so we printed enough at a low-enough cost that we could afford to go to wholesalers and bookstores. In 1991, we published *Simply Vegan*, with quick recipes and an easy-to-understand nutrition section based on science. There were few other vegan books at the time, and we sold 100,000. Debra did one of the first vegan cooking demos on *Good Morning America* from another of her cookbooks.

Our work today feels important, even more so when we see how much false information and meanness is circulating in the United States and the rest of the world. We feel good that we have planted a few seeds and have given many people an opportunity to contribute their skills. Introducing interns to new experiences and connections is one of our favorite parts of VRG. It is nice to have met so many people in the various related movements, and gratifying to give new writers an opportunity to publish.

When we started there were only a few vegan books. Of course, today it's very different, with so many vegan books and with the Internet. To be successful, you generally have to make yourself the center of attention or be a guru, which is a little counter to many of the reasons to be vegan. It's been said that today a book is your business card. It's not so much about publishing a book or magazine or social media, but the brand you build around it.

In the past, when we received books to review in *Vegetarian Journal*, likely it would get reviewed or sold at our booths if it was vegan. Today, there are so many vegan books that there is only room for a select few reviews in our magazine. People at booths don't buy as much because of "free" information on the Internet and the multitude of books, so you have to have different strategies, just as publishing quick-and-easy vegan information was a new strategy a few decades ago.

Bob Holzapfel, Book Publishing Company (founded 1974): <bookpubco.com>

Book Publishing Company was begun at The Farm, an intentional community based in Summertown, Tennessee. Although the community was vegan, we discovered that there was very little literature available. We decided to publish books on being a healthy vegan. Some of us went to work in a publishing house to learn the business, and we published Louise Hagler's *The Farm Vegetarian Cookbook* in 1975.

At that stage, the company was at a subsistence level. Nobody really knew how much money we were spending and we'd spend gobs of time creating. By the mid-1980s, when The Farm changed from being a commune to a cooperative community and we received an endowment, we became more professional. However, even today, we are certainly not rolling in dough. We're fortunate in that some of our other classic titles, like Ina May Gaskin's *Spiritual Midwifery* (1975), which has sold several hundred thousand copies and still sells well to this day, help boost the vegan publishing side of the business.

We always felt that vegetarianism was an important subject, which in the mid-1980s, wasn't being covered by mainstream media. We wanted people to know there was an alternative to the Standard American Diet that was better for your health, the environment, and animals. Up to the early 1990s, we only published books on vegetarianism. However, we then realized that dairy and eggs were only a quarter-step better than killing the animal.

In recent years, veganism has gone mainstream, with books like Michael Greger's *How Not to Die* (2015) selling hundreds of thousands of copies. The big publishers realized there were big hits out there and started scouring the country for popular bloggers and vegan chefs. That meant BPC had to adjust our focus. We now sell cookbooks that are specific and/or health-related: We have a FODMAP cookbook;[12] Miyoko Schinner's *Artisan Vegan Cheese: From Everyday to Gourmet* (2012) is a great seller; and our next cookbook focuses on seitan. We've branched out to publish more books outside of the food world, and we also have about a hundred titles for and by Native Americans.

To those thinking of entering vegan publishing today, I'd suggest making connections with specific authors who have the ability to move books. An unknown author with a limited platform who isn't pounding the pavement or doing gigs isn't going to work. There's too much competition from people doing all those things. Distribution of content is both easier and harder, since there are many more outlets than before. However, Amazon has crushed the business and publishing worlds, because it consistently exacts more from everybody it buys from.

The same is the case with vegan authors. If you land a large publisher and get a huge advance and things don't go right for you, you're gone immediately. A small publisher tends to publish books we believe in and you get a working relationship with us. We can still sell fifty or one hundred thousand books. So, authors need to be honest with themselves, which is difficult, because we all believe we're writing something that's never been seen before or is the next big hit.

But there's a bigger picture. All of us publishers need to see that veganism is an evolution that may take fifty or even a hundred years. Our task is to remind ourselves that we're lucky to be part of this effort, because we got to spend our professional lives doing work we believe in. And there aren't many folks that can say that.

Conclusion

So what lessons can be drawn about book publishing and veganism from the above? There are commonalities. Both are currently minority pursuits within a general society that is largely indifferent to their presence, except perhaps as signifiers of a kind of personal virtue or ambition ("I'm thinking of writing a book"; "I don't eat a lot of meat"). Both have been commercialized, commodified, and depoliticized, although both possess thriving grassroots communities exploring the possibilities of sustainable production and consumption. Both could continue to be consolidated in vertically integrated networks, or they could be radically democratized into artisanal, bio-regional, non-hierarchical sources of community and cultural knowledge transfer. And both are currently subject to technological innovation that might change the very identity of each (cultivated meat; interactive digital content).

That said, it would be hard to indicate a specifically *vegan* dimension to publishing, except to welcome more voices from self-proclaimed vegans, more arguments for veganism, and more diversity within the industry, the content it produces, and the readers who feel addressed and heard. Indeed, to project *Sistah Vegan* forward another decade or two, it is to be hoped that "veganisms" are no longer addenda or alternatives to our lives but the conceptual frames within which civilization, ecosystems, and diverse communities of human and nonhuman life not only survive, but thrive.

Notes

1. For a further discussion of *Sistah Vegan*, see Armin Langer's essay in this volume.
2. For more on the racial politics of mainstream publishing see De León et al.
3. For more on ONIX, visit <https://bookpublishingsoftware.com/onix>
4. BISAC stands for Book Industry Standards and Communications. For more on BISAC, see <https://bisg.org/page/BISACFaQ>
5. See, for instance, Adams and Messina, *Protest Kitchen*. A search of Google images under "vegan cookbook" will show you how rare such a cookbook is.
6. For a critique of this position, see Jamieson.
7. For more on this division, see Ali Ryland's essay in this volume.
8. University of Georgia Press (Animal Voices, Animal Worlds); Columbia University Press (Animal Studies); University of Illinois Press (Animal Rights); University of Chicago Press (Animal Lives); NYU Press (Animals in Context); University of Minnesota Press (Theory and Philosophy: Posthumanism).
9. Reaktion Books (Animal); Routledge (Human-Animal Studies Series); Lexington (Critical Animal Studies and Theory); Brill (Human-Animal Studies Book Series); Palgrave Studies in Animals and Literature.
10. For more on this problematic collaboration, see Anonymous Academic.
11. See Ali Ryland's essay in this volume for a close reading of the *Lithia* trilogy published by Ashland Creek.
12. Fermentable oligo-, di-, mono-saccharides and polyols.

Works Cited

Adams, Carol J., and Virginia Messina. *Protest Kitchen: Fight Injustice, Save the Planet, and Fuel Your Resistance One Meal at a Time*. Conari, 2018.

Albanese, Andrew, and Annie Coreno. "University Presses Are Not in Crisis." *Publishers Weekly*, 27 April 2018.

American Booksellers Association. "Independent Bookstores Are Thriving: Recent Stories and Profiles." n.d.

Anonymous Academic. "Academics Are Being Hoodwinked into Writing Books Nobody Can Buy." *The Guardian*, 4 September 2015.

Bowker. "Self-Publishing Grew 40 Percent in 2018, New Report Reveals." *Bowker.com*, 15 October 2019.

Brooks, David G. *The Grass Library: Essays*. Ashland Creek Press, 2020.

CBS News. "Michelle Obama's Book Sells 1.4 million Copies in a Week." *CBS*, 21 November 2018.

De León, Concepción, Alexandra Alter, Elizabeth A. Harris, and Joumana Khatib. "'A Conflicted Cultural Force': What It's Like to Be Black in Publishing." *New York Times*, 1 July 2020.

Echevarria, Gina, and Jordan Bowman. "Almost 80% of the Textbook Industry is Dominated by 5 Publishing Companies that Make Books So Expensive Most Students Skip Buying Them." *Business Insider*, 4 December 2018.

Gaskin, Ina May. *Spiritual Midwifery*. Book Publishing Company, 1975.

Godin, Seth. "Advice for Authors." August 2006. <https://seths.blog/2006/08/advice_for_auth>

Grady, Constance. "The 2010s Were Supposed to Bring the Ebook Revolution. It Never Quite Came." *Vox*, 23 December 2019.

Greger, Michael, and Gene Stone. *How Not to Die: Discover the Foods Scientifically Proven to Prevent and Reverse Disease*. Flatiron, 2015.

Greenfield, Jeremy. "Why Amazon is Going after Publisher Profit Margin." *Forbes*, 16 June 2014.

Hagler, Louise. *The Farm Vegetarian Cookbook*. Book Publishing Company, 1975.

Hess, Abigail. "24 Percent of American Adults Haven't Read a Book in the Past Year – Here's Why." *CNBC*, 29 January 2019.

Houser, A. Marie (ed.). *After Coetzee: An Anthology of Animal Fictions*. Faunary Press, 2017.

Jamieson, Dale. "Animal Liberation is an Environmental Ethic." November 1997. <https://acad.carleton.edu/curricular/ENTS/faculty/dale/dale_animal.html>

Lévi-Strauss, Claude. *Totemism*. Merlin Press, 1964.

Merry, Stephanie. "Michelle Obama's 'Becoming' Could Become the Best Selling Memoir Ever." *Chicago Tribune*, 26 March 2019.

Peterson, Valerie. "Types of Booksellers: A Survey of Where Books Are Sold." *The Balance Careers*, 25 June 2019.

Piersanti, Steven. "The 10 Awful Truths about Book Publishing, #1." *Berrett-Koehler Publishers*, 26 September 2016.

Regan, Tom. "The Case for Animal Rights." *In Defense of Animals*, edited by Peter Singer, Basil Blackwell, 1985, pp. 13–26.

Reingold, Jennifer. "Everybody Hates Pearson." *Fortune*, 21 January 2015.

Schinner, Miyoko. *Artisan Vegan Cheese: From Everyday to Gourmet*. Book Publishing Company, 2012.

Somin, Ilya. "University Presses Shouldn't Have to Make a Profit." *Atlantic*, 11 May 2019.

Stole, Jacki. *Dogland: A Journey to the Heart of America's Dog Problem*. Ashland Creek Press, 2015.

Streitfield, David. "Web Fiction, Serialized and Social." *New York Times*, 23 March 2014.

Thompson, Roger. *No Word for Wilderness: Italy's Grizzlies and the Race to Save the Rarest Bears on Earth*. Ashland Creek Press, 2018.

Wahba, Phil. "Why Barnes & Noble May Soon Look Like the Local Bookstores it Killed Off." *Fortune*, 23 June 2019.

Wasserman, Debra, and Reed Mangels. *Simply Vegan: Quick Vegetarian Meals*. Vegetarian Resource Group, 1991.

Wasserman, Debra, and Charles Stahler. *Vegetarianism for the Working Person*. Vegetarian Resource Group, 1983.

Watson, Amy. "Share of Adults Who Have Read a Book in Any Format in the Last 12 Months in the United States from 2011 to 2019, By Format." *Statista.com*, 10 October 2019.

Yunker, John. *The Tourist Trail*. Ashland Creek Press, 2012.

Notes on Contributors

Carol J. Adams's first book, *The Sexual Politics of Meat*, celebrated its 30th anniversary in 2020. *Neither Man nor Beast: Feminism and the Defense of Animals* (1994), and *The Pornography of Meat* (2004), were recently released in new editions. She is also the author of *Burger*, *Living among Meat Eaters*, and co-author with Virginia Messina of *Protest Kitchen: Fight Injustice, Save the Planet, and Fuel Your Resistance One Meal at a Time*. With Josephine Donovan, she is the editor of *Women and Animals* (1996) and *The Feminist Care Tradition in Animal Ethics: A Reader* (2007). With Lori Gruen, she is the editor of *Ecofeminism: Feminist Intersections with Other Animals and the Earth* (2022). With Alice Crary and Lori Gruen, she has edited *The Good It Promises, The Harm It Does: Critical Essays on Effective Altruism* (forthcoming, 2023), and with Michael Wise, she has edited *Pedaling Resistance: Sympathy, Subversion, and Veganism* (forthcoming, 2023).

Sune Borkfelt has a PhD in English literature from Aarhus University, Denmark, where he has lectured since 2007. He is author of *Reading Slaughter: Abattoir Fictions, Space, and Empathy in Late Modernity* (Palgrave, 2022). His work on topics such as nonhuman otherness, the naming of nonhuman animals, postcolonial animals, and the ethics of animal product marketing, has appeared in *English Studies*, *Animals*, and *Journal of Agricultural and Environmental Ethics* as well as in a number of edited collections. He is also editor of a 2016 special issue of the journal *Otherness: Essays and Studies* focused on animal alterity.

Catherine Brown is Associate Professor of English and Head of English Faculty at New College of the Humanities at Northeastern (London). Her research is mainly in the fields of D. H. Lawrence studies, Anglo-Russian literary relations, and (more recently) vegan literary studies. She is a Vice-President of the Lawrence Society, and in 2020 co-edited with Susan Reid *The Edinburgh Companion to D.H. Lawrence and the Arts*. She is the author of the monograph *The Art of Comparison: How Novels and Critics Compare* (Bloomsbury, 2011), and co-editor with Elinor Shaffer of *The Reception of George Eliot in Europe* (Bloomsbury, 2015).

Joshua Bulleid is a PhD graduate of Monash University in Melbourne, Australia, whose research broadly focuses on engagements with vegetarianism and animal ethics in science fiction and utopian literature. He is currently preparing his monograph *Vegetarianism and Science Fiction* for publication and also hosts the Terry Pratchett podcast *Unseen Academicals*.

Stewart Cole is Associate Professor in the Department of English and the Environmental Studies Program at the University of Wisconsin Oshkosh. His book *The Poetics of Utopia: Shadows of Futurity in Yeats and Auden* will be published by Bloomsbury in 2023. He is also the author of two poetry collections, *Questions in Bed* (2012) and *Soft Power* (2019).

Amy-Leigh Gray is a PhD candidate at the University of Manitoba in the Department of English, Theatre, Film, and Media Studies. She is currently writing her dissertation, which is tentatively titled *"The eye could literally not follow her": Deviant Girlhood, Reproduction, and Meat Animals in Twentieth-Century American Literature and Film*.

James Gregory is Associate Professor of Modern British History at the University of Plymouth. He published *Of Victorians and Vegetarians: The Vegetarian Movement in Nineteenth-century-Britain* in 2007 and is the author of a number of other monographs in British history, including *Mercy and British Culture, 1760–1960* (2021).

Alexandra Isfahani-Hammond is Associate Professor Emerita of Comparative Literature and Luso-Brazilian Studies at the University of California, San Diego. She works at the intersection of critical animal studies, decolonial studies, and comparative race and slavery studies, with publications including "A Pale Shade of Violet: Animals and Race in Machado de Assis" (2022), "Akbar, My Heart: Caregiving for a Dog During Covid-19" (2021), "Haunting Pigs, Swimming Jaguars: Mourning, Animals and Ayahuasca" (2020), "Slave Barracks Aristocrats: Islam and the Orient in the Work of Gilberto Freyre" (2014), "Akbar Stole My Heart: Coming Out as an Animalist" (2013), *White Negritude: Race, Writing and Brazilian Cultural Identity* (2008) and *The Masters and the Slaves: Plantation Relations and Mestizaje in American Imaginaries* (ed., 2005). In addition to her scholarly publications, Isfahani-Hammond has contributed to popular media including *The Advocate, The Conversation, CounterPunch, Folha de S. Paulo, Leia, Ms. Magazine, Persianesque*, and *Truthout*.

Sangamithra Iyer received a Whiting Creative Nonfiction grant for her first book, a lyrical manifesto and an ethical reckoning of the ways earthly bodies are controlled and liberated, which will be published by Milkweed Editions. Sangu was an Emerging Writer Fellow at Aspen Summer Words, a finalist for the Siskiyou Prize for New Environmental Literature, and a recipient of a Pushcart Prize. She served as an editor of *Satya*, and as an associate for Brighter Green. Her work has been published by *The Kenyon Review, Newtown Literary, n+1, Creative Nonfiction, Hen Press*, and *Hippocampus Magazine*. Her writing about animals has also been anthologized in *Primate People, Sister Species, Letters to a New Vegan*, and *Writing for Animals*.

Lisa Kemmerer is internationally known for her work on behalf of anymals, the planet, and disempowered human beings. She has authored more than 100 articles and ten books, including *Eating Earth: Environmental Ethics and Dietary Choice, Animals and World Religions*, and *Sister Species: Women, Animals, and Social*

Justice. She recently founded an educational non-profit, Tapestry, for scholars and activists working to build peace and compassion in the world. For more information, please visit <lisakemmerer.com>

Armin Langer holds a PhD in sociology from the Humboldt University of Berlin and an MA in Jewish Studies from the University of Potsdam. He has authored two monographs and dozens of articles in peer-reviewed journals, edited volumes and popular magazines on immigrants and minorities in Europe and the US, and edited a volume on Jewish-Muslim relations. Since 2019, he has been a visiting research scholar at Brandeis University in Waltham, MA. In 2019, he was a visiting fellow at the University of Virginia in Charlottesville, VA. Personal website: <arminlanger.net>

Dana Medoro is Professor of English at the University of Manitoba. Her publications include chapters and articles on industrialized pork production, eighteenth-century veganism, nineteenth-century theories of animal souls, and antebellum representations of plantation livestock. For almost two decades, she has worked with other activists to ban the intensive-confinement of pigs and chickens in Manitoba. She also volunteers in pop-up clinics that help bring veterinary services to the companion animals of under-waged, impoverished families.

Josh Milburn is a Lecturer in Political Philosophy and a British Academy Postdoctoral Fellow at Loughborough University. He is the author of *Just Fodder: The Ethics of Feeding Animals* (McGill-Queen's University Press, 2022) and *Food, Justice, and Animals: Feeding the World Respectfully* (Oxford University Press, forthcoming).

John Miller is Senior Lecturer in Nineteenth-Century Literature at the University of Sheffield, President of ASLE-UKI (Association for the Study of Literature and the Environment, UK and Ireland) and co-editor of Palgrave Studies in Animals and Literature.

Jovian Parry has a PhD in Science and Technology Studies from York University.

Samantha Pergadia is an Assistant Professor of English at Southern Methodist University. Her research and teaching interests include post-1945 American literature, African American literature, animal studies, and feminist theory. Her current book project, *Race and Species*, examines how contemporary American artists of color reformulate the relationship between race and species in the service of a multispecies ethics. Her essays and reviews have appeared or are forthcoming in *American Quarterly*, *African American Review*, *Feminist Studies*, *Eighteenth-Century Studies*, and *Contemporary Literature*.

Emelia Quinn is Assistant Professor of World Literatures & Environmental Humanities at the University of Amsterdam. She is author of *Reading Veganism: The Monstrous Vegan, 1818 to Present* (Oxford University Press, 2021) and co-editor of *Thinking Veganism in Literature and Culture: Towards a Vegan Theory* (Palgrave Macmillan, 2018).

Ruth Ramsden-Karelse recently completed her DPhil in English at the University of Oxford, where she held the inaugural Stuart Hall Doctoral Scholarship. She is a Research Associate at the University of Manchester's Centre on Dynamics of Ethnicity (CoDE). Her writing has appeared in *GLQ: A Journal of Lesbian and Gay Studies*.

Martin Rowe is the co-founder of Lantern Books and Lantern Publishing & Media, a senior fellow at Brighter Green, and the executive director of the Culture & Animals Foundation. He lives in Brooklyn, NY.

Ali Ryland is a researcher in the fields of animal studies and gender studies. She is currently completing her PhD in English at the University of Strathclyde, investigating the relationship between women and cows across early modern and nineteenth-century England: "from milkmaid to milking machine". She has previously worked for The Vegan Society, both as a trustee and as the charity's Digital Communications Officer.

Christopher Sebastian is a digital media researcher, author, and journalist. He sits on the advisory council for Encompass, a non-profit dedicated to addressing racial inequality in animal rights advocacy. He is the Director of Social Media on the board of Peace Advocacy Network. He is a recurring guest lecturer at Columbia University for the Department of Social Work, and he teaches social media theory and criticism while publishing on topics related to animality, food, politics, and pop culture.

Nicole Seymour works at the intersection of queer studies and environmental studies. She is Associate Professor of English and Graduate Advisor in Environmental Studies at California State University, Fullerton. Her academic monographs include *Strange Natures: Futurity, Empathy, and the Queer Ecological Imagination* (University of Illinois Press, 2015) and *Bad Environmentalism: Irony and Irreverence in the Ecological Age* (University of Minnesota Press, 2018). She is currently working on a public-facing book about glitter.

Rasmus R. Simonsen is senior lecturer of communication design and media at the Copenhagen School of Design and Technology. He has published on different aspects of veganism, and his publications in this field include "A Queer Vegan Manifesto" (2012), "Eating for the Future: Veganism and the Challenge of In Vitro Meat" (2015), and the collection *Critical Perspectives on Veganism* (2016), which he co-edited with Jodey Castricano. In addition to veganism, he publishes on topics related to American literature, queer theory, design, fashion, and photography.

Glenn Willmott is Professor of English and Cultural Studies at Queen's University in Canada. He works with cultural critique, ecocriticism, modernism, and comics in order to explore the subversive and symptomatic aspects of avant-garde and popular arts. He is past president of the Association for Literature, Environment, and Culture in Canada and of the Canadian Society for the Study of Comics. Recent books are *Reading for Wonder: Ecology, Ethics, Enchantment* (Palgrave Macmillan, 2018) and *Modern Animalism: Habitats of Scarcity and Wealth in Comics and Literature* (University of Toronto Press, 2012).

Corey Lee Wrenn is a Lecturer of Sociology with the School of Social Policy, Sociology and Social Research (SSPSSR) and Co-Director of the Centre for the Study of Social and Political Movements at the University of Kent. She served as council member with the American Sociological Association's Animals & Society section (2013–2016), was elected Chair in 2018, and co-founded the International Association of Vegan Sociologists in 2020. She serves as Book Review Editor for *Society & Animals* and

Editor for *The Sociological Quarterly*, is a member of The Vegan Society's Research Advisory Committee, and hosts the Sociology & Animals podcast. She is the author of *A Rational Approach to Animal Rights: Extensions in Abolitionist Theory* (Palgrave MacMillan, 2016), *Piecemeal Protest: Animal Rights in the Age of Nonprofits* (University of Michigan Press, 2019), and *Animals in Irish Society* (SUNY Press, 2021).

Laura Wright is Professor of English Studies, Director of English Graduate Studies, and Chair of the Faculty at Western Carolina University. Her monographs include *Writing Out of All the Camps: J. M. Coetzee's Narratives of Displacement* (Routledge, 2006 and 2009), *Wilderness into Civilized Shapes: Reading the Postcolonial Environment* (University of Georgia Press, 2010), and *The Vegan Studies Project: Food, Animals, and Gender in the Age of Terror* (University of Georgia Press, 2015). She is editor of *Through a Vegan Studies Lens: Textual Ethics and Lived Activism* (University of Nevada Press, 2019) and *The Routledge Handbook of Vegan Studies* (Routledge, 2021).

INDEX

abattoir *see* slaughterhouse
abolitionist approach, 24, 89; *see also* animal rights
Abolition movement, 32, 337; *see also* slavery
absent referent, the *see* Adams, Carol J., the absent referent
Abstinence from Animal Food a Moral Duty see Ritson, Joseph
activism
    animal, 12, 20, 26, 79, 87, 88, 128, 154, 171, 232, 237–40, 280, 333, 360; *see also* animal rights
    eco-, 95, 171, 213; *see also* environmentalism
    food, 287
    Irish, 27
    resource, 357
    theory and, 3, 155, 228
    vegan, 9, 13, 14, 26, 88, 108–9, 114–15, 338–9, 344–6, 359
    vegan and anti-racist, 21–2, 24–5, 108–9, 118, 251
    vegetarian, 47, 78, 243
Adams, Carol J., 7, 8, 20, 29, 31, 35, 263
    The Sexual Politics of Meat, 3, 8, 17, 23, 67 84, 102, 122, 152, 154, 195, 242, 267, 318
    on *Frankenstein*, 79, 126–7, 155; *see also* Shelley, Mary, *Frankenstein*
    the absent referent, 9, 17, 30, 100, 115, 155, 161, 175, 186, 268
Adams, Richard *see Watership Down*
Agamben, Giorgio, 143
ahimsa, 302–5, 344
Ahimsa (magazine), 340, 342, 346
Alcotts, the, 32, 320, 324, 337
Alexis, André *see Fifteen Dogs*
American Vegan Society, 333, 340–2, 344
American Vegetarian Society, 32, 321, 337–8; *see also* Vegetarian Society of America
American Vegetarian and Health Journal, 321, 323
Amstell, Simon, 269–70, 272
    Carnage, 278
An Act of Worship see Thompson, Kate

analytic philosophy *see* philosophy
animality, 25, 63, 68, 97, 125, 129, 194–5
Animal Liberation see Singer, Peter
animal products
    bone, 326, 328, 339; *see also* animal products, ivory
    dairy, 17, 31, 81, 84, 96, 218, 232–4, 237, 252–3, 254, 269, 282, 301–4, 306, 311, 312, 319, 321, 323, 328, 362; butter, 78, 322–4; cheese, 29, 95, 126, 234, 268, 270, 282, 323; milk, 29, 45, 51, 96, 123, 126, 188, 218, 234, 252, 278, 282, 291, 303, 318, 319, 321, 323, 324, 328, 336; yoghurt, 144
    eggs, 17, 29, 31, 63, 68, 78, 95, 96, 232, 234, 269, 278, 301, 303–4, 306, 311, 313, 319, 320, 321, 322–4, 328, 329, 336, 362
    fur, 50, 255, 273, 324, 326, 339
    honey, 51, 268, 321, 323
    ivory, 321, 325
    leather, 187, 216, 268, 269, 273, 319, 324, 325–6, 327, 339
    silk, 268–70, 326–7
    wool, 269, 319, 323, 324–5, 327
    see also vegan alternatives
animal rights, 16, 18, 22, 24, 25, 26, 27, 83, 88, 108, 113, 115–16, 129, 162, 213, 214, 215–16, 223–7, 237, 240, 242, 250–1, 255, 256, 268, 311, 328, 336, 343, 344, 349, 350, 353, 354, 356, 359, 360; *see also* activism, animal
animals
    baboons, 139
    bats, 71, 73, 194
    bears, 308, 354
    butterflies, 73, 197, 354
    cats, 94–6, 116, 138, 143, 144, 197, 200, 206, 207, 262
    cattle, 45, 52, 67, 69, 81, 86, 95–6, 233, 235, 245, 247, 248, 306, 307, 312; *see also* animals, cows
    chickens, 26, 51, 82, 96, 138, 139, 234, 247, 260, 278, 279, 305, 308n7, 309, 354; *see also* animals, fowl

chimpanzees, 263–4
cows, 13, 44, 49, 51, 81, 95, 99–100, 102, 116, 140, 160, 175–6, 218, 233, 235–7, 243, 245, 246–7, 260, 268, 302, 303, 308, 354; *see also* animals, cattle
crabs, 65
deer, 46, 48, 54, 72, 260, 261, 273, 274–5, 304
dogs, 9, 66, 71, 72, 73, 74, 130, 138–49, 161, 187, 191, 225, 255, 262–3, 272, 302, 305
ducks, 47
fish, 48, 52, 65, 71, 80, 84, 174, 189, 198–201, 217, 278, 301, 303, 304, 309, 337
fowl, 47, 72, 274, 303; *see also* animals, chickens
goats, 173, 174, 214
hedgehog, 115
hyenas, 207–8
lions, 24, 212, 215–16, 219, 308
mice, 71, 94–5, 96, 143, 173
monkeys, 140, 173, 217
moths, 354
otters, 70–5, 305
owls, 71
panthers, 193–4
pigs, 63–9, 74, 81, 96, 101, 139, 175, 218, 225, 226, 234, 242, 247, 260, 272, 308n7, 354
porcupines, 73–4, 196–7
rabbits, 44, 49, 70, 71, 72, 80, 147, 216, 308n7
reindeer, 29
sharks, 214
sheep, 52, 101, 173n6, 175, 195, 218, 278, 319, 327
snails, 138
squirrels, 147, 148
tigers, 54, 204
toads, 70, 71
turkeys, 54–5, 109–10, 116, 117, 237–9, 312
weasels, 71, 72
whales, 83
wolves, 72, 308, 354
animals (fictional)
  dragons, 354
  genetically engineered, 82, 87
  unicorns, 354
Animals, Men, and Morals, 224; *see also* Oxford vegetarians
animal studies, 3, 16, 17, 18, 19, 78, 93, 155, 193, 222, 224, 355; *see also* critical animal studies
anorexia, 168
  mirabilis, 170
  nervosa, 169, 175, 178, 179
  see also bulimia nervosa; orthorexia
anthropocentrism, 10, 20, 68, 116–17, 132, 139–40, 143, 154, 163, 193, 195, 197, 199, 201, 206, 269, 279, 285, 290, 321

anthropomorphism, 22, 66, 71, 86, 116, 200, 206, 264–5
anthropophagy *see* cannibalism
anti-capitalism, 108–9, 264, 357; *see also* capitalism
anti-racism, 2, 23, 24–5, 251, 290; *see also* racism
anti-vivisection, 62, 218, 326; *see also* vivisection
artificial meats *see* vegan alternatives
asceticism, 122, 169–70, 336
Ashland Creek Press, 14, 260, 355, 360–1
Atwood, Margaret, 18, 78, 178
  Edible Woman, The, 8, 10, 48–9, 55–6, 168–9, 174–6, 178
  MaddAddam trilogy, 19, 82, 86–7, 88, 174, 281
Australia, 31, 66, 245
autobiography, 5, 6, 12, 21, 54, 126, 156, 161, 242, 252, 255
autotheory, 22, 138

Baum, Frank L., 10, 212–14
Begbie, Harold, 327–8
Belly of Paris, The see Zola, Émile
Berger, John, 96
Birds of America see McCarthy, Mary
BISAC Codes, 349, 352–6
BISG (Book Industry Study Group), 354
Black Lives Matter, 24, 114, 256
bloodsports *see* hunting
Bloch, Ernst, 196
Book Publishing Company, 362
Brief Account of the First Concordium, A see Concordium, the
Brindel, June, 51–2
Brophy, Brigid, 50–2, 55, 224
Brontë, Charlotte, *Jane Eyre*, 176
Brotherton, Martha, 322
Brueck, Julia Feliz, 21, 128, 357–8
Bryant, Dorothy, 52–3, 84
BSE crisis, 86, 95
Buddhism *see* religion
bulimia, 168–9, 176–7
Butler, Judith, 116–17
Butler, Octavia E.
  Parable series, 85
  Xenogensis trilogy, 5–6, 11, 85, 153, 287, 289–94
Butler, Samuel *see Erewhon*

Calarco, Matthew, 16, 29, 31, 195, 275
Callenbach, Ernest, 85, 88
Call of the Wild, The see London, Jack
Canada, 18, 55, 66, 223
  Toronto, 139, 142
cannibalism, 32, 49n37, 70, 80–2, 96–7, 101, 159, 288–93, 304

capitalism, 1, 9, 22, 32, 67, 78, 110, 122, 139, 170, 213, 233, 253, 280, 285; *see also* anti-capitalism
Carnage see Amstell, Simon, *Carnage*
carnism, 21, 30, 31, 77–8, 79, 80, 82–8
carnophallogocentrism *see* Derrida, Jacques, carnophallogocentrism
cheese *see* animal products
Christianity *see* religion
Clarke, Arthur C., 77–8, 82–4, 86
climate change, 31, 66, 75, 86, 87, 250, 309
  denial of, 134, 240
Clubb, Henry S., 321, 338–9
Cobbett, William, 325
Coetzee, J. M., 18, 22
  The Life & Times of Michael K, 7, 10, 168–9, 172–4, 179
  The Lives of Animals, 69, 193–7, 199, 223, 273
Cole, Matthew, 27, 31, 162, 169
Colegate, Isabel, *The Shooting Party*, 8, 47–8, 55
comics, 5, 10, 186, 189, 203–10, 267, 269, 272
Concordium, the, 320, 322, 324–5
  Brief Account of the First Concordium, A, 322–3
continental Philosophy *see* philosophy
cookbooks, 11, 12, 49, 175, 333, 340–2, 350, 354, 359, 360, 361, 362
  Artisan Vegan Cheese, 362
  Dirt Candy: A Cookbook, 270
  Farm Vegetarian Cookbook, The, 362
  Golden Rule Cookbook,The, 43, 45, 50, 52
  How to Be Vegan and Keep Your Friends, 270
  Meatless and Wheatless Menus, 44, 45
  Penny Vegetarian Cookery, 323
  Science of Cooking Vegetarian Food, The 321, 323
  Thug Kitchen, 22, 271–2
  Vegan Junk Food, 271
  Vegan Kitchen, The, 340–1
  Vegan Stoner Cookbook, The 270
  Vegetable Cookery, 322
COVID-19, 1, 312, 356
Cowherd, William, 322, 337
Cowherdites, 323; *see also* Simpson, James
cows *see* animals
critical animal studies, 3, 16, 19, 22, 26–7, 31, 78, 139, 155
critical race studies, 3, 28, 154n3, 162, 251
cyborgs, 129, 205–6; *see also* Haraway, Donna

dairy *see* animal products, dairy
Dangarembga, Tsitsi, *Nervous Conditions*, 5, 10, 168–9, 176–9
Danielite Star, 326
Darwinism 67, 72, 73, 74
  On the Origin of Species, 63
Davis, Angela, 116
Dear Green Place, The, 9, 99–100

Deckha, Maneesha, 139, 178
Derrida, Jacques, 16, 31, 116, 154, 160, 222
  carnophallogocentrism, 74
Diamond, Cora, 223, 269, 274
Dickinson, Peter, *Eva*, 5, 260, 263–5
Dick, Philip K.
  "Beyond Lies the Wub", 83–4
  Do Androids Dream of Electric Sheep?, 22, 78, 83–4, 85
Diet for a New America, 342
Dinshah, Freya, 340; *see also* cookbooks, *The Vegan Kitchen*
Dinshah, Jay, 340, 344
D'Lacey, Joseph, *Meat*, 9, 96, 99
Do Androids Dream of Electric Sheep see Dick, Philip K.
dogs *see* animals
Donaldson, Brianne, 29–30, 139
Donovan, Josephine, 16, 98
Doukhobors, the, 55
Drive your Plow over the Bones of the Dead see Tokarczuk, Olga
dub poetry, 9, 108, 112
Duncan, Isadora, 54–5
Duncan, James Elmslie, 320
Durrell, Gerlad, 68
dystopia, 78, 82–4, 96, 209, 281, 360

Earthlings, 139
Eating Animals see Foer, Jonathan Safran
ecocriticism, 3, 16, 31, 193, 203, 242; *see also* Fromm, Harold; Schuster, Joshua
ecofeminism, 1, 2, 3, 16, 19, 20, 31, 85, 94, 98, 99, 162, 196, 261, 290, 292, 293; *see also* Adams, Carol J.; Donovan, Josephine; Gaard, Greta; Gruen, Lori
Edible Woman, The see Atwood, Margaret
eggs *see* animal products
empathy, 1, 12, 80, 83–5, 115, 123n1, 128–9, 174, 176, 178–9, 194, 218, 264–5, 290
entanglement, 5–6, 11, 23, 109, 129, 132, 160–2, 203–4, 206–10, 287, 289, 293–4; *see also* Haraway, Donna
environmentalism, 86, 172, 213, 252, 260, 268, 309, 359; *see also* activism, eco-
Erewhon, 47, 278
eugenics, 11, 81, 127, 154, 224, 284–5, 290
eurocentrism, 18, 109
Eva see Dickinson, Peter
extinction, 72, 85, 88, 264, 283–4, 292–3, 309

Faber, Michel, *Under the Skin*, 31, 88
factory farming, 31, 75, 84, 124, 130, 194, 232–3, 237–9, 244, 246, 267, 311
Fanon, Frantz, 176–7
Faunary Press, 14, 355, 358–9

Fiddes, Nick, 30, 85
Fifteen Dogs, 9, 138–9, 142–3, 145–8
Foer, Jonathan Safran, 11–12, 23, 231–2, 237–40
Food, Home and Garden, 325, 333, 338, 346
Francione, Gary, 2, 22, 24, 25
Frankenstein see Shelley, Mary
Frankissstein see Winterson, Jeanette
fregans, 86
Fromm, Harold, 97, 154, 162
fruitarianism, 65, 80, 323
Fruitlands, 32, 324
fur *see* animal products, fur
Furniss, Harry, 327

Gaard, Greta, 16, 31
Genesis, 74, 103, 306–7, 309; *see also* religion, Christianity
Gillespie, Kathryn, 138–9, 231, 233–7, 240
Gilman, Charlotte Perkins, 281
    Herland, 52–3, 81
    His Religion and Hers, 46
    Moving the Mountain, 81
    With Her in Our Land, 81
Giraud, Eva, 1, 2, 6, 22
Godin, Seth, 350, 356
Godlovitch, Ros, 223
Golding, William, *Lord of the Flies*, 62–3, 65–8, 70–3, 74
Gompertz, Lewis, 328
Gothic (genre), 124, 126, 131, 133, 153
Graham, Sylvester, 32, 322–3, 336
Grahame, Kenneth *see The Wind in the Willows*
graphic novels *see* comics
Greaves, James Pierrepont *see Concordium, the*
Greger, Michael, 350, 362
grief *see* mourning
grotesque (aesthetic tradition), 203–4, 206, 220
Gruen, Lori, 16, 28, 123n1
Gulliver's Travels, 67

Halberstam, Jack, 124, 127–8, 130–3, 153, 157–8, 264–5
Hamilton, C. Lou, 1, 22–3, 122, 124
Hamsun, Knut, 172
Haraway, Donna, 5–6, 11, 96n2, 129–30, 160, 203n3, 287, 288, 290, 293–4
Hardy, Thomas, *Jude the Obscure*, 8, 62, 63–5, 67, 69
Harper, A. Breeze *see Sistah Vegan*
Herland see Gilman, Charlotte Perkins
heteronormativity, 2, 259–60, 262–3, 264
heterosexism, 2, 130, 262–3; *see also* sexism
Hind, Archie *see Dear Green Place, The*
Hinduism *see* religion
Hitler, Adolf, 154, 159; *see also* Nazism
Holzapfel, Bob, 362

homophobia, 12, 123, 134, 156, 217, 235, 262, 290n6; *see also* transphobia
honey *see* animal products
hooks, bell, 138
Horsell, Elizabeth, 323
Horsell, William, 318, 320, 321, 323; *see also* cookbooks, *Science of Cooking Vegetarian Food, The*
Houser, A. Marie, 358–9; *see also* Faunary Press
Hughes, Ted, 172n5, 193–6, 199
humanitarinism, 25, 63, 328
humour, 46, 68, 157, 163, 267–72, 318, 326–7, 329; *see also* satire
Hunger see Hamsun, Knut
"Hunger Artist, The" *see* Kafka, Franz
hunting, 45–9, 54, 62, 65–6, 70–5, 81, 83–6, 104, 147, 178, 207–8, 219, 233–4, 246, 273, 275

India, 29, 34, 128, 140, 178, 301–2, 304, 323, 328, 340
Indigenous cultures, 29, 85, 88, 117, 178–9, 213, 250–1, 254, 337, 357; *see also* Native Americans
inedia (breatharianism), 170
International Vegetarian Union, 336, 342
intersectionality, 2–3, 12, 18, 21–2, 23, 25, 26, 27, 28, 29, 114, 118, 124, 128–9, 173, 209, 240, 253, 268
in vitro meat *see* lab-grown meat
Ireland, 27, 31, 95–6
irony, 11, 67, 102, 134, 143, 145, 146, 158, 267–8, 271, 273–4, 351
Ishiguro, Kazuo, *Never Let Me Go*, 88
Islam *see* religion
Island of Doctor Moreau, The see Wells, H. G.

Jameson, Fredric, 77, 280
Japan, 31–2, 78, 242–6, 305
jones, pattrice, 16, 352
Joy, Melanie, 21, 30, 31, 85; *see also* carnism
Joyce, James, 32, 70
Jude the Obscure see Hardy, Thomas
Jungle, The see Sinclair, Upton

Kafka, Franz, 31, 69n8
    "A Hunger Artist", 10, 19, 168–9, 171–4
Kang, Han *see Vegetarian, The* (Kang)
Kin of Ata are Waiting for You, The see Bryant, Dorothy
Kingsford, Anna, 44, 50, 55, 319, 326, 327
Ko, Aph and Syl, 24–5, 109

lab-grown meat, 5, 11, 82, 174, 278–5
Lambe, William, 320, 322
Lane, Mary E. Bradley *see Mizora*
Lantern Books, 13, 251–2, 349–52

Lawrence, D. H., 7, 63, 68, 75
  "Fish", 10, 71, 193, 198–201
  Lady Chatterley's Lover, 176
  "Man and Bat", 73
  "Reflections on the Death of a Porcupine", 73–4, 196–8
leather *see* animal products, leather
Le Guin, Ursula K., 84–5, 88, 103–4
LePan, Don, *Animals*, 88
Levitas, Ruth, 196
Life & Times of Michael K, The see Coetzee, J. M.
Lithia (trilogy) *see* Richmond, Blair
Liu, Marjorie *see Monstress*
Lives of Animals, The see Coetzee, J. M.
London, Jack, 74
  The Call of the Wild, 71–2
  White Fang, 66, 71
Lord of the Flies see Golding, William

McCarthy, Mary, *Birds of America*, 8, 54–5
McCorry, Seán, 30–1, 101
Macdonald, William Allan, 328
mad-cow disease *see* BSE crisis
Maguire, Gregory, *Wicked*, 5, 7, 153, 212–20
Mare, Walter de la, 43
meat (types of)
  bacon, 82, 87, 272, 312
  beef, 29, 67, 69, 101, 178, 234, 242–3, 245–7, 280, 325
  chicken, 247
  meat loaf, 48
  mutton, 80, 101
  pork, 68, 70, 87, 96, 101–2, 157, 167, 218
  sausage, 68, 70, 172
  steak, 45, 46, 49, 86, 123, 175, 261, 279
  turkey, 54–5
  veal, 17, 101, 218
  see also lab-grown meat
Meat (D'Lacey) *see* D'Lacey, Joseph
menstruation, 51, 190
Midgley, Mary, 16, 45, 53
milk *see* animal products
Milton, John *see Paradise Lost*
misanthropy, 157, 159, 275
Mizora, 5, 11, 81, 278, 281–5
monsters, 4, 18, 124, 131–4, 152–65, 206–7, 212–17
Monstress (Lui and Takeda), 203–10
monstrous vegan, the *see* Quinn, Emelia
mourning, 43–4, 131, 138, 140, 142, 148, 243, 273
Mwangi, Evan Maina, 4–5, 18, 62n1, 164, 177, 179, 212, 218, 318
My Year of Meats see Ozeki, Ruth

Nabokov, Vladimir
  Lolita, 161
  Pale Fire, 9, 152, 154, 155–65
Nagel, Thomas, 71, 194

Narayanan, Yamini, 139–40, 144
Native Americans, 85–6, 88, 115, 213, 252, 255, 362; *see also* Indigenous cultures
Nazism, 154, 158–9; *see also* Hitler, Adolf
Nervous Conditions see Dangarembga, Tsitsi
Newkirk, Ingrid, 350; *see also* PETA
Newman, Francis W., 319, 324
Newton, John Frank, 320, 322
Nicholson, Asenath, 323
nut milk *see* vegan alternatives, milks

Omnivore's Dilemma, The see Pollan, Michael
organic produce, 96, 116, 126, 254
orthorexia, 63, 69, 169; *see also* anorexia
Orwell, George, 31
  Animal Farm, 65
  Nineteen Eighty-Four, 82
Owen, Wilfred, 48
"Oxford Vegetarians", 223–4; *see also* Singer, Peter
Ozeki, Ruth, *My Year of Meats*, 5, 12, 241–8

Pachirat, Timothy, 231, 233–6, 240
pacifism, 8, 41–56, 63, 66, 133
Pale Fire see Nabokov, Vladimir
Pan (god), 70, 72, 74
Paradise Lost, 80; *see also* genesis
PETA, 109, 114–16, 250, 255, 350
philosophy, 2, 6, 27
  analytic, 11, 22, 24, 222–3, 225–8
  Buddhist, 232, 304–5; *see also* religion, Buddhism
  continental, 16, 222; *see also* Derrida, Jacques
  moral, 3, 16, 24, 25, 28, 83, 88; *see also* Singer, Peter
  posthuman, 16, 18, 126; *see also* posthumanism
  utilitarian, 63, 223
  vegan and vegetarian 3, 24, 33, 34, 79, 81, 259, 263, 301, 322, 333–4, 344–6
  see also Diamond, Cora; Plato; Plutarch
Piercy, Marge, 78
  He, She and It, 84
  Small Changes, 8, 48–50, 84
  Woman on the Edge of Time, 84
Plato, 34, 197, 199, 201
  Republic, 52, 77, 228
Plutarch, 156–60, 320
Pollan, Michael, 11–12, 20, 231–5, 239
Pope, Alexander, 97–9
postcolonialism, 4–5, 9, 10, 18, 20, 138, 140, 169, 178–9, 255
posthumanism, 3, 5, 9, 16, 18, 19, 68, 79, 86, 124–6, 130, 173, 204, 264; *see also* transhumanism
postmodernism, 152, 279
Potts, Annie, 2, 31, 261; *see also* vegansexuality
Power, Richard, *The Echo Maker*, 20, 171–2, 174
Prosser, Jay, 132–3
Punch, 327, 328

Pure Food and Drug Act of 1906, 242
Pythagoras, 34, 156, 232, 320, 336

Queen Mab see Shelly, Percy Bysshe
queerness
   homosexuality, 152, 156, 171, 262
   lesbianism, 48, 243
   queer sexuality, 124, 134, 205, 209, 262, 263
   queer subcultures, 23
   queer theory, 12, 19, 28–9, 267, 285;
     see also Halberstam, Jack; Sedgwick, Eve Kosofsky
   species-queer, 70, 264
   veganism as queer, 5, 9, 117, 122–34, 171, 259–60, 265; *see also* vegansexuality
   see also transgenderism
Quinn, Emelia, 2, 3, 4, 18, 19, 78, 80, 93, 94, 104, 117–18, 129, 133, 163, 195, 196, 207, 212–13, 216–17, 260, 269

racism, 11, 21, 25, 29, 31, 108, 117, 209, 217, 224, 250–6, 353
   white supremacy, 21, 25, 108, 110, 139, 215, 217, 220, 256
Rakshit, Doel, 128, 130
Rastafarianism *see* religion
Realism (genre), 5, 12, 69, 70, 71, 204, 207, 242–8
Regan, Tom, 16, 83, 223, 355
religion
   Buddhism, 20, 83, 171, 232, 301, 304–6
   Christianity, 34, 64, 65, 74, 301, 306, 308–10, 322; *see also* Genesis
   Hinduism, 170, 301–4
   Islam, 108, 147, 301, 306, 310–12
   Rastafarianism, 107–8, 112–13
Republic (Plato) *see* Plato
Return to Nature, or Defence of a Vegetable Regimen, The see Newton, John Frank
Richardson, Thomas Wilson, 325–6, 328
Richmond, Blair, *Lithia* trilogy, 12, 260–3, 265
Rilke, Rainer Maria, 193–4
Ritson, Joseph, 322
Robinson, Kim Stanley, 85–6, 88
Rohman, Carrie, 62, 74, 199
Romantic period, 66, 79–81, 122, 126–7, 133, 283–4, 318, 320
Romantic poets, 107, 113, 198; *see also* Shelley, Percy
Routledge Handbook of Vegan Studies, The, 2, 27–8, 162, 178
Ryan, Agnes, 41, 43, 46, 49–50, 53, 55
Ryder, Richard, 26, 83, 224; *see also* speciesism

sadism, 66
Salih, Sara, 26, 222–3, 225, 227, 228–9
Salt, Henry S., 35, 45, 46, 53, 55, 224, 232, 325, 326, 336

Sanctuary Press, 355, 357–8
Sassoon, Siegfried, 46
satire, 11, 13, 46, 79, 80–1, 85, 152, 155, 158–9, 163, 174, 203, 242, 267–75, 278, 317, 318, 321, 326–8; *see also* humor
Satya, 235, 349, 354
Schreiner, Olive, 43
Schuster, Joshua, 7, 22, 77, 83, 195, 196
science fiction (genre), 6–7, 8, 77–89, 281, 287–9, 293
Science of Cooking Vegetarian Food, The see cookbooks
Sedgwick, Eve Kosofsky, 122
sentience, 129, 216, 225–7, 322, 354
sexism, 31, 108, 133, 217, 224, 253; *see also* heterosexism
Shakespeare, William, 131
   Timon of Athens, 159–61
   Macbeth, 64
Shaw, George Bernard, 27, 45, 50, 53–5, 172n5
Shelley, Mary, 80, 85, 107–8, 112–13, 131, 318
   Frankenstein, 9, 17, 18, 41–2, 78–80, 83, 124, 126–7, 129, 132–4, 155, 158, 282–3
   The Last Man, 79–80
Shelley, Percy Bysshe, 41, 44, 53, 55, 78–9, 85, 107, 110, 112–13, 172n5, 197, 320
Shooting Party, The see Colegate, Isabel
Simpson, James, 323, 325; *see also* cowherdites
Sinclair, Upton, *The Jungle*, 32, 63, 67–70, 74, 236, 242
Singer, Peter, 11, 16
   Animal Liberation, 83, 222–8, 234
Sistah Vegan, 2, 5, 12, 13, 23–4, 108, 114, 250–6, 349, 352–6, 363
slaughterhouse, 45, 67–9, 74, 79, 95, 99, 115, 231, 234–6, 238, 242–8, 303, 311, 340
slavery, 113–14, 139, 206, 209, 233, 253, 290, 253; *see also* Abolitionism
Smith, James Elimalet, 325
socialism, 69, 320
social media, 256, 272, 317, 344, 361
South Africa, 18, 172–3
South Korea, 9, 31, 167, 185
"Soy boy", 123n3, 260, 262
Soylent Green, 82
Space Merchants, 82
speciesism, 27, 74, 79, 83, 88, 108, 115, 129, 133, 140, 213, 217, 219, 224, 225, 255, 339, 345; *see also* Ryder, Richard
Stahler, Charles, 361
steampunk, 205
Steiner, Gary, 162
Stevens, Henry Bailey, 43, 50–1, 53
Stryker, Susan, 132
supernatural, the, 206
Swift, Jonathan *see Gulliver's Travels*

Taft, Casey, 359
Takeda, Sana see Monstress
Tarka the Otter see Williamson, Henry
temperance movement, 268, 317–18, 320
theosophists, 329
Thinking Veganism in Literature and Culture, 19, 129, 223; see also Quinn, Emelia; Westwood, Benjamin
Thompson, Kate, An Act of Worship, 94–7, 99
Third Eye, The, 205, 207–8
Thug Kitchen see cookbooks
Timon of Athens see Shakespeare, William
tofu, 1, 234, 261, 268
Tokarczuk, Olga, Drive your Plow Over the Bones of the Dead, 11, 267, 273–5
Tolstoy, Leo, 35, 67, 69, 74, 231–2, 234–5
transgenderism, 9, 123–34
   non-binary gender, 209
   transphobia, 123, 130–1
   trans rights, 116
transhumanism, 123–35; see also posthumanism
True Blood, 153; see also vampires
Twine, Richard, 26–7, 31, 110
   "the vegan killjoy", 154, 218, 268–9, 271
Twilight, 153, 260, 262–3, 265; see also vampires

Ulysses see Joyce, James
utilitarianism see philosophy
utopianism, 4, 5, 8, 9, 10, 11, 18, 41, 52, 63, 75, 77–9, 80–1, 83–7, 118, 125, 133, 153, 162–4, 174, 193, 196, 198, 201, 209, 242, 247, 278–85, 287, 289, 293

vampires, 4, 20, 153–4, 207n7, 260–3, 290
Vegan, The, 333–40, 343–6
vegan alternatives
   cheese, 30, 96, 282, 326, 362
   fur, 328, 339
   ivory, 323, 339
   leather, 318, 321, 325–6, 328, 339
   meat, 1, 81–3, 86, 261, 280, 282–3; see also lab-grown meat
   milks, 1, 29, 123, 282, 324, 326
   wool, 318, 324–7
   see also tofu
Vegan Junk Food (Gold) see cookbooks
vegan killjoys see Twine, Richard
vegansexuality, 2, 261
Vegan Society, The (UK), 1, 27, 108, 265, 270
Vegan Studies Project see Wright, Laura, The Vegan Studies Project
vegan unconscious, the see Mwangi, Evan Maina
Vegetable Cookery see cookbooks
Vegetarian, The (London), 80, 336
Vegetarian, The (Kang), 6, 10, 19, 167–8, 178–9, 185–91, 245

Vegetarian Advocate, 320–1, 323
Vegetarian Messenger, 319, 320, 323, 325–6, 334, 338, 345–6
Vegetarian Resource Group, 361
vegetarian restaurants, 33, 64, 87, 267, 270, 317, 328
Vegetarian Society (UK), 34, 97, 319, 320, 321, 323, 324, 325, 333–4, 336, 337, 342
Vegetarian Society of America, 336, 338, 345
Vegetarian Voice, 342
Verne, Jules, 80
Vindication of a Natural Diet see Shelley, Percy Bysshe
Vint, Sherryl, 6, 78
vivisection, 80, 139, 216, 309, 326; see also anti-vivisection

Water-Cure Journal, 321
Watership Down, 71
Watson, Donald, 334–6
Wells, H. G., 18, 78, 80–2, 127, 318
   The Island of Doctor Moreau, 80–1
Westwood, Benjamin, 19, 93, 100, 104, 117, 122–3, 129, 195, 196, 207, 259
White Fang see London, Jack
white supremacy see racism
Wicked (Maguire) see Maguire, Gregory
Williams, Howard, The Ethics of Diet, 35, 67, 232
Williamson, Henry, Tarka the Otter, 8, 63, 71–5
Wind in the Willows, The, 63, 70–1, 74
Winterson, Jeanette, 5, 9, 122–34
witches, 64, 206, 212–20
Wollstonecraft, Mary, 55
Women's Vegetarian Union, 326
Woolf, Virginia, 31, 43, 53
World Vegetarian Congress, 342
World War I, 8, 41–56, 67, 73
World War II, 68, 273; see also Hitler, Adolf; Nazism
Wright, Laura, 2, 4, 100, 163, 185, 220, 260, 263
   The Vegan Studies Project, 4, 19–20
   Through a Vegan Studies Lens: Textual Ethics and Lived Activism, 20
   see also Routledge Handbook of Vegan Studies, The

Xenogenesis (trilogy) see Butler, Octavia E.

Yunker, John, 360–1

Zephaniah, Benjamin, 5, 9, 107–18
Zola, Émile, The Belly of Paris, 9, 101–3
zombies, 4, 20
zoos, 27, 81, 86, 290

EU representative:
Easy Access System Europe
Mustamäe tee 50, 10621 Tallinn, Estonia
Gpsr.requests@easproject.com

www.ingramcontent.com/pod-product-compliance
Lightning Source LLC
Chambersburg PA
CBHW081534300426
44116CB00015B/2628